ORGANIZING
VICTORY

Press briefing, Trident Conference, Washington DC, 25 May 1943:

Question: Mr. Prime Minister, would you make a prediction on the progress of the war for the rest of this year? I have in mind the statement you and the President made at Casablanca, on new and heavier blows against all of the Axis members in 1943.

Churchill: Well, I think that seems to be a very sound prediction, and couched in terms which are unexceptionable from the point of view of military security. (Laughter).

Roosevelt: May I say one word, please? Don't get the idea the conferences are concluded. They are not. They are continuing.

Churchill: We have a lot of ground to cover.

Roosevelt–Stalin meeting, 4 February 1945:

Roosevelt said he would now tell the Marshal something indiscreet, since he would not wish to say it in front of Churchill. For two years the British had had the idea of artificially building up France into a strong power, which would have 200,000 troops on her eastern border, to hold the line for the period required to assemble a strong British army. He said the British were a peculiar people and wished to have their cake and eat it too.

Terminal Conference, 17 July 1945:

Stalin had one question before they adjourned. Why did Churchill refuse to give Russia her share of the German fleet? Churchill exclaimed, "Why, because the fleet should be destroyed *or* shared; weapons of war are horrible things." Stalin replied, let us divide it. "If Mr Churchill wishes, he can sink his share."

The meeting adjourned.

ORGANIZING VICTORY

THE WAR CONFERENCES 1941–45

ANDREW RAWSON

Praise for Andrew Rawson's companion volume, *Eyes Only: The Top Secret Correspondence betweeen Marshall and Eisenhower*:

A fascinating insight into the war in Europe – *Britain at War*

History as it occurred – not as it has been retold time and again through liberal interpretations and pundit opinions. After four years research for a biography of a former OSS operative at SHAEF, it opened my eyes to the reality of that War. I wish I had read it first, before studying 50 others. Forget the rest until you've read it. *Eyes Only* should be required reading for every World War II American history student studying the European theater for 1938 to 1945. Yes … It's that important –Vic Currier

First published 2013

The History Press
The Mill, Brimscombe Port
Stroud, Gloucestershire, GL5 2QG
www.thehistorypress.co.uk

British Library Cataloguing in Publication Data.
A catalogue record for this book is available from the British Library.

ISBN 978 0 7524 8925 4

Typesetting and origination by The History Press
Printed in Great Britain

CONTENTS

INTRODUCTION

Between December 1941 and July 1945 the Allies had ten main conferences where the Heads of State and their advisors gathered to discuss the conduct of the war. Within these pages you will read the edited minutes of these meetings.

To begin with, it was only President Franklin D. Roosevelt of the United States and Prime Minister Winston S. Churchill of Great Britain making the decisions about strategy, aided by their Chiefs of Staff. Later on, Premier Joseph Stalin of the Soviet Union and Generalissimo Chiang Kai-shek of China joined the conferences.

The first meeting, codename ARCADIA, was held in Washington just after the attack on Pearl Harbor on 7 December 1941 and it was a meeting of the two new Allies, the United States and Great Britain. The main decisions taken were to secure Great Britain and to attack Germany first rather than Japan, which involved securing a supply line across the Atlantic. The Declaration of the United Nations was also signed on 1 January 1942 by 26 governments. It stated "that complete victory over [their] enemies is essential to defend life, liberty, independence and religious freedom, and to preserve human rights and justice in their own lands as well as in other lands, and that [they] are now engaged in a common struggle against savage and brutal forces seeking to subjugate the world." The words "complete victory" established the Allied precedent for obtaining unconditional surrender from the Axis powers later on.

There were many questions raised at ARCADIA and while Churchill returned to Britain, his Chiefs of Staff worked on with their American counterparts until May. They dealt with a host of issues in time for the Prime Minister's return in June. The hastily organized conference had no name but important strategies were agreed. The main one was to make a landing on the North Africa coast before making a cross-channel attack against northern France.

The SYMBOL Conference was held on captured territory in Casablanca, Morocco, in January 1943 and it was the first time a President of the United States had left his country in time of war. The main topic was the Mediterranean campaign, particularly the invasion of Sicily, codename HUSKY, and where to go afterwards; Sardinia, Greece or the Italian mainland. The continuing build up of American troops in the United Kingdom, codename BOLERO, and the projected channel crossing were also discussed. Attempts to unify the French leaders, General Charles de Gaulle and General Henri Giraud, were also made.

The TRIDENT Conference was held in Washington in May 1943 and news that the Axis troops in Tunisia had surrendered, completing the capture of the North African coast, intensified planning for the Italian campaign. Now that the American air forces were concentrating in the United Kingdom plans were put in place to increase the bombing attacks on occupied Europe and Germany. Plans to step up the Pacific campaign were also discussed.

The QUADRANT Conference was held in Quebec in August 1943 because the climate was cooler than Washington. With Sicily taken and plans for the Italian campaign well underway, it was time to focus on the invasion of France the following spring. The reorganization of Southeast Asia command was also agreed.

Starting at the end of November 1943 there were three conferences in quick succession. The first SEXTANT conference was held in Cairo where Roosevelt and Churchill met Generalissimo Chiang Kai-shek to discuss aid for China and postwar Asia. Roosevelt and Churchill then headed to Tehran in Iran to meet Stalin for the EUREKA conference, the first time the Big Three came together. Marshal Joseph Stalin, as Premier of the Soviet Union, had been unable to attend the previous conferences because he was too involved with the campaigns on the Eastern Front. By the end of 1943, the tide had turned in favour of the Red Army and he was able to meet Roosevelt and Churchill.

They agreed a final strategy for the defeat of Nazi Germany including a date for the invasion of Northwest France and a simultaneous attack on the Eastern Front. Stalin also suggested conducting a simultaneous attack against southern France, an idea the Allies eventually adopted. The third meeting, an extension of EUREKA, was again at Cairo and Roosevelt and Churchill took the opportunity to meet President Inonu of Turkey. They also reviewed a hectic two weeks of meetings.

In September 1944 it was back to Quebec for OCTAGON. By now the Allies had been ashore in France for two months but after a difficult campaign in Normandy, their troops had liberated most of the country. The end of the war in Europe was in sight and plans for postwar Germany were discussed. The Pacific campaign was also high on the agenda because it was increasing in momentum.

ARGONAUT involved two meetings in February 1945, just as the Allies were beginning their final offensive on Nazi Germany. Roosevelt and Churchill met briefly in Malta on 1 February before heading for Yalta in the Crimea to meet Stalin. They discussed the final offensive on Germany as well as developing their plans for postwar Europe. The conditions for the Soviet Union's entry into the war on Japan were also discussed. The Yalta Declaration laid down the foundations for a postwar world and set an April date for the United Nations Conference.

The final conference was aptly named TERMINAL and it was held in Potsdam, in the outskirts of Berlin. With Germany defeated, there was plenty to discuss about postwar Europe and the final attack on Japan. Borders had to be decided, reparations had to be calculated, diplomacy had to be re-established and populations had to be fed. There were also old problems to solve, many of them caused by the Treaty of Versailles.

The United States and British Chiefs of Staff worked hard, before, during and after the conferences, performing many functions on behalf of the Heads of State. They reported on the current conduct of campaigns and suggested future operations. They also conducted assessments of the enemy capabilities and possible strategies. However, they had to consider their strategies as a whole because this was a global war the likes of which had not been seen before. Consultation with the air, army and navy chiefs of staff brought together a great deal of information and views. For example, what may have been a strong amphibious operation from an army point of view may have been a problem from the naval chief of staff's point of view. All military factors had to be considered. Of course, the political circumstances then had to be considered by the Heads of State.

The Chiefs of Staff then had to decide if they were feasible from a manufacturing point of view; could they build the weapons and make the supplies needed? Then they had to consider what were usually the most difficult questions; how to get the men and equipment to the theatre of war and then how to get them into contact with the enemy. That involved consultations with a host of experts covering shipping, manufacturing and munitions.

During the final year of the war, the need for new military strategies waned but the need for political solutions increased and a Committee of Foreign Ministers of the three nations was formed to deal with them. The Foreign Ministers often had preliminary discussions on political matters, deciding areas of agreement and disagreement before they were referred to the Heads of State. In turn, the Foreign Ministers were sometimes called upon to look at new solutions raised by the Heads of State. The Foreign Ministers then set up subcommittees to investigate particular problems. One in particular was the Economic Subcommittee, which investigated the economic impact of decisions on a Europe in turmoil.

In case you are wondering what the editing of the raw material involved, it entailed several processes. A lot of procedural matter, which was necessary during the conferences but is irrelevant 70 years later, was removed. Items would sometimes be discussed but the only agreement made was to talk about it another day, the second discussion would then repeat the first before moving on. In such cases the original discussion is omitted while references to it are made in the footnotes.

The original text was written in the present tense and while it was relevant at the time, the conferences and events happened a long time ago and the text reads much better in the past tense. A lot of the text was also written in the passive form and changing it to the active form simplified and shortened sentences, making them clearer without changing the facts.

Altogether the editing process reduced the length of the text by about a third, without removing any relevant discussions. I hope it has clarified what are world-changing discussions between some of history's most interesting leaders. The plan was to concentrate on the facts, bringing out the important information, so the reader can understand the significance of the conferences.

Finally, the footnotes explain who people are, what codenames mean and what events are being discussed. They give background information to discussions if needed and facts and figures to illustrate the importance of the conversations. They also detail the outcome of decisions made, giving the reader the benefit of hindsight, something the men around the table did not have.

In the course of editing and researching this book I discovered far more about the Second World War and the establishment of the postwar world than I ever thought possible. It has been an enjoyable and thought provoking journey. I hope the reader enjoys the same journey of discovery.

The Arcadia Conference, 23 December 1941–14 January 1942

By December 1941 the war in Europe had been fought for two years. Germany invaded Poland on 1 September 1939 and two days later Great Britain and France declared war. Poland soon capitulated and a period known as the Phoney War followed, as Germany gathered its troops for an attack on France. It came on 10 May 1940 and in less than a month the shattered British Expeditionary Force was rescued from Dunkirk. An armistice was brokered between France and Germany on 22 June and the country was divided into occupied territories and Vichy France.

Great Britain was next but after the Luftwaffe failed to beat the Royal Air Force in the Battle of Britain, Nazi Germany turned its attention to the east. Elsewhere, the Italians invaded British-controlled Egypt in September 1940 and Greece in October. However, the Italians met their match in North Africa and the German Afrika Korps were sent to help in February 1941.

Germany, Italy, Hungary and Bulgaria dismembered Yugoslavia in the spring of 1941. The focus of the war changed when the Axis forces invaded the Soviet Union on 22 June 1941. The Red Army was severely mauled over the next six months but on 6 December it struck back at the gates of Moscow. The following day, Japanese planes attacked Pearl Harbor and the Philippines. Over the days that followed Germany and Italy declared war on the United States turning the European war into a global war.

On 14 December 1941 the Prime Minister and the British Chiefs of Staff sailed for the United States on HMS *Duke of York*. Four days later, several US War Department planners began working on a five-point agenda suggested by the British Chiefs of Staff:

a) Agreeing a basis for a joint strategy.
b) Immediate military measures and redistribution of forces to implement the joint strategy.
c) The allocation of forces to carry out the joint strategy.
d) A long-term programme for carrying out the strategy, including agreement on the forces to be trained and the equipment to be built.
e) The setting-up of joint committees and boards to implement the distribution, allocation and raising of troops, and the equipment they required, to implement the strategy.

Churchill and his Chiefs of Staff arrived in Washington on 22 December and they immediately started talking. The first formal meeting with the Chiefs of Staff took place the following day, with the second on 26 December. The Chiefs of Staff kept busy while the Prime Minister visited the Canadian Prime Minister in Ottawa and they had plenty of answers during the next two meetings on 1 and 4 January. The Prime Minister then rested in Florida for several days. There were two more meetings with the President and the Chiefs of Staff on 12 and 14 January.

The two heads of state were supported by Harry Lloyd Hopkins and Lord Beaverbrook; the Secretary of War and the Secretary of the Navy sometimes attended. The meetings gave the US Chiefs of Staff the opportunity to explain their reactions to the Japanese attacks. The meetings concluded with the President and the Prime Minister confirming their military decisions with a review of the conclusions of the Chiefs of Staff.

First Arcadia Meeting, 23 December 1941[1]

The President[2] had discussed general questions with the Prime Minister the previous night.[3] They had covered the initial situation, the present status, and relations with the Vichy Government[4] and with Portugal;[5] but no army and navy details had been considered. A declaration had been prepared covering their joint intentions and the point that no one power would make peace without an agreement with the associated powers. He noted his statement regarding the North Atlantic ferrying problem and the protection of the British Isles:

1)   The presence of a small number of American bombers in England would have an important effect on the French people and on Germany.

2)   The next thing was to have three American divisions take over defences in the North Atlantic.

3)   A mixed command in Iceland was a disadvantage and they should be regulated.[6]

Roosevelt and Churchill discussed the relative importance of the Azores versus the Cape Verde Islands.[7] They agreed it would be a mistake to send American troops into the Near East at this time. They also thought it was important to keep a flying route open across Africa, referring to the Brazilian situation[8] and the threat from Dakar.

Roosevelt said England would hold Singapore in the Southwest Pacific[9] while the United States would build up in Australia towards operations to the north, including the Philippines.[10] In China they were endeavouring to effect arrangements to utilize Chinese territory for air operations against Japan. Roosevelt felt

---

1   President Roosevelt and Prime Minister Churchill met their military advisors to discuss General Marshall's memorandum.
2   President Franklin D. Roosevelt (1882-1945), President of the United States from 4 March 1933 until his death on 12 April 1945.
3   Prime Minister Winston L. Spencer-Churchill (1974-1965), Prime Minister of Great Britain 1940-1945 and 1951-1955.
4   The Vichy government of France, headed by Marshal Philippe Pétain, which collaborated with the Nazis between July 1940 and August 1944.
5   António de Oliveira Salazar (1889-1970) was Prime Minister of Portugal from 1932 to 1974.
6   Iceland was Danish but when Germany invaded Denmark on 9 April 1940, Britain took action. Over 700 Royal Marines invaded on 10 May 1940 and before long there were 25,000 troops on the island. Defence of Iceland transferred to the United States on 7 July 1941 and before long there were 40,000 troops on the island.
7   The Azores were a Portuguese colony of small islands 930 miles west of Lisbon, (now the 'Autonomous Region of the Azores'). The Cape Verde Islands were another Portuguese colony of small islands 350 miles off the coast of West Africa.
8   President Getúlio D. Vargas (1882-1954) was the dictator of Brazil and there had been an increase in military and civilian trade with Germany. Hitler had invited Brazil to join the Axis in 1937 but Vargas had refused. Starting in 1940 the US had reached out to the Brazilians, offering large loans. Vargas would eventually break off diplomatic relations with Germany in January 1942 and, after naval attacks, declared war on Germany and Italy on 22 August 1942.
9   Singapore surrendered on 15 February 1942, at the end of the Japanese offensive through Malaya; 130,000 British and Commonwealth troops were captured during the campaign. Churchill called it "the worst disaster and largest capitulation in British history".
10   Japanese troops had landed in the Philippines on 8 December 1941. They would capture the main islands by 10 April 1942 and the final outpost on Corregidor on 8 May.

no attack on Japan was indicated now and would not be probable before March or April, unless Japan attacked Russia. Diplomatic representatives in Switzerland reported the Germans were planning an attack on the Spanish mainland on 27 December. Other sources of information did not indicate this.

Roosevelt then discussed the importance of Dakar,[11] with reference to the deficiencies in shipping, the lack of anti-aircraft ammunition and planes. He said the transports now being used by British troops (approaching Bombay) were to be used for what was most important at the time, British or American. He was not in favour of converting transports into airplane carriers.

Roosevelt then mentioned several questions which had been raised:

1) Were they to put PBY naval planes[12] in Ireland?
2) Could they induce South Ireland to make naval bases available?[13]
3) How soon could the commercial airlines take over the transportation to Foynes?[14]

Roosevelt said there was no reason to transfer North American flag ships to the British flag for Atlantic runs under the Lend-Lease.[15] Admiral Stark[16] wanted more time to consider this because of the scarcity of trained crews. The general question of supply and additions to munitions production were to be considered in one or two days by Lord Beaverbrook,[17] Knudsen,[18] and others. As an example of increases, he mentioned the doubling of plane production. He specifically mentioned planes, tanks, antiaircraft material and ammunition. He thought the overall estimate should carry on into 1944.

Churchill voiced his appreciation of Stimson's[19] statement and said the preservation of North Atlantic communications with the British Isles fully justified their trip, if nothing else. He referred to the Unites States' appreciation of the British present situation and their desire to help them in the Pacific and expected his Staff to be kept informed. He was very impressed by the American attitude during the immediate crisis, planning ahead in years instead of weeks.

---

11 Dakar is on the westernmost tip of Africa, and was in French West Africa; it is now the capital of Senegal.
12 Consolidated PBY Catalinas were American flying boats used for anti-submarine patrols, convoy escorts, patrol bombing and air-sea rescue.
13 Eamon de Valera (1882-1975), as head of the Republic of Ireland's government, saw that the country remained neutral throughout World War II (known in Ireland as 'The Emergency').
14 During the late 1930s and early 1940s land-based planes did not have the range to make Atlantic crossings. Foynes in Country Limerick, Ireland, was the last port of call for seaplanes and would become one of the largest civilian airports in Europe during World War II.
15 The Lend-Lease Act had been signed on 11 March 1941 and the United States shipped supplies to the United Kingdom, Soviet Union, China and Free French troops under the program. $50.1 billion (equivalent to $647 billion today) of supplies were shipped.
16 Admiral Harold R. Stark (1880-1972), Chief of US Naval Operations; nickname Betty.
17 Lord William Maxwell Beaverbrook (1879-1964), British Minister of Supply; nickname Max.
18 William S. Knudsen (1879-1948) worked for Roosevelt on war production. He was commissioned a Lieutenant General in the US Army In January 1942, the only civilian ever to join the Army at such a high rank. He worked as a consultant and trouble shooter for the War Department.
19 Secretary of State Henry L. Stimson (1867-1950).

Churchill said they were short of manpower and agreed with the proposal to replace the three British divisions in Ireland[1] with American divisions. He thought they should hold better trained American divisions for other tasks as it was unlikely they would be actively employed, so they could continue training. Their presence would have an excellent effect in many directions and he was highly pleased with the American willingness to go ahead with the relief.[2] He and Beaverbrook said they could furnish the Americans with anti-aircraft weapons. The tonnage issue was not elaborated on. Churchill wanted the Americans to take over Iceland, merely leaving airfields and shipping facilities sufficient for them to protect the northwest approaches.

North Africa

Roosevelt felt matters in North Africa were coming to a head quickly. French minds were fomenting over the United States entry into the war and the reverse in Russia.[3] Supposing the British pushed beyond Cyrenaica[4] to the frontier of Tunis in a month or six weeks, the situation would be 'pregnant'.[5] How would the Germans get into North Africa? Maybe that was the moment when the French or African people would not accede to the German demands. That was the moment for the British and the Americans.

Churchill said the British had 55,000 men with transports ready for shipment for such a purpose and they could be in Africa in 23 days. Two or three air squadrons from Malta[6] could also proceed to Bizerte.[7] Assuming French agreement, United States forces should land on the Moroccan coast by invitation at the same time. They could promise supplies, the assurance France's future would be protected at the peace table and conversely, she could be ignored entirely in the peace settlement.

Roosevelt commented on an expedition against Agadir and Casablanca.[8] Churchill said Spain[9] should not be irritated if possible. Assuming an invitation from the French, possibly the American expedition should move first but the British were ready to go into it abreast, or to follow, as might be deemed advisable in relation to French reaction. Their expedition was ready and he asked for it to be studied. Roosevelt agreed.

Roosevelt commented on the use of colonial troops against Dakar. It was very important to morale as it would give his country a feeling they were in the war; it would put American troops in active fighting across the Atlantic. Churchill agreed and said it was not wise to send American troops into the Middle East, it

---

1   In Northern Ireland.
2   The Prime Minister understood the limitation was tonnage and anti-aircraft weapons.
3   After six months on the retreat, Soviet troops stopped in front of Moscow. Fresh troops from Siberia counterattacked on 6 December and by 7 January the freezing and exhausted German troops began withdrawing. It was the turning point in the Eastern Front campaign.
4   Cyrenaica is eastern Libya.
5   Ripe; a moment of opportunity.
6   Malta is 75 miles south of Sicily and 200 miles east of Tunisia.
7   Bizerte at the northern tip of Tunisia, 50 miles north of Tunis.
8   Two ports on Morocco's coast; Agadir is 250 miles southwest of Casablanca.
9   Spain had just come out of a civil war (1936-1939) and was ruled by dictator General Francisco Franco (1892-1975), a regime close to Germany and Italy.

was better to deploy Indian Army and Australian troops there.[10] He also wanted to consider the question of landing troops in Norway in 1943.

The Secretary of War[11] spoke of the importance of timing the movements into Ireland and the Mediterranean, with relation to its effect on the French people. The American movement into Ireland would have a very definite effect on the French mind, facilitating a British and French movement into Tunis and Morocco. Churchill said the Mediterranean issue might arise at any moment.

Pacific

Churchill wanted his staff officers to have a full view of the situation in the Philippines, Hawaii and the West Coast.[12] Roosevelt interrupted to comment on the decentralization of aircraft plants.[13] Churchill offered Beaverbrook's services to show how to move them without interfering seriously with production.

Churchill said his staff felt Hawaii need not be a fleet base; it could be approached from so many directions that it should be supplied. It appeared it could be defended.[14] The United States had the greatest need in this emergency and required the supplies at the moment.

Churchill understood two new battleships would be ready in May and Admiral King[15] confirmed some time in March. Admiral Stark said there would be three and possibly four more battleships this year. Churchill continued, "We will do our best to look out for the Atlantic so far as battleships are concerned" and commented on the conditions of certain battleships. The *King George V*[16] and another very good one he had missed, the *Renown*[17]; the *Nelson*[18] had recently been torpedoed but it would be ready for action in February; and the *Rodney*.[19] He spoke of the *Anson*[20] being ready for service in May and another one later. Churchill said they might be able to help the United States restore superiority in the Pacific. While they wanted United States destroyers for Atlantic convoy duty, the distribution of battleships was open.

Syria and Persia

Churchill thought Hitler might feint at Russia in the spring and then thrust out in the southeast.[21] They would probably be able to hold the Nile Valley and they

---

10 Owing to the problems with the climate and terrain. It was also closer to the two countries, requiring fewer transport ships.

11 Henry Stimson.

12 The West Coast of the United States.

13 To stop aircraft plants being easy targets for bombing raids. Britain had experience of decentralising industrial plants during the Blitz.

14 Used as a supply base for operations in the Pacific.

15 Admiral Ernest J. King (1878-1956), Commander-in-Chief, United States Fleet, and Chief of Naval Operations (COMINCH-CNO).

16 HMS *King George V* (41) was a 1939 ship and the lead ship of the King George V class battleships and had been involved in the pursuit and sinking of the *Bismarck* in May 1941.

17 HMS *Renown* was a World War I era battle cruiser and had also been involved in the pursuit of the *Bismarck*; she spent most of 1940-1941 based at Gibraltar.

18 HMS *Nelson* (28) was a 1930 battleship and she had been torpedoed by an Italian airplane on 27 September 1941; she would be ready for action in May 1942.

19 HMS *Rodney* (29), *Nelson*'s sister ship, played a major part in the sinking of the *Bismarck*.

20 HMS *Anson* (49) was another King George V class battleship and she would be ready for action in May 1942.

21 Hitler had attacked Russia on 22 June 1941, codename BARBAROSSA, and his armies had captured most of the Ukraine and Belorussia. Churchill was correct because Plan BLUE was an advance southeast by Army Group South towards Stalingrad and the Caucasus.

now felt more secure because of improved conditions. Storms could come again but it would be a tremendous disaster to give up the Suez Canal; Turkey would go and Africa would be overrun. Churchill was not asking America to do anything in the region except furnish supplies and build up bases. They were making no request for an American presence in the Near East.[1] They hoped to have four armoured divisions, the 1st, 2nd, 7th and one other available there.

To sum up, Churchill said there were the questions of Iceland, Ireland, French North Africa and the holding of forces available for operations against small islands. He spoke of an in and out expedition against Dakar, leaving other troops to hold the place.[2] In the Far East, he spoke of possible retirement towards Johore and fighting there.[3] Singapore had to hold out. It ought to be a matter of six months before the Japanese could close in.[4]

The Burma Province[5] had been reinforced a fortnight earlier. 17th Indian Division, a very good division, was en route to Burma.[6] Wavell[7] was in command, having released Iran and Iraq to Auchinleck.[8] 18th Division was routed for Bombay and Ceylon in a convoy on American ships.[9] It might be possible for the Australians to move their troops closer to the theatre but it would take considerable tonnage. They would do their best to keep the Burma Road open.[10] Churchill said the Indian Army had twelve divisions. Churchill and Beaverbrook mentioned they had 25-pounders and other guns with ammunition the Americans could use in Ireland, however, they could not help them with rifles.[11]

24 December
First Combined Chiefs of Staff Meeting
The defence of the British Isles; the relief of British troops in Northern Ireland and Iceland; Greenland; the U-boat war; Naval Dispositions in the Atlantic; Guns for merchant ships; Deployment of heavy bombers; PBYs for the British;[12] Airplane carriers; The Portuguese and Spanish Islands in the Atlantic; British crews for American ships; West African Situation; the occupation of Africa; Brazil and the Curaçao-Aruba area; The Russian Situation; Spain and Portugal; Priorities in Expeditions; Troops for an attack on the Continent; The Bombardment of Japan.

---

1   The Near East as in Egypt. Eighth Army was just about to finish Operation CRUSADER, having advanced across Libya and relieved Tobruk.
2   Note: "I assume this was on a basis of some agreement with the French."
3   Johor is the area immediately north of Singapore.
4   It would be less than two months.
5   Burma (now Myanmar) is east of India and north of Malaysia.
6   Two of the 17th Indian Division brigades surrendered at Singapore six weeks later.
7   General Archibald Wavell (1883-1950) had just become Commander-in-Chief, India.
8   General Sir Claude J.E. Auchinleck (1884-1981) had just become Commander-in-Chief, Middle East; nickname the Auk.
9   Two of 18th Division's brigades reached Singapore on 13 January 1942 and surrendered four weeks later.
10 The supply route for all campaigns into northern Burma started at Ledo on the border with India.
11 For use by the American divisions destined for Northern Ireland. By supplying artillery it meant that the divisions took up less space on ships. The same had been done in World War I to get American divisions into battle as quickly as possible.
12 The Consolidated PBY Catalina American flying boat.

25 December
Second Chiefs of Staff Meeting[13]
The program of planning; Unified Command; Disposition of USS *Mount Vernon* (AP22); A Diversion of Reinforcements; Forces destined for the Far East; Priorities for Expeditions in the Atlantic; The Northwest African Project.

Roosevelt Meeting with his Chiefs of Staff
Although there is no record of the discussion Stimson recorded his feelings in his diary. Generals Marshall, Eisenhower and Arnold visited Stimson with a rather astonishing memorandum from the White House, concerning a meeting between Churchill and the President.[14] Roosevelt proposed to turn over reinforcements destined for MacArthur to the British.[15] The paper made Stimson extremely angry and he called Hopkins to say the President would have to accept his resignation if he persisted.

Hopkins thought it was very improper to discuss the matter of reinforcements with another nation while the fighting was going on. He was surprised and shocked by Stimson's reaction and spoke to the President in the presence of Churchill about the matter; they both denied any such propositions had been made. Hopkins called Stimson back and he read out the paper, which bore out his view.

Stimson met Marshall and Arnold, Secretary Knox, Admirals King and Stark, and Hopkins at the White House. After Roosevelt's had discussed reports and the campaign in the Far East, he "incidentally and as if by aside, flung out the remark that a paper had been going around which was nonsense and which entirely misrepresented a conference between him and Churchill." Stimson did not reply because the President had given up, if he had ever entertained, the idea of discussing the surrender of MacArthur's reinforcements.

"This incident shows the danger of talking too freely in international matters of such keen importance without the President having his military and naval advisors present. This paper, which was a record made by one of Churchill's assistants, would have raised any amount of trouble for the President if it had gotten into the hands of an unfriendly press. I think he felt he had nearly burned his fingers and had called the subsequent meeting to make up for it. Hopkins told me when I talked with him over the telephone that he had told the President to be more careful about the formality of his discussions with Churchill."[16]

26 December
The President met Lord Beaverbrook
The British asked the United States for ships, planes, ordnance and tanks.

---

13 Held in two parts.
14 Recorded by one of Churchill's assistants.
15 General Douglas MacArthur (1880–1964) would continue to fight in the Philippines until March 1942.
16 The incident illustrates the danger of the President and the Prime Minister talking off the record, when someone was taking notes. While the two Heads of State could clear up what they had said, rumours could quickly spread and the press could cause a lot of trouble if they published their private exchanges. None of the dinner meetings between Roosevelt and Churchill were recorded. The meetings with their Chiefs of Staff were.

26 December: Second Arcadia Meeting
Tonnage

Field Marshal Dill[1] reviewed the proposition of sending troops to North Africa, it was at a hypothetical stage and it depended on an invitation. There were studies of the forces required but the biggest problem was tonnage. Roosevelt asked if the convoys going to Great Britain would be impaired if the operation was undertaken. Marshall understood they would not.

Both the British and Americans were in agreement on the general plan and details were being worked out by a Joint Planning Committee. The tonnage situation meant they could not proceed with the North African Expedition[2] and relieve British units both in Iceland and Ireland at the same time. One question was how large a force was needed to appeal to the French to help the occupation and that was a political matter for the President and the Prime Minister to decide. Even so, the shipping should be collected and made ready for contingent use.

Roosevelt said the time for the movement was not ripe but it might be at any moment, or in three months time. They had to consider collecting transports for the movement of troops to Northern Ireland and the tonnage could be diverted to the North African move if necessary. General Marshall said this would be feasible. Churchill said the North African Expedition would have to be carried through if started, while the Ireland Expedition could be interrupted at any time without difficulty.

Churchill placed tremendous importance on the Ireland and Iceland reliefs, the French African Expedition and the situation in the Far East. He approved them all but the question was, how could they all be fitted in? The relief of Northern Ireland could be fitted in at any time. He recalled how two million men were shipped to France in a comparatively short time in the First World War.[3] What had become of the ships they used then? He was reluctant to take no for an answer because of shipping and asked why it was the bottleneck. Shipping could be obtained if they tried harder – he would be frightfully unhappy if he had to choose between expeditions. He also thought there was no possibility of an invasion of Great Britain before April.[4]

Roosevelt said they involved the State Department when it came to additional shipping. They had three large ships plying back and forth between North and South America[5] but they had not been considered for troop transportation because of the 'Good Will' feature.[6] They could utilize them, plus three other Grace Line boats if they had to.[7] Admiral Turner[8] said large ships could not go

---

1   Field Marshal Sir John G. Dill (1881–1944), Chief of British Joint Staff Mission in Washington DC having just been moved from the post of the Chief of the Imperial General Staff by Churchill.
2   What would become Operation TORCH in November 1942.
3   Following the United States entry into World War I in April 1917.
4   Owing to bad weather in the English Channel. Germany would have its hands full in Russia in April 1942.
5   They were the only access between South America and the United States.
6   The United States' 'Good Neighbour Policy' was Roosevelt's foreign policy towards Latin American countries. It was a policy of non-intervention, non-interference and of creating economic opportunities. This involved shipping of exports and imports.
7   The Grace Line (or W.R. Grace and Company) operated a shipping service between North and South America.
8   Admiral Richmond Kelly Turner (1885-1961), Assistant Chief of Staff to the Commander-in-Chief, United States Fleet.

into certain Irish ports or Casablanca. Churchill replied that as far as Ireland was concerned, they could go into the Clyde and the troops could be moved across.[9]

Roosevelt said Admiral Turner[10] should discuss turning over the South American ships to the State Department if it meant delaying moving troops to Ireland. Churchill said two million troops were moved in five months during 'the World War' while the present plan only called for the movement of ¼ million men in three months; he did not feel it was too great a problem to be solved. The Secretary of War[11] understood the movement of troops to Ireland was merely a passage of personnel and they would not require all their combat equipment.[12]

Lord Beaverbrook said the British were turning out ten cargo class ships each month while the conversion of five armed merchant ships to cruisers could be stopped. There was also the possibility of utilizing some large ships, such as the *Queen Mary* or even the *Queen Elizabeth*.[13]

Churchill said one solution might be to use a large battleship to carry troops. 10,000 men could be transported in a vessel moving at a speed of 25 knots. The only danger was it would be a large number of eggs in one basket and difficult to provide adequate protection for the battleship during part of its trip.[14] Roosevelt thought they might be able to dig up more ships in some way and gave instructions to consult Admiral Land[15] and Captain Vickery[16] of the Maritime Commission.

Roosevelt suggested sending small groups of men, possibly 50 to a boat, on the convoys carrying food and raw materials continuously back and forth between the United States and Britain. A 40-ship convoy could carry 2000 men.

Churchill asked if Marshall had looked into the artillery matter and he said they intended to send several key men who would be introduced to the British equipment. These cadres would be followed by personnel who would take over the equipment.

Churchill asked if rationing had been looked into. Marshall said it was still being studied. It was feasible to standardize some things but not all, since the Americans were strongly antagonistic to 'plum and apple' and not enthusiastic over British tea. Their World War experience had been both amusing and disturbing. Churchill was very anxious to get the American troops into Northern Ireland.

---

9   The ships were too big for Irish ports so they would have to dock on the river Clyde, Glasgow, and the troops would have to be shipped across the Irish Sea to Northern Ireland on smaller vessels.

10   Admiral Richmond K. Turner, recently appointed Assistant Chief of Staff to the CiC, United States Fleet, had the nickname Terrible Turner.

11   Secretary of State Stimson.

12   The troops only had to take their personal equipment because artillery was being supplied by the British.

13   RMS *Queen Mary* and RMS *Queen Elizabeth* would be converted into the largest troopships in the war, often carrying 15,000 men in a single voyage. They were also the fastest and often sailed out of convoy because it was difficult for U-boats to catch them.

14   Air cover did not protect the centre section of the Atlantic and the battleship would need a small fleet of cruisers and destroyers to protect it from U-boats.

15   Vice Admiral Emory S. Land (1879-1971), chairman of the US Maritime Commission, would oversee the design and construction of 4000 Liberty ships and Victory ships during World War II. Land would soon be Administrator of the War Shipping Administration (WSA), responsible for allocation of non-combatant ships.

16   Captain (later Vice Admiral) Howard L. Vickery (1892-1946), assistant to Vice Admiral Land.

The Far East

Roosevelt asked if everything was being done to get troops and planes to the Far East and Marshall said it was. There had been some delay in the movement of the *Kitty Hawk*[1] but planes and personnel could to be moved as fast as ships could take them.[2] Roosevelt asked if the unity of command had been solved because it was most desirable, since there were four forces involved in the Far East.[3] Marshall had raised the matter the day before. Roosevelt wanted it considered because he did not think they were getting the most out of the forces in the Far East.

Churchill said in some cases the troops were separated by 1000 miles and it was necessary for the person on the spot to play his own hand because a commanding officer could not be a true commander if he was so far away. He thought the disposition of forces should be taken care of in Washington, the clearing and disposing house. Churchill believed unity of command was all right where there was a continuous line of battle, such as existed in France in the First World War, but the situation in the Far East was not the same. Command would be best exercised from Washington.

Roosevelt said reports from the Far East were very sketchy. His idea was for the commander to have his headquarters in a plane and to go from place to place. Churchill wanted to discuss the matter with Roosevelt. He also said the British were very happy that the United States considered Germany to be the Number One enemy.[4]

Roosevelt said they were not getting good information from the Far East and asked if the naval commanders were working together. Admiral King said they were working in the sphere of action previously arranged. The Dutch and British were generally in the Singapore area while the United States forces were farther to the East. Churchill thought Admiral Phillips had worked out an agreement prior to his death.[5] Roosevelt asked if the Dutch had a good man in command of their forces. Marshal Dill replied there had been a recent change but he understood the new man was good.[6]

Admiral Pound[7] said Admiral Layton[8] reported cooperation between naval forces had weakened since the outbreak of war and he thought it could be improved. The Secretary of the Navy[9] said Churchill's belief that a scattered

---

1   USS *Kitty Hawk* (APV-1) was taking planes to Pearl Harbor to replace those destroyed in the Japanese air attack on 7 December; it was her maiden voyage.

2   The first P-40 Tomahawk single engine fighter planes had seen action with British Commonwealth squadrons in the Middle East and North African campaigns in June 1941. The P-40D was known as the Kittyhawk.

3   Referring to the huge area between Australia and China, including Burma, Malaysia, Philippines and the Dutch East Indies. It would soon become the American-British-Dutch-Australian (ABDA) Command area and commanded by General Wavell.

4   After all, Japan had attacked and captured American territories.

5   Admiral Sir Thomas S. V. Phillips, RN (1888-1941), commander of Z Force during the invasion of Malaya. Phillips was killed in action when his flagship, HMS *Prince of Wales*, was sunk on 10 December 1941. His nickname was Tom Thumb because of his short stature.

6   General Hein ter Poorten (1887-1968). He would have to surrender the island of Java on 8 March 1942 and spent the rest of the war in captivity.

7   Admiral of the Fleet Sir A. Dudley P. R. Pound, RN (1870-1943) First Sea Lord.

8   Rear Admiral Edwin T. Layton (1903-1984), Combat Intelligence Officer for the Pacific Ocean area.

9   William Franklin 'Frank' Knox (1874-1944), Secretary of the US Navy from July 1940 to April 1944.

command was an argument against unity of command, was wrong. This scattered condition was an argument for it.

Roosevelt said after the Japanese invaded Borneo, the Dutch and United States elements might attain success if they worked together; if they worked individually it would be impossible.[10] The Secretary of the Navy believed there should be one commander, working under a directive from Washington. The President said it was well worth studying. The conference adjourned.[11]

27 December
General Meetings
Churchill met General Marshall met to discuss Unified Command and the Far East situation.

Roosevelt met Secretary of War Stimson, General Marshall and Lieutenant General Arnold.

Secretary Hull met Prime Minister Mackenzie King.

Roosevelt and Churchill met Maxim Litvinov.[12]

Roosevelt and Churchill met the chiefs of various diplomatic missions.

Roosevelt and Churchill met the Latin American Chiefs of Mission.

Roosevelt met Maxim Litvinov a second time.
Third Combined Chiefs of Staff Meeting
Priorities for expeditions in the Atlantic; the Northwest African Project; American-British Strategy; Unity of command; US transports in the Indian Ocean.

29 December
Roosevelt met ex-Dutch Minister Loudon.[13] US Supply ministers met Lord Beaverbrook.
Fourth Combined Chiefs of Staff Meeting
Priorities for expeditions in the Atlantic; Northwest African Project; American-British Strategy; Reinforcements in the Southwest Pacific; Unity of Command in the Southwest Pacific; Communication with General Chiang Kai-shek.

30 December
Fifth Combined Chiefs of Staff Meeting
Direction in the ABDA area; Directive to the commander in the ABDA area.

31 December
Sixth Combined Chiefs of Staff Meeting
Withdrawal of US Marines from Iceland; US troops to Northern Ireland;

---

10 The Japanese invaded Borneo on 16 December and by the end of the month they had driven the garrison into the jungle; it eventually surrendered on 1 April 1942.

11 There was a dinner meeting between President Roosevelt, Prime Minister Churchill and Prime Minister Mackenzie King after the meeting.

12 Maxim Litvinov (1876-1951) ex-People's Commissar for Foreign Affairs; Litvinov was sacked by Stalin in May 1939 (the Germans refused to deal with him because he was Jewish) and replaced by Vyacheslav Molotov (1890-1896).

13 John Loudon (1866-1955) Dutch Minister for Foreign Affairs in the First World War.

American–British Strategy; Northwest African Project; Naval dispositions; Reinforcements for the southwest Pacific; Directive to the commander in the ABDA area.

1 January 1942: Third Arcadia Meeting

Roosevelt and Churchill met Litvinov. The President and the Prime Minister approved the directive to the Supreme Commander in the Far East.[1] There was a discussion about Burma's place in the war theatres. The propositions were:

1)   Burma as part of the Indian Command.
2)   Burma as part of Chiang Kai-shek's Theatre.[2]
3)   Burma as part of the ABDA Theatre.[3]
4)   Burma as an independent command.

Burma as part of the Indian Theatre would be impossible while Burma could not be a part of Chiang Kai-shek's command. Burma as an independent command would gum up the works for everybody, so there was only one other solution – to make Burma a part of Wavell's ABDA theatre, which was done. Roosevelt then OK'd the directive to the Supreme Command.

Churchill raised the question of the application of the ABDA agreement to the entire war. The powers of primary interest were the British and the United States because they controlled the sea. They supplied most of the weapons of war such as airplanes and munitions for ground forces. While Russia was doing a masterful job, their activities were in one theatre only, making them a secondary power rather than a primary power.

Churchill then asked about the dividing line between the operations directed from the west coast of the United States and the eastern operations directed from Australia.[4] He also asked about the dividing line between the Australian and New Zealand operations in the Fiji Islands.[5] Some provision had been made to take care of the area between the ABDA, Australia and New Zealand areas. Admiral King thought the Australian and the New Zealand Navies might take care of the triangle but the matter had to be considered.[6]

Roosevelt thought the French Fleet at Alexandria would probably prefer to be transferred to the United States rather than the British Flag.[7] Churchill replied the ships were not in very good repair and he preferred to keep them in cold storage in Alexandria. The only ammunition was in the holds of the ships and they had no repair parts. Roosevelt thought they ought to take them over if they wanted to come into the war. Admiral Pound said the French Admiral was

---

1   Approved with a few changes.
2   Generalissimo Chiang Kai-shek (1887-1975), Chairman of the National Government of China from October 1928 to December 1931 and August 1943 to May 1948.
3   The American-British-Dutch-Australian (ABDA) Command area.
4   The dividing line across the Pacific Ocean.
5   1100 nautical miles north of New Zealand's North Island.
6   The area was to the east of the ABDA command area.
7   Alexandria, Egypt. The French squadron included the battleship *Lorraine*, three heavy cruisers, a light cruiser, three destroyers and a submarine. They would be used by the Allies after May 1943 following negotiations with General Henri Giraud (1879-1949) of the Free French Forces.

loyal to Vichy and had made plans to scuttle his fleet and rebel against orders. Churchill had no objection if they wanted to move to the United States of their own free will.

Roosevelt then read a telegram from Bullitt[8] and Lyttelton[9] covering the invasion of Tunisia:[10]

1) French resistance was certain.
2) It would be impossible to get supplies in North Africa if the French in Morocco were hostile.
3) It was certain the Germans would send air units against any invasion troops.
4) The operation could not be a success unless the US movement into North Africa was simultaneous with the British invasion of Tunisia.
5) They believed there would be resistance against the US invasion unless French leaders were brought into the plan.

They recommended

1) Reinforcing the British in the Near East.
2) The United States to start action to create a force for Casablanca operations at once.
3) Start the necessary propaganda machinery to secure as much aid as possible in all countries prior to the invasion.
4) Provide for the taking over of the Canaries and the Azores.

Churchill said it was not necessary to take over the Canaries[11] and the Azores first but it was remarkable these two men, quite independent from the rest of them, agreed in principle with the British. Roosevelt said they had to consider the case while Churchill was in Washington.

It was agreed to make plans and start the movement of troops to North Africa and towards replacing the Marines in Iceland at once.[12]

Signing the Declaration by the United Nations, January 1, 1942

Roosevelt devised the name United Nations in December 1941 and the Declaration was agreed by 26 governments.[13] The text affirmed the signatories' perspective "that complete victory over their enemies is essential to defend life, liberty, independence and religious freedom, and to preserve human rights and justice in their own lands as well as in other lands and they were now engaged in a common struggle against savage and brutal forces seeking to subjugate the world."

8　William C. Bullitt (1891-1967), US ambassador to France; the only ambassador to remain in Paris after the German invasion of France in May 1940 (much to Roosevelt's annoyance, he wanted him to follow the French government to Bordeaux).
9　Oliver Lyttelton, 1st Viscount Chandos (1893-1972), Minister of State in the Middle East, based in Cairo.
10　Codename TOKYO.
11　The Canary Islands are a group of small Spanish islands 80 miles off the coast of Africa; opposite the border of Morocco and what is now the Western Sahara.
12　US Marines occupied Iceland after the British. They were needed for amphibious operations in the Pacific, so they were replaced by Army troops who still had to complete their training.
13　The Allied Big Four, nine American allies in Central America and the Caribbean, the four British Dominions, British India, and eight Allied governments-in-exile.

Roosevelt, Churchill, Soong[1] and Litvinov[2] signed the declaration together. Hopkins[3] signed it later.

2 January

Roosevelt and Churchill met their shipping advisors.

3 January

Roosevelt and Churchill met their war production advisors.

4 January: Fourth Arcadia Meeting

Roosevelt and Churchill met General Arnold,[4] commander of the US Army Air Forces. Roosevelt said there were one or two matters he wanted clarifying because certain Army-Navy actions depended on political considerations. Firstly, what would happen to the French, both in France and in West and North Africa? Plans also had to be prepared for any situation which might arise. The second consideration was the Brazil situation – at the present time they could do no more than guess – but it was of great importance to keep their lines of communication with Europe open.[5] Thirdly, they had to be prepared to take Army-Navy action if there were no additional developments in either area and the situation appeared to be working in their direction.

They had to work on the basis that the Ireland and Iceland expeditions were ready to proceed without delay, but in such a way they could be halted if other considerations intervened. They could not make a decision about Africa and Brazil but they had to be ready to take proper action if both situations blew up in their faces. They also had to be ready if nothing happened in either. The Secretary of War[6] was correct in saying they could take no chances on the possibility of their first major expedition being a failure. If the risk looked great, they had to think twice before they went ahead.[7]

Relief of British Troops in Northern Ireland

Stimson said the expedition to Northern Ireland had been agreed upon and the sailing date had been set. The question was, were the British ready for them? Field Marshal Dill said he would see all arrangements were made to receive the American troops. Stimson wanted to be certain they would not have to 'roost on the rocks' when they arrived. Churchill said the British would take full responsibility for accommodating them when they arrived. The three divisions being

---

1   Dr. Soong Tse-ven (1891-1971), China's Minister of Foreign Affairs.
2   Maxim Litvinov (1876-1951) Soviet Deputy Commissar of Foreign Affairs and Ambassador to the United States.
3   Harry L. Hopkins (1890–1946) was one of President Roosevelt's closest advisors and administrator of the Lend Lease program to the UK and the Soviet Union. He had first met Stalin in July 1941 and accompanied the President to the meetings at Cairo, Tehran, Casablanca and Yalta. He wanted to resign after Roosevelt's death but made one final visit to Moscow for President Harry S. Truman.
4   General Henry H. Arnold (1886–1950), nicknamed 'Hap', Commander-in-Chief of the US Army Air Forces.
5   The action to be taken in Africa depended on the Vichy French, while the Brazilian situation was still an unknown quantity.
6   Henry Stimson.
7   The political repercussions from a military failure would make Roosevelt's position very difficult.

relieved could be moved to England and it was of tremendous importance to begin this movement at once.

Roosevelt asked how many American planes were being sent to Northern Ireland. General Arnold replied, "Two pursuit groups; about 160 planes." Roosevelt asked if the British were going to withdraw their planes from Northern Ireland. Air Marshal Portal[8] replied they had none there. The presence of American planes in Ireland would be of great assistance to the British because they would not have to dispatch planes to Ireland if it was invaded.[9] He added accommodation would be provided for the air units.

GYMNAST

It was agreed the British plans for the occupation of Northwest Africa would be known as GYMNAST, while British plans with American participation would be known as SUPER-GYMNAST.[10] Stimson said the Army representatives had just met the Navy but the situation depended on political considerations:

1)   Would the French invite them to land?
2)   Would the Spanish be able to delay a German invasion of the Iberian Peninsula long enough to permit the occupation to be completed?

Roosevelt discounted any idea that the Spanish would offer opposition to the Germans.[11]

Stimson stated:

1)   The crucial matter was whether the American-British forces could establish a canopy of air protection until the landing was completed.
2)   This meant the employment of considerable carrier forces; a matter still under discussion.
3)   He was concerned the Germans could quickly establish themselves in the Iberian Peninsula and from there employ a dangerous force against the operation.
4)   The Germans were already on the ground.[12]
5)   The Germans had considerable knowledge of the situation in Africa.
6)   They needed a fifth column[13] in the North African area.
7)   The chances of the plan being a success would fade as time went on.

Roosevelt stated:

1)   If the Germans moved in immediately, it would take them as long to complete the occupation as it would the Allied troops.
2)   The Germans would have the same problems as they had.
3)   He did not think they could stand idly by and permit them to become established.

---

8   Air Chief Marshal Charles F.A. Portal, 1st Viscount Portal of Hungerford, RAF (1893–1971), Chief of the Air Staff.
9   The Germans had prepared Plan GREEN, the invasion of Ireland; some say it was real while some say it was a plan circulated to worry the British. Either way, it was never carried out.
10   The British-American invasion of French North Africa would later be called Operation TORCH.
11   The scenario under consideration is if the Wehrmacht invaded Spain, they could overrun airfields and the Luftwaffe would use them to attack the landing.
12   Meaning the Afrika Korps was already in North Africa.
13   A clandestine group who could capture or sabotage key installations.

Churchill said it had not taken the Japanese four months to get ashore in Luzon.[1] Admiral Turner replied Casablanca was the only suitable port and it was small; it would take each convoy two weeks to unload. There were other small ports along the coast but they could only furnish air protection for one of them. Churchill said opposition would undoubtedly be small if they could complete the movement in one month but they would be blasted out if it took four months.

Stimson said only one port was available; the force would have to land from an open roadstead elsewhere.[2] But he could not understand why it would take four months, even if the British were landing at Algiers, not at Casablanca.[3] Roosevelt asked if the Rio de Oro had been investigated.[4] Admiral Turner replied communications were very bad there and it involved a movement over 700 or 800 miles of desert road.

Churchill said the unloading time would have to be reduced if carriers were involved. If not, the Germans could assemble a strong U-boat concentration, and they could not afford to lose carriers at this time. Stimson said the carriers would be moving out without delay and two possibilities were being studied. One was to carry assembled army planes on the carriers, and the other was to use navy planes.[5]

Admiral Turner said carriers could not remain more than ten days in the Casablanca area and he believed two plans were possible. The first was to carry army planes and have them fly off the carrier and immediately establish themselves on landing fields adjacent to Casablanca. This plan did not appear to be feasible because the navy planes had to furnish the initial air canopy while the airfields were being established. They could then return to the carriers, something the army planes could not do. The army planes could land on the airfields once they had been established.[6]

Admiral King proposed using three carriers; one to carry navy fighters, the other army fighters, and the third, heavy army bombers. While the navy fighters were furnishing the canopy, the army bombers would carry supplies, such as gasoline, bombs, etc., to the airfields where they intended to base the army fighters. This would avoid a delay in moving supplies to these airfields. He thought it could be done in three weeks and then the carriers could move out.

Stimson said it had been of vital importance to have several dispersed fields in the Philippines,[7] while the basic necessity was to immediately establish a canopy of air protection as soon as the operation started. Churchill said the first wave should be accommodated in two or three days. Even if the Germans heard about

1   The first Japanese troops landed on Luzon, the largest of the Philippine Islands, on 12 December. But the main attack was made on 22 December as 48,000 troops landed at three points; another 7000 landed the following day.
2   In other words, across the beach, which required specialist landing craft to make the journey from ship to shore.
3   There would be three task forces; the Western Task Force landed at Safi, Casablanca and Mehdia; the Centre Task Force landed at Oran/Arzew; the Eastern Task Force landed at Algiers.
4   The Rio de Oro (Spanish for Gold River) was the coastal area south of Morocco, now the northern part of the Western Sahara. In other words, a landing in the Spanish possession was contemplated.
5   Part of the plan was to seize airfields early on, so carrier-based planes could transfer to them.
6   Army pursuit planes cannot land on the decks of a carrier.
7   If one was attacked, the planes could land at another.

the movement, it would take them at least ten days to move supplies and get ready for an attack from Spain.

Stimson asked how many ships could unload at Casablanca at once. Admiral Turner replied not more than ten or twelve. The first convoy would have 22 or 23 ships and it would take two weeks for each convoy to unload. While the Americans thought it could be done in ten days, the British believed two weeks. Roosevelt asked if it could unload in one week instead of two, if ordered to. Admiral Turner replied two weeks was the best estimate they could make.

Roosevelt said two weeks to completely unload one convoy seemed awfully slow for people who were in a hurry. Churchill suggested practising the landing at some place similar to the anticipated conditions to determine how long it would actually take. The general plans could go forward while this was being done. Marshall said amphibious exercises were being undertaken at the present time.[8] Roosevelt asked how long had it taken to unload and Admiral King replied 48 hours to unload 12,000 men without their heavy equipment.

Stimson quoted 'Hap' Arnold as saying German fighters could not operate over Casablanca from bases in Spain. Colonel Donovan's[9] organization was also attempting to get detailed information on the Casablanca area. Roosevelt said he, Churchill and the two Staffs knew very little about the region, while the possibility of the Germans moving into the area first had not been discussed.

Stimson could not understand the lack of military intelligence concerning this area. Admiral Turner said the Joint Planning Committee had a mass of information available, but certain factors could only be obtained by inspecting the ground.[10] Stimson said the essential points should be boiled down to whether it would be possible to get and then keep air control, and whether it would be possible to land and disperse on fields around Casablanca. Roosevelt asked about the sea conditions and Admiral Turner replied there was large surf with a heavy roll at that time of the year.

Roosevelt said while an invitation was in the lap of the gods,[11] they had to have the transports ready to sail within one week after it was received.[12] Marshal Dill said if they did, it would hold up transportation needed for other purposes. Admiral King said they could hold the ships in readiness.

Marshall said the present plans contemplated the Ireland relief expedition sailing on 15 January. If they wanted to initiate SUPER-GYMNAST and the convoy had already sailed, it would require three or four weeks to get it back. Meanwhile, an effort would be made to figure out every possible way to put across the North

8   An exercise had been planned for December 1941 at New River, North Carolina, but the U-boat menace forced it to be moved to the southern shores of Chesapeake Bay.
9   William Joseph Donovan (1883-1959), Coordinator of Information (COI) since June 1941, attempting to bring together intelligence from the Army, Navy, Federal Bureau of Investigation (FBI) and the US Department of State. In 1942 he became head of the new Office of Strategic Services (OSS). Nickname Wild Bill.
10 Mieczyslaw Slowikowski (codename Rygor, Polish for Rigour) headed Agency Africa, gathering information used to plan Operation TORCH.
11 An invitation by the French to land.
12 Note: "if it is received."

Africa expedition. Everyone agreed on the strategic importance of the expedition and they had to push for information and explore all possibilities.

Churchill attached tremendous importance to the 15 January movement because it would be a morale boost to the British to have American troops move into Ireland. He suggested the planners push ahead with their plans for SUPER-GYMNAST but not to divert shipping from the Ireland relief; they should not take real ships from real jobs. They could talk about the matter again in a few days. Admiral Pound said if the Ireland relief was undertaken, there would not be enough ships for SUPER-GYMNAST.

Churchill asked if some of the fast, large ships allocated for MAGNET[1] could sail unescorted. Admiral Pound agreed the risks were not too heavy, but the price was frightful if the ship was sunk. Admiral King believed a fast ship moving unescorted had a better chance of reaching its destination than slow moving convoys.

Stimson then made the following summary. Assuming the MAGNET force went ahead as planned, they should try and get 22 or 23 ships for the first convoy of SUPER-GYMNAST. If it became feasible to put SUPER-GYMNAST into operation, the MAGNET force would not be interfered with. The first expedition on SUPER-GYMNAST would consist of certain Marine and Air Corps units but would not contain armoured forces. Even if the British made a landing at Algiers, some armoured forces should be provided for the first SUPER-GYMNAST convoy.

Admiral Turner thought they could get enough ships for the first SUPER-GYMNAST convoy but they could not dispatch the second SUPER-GYMNAST convoy until the MAGNET ships returned. Churchill replied under no circumstances should they delay MAGNET. Admiral Pound said the *Queen Mary* would be ready in a week, while the *Queen Elizabeth*, the *Aquitania* and the *Normandie* would also be available.[2] Admiral King suggested sending a token force on the *Queen Mary* while leaving the other ships to wait on events. Admiral Turner replied they were all set for 21,000 men to sail to Ireland on 15 January.

Marshall said the troops were ready to go as fast as the ships were ready to carry them. Roosevelt said they could transport 6000 men on the *Queen Mary* for MAGNET and use the rest of the available space for cargo but the matter needed further study. He also asked for more information regarding Northwest Africa. Churchill then asked "Then you rule the *Queen Mary* can be used for this transportation?" The President agreed.

Admiral Pound asked if additional use could be made of American ships that had been turned over to the British for convoys from the Middle East to the Far East. Admiral King said the British could make emergency use of these ships. Admiral Stark said he would talk to Admiral Pound about the matter. The meeting adjourned.

---

1   MAGNET was the codename for shipping troops from the United States to Northern Ireland.
2   The four liners were stripped of their plush interior decor, painted navy grey for camouflage and fitted with degaussing coils to protect against magnetic mines. The *Queen Mary* often carried over 15,000 troops at a time and on occasions carried a special passenger, Colonel Warden, Prime Minister Churchill's codename when crossing the Atlantic.

10 January
Seventh Combined Chiefs of Staff Meeting
Operation GYMNAST; Directive to commander of ABDA area; General Wavell taking command of ABDA; Immediate assistance to China; Post Arcadia collaboration.

11 January
Eighth Chiefs of Staff Meeting
Command and situation in the ABDA area; Port Darwin in the ABDA area; Defence of the island bases between Hawaii and Australia; US forces in Northern Ireland.

11 January
Roosevelt and Churchill met their war production advisors.

12 January
Ninth Combined Chiefs of Staff Meeting
Shipping for reinforcing the Far East; Defence of the island bases between Hawaii and Australia.

12 January: Fifth Arcadia Meeting
SUPER-GYMNAST
Churchill understood the Staff had produced a timetable which had been approved in principle. However, it looked as if Rommel[3] might get away but there would be a determined chase if he was defeated.[4] The British were getting a new armoured brigade into the Near East and there would be a battle soon but information had been received about a convoy arriving at Tripoli with additional German materiel. It was possible the date the Germans would be pushed back to Tripoli would be delayed, but it gave more time for the completion of SUPER-GYMNAST.

Roosevelt said there was more time available politically and there was a tendency on the part of Vichy[5] to say no to German demands. He had reports about a growing number of French Army officers asking whether their overtures would be accepted if they did something. Admiral Darlan[6] had asked if he would be accepted into a conference and the answer had been, not under the present circumstances, but the situation would change if he brought the French Fleet over to the Allies.

However, more time existed for SUPER-GYMNAST and it was desirable to get a settled timetable that fitted into the negotiation timetable. The Germans

---

3   Field Marshall Erwin J. E. Rommel (1891-1944), Commander-in-Chief of the Afrika Korps; nickname the Desert Fox.
4   Operation CRUSADER was just coming to a close. Eighth Army had advanced 500 miles since 18 November, from the Egyptian border across Libya to El Agheila.
5   The Vichy government of France that collaborated with the Nazis.
6   French Admiral Jean Louis Xavier François Darlan (1881-1942) and Marshal Henri Pétain's deputy in the Vichy Government. The majority of the French fleet was in North Africa and there were fears it could fall into German hands.

would know as soon as the negotiations commenced and they should have the Army aboard ships ready to land in a week or ten days.[1]

Roosevelt then asked about transports. Marshall said the Staffs had reached a tentative agreement about the reduction of the schedule of troops to Northern Ireland the night before. They had also agreed a reduction of cargo ships available for the expedition, which brought up the question of quarters and supplies for the troops. Churchill said there was no question about the quarters; one British Division was being moved out of Northern Ireland and the British would have quarters ready for the American troops.

Marshall briefly explained the substance of the Joint Chiefs of Staff plan as follows: 21,800 American troops would sail from the East Coast on 20 January, set to arrive in the ABDA area around 14 February. The convoy would consist of 10,000 ground troops for New Caledonia, which, with the artillery brigade now in Australia, would furnish approximately a division for New Caledonia.[2] The remainder of the expedition would consist of engineers and other ground service troops for the bombers now arriving in the ABDA area. Also moving out were 20 cargo ships carrying 250 pursuit planes, 86 medium bombers, 57 light bombers, 220 ship tons of cargo, and 4½ million gallons of gasoline. The aircraft were to replace attrition.

Marshall said the following changes had to be made to permit the expedition to depart. The troops scheduled for Iceland on 15 January would be reduced to 2500 in the first MAGNET convoy; the 16,000 scheduled for Ireland would be reduced to 4000. The *Queen Mary* could carry 7000 troops to Ireland on 1 February and then transport whatever British troops were desired to the Middle East. Three navy transports[3] being used to transport troops from the Middle East to the Far East via the Suez Canal would be available to move British troops over the same route. In addition, 4400 more troops could be moved to Ireland on the *George Washington*[4] early in February. This procedure would result in approximately 24,000 troops being in Ireland by 25 February. However, the plan entailed the following:

1)   Cancellation of the arranged movements to Ireland and Iceland.

2)   Confusion in the port of New York, due to the necessity of unloading ships.

3)   The utilization of the *Kungsholm*, which was being held for the State Department.[5]

---

1   It had been figured that a period of three weeks grace could be obtained from the time the Germans commenced their movement into Spain.

2   New Caledonia is a group of islands 750 miles east of Australia's northeast coast. It was a French colony in 1941.

3   USS *Mount Vernon* (AP22) disembarked British and Commonwealth troops at Singapore on 13 January. USS *Wakefield* (AP21) and USS *West Point* (AP23) did the same on 29 January 1942. They were captured by the Japanese only a month later.

4   The British had taken over the ageing steam powered *George Washington* on 29 September under Lend Lease. However, her boilers could not drive her and she was returned to the US War Shipping Administration in April 1942.

5   US Authorities seized the Swedish-American Line passenger liner SS *Kungsholm* on 12 December 1941 and operated it as a troopship under the name *John Ericsson*.

4) Difficulties in crating the medium bombers scheduled for the ABDA convoy.

5) Two vessels needed on the South American route

6) The loan of three British ships.

Roosevelt asked about refuelling the ABDA convoy and Admiral King replied it would not be necessary en route. Marshall said another serious consideration was that the ABDA convoy resulted in a 30% reduction of lend-lease[6] to Russia for four months and a reduction of lend-lease materiel going to Basra.[7] Roosevelt said the plan sounded good.

Churchill asked how the *Queen Elizabeth* and the *Aquitania* were going to be used.[8] Marshall replied the *Queen Elizabeth* was being used for a third convoy to the Far East, involving the movement of three anti-aircraft regiments. The following troops were also being moved from the West Coast; 7000 on 12 January; 14,000 on 30 January and 11,000 early in February. It was understood the *Aquitania* would not be available until the end of February.

It would take three weeks to assemble the freight boats for the ABDA convoy and the American troops would arrive on 20 January before their equipment. This involved some complications in the convoy but it was the best arrangement they could make.

Roosevelt asked about troop accommodations in New Caledonia. Marshall said there would be little difficulty in finding shelter for the troops due to the tropical climate; they could take tents.

Churchill said the plan would result in some confusion and the delay of shipments to Russia would undoubtedly cause disappointment. He asked if the Chiefs of Staff had discussed the plan. Marshall replied they had and the Russian question had been brought up. But there was no use sending troops to the ABDA area without their equipment. If a cut became necessary, the New Caledonia increment should be eliminated. It was of urgent necessity to send air reinforcements.

Admiral Pound said the Joint Chiefs of Staff had discussed the matter. The people in London were working on a slightly different shipping schedule for the American transports to the Middle East, to the Far East, and the possible use of the *Queen Mary* from England to the Middle East. However, an answer could be received by noon the next day.

Roosevelt asked if the occupation of New Caledonia was off the agenda if they carried out their Russian promises. Marshall could not be sure, but if anything was to be spared, the New Caledonia occupation should be first. Hopkins[9] noted 30% of the shipping to Russia involved only seven ships, and they should

---

6   Lend-Lease was a United States program of supplies to her Allies, including Britain, the Soviet Union, China and France. It was signed into law in March 1941 and lasted until the end of the war. Supplies were sold to Britain at a heavy discount at the end of the war.

7   Supplies for the British and Commonwealth troops engaged in Iraq. They were delivered to the port of Basra, at the head of the Persian Gulf.

8   RMS *Queen Elizabeth* was a 1938 luxury liner while RMS *Aquitania* was a 1913 Cunard liner.

9   Harry Hopkins (1890-1946), Roosevelt's chief diplomatic advisor and trouble shooter; also Roosevelt's unofficial emissary to Prime Minister Winston Churchill.

be able to find seven ships, even if it involved stopping the shipment of some reserve equipment to England. It should not be too difficult to locate seven ships amongst the 1200 merchant ships they had available.

Admiral King asked if Russia could absorb the shipments if Archangel[1] was closed and Roosevelt replied the Russians denied it was closed. Admiral Stark said the main question was which was more important: the 30% reduction of lend-lease to Russia or immediate reinforcements for the Far East?

Churchill said the Far East and the Russians should take priority over other things and the Ireland and Iceland reliefs were secondary. He was sorry about reducing MAGNET, but he understood the need for it.

Marshall said an early decision had to be reached, so the MAGNET shipment could be delayed. General Arnold[2] noted it was no use sending planes to the Far East without their ground service crews. Admiral Pound said the only immediate commitment was the unloading of the MAGNET convoy. Marshall replied if they unloaded it, they had to load the Australian convoy immediately. Churchill asked whether this matter had been taken up with the British Chiefs of Staff and Marshall replied they had worked most of the night together on it.

Roosevelt liked Marshall's program, if only some means could be found to take care of the Russians. Hopkins did not think Marshall should be held up by the necessity for Russian lend-lease and suggested directing Admiral Land to find six or seven more ships a month for Russia.

Lord Beaverbrook[3] said he would be very sorry to see ships diverted from the Atlantic because of the increased strain that would result. It was important to maintain the supply of certain items to England to keep up production schedules; but he also hated to stop the Russia shipments.

Roosevelt agreed there might be unfortunate repercussions in Russia if they let them down at the very time they were pinched, as they were at the time. He asked how important the occupation of New Caledonia was. Admiral King said the island was on the line of naval communication and a potential target for Japanese occupation.[4] Roosevelt asked if it would be easy to re-conquer. King replied no island was easy to re-conquer once it had been occupied. Arnold said as far as flying routes were concerned, both New Caledonia and the Fiji Islands could be jumped if necessary.

King said the urgent question was assistance to the Far East and Churchill agreed it should come ahead of New Caledonia. Roosevelt replied that only the seven cargo ships were holding up Marshall's plan. Hopkins asked if Marshall's plan would be approved if Russia were not involved. They agreed it would be.

Hopkins then suggested Roosevelt and Churchill take the responsibility of reducing lend-lease materiel to Russia rather than holding up Marshall's plan. Churchill suggested keeping the ships on the Russian run and finding other ships to make up the deficit. He asked if the Chiefs of Staff agreed on the mechanics of

---

1   Archangel (now Arkhangelsk) is on the north coast of European Russia. Closed due to the winter ice.
2   General Arnold, commander of the US Army Air Force.
3   Lord Beaverbrook, British Minister of Supply.
4   The line of communications between the United States, Australia and the whole ABDA area.

the plan. Admiral Pound said it had to be approved in London, because they had been working on a slightly different arrangement. Roosevelt asked Hopkins[5] if he could get enough ships to take care of the Russians. Hopkins was sure it could be done if he explained the situation to Admiral Land and Salter.[6] Marshall said Land had told him they were behind in furnishing materials under their present protocol agreement with Russia earlier in the day.

Churchill suggested accepting the plan and making a search for the seven ships. He also asked if the British were behind in their deliveries to the Russians and Beaverbrook replied they were in some items but he expected they would catch up. Marshall added what they were doing in the Far East would help the Russians anyway.

Churchill said there was a possibility, if Japan continued to succeed in the Far East, of a Pan-Asiatic movement including all the brown and yellow races, which might complicate the situation. He also said a symbolic landing in Ireland would be satisfactory but he hoped materiel for England would not be piled up on the docks in New York awaiting ships.

Beaverbrook said additional shipping had been scraped up for convoy movements to the ABDA area and he thought more could be found. Churchill replied the ABDA plan made no provision for SUPER-GYMNAST. Marshall said no ships arranged for combat loading were being used for ABDA.

Roosevelt asked when could they do SUPER-GYMNAST if they went ahead with the ABDA plan and found enough shipping for Russia. Churchill said the Joint Staffs had already established some planning days would be required. If 7 January was established as the beginning of planning, D-Day[7] would be 4 February and the earliest arrival in Casablanca would be 23 March. Marshall replied the shortage was not in troop carriers but in cargo carriers.

Churchill said the Staffs should get data about the effect of this plan on GYMNAST. Admiral King said for purposes of a round calculation, the date which the ships could be available for GYMNAST would be determined by the turn around between the East Coast[8] and Australia; approximately three months. It would set back the possible date of loading for GYMNAST to about 15 April. Admiral King also said 15,000 combat loaded troops[9] could be embarked for GYMNAST without delay at any time. Churchill said the whole problem was to get planes to the Far East. Arnold agreed it was the only way to stop the Japanese advancing south. Roosevelt then said; "We approve General Marshall's plan. We will make Beaverbrook and Hopkins find ships and we will work on SUPER-GYMNAST at the earliest possible date."

---

5   Hopkins was also administrator of the Lend Lease program to the UK and the Soviet Union.
6   Admiral Emory S. Land, US War Shipping Administrator, and Sir Arthur Salter (1881-1975), head of the British Shipping Mission, representatives of the United States and Great Britain on the Combined Shipping Adjustment Board.
7   D-Day was the day loading would commence.
8   East Coast of the United States, including the passage of the Panama Canal in Central America.
9   Combat loaded meant armed and ready to step ashore and fight.

Air Marshal Portal[1] said the Chiefs of Staff had agreed the ABDA movement would not interfere with the movement of pursuit ships to the Far East. Churchill said the Staff had to check on the impact of the plan on GYMNAST and establish the earliest possible date. They also had to investigate what would be available for the expedition if an invitation arrived suddenly. The meeting adjourned.

13 January
Tenth Chiefs of Staff Meeting
Post Arcadia collaboration; Atlantic projects early in 1942; Operation SUPER-GYMNAST.

14 January
Eleventh Chiefs of Staff Meeting
Post Arcadia collaboration; Reinforcing the Far East; Operation SUPER-GYMNAST.

14 January: Sixth Arcadia Meeting
Roosevelt thought a public statement about the conference accomplishments should be issued at an appropriate time in both Great Britain and the United States.[2]

New Agencies for American-British Collaboration
Roosevelt was opposed to creating additional boards but it was desirable to create certain agencies to ensure a more efficient prosecution of the war. One would be a Combined Raw Materials Board, to allocate raw materials.[3] Twenty-six nations were involved and he did not want the smaller nations to feel they were being left out. Lord Beaverbrook said the British had already nominated Sir Clive Baillieu[4] as the British representative; Roosevelt and Hopkins had not decided on the American representative.

Roosevelt said the Board would have an appropriate sized staff to ensure efficient planning and the speediest development of raw materials. It would make recommendations to the heads of government in collaboration with the other nations. The Board would also confer with Russia and China. Admiral King asked who the Board would make recommendations to. Beaverbrook replied, "The President and the Prime Minister."

Roosevelt said it was proposed to establish an Anglo-American Combined Shipping Adjustment Board,[5] with agencies in London and Washington. The

---

1　Air Chief Marshal Portal, RAF, Chief of the Air Staff.
2　The announcement was made after Churchill arrived back in England, on 17 January.
3　The Combined Raw Materials Board would source raw materials to meet the needs of the war industries, which in turn had to meet the requirements of the armed forces and civilians. Foodstuffs, oil and metal ores are just a few items that had to be sourced around the world and then shipped to the factories.
4　Sir Clive L Baillieu, 1st Baron Baillieu (1889-1967), Director-General of the British Purchasing Commission in Washington from 1941 to 1942, as Head of the Raw Materials Mission in Washington and as Representative on the Combined Raw Materials Board from 1942 to 1943.
5　The Combined Shipping Adjustment Board would unify the work of the US War Shipping Administration and the British Ministry of War Transportation to maximise use of shipping.

Board's executive power would be exercised by the United States Maritime Commission,[6] in coordination with the British Minister of War Transportation.[7] The Board would also confer with Russia, China and other interested nations.

Roosevelt said the assignment of munitions was a primary interest and all munitions should be placed in a common pool. Marshall and Arnold believed the Board should be a subcommittee of the Joint Chiefs of Staff Committee.[8] It would have a civilian chairman[9] and would advise on all assignments and priorities of finished munitions.

Beaverbrook asked who would advise him on apportioning.[10] Roosevelt replied it would be handled the same as the arrangements for the ABDA area while disagreements could be referred to the President and the Prime Minister. Beaverbrook asked who to speak to obtain goods for Russia. Roosevelt said the Joint Chiefs of Staff, except he would nominate a civilian chairman. The munitions subcommittee would invite comments on their allocations from representatives of the State Department and production agencies in both countries.

Beaverbrook asked where the decision would rest if he went to the British civilian chairman. Churchill said the two committees would discuss the matter through the Chiefs of Staff, although their arrangement would be different due to the difference between the British and American set-ups. Admiral Pound asked who would be the British representatives in Washington and Churchill replied they would be members of the Combined Chiefs of Staff, Hopkins as chairman.

Marshall said the Prime Minister's suggestion was not his understanding. He understood the Munitions Allocation Committee would deal purely with munitions while its civilian chairman would report to the Joint Chiefs of Staff. It would have Army, Air and Navy representatives, plus British representatives, with Hopkins as chairman. Stimson felt it was important that Great Britain had representatives on the committee, so the economic resources of the two countries would be combined.

Stimson said the War Department had been dealing with ten or twelve buyers from foreign nations before the Lend–Lease Act was passed.[11] He understood this proposed plan was one step nearer to ensuring allocations would optimize the associations with their Allies.

Hopkins said the movement of tanks and airplanes, even if they were not given to American troops, was an operational problem and a subject for the Joint Chiefs of Staff. The munitions committee would recommend the distribution of munitions and report through the Joint Chiefs of Staff to the President. The Joint Chiefs of Staff could alter or throw out its recommendations. However, room was left open for the agencies to appeal to the President.

---

6   The United States Maritime Commission had been set up in 1936 to formulate a merchant ship building program to replace aging World War I era ships belonging to the US Merchant Marine.

7   Frederick Leathers, 1st Viscount Leathers (1883-1965), Minister of War Transport 1941-1945.

8   The US Army and Navy Munitions board needed a committee to decide where munitions would be sent to around the world.

9   One group operating in London and one in Washington.

10   Deciding where to send ammunition, because each area commander would be asking for more than could be supplied.

11   The Lend Lease Act was signed on 11 March 1941.

Marshall did not want to duplicate the Chiefs of Staff Committee in London; the purpose was to set up a command post in Washington. At the present time, strategy was dominated by materiel,[1] and proposals regarding materiel should come from the same source.[2] The President or the Prime Minister could reverse the decision if the Chiefs of Staff did not appreciate the munitions committee's recommendations. It was illogical to have an agency independent of operations, controlling the basic material required for successful operations.[3]

Churchill said the London Committee would be able to survey available materiel, and as Minister of Defence,[4] he could tell the British Staff what line to take. Roosevelt said the reason for having the civilian chairman was to permit Beaverbrook and similar individuals to raise the political viewpoint on certain allocations.

Admiral King said if the Chiefs of Staff had representatives in London, it would duplicate the present set-up and that was not the intended idea. Marshall replied there would be a British committee in London. A similar committee would exist in the United States and the two would forward their recommendations to the Joint Chiefs of Staff. Marshall did not see how it would be possible to conduct a war properly with two independent agencies making allocations. Churchill thought the military representatives would take the purely strategic view.

General Marshall said there are two lots of munitions – British and American – under the present situation and they should be merged. Churchill suggested trying out the new method of handling allocations for a month without an announcement. Roosevelt suggested announcing the pooling of resources and the exchange of information on materials but not the procedure. Beaverbrook said the system should be trialled first because he envisaged many difficulties in England.

Churchill said the British were counting on lots of allocations from the United States and wanted to know what the situation was. They would be deeply interested in the margin or balance over and above 80% of the munitions. Marshall said there was more to the matter than this 15 or 20 per cent margin, actual requirements had been the basis for most allocations. For instance, many American units had been kept below full equipment so it could be used where it was needed more urgently. At the present time, the Army was planning to increase the number of divisions while only supplying them with about half of their equipment. Roosevelt stated, "We will call it a preliminary agreement and will try it out that way."

Both Churchill and Admiral Pound agreed the system should be given a trial. Admiral King was concerned the Chiefs of Staff Committee in Washington would be duplicated in London. It was agreed the proposed system did not involve this.

---

1   They had the troops but munitions were scarce and once made, they had to be shipped to a theatre.
2   Strategy around the world could not be agreed until the Chiefs of Staff knew if the equipment, munitions and supplies were available.
3   On the other hand, the Munitions Allocation Committee had to understand the Chiefs of Staff plans for strategy, so that they sent ammunition to the right commands.
4   Churchill was both Prime Minister and Minister of Defence.

Communications with London

Roosevelt wanted to work out a better system of communications with London. Marshall said the Signal Corps had advised him there was no way secret messages could be sent by telephone. The so-called scrambler system merely assured privacy. Admiral Stark added the longest cable line for telephone purposes was between Miami and Cuba.[5]

Roosevelt thought it should be possible for the two Governments to have the full use of one cable. Marshall replied one trunk cable was under lease at present. Roosevelt said the Government could not be cut in on if it had its own line. Marshall replied complete secrecy would be difficult because the transmission had to go through the hands of a certain number of individuals. He would check and advise the President at the earliest practicable date.[6]

Roosevelt also said a study should be made into improving communications between Washington and London. Admiral Stark said direct connections existed but messages could not be sent by telephone. Air Marshal Portal replied the British were working on an instrument which would ensure secret radio telephonic transmission and he felt it would be available in four months.

GYMNAST

Churchill asked if there was anything further to be said about GYMNAST. Dill said the merchant shipping necessary for GYMNAST operations would be delayed until May under the present plans. Marshall estimated there would be enough shipping to send another 12,500 men from the United States,[7] four weeks after GYMNAST's D-Day, regardless of the ABDA reinforcement. Roosevelt asked if the operation would be put into effect if the political situation could be kept stable until May. It was agreed it could be.

Roosevelt said if the Germans should move into the GYMNAST area in the interim, the thing to do would be to utilize whatever forces were available.[8] Churchill replied they should make a 'slash' with whatever forces were available and operate on a guerrilla basis if necessary.[9] The Secretary of the Navy[10] suggested taking advantage of the delay to soften up the GYMNAST area. Roosevelt said he had taken steps to accomplish this. The meeting adjourned.

Roosevelt and Churchill Dinner Meeting, 14 January 1942[11]

On the last evening of Churchill's visit Roosevelt, Churchill and I [Hopkins] had dinner together. They finalised the agreements on shipping raw materials and the

---

5   It is 90 miles from the end of Florida (Key West) to Cuba. It is nearly 3500 miles from Cornwall, England, to Washington DC.
6   It was a case of balancing secrecy with availability.
7   In addition to the original 12,000 to go combat loaded.
8   If Rommel moved his Afrika Korps troops into Algeria or Morocco.
9   The No.1 Long Range Patrol Unit had been operating on a guerrilla basis since July 1940 and in November it was renamed the Long Range Desert Group. Patrols operated behind enemy lines, keeping a watch on Axis movements and working with men of the Special Air Service, carrying them on hit and run raids.
10   William F. Knox.
11   Notes by Harry Hopkins.

allocation board. It was agreed the text would not be given out but the President would release a general statement at the appropriate time.

Roosevelt and Churchill reviewed the work of the past three weeks and Churchill expressed his warm appreciation of the way he and his associates had been treated and his confidence that great steps had been taken towards the unification of the prosecution of the war. Churchill had not decided whether to fly from Bermuda or to go in a battleship. The President did not know until later that Churchill had flown to England.

They were supposed to leave at 20:45 but it was 21:45 before the President and I drove with Churchill to his train to Norfolk, Virginia. A special train had been put on the siding at Sixth Street. The President said goodbye to Churchill in the car and I walked with him and put him on the train and said goodbye to him, Pound and Portal. On the way back, the President made it clear he, too, was very pleased with the meetings. There was no doubt he had genuinely grown to like Churchill and I am sure Churchill equally liked the President.

Note: Arcadia Informal Meetings

The Prime Minister stayed in White House guest quarters during the Arcadia Meetings and had many private meetings with Roosevelt; they always lunched together with Harry Hopkins. No formal minutes were taken and while many of the subjects were covered in formal meetings, a few were not. For example:

1) Opening a second front on the continent in the summer of 1942 if the Russian front was in serious difficulties.
2) Maintaining their position against the Soviet Government.
3) Sending relief supplies to the Greek people.
4) India's political situation.
5) Cooperation on atomic energy research.

Post Arcadia Meetings: 23 January to 19 May

While the Arcadia meetings had addressed immediate problems, they raised more questions than they answered. The Combined Chiefs of Staff had plenty to study and they held twenty meetings over sixteen weeks, determining a world-wide strategy for the prosecution of the war. The meetings were held in the Federal Reserve Building in Washington DC. The following list illustrates the wide range of topics discussed.

23 January: First Meeting
General Wavell's appreciation of the ABDA area; Naval reinforcements for ABDA area; Situation in the Philippines area; Free French forces in the Pacific; Employment of American Volunteers Group (the AVG or Flying Tigers) in Burma and China; SUPER-GYMNAST; Division of the Western Atlantic Area; US Transports in the Indian Ocean; Supplies for the Dutch in the ABDA Area.

27 January: Second Meeting
Naval Reinforcements for the ABDA area; Anzac area; Modified SUPER-GYMNAST; Support of Chiang Kai-shek; Defence of Tahiti; Inclusion of Darwin in the ABDA area; Supplies for the Dutch in the ABDA area; Malaya and

New Guinea Situation; Employment of AVG in Burma and China; Russian attitude to Japan; Allocation of United States Heavy Bombardment Groups.

3 February: Third Meeting
US Naval Operations in the Western Pacific; Naval Reinforcements for the ABDA Area; Representation of the British Dominions and Dutch; Relations with Vichy France; Possible Japanese action against Australia and New Zealand; Defence of northeast approaches to Australia; Review of the ABDA area; Munitions Assignments Board; Movement of US troops to North Ireland; Cooperation with Generalissimo Chiang Kai-shek; Naval Action in the Pacific; Portuguese Timor; Communications between General Wavell and Chiang Kai-shek.

10 February: Fourth Meeting
Appointments of British flag officers; Collaboration between United Nations; Combined Military Transportation Committee; Bolstering Chinese morale; Employment of air forces against Japan; Air Requirements for Australia and New Zealand; Extra fighter aircraft for the Dutch East Indies; Situation in the Dutch East Indies; Naval Command in the ABDA area; Mining the Torres Strait.

17 February: Fifth Meeting
Situation in the ABDA and Anzac areas; Armed forces in the ABDA and Anzac areas; Naval reinforcements for the ABDA area; Defense of West African air route; Predicted Merchant Shipping Losses; Munitions priorities; Tank production; Deploying two USAAF Heavy Bombardment Groups to the United Kingdom.

18 February: Sixth Meeting
Situation in the ABDA area.

21 February: Seventh Meeting
Situation in the ABDA area; Excluding Burma from the ABDA area; Command in New Caledonia.

23 February: Eighth Meeting
Situation in the ABDA area; Transferring British Submarines to the Eastern Fleet; Policy for Disposition of US and British Air forces; Madagascar; Command in New Caledonia; Combined Meterological Committee.

3 March: Ninth Meeting
Situation in the ABDA area; Demarkation of strategic areas in the Japanese War Zone; Deploying heavy bombers to Australia; Air transportation units for Burma; Assignment of munitions, Ground forces; Defence of the Caucasus.

7 March: Tenth Meeting
Bases in the Indian Ocean; Control and commands in the Anzac area; Personnel Shipping; Deployment of air forces.

10 March: Eleventh Meeting
Situation in the Dutch East Indies; Burma situation; US Aircraft deployed to the Dutch East Indies; Control and Commands in the Anzac Area; Demarkation of strategic areas in the Japanese War Zone; British troops in Java; Situation in New Guinea; Japanese intentions; Situation in the Middle East.

17 March: Twelfth Meeting
Assignment of Munitions; Arrival of General Macarthur in Australia; Merchant Shipping Losses; Movement of aircraft and air formations; Command in Iceland;

Naval bases in the Indian Ocean; President's proposals on the division of strategic responsibility.

24 March: : Thirteenth Meeting
Australian views on strategic control in the Pacific Area; Strategic responsibility of the United Kingdom and the United States; Command in Iceland; Relief of British Troops in Iceland; Ascension Island; Assignment of munitions; Offensive operations in Europe; British Combined Operations Staff.

31 March: Fourteenth Meeting
Strategic responsibility of the United Kingdom and the United States; Relief of British Troops in Iceland; US aircraft allocated to the Dutch East Indies; Escort vessel requirements; Allocation of air forces.

7 April: Fifteenth Meeting
German capabilities in Turkey, Syria and Iraq; United States and British Strategy; Aircraft Situation; US aircraft allocated to the Dutch East Indies; Provision of Fighter Aircraft for Australia; Aircraft for India; Landing craft production.

21 April: Sixteenth Meeting
Naval bases and repair facilities; Rapid military communications for the United Nations; Allocation of Transport Airplanes for USSR; British use of US aircraft carriers; Supplies to Russia; Situation in the Indian Ocean; General Marshall's visit to London; Admiral Stark's review of the situation.

28 April: Seventeenth Meeting
Transport aircraft for Burma and India; Auxiliary aircraft carriers; Transporting troops on cargo vessels; Preparation for war; BOLERO;[1] Assignment of munitions; Requisition of materiel for the Southwest Pacific Area; Vichy France possessions in the Caribbean.

5 May: Eighteenth Meeting
Requisition of material for Southwest Pacific Area; Transport aircraft for India; Situation in the Philippines; Enemy intentions.

12 May: Nineteenth Meeting
Requisition of material for the Southwest Pacific Area; Troop movements for BOLERO; Allocation of Aircraft of the United Nations.

19 May: Twentieth Meeting
BOLERO; Adequacy of combined communications; German Capabilities in Syria and Iraq; New type of German gas; Air offensive against submarine bases, building yards and heavy ships.

Second Washington Conference: 19–25 June 1942

The conference was hastily arranged to deal with strategic questions that had arisen out of the post-Arcadia Combined Chiefs of Staffs meetings. Prime Minister Churchill flew from Scotland on 17 June in a flying boat, landing in

---

1   The US military build-up in the United Kingdom.

Washington DC the following evening. He was only accompanied by five staff, including General Alan Brooke and Major General Ismay.

The President held his first meeting in the British Embassy and then flew to the President's home at Hyde Park, New York, on 19 June. The two Heads of State headed to Washington two days later to continue the rest of the conference. Very little documentation relating to the Conference has been found.

17 June

President meets with his Senior Military Advisors.

19 June

Churchill meets Marshall.

First Combined Chiefs of Staff Meeting
Offensive plans for 1942–1943.

Informal Chiefs of Staff Meeting
BOLERO and GYMNAST.
Roosevelt and Churchill Meeting.

20 June

Second Combined Chiefs of Staff Meeting
Offensive plans for 1942–1943.
Roosevelt and Churchill Meeting. The atomic bomb project.

21 June

Roosevelt and Churchill Meeting
Plans and preparations for operations on the continent of Europe in 1943 must be pushed forward with all speed and energy on as large a scale as possible. The United States and Great Britain should be prepared to act offensively in 1942.

Operations in Western Europe in 1942, would, if successful, yield greater political and strategic gains than operations in any other theatre. Plans and preparations for the operations in this theatre are to be pressed forward with all possible speed, energy and ingenuity. The most resolute efforts must be made to overcome the obvious dangers and difficulties of the enterprise. If a sound and sensible plan can be contrived, we should not hesitate to give effect to it. If, on the other hand, detailed examination shows that despite all efforts success is improbable, we must be ready with an alternative.

Provided political conditions are favourable, the best alternative in 1942 is Operation GYMNAST. Accordingly, plans for this operation should be completed as soon as possible. The forces for GYMNAST would be found from BOLERO units which had not yet left the United States.

BOLERO planning will be centred in London. GYMNAST planning will be centred in Washington.

As a further alternative, the possibility of operating in Spain and Portugal in the autumn and winter of 1942 should also be considered by the Combined Chiefs.

Roosevelt and Churchill Meeting with Senior Staff Officers

Naval cooperation in the South Pacific.

22 June

Roosevelt and Churchill Meeting[1]

North African situation; BOLERO; speculation about an American force in the Middle East.

Roosevelt, Churchill and Soong Meeting.

23 June

Roosevelt and Churchill meet Shipping Advisors.

Escort ships; Merchant ships construction program.

Roosevelt and Churchill meet with Duke of Windsor.

24 June

Roosevelt and Churchill meet with King Peter of Yugoslavia.

25 June

Third Combined Chiefs of Staff Meeting

US reinforcements for the Middle East.

Twelfth Meeting of the Pacific War Council.[2]

Roosevelt, Churchill and Prime Minister MacKenzie King.

The Symbol Conference, 15–23 January 1943

Following the Arcadia Conference, 1942 started badly with the unexpected surrender of Singapore on 15 February. While there was stalemate in Burma, the Allies worked to establish a line of supply across the Atlantic to secure the British Isles.

The first good news came at the beginning of June when the United States Navy defeated the Japanese Navy at the Battle of Midway; it would mark the highpoint of Japanese aspirations in the Pacific. Meanwhile, US and Australian troops were holding their own against the Japanese on Guadalcanal, New Guinea and the Solomon Islands by the end of the year.

In the Mediterranean Theatre Rommel had forced the British back along the North Africa coast, nearly to Cairo. They struck back at the end of October in the Second Battle of El Alamein, the turning point in the Western Desert campaign. Operation TORCH, the Allied invasion of Vichy-held North Africa, began on 8 November, bringing US troops into action in the Mediterranean. By the time

---

1   They had just heard about the fall of Tobruk, depressing Churchill.
2   The Council was established on 30 March 1942 and held its first meeting on 1 April. It discussed the war effort against Japan. Meetings were held almost weekly.

of the SYMBOL meeting in Casablanca in February 1943, the battle to clear the North African coast was well underway.

President Roosevelt left Miami, Florida, on 11 January and flew the 5000 miles across the Atlantic to the North African port of Casablanca. It was the first time a president had flown while in office and the first time a president had left the United States in time of war.

The conference was held on the outskirts of Casablanca in the large ANFA hotel overlooking the ocean. The building was surrounded by villas and palm trees and protected by barbed wire, armed guards and secret service men. While Prime Minister Churchill attended, Marshal Stalin turned down his invitation because the critical battle of Stalingrad demanded his full attention. General Henri Giraud, High Commissioner of French Africa, and General Charles de Gaulle, leader of the Fighting French forces, attended but they did not take part in the main meetings. There were three main conferences and 15 Chiefs of Staff conferences between 14 and 24 January 1943.

14 January
First Combined Chiefs of Staff Meeting
A discussion of the general war situation.
Second Combined Chiefs of Staff Meeting
A discussion over combined strategy.
Third Combined Chiefs of Staff Meeting
The U-boat War; the war in North Africa and strategy in the European Theatre.

15 January: First Symbol Meeting
The Situation in North Africa
General Eisenhower reviewed the situation on his front. The Allied forces who had landed in French North Africa were equipped to capture three ports.[3] They were not a mobile army and had little strength for offensive operations. This arrangement had been necessary since the French attitude was an unknown quantity.[4] General Anderson[5] had advanced with great boldness and rapidity, taking every kind of risk in an attempt to get into Tunis and Bizerte in the first rush.[6] He had finally been stopped by dive bombing when he got into the open country near Tunis and by wet weather, which hampered movement off the roads. Every effort was made to reinforce the forward troops, units being moved from Oran and from Casablanca.[7]

---

3   Operation TORCH, the Anglo-American invasion of French North Africa, began on 8 November 1942. Three amphibious task forces seized the key ports and airports of Morocco and Algeria; the three ports mentioned were Casablanca, Oran and Algiers.

4   Vichy France had 125,000 troops in North Africa as well as 10 warships and 11 submarines at Casablanca; German planes were on call to give support. The belief was the French would not fight and American troops were instructed not to fire first.

5   General Sir Kenneth A. N. Anderson, KCB, MC (1891-1959) was the British Army officer in command of First Army during Operation TORCH. Outwardly reserved, he did not court popularity from his superiors or the public; Eisenhower wrote that he was "blunt, at times to the point of rudeness".

6   Tunis and Bizerte are the main ports on the northeast coast of Tunisia.

7   Oran, Algeria, and Casablanca, Morocco.

It was hoped to launch an offensive on 22 December to capture Tunis, making use of superior gun power, but the weather had turned against them and they had to call off the offensive. A means of carrying out operations in the drier country in the south had been sought and an operation was now been planned for the capture of Sfax[1] which would begin on 24 January.[2] Eisenhower had been waiting for a chance to coordinate action with General Alexander[3] because it was important the timing should fit in with the movements of the Eighth Army.[4]

Eisenhower then gave details of the forthcoming operation and the forces to be employed. It was intended to use the American 1st Armored Division,[5] a regimental combat team and additional units of artillery; they would also use the Gafsa and Tebessa airfields[6] for supporting aircraft. The Germans had disposed their armour northeast of Pont du Fahs[7] and it would be necessary to guard against a counter stroke towards the rear of the forces attacking Sfax. It was hoped to put supplies into Sfax by sea to ease the maintenance problem.

It was hoped this operation would be of real assistance to the Eighth Army,[8] because the Germans were sending supplies by rail to Sfax and then using small coastal vessels to move them to Rommel. The Sfax force would be separated by 75 miles of rough country from the British First Army and there were two critical points, Pont du Fahs and Foudouk,[9] which were held by the French. Apart from one regiment in Algiers, and part of a division in Oran, there was virtually nothing between the troops in the front line and Morocco.[10] Troops in Morocco were too far away to move up the long and difficult line of communications.

First US Army had seven to ten days supplies of all kinds but they could launch an attack if the Germans offered an opening. In the whole theatre of war there were now about 320,000 troops. Supplies were ample in the Casablanca area but again, transportation difficulties prevented much being moved forward.

Eisenhower described the airfields being used by the Allied Air Forces and the difficulties of keeping them serviceable. He said the political situation was very closely related to the military situation in view of the very vulnerable nature of the line of communications, which French troops were guarding. Eisenhower said Air Chief Marshal Tedder[11] had twice visited Algiers and detailed plans had been worked out to ensure the coordinated action of the Air Forces from the Middle

---

1 Sfax on the east coast of Tunisia, 200 miles south, southeast of Tunis.
2 Eighth Army captured Tripoli, Libya on 23 January 1943. By February it was facing the Mareth Line; Sfax would not be taken until 10 April.
3 General Harold Alexander (1891-1969), Commander-in-Chief of Middle East Command.
4 Eighth Army came under command of General Alexander's new 18th Army Group on 20 February for the combined offensive into Tunisia.
5 Commanded by Major General Orlando Ward; the division was nicknamed the 'Old Ironsides'.
6 60 miles south and 40 miles west of Kasserine.
7 40 miles southwest of Tunis.
8 Lieutenant General, later Field Marshal, Bernard L. Montgomery, 'Monty' (1887-1976), Eighth Army's commander.
9 Foudouk is on the Bay of Tunis, 15 miles southeast of the capital.
10 In a direct line, around 800 miles to the Moroccan border and another 400 to Casablanca.
11 Air Chief Marshal Sir Arthur Tedder (1890-1967) Marshal of the Royal Air Force, head of RAF Middle East Command. He had built up an air force in North Africa, a key factor in the Battle of El Alamein and the battles that followed.

East, Malta and French North Africa. Medium bombers based on Philippeville[12] were also being used against shipping.

General Alexander gave an account of Eighth Army operations. The El Alamein position was about 40 miles long and occupied by four full strength German divisions[13] and ten Italian divisions. The position had no open flank, so the problem was one of punching a hole through which the armour could be launched.[14] The attack went in under a very heavy barrage of 500 guns on 24 October.[15] Infantry advanced through deep minefields for 4,000 to 6,000 yards. For the next ten days there was severe fighting designed to eat up the enemy's reserves and prepare the way for the final breakthrough. On 4 November the front was broken and the opportunity came for the fine American Sherman tanks to pour through.[16]

Tobruk was reached in two weeks and the army was at El Agheila by the end of the month.[17] They had the satisfaction of advancing twice as fast as Rommel had moved during their retreat. The Germans did not have enough transport to go round but they had made certain it was used to move German units.[18] Their casualties in twelve days were 15,000; the enemy's must have totalled between 60,000 and 70,000 and Rommel must have lost nearly 5,000 vehicles.[19] None of this would have been possible had it not been for the air superiority gained by the air forces who had done magnificent work throughout.

Everything depended upon the use of Benghazi for the advance beyond El Agheila.[20] The Germans had left the harbour in a terrible mess. However, by dint of fine work on the part of the Navy, a flow of 3000 tons per day was reached. A severe gale had breached the mole and sunk several ships, interrupting the flow, but it was now back up to 2000 tons per day. Sirte[21] was useless but there was a small place near El Agheila where 400 tons per day had been unloaded.[22] The current operation was an attack by the 7th Armoured Division,[23] the New Zealand Division and the 51st Highland Division, who were carrying ten days' supplies

---

12 Now Skikda, on Algeria's northeast coast.
13 15th Panzer, 21st Panzer, 90th Light and 164th Infantry Divisions.
14 The sea was to the north and the Qattara Depression, an impassable area of sand dunes and salt flats, to the south.
15 The Second Battle of El Alamein, codenamed Operation LIGHTFOOT, was led by infantry who crossed the anti-tank minefields without detonating them (hence the name light foot), allowing minesweepers to follow. Lieutenant-General Georg Stumme died of a heart attack on 24 October and Field Marshall Erwin Rommel, nickname Desert Fox, returned to command Panzerarmee Afrika.
16 4 November was the culmination of Operation SUPERCHARGE, the destruction of the German armour, supplies and lines of communication. 300 Shermans had been donated to the British.
17 Tobruk is 350 miles west of El Alamein and El Agheila is another 400 miles along the coast via Benghazi (300 miles southwest in a direct line).
18 Abandoning their Italian Allies.
19 Later reported as Allies; 13,560 casualties, around 400 tanks, 110 guns and 97 aircraft: Germans; 30,540 casualties, 500 tanks, 254 guns and 84 aircraft.
20 Benghazi is the second largest city in Libya and over 200 miles west of Tobruk. El Agheila is 200 miles south-southwest of Benghazi.
21 Sirte is 300 miles west along the coast from El Agheila.
22 The Allies needed to open ports along the coast to maintain supplies to the fighting troops.
23 7th Armoured Division was nicknamed the Desert Rats while 51st Division was nicknamed the Highway Decorators because their road signs had the divisional symbol HD on them.

and 500 miles of petrol with them.[1] It was hoped to reach Tripoli[2] by 26 January. The enemy's fighting value was hard to assess but he was believed to have at his disposal the following forces:

15th Panzer Division with 30 tanks and 21st Panzer Division with about 27 tanks.[3] (50 additional tanks were believed to be ready in Tunisia);

90th Light Division and 164th Division, both weak in strength and short of artillery;

About 9 Italian Divisions.

The total strength might be assessed at 50,000 Germans and 30,000 Italians, although only about 20,000 of the former were strictly fighting troops. The enemy's organization was very broken up and he was very short of artillery. Furthermore, his army had retreated 1000 miles, which must have had an effect on morale. The British superiority rested in tanks and guns, of which they had ample. General LeClerc's[4] advance through Fezzan had been a fine piece of work but it would not influence the present battle.

If Eighth Army got to Tripoli according to plan, it would be quite immobilized until the port was open. This would probably take seven or ten days, though in the worst case it might take three months.[5] It was hoped to work it up to 3000 tons a day and if this was achieved it would be possible to attack the Mareth Line[6] towards the middle of March with two armoured and four infantry divisions. They were getting photographs of the Mareth Line, which was certainly a prepared position, though it lacked depth.[7] It had to be realized the distances involved were very great. From Buerat to Tripoli was 248 miles and from Tripoli to Gabes was 220 miles. Of course it would be possible, if the enemy's resistance proved weak, to advance to the Mareth Line with very light forces somewhat earlier.

Discussion then turned to the coordination of Eighth Army's operations with those of Eisenhower's command. Eisenhower asked what Rommel's position would be if Eighth Army captured Tripoli and if he captured Sfax. Could the Eighth Army keep Rommel engaged so the forces at Sfax could neglect their right flank and turn all their attention towards the North?

Alexander said Rommel was living very much from hand to mouth for supplies and if he lost all his ports he would certainly be trapped. Nevertheless, it would

1 On 15 January 1943 51st Division attacked the Axis while 2nd New Zealand Division and 7th Armoured Divisions went around the inland flank.

2 Capital of Libya and only 100 miles from the Tunisian border. It was a 700-mile drive from Benghazi to Tripoli. The capital was taken on 23 January.

3 21st Panzer Division had actually been moved to Tunisia to help Fifth Panzer Army.

4 General Philippe F. M. LeClerc de Hautclocque (1902-1947), commander of French troops advancing from Chad through the Fezzan area of southwest Libya.

5 The winter weather and enemy action could delay the opening of the port. In addition, the Allies did not know if it had been damaged by the retreating Axis troops.

6 The Mareth Line was a defensive line 100 miles south of Sfax and 300 miles south of Tunis.

7 The French built the line of fortifications before World War II as protection from the Italians in Libya. It stretched 22 miles between Medenine and Gabès in southern Tunisia. It was built along Wadi Zigzaou, covering the gap between the Mediterranean Sea and the Matmata Mountains.

be necessary to give the Sfax operation a very careful study. Rommel would react like lightning if a force advanced on Sfax and his plan would be the best possible. Great care would be necessary to ensure undue risks were not taken.[8]

Brooke said a great deal depended upon the timing of the Sfax operation. It might be unfortunate if the force arrived at Sfax just as the Eighth Army reached Tripoli, immobilized for lack of supplies.[9] It was agreed the coordination of the action of the two armies was a matter of the highest importance and the present opportunity had to be utilized to the full.[10]

Discussion then turned to the strength required to hold the North African shore after it had been completely cleared of the enemy. Alexander calculated two divisions with a mobile reserve would be sufficient for Cyrenaica and Tripolitania.[11] Eisenhower believed four divisions should be held to watch Spanish Morocco, while one infantry and one armoured division would certainly be necessary in Algeria and Tunisia.

There were six US divisions in French North Africa and three more were due to come in the original plan. If these were shipped there would be three US divisions over and above defensive requirements. He thought it would be unwise to hand over the defence of Tunisia to the French too early. Churchill agreed; it appeared there would be some thirteen divisions in the whole North African theatre available for future operations.[12]

Tedder believed convoys could be passed through the Mediterranean once airfields had been established and the Tunisian tip had been cleared.[13] Admiral Pound[14] agreed and reckoned all the Cape traffic could be done away with if 30 ships could be passed through every ten days, releasing 225 ships for other uses.[15] But it was hard to estimate the relative losses which might be incurred. Although the percentage loss might be slightly higher through the Mediterranean, the total would be lower, as fewer ships would be involved. The Mediterranean route would be more expensive in escorts, but there would be a saving in voyage time.[16]

Churchill said the opening of the Mediterranean would have its effect on the Turkish attitude. Moreover, the six divisions of the British Tenth Army in Persia,

---

8 General Alexander is acknowledging the Allies' respect for Rommel, nicknamed the 'Desert Fox', and his Afrika Korps.
9 First US Army would be attacking Sfax from the west while Eighth Army advanced from the south.
10 Eighth Army would not be ready to attack the Mareth Line until 19 March 1943.
11 Cyrenaica is eastern Libya and Tripolitania is western Libya. The two divisions would have to guard against seaborne and airborne raids.
12 Vichy French troops had put up a strong resistance when Allied troops landed in North Africa on 8 November 1942. It had taken three days of negotiations to get General Alphonse Juin and Admiral François Darlan to stop resistance. Eisenhower was concerned there could be an uprising if the Allied troops were overstretched.
13 The Tunisian tip was the headland east of Tunis that faced Sicily.
14 Admiral of the Fleet Sir (Alfred) Dudley P. R. Pound.
15 Ships would be able to pass through the Mediterranean Sea and the Suez Canal, a journey of 5,000 miles, rather than sailing around the Cape, a journey of 15,000 miles. While the Mediterranean route was more dangerous, the potential loss in sinkings was far outweighed by the number of ships freed up by the shorter journey.
16 Axis planes based on Italian and Sicilian airfields would be able to attack the Mediterranean convoys.

ready to meet any threat through the Caucasus, were now available to encourage and support the Turks.[1]

It was then suggested it might be worthwhile calculating what specialized units would be required to round out the Turkish Army.[2] Brooke said the Turks had already been supplied with technical material and arms and although their Army had first rate infantry they tended to misuse technical equipment and allow it to deteriorate.[3] He did not think their army would ever be fit to operate offensively outside Turkey. But it might hold Turkey as a base from where their forces could operate.[4]

Tedder said the Turks had a small air force and although they had given it a limited number of aircraft, it would never be fit to fight. Their plan was initially to operate some 25 fighter and bomber squadrons from Turkish airfields. More airfields would be required if they were to operate offensively and plans had been drawn up for their preparation. They intended to move anti-aircraft units in with the squadrons.[5] Tedder then gave an account of the part played by the Air Force in the recent victories in the Middle East. He emphasized their task began during the British retreat from Gazala.[6] Since then the enemy air force had been beaten down and great efforts had been made to stop Rommel's supplies. The action of an air force in operations of this kind was difficult to explain concisely, because it extended over great areas and had diverse tasks. The Middle East Air Forces had first struck at Rommel's supplies.[7] Malta had been reinforced to the utmost to attack the Axis supply route across to Tunisia and aircraft had been transferred to Tunisia.[8] The coordination of the air forces of the Middle East, Malta and Tunisia was a complex problem and he was pleased to have the opportunity to meet General Eisenhower to discuss it.

Eisenhower explained the difficulties under which the air forces in Tunisia were operating in support of the Army. There were only two airfields available for fighters and even these were 100 miles from the front line. The Germans, on the other hand, had two all-weather airfields in Tunis. In the early stages US units from the Western Zone had been moved up and placed under British command;

1　British and Indian troops had been deployed from India to Iraq to protect British interests, in particular oil concessions. They were known as Iraqiforce and commanded by General Sir Edward Quinan (1885-1960). They later took part in the Anglo-Soviet invasion of Iran to stop Axis troops entering Persia. The force was renamed Tenth Army and it maintained communications to the Soviet Union through the Persian Gulf.
2　Round out meant support. While the Turkish Army had infantry, it needed artillery, tanks, anti-aircraft guns and other support equipment.
3　Turkish troops were not negligent; they were not technically trained and did not understand maintenance.
4　Brooke was right, Turkish troops would never fight outside their borders.
5　The entry of Turkey into the war would allow Allied planes to fly from its airfields and attack targets across southeast Europe, particularly the Romanian oil fields, the main Axis supply.
6　Gazala, Libya, 200 miles east of Benghazi and 50 miles west of Tobruk. Rommel's Panzer Army Afrika drove back Lieutenant-General Neil Ritchie's Eighth Army starting on 26 May 1942 and by 21 June it had captured Tobruk.
7　The first attacks would be made against targets along the north coast of Africa and then at shipping crossing from Italy and Sicily to Tunisia.
8　King George VI awarded the George Cross to Malta on a collective basis on 15 April 1942, "to bear witness to a heroism and devotion that will long be famous in history."

Air Marshal Welch[9] had deployed them in the Tebessa area.[10] For the operation now contemplated, the British fighter force would operate from Souk-el-Arba under Lawson[11] while the US fighters would operate in the south under General Crane.[12]

Eisenhower believed the British Army Commander[13] should control this front since there was no sound arrangement for dividing the front. However, the French had refused to serve under British command.[14] He hoped to overcome this kind of difficulty in the near future.

Churchill asked if there was any danger of the Germans striking through General Anderson's left flank rather in the manner adopted by the Eighth Army at El Alamein.[15] Eisenhower said First Army had such superiority over the enemy in artillery, he did not think there was much fear of this. Though the enemy's specialist and tank units were good, his infantry had not seemed to be up to the same standard.[16]

In conclusion, events had reached a crucial stage in the North African Theatre and the events over the next two or three weeks would be of vital importance.[17] Now was the time to consider what action should be taken once the North African shore had finally been cleared.

16 January
Fourth Combined Chiefs of Staff Meeting
The war in North Africa; Strategy in the European Theatre; Supplies to Russia.

17 January
Fifth Combined Chiefs of Staff Meeting
The Eastern Theatre; Iceland; Russian air cover for convoys.

The President and General Noguès
The President and Major General George S. Patton Jr., Commanding General of I Armored Corps, met Major General Chas. A Noguès, the resident General in Rabat.

The President and General Giraud
The President and Lieutenant General Mark W. Clark met General Henri Giruad, Commander of the French Armies in North Africa.

---

9 Air Marshal Sir William L. Welsh KCB, DSC, AFC (1891-1962), the Royal Air Force officer in command of British air operations during Operation TORCH.
10 Tebessa, near the Algerian-Tunisian border, 200 miles southwest of Tunis.
11 Air Commodore George M. Lawson (1894-1965); his fighters operated from Souk-el-Arba in northwest Tunisia, 80 miles west-southwest of Tunis.
12 Possibly Brigadier General William C. Crane.
13 Eighth Army commander Lieutenant General Montgomery.
14 XIX Corps commanded by General Alphonse P. Juin (1888-1967).
15 Rommel's Afrika Corps attacked General Anderson's First Army at Kasserine Pass, a gap in the Atlas Mountains on 19 February 1943. II US Corps bore the brunt of the attack and was pushed back 50 miles before it stopped the German onslaught.
16 It was the American troops who suffered, owing to inexperience and poor leadership. As a result, commanders were replaced and units were reorganised. They were far more effective in future battles.
17 Indeed they were, when the Afrika Korps nearly broke through the Kasserine Pass.

18 January
Sixth Combined Chiefs of Staff Meeting
Burma campaign; Polish forces, Air raids on Berlin; the Mediterranean naval situation; Escort vessels.

18 January: Second Symbol Meeting
The President and the Prime Minister asked the Chiefs of Staff for a progress report on the current conferences. General Brooke felt definite progress had been made after seven days of argument. A document setting forth the general strategic policy for 1943 was now being prepared. It would be discussed in detail at the Combined Chiefs of Staff meeting the following morning. Brooke summarized it as follows:

1.   Measures to combat the submarine menace were the first charge on the United Nations' resources because it would provide security for all their operations.
2.   They would concentrate on the defeat of Germany first, followed by the defeat of Japan.
3.   They would first concentrate on forcing Germany to withdraw ground and air forces from the Russian front through operations from North Africa.[1] Southern Europe, the Dodecanese Islands,[2] Greece, Crete, Sardinia, and Sicily would all be threatened, forcing Germany to deploy her forces to meet each threat. The operation decided upon was the capture of Sicily.[3]
4.   Simultaneously, they would continue to prepare forces and assemble landing craft in England for a thrust across the Channel in case the German strength in France decreased, either through the withdrawal of her troops or an internal collapse.[4]
5.   The maximum combined air offensive would be conducted from the United Kingdom against Germany. Attempts would be made to undermine Germany's morale by this and every other available means.
6.   Every effort would be made, political and otherwise, to induce Turkey to enter the war so they could establish air bases there for operations against Romania.
7.   Plans and preparations for ANAKIM were to be undertaken immediately and the United States would make up the deficiencies in landing craft and naval vessels. The operation was planned for December of

---

1   Sixth Army and Fourth Panzer Army had been engaged in Stalingrad for three months when the Soviets struck back with Operation URANUS on 19 November 1942. Three days later they had encircled the Stalingrad position, trapping over 250,000 German and Romanian troops. 90,000 survivors surrendered on 31 January 1943; few would survive in captivity. Meanwhile, the Soviet Armies advanced 300 miles west through Kursk and Kharkov.
2   The Dodecanese Islands are 12 large and 150 smaller islands off the southwest coast of Turkey; the largest is Rhodes. They define the eastern limit of the Sea of Crete.
3   Codename HUSKY, which would take place on 9-10 July 1943.
4   During COSSAC's planning of what would become Operation OVERLORD, RANKIN was prepared in case there was a change in the German situation in northern Europe. There were three scenarios; (A) the weakening of German forces, (B) the withdrawal of German forces, (C) the surrender of German forces.

1943 with a view to capturing Burma and opening the Burma Road before the monsoon season of 1944.[5]

8.   RAVENOUS[6] would establish bridgeheads over the Chindwin River, preparing roads and airfields in northern Burma to facilitate the mounting of ANAKIM. CANNIBAL was now being undertaken with a view to securing air bases in the Akyab area.[7]

9.   Operations in the Pacific were to be continued. They included the capture of Rabaul and Eastern New Guinea while plans were to be prepared to extend operations into the Marshall Islands and the capture of Truk.[8]

The U-boat War

Marshall said they had to coordinate and improve their methods in combating the submarine menace and it would be a subject of discussion during the conferences.[9]

The Arctic Convoys

Another vital question was how to maintain the Russian forces at their maximum effort both by forcing a withdrawal of German pressure on their front and also by insuring the flow of munitions to them. It was questionable if the United Nations could take the losses of tonnage incidental to escorting the northern convoys. It might be possible to decrease the intervals between convoys or to add to the strength of their escorts. However, it was entirely within the power of Germany to administer such losses to close this route to Russia. Marshall did not believe it was necessary to take excessive punishment in running these convoys simply to keep Stalin placated. In any event, they would have to tell Stalin the convoys would have to be discontinued during HUSKY.

The Combined Bomber Offensive[10]

Marshall thought the US bombers in England should be under British operational direction and they should prescribe the targets and timing of attacks. Control of operational procedures and techniques would remain under the United States Commanders. The Combined Chiefs of Staff would attempt to prescribe general

---

5   ANAKIM was to include a British amphibious assault on Rangoon and an offensive into central Burma, plus an American-sponsored Chinese offensive in the north involving convergence of forces operating from China and India.

6   RAVENOUS would be carried out by IV Corps, commanded by General Sir Geoffrey A. P. Scoones (1893-1975).

7   There was a port and airfield on Akyab Island, at the end of the Mayu Peninsula and while fighters could reach all of Central Burma from it, bombers could reach Rangoon.

8   The Marshall Islands are a group of over 1150 islands over 2000 miles north east of Papua New Guinea. Truk is 1000 miles west of the Marshalls.

9   Sir Dudley Pound recommended four U-boat targets; factories and building yards, operating bases and routes to the hunting grounds. It was estimated that 20 U-boats a month were being built. In November 1942 16 had been sunk and 21 damaged; in December 1942 8 had been sunk and 15 damaged; mainly by air attack.

10 After hearing that the British Ministry of Economic Warfare had identified the bottleneck German industries of oil, communications and ball bearings, the Combined Chiefs of Staff agreed to conduct the Bomber Offensive from the United Kingdom.

priorities of bombing objectives.[1] General Arnold[2] said the agreements would be very helpful from the air point of view because they would facilitate the allocation of aircraft and the development of procedures and techniques.

Operations in Northwest Europe

Churchill thought Operation SLEDGEHAMMER[3] should be given a 'sharper point' and they should appoint a Commander and fix a target date. He had not been in favour of such an operation in 1942 but it was their duty to engage the enemy on as wide a front and as continuously as possible. As the only way of staging an operation with the full force of the British Metropolitan air forces[4] and the US air forces in Great Britain was SLEDGEHAMMER, he thought they should do everything they could to make the operation possible that summer.

Roosevelt agreed and suggested they joined together to build up forces in the United Kingdom. It would be desirable to prepare a monthly schedule of the build-up of forces so they knew the potential effort at any time. Plans should be made so they could utilize this potential at any time that Germany showed signs of deterioration.[5]

Operations in the Mediterranean

Churchill discussed possible operations from the Mediterranean against the Dodecanese. He thought they might be developed either as feints, to conceal the main effort against Sicily, or as a real attack.[6] He had received a message from the three Commanders-in-Chief in the Middle East confirming plans were underway. He wanted the Chiefs of Staff's final document for 1943's strategy to include some mention of the Dodecanese.

Roosevelt said they had been extremely fortunate in Operation TORCH but he was worried news concerning the operations against Sicily might reach Germany. To prevent this, they should give the operations in the Mediterranean some such name as UNDERBELLY and continually think of them as being aimed at any one of a number of objectives, knowing secretly all the while it was Sicily. Admiral King[7] said deception could be well achieved by the use of cover plans.

King said the document being prepared for discussion on 19 January went a long way towards establishing a policy of how they were to win the war. It had taken some days for the Chiefs of Staff to express themselves but they all agreed in principle and he believed the document would be approved after a short

---

1   The British Air Ministry issued a directive on 4 February to carry out "the progressive destruction and dislocation of the German military, industrial and economic systems and the undermining of the morale of the German people to a point where their capacity for armed resistance is fatally weakened. Every opportunity to be taken to attack Germany by day to destroy objectives that are unsuitable for night attack, to sustain continuous pressure on German morale, to impose heavy losses on German day fighter force and to conserve German fighter force away from the Russian and Mediterranean theatres of war."
2   General Arnold, Commanding General of the US Army Air Forces.
3   SLEDGEHAMMER had been the plan to capture Cherbourg in the autumn of 1942 and then build up troops on the Cotentin Peninsula over the winter ready for a spring 1943 offensive.
4   Another name for the Royal Air Force.
5   Chief of Staff, Supreme Allied Commander Headquarters (COSSAC) would eventually prepare the three RANKIN plans.
6   The Dodecanese would be attacked following the capitulation of Italy in September 1943. German troops would defeat the British invasion force.
7   Admiral King, Commander-in-Chief, US Fleet, and Chief of Naval Operations (COMINCH-CNO).

discussion. He personally wanted it expanded to present a complete concept for concluding the war but he was very pleased with it as it was.

ROUNDUP versus HUSKY

Marshall said the US Chiefs of Staff had preferred ROUNDUP[8] when they came to the conference. However, the decision had been made to undertake HUSKY because they had a large number of troops in North Africa and it would result in an economy of tonnage, which was the major consideration.[9]

It was estimated the possession of the north coast of Africa and Sicily would release approximately 225 vessels, facilitating operations in Burma, the Middle East and the Pacific. He felt the capture of Sicily would do much to improve the air coverage for their shipping in the Mediterranean, making the passage considerably safer.

Marshall said Admiral Cunningham[10] and other naval officers believed the capture of Sicily would not be of great benefit in protecting their convoys; Cunningham stated it would only make them 5 per cent more effective. Air Marshal Portal thought there had been a misunderstanding of Cunningham's views. They would lose 15 ships out of 100, or be 85 per cent effective, without Sicily. They would lose 10 ships out of 100, or be 90 per cent effective, if they held Sicily. So the number of ships lost was 50 per cent greater with Sicily in possession of the Axis.[11] Marshall said the second reason for operating against Sicily was the possibility of eliminating Italy from the war; making Germany take over Italian commitments.[12]

Marshall emphasized ROUNDUP would be a difficult, if not impossible, operation to undertake once they had committed themselves to HUSKY. The United Kingdom maintained a 20,000-strong spearhead of amphibious forces, which were available at all times for an operation across the Channel. This force could be strengthened by follow-up troops carried in small craft.[13] But operations across the Channel had to be extremely limited unless there was a complete crack in German morale. After HUSKY it would be as difficult to assemble landing craft and send them to England as it would be to assemble them after the capture of Rabaul[14] and send them to Burma. Probably three months would be required in each case.

---

8   ROUNDUP replaced SLEDGEHAMMER as an invasion of Normandy planned for the spring of 1943. Both were later considered to be impractical and replaced by OVERLORD, timed for the spring of 1944.
9   There was no need to move troops and equipment from North Africa to England if Sicily was attacked. It was only a short distance from Tunisia to Sicily.
10   Admiral of the Fleet Andrew Browne Cunningham, (1883-1963), First Sea Lord of the Admiralty and Chief of the Naval Staff, nickname ABC.
11   Losing 5 per cent fewer ships of the total but halving the number of ships lost. Two very different ways of looking at the same figures.
12   To give an idea of size of Italy's armed forces when it declared war on France and the UK in June 1940, the army had 59 infantry divisions (6 million men); the navy had six capital ships, 19 cruisers, 59 destroyers and over 100 submarines; the air force had 2000 planes, most of them outdated.
13   Operation JUBILEE on 19 August 1942 was a failed attack on Dieppe, launched with the intention of seizing a major port for a short time. Over 3600 of the 6085 men who went ashore were casualties or captured. The raid would have been on everyone's minds.
14   Rabaul in Papua New Guinea.

Marshall said sudden signs of deterioration of the Axis forces might take two forms; firstly, a collapse in the interior with the troops initially holding fast and, secondly, a withdrawal of troops from France. In the latter case, they should make every effort to cross the Channel and utilize any means available. The lack of escort vessels and landing craft was the greatest difficulty in setting up the strength for ROUNDUP in addition to HUSKY.

A Question of Command

Roosevelt said ROUNDUP[1] should be under British command if it was undertaken. Churchill replied it could be determined later but agreed it would be advisable to designate a British commander to undertake the planning. In his view, the command of an operation should, as a general rule, be held by an officer of the nation that furnished the majority of the forces.[2]

Churchill said six divisions of the Eighth Army would enter Tunisia in perhaps five weeks and they would come under command of General Eisenhower. But he thought it would be advisable to designate Alexander the Deputy Commander of the Allied Forces. Roosevelt and Marshall agreed. Marshall said it would be particularly desirable because there would be two British Armies involved on the Tunisian front. Admiral King suggested the possibility of unifying command before Eighth Army's entry into Tunisia, because there were many matters common to both the Allied Expeditionary Forces and the Eighth Army which should be coordinated.[3] After discussion, they agreed the date of appointment should be decided later.[4]

Marshall informed Churchill and the Chiefs of Staff of the great contribution Cunningham had made to TORCH. He wished to express the appreciation of the US Chiefs of Staff, not only for the skill Cunningham had displayed but his spirit of helpfulness and cooperation. Churchill thanked Marshall and asked him to include his comments in the minutes so he could present them to the Cabinet.[5]

After hearing the agreements arrived at the conference would be included in a paper, Churchill suggested submitting one to Premier Stalin. While he felt the Soviets were entitled to know what they intended to do, they had to make it clear the paper expressed their intentions and did not constitute promises.

Turkey

Churchill said the British had some right to expect Turkey to enter the war after the Balkans had been invaded. They did not press it in view of their own weakness to help Turkey but she would be in a weak position at the peace table following

1   The invasion of the north coast of France.
2   At this stage only British divisions were available to invade Northwest France; the number of American divisions would increase as the months passed.
3   The Allied Expeditionary Forces were approaching Tunisia from the west, while Eighth Army was approaching from the southeast.
4   General Eisenhower's Allied Force Headquarters would assume control of Eighth Army in February 1943. General Alexander became Eisenhower's deputy at the same time.
5   Eisenhower wrote in his diary of Admiral Sir Andrew Browne Cunningham, "He remains in my opinion at the top of my subordinates in absolute selflessness, energy, devotion to duty, knowledge of his task, and in understanding of the requirements of Allied operations. My opinions as to his superior qualifications have never wavered for a second." Cunningham was promoted to Admiral of the Fleet three days later.

the war if she did not participate.[6] It was impossible to give them a guarantee for existing territory and for their rights over passage through the Dardanelles.[7]

The United Nations had to be prepared to provide Turkey with anti-aircraft guns, tanks and other mechanized vehicles. They also had to be prepared to send some of this equipment manned with units, because Turkish troops did not handle machinery particularly well.[8] He felt Turkey could be influenced to enter the war by Russian successes in the north and United States–United Kingdom successes in the south. At present, Turkey was angry with the Bulgarians and it would not be surprising if they did enter the war.[9]

Churchill asked that the British be allowed to play the Turkish hand since most of the troops involved in reinforcing Turkey would be British, just as the United States was handling the Chinese situation. The British would advise the United States on progress at all times.[10] Roosevelt agreed.

The Defeat of Japan

Marshall said the Combined Chiefs of Staff had agreed to adopt effective measures to improve the situation in the Pacific. He hoped they were sufficient to ensure they would not be threatened by a series of crises again, since sufficient forces would be made available to maintain pressure on Japan. Marshall said the Combined Chiefs of Staff should meet again as summer approached to make the necessary readjustments to the decisions made now.

Churchill made it clear that if and when Hitler broke down, all the British resources and effort would be turned toward the defeat of Japan. Not only were British interests involved; her honour was engaged.[11] The British Government would enter into a treaty or convention with the US Government to this effect if it had a positive effect on the people of the United States. Roosevelt replied a formal agreement was entirely unnecessary.

Roosevelt stressed efforts should be made to obtain an engagement from Russia to concentrate on the defeat of Japan after Germany had been eliminated from the war. He thought Russia would probably want to come in with the United Nations, but he wanted to have an expression as to whether they would come in and how.[12]

---

6   Churchill secretly tried to persuade Turkish President Ismet Inonu (1884-1973) to enter the war at the Yenice Station near Adana on 30 January 1943. Churchill promised military help under codename Operation HARDIHOOD in return for the use of Turkish airfields.
7   Churchill made it clear that if Turkey did not join the Allies, they would not stop the Soviets if they went on to control the Dardanelles.
8   The Americans were concerned Turkey would become a black hole for supplies.
9   Bulgaria had joined the Axis on 1 March 1941 and in December she was later forced to declare war on the United Kingdom and the United States. She did not declare war on the Soviet Union or join the invasion in June 1941. Her troops were engaged in the Balkans.
10 The British delegation arrived in April 1943 only to find itself stopped by red tape and stalling. President Ismet was concerned about the German presence in Bulgaria.
11 An honour to be restored because of the defeats in the Far East such as the fall of Singapore in February 1942, which Churchill called the "worst disaster" and "largest capitulation" in British history.
12 Stalin agreed that the Soviet Union would enter the war against Japan once Nazi Germany was defeated at the Tehran Conference (codename EUREKA) in November 1943.

Operations in the Far East

Brooke said Chiang Kai-shek[1] wished to postpone his part of RAVENOUS[2] until there was more naval support in the Bay of Bengal.[3] This was strategically sound because the Chinese operation would be more effective if it was coordinated as a part of ANAKIM.[4] RAVENOUS required no naval support.

Marshall said the Chinese advance from Yunnan[5] could be advantageously postponed. But the advance from Ramgarh[6] could well be initiated as part of RAVENOUS, to provide security for the construction of a road southward from Ledo.[7] However, this needed the Generalissimo' approval.

Marshall said the United States had an agreement to increase the Chinese air force as far as it could be supplied. They contemplated sending a group of heavy bombers that could shuttle back and forth from China to India.[8] There would be another 25 to 30 medium bombers, with appropriate fighter protection. While they were committed to the build-up of the Chinese air forces, it was a tremendously expensive operation. The air transport planes needed to supply them could be used elsewhere with great effect.

Churchill said General Chennault's[9] air force in China should be reinforced and General Wavell agreed. Roosevelt said the effects of helping China would be largely political. A small effort to send aid would have a tremendously favourable effect on Chinese morale. The Generalissimo had been disappointed about the Burma operations and he had considerable difficulty in maintaining the loyalty of some of the Chinese provinces. Anything they could do to help China and hurt Japan would have a heartening effect on him.

Roosevelt said reinforcing their air power in China would be a severe blow to Japan because the Japanese people panicked easily. This had been especially true at the time of their earthquake.[10] The US Ambassador, Mr. Grew,[11] said it had been necessary for Japanese broadcasts to adopt every means possible to quieten the people.

Roosevelt believed they should send 200 to 250 planes to China, including heavy bombers based in India.[12] They could operate over Japan proper by refuel-

---

1 Generalissimo Chiang Kai-shek, Chairman of the National Military Council of China.
2 An advance to the banks of the Chindwin River.
3 The largest bay in the world, between India and Burma.
4 ANAKIM was to be launched in the fall of 1943 to retake Burma and reopen the supply line to China. It included a British amphibious assault on Rangoon and an offensive into central Burma. There would also be an American-sponsored Chinese offensive in the north. ANAKIM proved to be too ambitious and was cancelled.
5 The southwest Chinese province next to the Burma border.
6 Ramgarh was an army camp in northeast India where Chinese troops were trained.
7 The Burma Road connected Burma to China. The Ledo Road was a new extension linking India to the Burma Road.
8 Referring to as flying over the Hump, the dangerous air route over the eastern end of the Himalayas, which started in April 1942. The only way of getting supplies into China until a road was cut across the mountainous terrain of northern Burma. 650,000 tons of supplies were flown over the Hump by the time the airlift ended in November 1945.
9 General Claire L. Chennault (1893-1958), commander of 1st American Volunteer Group (the Flying Tigers), Chief of the US Air Force in China and then Fourteenth Air Force.
10 Following a major earthquake and tsunami in March 1933.
11 Joseph C. Grew (1880-1965), ambassador to Japan since 1932. Interned after Pearl Harbor in December 1941 but released after nine months.
12 Because of the difficulties of supplying them with fuel and bombs.

ling in China. He thought the United Nations should commit themselves to this line of action and whoever of the Chiefs of Staff was due to see the Generalissimo next should inform him.

The Free French Forces

Field Marshal Dill asked Roosevelt if there was any information concerning General de Gaulle.[13] Churchill had arranged for General Giraud[14] to come for a conference but so far he had been unable to make arrangements with General de Gaulle. De Gaulle had refused, saying if the President wished to see him, he would no doubt invite him to come to Washington. De Gaulle would not meet Giraud in an atmosphere dominated by the High Command of the United Nations. Churchill had sent an invitation to de Gaulle to come, in the name of the President and himself. But if he refused, it would be necessary to consider whether or not he was a leader who merited their support.[15]

Roosevelt said General Giraud told him there were sufficient French officers and non-commissioned officers in North Africa to enable the French to raise an army of 250,000 men. He thought General Giraud should be instructed to raise such an army and they should make every effort to provide him with equipment. General Giraud also wanted to be relieved of some of his civilian responsibilities.

Churchill thought the political representatives of the United States and the United Kingdom should always be represented in whatever controlling machinery was set up. Even Eisenhower should present his demands to the French Government through civilian representatives, except when he wished to exercise his prerogatives as a military commander of an occupied country.

Brooke said the French had a considerable number of French 75 mm guns on hand, together with ammunition. They would receive tanks from the British 6th Armoured Division when it received new Sherman tanks from the United States. There were also some anti-aircraft weapons available that could be given to the French.

Marshall proposed giving the French the best equipment obtainable from United States resources, subject to shipping limitations. But if they were to equip the French, they had to make good units of them. Roosevelt thought it would be desirable to utilize some French units in HUSKY, even if only as a reserve.

Churchill hoped the United States would bring to North Africa the remaining three divisions scheduled to come over. Marshall replied there had been no change in the schedule yet, but after the complete details for HUSKY had been worked out, a determination could be made about what divisions should be brought or what other changes might be made.

---

13 General Charles A. J. M. de Gaulle (1890-1970), leader of the French Free Forces.
14 General Henri H. Giraud (1879-1949) had escaped from a German prisoner of war camp in April 1942. While he supported Marshal Philippe Pétain (1856-1951) and the Vichy government, he refused to cooperate with the Germans and instead supported the Allied landing in French North Africa. Following Admiral Francois Darlan's (1881-1942) assassination in December 1942 Giraud became his successor with Allied support. While de Gaulle wanted to pursue a political position in France, he agreed to have Giraud as Commander-in-Chief.
15 General de Gaulle mistrusted both British and US intentions for France. The US political leadership in turn mistrusted the Free French and for a long time refused to recognise de Gaulle as the representative of France.

A Summary of Strategy

Churchill said they had surveyed the whole field of strategy and it was necessary for the Chiefs of Staff to go into the ways and means to accomplish the adopted strategy. They had to determine where risks should be taken and where the reduction of forces was necessary. It might take several days and it would involve the broad distribution of their resources. He agreed with Marshall that another meeting should be held before the summer. Finally, he expressed his thanks to the President of the United States, and to the US Chiefs of Staff, for arranging the conference. Roosevelt appreciated having Marshal Dill[1] at the conference since he was the indispensable link between the Chiefs of Staff in London and the Chiefs of Staff in Washington.

Admiral Pound said they had to go into the ways and means of implementing their agreed decisions. The two problems were the security of the Atlantic convoys and how much they needed to decrease the security during HUSKY. They had to maintain pressure against the submarine menace by adequate coverage of the convoys and by striking where submarines were manufactured and assembled. It might improve the situation considerably by the time HUSKY was undertaken.

Pound agreed it would be necessary to discontinue the northern convoys during HUSKY. Churchill said this was another reason for increasing the tonnage sent to Russia before it. Pound said it could be done if the United States helped with the escort problem.

Roosevelt then discussed the possibility of assembling a large number of river and lake craft in the United States and sending them quietly to Europe, ready to transport troops across the Channel in case Germany cracked. Lord Mountbatten[2] confirmed five Great Lakes steamers had already been sent. Roosevelt told Admiral King to survey the situation and see what could be done. Marshal Dill expressed his satisfaction over the progress of the conferences.

Press Releases

Roosevelt brought up the subject of press releases. He said a photograph should be taken of the conference participants and be given out, to be released on the day he and the Prime Minister departed. Churchill suggested releasing a statement at the same time to the effect that the United Nations were resolved to pursue the war to the bitter end; neither party relaxing its efforts until the unconditional surrender of Germany and Japan had been achieved. He wanted to consult with his colleagues in London before issuing such a statement. The meeting then adjourned.

19 January

Seventh Combined Chiefs of Staff Meeting

The conduct of the war: French West Africa.

Eighth Combined Chiefs of Staff Meeting

Axis oil situation, Turkey, General Giraud.

---

1   Field Marshal Sir John G. Dill (1881-1944), Senior British Representative on the Combined Chiefs of Staff.
2   Vice-Admiral Lord Louis Mountbatten (1900-1979) Chief of Combined Operations.

20 January

Ninth Combined Chiefs of Staff Meeting
US aid to Russia, Turkey, Bombers in North Africa; Mediterranean command.

Tenth Combined Chiefs of Staff Meeting
Operation HUSKY.

21 January

Eleventh Combined Chiefs of Staff Meeting
The U-boat war; Bombers in the UK; A telegram to Stalin; Operation ANAKIM; Operation BOLERO.

22 January

Twelfth Combined Chiefs of Staff Meeting
A telegram to Stalin; HUSKY.

Thirteenth Combined Chiefs of Staff Meeting
The Pacific war; Continental operations in 1943; Command of the Cross Channel attack; Landing craft; Combined US/UK command.

The President and General de Gaulle
Roosevelt found General Giraud wanted to "get on with the war", while General de Gaulle "placed too great an emphasis on French national politics, forgetting the need for a military victory as a precedent to any French political settlement."

23 January

Fourteenth Combined Chiefs of Staff Meeting
Operation BOLERO; Continental operations 1943; Operation HUSKY directive; landing craft; Final Report to the President and Prime Minister.

23 January: Third Symbol Meeting

The President suggested discussing the Chiefs of Staff report. Both Roosevelt and Churchill congratulated the Chiefs of Staff on their work. Churchill said it was the first time he knew of when military leaders had remained together so long, free from political considerations, and had devoted their full thought to the strategic aspects of the war. Roosevelt agreed and recalled an incident in the last war when Marshal Foch, Field Marshal Haig and General Pershing had had a similar conference, which lasted five hours.[3]

Security of Sea Communications
A close examination of the minimum escort requirements to maintain the sea communications of the United Nations had been completed.[4] They had laid down certain scales of ocean-going escort vessels as the minimum acceptable but the conclusion was that this minimum would not be met until about August or September 1943. They should not count on the destruction of submarines at a

---

3   Four Allied commanders (General, later Marshal, Philippe Pétain was Commander-in-Chief of the French Army) met on 24 July 1918 to discuss going over to the offensive, following the failure of the German spring offensives.

4   C.C.S. 160 recommended extra air cover if the number of surface escorts was kept to a minimum but both the US and the UK had to reduce the deficiency of 65 surface escorts and provide auxiliary escort carriers for the protection of Atlantic convoys.

rate in excess of the production rate before the end of the year.[1] The acceptance of increased losses had to be balanced against the importance of the operations if they wanted to provide escorts for offensive operations. They had adopted certain resolutions on measures necessary to intensify the anti U-boat war.[2]

Assistance to Russia

They had examined the obligations to Russian shipments throughout 1943, estimating the effect they had on other commitments. The conclusion was that they could meet the full commitments by the end of 1943.[3] They had approved a shipment program, providing supplies to Russia would not be continued at a prohibitive cost.[4] It was essential to agree a loss rate for 1943 in order that the British and American calculations could be made on the same basis. The Combined Military Transportation Committee had therefore been directed to make an estimate.

They agreed on a new clause in the next Protocol with Russia.[5] It would state commitments might be reduced if shipping losses or the necessities of operations made it prohibitive to fulfil.[6]

Discussion about Assistance to Russia

Roosevelt had to extend the Russian Protocol in March. He believed the statement "The supply to Russia will not be continued at prohibitive cost to the United Nations' efforts" should be added. Mr. Hopkins said the present Protocol had such a clause but it could not be exercised without violent objections from Stalin.

Churchill said they had to push aid to Russia because no investment paid a better military dividend; they could not let Russia down. The Chiefs of Staff had considered whether or not sixteen destroyers could be made available from the United States, to reduce the convoy turnaround from 40 to 27 days.[7]

Admiral King said the destroyers were simply not available. The escort vessel situation was so tight they had to stop the Russian convoys around 14 June to take care of HUSKY's needs.[8] The Atlantic convoys were already 65 escorts short and HUSKY would increase the shortage.[9] Hopkins suggested they could stop

---

1   There would be intensified bombing of U-boat construction yards and operating bases. Air cover for North Atlantic convoys would come from both sides of the Atlantic. Air cover for Dutch West Indies oil convoys would come from the West Indies and UK air cover for TORCH oil convoys would come from the West Indies and Gibraltar. Air cover for convoys from the UK to Freetown would come from Northwest and West Africa.

2   The Prime Minister indicated that he wished German submarines to be referred to as U-boats rather than dignifying them by calling them submarines.

3   Providing the monthly shipping loss rate was not more than 2.4 per cent.

4   Four convoys would sail to the northern Soviet ports in November and December (each around 17 ships); all the ships arrived safely. A German force led by the *Scharnhorst* battleship tried to attack the fourth convoy. The convoy escorts, led by HMS *Duke of York*, stopped them, sinking the *Scharnhorst*.

5   Covering the period after 1 July 1943.

6   It was noted that an additional troop lift of 500,000 men to England would be possible if losses in shipping were reduced from 2.6 to 2 per cent a month in 1943.

7   Rather than one convoy making a complete round trip, two convoys would operate back to back. This doubled the number of escorts required.

8   The invasion of Sicily.

9   The minimum import requirements for the United Kingdom during 1943 were 27 million tons.

the convoys if they could give Russia something she had not previously expected and suggested aircraft.

Roosevelt asked what new escort construction would be available by June of 1943. Admiral King replied 100 escort vessels but it was only a small net gain if the present loss rates continued.[10] Admiral Pound said there was no substitute for destroyers in protecting convoys and they were utilizing sixteen destroyers and eight other ships on the 40-day convoys. The force would have to be doubled to operate two convoys on the 27-day cycle. Hopkins asked whether the destroyers and escort vessels could be used elsewhere if the convoys were stopped. Pound said the escort vessels would be released, except for the Home Fleet destroyers, which had to watch for the German fleet breaking out into the Atlantic.[11]

Hopkins said the Chiefs of Staff should consider eliminating the Russian convoys via the northern route.[12] It might be possible to increase the delivery of munitions to Russia over the Persian route and via Alaska,[13] although the Russians objected to handling some types of munitions over these routes. They could also increase the Protocol in certain types of munitions such as aircraft. This would save 500,000 tons of shipping from the Russian convoys. The considerable losses of shipping connected with the northern convoys[14] would be eliminated, as well as the cargoes lost when ships were sunk. The Chiefs of Staff had been inclined to consider aid to Russia as a political expedient but the question needed to be viewed from the standpoint of military necessity.

Churchill said it would be a great thing if they could continue the Russian convoys throughout the HUSKY period. It was better to continue on the 40-day cycle rather than attempt the 27-day cycle before HUSKY and then stop the convoys during HUSKY. They had never promised to take supplies to Russia; they had merely committed themselves to making munitions available to them at their ports. General Somervell[15] said they would be able to send 30 ships a month to the Persian Gulf ports by 1 July, offering good prospects for increasing the supply to Russia.

Roosevelt said supplying Russia was a paying investment. Stopping the convoys in July and August would occur when the Russians would be engaged in their most severe fighting.[16] It was difficult to predict what the shipping losses situation would be at that time, or the conditions along the route of the northern convoys.[17] Admiral King said they were definitely committed to HUSKY and everything had to be done to ensure its success, including the elimination of the Russian convoys if necessary.

---

10 In other words, nearly 100 escort vessels would be sunk in the same period.
11 The German fleet had been holed up in Norwegian waters since February 1942, occasionally attacking the Arctic Convoys, in particular at the Battle of the Barents Sea in December 1942.
12 With the increasing hours of daylight and the ice moving south in the spring, it was essential to increase the number of escorts to the North Russia convoys.
13 Through the Persian Gulf into Iran or from Alaska to Siberia; neither was ideal and both were heavy on shipping.
14 The convoys to Murmansk and Archangel.
15 Lieutenant General Brehon B. Somervell (1892-1955), Commanding General of the Army Service Forces, responsible for logistics.
16 The Battle of Kursk, the largest tank battle in history, would take place in the summer of 1943.
17 It was light most of the time in July and August, making it dangerous for shipping.

Roosevelt said the United States had been suffering great shipping losses along her East Coast at the time of the last conference.[1] The area had almost been cleared of submarines and the greatest losses were now occurring off the coast of South America.[2]

Marshall said the first charge against the United Nations was the defeat of the submarine menace while aid to Russia came next.[3] If they had to suffer the losses in the Murmansk convoys, they hurt Russia as much as the US and UK. Such losses made it impossible to attack on other fronts, eliminating the possibility of forcing the Germans to withdraw ground and air troops from the Russian front. Last year's losses came just as they were labouring to build up BOLERO.[4] It must be made certain they did not endanger HUSKY's success.

Churchill agreed the passage of convoys on the northern route had to be stopped if their cost became prohibitive. But it was right to consider continuing the convoys through the HUSKY period, while making no promises to Stalin. Admiral Pound said this had to be the case because the Royal Navy could not play its part in HUSKY if they were committed to the convoys.

Churchill said the discontinuance of these convoys would depend upon the losses suffered. They had to tell Stalin the facts; he had to rely on a 40-day schedule[5] and they could not promise to continue the convoys while HUSKY was being undertaken.[6] It had to be made clear the US and UK were under no obligation to continue the convoys. Roosevelt said the draft message to Stalin required some revision. It also had to be remembered the Russian General Staff would be making plans on the assumption the munitions in the Protocol would be available. In fairness to them, they needed to know what was intended.

Roosevelt asked how a 2.4% per month loss rate would relate to the 700,000 tons loss of shipping per year. Admiral King thought the loss rate of 2.4% would reduce the losses in shipping to less than 700,000 tons. The Prime Minister had said before the House of Commons that the shipping situation would be satisfactory if their losses could be reduced below 500,000 tons per year.

Roosevelt said the shipping situation was bound to improve during the coming year because they had nearly doubled the construction program and introduced more effective anti-submarine measures. Admiral King agreed and said the great losses on the East Coast of the United States were possibly in large measure

---

1   A number of military meetings called between Roosevelt and Churchill at short notice in June 1942. The conference had no codename.
2   Oil supplies had to be transferred from the Caribbean oil fields to the eastern seaboard. A lot of bauxite, the ore for aluminium, came from South America.
3   U-boats had increased the size of their packs to 12 to 18, required stronger surface and air support. It was estimated a convoy needed three plus one escort for every 10 ships in the convoy in dangerous areas and one plus one for every 10 ships elsewhere. Stronger air cover worked if the U-boats were not operating in packs.
4   The movement of one million US troops to Britain was planned by General Henry H. Arnold; the word BOLERO was substituted for Great Britain in correspondence.
5   The 40-day schedule involved an 11-day voyage in each direction and three days to unload in the Russian port. The remaining 15 days were used to load the ships and check them over.
6   The convoys stopped at the end of February and started in November.

because of a lack of effective means to combat the submarines; great improvements had been made in this respect.

Churchill suggested they should continue the 40-day convoy throughout HUSKY if the shipping situation was better than expected, but they should not commit themselves either way. While it might be possible to continue the convoys, they had to be stopped if the losses were too great. Admiral King suggested reviewing the situation on 1 May before deciding whether or not to discontinue the convoys.[7]

Operations in the Mediterranean

The Chiefs of Staff had carefully examined possible operations in the Mediterranean Theatre and they recorded the following conclusions:

(1) Attack Sicily in 1943 with the favourable July moon as the target date.[8]

(2) Instruct General Eisenhower to report (not later than 1 March), firstly, whether any insurmountable difficulties regarding resources and training would delay the date of the assault beyond the favourable July moon; secondly, in that event to confirm the date would not be later than the favourable August moon.

(3) The following should be the command set-up for the operation:

a)   General Eisenhower to be in Supreme Command with General Alexander as Deputy Commander-in-Chief. They were responsible for the detailed planning and preparation and for the execution of the operation.

b)   Admiral Cunningham to be Naval Commander and Air Chief Marshal Tedder to be Air Commander.

c)   General Eisenhower to submit recommendations for the Western and Eastern Task Force Commanders in due course.[9]

(4) General Eisenhower should be instructed to set up[10] a special operational and administrative staff, with its own Chief of Staff, for planning and preparing the operation.

Discussion on the Invasion of Sicily

Marshall said training and other features in connection with the preparations for HUSKY had to be considered. Training and preparations had to be scheduled but if an impossible or improbable target date was set and later changed to a practical one, they would be out of adjustment and might compromise every aspect of the operation. The target date had been exhaustively studied and it was going to be difficult to mount HUSKY with properly trained forces even in July.

Roosevelt asked if the target date in July was made on the assumption the Axis forces would be driven from Tunisia by the end of April. He asked what the effect would be if they were eliminated from Africa by the end of March.

---

7   Giving time to assess the impact on Operation HUSKY, which was due to begin on 10 July 1943.

8   It was agreed that efforts would be made over the next three weeks to make it possible to launch the operation during the favourable June moon period. Churchill wished to set the target date as the period of the favourable June moon rather than that of July.

9   The Western Task Force would be Seventh US Army, commanded by General George S. Patton (1885-1945); nickname Blood and Guts. The Eastern Task Force would be Eighth British Army, commanded by General Bernard L. Montgomery.

10 After consultation with General Alexander.

Marshall replied success in Tunisia at the end of March would improve the situation somewhat but it was not the limiting factor.[1] This was organizing naval crews and assembling landing craft. When they were ready, the naval crews and landing craft had to be made available for the training of troops. The situation in Tunisia might result in delaying HUSKY but an earlier success would move the target date forward. Admiral King said it was a question whether the assault on Sicily should be made by partially or fully trained forces.

Roosevelt suggested the operation might be easier than TORCH in view of the better weather in the Mediterranean.[2] Lord Mountbatten said the weather was not HUSKY's expected difficulty; it was the excellence of the enemy's defences.[3]

Marshall pointed out some of the errors made during TORCH were owing to lack of adequate training. Some landing boats went to the wrong place and one Ranger unit landed 18 miles away from the shore battery it was supposed to take. Roosevelt said this might have been poor navigation rather than inadequate training.[4] Marshall replied while they had divisions with amphibious training, they did not have the landing craft or crews. The craft had to be built and the crews had to be trained.

Churchill agreed the point that HUSKY's target date did not depend on the Tunisian operations but on training was a good one. However, the British were going to send their overseas assault force, with a capacity of seven brigade groups, to participate in HUSKY. He had been told it could not leave England until 14 March and then had to undergo some training in the eastern Mediterranean. Surely the force could be sent earlier and Lord Mountbatten said he had been told it could be sent by the end of February. Churchill said this would be done.

Churchill said no effort should be spared to obtain capable navigators for HUSKY and suggested combing the navy, particularly the R class battleships, to set up a special group of navigators.[5] Admiral Pound said skilled navigators could not be taken from the navy without serious effects; they would have to be supplemented by inexperienced men and so the training period could not be shortened.

Churchill feared the gap of perhaps four months during the summer when no US or British troops would be in contact with the Germans.[6] Roosevelt agreed and said it might have a serious effect all over the world. Brooke said the Combined Chiefs of Staff had examined the timing of the operation most carefully. September was the date first put forward and they had rejected it. Further study had brought the date back to the end of August. The Combined Chiefs of Staff had then put on the pressure and July had been tentatively fixed, although

---

1   The Axis forces did not capitulate in Tunisia until 13 May; however, over 275,000 German and Italian soldiers (many of whom had just arrived from Sicily) surrendered. Operation HUSKY was launched on 9/10 July.
2   The weather was more predictable and the seas calmer in July in the Mediterranean than on Morocco's Atlantic Coast in November.
3   Not so much beach defences, but air defences.
4   In other words, a naval problem rather than a Ranger problem.
5   Five Revenge class battleships fuelled by a mixture of coal and oil, launched between 1914 and 1916.
6   Between the capture of Tunisia in March and the Sicily landings in July.

August remained a more likely date. Brooke agreed trying to fix too early a date would prejudice the preparations. It was impossible to shorten the loading period, and training was the only process that could have time lopped off. But the result might be disastrous if it was curtailed.

Churchill thought the loading might be accelerated by intense efforts. Similarly, if the landing craft used to maintain Eighth Army[7] could be recovered, training might start earlier. All these points had to be rigorously examined before the July date could be accepted. Marshall said if the date was going to be earlier it had to be by a complete four weeks, unless the added risks of moonlight were acceptable.

Roosevelt said the present proposals were based on a large number of factors, which might well prove correct, but they were estimates, for example the state of morale in Italy, which recent reports indicated was deteriorating. If this process continued, the Germans might face an Italy in revolt. It was essential for them to have their preparations far enough advanced to be able to act, not necessarily in Sicily but perhaps in Sardinia, or even in Italy. For this reason he would like to set the date for June, but it was understood it might have to be carried out in July if the enemy's strength remained as at present.

Marshall pointed out to bring back the date at the expense of adequate preparation would not make it any easier to stage an improvised operation during the intervening months. The troops would have been moved into place quite early in the preparatory period, so they would be standing ready if required.[8] Brooke agreed and said they would probably get some advance indication of an Italian collapse, which would enable them to speed up the launching of a smaller force. It would be quite wrong to risk a costly failure by unduly curtailing the period of preparation.

Churchill said Marshall was pleading for the integrity of the operation and his arguments were most convincing. Nevertheless, he was not convinced the integrity of the operation would be compromised with a June date. Some quicker methods for moving troops into place might be found. Marshall said this had also been examined.[9]

The period after the fall of Tunis would not be one of inactivity, as a growing air bombardment of Italy would be launched. They ought to place themselves in a position to do the hard operation against Sicily while being ready to improvise if the enemy weakened.[10] The initial landing in Sicily was larger than envisaged for ROUNDUP.[11] Roosevelt asked if the pressure could be eased if the Spanish situation cleared during the spring. Marshall said the troops standing ready to move into Spanish Morocco would be simultaneously training for Sicily.

Admiral King said one of the innumerable items which had to be considered was the provision of armoured landing craft. He and Mountbatten agreed they

---

7 Used to move supplies along the North African coast.
8 Preparation for the operation involved training the soldiers and sailors; it also involved stockpiling supplies and ammunition. Then there was the problem of security to consider.
9 There is a real clash of ideology between Churchill the British politician and Marshall the American soldier.
10 There were many unknowns, including the state of the Tunisian airfields and ports after the Axis withdrew or surrendered.
11 Seven assault divisions (three British, three American and one Canadian) were ashore by the end of the first day.

were essential but there were none available for the US forces. He agreed the ideal method for launching the operation would be to follow on the heels of the Germans fleeing from Tunis. But he was convinced the closest they could come to this ideal was July. He would have liked June, but he felt it was impossible to promise such a date.

Roosevelt said the important point was to retain a flexible mind, so advantage could be taken of every opportunity. Marshall felt embarrassed over the date of the operation, remembering the incentive for hastening TORCH in view of the US elections.[1] In spite of that, it had not proved possible to advance the date. Churchill said there had been a lot of admiration in England because the election had not been allowed to influence the course of military events in the slightest.

After some further discussion, it was agreed the July date should stand, subject to an instruction. Over the next three weeks, without prejudice to the July date, an intense effort should be made to try and achieve the favourable June moon as the date of the operation. Eisenhower's instructions could be modified to conform if the June date could be fixed at the end of the three weeks.

Mediterranean Cover Plans
The Chiefs of Staff intended to instruct the appropriate agencies in Washington and London and the Commander-in-Chief, Allied Expeditionary Force in North Africa, to draw up a comprehensive cover plan for the Mediterranean. The possibility of carrying out feints or minor operations in the eastern Mediterranean would be examined.[2]

Command in the Mediterranean Theatre
The Chiefs of Staff had agreed to the following command arrangements in the Mediterranean.

Sea Operations: The Naval Commander of Force X designated for HUSKY would become Commander-in-Chief, Mediterranean.[3] The Commander-in-Chief, Mediterranean, would become Commander-in-Chief, Levant.[4] The Commander-in-Chief, Mediterranean, would be responsible for naval matters affecting the Mediterranean as a whole.

Land Operations: At a predetermined moment after Eighth Army crossed the Tunisian border, Alexander would become Deputy Commander-in-Chief to Eisenhower; Eighth Army would transfer to Eisenhower's command at the same time. Subject to the concurrence of Eisenhower, Alexander's primary task would be to command the Allied forces on the Tunisian front with a small headquar-

---

1   The US congressional elections had been on 4 November 1943, a few days before the TORCH landing. The original date for the landing had been October but Roosevelt made no reference to tying the two together. Roosevelt is quoted as saying "this was a decision that rested with the responsible officer, Eisenhower, and not with the Democratic National Committee."
2   Churchill suggested including Norway in cover plans but General Brooke pointed out it might add to the difficulties of the Russian convoys if the Germans reacted by reinforcing Norway. He suggested active preparations all over the North African shore to disguise the objective and disperse the Axis forces. Roosevelt thought the creation of General Giraud's French army might make the Axis think the southern coast of France was a target.
3   Admiral Sir Andrew Cunningham with the Western Naval Task Force commanded by Vice Admiral H. Kent Hewitt and the Eastern Naval Task Force commanded by Vice Admiral Bertram Ramsay.
4   The boundary between the two Commands would be from Zanti to Bardia at the Libyan–Egyptian border on the North African coast.

ters of his own. After the conclusion of these operations, he would take charge of HUSKY.[5]

Air Operations: Air Chief Marshal Sir Arthur Tedder would be appointed Air Commander-in-Chief of the whole Mediterranean theatre with his Headquarters at Algiers. Under him would be the Air Officer Commanding in Chief, Northwest Africa,[6] and the Air Officer Commanding in Chief, Middle East.[7]

The Bomber Offensive from North Africa

The Chiefs of Staff laid down the following objectives for the bomber offensive from North Africa:[8]

1) Continuing operations to evict all Axis Forces from Africa.
2) Inflict the heaviest possible losses on the Axis air and naval forces in preparation for HUSKY, including the bombing required by their cover plans.
3) Operation HUSKY.
4) The destruction of the Ploesti oil refineries.

Bombing objectives would be chosen with a view to weakening the Italian will to continue the war.

Operations from the United Kingdom

The Chiefs of Staff agreed the US Heavy Bombardment Units in the UK would operate under the strategical direction of the British Chief of the Air Staff. The United States Commanding General would decide upon the technique and method to be employed.[9]

Operation BOLERO

The Chiefs of Staff had studied the shipping capabilities for the BOLERO build-up in 1943. They had checked the available data and made a number of assumptions, to compile the following table of US forces available for Continental operations in the UK. They were the minimum and every effort would be made to increase their number before 15 August:[10]

By 15 August	384,000 (4 divisions)	15 November	759,000 (12 divisions)
15 September	509,000 (7 divisions)	31 December	938,000 (15 divisions)
15 October	634,000 (9 divisions)[11]		

The overall number of men per division would decrease as the movement continued and it might be down to 40,000 by the end of the year, in which case the number of divisions available on 31 December might be 19 instead of 15.

---

5   The boundary between the North African and Middle East Commands would be the Tunisian-Tripolitania frontier (the northwest region of Libya).

6   General Carl A. Spaatz (1891-1974), nickname Tooey, was commander of Twelfth Air Force in North Africa in December 1942 and promoted to commander of the Allied Northwest African Air Force in February 1943.

7   Air Chief Marshal Sir Sholto Douglas (1893-1969) was Air Officer Commanding in Chief of Fighter Command before he was appointed Air Officer Commanding in Chief, Middle East.

8   The Prime Minister said it would be advisable to maintain the threat of bombardment against Rome but not to carry it out without further consultation. The President agreed.

9   US 8th Bomber Command had U-boat targets at the top of their list and attacked them on every possible occasion, with good results. However, there had been considerable criticism in the UK because they never attacked targets across Germany.

10 Based on 50,000 combat and service troops per division and 45 days between sailing and availability dates.

11 All figures include the build-up of the air contingent to 172,000.

But the number of divisions earlier in the year was unlikely to be increased. The Chiefs of Staff had examined the problem of amphibious operations from the United Kingdom in 1943. Plans and preparations had to be made for three types of operation:

1) Raids with the primary object of provoking air battles and causing enemy losses.[1]

2) Operations with the object of seizing and holding a bridgehead and exploiting success, if the state of German morale and resources permitted.[2]

3) A return to the Continent to take advantage of German disintegration.[3]

Plans and preparations for the raids would proceed as at present. An attack on the Channel Islands was an example of the type of operation they had in mind.

The Chiefs of Staff proposed preparation for an operation against the Cotentin Peninsula with the available resources, the target date being set as 1 August, 1943. This operation came under type (2).

The Chiefs of Staff agreed to establish a Combined Staff under a British Chief of Staff until a Supreme Commander was appointed.[4] A directive to govern the planning was being prepared and it was intended to include provision for a return to the Continent under (3), with the forces available in the United Kingdom month by month. The directive would also make provision for the planning of an invasion of the Continent in force in 1944.

Operations in the Pacific Theatre

The following was an outline of operations intended to be carried out in the Pacific:

(1) Make the Aleutians as secure as could be.[5]

(2) An advance from Midway[6] towards Truk–Guam and particularly in conjunction with the operations now in hand for the capture of Rabaul.

(3) An advance along the line Samoa–Jaluit.[7]

(4) An advance on the Malay Barrier on a limited scale to counter enemy capabilities and divert his forces.[8]

It was not intended to advance from the Rabaul area towards the Truk-Guam line unless, and until, forces were in hand to enable the advance to be carried through and followed up.[9]

---

1   Raids across the English Channel to entice the Luftwaffe into the air.

2   Operation ROUNDUP.

3   Operation RANKIN.

4   General Sir Frederick E. Morgan (1894–1967) would be appointed Chief of Staff to the Supreme Allied Commander (Designate) (COSSAC) in March 1943.

5   A Japanese task force seized the chain of islands between northeast Russia and Alaska in June 1942. A US Task Force invaded Attu Island in May 1943 and an abandoned Kiska Island in August 1943.

6   The Battle of Midway in June 1942 was a victory for the US Navy. The island was over 1500 miles west-northwest of Hawaii. Guam is over 200 miles west-southwest of Midway.

7   The Samoan Islands are 1500 miles north-northeast of New Zealand. Jaluit is in the Marshall Islands 2000 miles northnorthwest of the Samoan Islands.

8   The Indonesia Islands, running west from East Timor, 400 miles north of Australia.

9   Rabaul in Papua New Guinea.

Operations in China

The Chiefs of Staff intended to support the Chinese war effort, provide the means for intensifying attacks on Japanese shipping and to strike at Japan herself when the opportunity offered. They would improve air transportation into China by supplying additional transport aircraft. They would also build up the US Air Forces now operating in China to the maximum extent logistical limitations and other important claims would permit. They hoped more sustained operations with increased Air Forces could begin in the spring, and this development was of great importance in the general scheme.[10]

Reconquest of Burma and Opening of the Burma Road

The Chiefs of Staff approved 15 November 1943 as the provisional date for the ANAKIM assault. In July 1943 they had to decide whether to undertake the operation or postpone it.[11] They had prepared a provisional schedule of the forces required for the operation but while the land and air forces could be provided, naval forces, assault shipping, landing craft and other shipping could not be guaranteed so far in advance. It would depend upon the situation existing in the late summer of 1943.

The Axis Oil Position

The Chiefs of Staff had information from British sources on the Axis oil position[12] but additional information available in Washington could modify the British conclusions. They had directed the Combined Intelligence Committee to submit as early as possible an agreed assessment of the Axis oil situation based on the latest information available from both British and United States sources.[13]

In the meanwhile, they had noted the Axis oil situation was so restricted it was decidedly advantageous to make bombing attacks on their oil sources, as soon as other commitments allowed; namely, against the Romanian oil fields and oil traffic via the Danube, and the synthetic and producer gas plants in Germany.[14]

Naval and Air Command in West Africa

The Chiefs of Staff had agreed upon the following naval and air arrangements to cover the French West African Coast:

(a)   The West African Coast from Cape Bojador[15] south would be under the command of a British naval officer for naval operations and a British air officer for air operations.[16]

---

10 Increasing the number of aircraft flying supplies over the Hump.
11 The amphibious assault designed to help retake Burma and open the supply route to China. It was timed for the autumn of 1943, after the monsoon; it would be cancelled.
12 Germany depended on the Ploesti oil fields in Romania for one-third of her oil. It was suggested to wait for Turkish bases before attacking it because of the long range and unreliable weather. Synthetic oil plants were also essential to the German war effort but they were small targets, requiring improvements in daylight precision bombing. Attacks on Danube oil traffic were also suggested.
13 The Combined Intelligence Committee brought together the US Joint Intelligence Committee and the British Joint Intelligence Subcommittee.
14 Airplanes equipped with the new H2SL device, the forerunner of the latest precision bombing by radio beam equipment, were starting to be used. It would permit precision bombing regardless of weather.
15 Rio d'Oro.
16 The coastline south of Morocco, now the Western Sahara.

(b) A sub-area extending from Cape Bojador to the western boundary of Sierra Leone would be under French Command.[1] French air units would take over air duties as soon as equipment and training permitted.

Turkey

The Chiefs of Staff had agreed the necessary administrative measures so the British could handle all matters connected with Turkey.[2]

Fifteenth Combined Chiefs of Staff Meeting

Operation HUSKY directive; Assault shipping; Final report to the President and Prime Minister; Conclusion of the conference.

24 January

The President meets General Giraud

Roosevelt found Giraud "reluctant to cooperate with de Gaulle, but [he] eventually agreed to do so."

The President meets General De Galle

Roosevelt could not "persuade de Gaulle to accept the text of a draft joint statement or communiqué regarding his meeting with Giraud."

The President and Prime Minister met General de Gaulle and General Giraud

The four discussed a joint statement to be made by the two French generals.

The Symbol Press Conference[3]

The President: This meeting goes back to the successful landing operations last November, which as you all know were initiated as far back as a year ago and put into definite shape shortly after the Prime Minister's visit to Washington in June.

After the success of the operations of last November, it became perfectly clear the time had come for another review of the situation and planning for the next steps, especially the steps to take in 1943. That is why we came here, and our respective staffs came with us, to discuss the practical steps to be taken by the United Nations for prosecution of the war. We have been here about a week.

I might add we began talking about this after 1 December and at that time we invited Mr. Stalin to join us at a convenient meeting place. He very greatly desired to come, but was precluded from leaving Russia because he was conducting the new Russian offensive against the Germans along the whole line. We must remember he is Commander-in-Chief and responsible for the very wonderful detailed plan which has been brought to such a successful conclusion since the beginning of the offensive.

In spite of the fact Mr. Stalin was unable to come, the results of the staff meeting have been communicated to him, so we will continue to keep in very close

---

1   The west coast of Africa (south of the British zone) covering what is now Senegal, The Gambia, Guinea and Sierra Leone.

2   While all matters connected with Turkey were handled by the British, all matters connected with China were handled by the United States.

3   The press conference was held on the lawn behind the President's villa. Around 50 pressmen sat cross-legged on the lawn, while the President and Prime Minister sat on chairs.

touch with each other. I think it can be said the studies during the past week or ten days are unprecedented in history. Both the Prime Minister and I think back to the days of the First World War when conferences between the French and British and ourselves very rarely lasted more than a few hours or a couple of days. The Chiefs of Staffs have been in intimate touch; they have lived in the same hotel. Each man has become a definite personal friend of his opposite number on the other side.

Furthermore, these conferences have discussed, I think for the first time in history, the whole global picture. It isn't just one front, just one ocean, or one continent – it is literally the whole world; and that is why the Prime Minister and I feel the conference is unique in this global aspect.

The Combined Staffs, in these conferences and studies during the past week or ten days, have proceeded on the principle of pooling all of the resources of the United Nations. And I think the second point is they have reaffirmed the determination to maintain the initiative against the Axis Powers in every part of the world.

These plans cover certain things, such as united operations conducted in different areas of the world. Secondly, the sending of all possible material aid to the Russian offensive, with the double object of cutting down the manpower of Germany and her satellites, and continuing the very great attrition of German munitions and materials of all kinds, which are being destroyed every day in such large quantities by the Russian armies.

And, at the same time, the Staffs have agreed on giving all possible aid to the heroic struggle of China – remembering China is in her sixth year of the war – with the objective, not only in China but in the whole of the Pacific area, of ending any Japanese attempt in the future to dominate the Far East.

Another point; I think we have all had it in our hearts and heads before, but I do not think it has ever been put down on paper by the Prime Minister and myself, and that is the determination that peace can come to the world only by the total elimination of German and Japanese war power.

Some of you Britishers know the old story – we had a General called US Grant. His name was Ulysses Simpson Grant, but in my, and the Prime Minister's, early days he was called "Unconditional Surrender" Grant.[4] The elimination of German, Japanese and Italian war power means the unconditional surrender by Germany, Italy, and Japan. That means a reasonable assurance of future world peace. It does not mean the destruction of the population of Germany, Italy, or Japan, but it does mean the destruction of the philosophies in those countries based on conquest and the subjugation of other people.

While we have not had a meeting of all of the United Nations, I think there is no question – in fact we are both confident the same purposes and objectives are in the minds of all of the other United Nations – Russia, China, and all the others.

---

4   Ulysses S. Grant (1822-1885) a highly effective general for the Union forces during the second half to the American Civil War and then 18th President of America. He would only accept "unconditional and immediate surrender" from the Confederates.

And so the actual meeting has come to a successful conclusion. I call it a meeting of minds with regard to all military operations, and, thereafter, the war is going to proceed against the Axis Powers according to schedule, with every indication that 1943 is going to be an even better year for the United Nations than 1942.

The Prime Minister: I agree with everything the President has said, and I think it was a very happy decision to bring you gentlemen here to Casablanca to this agreeable spot, Anfa Camp, which has been the scene of much the most important and successful war conference which I have ever attended or witnessed. Nothing like the continuous work has occurred in my experience, which is a long while. Hours and hours every day from morning until often after midnight, carried on by the Staffs of both sides, by all the principal officers of the two nations who are engaged in the direction of the war.

This work has proceeded with an intensity, and thoroughness, and comprehensiveness, the like of which I have never seen, and I firmly believe you will find results will come from this, as this year unfolds. You will find results will come from it which will give our troops, and soldiers, and fliers, the best possible chance to gather new victories from the enemy. Fortune turned a more or less sombre face upon us at the close of last year and we meet here today at this place; which in a way is the active centre of the war direction.

We wish indeed it was possible to have Premier Stalin, and the Generalissimo and others of the United Nations here, but geography is a stubborn thing; and the difficulties and pre-occupations of the men engaged in fighting the enemy in other countries are also very clear obstacles to their free movement, and therefore we have had to meet here together.

Well, one thing I should like to say, and that is, and I think I can say it with full confidence, nothing which may occur in this war will ever come between me and the President. He and I are in this as friends and partners, and we work together. We know our easy, free conversation is one of the sinews of the Allied Powers. It makes many things easy that would otherwise be difficult, and solutions can be reached when an agreement has stopped (which would otherwise be impossible), even with the utmost goodwill, of the vast war machinery which the English-speaking people are operating.

I think the Press have had rather a hard, provoking time, because it isn't possible to have everything organized at once when you throw yourselves on a shore. Some of our earliest and brightest hopes have not yet been fulfilled, and you gentlemen have no doubt felt baffled in the work you want to do, and therefore a trial is imposed upon you. I beg you to rise to the level of that; namely, not to allow the minor annoyances of censoring make you exaggerate these details. To keep your sense of proportion is a patriotic duty.

Tremendous events have happened. This enterprise which the President has organized, and he knows I have been his active Lieutenant since the start, has altered the whole strategic aspect of the war. It has forced the Germans to fight under the very greatest difficulties. And I think it gives us the initiative in a very marked way. Once we have got that precious treasure into our hands, we must labour hard to keep it. Hitler said you never could tell what would happen, because he was not dealing with competent military experts but with military idiots and drunkards. He said he did not know where he was, and that was a preliminary forecast of the explanation which he will no doubt offer to the Nazi Party for the complete manner in which he has been hoodwinked, fooled, and out-manoeuvred by the great enterprise which was launched on these shores.

We are still in full battle, and heavy action will impend. Our forces grow. The Eighth Army has taken Tripoli, and we are following Rommel – the fugitive of Egypt and Libya – now wishing, no doubt, to represent himself as the deliverer of Tunisia. The Eighth Army have followed him a long way – 1500 miles – from Alamein, where I last saw them, to Tripoli. And Rommel is still flying before them. But I can give you this assurance – everywhere Mary went the lamb is sure to go.

I hope you gentlemen will find this talk to be of assistance to you in your work, and will be able to build up a good and encouraging story to our people all over the world. Give them the picture of unity, thoroughness, and integrity of the political chiefs. Give them that picture, and make them feel there is some reason behind all that is being done. Even when there is some delay there is design and purpose. As the President has said, the unconquerable will to pursue this quality, until we have procured the unconditional surrender of the criminal forces who plunged the world into storm and ruin.

The President: I think – the Prime Minister having spoken of the Eighth Army – that you should know that we have had a long talk with General Alexander, Admiral Cunningham and Tedder. General Eisenhower has been here, as has General Spaatz and General Clark too. We have had a pretty good picture of the whole south shore of the Mediterranean, at first hand.

This afternoon a communiqué will be given to each of you from the Prime Minister and myself. It is really the formal document stating the history of this conference, and the names of all the people who have taken part; nothing very much in it in addition to what we have talked about as background for you all.

You will want to know about the presence of General Giraud and General de Gaulle. I think all that should be said at this time is that the Prime Minister and I felt here we were in French North Africa and it would be an opportune time for those two gentlemen to meet together, one Frenchman with another Frenchman. They have been in conference now for a couple of days, and we have emphasized one common purpose, and that is the liberation of France. They are at work on that. They are in accord on that, and we hope very much that as a result of getting to know each other better under these modern, new conditions, we will have French armies, and French navies, and French airmen who will take part with us in the ultimate liberation of France itself.

I have not got anything else relating to the United Staffs conference, but, it is purely personal, I might as well give it to you as background. I have had the opportunity, during these days, of visiting a very large number of American troops. I went up the line the other day and saw combat teams and the bulk of several divisions. I talked with the officers, and with the men. I lunched with them in the field, and it was a darn good lunch. We had to move the band, because it was a very windy day, from leeward to windward, so we could hear the music.

From these reviews we went over to a fort – I don't know whether you can use the name or not – that is up to General McClure.[1] Actually, it was at the mouth of Port Lyautey[2] where the very heavy fighting occurred and where a large number of Americans and Frenchmen were killed. Their bodies, most of them, lie in a joint cemetery – French and American. I placed a wreath where the American graves are and another wreath where the French graves are.

I saw the equipment of the troops ready to go into action at any time; and I wish the people back home could see it, because those troops are equipped with the most modern weapons we can turn out. They are adequately equipped in every way. And I found them not only in excellent health and high spirits, but also a very great efficiency on the part of officers and men, all the way from top to bottom. I am sure they are eager to fight again, and I think they will.

I would like to say just a word about the bravery and the fine spirit of the French whom we fought, many of whom were killed. They fought with very heavy losses, as you know, but the moment the peace came and fighting stopped, the French Army and Navy, and the French and Moroccan civil population gave to us Americans wholehearted assistance in carrying out the common objective that brings us to these parts – to improve the conditions of living in these parts. Which you know better than I do have been seriously hurt by the fact that during the last two years so much of the output, especially the food output of French North Africa, has been sent to the German Army. That time is ended and we are going to do all we can for the population of these parts, to keep them going until they can bring in their own harvests during this coming summer.

Also, I had one very delightful party. I gave a dinner party for the Sultan of Morocco[3] and his son. We got on extremely well. He is greatly interested in the welfare of his people, and he and the Moroccan population are giving to us the same kind of support the French population is.

So I just want to repeat I saw with my own eyes the actual conditions of our men who are in this part of North Africa on this trip. I think their families back home will be glad to know we are doing all we can, not only in full support of them, but in keeping up the splendid morale with which they are working at the present time. I want to say to their families, through you people, that I am mighty proud of them.

This is not like a Press Conference in Washington where we have 200 to 250 crowded into one rather small room, and it is almost impossible to meet everyone personally. You are an elite group, and because it is not too big a group, the Prime Minister and I want to meet all of you.

One thing, before we stop talking, is the release date of this thing. Sometimes I also am under orders. I have got to let General McClure decide the release date. There are certain reasons why it cannot be for a few days, but as I understand

---

1   Brigadier General Robert A. McClure.
2   Now called Kenitra in Morocco.
3   Sidi Mohammed be Yusef (1909-1961), Sultan of Morocco from 1927-1953. Exiled 1943-1955 and returned as Sultan and then King 1957-1961.

it, one of your problems is the bottleneck at Gibraltar. I think you have enough background to write your stories and put them on the cables, and General McClure will decide what the actual release date will be. I told him it should be just as soon as he possibly could.

The Trident Conference: 12–25 May 1943

The Prime Minister and around 100 staff crossed the Atlantic Ocean on the *Queen Mary* to attend TRIDENT, the largest assembly of Anglo-American staff so far in the war. Churchill was named Colonel Warden on the passenger list and insisted being put in a lifeboat armed with a machine gun if the ship was torpedoed, so he could "resist capture at all costs". Harry Hopkins met the party at Staten Island and escorted Churchill directly to Washington by train, where he was taken to the White House.

The conference began in the White House on 12 May with a mood of great optimism for the future. So far, Allied campaigns had been successful and they had virtually completed their transition to the initiative. News that organized resistance had ended in North Africa on the second day of the conference increased the optimistic mood.

In the Pacific, US forces had completed the Guadalcanal and Papua Campaigns and they were engaged in seizing Attu. On the Eastern Front the Soviet forces, having withstood the siege of Stalingrad, were continuing their counteroffensives. The Battle of the Atlantic was also turning in favour of the Allies while preparations were going forward for HUSKY in the Mediterranean.

For two weeks, the delegations debated strategic issues. The President and the Prime Minister met six times with the Combined Chiefs of Staff at the White House. The Combined Chiefs of Staff held almost daily in the Board of Governors room close by, in the Federal Reserve Building on Constitution Avenue.

12 May: First Trident Conference

The President welcomed the Prime Minister and the British Chiefs of Staff. He recalled they had all met in the White House, it was less than a year ago and had begun the moves leading up to TORCH. It was very appropriate they should meet again just as that operation was coming to a satisfactory conclusion. The meeting at Casablanca[4] had set on foot Operation HUSKY, and he hoped this would meet with similar good fortune.

He thought the keynote of their plans should be an intention to employ every resource of men and munitions against the enemy. Nothing that could be brought to bear should be allowed to stand idle. He then asked the Prime Minister to open the discussion.

---

4 The SYMBOL meetings in January 1943.

Churchill recalled the striking change in the situation since he had last sat by the President's desk, and had heard the news of the fall of Tobruk.[1] He could never forget how the President had sustained him and how the Shermans[2] that had been handed over so generously had made their reputation in Africa.

The British came to the present meeting adhering to the Casablanca decisions but there might have to be adjustments made necessary by their success, which allowed them to take a longer forward view. TORCH was over, HUSKY was near, what should come next? He would put forward views formed by careful study. They would not be in the shape of fixed plans, but rather of ideas for the common stock.

They had been able to produce a succession of brilliant events, which had altered the whole course of the war. They had the authority and prestige of victory. It was their duty to redouble their efforts, and grasp the fruits of their success. The only questions outstanding between the two Staffs were questions of emphasis and priority. He felt sure they could be solved by mutual agreement.

Churchill did not propose to deal with the U-boat war and the aerial bombardment of Germany. There were no differences of opinion on these subjects, although there might be a few points of detail to be cleared up between the two Staffs. He wanted to put forward a number of objectives and questions for consideration that might focus subsequent study.

The first objective was in the Mediterranean. The great prize there was to get Italy out of the war by whatever means was best. He recalled how in 1918, when Germany might have retreated to the Meuse or the Rhine and continued the fight, the defection of Bulgaria brought the whole of the enemy structure crashing to the ground.[3]

The collapse of Italy would cause a chill of loneliness over the German people and might be the beginning of their doom. Even if not immediately fatal to Germany, the effects of Italy coming out of the war would be very great; first of all on Turkey, who had always measured herself against Italy in the Mediterranean. The moment would come when a joint American-Russian-British request might be made to Turkey for permission to use bases in her territory from which to bomb Ploesti[4] and clear the Aegean Sea. Such a request could hardly fail to be successful if Italy was out of the war and the moment was chosen when Germany could take no powerful action against Turkey.

Another great effect of the elimination of Italy would be felt in the Balkans, where patriots of various nationalities were, with difficulty, held in check by large Axis forces, including 25 or more Italian divisions. If these withdrew, Germany

---

1   The Battle of Gazala was fought around the port of Tobruk between 26 May and 1 June 1942. The Allies lost over 50,000 casualties, 35,000 captured; material losses were also high.

2   The British had been using Cruiser tanks and heavier Matilda tanks. However, the arrival of the German Afrika Korps, and their 88mm anti-aircraft guns, which were used as anti-tank guns, had accounted for most of the Matildas. 300 American Sherman tanks took their place in September and October 1942, in time for the Battle of El Alamein.

3   The signing of the Armistice of Thessalonica and Bulgaria's armistice on 29 September 1918 had been the beginning of the end for the Central Powers.

4   Ploesti oil fields in Romania produced a third of the oil for the Axis.

would either have to give up the Balkans or withdraw large forces from the Russian Front to fill the gap. In no other way could relief be given to the Russian Front on so large a scale this year. The third effect would be the elimination of the Italian fleet. This would immediately release a considerable British squadron of battleships and aircraft carriers to proceed either to the Bay of Bengal or the Pacific to fight Japan.

Certain questions presented themselves in relation to the Mediterranean. Need they invade the soil of Italy, or could they crush her by air attack? Would Germany defend Italy? Would Italy be an economic burden to them? He did not think so. Would arguments against a general conquest of Italy apply equally against a toe and heel operation to establish contact with Yugoslavia?[5]

Finally, there was a large political question for the British and United States Governments. What sort of life after the war should they be willing to accord to Italy if she placed herself unreservedly in their hands? If Italy made a separate peace, they might have the use of Sardinia and the Dodecanese without having to fight for them.

The second objective was taking the weight off Russia. He was much impressed by Stalin's attitude, in spite of the stopping of the Arctic convoys.[6] For the first time, in his recent speech, Stalin had acknowledged the efforts and victories of his Allies. But they should never forget there were 185 German divisions on the Russian Front. They had destroyed the German Army in Africa, but soon they would not be in contact with them anywhere. The Russian effort was prodigious and it placed the United States and the United Kingdom in their debt; a position from which Churchill wanted to emerge. As he had already mentioned, the best way of taking the weight off the Russian Front in 1943 was to get, or knock, Italy out of the war, forcing the Germans to send a large number of troops to hold down the Balkans.

The third objective had already been mentioned by the President in his opening remarks. It was to apply to the greatest possible extent their vast armies, air forces, and munitions to the enemy. All plans had to be judged by this test. There was a large army, and the Metropolitan Fighter Air Force[7] in Great Britain. They had their finest and most experienced troops in the Mediterranean. The British alone had thirteen divisions in that Theatre.

Supposing HUSKY was completed by the end of August, Churchill asked what these troops should do for the next seven or eight months, when the cross-Channel operation might first be mounted. They could not possibly stand idle, and he could not contemplate so long a period of apparent inaction. It would have a serious effect on relations with the Russians, who were bearing such a disproportionate weight.

The objectives he had so far mentioned all led up to BOLERO, SLEDGE-HAMMER, and ROUNDUP.[8] He could not pretend the problem of landing on

---

5   The capture of the foot of the Italian mainland could be followed by an invasion of Yugoslavia.
6   As mentioned earlier, they stopped at the end of February and resumed in November.
7   The Royal Air Force.
8   BOLERO was the build-up of US troops in the United Kingdom. ROUNDUP and SLEDGEHAMMER were the original plans to invade northwest France.

the Channel coast had been solved. The difficult beaches, with the extreme tides, the strength of the enemy's defences, the number of his reserves and the ease of his communications, all made the task one which must not be underrated. Much, however, would be learned from HUSKY.

The question arose whether anything could be done this year, before the weather broke in August or September. All the British landing craft had gone from the United Kingdom to HUSKY, and owing to priority having been rightly given to SICKLE,[1] only one US Division was so far available in the UK. Nevertheless, plans were being made for an operation to provoke an air battle, and they were standing ready to exploit a German collapse, should it by any chance take place.[2] He wished to make it absolutely clear the British Government earnestly desired to undertake a full-scale invasion of the Continent from the United Kingdom as soon as possible. They certainly did not disdain the idea if a plan offering reasonable prospects of success could be made.

The fifth objective was aid to China. As a result of Casablanca, Field Marshal Wavell had prepared the best plan he could for Operation ANAKIM[3] and he thought it had some prospect of success. The difficulties of fighting in Burma were apparent. The jungle prevented the use of their modern weapons. The monsoon strictly limited the length of the campaigning season and there was no means of bringing sea power to bear. Should, however, ANAKIM be carried out successfully, he was advised the Burma Road could not be reopened until 1945 and even then its capacity would not be more than 20,000 tons a month.[4] Nevertheless, he had not gone back on the status of ANAKIM.

Churchill attached the same degree of importance as before to activity in the Indian Ocean Theatre of war. Was there any way of helping China in 1943 other than the air route? How could this be improved? The British readily shouldered their responsibility to establish and guard the air facilities required in Assam.[5] If further study showed it would be better to bypass Burma, he was anxious to find another means to utilize the large forces standing in India. He thought this alternative might well be found in an operation against the tip of Sumatra and the waist of Malaya at Penang.[6]

Churchill was anxious for them to find some means of making use of the advantages which had been so valuable in TORCH. In that operation, sea power had played its full part and complete surprise had been possible. They had seized a territory of importance, which brought in a new army on their side and forced the enemy to fight in a place most disadvantageous to him. These conditions might apply to an attack on Sumatra. The fleet to cover the operation would come from the Mediterranean after the elimination of Italy. This meant the oper-

---

1 The delivery of US infantry and armoured divisions, along with strategic and tactical air formations to the UK.
2 Operation RANKIN.
3 An amphibious assault on Rangoon, a land offensive in central Burma and a Chinese attack in the north.
4 The Burma Road needed repairing. It traversed very difficult terrain, which made reconstruction difficult.
5 The airfields in northeast India that American planes were using as they flew supplies over the eastern Himalayas (known as the Hump) into China.
6 On the island west of the Malaysian Peninsula and on the peninsula itself, north of Singapore.

ation could not be launched before March 1944, which would, however, be a suitable moment from the point of view of weather.[7]

Churchill felt the time had come to study the long-term plan for the defeat of Japan. He wanted once more to state the British determination to carry the struggle home to Japan. The only question was how best to do it. Churchill thought the US Chiefs of Staff should lead in a joint study, on the assumption Germany would be out of the war in 1944 and they could concentrate on the great campaign against Japan in 1945. If the underlying strategic conception was agreed, operations could be planned to fit in and the requisite specialized apparatus could be got ready in time. If, of course, Russia could be brought in against Japan, that would prove the best solution of all. Stalin had shown plain indications that Russia wanted to be in at the death, but the timing of Russian action would obviously depend upon what happened to Hitler, and when.[8]

In conclusion, Churchill hoped his remarks would be of use in framing an agenda for the Combined Chiefs of Staff Conferences, and would be some guide to the emphasis and priorities which should be assigned to the various theatres of operation, as well as to their relationship and reciprocal reactions.

Roosevelt expressed his gratitude to Churchill for the open manner in which he had presented his views. He said the Combined Staffs must approach their problems with open minds, giving full consideration to the priorities and relative importance of the many problems which they would consider in the course of the conferences. Roosevelt had always been a firm believer in attrition as an effective weapon. He pointed to the North African campaign and suggested it might have been less successful if sufficient forces had been sent to capture Tunisia on the initial landing. As a result of the Tunisian campaign there had been perhaps some 200,000 enemy casualties.[9] There would have been considerably less had Tunisia been taken at the outset. The United Nations were now out-producing both the Germans and the Japanese and if they broke even in their losses of airplanes and other munitions, they were, in effect, forging ahead. Roosevelt said every effort should be made to keep the large armies and naval forces available to the United Nations engaged with the enemy. The United Nations were losing ground when their forces remained idle.

Roosevelt expressed optimism as far as the situation in Turkey was concerned. When the Prime Minister went on his fishing trip after the Casablanca Conferences Roosevelt had been surprised by the cordial reception the Prime Minister had received.[10] He felt Turkey was now in a better political position than

---

7 After Sicily had been taken and the fleet had sailed to the Indian Ocean but before the monsoon season began in May.

8 The Soviet Union needed all her forces to hold the Germans on its Western Front, only when Germany had capitulated could she shift her armies east.

9 Roosevelt's point is that the small deployment of Allied troops to begin with and a slow build-up to the campaign had drawn more Axis troops into North Africa, particularly German troops. Over 230,000 German and Italian troops were taken as prisoners of war, including most of the German Afrika Korps.

10 Churchill met Turkish President Inonu at Yenice near Adana on 30 and 31 January 1943 and tried to persuade him to join the Allies. Churchill made promises of military help, codenamed HARDIHOOD, and asked to use Turkish airfields to bomb Ploesti. Churchill warned he would not stop the Soviets if they tried to control the Dardanelles but Inonu did not commit his country to the Allied cause.

she had ever been before. Perhaps Turkey could be brought to a favourable attitude toward the United Nations by diplomacy alone. If so, this would permit the use of her airfields for combined air operations against Ploesti, the German right flank and lines of communication.

If Turkey could be brought into the war there would be the possibility of combined operations toward the Adrianople line,[1] inducing Bulgaria to withdraw from the war. He felt the Russians would welcome any effort on the part of the United Nations which resulted in breaking the German lines of communication.[2] Attrition would also be at work during operations from Turkey.

Roosevelt asked "Where do we go from HUSKY?" He had always shrunk from the thought of putting large armies into Italy because it might result in attrition for the United Nations and play into Germany's hand.[3] He wanted a thorough investigation of what an occupation of all of Italy, or of the heel or toe of Italy, would mean as a drain on allied resources. But the Mediterranean area contained large armies of the United Nations, perhaps 25 divisions, and they had to be kept employed. There was not much time in 1943, because planning future operations was a lengthy procedure so the question to be decided quickly was how to use the Mediterranean troops that year.

Roosevelt said conditions in Italy were precarious. Italy might drop into the lap of the United Nations but they would then have the responsibility of supplying the Italian people. Everyone was agreed Italy must be reconstituted, but the mistakes regarding possession of the northern Adriatic, which occurred at the peace table after the last war, could not be repeated.[4]

Roosevelt said a survey should be made to determine the cost of occupying Italy or parts of it as opposed to the cost of achieving the same results by air offensives from Sicily or the heel and toe of Italy. The United Nations had to continue with a strategy which compelled the Germans to fight to take weight off Russia.[5] It was for this reason he questioned the occupation of Italy, feeling it might result in the release of German troops from that country.[6] The most effective way of forcing Germany to fight was by carrying out a cross-Channel operation.

Churchill did not feel an occupation of Italy would be necessary. In the event of an Italian collapse, the United Nations would occupy the necessary ports and air bases from which to carry on operations against the Balkans and southern

---

1   Adrianople, now Edirne, is in northwest Turkey, close to the borders of Greece and Bulgaria.
2   The lines of communication between Germany and Army Group South, operating in the Ukraine.
3   Roosevelt's fears were correct. The Germans dug in across the Italian Peninsula and the Allies were forced to break them, taking five months to break the Gustav Line south of Rome.
4   Istria was given to Italy following the dissolution of Austria-Hungary at the end of World War I. When Mussolini's regime took control, Croatians and Slovenes were subjected to forced Italianization and cultural suppression. They lost their right to education and religious practice in their own language. The TIGR (Trieste, Istria, Gorizia, Rijeka) formed in 1927 and it was one of the first anti-fascist resistance groups in Europe.
5   Fight anywhere but on the Eastern Front.
6   Forcing the Germans out of Italy would allow them to deploy troops against the Russians, while the Allies had to deploy troops to occupy the country.

Europe, but they should let an Italian Government control the country, subject to supervision on the part of the United Nations.[7]

Roosevelt said regardless of operations undertaken in the Mediterranean, there would be a surplus of manpower and it should be used to build up BOLERO.[8] Preparations for such a build-up should begin at once. All were agreed that ROUNDUP or SLEDGEHAMMER were not possible that year, but preparations had to begin now if one or the other were going to be mounted in the spring of 1944.[9] ROUNDUP and SLEDGEHAMMER had been talked about for two years but they had not been accepted as a concrete plan to be carried out at a certain time. Therefore he wished to emphasise that SLEDGEHAMMER or ROUNDUP should be decided upon definitely as an operation for the spring of 1944.[10]

Roosevelt then spoke about the Pacific. At the present time approximately 3000 men had been put ashore on Attu Island in the Aleutians.[11] It was hoped to put Kiska in a box between Attu and Amchitka, imposing attrition on the enemy.[12] So far, the operations in the Aleutians had resulted in a net gain to the United Nations; operations in the Solomons[13] and in New Guinea[14] had had the same result.

Roosevelt said while things were apparently going along all right in the Pacific, attention must be devoted to the Japanese supply lines. He likened them to a segment of pie in which Japan was at the apex while the line from the Solomons through the Dutch East Indies to Burma represented the outer crust.[15] Attrition against the outer crust was going on but the most effective way to get at the Japanese shipping was to strike at the apex.

So far the United Nations had done well in sinking Japanese merchant tonnage. The Japanese had needed to take shipping from the Yangtze[16] and use it for coastal runs, to release coastal shipping for ocean work.[17] Since the war started, the Japanese had suffered a net loss of one million tons[18] of shipping. If they continued to lose shipping at the same rate they could not maintain the outer rim of the pie

---

7   In September Italy switched sides to the Allies after ousting Mussolini and closing down the Fascist party in southern areas controlled by the Allies. Loyalist Fascists fought on against the Allies in northern Italy as the Italian Social Republic, a puppet state of Nazi Germany.

8   The build-up for the invasion of Northwest France.

9   In other words, begin preparations for the invasion of northwest Europe.

10   They would become known as Operation OVERLORD, the invasion of Normandy. The landings would be codenamed NEPTUNE.

11   Attu is the largest of the Near Islands group of the Aleutian Islands of Alaska. It was the site of the only World War II land battle fought on an incorporated territory of the United States. The landings began in 11 May and organised fighting ended on the 29th.

12   The Japanese evacuated the rest of the Aleutians three months after the capture of Attu.

13   The six-month land, air and sea campaign for Guadalcanal, Operation WATCHTOWER, came to an end on February 9. It was the first major Allied offensive against the Japanese.

14   After a two-month battle Australian and United States forces secured Buna, Sanananda and Goa, the main Japanese beachheads on New Guinea.

15   An arc north of Australia, curving north to the west of Burma.

16   The shipping sailing up the river from Shanghai on the South China Sea.

17   They were also launching cheap and easy-to-build junks to carry supplies along coastal waters.

18   Approximately one-seventh of Japan's shipping.

and would have to contract their operations.[1] Roosevelt said the same was true with regard to aircraft. Attrition suffered by the Japanese air forces had resulted in their having less available strength now than at the beginning of the war.[2]

Roosevelt repeated the most effective way to strike the Japanese shipping was as it was leaving Japan. This was best done from bases in China or Russia. Therefore, a lot depended on keeping China a going concern. He did not believe the Chinese were crying wolf when they reported the current critical condition in their country and they could not justify overlooking the possibility of a Chinese collapse. This brought up the question of the priority for aid to China in 1943 and 1944.

ANAKIM and similar plans proposed at Casablanca might not have an immediate enough effect to keep China in the war. The results of ANAKIM would not be felt until March or April 1944 and the Burma Road would not fully open to traffic until 1945.[3] They needed to do something for China now.

Roosevelt said the question resolved itself to assisting China by air; but it was essential to reconstruct and maintain the security of the airfields in Assam to the west of the mountains.[4] They must be made secure regardless of the cost in manpower and materiel and they must also be protected. On the east side of the mountains the Chinese were building landing fields and had five or six fields in good condition. General Stilwell[5] had two divisions in training for the protection of these fields while the Generalissimo did not fear a ground attack in Yunnan.[6]

Roosevelt said air units in China would accomplish three objectives:

1) Harass Japanese troops south of Hankow[7] or advancing north towards Chungking;[8]

2) Harass Japanese troops advancing against Chungking from the north;

3) Stop Japanese troops advancing up the Yangtze towards Chungking.

Roosevelt doubted if reliance could be placed on the Chinese army, except those troops being trained in Yunnan[9] and Ramgarh.[10] But he thought it was important to give the Generalissimo what he wanted: a strong build-up of the American-Chinese Air forces. Such an air force could be built up to strike Japanese shipping and Japan itself. The Chiefs of Staff had to bear in mind the political fact that China was in danger of collapse.

---

1   Without shipping, the Japanese could not maintain their forces at the edge of the territory they had conquered, along what President Roosevelt refers to as the 'rim of the pie'.

2   The war between the United States and Japan.

3   The Ledo Road, would cross northern Burma, connecting Ledo in northeast India to the Burma Road, which continued into the Yassam Province of China.

4   The Himalayas, referred to as the Hump.

5   General Joseph W. Stilwell (1883-1946), Commander of the China Burma India Theatre, Chief of Staff to Generalissimo Chiang Kai-shek and responsible for Lend-Lease supplies going to China; nickname Vinegar Joe.

6   The Chinese province bordering Burma (which is now Myanmar) to the southwest and French Indochina (what is now Laos and Vietnam) to the southeast. The Japanese attack would come on the east coast.

7   Hankow, or Hankou, now forms part of Wuhan, capital of the Hubei Province in eastern China.

8   Chungking, or Chongqing, was Generalissimo Chiang Kai-shek's provisional capital.

9   The Chinese end of the Burma Road.

10 The Ramgarh U.S. Army Chinese Training and Combat Command in northeast India.

Roosevelt said aid to China did not immediately take the weight off Russia but it would have an ultimate effect when Russia joined the United Nations in their war against Japan. He predicted this would take place 48 hours after Germany had been defeated.[11]

Roosevelt and Churchill then said they were considering the possibility of securing the Azores.[12] An attempt would be made to accomplish this by diplomacy, with threats or a surprise arrival of forces. They also thought an arrangement with Portugal could be made where they obtained the Azores on a rental basis. However, the question was largely political.

Field Marshal Dill[13] asked if they had considered Spain's present attitude. Both Roosevelt and Churchill felt Spain was very relieved by the turn of events in Africa. It was becoming more favourably disposed toward the United Nations and it now had the threat of the American forces facing Spanish Morocco constantly in mind.[14]

13 May

Roosevelt and Churchill met President Beneš[15]
Beneš explained his views on the partition of Germany, German war criminals, re-educating the German people, decentralising German administration and changing the German social structure.

First Combined Combined Chiefs of Staff Meeting
Conduct of the War; Mediterranean air and naval war; Operation HUSKY; Operation BOLERO; Operation ROUNDUP.

The Prime Minister met Secretary Hull[16]
Churchill and Secretary Hull discussed Russia, trade agreements and General de Gaulle.

Second Combined Combined Chiefs of Staff Meeting
Global strategy; Burma campaign.

14 May: Second Trident Meeting

The President said the meeting had been called to talk about the situation in the India-Burma-China Theatre because it presented extremely difficult problems. The thoughts on the subject must be simplified.

Roosevelt said the problem should be divided into two: operations to be carried out immediately and operations to be carried out at the end of the monsoon

---

11 Germany surrendered on 8 May 1945; Russia declared war on Japan on 8 August 1945, two days after the atomic bomb was dropped on Hiroshima.
12 The Azores are a Portuguese colony of islands off the west coast of Africa. An airfield on the island would allow Allied plans to cover convoys all the way across the Atlantic. Aerial cover was by far the most effective deterrent against U-boats. However, Portugal was a neutral country bordered by Spain, a country favourable to the Axis.
13 Field Marshal Dill, Chief of British Joint Staff Mission in Washington DC.
14 The clearing of the North African coast by the Allies meant there were no Axis troops in striking distance of southern Spain.
15 Edvard Beneš (1884-1948), President of the Czechoslovak Government-in-exile.
16 Cordell Hull (1871-1955), Secretary of State 1933-1944. He was awarded the Nobel Peace Prize in 1945 for his role in establishing the United Nations.

season.[1] The two should not be confused. Preparations for operations in November and December of 1943 had to start now.

Roosevelt said China was in a dangerous political condition and the United Nations could not let it go to pieces. It had to be remembered the Generalissimo was both head of the Army and of the State when discussing his demands. It was imperative the United Nations was not responsible in any way for the collapse of China. It was no longer possible to tell China to take what she was given, there had to be active cooperation on the part of the United Nations; something certainly had to be done. There would have to be a 1943 affirmative. Churchill replied there had to be a 1943 *and* a 1944 affirmative.

Roosevelt asked them to express their convictions freely on the subject of China and asked the Prime Minister to present his views. Churchill felt the President had put the case very clearly. He himself had once been keen on action of the ANAKIM type and two years ago had written a memorandum on the subject,[2] proposing an operation through Rangoon on Bangkok. The decision to mount ANAKIM was taken at Casablanca and Field Marshal Wavell[3] had prepared a plan, which was in his opinion the best method for accomplishing the recapture of Burma. Churchill replied he now understood Wavell believed the plan had a bleak outlook, but it was feasible still, if and when the necessary material was provided.

Churchill said operations in Burma had so far not been effective but they had taught them lessons. He did not like the look of Wavell's plan in the light of results to date.[4] He questioned the value of trying to retake Burma now and asked if it could not be bypassed. If so, would not the construction and defence of airfields be sufficient to ensure a flow of supplies into China? The question was how to construct these airfields quickly and to ensure their protection. He had little inclination to go into swampy jungles where operations could only be conducted for five months of the year, into country infested with malaria where modern equipment could not be used.

The idea of making four attacks from the sea, while under attack from shore defences of various kinds, did not present a favourable outlook.[5] All of these factors, together with the long lines of communications, made the prospects for ANAKIM extremely gloomy, a view shared by his military advisors. Churchill could not see how operations in the swamps of Burma would help the Chinese. The one factor more than any other which had turned him against the plan was that only 20,000 tons could be transported over the Burma Road, and then only in early 1945; even if ANAKIM was completely successful.[6] What would happen

---

1   The monsoon would finish at the end of October.
2   A copy of which was given to Admiral King during the Casablanca Conference.
3   Commander-in-Chief India, recently promoted to Field Marshal.
4   There had been an offensive in the coastal area around Arakan, while the Chindits of General Wingate (1903-1944) had made a deep march behind Japanese lines to attack the railway.
5   Excluding the advance up the Rangoon River to Rangoon.
6   The Burma Road had opened in 1938; it crossed over 700 miles of inhospitable terrain. The Ledo Road was a new section connecting India to the Burma Road. It was not completed until January 1945.

to the Chinese in the interval? All the above considerations indicated the objectives for 1943 should be a passionate development of air transport into China and a build-up of air forces in China.

Churchill then turned to 1944. He indicated an Asiatic TORCH should be sought.[7] A blow had to be struck where it could be accomplished with complete surprise. The operation had to attract enemy reaction, taking the pressure off China and the South Pacific. He suggested seizing the northern tip of Sumatra.[8] It would be much better to baffle the enemy by surprise than to continue with the development of the obvious.

Roosevelt said the objective of the TORCH operation had been to drive the Axis forces out of Africa, or at least to form a junction between Alexander and Montgomery in the east and Eisenhower in the west. Their objectives in China should be firstly, to save China and keep it going and secondly, to increase the rate of attrition on Japan's ships and aircraft. The United Nations had met with considerable success in their battle of attrition against Japan but the pace had to be stepped up.

Roosevelt asked Wavell to express his views on the Burma and ANAKIM operations. Wavell said the Burma campaign had been constantly on his mind for two years and he considered it to be the most important pivot in the war against Japan. After war had been declared, it became impossible to defend Burma once the United Nations had lost control of the seas. He had been thinking of the reconquest of that country ever since. But Wavell was convinced reconquest could not be accomplished by land operations alone: it had to be combined with amphibious operations and naval action. He had always realized the political effect the loss of Burma had on China and India. The morale effect on both countries was also of extreme importance.

Wavell said the more he had planned for the reconquest, the more difficult it became. Communications to northeast India, the base for land operations, were extremely difficult. They were dependent upon a small-capacity railroad, which was often out of operation for long periods. Airfields had to have metal or concrete surfaces. To illustrate the difficulties in communications, Wavell said his troops at Manipur[9] had not been on full rations during the last monsoon period because of the effect the rain had on the roads. Current operations had shown the Japanese troops were good at defensive fighting, whereas the Indian forces were accustomed to the open plains and required intensive training for jungle warfare.

When Wavell was asked to produce a plan to conquer Burma in the next dry season, he had prepared what he thought was the best plan possible. It was a hazardous one and difficult to accomplish but he felt it had a reasonable chance of success if his troops were fully trained and equipped.

The plan required an immediate increase of supplies to the theatre. 180,000 tons per month had to be sent to India but in fact only 65,000 and 70,000 tons

---

7 An Asiatic amphibious invasion.
8 The island on the west side of the Malaysia Peninsula.
9 Manipur state is in northeast India, on the border of Burma; the capital is Imphal.

respectively had been shipped in March and April. So the operation could not start in November[1] as originally planned. But if it did not start then, it could not succeed in the coming dry season. It would be necessary to get land-based air cover on the Arakan coast first and then capture Rangoon.[2]

At the same time they had to conduct operations in the north alongside the British and Chinese troops. The Chinese forces from the north and the British-Indian forces from the south would attempt to form a junction. Then it would be necessary to repair the railroads and bring supplies in through Rangoon and ship them north to repair the Burma Road. His administrative experts told him the road could not be fully opened to traffic until the middle of 1945.[3]

Wavell said while the relief to China would not be effective until 1945, the immediate morale effect would be considerable to both China and India. If success was assured, it would be worth hazarding the losses and his planners had examined the alternatives. However, an unsuccessful expedition would be much worse than none at all. In the long run, it was probable more supplies could be flown into China over the next 18 months than could be supplied if most of the air transport was used to support operations leading to the construction of the Burma Road.[4]

The possibility of using troops in the India Theatre for another operation was being examined. An effort was being made to determine the effect of creating a break or landing somewhere in the semi-circle from Burma through the Malay Peninsula, Sumatra, and Java. Possible objectives were Bangkok via the Kra Isthmus,[5] northern Sumatra,[6] and Malaya or the Sunda Straits.[7] Bangkok was impracticable because there were no adequate port or routes across the Kra Isthmus. The Sunda Straits was an attractive objective because it threatened the Palembang oil fields[8] but they did not have the resources available.

One promising operation was to seize three or four airfields in northern Sumatra and then drive into the Malayan Peninsula at Penang,[9] where there were another four or five airfields. The expedition would place large air forces in Sumatra and Malaya so they could attack Bangkok, Singapore, the Palembang oil fields, and Japanese shipping. If they could place and protect strong air forces on northern Sumatra, the Japanese faced a bad situation which could cause them considerable air losses. The expedition would probably require about the same forces as ANAKIM[10] and it did not depend on the monsoon. But it would be an

---

1   November was the start of the dry season after the six-month monsoon season.
2   Arakan state is on the northwest coast of Burma. Rangoon (now Yangon), Burma's former capital, is on the southwest coast.
3   It would open at the beginning of 1945 and the first trucks reached the Chinese border on 28 January 1945.
4   Planes flew 650,000 tons of supplies to China between May 1942 and November 1945. President Roosevelt ordered USAAF's Air Transport Command to deliver 5,000 tons a month to China by July; 7,500 tons by August; and 10,000 tons by September 1943.
5   The northwest part (the Burmese part) of the Malaysian Peninsula.
6   The island southwest of the Malaysian Peninsula.
7   The Sunda Straits separate Sumatra and East Java.
8   The Palembang oil fields in Sumatra. When British and US embargoes were put in place following Pearl Harbor, Japanese oil imports fell by 90 per cent. It meant they had to take and hold new sources.
9   State on the northwest coast of Malaysia.
10   The amphibious landing planned on the west coast of Burma.

expensive operation in aircraft because of the distance from air bases in India and it would also require considerable shipping.

The operation would cause considerable attrition to Japanese air power and shipping because they would have to react and this would bring on air battles.[11] Considerable further study would be required before an opinion could be given as to the possibility of the operation. Churchill asked when could it take place and Wavell replied 1944.

Roosevelt said there were many naval problems involved in the capture of Rangoon and asked if sufficient carriers could be made available. Admiral Somerville[12] said the Rangoon operation was not attractive. Carriers would have to stand off for one to three weeks to seize the airfields on the Arakan coast and that was too long against a land-based Japanese air attack. Seizure of Rangoon was not feasible unless it could be covered to some extent by land-based aircraft from the Arakan coast.

Admiral Pound said carriers would not be available until they had been released from the Mediterranean.[13] Somerville[14] said the naval approach to Rangoon was narrow and could be easily defended.[15] He doubted if the operation was feasible from the naval point of view.

Air Chief Marshal Peirse[16] said air development appeared to meet the requirements from an airman's point of view, which were firstly, to defeat the enemy air forces; secondly, to assure military aid to China; and thirdly, to bring in supplies at the earliest date.

It was essential to have adequate air forces operating from India to neutralize Japanese air forces that might interfere with the air route. But it was clear the development of land operations through Assam into China[17] and the development of the Royal Air Force and the American Ferry Command[18] facilities were mutually antagonistic.

Peirse said much more could be done if all the effort was put into building up the air forces operating under General Chennault[19] and the air transport into China. The tonnage over the air transport route to China could be considerably increased. It was not necessary to re-conquer Burmese territory to defend this air route, provided Allied Air Forces were able to neutralize the enemy air forces. Peirse had never considered ANAKIM to be sound, because the seaborne expedition and landings could not be supported by land-based aircraft. The plan assumed the enemy might have 300 to 350 aircraft and around 100 might attack

---

11 If the Allies could take on the Japanese air force, it would leave their shipping vulnerable, which in turn left their armies short of supplies.
12 Admiral Sir James F. Somerville (1882-1949).
13 Carriers were needed to provide air cover until onshore airfields could be seized and opened.
14 Admiral Somerville was Commander-in-Chief, Eastern Fleet.
15 Ships would have to sail 30 miles along the Rangoon River to reach Rangoon.
16 Air Chief Marshal Sir Richard Edmund Charles Peirse (1892–1970), Air Officer Commanding-in-Chief RAF India.
17 From northeast India into China.
18 Ferry Command transferred new aircraft from the factory to the operational airfield.
19 General Chennault of the Fourteenth USA Air Force.

any landing operation. Clearly, one or two carriers were inadequate to oppose an attack of this order.

Roosevelt asked how many airports there were between Assam and Chittagong.[1] Peirse was operating fourteen squadrons from forward airdromes in the area at the time.[2] Roosevelt asked if the runways were long enough for bombers. Peirse replied medium and heavy bombers could operate from six airfields with hard runways; heavy bombers usually operated from airfields farther back. Peirse said the plan to capture Sumatra had considerable merit because it extended their air cover east and interfered with the Japanese shipping lanes. The radius of bomber aircraft operating from Malaya to northern Sumatra would extend far enough to meet the bombers operating from southern China.[3] Combined air operations from Malaya and China were bound to draw considerable enemy air forces into these areas to oppose them; such air forces the enemy could ill afford.

General Stilwell said the weight of opinion was apparently against him. To his mind, China represented a base the United Nations wanted. They wanted it both for its geographic position and for the use of Chinese manpower. He felt the United Nations must ultimately meet the Japanese Army on the mainland of Asia. If China were allowed to fall now, it would be a long road back before the United Nations would be able to meet Japan on Chinese soil. It was essential to retain control of Yunnan to keep China in the war.[4] Stilwell had been worried about the possibilities of a Japanese attack against Kunming for a long time, particularly one from the south.[5] The Japanese had the forces available in Indochina to make such an attack. Ground forces had to be trained if they were to hold Yunnan and they must be Chinese forces. There were 32 divisions in training and they would be available to defend the province. At the present time, they were about 8100 strong but it was planned to deactivate one in three divisions to bring the remainder to a total strength of 10,000 each. This would result in 22 available divisions as soon as their equipment arrived and the others would be brought up to strength later. If the force could be trained and equipped, it would be capable of defending Yunnan Province. Sufficient equipment would be available if 10,000 tons capacity of the air transport route was utilized for this purpose between now and September.

Stilwell said it was absolutely essential to open land communications to China.[6] Even though the initial supplies would be small, they would have a tremendous morale effect on China. The extra munitions would be used to build up a second group of 30 divisions which had been promised by the Generalissimo. Under this program there would ultimately be a force capable of fighting the Japanese. If supplies for these ground forces were not sent at once, it would be impossible to train and equip the Chinese Yunnan forces and the Chinese Army would disappear.

---

1   Along the India-Burma border.
2   Exclusive of those used by the American Air Force.
3   Providing complete air coverage.
4   The southwest Chinese Province next to the Burmese border.
5   Kunming, capital of the Yunnan Province.
6   Referring to the Ledo Road connecting northeast India to the Burma Road. Work had started in December 1942 and 15,000 Americans and 35,000 local workers were employed on it. It would not open until January 1945.

Stilwell admitted if all their supplies were devoted to building up the Chinese Air Forces, it would have an effect on the Japanese shipping lanes and it would be a shot in the arm to Chinese morale; but he felt it would not lead to decisive results. As soon as the build-up of American forces began to sting the Japanese too much, they would launch an attack from Indochina to capture the Kunming Area. The eastern terminal of the air route would disappear and China would be out of the war. It was imperative to defend Yunnan Province and the only way to accomplish this was by the build-up of Chinese ground forces.

Roosevelt had never accepted such a low tonnage figure for the air route. It had to be divided between air and ground equipment, so why not convey sufficient for both? Stilwell said 3400 tons had been the maximum conveyed in any one month up to present. Increased quantities were certainly possible on paper, but it had to be always remembered they were fighting the conditions of the country, the monsoon, and inadequate airfields, and there was always the danger the Japanese would interfere with the route.

Wavell said there was no great danger to the Assam airfields from land attack. The warning system was reasonably adequate, giving thirteen minutes warning.[7] Stilwell believed the warning system required improvement but he thought Wavell had taken all possible steps to speed up the development of the airfields; labour had already been switched from the Ledo Road.

Stilwell said the Chinese Army in Yunnan required 2000 tons a month over the next five months. General Chennault needed 4700 tons a month over the next four months and then 7000 tons a month. Roosevelt suggested the immediate objective should be 7000 tons a month. However, the plan was to achieve 10,000 tons per month by November, although something could be done to speed up matters to try to achieve 7000 tons a month by July. Stilwell said the only way of getting large quantities of material into China was by road. They might achieve 10,000 tons by air through great effort but a land route was ultimately essential.[8]

Roosevelt reminded them the Generalissimo was head of State and Commander-in-Chief and both Stilwell and Chennault were, in a sense, under him when in his territory. From the psychological point of view it was difficult to tell the Generalissimo they thought things should be done differently to his ideas. Chennault agreed it was necessary to listen to what the Generalissimo said. His own plan was to use his air forces initially to protect the terminal base in Yunnan, and then to operate from another area farther east to attack Japanese shipping in the Hong Kong–Formosa area.[9]

Chennault doubted whether the Japanese could advance across country and capture Yunnan, they had never yet succeeded in such an operation. They had always advanced up rivers, using them for their line of communication, and their

---

7 The air warning system, giving pilots time to scramble and meet the Japanese planes.

8 Stilwell's assessment would prove to be incorrect. In July 1945 71,000 tons of supplies would be flown over the Hump, compared with only 6,000 tons carried along the Ledo Road. 650,000 tons were eventually airlifted, compared to 147,000 by road.

9 Formosa (now Taiwan) is 400 miles east of Hong Kong, on China's southeast coast. The stretch of water is on the shipping route between Japan and the South China Sea, the supply route to Malaysia and Burma.

river traffic was open to air attack. The Generalissimo certainly feared an attack up the Yangtze,[1] but quite a small force, say, two fighter squadrons and one bomber squadron, would be enough to prevent one.

Churchill said if all efforts now concentrated on the Ledo Road and the troops in Burma were switched to developing the airfields, progress might be more rapid and the higher tonnage might be achieved earlier. Wavell said a certain amount of resources might be saved from the Ledo Road, though it was in itself important for improving the warning system.[2] Airfields already had first priority. Marshall said several steel mats for airfields were on their way and General Wheeler's[3] demand for two or three more engineer battalions was under examination; it might be possible to supply them from the Middle East.

Roosevelt asked about the effect on the Generalissimo if ANAKIM was cancelled. Stilwell said it was unpredictable but there was no doubt he was relying on it. Chennault said the Generalissimo always wanted definite commitments on dates and size of forces but he would be satisfied if 7000 tons a month were flown in. Dill said the Generalissimo knew about the plan for 10,000 tons a month and was expecting it to be carried out in addition to ANAKIM. A 7000-ton project would not be anything new to him.

Stilwell said the Generalissimo felt he had been involved in the making of the ANAKIM plan and was committed to it. He expected it to be carried out and would feel deserted if it was not. Operations against Sumatra or Malaya would have no bearing on the opening of the Burma Road and would prolong the period during which no steps were being taken to reopen it.[4] The Chinese were suspicious of the British and they had to prove to the Chinese they were in earnest. The effect of the cancellation of ANAKIM would be very bad on the Chinese people and the development of the air supply route would not be regarded as an adequate substitute.

Churchill was not prepared to undertake something foolish purely to placate the Chinese. He was not prepared to make war that way. He would do anything sensible to help the Chinese; in exactly the same way he would do anything sensible to help the Russians. But he did not see any particular value in carrying out costly operations to no purpose. Admiral King said the Burma Road was a symbol to the Chinese and operations in Burma would make them feel the reopening was on the way.

Roosevelt was sorry to hear the Chinese were suspicious of the British, they had asked nothing of the Chinese and were prepared to do anything to contribute to their safety. He was not prepared to undertake months of unprofitable operations to remove the unfounded suspicions of the Chinese. The United States would

---

1   The Yangtze River is the longest river in Asia, running through Nanking and Shanghai.
2   It allowed them to build warning stations farther east.
3   General Raymond A. Wheeler, US Army (1885-1974), Commander of Services and Supply for US forces in China, Burma and India.
4   ANAKIM would lead to direct support for China while operations farther south would only be indirect support. Unfortunately, any operation in northern Burma was subject to the monsoon, which stopped operations between May and October.

realize it was not a question of saving the expenditure of British blood; the British were perfectly prepared to fight in true brotherhood with their Allies.

Roosevelt said an alternative solution would be to use the forces designed for ANAKIM for an advance towards China, opening the Burma Road as the advance progressed. Wavell said this had been carefully studied. The question was how to sustain the force because the Assam railhead was already overloaded. There were 200 miles of completed hill road beyond that and then 80 miles of partly made hill road to a point still west of the Chindwin River.[5] Then there was no all-weather road at all in Upper Burma north of Mandalay.[6] Meanwhile, the Japanese had a dry-weather road towards the Chin Hills[7] but it was separated from the end of their road by 120 miles.[8]

They had to build 250 miles of all-weather road in four to five months; an engineering effort beyond the capacity of the Assam line of communication. Upper Burma was the most malarial country in the world and 25% casualties per month had to be expected if operations continued there in the rainy season.

Wavell said it might be better to go down to Mandalay, rather than try to go due east.[9] But after they got to Mandalay, they had to maintain their forces over 300 miles of road, of which 150 miles were not all-weather. They could not possibly meet the Japanese on even terms because they had the railway, the road, and the river behind them. He did not think they could cut their line of communication decisively by air.

Stilwell agreed an attack on Rangoon would be very hazardous and it might be better to go in through Bassein.[10] Somerville said an attack on Bassein was open to the same objection; carriers would have to provide air support for two or three weeks. Stilwell explained it was only necessary to undertake operations to open the way into China because it was ultimately essential as a base. Churchill was not convinced but he saw no reason to abandon the operation. Preparation moves should continue provided they did not hamper the development of the air route. Further study would be necessary before a decision could be taken.

Roosevelt thought the two objectives should be to get 7000 tons a month into China by air by July and to open land communication with China. It was for the military advisors to suggest the best way to carry out the latter objective. Admiral Leahy thought the staffs had to find out the most promising operation to open the way to China irrespective of any agreement to carry it out in the immediate future. Marshall did not want a suggestion to be made to the Generalissimo that

5   The Chindwin River runs on the Burma side of the Burma-India border.

6   Mandalay is in the centre of Burma. So there was no all-weather road (only dirt tracks) in the 80,000 square miles of Burmese territory.

7   The Chin Hills are a range of mountains inland of the west coast Burma and on the Burmese side of the border with India.

8   The Japanese employed forced labour (many of them prisoners of war) to build their roads and railways and thousands died due to malnutrition, diseases and the cruelty of their guards. The famous example is the 258 mile long 'Death Railway' connecting Bangkok in Thailand and Rangoon in Burma.

9   That is advance southeast to Mandalay rather than east to the Chinese border. But as the Allies advanced, their line of communication grew longer and more tenuous while the Japanese line of communication grew shorter and was over railways and roads.

10   Bassein (now called Pathein) is on the western branch of the Irrawaddy River, in southwest Burma.

7000 tons per month was the target, as this would appear to be a reduction from the objective of 10,000 tons.

Marshall said RAVENOUS had been the first approach in the development of ANAKIM.[1] Wavell objected to RAVENOUS because it had unsound supply, Brooke objected because of the insecure south flank and the Generalissimo objected because it was not coupled with naval action. Finally, ANAKIM had been agreed upon by all.[2] This was now considered to be impracticable. The plan proposed by Stilwell to get supplies into China by air and land was new in many of its features and had to be thoroughly explored.

14–17 May

The President and the Prime Minister spent the weekend at Shangri-La, the President's mountain camp in Maryland.

15 May

Third Combined Chiefs of Staff Meeting

Operations in Europe; Azores; Burma Campaign; Directive to the Allied Authorities in the Far East.

17 May

Fourth Combined Chiefs of Staff Meeting

The situation in China; the Azores; Agreed essentials for conducting the War; Operation HUSKY; Operation UPKEEP.

18 May

Fifth Combined Chiefs of Staff Meeting

Defeat of the Axis powers in Europe; Rearming the French in North Africa; the Azores; The Combined Bomber Offensive from the UK; Bombing of Ploesti; Operation UPKEEP.

18 May: President's Press Conference

The President: I don't think I have anything of any importance. I have just had a very satisfactory conference with the Duke of Windsor. As you probably know, we are bringing several thousand labourers from the Bahamas and others from Jamaica, to help out the farm labour this summer and autumn. And I think it is progressing very well. The talks with the Prime Minister are going along very satisfactorily but they are not finished yet. I think that is about all.

Question: Is the Prime Minister going to be subjected to the tender mercies of a Press Conference? *Roosevelt*: Yes, I think so. He doesn't worry about it any more than I do (laughter).

Question: Has Prime Minister Mackenzie King joined the conferences yet?

---

1   The planned attack into Burma had started with RAVENOUS, an advance to the Chindwin River, just across the Burmese border.

2   RAVENOUS expanded into ANAKIM, a three-pronged attack including a British amphibious assault on Rangoon, a British overland offensive into central Burma and an American-sponsored Chinese offensive from the north.

Roosevelt: No. I understand he just got into town this afternoon and he is coming to the White House in the morning, to spend the night.

Question: I did not understand you a moment ago; did you say the Prime Minister met the Duke of Windsor?

Roosevelt: No, I met him.

Question: The Prime Minister did not meet him?

Roosevelt: I did not know this was society column (laughter). The Prime Minister lunched at the British Embassy. The Duke and Duchess were there, I think, and the Prime Minister brought the Duke of Windsor down afterwards. The Duke and I talked for about an hour and we would have talked longer if I hadn't noticed it was four o'clock.

19 May
Sixth Combined Chiefs of Staff Meeting
The defeat of the Axis in Europe.
Churchill at the Capitol
Churchill addressed a joint meeting of the Houses of Congress and then met members of the Senate Foreign Relations Committee and the House Foreign Affairs Committee. He was accompanied by Prime Minister Mackenzie King.
Seventh Combined Chiefs of Staff Meeting
The defeat of the Axis in Europe; Operations from India; Transport aircraft for Operation HUSKY.

19 May: Third Trident Conference
Roosevelt asked what progress the Chiefs of Staff were making. Admiral Leahy hoped it would be possible to furnish the President and the Prime Minister with some tentative conclusions before the weekend. ANAKIM had been dealt with in a general way but would be considered in more detail the following day.

Churchill was entirely in favour of carrying out whatever operations might be possible in Burma without trenching[3] too deeply on shipping and naval resources. Of course any troops who could be placed in contact with the enemy should not be allowed to stand idle. General Brooke agreed.

Churchill hoped it would be possible to arrange for British squadrons to take part in the China operations and Air Marshal Portal agreed. General McNarney[4] said logistical difficulties would prevent any employment of British squadrons in the near future. The President drew attention to the importance of political and personal considerations in planning action in China.

The U-boat War and the Azores
Roosevelt asked Admiral Pound whether the U-boat war was proceeding reasonably well. Pound replied recent results had been fairly satisfactory. Air Marshal Portal said air operations against submarines were being extended and it was

---

3   Digging into or using up.
4   General Joseph T. McNarney USAAF (1893-1972), Deputy Chief of Staff, US Army (1942-1944).

hoped to increase not only the total sinkings but the rate of sinkings per air-craft employed.

Marshall asked if Roosevelt had considered the securing of the Azores. Roosevelt said one method might be to ask President Vargas of Brazil[1] to make a secret approach to the Portuguese Government.[2] Roosevelt then read the Secretary of State's telegram to President Vargas. The last time he had seen President Vargas, he suggested sending a token Brazilian force to the Islands so the Portuguese could transfer some of their effective troops back to the mainland. It might encourage the Portuguese to allow the United Nations to use the islands.[3] The Combined Chiefs of Staff were all agreed about the great military advantages of occupying the Azores and considered no time should be lost carrying it out.

Hopkins thought the chance of the Portuguese willingly conceding the use of bases was extremely remote. Before any approach was made, they should be quite sure they would occupy the islands by force if their request was refused. On the face of it, the action savoured somewhat of a German or Japanese tech-nique. However, the occupation could hardly be condemned if they remembered Portugal depended for her very existence upon the victory of the United Nations.

As long as the United Nations were debarred from using the Azores, their ship-ping was subjected to damaging attacks, against which a proper defence could not be provided. In the last war it had been found necessary to make a technical breach of neutrality by occupying the Piraeus,[4] but the incident had eventu-ally been settled to everyone's satisfaction. It should not be forgotten the Allies depended on the margin of shipping for their war-making capacity.[5]

Probably the best way of handling the matter would be to have ample force available off the Islands. They would then inform the Portuguese government the Islands would be occupied the following morning and resistance would be hopeless. Solid inducements would be offered and the Brazilians could ostensibly provide the occupying troops, if the Portuguese wanted.

In conclusion, it was agreed the Prime Minister would telegraph proposals along these lines to the British Government for their comments. In the meantime, the Combined Chiefs of Staff had to plan an operation ready for examination by the President and Prime Minister.[6]

---

1   President Getulio Vargas (1882-1954), president and dictator of Brazil from 1930. He would be elected president in 1951 but committed suicide in 1954 following his implication in the assassination of a political opponent.
2   Brazil had sided with the Allies, declaring war on Germany and Italy on 22 August 1942.
3   The establishment of an airfield on the Azores would mean that the Convoys could get air cover all the way across the Atlantic.
4   The Port of Athens; Greece's major port at the time in the Attica region in the southeast of the country. It was occupied by Allied forces in November 1916 to make the Greek government surrender supplies.
5   Margin of shipping was a technical way of saying shipping losses; or how many ships survived the crossing.
6   Churchill used a 1373 friendship treaty between England and Portugal to get Portuguese Prime Minister Salazar onside. The British occupation of the islands in October 1943 was codenamed Operation ALACRITY. The Portuguese leased air and naval bases in the Azores to the British. It was agreed that US warships would fly the Royal Navy's White Ensign and US aircraft would have the RAF's markings, so there was no reaction from the Axis.

The Mediterranean

Churchill asked how discussions about the Mediterranean and BOLERO were progressing.[7] Brooke said the Chiefs of Staff had agreed on the build-up of a sufficient force in England to secure a bridgehead on the Continent from which further offensive operations could be carried out. It would involve approximately nine divisions in the assault and a build-up of 20 additional divisions.

At the same time, the Chiefs of Staff agreed the Commander-in-Chief, North Africa[8] should be instructed to mount operations to exploit HUSKY, subject to the Combined Chiefs of Staff approval. They would be calculated to eliminate Italy from the war and to contain the maximum number of German forces.

Eisenhower was to be told he could use all forces available in the Mediterranean except for four American and three British divisions ready to move after 1 November; they would take part in the operations from the United Kingdom. Brooke said these decisions would be reviewed by the Combined Chiefs of Staff in July or early in August, in the light of HUSKY's results and the Russian situation.

Brooke told the President there were not many available divisions in Syria; most were being trained for HUSKY, either in Syria or in Egypt. There were two Polish divisions now in Iraq. Churchill said the Polish troops would be much improved if they could be actively engaged. Roosevelt asked what use could be made of Yugoslav troops. Brooke said there were only a handful; about a battalion. He said the Greeks had also organized a brigade.

Turkey

Churchill thought September would be a good time to urge Turkey to permit the United Nations to use their air bases. Relations with Turkey would have been considerably strengthened because they would have supplied them with considerable munitions of war and they might be receptive to such an approach.

Portal told the President that flying conditions out of Turkey were not too reliable after the late summer. Churchill said it would be desirable to obtain Turkey's permission to use her air bases before September and thought it might be possible if Italy was eliminated from the war; they should also get free access to Rhodes and the Dodecanese.

Roosevelt then mentioned a message he had sent to Marshall concerning the inclusion of a promise of peace with honour to Italy in the pre-HUSKY propaganda in the proposals to Eisenhower. Roosevelt and Churchill agreed the promise should not be made.

Churchill was pleased the Conference was progressing so well and that a cross-Channel operation had finally been agreed upon. He had always been in favour of such an operation and had to submit to its delay in the past for reasons beyond control of the United Nations. He thought Stalin would be disappointed at not having an invasion of northern France in 1943 but was certain he would be gratified by HUSKY's results and other events that would take place later in the year.

---

7   The discussion was about the transfer of divisions from the Mediterranean.
8   General Eisenhower.

20 May

Eighth Combined Chiefs of Staff Meeting

Propaganda and Subversive Activities; Strategy for the Defeat of Japan; Burma Operations to open an overland route to China; Air Route from India to China.

31st Meeting of the Pacific War Council[1]

The President said the Prime Minister's address to Congress was the clearest and best exposition of global war ever given. There was general agreement.

Roosevelt explained the operations in progress on Attu.[2] He described the physical difficulties and laid special stress on the almost continuous bad weather during the month of the year when the best weather was to be expected in the Bering Sea. The attack had to be delayed several days because of fog and gales and they had kept up ever since. They had rarely been able to use aerial or gun support while the physical difficulty of moving through the tundra was great. Snow impaired progress in the high spots and more men have been hospitalized with frozen feet than from enemy bullets. Nevertheless they had progressed and had now squeezed the defending forces into the high land surrounding Chicagof Harbor, where they were making a final stand.[3]

Roosevelt said so much misinformation had been written and expressed about Attu Island's significance. The Council should remember its capture and the establishment of an airfield would not open the way to bombing the Japanese homeland, even though they had moved appreciably nearer their final objective. The tremendously uncertain weather meant even if they launched attacking squadrons, the chances of their return would be very slim.

The occupation of Attu would secure and neutralize the value of enemy bases at Kiska.[4] This should enable them to push the Japanese out of the Aleutians. When and if Russia should join in the war against Japan, their position in Attu would help them to take full advantage of Siberian bases.

Mackenzie King said the Japanese occupation of the Aleutians had been a matter of grave concern to Canada and it welcomed and applauded every measure to evict the Japanese from the Aleutians.

Roosevelt had no further information to give the Council except to say they were assiduously continuing their pressure on their enemies and weakening their position throughout the world by daily attrition of their land, sea and air forces. In the case of Japan, the combined submarine and air action was steadily reducing the Japanese merchant marine to the point where the maintenance of her outlying stations would become more and more difficult. Roosevelt told Dr. Soong that Churchill planned to lend material to help revitalize the air forces in China.

---

1   President Roosevelt, Prime Minister Churchill, Prime Minister Mackenzie King (Canada), Foreign Minister Soong (China), Minister for Australian External Affairs Herbert V. Evatt (1894-1965), First Secretary of the New Zealand Legation Geoffrey Cox (1910-2008), Ambassador Alexander Loudon (Netherlands), President Manuel Quezon of the Philippines (1878-1944).
2   The westernmost of the Aleutian Islands.
3   The battle of Attu lasted from 11 to 30 May 1943. 15,000 Americans fought 2900 Japanese in atrocious weather. There were nearly 1700 US casualties while only 29 Japanese were captured; the rest were killed. 2100 US troops were evacuated suffering from disease and the effects of the weather.
4   Kiska is in the Aleutian Islands off the coast of Alaska.

British air squadrons would be added to the American and Chinese air forces to create a united Allied force in China so they may learn by experience to work together effectively. Soong said the aid would be highly valued by China.

Roosevelt said everyone realized the principal difficulty of building up a powerful air force in China was providing sufficient petrol; but General Chennault[5] was confident it could be brought in by air. If they gave him sufficient planes he could accomplish two very positive things:

a) Break up any extensive Japanese land offensive aiming to demolish Chinese air fields;[6]

b) Destroy 500,000 tons of Japanese shipping within a year by raiding their sea lanes and river boat supplies.

Soong said the people of China were very much heartened by Churchill's speech and they were very hopeful the difficulties of maintaining a strong air force in China would be solved. However, his government and of all the Chinese wanted them to continue the offensive in Burma to restore the Burma Road. Sufficient supplies could be brought into China via the Burma Road alone to enable her to drive out her invaders.

Soong was sure everyone would agree air forces alone could not win the war and they had to provide a land route to equip the Chinese armies. To do this they had to carry out the promises made at Casablanca and send a combined naval and land expedition to recapture Burma.

Churchill understood the Burma Road had been so damaged by the Chinese and Japanese it could not possibly be restored to a point where supplies could be brought in until 1945. Soong replied that although the road had been badly damaged, the Japanese and Chinese were repairing their respective parts and the road could be restored very soon after they gained physical control.

Dr. Evatt[7] thought the Council failed to realize what extremely heavy casualties were involved in tropical warfare. In New Guinea, the combined Australian and American forces had suffered nearly 45,000 casualties up to February. Of the 50,000 Australians who had fought in New Guinea, over 7,000 had been lost in action, killed or missing, but malaria brought the combined casualties to above 40,000. Roosevelt agreed the casualties in the New Guinea campaign had amounted to nearly 50 per cent of the forces involved. This was a terribly high rate but on the other hand, they had to remember the Japanese losses had been very much greater; nearly three to one. While Roosevelt and Evatt agreed the bad cases of malaria should not be sent back into malaria countries, they could be used to garrison important non-malarial stations, releasing other men to fight who had not been exposed to malaria.

---

5   General Claire Chennault (1893-1958) retired in 1937 and went to work as an aviation trainer and advisor in China. He led the American Volunteer Group (AVG) otherwise known as the Flying Tigers.

6   The land offensive would come in April 1944. Operation ICHI-GO involved three battles for Henan, Hunan and Guangxi, designed to open a land route to French Indochina and seize the airfields used by American bombers. While 400,000 Japanese troops forced the American Air Force to move inland over the next six months, the bombing of Japan and her shipping continued unabated.

7   Australian Minister of State for External Affairs.

Churchill told the Council he had several problems very much in mind. He briefly stated his theory of the general strategy the Allies should follow, now they had gained the initiative and were building up an overpowering superiority in all weapons. Churchill said they had to recognize they were limited by the number of ships available to carry men and supplies to the chosen theatres. They had to force the enemy to fight where it was advantageous to the Allies and disadvantageous to the enemy.

Tunisia was a fine example of what Churchill considered a sound strategy. The enemy was compelled to lengthen his line of communications and overstrain his line of supply, which led to eventual collapse because of his inability to maintain and reinforce his armies. Churchill believed an extensive campaign in Burma would place all of these burdens on the Allies, instead of putting the enemy at a disadvantage. The rainy season only gave them six months to gain their objective, while the jungle heat decimated their forces, as had been demonstrated by the fighting in New Guinea. The Allied supply problem would be tremendous.

Churchill noted how an American Senator had said the British had two million men in India who were apparently unable to drive a few thousand Japanese out of Burma. Such a declaration completely ignored the practical problems of logistics. The forest and swamps of Burma only allowed a limited number of men to work and fight in any given area; it was a question of quality rather than quantity. When they put troops into Burma, they had to be experienced fighters who could overcome difficulties and defeat superior numbers of the enemy. It was for that reason he offered British air squadrons to fight in China as the most effective assistance Great Britain could contribute. This supported the view the President had held and enforced for the past few months.

Churchill wished to put on record his belief the President had a penetrating insight into the sound strategy of the present world war, and his instinct for lending immediate air support to China was wholly sound. Churchill was pleased to announce at least 450 planes would be added to the Australian Air Force. Everyone knew Australian fliers were among the best in the world and the planes would be provided for the Australians to man, so they could take a more active part in the defence of their homeland.

Churchill finally commented on a disturbing rumour that had reached him about China massing troops on the borders of Tibet. He hoped it was in error because the borders of Tibet had been secure for many years and it would mean diverting forces away from the true enemy – Japan. He would regret to see the Chinese take offensive action against a neutral.[1]

Soong stated emphatically there was no truth whatsoever to the rumour. Tibet was not a separate nation, it was a part of China. China might eventually have to

---

1   The Tibetan government signed the Simla Accord with Britain in 1914, ceding the South Tibet region to British India. The Chinese government denounced the agreement as illegal. The regents in the 1930s and 1940s were negligent and the Kuomintang Government of the Republic of China used this to their advantage to expand their influence into the territory.

take necessary action to maintain her sovereignty, but she had no intentions of taking such action at the present time.[2]

Soong could not accept the Prime Minister's statement about the impossibility of undertaking a campaign in Burma. His people were greatly cheered by Allied successes in Tunisia and it had demonstrated the Allies were able to defend their own. In his country the question was often asked, "How can the Englishmen, who were so feeble in their conduct of the war in Malaya, fight such magnificent battles in Africa?" Soong's answer was the Briton was always a good soldier when properly led and perhaps the difficulty in Burma rested with the leadership.

Churchill interrupted to say he hoped no country would feel it was their privilege to select the generals for the armies of their allies and he believed the leadership in Burma left little to be desired. Soong said China expected and hoped the United States and Great Britain would live up to their commitments. Churchill emphatically denied any commitments had ever been made.

Soong believed the military discussions at Casablanca, Calcutta and Chungking were definite commitments. Churchill argued the Allied governments had never made any pledges to recapture Burma but they had lent their full support to military studies which had to be modified from time to time. He had not seen the plan of attack until February. Soong did not understand how that could be so.[3]

Churchill said it would be of no help to an ally to do anything foolish and it would be a very foolish thing to consider pushing troops into Burma at the present time. Roosevelt said perhaps they were talking at cross purposes and about different things. Soong was wrong if he believed they had abandoned all thought of a Burma campaign. They expected to prosecute the campaign as soon as conditions permitted, but their present need was to provide something to benefit China at once. There was agreement air power would do this more effectively than any other way.[4] Roosevelt repeated there was no change in intention and the general policy remained the same, but the tactics had been modified since the studies were initiated at Casablanca.

President Quezon[5] said when an authority like Churchill told him an invasion of, and the restoration of, Burma was not practical at this time, he accepted the statement. He was pleased to support the request for additional aircraft for the Western Pacific as the best step that could be taken.

Evatt wanted to know the Japanese troop strength in China. The Japanese had been withdrawing troops from China for some time and it appeared the threat to China was not as great as it had been. Soong believed Japan would try to finish China in the summer. Rather than removing troops from China they were

2   Following the Chinese Civil War, the People's Republic of China invaded Tibet in October 1950, dethroning the 14th Dalai Lama. Following a rebellion in 1959, 200,000 Tibetans died and 6000 monasteries were destroyed as part of what the Chinese called the Great Leap Forward.
3   Britain had limited resources and concentrated on the Middle East rather than the Far East as part of the Grand Strategy to attack Germany first.
4   Air power provided instant aid and would support China until the Burma Road could be opened.
5   President Luis Quezon (1878-1944), president of the Commonwealth of the Philippines 1935-1944.

replacing troops who had been there for some time, while using China as a training ground for inexperienced troops.

Churchill stated Russia was the real answer to bringing about the coup de grace of Japan but it was already bearing a tremendous burden. Neither the Prime Minister nor the President had ever asked Russia to join the war against Japan because she was already doing her full share. Churchill's personal opinion[1] was the Russians would be glad to join in the final defeat of Japan when Germany had been defeated. Russia disapproved of Japan's treachery and her menace to stability as much as any other country.

Soong said China situation's was desperate and she required help by land and air. The recovery of the Burma Road was not only a material necessity; its recovery was necessary for the psychology of the Chinese people because they saw it as a symbol of their allies' armed support.[2]

Churchill made it clear the British Empire would do everything humanly possible to support China but he was convinced the only effective aid they could give to China that summer was an increase of her air power and this would be pressed with every possible atom of energy. He hoped Soong would not send a discouraging report home. They all had to try to maintain the morale of all their allies.

Soong appreciated Churchill's assurances; he had the highest respect for his great ability as a strategist and an authority on war. He begged Churchill to devote his great talent to the relief of the people of 'Tortured China' he had referred to in his speech the day before. Soong confirmed the people of China were indeed a tortured people after four years of war and the results of the failure to help them in time could not be predicted.[3]

Roosevelt reminded them one of their most serious problems had been the German submarines in the North Atlantic. Recent measures to increase offensive action by surface craft and by aircraft encouraged them to hope the situation would improve and they could then develop more ambitious plans of action. However, Japanese submarines had had marked success against shipping in the South Pacific during the past month and it required more planes and escort vessels to keep the lines of communication open.

Evatt said Australia also felt seriously threatened and the Japanese had to be pressed on all fronts in order to stop them assuming the initiative again. He expressed his sincere thanks to the soldiers, sailors and airmen of Holland who

---

1   He gave it only as a personal opinion, without any suggestion he had received any assurances.

2   The Burma Road was built by 200,000 Burmese and Chinese labourers during the Second Sino-Japanese War in 1937–38. Supplies landed at Rangoon were moved by rail to Lashio and then by road in China. The Ledo Road (or Stilwell Road, after General Stilwell) would be built from Ledo in northeast India, through Myitkyina, connecting to the Burma Road at Wandingzhen in Yunnan, China.

3   Japan attacked China in July 1937 and captured the capital Nanking at the end of the year, resulting in the notorious Rape of Nanking, when around 300,000 civilians were tortured, raped and murdered. While Tokyo wanted to scale down attacks, the generals increased them, overstretching their armies. A bombing campaign caused thousands of casualties, while many more were made homeless. A Chinese counterattack early in 1939 forced the Japanese on the defensive and they had difficulty administering their conquered territories. Their attentions turned elsewhere following the attack on Pearl Harbor and the Philippines on 7 December 1941.

had continued to render outstanding services in the war against Japan. The Council adjourned to allow news photographers to take a group photograph.

Ninth Combined Chiefs of Staff Meeting
Burma operations; Air supply for China; the Air Force in China.

21 May

Tenth Combined Chiefs of Staff Meeting
Selection of codenames; military supplies for Turkey; Operations in the Pacific and Far East.

21 May: President's Press conference

Question: Mr. President, you have had a number of recent conferences with Dr. Soong. Is there anything you can tell us?

Roosevelt: I don't think so. There isn't any particular news, one way or another.

Question: I wondered if there was anything special you had up between you.

Roosevelt: No. I suppose the principal thing relates to getting war materials of all kinds into China.

Question: Did you say more material?

Roosevelt: War materials and medical things, things of that kind. That is going along pretty well.

Question: Mr. President, is there anything you can tell us about the visit of Prime Minister Mackenzie King?

Roosevelt: I don't think so. He is just down here on the same thing everybody else is here for, the furtherance of the war. I am seeing him again this morning.

Question: Mr. President, back to Dr. Soong, he has been here since Prime Minister Churchill arrived. Could you say if your talks with the Prime Minister concerned something about China?

Roosevelt: Oh, sure. We talked about China. It isn't the only place we have been talking about.

Question: Mr. President, when you referred to the majority of our forces, were you speaking of those outside the continental United States?

Roosevelt: Yes.

Question: Mr. President, any sort of progress report you can give us on your talks with the Prime Minister?

Roosevelt: Well, I suppose the best way to put it is this: so far, most of the work has been done by the Combined Staffs. And they have been at it, and we expect to get some preliminary recommendations from the Combined Staffs – you might call them tentative recommendations – probably in tonight's meeting. Then those will be gone over – and I might say the Combined Staffs have been getting along extremely well. Then over the weekend we will be going over them, and take up the preliminary recommendations next week and iron out any kinks that are in them and make them final.

Question: Mr. President, has any consideration been given to the political future of Italy?

Roosevelt: Unconditional surrender. I think that speaks for itself.

21 May: Fourth Trident Meeting

The meeting had before them a draft of the Combined Chiefs of Staff's agreed decisions.[1]

Overall Objective

To bring about at the earliest possible date, the unconditional surrender of the Axis powers, in conjunction with Russia and other Allies.

Overall Strategic Concept for the Prosecution of the War

1) To bring about the unconditional surrender of the Axis in Europe at the earliest possible date.

2) Simultaneously[2] to maintain and extend unremitting pressure against Japan with the purpose of continually reducing her military power and attaining positions from which her ultimate surrender could be forced.

3) Upon the defeat of the Axis in Europe[3] to direct the full resources of the United States and Great Britain to bring about, at the earliest possible date, the unconditional surrender of Japan.

Basic Undertakings in Support of the Overall Strategic Concept[4]

Whatever operations were decided on, the following undertakings would be a first charge against resources, subject to review by the Combined Chiefs of Staff and in keeping with the changing situation.

1. Maintain the security and war-making capacity of the Western Hemisphere and the British Isles.

2. Support the war-making capacity of our forces in all areas.

3. Maintain vital overseas lines of communication, with particular emphasis on the defeat of the U-boat menace.

4. Intensify the air offensive against the Axis Powers in Europe.[5]

5. Concentrate maximum resources in a selected area as early as practicable for the purpose of conducting a decisive invasion of the Axis citadel.[6]

6. Undertake such measures to aid the war effort of Russia.[7]

7. Undertake such measures to aid the war effort of China as an effective Ally and as a base for operations against Japan.

8. To prepare the ground for the active or passive participation of Turkey in the war on the Allied side.

9. To prepare the French Forces in Africa to fulfil an active role in the war against the Axis.

---

1 The Final Report to the President and Prime Minister, C.C.S. 242. The opening statements regarding the Overall Objective and Strategic Concept would be reaffirmed at future conferences.
2 In cooperation with other Pacific Powers.
3 In cooperation with other Pacific Powers and, if possible, with Russia.
4 These Basic Undertakings would be updated and reaffirmed at future conferences.
5 The Combined Bomber Offensive, codename POINTBLANK.
6 Meaning the Third Reich.
7 Continue the Atlantic Convoys and move supplies through the Persian Gulf and through Iraq.

Specific Operations for 1943-44[8]

The U-boat War: The Azores Islands[9]

The Combined Chiefs of Staff agreed the occupation of the Azores was essential to the efficient conduct of the anti–U-boat war. The preparation of the plan was the responsibility of the British Chiefs of Staff and they had made a preliminary examination. The expedition should be mounted from the United Kingdom and the islands of Faial and Terceira should be seized first.[10] It was expected a force of about nine battalions would be required. The availability of landing craft was likely to be the limiting factor while the earliest date would be about the end of August.

It was agreed the land, air and sea facilities of the Azores would be available to all United Nations forces. The possibility of an earlier move on the Azores would be studied while the two governments settled the political decision.

Discussion on the Azores

Churchill said nothing would be gained by a diplomatic approach unless it was backed up by force. The Portuguese should be presented with an imminent occupation with only sufficient time to send a message ordering no resistance.[11] The question of the diplomatic approach should be left to the President and himself and he hoped to have the views of the British Government shortly. At the same time they needed a statement by the Combined Chiefs of Staff showing why it was important to occupy the Islands without delay.

Combined Bomber Offensive from the United Kingdom

The Combined Chiefs of Staff had approved a plan to accomplish (through a combined US–British air offensive) the progressive destruction and dislocation of the German military, industrial, and economic system, and the undermining of the morale of the German people to a point where their capacity for armed resistance was fatally weakened.[12] It would be accomplished in four phases between June 1943 and 1 April 1944. Their increased strength would allow a deeper penetration into enemy territory in each successive phase.[13] An intermediate objective of particular importance was the continued reduction of German fighter strength.[14]

---

8 No order of priority was given because there were enough resources to accomplish them all. Any conflict of interests would be referred to the Combined Chiefs of Staff.

9 It was also agreed to investigate increasing the number of flying boats (VLRs) for convoys and the air forces engaged in the Bay of Biscay.

10 The two main islands of the Azores.

11 Take the Azores by force after a pretence of diplomacy.

12 For example, "The critical condition of the ball bearing industry in Germany is startling." If ball bearing production capacity could be reduced, every type of engine would be compromised. 50 per cent of the synthetic rubber capacity and nearly all of the tyre production would be targeted.

13 A committee led by General Ira C. Eaker, USAAF (1896-1987), Commander-in-Chief of the Eighth Air Force, completed the Combined Bomber Offensive Plan (CBO Plan) in April 1943. It recommended 18 operations during each three-month phase (12 in each phase were expected to be successful) against a total of 76 specific targets. The plan also projected the US bomber strength for the four phases at 944, 1192, 1746, and 2,702 bombers.

14 The primary objectives were: a) German submarine yards and bases, b) German aircraft industry, c) Ball bearings, d) Oil (contingent upon attacks against Ploiesti). The secondary objectives were: a) Synthetic rubber and tyres, b) Military motor transport vehicles. The intermediate objective was to reduce German fighter strength.

General McNarney[1] gave a short account of how the plan for the Combined Bomber Offensive had been built up. In view of the expansion of the German fighter force, it had been found necessary to include attacks on the manufacturing plants. According to a conservative estimate based on experience, it was hoped to reduce the German fighter strength down to 500, rather than the projected figure of 3000, by the middle of 1944.[2] 25% of the bomber effort would go on submarine targets.[3]

About 425,000 ground personnel were required and Air Marshal Portal said this included ground personnel for ROUNDHAMMER. Churchill asked if the figure could be reduced. He recalled when he had asked Monsieur Maisky[4] why the Russians had refused twenty squadrons for the Caucasus, Maisky had pointed to the large number of ground personnel who had to accompany the aircraft and the complication it presented to Russian communications. Every man brought to the UK on the ground staff of the Air Force excluded a soldier and he earnestly hoped there could be a reduction.

Marshall had appointed a special group to survey the establishments of the Army and Air Corps.[5] General Arnold had already made an arbitrary cut in the numbers of ground personnel for the United Kingdom and although the figure was already lower, it was hoped a further reduction might be secured.

Churchill attached the greatest importance to this combined plan. There had not been an opportunity to apply the American scheme of daylight bombing.[6] From time to time he had been critical of the few occasions when the bombers had gone out to deliver comparatively small loads on Germany. But he could see in the future, when several raids could be made in one day and most deadly results would be produced. He therefore welcomed the plan and hoped it could be developed to the full.[7]

Marshall said in the latest raid by US B-17s[8] from England, three separate forces had been employed on three different objectives. One had 5% casualties and another had none; the overall loss had been 3.5%. This was as indication of what could be achieved in the future. He assured Churchill he was just as anxious to reduce the number of ground personnel in the United Kingdom. Churchill thanked Marshall for his assurance.

Roosevelt drew attention to the value of occasional raids on smaller towns, where factories were known to exist. It would greatly depress the Germans if they felt even small towns could not escape. There was general agreement.

---

1   General McNarney, Deputy Chief of Staff, US Army.
2   Destruction of 43 per cent of the German fighter capacity and 65 per cent of the bomber capacity would give the necessary domination of the air.
3   Destruction of the selected submarine building yards would reduce submarine construction by 89 per cent.
4   Ivan M. Maisky (1884-1975), Soviet Ambassador to London until 1943.
5   The United States Army Air Corps had been renamed the Army Air Forces in 1941. It dealt with the Army's aviation units.
6   While daylight bombing allowed precision bombing missions to be carried out, losses were higher.
7   The results were indeed deadly. RAF Bomber Command and US Air Forces would drop over 1.5 million tons of bombs on Germany during the war, 90 per cent of them between January 1943 and May 1945. There were over 1 million civilian casualties, while 7.5 million Germans were left homeless. Over 160,000 Allied airmen were killed.
8   Boeing B-17 Flying Fortresses would drop 640,000 tons of bombs during the war.

Cross-Channel Operations[9]

The Combined Chiefs of Staff agreed forces and equipment would be established in the United Kingdom. The object was to mount an operation, with target date 1 May 1944, to secure a lodgement on the Continent from which further offensive operations could be carried out. The operation would make the following forces present and available for use in the United Kingdom by 1 May:[10]

Assault: 5 Infantry Divisions simultaneously loaded in landing craft;

                2 Infantry Divisions to follow-up;

                2 Airborne Divisions;

Build-up: 20 Divisions available for movement into lodgement area.[11]

The possibility of adding one French Division would be considered at a later date. The expansion of logistical facilities in the United Kingdom would be undertaken immediately.

After the initial assault, the seizure and development of Continental ports would be expedited so the build-up forces could be augmented by follow up shipments of additional divisions from the United States or elsewhere, at the rate of three to five divisions per month.[12]

The constant keeping up-to-date of plans for an emergency crossing of the Channel in the event of a German collapse would proceed in accordance with General Morgan's directive.[13]

Norway

The President called attention to a news report concerning the German evacuation of Norway and suggested the Staffs consider what action should be taken in the event the report proved true. Morgan would submit a plan to the Combined Chiefs of Staff for sending forces to Norway.

Mediterranean Operations

The Combined Chiefs of Staff agreed the Allied Commander-in-Chief in North Africa would be instructed as a matter of urgency to plan operations to exploit HUSKY, to eliminate Italy from the war and to contain the maximum number of German forces. The Combined Chiefs of Staff would decide which operations would be adopted. The Allied Commander-in-Chief in North Africa could use all the forces in the Mediterranean Area except for four American and three British divisions held in readiness from 1 November onward for withdrawal to the United Kingdom.[14] Additional air forces provided for HUSKY would not be available.

---

9   The British view was that it necessary to create a suitable situation by diversion of German forces from the beachhead area. The United States view was that the war could be won by cross-Channel operations in 1944. The question was how long would the Mediterranean operations delay the build-up of troops in the United Kingdom?

10 In addition to the air forces.

11 The Prime Minister wanted to see what the subsequent build-up would be. General Marshall said it was down to shipping and the probable rate would be three to four divisions per month.

12 The President asked if the forces could hold the Brest Peninsula and General Brooke said they should be able to hold and extend the beachhead to take more ports. The opening of Continental ports allowed ships to sail straight from the United States to France.

13 General Morgan, Chief of Staff to the Supreme Allied Commander (COSSAC) was planning RANKIN and OVERLORD.

14 Provided the required naval vessels were approved by the Combined Chiefs of Staff.

It was estimated 27 divisions[1] and 3648[2] aircraft would be available for garrisons and operations across the Mediterranean area following HUSKY.[3]

The air forces provided for HUSKY consisted of British and American air reinforcements specially lent to the Mediterranean Theatre from the United Kingdom. Churchill suggested including a statement outlining the army forces available in the Mediterranean Theatre after HUSKY. Roosevelt agreed because it would be good to know what was available to send into Salonika[4] if the Germans withdrew from the Balkans. They also wanted to know what could be done if Italy collapsed immediately after HUSKY. Brooke said a survey of the troops in the Mediterranean area and various garrisons had been drawn up. It was agreed to include a final report of the troops available in the Mediterranean Area after HUSKY.[5]

Churchill did not think it was right to leave North Africa in the hands of the French, some of them should certainly move forward in the general advance. Roosevelt said no French Division was included in the first attack on the Continent and it was politically desirable to include one.

Churchill said a new code word was needed to cover post-HUSKY operations. Admiral Leahy[6] said the security staffs had been instructed to propose code words for a number of different operations and the Combined Chiefs of Staff would put forward their final suggestions.[7]

The Bombing of Ploesti[8]

The Combined Chiefs of Staff agreed US Army Air Forces representatives should immediately present their plan for bombing the Romanian oil fields from bases in North Africa to the Commander-in-Chief, North African Theatre. He in turn would submit appropriate comments and recommendations to the Combined Chiefs of Staff.

Roosevelt asked how far the Ploesti oil fields were from North Africa. General McNarney replied Ploesti was 895 miles from Tobruk and 875 miles from Aleppo. Churchill asked when they envisaged conducting the operation. McNarney said it should be accomplished in June or early July because of the excellent weather conditions in those months. The blow struck would also coincide with the German summer campaign in Russia.

---

1   19 British and Allied, four United States, and four French divisions.
2   242 heavy bombers (day and night), 519 medium bombers (day and night), 299 light and dive bombers, 2,012 fighters, 412 transports, and 164 army cooperatives.
3   Excluding four United States and three British divisions to be transferred to the United Kingdom and two British divisions constituting the British commitment to Turkey.
4   Northeast Greece.
5   Excluding the American and British Divisions earmarked for the United Kingdom.
6   Admiral Leahy, Roosevelt's personal Chief of Staff.
7   The landings on the Italian mainland would be: main landing near Salerno on the west coast, Operation AVALANCHE; landing on the toe, Operation BAYTOWN; landing at Taranto on the southeast coast, Operation SLAPSTICK.
8   A third of the Axis oil supplies came from the Ploesti oilfields, north of Bucharest. Operation TIDAL WAVE would be planned for 177 B-24 Liberators to attack them on 1 August 1943.

McNarney said two B-24 groups had to be taken from the United Kingdom for about four weeks.[9] One B-24 group heading to the United Kingdom would be diverted to the operation and would arrive about two weeks late in Great Britain. Officers with special sights for low-level bombing were on their way to England and North Africa to give instructions on how to use them. Those going to North Africa would present the plan to the Commander-in-Chief, Allied Force Headquarters,[10] who would submit his comments to the Combined Chiefs of Staff.

Air Marshal Portal said there were two important considerations. Firstly, whether or not aircraft should be diverted from the pre-HUSKY preparation and the British Chiefs of Staff were doubtful if this should be done. Secondly, unless the operation was fully successful, it would make subsequent operations from closer bases, which might become available later, more difficult because the enemy would install additional defences.[11] But the prize was so great and the weather conditions good, so the operation had to be thoroughly explored before a decision was made.

Marshall said if an attack against Ploesti had a fair degree of success, it would be a staggering blow to the enemy; probably the greatest single blow that could be struck. Roosevelt said even if the operation were not successful, it would divert considerable German anti-aircraft equipment from the Russian Front. Churchill asked the Chiefs of Staff to reconsider the report and make appropriate amendments. Brooke replied the report included only the agreed decisions and they still had to be related to the available resources.

Rearming the French in North Africa

The Combined Chiefs of Staff agreed to rearm and reequip the French forces in North Africa as soon as the availability of shipping and equipment allowed.[12] The use of captured German equipment would be explored. Churchill said large quantities of captured material had been taken from the Germans and suggested investigating manufacturing a limited amount of ammunition of German calibres. Marshall said General Smith[13] was making a rapid survey of captured material to see what could be used to equip the French forces.

Churchill asked if munitions were being manufactured for use on the *Richelieu*.[14] King said it was and Churchill suggested something of similar nature might be accomplished. Marshall said he would have General Somervell[15] make an immediate investigation. Churchill asked how many French Divisions were to be armed and

---

9   Two weeks either side of the operation.

10 General Eisenhower.

11 It was too late. A raid by 13 B-24 Liberators in June 1942 had resulted in slight damage to the oilfields. The Germans had already put strong anti-aircraft defences around the area, including several hundred large calibre AA guns. The German signal station in Athens could pick up aircraft formations crossing the North African coast.

12 But as a secondary commitment to the British and US forces' requirements.

13 General Walter B. Smith (1895-1961), General Eisenhower's Chief of Staff at Allied Forces Headquarters; nickname Beetle.

14 The 35,000-ton French battleship *Richelieu* had left Brest in June 1940 to avoid being captured by the Germans. She had not been completed but served Vichy France until Allied forces captured French North Africa. It sailed to New York in April 1943 for a long-overdue refit and was upgraded with American armament and joined the British Home Fleet in October. The *Richelieu* served off Norway and was then renamed HMS *Nelson*, joining the British Eastern Fleet in April 1944.

15 General Brehon B. Somervell (1892-1955), Commanding General of the Army Service Forces, responsible for Army logistics.

Marshall replied a maximum of eleven. Three-and-a-half divisions had been re-equipped, including two-and-a-half infantry divisions and one armoured division.

Roosevelt asked if French pilots were being used. Marshall said the British had provided airplanes for one French squadron and the United States had equipped another. Admiral Portal noted the British had supplied the French with air-planes for patrolling off the West African coast. The project was in the hands of the United States apart from the one squadron given towards the build-up of a French Air Force.

Operations for the Defeat of Japan

They had directed the Combined Staff Planners to prepare an appreciation leading up to a plan for the defeat of Japan, including an estimate of the forces required.

Operations in the Burma–China Theatre

The Combined Chiefs of Staff had agreed on:

1) The concentration of available resources, as a first priority within the Assam-Burma Theatre.

2) To build up the air route to China to a capacity of 10,000 tons a month by early fall and the development of air facilities in Assam[1] with a view to:

   a) Intensifying air operations against the Japanese in Burma;

   b) Maintaining increased American Air Forces in China;

   c) Maintaining the flow of airborne supplies to China.

3) Vigorous and aggressive land and air operations at the end of the 1943 monsoon from Assam into Burma via Ledo and Imphal. Advance in step with Chinese forces from Yunnan, with the object of containing as many Japanese forces as possible, covering the air route to China and as an essential step towards the opening of the Burma Road.

4) The capture of Akyab and of Ramree Island by amphibious opera-tions, with possible exploitation.[2]

5) The interruption of Japanese sea communications into Burma.

6) The continuance of administrative preparations in India for the even-tual launching of an overseas operation of about the size of ANAKIM.[3]

Discussion on the Burma-China Theatre

Roosevelt questioned the Combined Chiefs of Staff's statement regarding the interruption of Japanese sea communications into Burma; did it imply an operation against Rangoon? Admiral King[4] replied it did not; it envisaged sub-marine operations against Japanese communications in the Bay of Bengal and the approaches to all the ports of Burma.

Churchill was in agreement with the Chiefs of Staff's report on the Burma operations, but was unhappy it did not mention offensive action against Kra, Sumatra, or Penang. King felt operations against these points depended upon the

1 Northeast India, along the Burmese border.
2 Akyab (now Sittwe) and Ramree Island on the west coast of Burma.
3 ANAKIM was to include a British amphibious attack on Rangoon, a land offensive into Burma and an American-sponsored Chinese attack from Yunnan. It proved to be too ambitious.
4 Admiral King, Commander-in-Chief and United States Fleet and Chief of Naval Operations.

availability of shipping but he doubted they could be mounted in conjunction with the operations planned in the report. King said the shortage of shipping also limited the use of troops from India in the Burma Theatre. An operation against Sumatra or the Kra Peninsula was eventually indispensable to induce the Japanese to split their naval forces. If this could be accomplished, a reinforced Indian Ocean Fleet, operating in coordination with the US Pacific Fleet, might inflect severe damage on the enemy.[5]

Churchill said as soon as the Italian Fleet had been neutralized,[6] the First Sea Lord[7] intended to send six or seven battleships, with necessary auxiliaries, from the Indian Ocean to operate in coordination with the United States Fleet in the Pacific.

Roosevelt was concerned about the failure to mention Rangoon. He thought the Chinese would be much happier if it was mentioned and thought it was wise to do so, if only for political reasons. Churchill suggested amending the wording to read: "The capture of Akyab and of Ramree Island by amphibious operations, with possible exploitation toward Rangoon."[8]

Churchill said the Chiefs of Staff had considered all the essential operations. He felt subsidiary plans should also be worked out, so they would be ready to take advantage of opportunities that might present themselves. Brooke said the whole conception for the defeat of Japan was now the subject of study by the Combined Staff planners. All the operations the Prime Minister referred to would be considered; the present report included only the proposed Burma operations.

Admiral Pound said the program under discussion would probably take all the available resources. The planners were investigating whether or not the operations envisaged could actually be carried out with the available resources. Brooke said the relating of resources to the operations would occur over the weekend and the results would be included in the final report to the President and the Prime Minister.[9]

Pacific Operations 1943-1944

The Combined Chiefs of Staff agreed the following operations:

1)   Conduct of air operations in and from China.
2)   Ejection of the Japanese from the Aleutians.
3)   Seizure of the Marshall and Caroline Islands.
4)   Seizure of the Solomons, the Bismarck Archipelago, and Japanese-held New Guinea.
5)   Intensification of operations against enemy lines of communication.

Roosevelt noted there was no mention of air coverage for US convoys or patrolling for enemy submarines. Admiral King said aircraft were being sent to the Pacific for this purpose as rapidly as possible but there were not enough to cover

---

5   Any naval operations in the Andaman Sea (the sea on the west coast of Burma and the Malaysian Peninsula) would force the Japanese to split their ships operating in the Pacific.
6   It would be neutralised when Italy surrendered in September 1943.
7   Admiral Pound.
8   The words "toward Rangoon" were deleted so it would not be interpreted as a promise by the Chinese.
9   Having agreed which operations were to be considered, the Chiefs of Staff had to check if the United Nations had, or could build, the resources required to carry them out.

everywhere; other operations, particularly HUSKY, absorbed many aircraft necessary for this work. Roosevelt said while everything possible was being done, it was not mentioned in the report.

King said the submarine situation in the Pacific was difficult to explain. He could not understand why the Japanese had not attacked the United States' West Coast. They had great potentialities which they were not using and he was constantly concerned about the possibility of a well conceived Japanese submarine effort.[1]

Admiral Leahy said the President had made a good point and suggested mentioning the protection of the US lines of communications. Brooke said the question of security to lines of communications would be covered in a paper on global strategy.[2]

Churchill thought it would be better to leave the protection of the lines of communications out of the report, as most decisions in it were about the offensive. Defensive measures should be included in the global strategy paper. He asked Admiral Pound how many submarines had been sunk in the last four days; the reply was an average of about one per day.

Summary
The President and the Prime Minister expressed their gratification regarding the work accomplished by the Combined Chiefs of Staff and the decisions reached. Churchill said what appealed to him most was the spirit of the offensive that permeated the paper and the provisions it made for the full utilization of their troops and resources.

22 May
Eleventh Combined Chiefs of Staff Meeting
Anti-U-boat warfare; Sonic warfare; The Queens' movement;[3] Propaganda and Subversive activities.

Churchill met General Stilwell
Discussions about the Burma campaign and giving China aid.

Churchill met Senior American Politicians[4]
Discussion about post-war world and regional councils and their relationship; Post-war Europe; The American hemisphere, the Pacific; Neutrality, lessons of the League of Nations; National and international forces; Fraternal association between Great Britain and the United States.

Churchill met 30 Junior American Politicians[5]
No official record of the meeting.

---

1   The Japanese did not conduct concerted submarine attacks in the Pacific Ocean, as the Germans did in the Atlantic Ocean.
2   The United States lines of communication had to extend across the Pacific.
3   The liners *Queen Mary* and *Queen Elizabeth* used as troopships.
4   Vice President Wallace (1888-1965), Secretary of War Stimson (1867-1950), Secretary of the Interior Ickes (1874-1952) and Senator Connally, the Under Secretary of State (1877-1963).
5   15 Senators and 15 Representatives.

23 May

Twelfth Combined Chiefs of Staff Meeting

Anti U-boat warfare; Movement of *Queen Mary, Queen Elizabeth*; Propaganda, subversive activities; Basic undertakings and specific operations; Moving US Service and Engineer troops to the UK; Operation BRISK;[6] The Third Soviet Protocol.

24 May

Thirteenth Combined Chiefs of Staff Meeting

A military government for Sicily; Provision of new LSIs;[7] Expanding the Air Route to China; Draft final report to the President and Prime Minister.

24 May: Fifth Trident Meeting

Report to the President and Prime Minister

The President said he and the Prime Minister were satisfied with the unanimity of opinion and the Combined Chiefs of Staff's satisfactory decisions. He was particularly grateful so much had been accomplished in such a short time. Churchill recalled decisions had been made with undue speed in the last war when there was no organized group corresponding to the Combined Chiefs of Staff able to provide continuity in the strategic direction of the war.

Churchill said "Today we meet in the presence of a new fact," one which might prove to be decisive progress in the anti-U-boat war. There were indications there might be as many as 30 sinkings in May. A striking change would come over the scene if this continued. Roosevelt then read the revised Final Report to the President and Prime Minister.

French Naval Forces[8]

Churchill said Admiral Godefroy[9] had received an order from the Vichy Government to scuttle his ships in Alexandria but he had definitely thrown in his lot with General Giraud's forces. The British Government would probably lift the pay ban on Godefroy's squadron. Admiral Godefroy wanted his heavy ships to sail around the Cape, call at Dakar and then proceed to the United States for refitting.[10]

Operation to Seize the Azores

Churchill said the political considerations still had to be considered. There was a possibility the islands could be secured without deploying a force as strong as nine battalions and a smaller force could approach the Azores in June. The Portuguese Government could be approached diplomatically seven to ten hours before its arrival and told the force was en route. The Portuguese Government

---

6   The seizure of the Azores.
7   The Landing Ship Infantry carried 800 troops, the LSI (L) carried 1800 troops. They transported troops close to the shore so they could load onto Landing Craft, Assault.
8   At Admiral King's suggestion, equipment would be supplied for all French Forces in Africa, not just French Army Forces.
9   Admiral Godefroy's Dusquesne Squadron was interned in Alexandria when France fell in June 1940. It consisted of the old battleship *Lorraine*, the cruisers *Suffren, Tourville, Duquesne* and *Dougay-Trouin*, the destroyers *Basque, Le Fortune* and *Forbin*, and the submarine *Protée*.
10   Sail through the Suez Canal, around the coast of Africa and then across the Atlantic, avoiding the Mediterranean.

would be reimbursed by whatever figure was set, if they were received without opposition. He thought the chances the Portuguese Government would submit were possibly three to one.

Churchill personally favoured an expedition in sufficient force to take the islands but his government had not authorized such action; the British Cabinet wanted to discuss the subject on his return. Marshall favoured a smaller force, as a threat to back up a diplomatic approach. He thought the present success in anti-submarine warfare made it even more imperative to get use of the islands as soon as possible.

Admiral King said if President Salazar refused to give his assent and the smaller force failed to attack, the Allied Forces would be in a bad position. They would have the humiliation of withdrawing; the Germans would know of the diplomatic approach and it would stiffen the resistance of the islands. Roosevelt had never liked the idea of being put in a position where Salazar could call their bluff. He favoured approaching with sufficient force to take the Islands in the event Salazar refused to permit a peaceful occupation.

General McNarney suggested reinforcing the bluff by timing it with the sailing of a HUSKY convoy from the United Kingdom.[1] Churchill said the earlier operation would have a good prospect of success, as the Portuguese would have no way of knowing how strong the force threatening them was. General Ismay[2] said they were examining a plan to see if something less than a full-scale operation could be mounted. Churchill would discuss the matter with his government upon his return to England and let the President know the outcome.

Roosevelt said Churchill would suggest the alternative of an approach to the Portuguese Government by the USA and Brazil to the British Cabinet. In any case, the idea Brazil might provide the occupying force would be a strong factor in influencing the Portuguese Government to submit.

Cross-Channel Operations

Roosevelt asked if the decision precluded the use of French Divisions in the assault on the Continent. Churchill suggested they might add "the follow-up divisions might come from the United States or elsewhere." Roosevelt considered having a French Division as either one of the nine assault divisions or as one of the first twenty build-up divisions. It was of great political importance to have the French represented in the first attempt to re-conquer French soil.[3]

Marshall asked if the decision should be communicated to the French but Churchill replied it would be extremely dangerous. General Giraud and General de Gaulle were soon to have another meeting and it might result in violent disputes. General Giraud had become stronger because of the Tunisian victories while de Gaulle would think he was about to regain control. The important thing was not to let these two French generals create discord between the United States and the British. He did not feel reassured regarding the outcome of the Giraud-de

---

1   Letting the Portuguese think the invasion fleet was heading for the Azores rather than North Africa.
2   General Ismay, Churchill's chief military advisor, who attended all the conferences.
3   Two Troops of French commandos landed on Sword Beach, while paratroopers serving with the British Special Air Service Brigade were assigned targets in the Brittany Peninsula.

Gaulle conference.[4] He thought it extremely important not to inform the French of their decisions when there was the prospect of a split.

Roosevelt said it was satisfactory to leave any mention of the French Forces out of the paper. But he wanted the fact recorded in the meeting minutes and wanted the Staffs to give serious consideration to the participation of French Forces early in the operation.

Admiral King said there was no mention of General Morgan's month-by-month planning for a troop build-up in the United Kingdom in case of a German crack-up. Roosevelt agreed it was a good idea to include Morgan's decisions in the report but it was impossible to tell when the German resistance might break. In the last war the first German forces to crack were the submarine crews[5] and at the rate they were now losing submarines, the crews would be unable to stick it.[6] German submarine losses in 1918 were not as great they were now experiencing, yet they had induced a break in German morale.

German aircraft had recently failed to reach their objective by ten or twenty miles in two theatres but the crew reports stated they had reached their objectives. Roosevelt thought this was indicative of a bad state of morale and efficiency in the German Air Force. These conditions were bound to spread. When the German ground forces learned they did not have adequate air protection and the U-boat campaign had failed, news would spread rapidly and a serious break in morale might come unexpectedly. It was essential the Allies were ready to take advantage of such conditions.

Roosevelt said there had been rumours of a German evacuation of Norway. He thought they should make plans to take advantage of such a contingency. Churchill suggested adding: "Meanwhile preparations will be continuously kept up-to-date to take advantage of a collapse of the enemy in France or, alternatively, for the occupation of Norway in the event of a German withdrawal."

Air Marshal Portal said air bases in Norway would not be of great assistance for bombing operations, because they would not extend the bombing range far. It would be more economical to utilize airfields in England than build new ones in Norway. However, it would be beneficial to base fighters on airfields in southern Norway.

Churchill said they would reopen their communications with Russia if Norway could be occupied, making it imperative to take immediate advantage of the situation. Churchill said the US authorities would be kept informed of General Morgan's studies.

Mediterranean Operations

Churchill asked to include the Poles in the forces detailed as available for garrisons and operations in the Mediterranean. Brooke confirmed they were included in the 19 British or Allied Divisions.

---

4   Discussions between de Gaulle and Giraud began in Algiers on 31 May. On 3 June an agreement provided for the unification of the French liberation movement and the establishment of the French Committee of National Liberation.
5   At the end of October 1918 Admiral Reinhardt Scheer (1863-1928) proposed a plan to launch suicide attacks against the Royal Navy. The submarine crews in Kiel mutinied and it was the start of a general mutiny across the German armed forces.
6   One U-boat a day was being sunk at this time.

Churchill hoped it was not the intention to commit the Allies to carry out particular operations. For example, he would be very much opposed to the capture of Sardinia after HUSKY. This would be an eccentric operation. It would have no influence on the securing of the great prize open to them if they could take the toe and heel of Italy, and gain touch with the insurgents of the Balkan countries. Admiral King said each operation would be subject to the Combined Chiefs of Staff approval.[1]

Brooke said Eisenhower would not know which operation to do after HUSKY until the situation had declared itself. So they would plan several operations and decide which to carry out after HUSKY. Roosevelt said it was certainly difficult to foretell what the conditions would be. For example, a movement in Sardinia to separate it from Mussolini's regime might gain sway, and comparatively small forces could gain possession of the island. Or again, as one report suggested, the Germans might decide to withdraw their forces behind the Po, making entry into southern Italy easy.[2]

Roosevelt said it might be better to widen the instructions to Eisenhower and to tell him to prepare operations against all parts of southern Europe. Marshall said Eisenhower would prepare a number of different operations and they would decide which to adopt when they saw how HUSKY went. Eisenhower had already put in summaries of plans against the heel and toe of Italy, and against Sardinia, and had expressed a preference for Sardinia. Tedder disagreed, on account of the difficulties of staging an attack against Sardinia without adequate air support.

Air Marshal Portal said Tedder had also thought the value of northern Italy as a base to bomb Germany had been underrated.[3] Churchill said the prime factor to keep in mind was the position in the Balkans, where 34 Axis divisions were held in play by rebels. They would become much more active if they could gain touch with them through Durazzo,[4] or any other suitable point. Of course, if Italy went out of the war, the Italian divisions would have to withdraw and Germany would either have to fill the gap, or retire to the Danube.[5] The effect on Turkey would be very important. None of these effects could possibly accrue from an operation against Sardinia.

Brooke said Eisenhower would be instructed to prepare the operations which had the highest chance of eliminating Italy. This would place these prizes within their grasp and the right operation to bring this about would depend upon the situation after HUSKY. A lot also depended upon events on the Russian Front. The presence of large numbers of Germans in the toe and heel might make a direct assault on this unprofitable – in which case Sardinia would be a better choice.

Churchill did not agree Sardinia could be an acceptable alternative. Operations in the general direction of the Balkans opened up very wide prospects, whereas the

---

1 Churchill wanted to move east following the capture of Sicily, not west.
2 The River Po in northern Italy, effectively abandoning the Italians.
3 Seizing the airfields around Rome would allow the Allies to fly bombing missions over the Alps to bomb targets in Southern Germany.
4 Durazzo, now Durres and the second largest city in Albania, is 125 miles east of the Italian coast.
5 Abandoning Yugoslavia and parts of Bulgaria and Austria.

capture of Sardinia merely placed a desirable island in their possession.[6] Nothing in the paper indicated to Eisenhower they had views on this matter. The politico-strategic aspect would not be present in his mind. Roosevelt said he was not ready to make up his mind. Certainly there were greater advantages in going to places other than Sardinia, but he did not think they were ready to say where yet.[7]

Discussion then took place on the exact meaning of the word 'mount' an operation. Brooke said they had to draw up plans, allocate forces and give them special training to mount an operation. For example, HUSKY had been mounted during VULCAN.[8] It was quite possible to mount more than one operation at a time, as considerable changes could always be made and indeed, had been made quite recently in the HUSKY plan. Churchill thought the word 'mount' meant the fixing on a particular operation for execution to the exclusion of others. He did not think more than one operation at a time could be mounted with the same resources.

The Bombing of Ploesti

Churchill hoped the bombing of Ploesti would not be carried out if it reduced the preparatory aerial bombardment for HUSKY. General McNarney said the bombers from the North African Theatre would only be away for four or five days while units from the United Kingdom would be absent for longer. Marshall said B-24 Liberator aircraft would be used, and they were not as valuable as the B-17 Flying Fortresses for the HUSKY preparatory bombardment.[9] It would be a blow of tremendous importance in support of Russian Front operations if Ploesti could be seriously damaged.[10] The decision depended upon the comments and recommendations of the Commander-in-Chief, North Africa.

Operations in the Burma Theatre

Roosevelt asked Mr. Hopkins what the Chiang Kai-shek's reactions would be to the proposals. Hopkins thought he should not be told the Conference decisions, he would not agree with them. Although he would secretly not be unhappy about them, he would resent not been consulted more than anything else. Hopkins suggested telling Soong about ANAKIM the following day.

Marshall thought the Chinese would have to be told a little more about the operations than Hopkins proposed. The Chinese were constantly asking him about decisions and he felt it wise to tell them everything except the details concerning the capture of Akyab and Ramree Islands.

Roosevelt said the Chinese should simply be told an occupation of a base on the Burma Coast by amphibious operations was included in the decision but the

---

6   It placed Allied troops within striking distance of the south coast of France.
7   The Allies had to make several plans and then wait to see what happened in the Mediterranean after the capture of Sicily.
8   The final attacks on German forces in Tunis, Cap Bon and Bizerte. While the British cleared Tunis, American troops took Bizerte; the operation ended on 6 May 1943. Operation FLAX followed in June, cutting supplies to North Africa, while Operation RETRIBUTION stopped the evacuation of Axis forces to Sicily and Italy. Air and naval operations resulted in nearly 240,000 German and Italian troops being captured.
9   The B-24 Liberator had a longer range and a heavier payload but its lightweight construction and extra fuel tanks in the upper fuselage made it vulnerable to enemy fire and it had a tendency to break up during crash landings.
10 If successful, it would reduce Axis oil stocks considerably during their summer offensive.

details still had to be worked out. Churchill proposed telling the Chinese that a further study of ANAKIM had led to the following plan:

1)   A large-scale build-up of air combat forces.
2)   A rapid build-up of the air transport route to China.
3)   A vigorous offensive in north Burma to open the Burma Road and regain contact with China.
4)   Amphibious operations against the Burma coast, to control communications in the Bay of Bengal.

Churchill said he would prepare a written suggestion as to what to tell the Chinese.

Equipment for Turkey

Churchill wanted to tell the Turks the origin of equipment given by the United States and the same rule should apply to equipment given to Russia. Marshall said the US Chiefs of Staff were more concerned about the equipment's availability and its effects on their training than they were about getting credit for giving it to the Turks. Churchill understood the situation perfectly.

Summary

The rest of the paper was agreed by the President and the Prime Minister. Churchill wanted to give it further consideration. He proposed to submit a suggestion regarding the post-HUSKY operations in the Mediterranean and also a proposal regarding the information to give to the Chinese concerning the Burma decisions. He suggested the meeting adjourned ready to meet again on the morning of 25 May. This was agreed to.

25 May

Fourteenth Combined Chiefs of Staff Meeting

Final Report to the President and Prime Minister; Implementation of Decisions taken at Trident; A Statement to the Chinese; Improving Combined Planning; Conclusion of the conference.

25 May: Sixth Trident Meeting

Employment of the Poles

General Sikorski had made a strong appeal to Churchill about the employment of Polish troops in battle in the near future. He hoped these good troops could be used. Brooke said the Polish troops in the United Kingdom[1] had been included in the forces earmarked for ROUNDHAMMER.[2] The two Polish Divisions and certain minor formations now in Iraq had been included in the 19 British and ·
Allied Divisions available for further operations in the Mediterranean.[3]

Final Report to the President and Prime Minister

The Combined Chiefs of Staff reported they were in entire agreement with Churchill's amendments and would incorporate them in the final report. Churchill said it would be necessary to give a version of the report to the Russians. It could

---

1   General Wladyslaw Sikosrki (1881-1943) had one armoured division and one brigade.
2   Also referred to as SLEDGEHAMMER, a plan to seize Brest or Cherbourg. If it was possible to secure the Cotentin Peninsula and ship troops to Cherbourg, they could break out when enough troops had been assembled.
3   They would take part in the Italian campaign, notably at Monte Cassino.

be drawn up in suitable form through the normal official channels. It meant they did not have to send an explanatory telegram. The message could say a full report would reach them through the American and British representatives in Moscow.

Communication with the Chinese

It was agreed Roosevelt and Marshall should use Churchill's suggested wording in their conversation with Dr. Soong and General Chu regarding Burma-China Theatre operations.

General Stilwell and General Chennault to Visit the United Kingdom

Churchill said it would be of great value if Stilwell and Chennault could return to their posts via London so they could share their unrivalled knowledge of the Burma-China Theatre. The London route was three days shorter than the South Atlantic route. Field Marshal Wavell and Admiral Somerville were also going to London and a visit by the two generals would give a great impetus to the decisions of the Combined Chiefs of Staff regarding the Burma-China Theatre. Marshall agreed.

Post-HUSKY Operations

Roosevelt said Churchill would soon talk to the Commanders-in-Chief in North Africa about post-HUSKY policy and suggested it would be of great value if Marshall could accompany him. Roosevelt asked Marshall to defer his visit to the Southwest Pacific and Marshall agreed.

Churchill would feel awkward discussing the matters with General Eisenhower without the presence of a United States representative on the highest level. If decisions were taken, it might be thought he had exerted undue influence. It was accordingly a source of great gratification to him to hear Marshall would accompany him. He was sure they could arrange everything satisfactorily in Algiers, and for a report to be sent back to the Combined Chiefs of Staff for their consideration.[4]

Code Names for Future Operations

Admiral Leahy said the Combined Chiefs of Staff recommended the adoption of certain code names, a list of which he handed to the President. Certain modifications were agreed.

The PLOUGH Scheme

Marshall read a report on the state of training and readiness for action of the force specially set aside and trained for the PLOUGH scheme. It was the firm opinion of all the United States and British officers concerned that this force of some 2,500 men should be given battle experience as soon as possible.[5]

The force, which had been given amphibious training in addition to special training for the PLOUGH scheme, had been worked up to a high pitch of readiness, and provided it was not uselessly dissipated, it would greatly benefit by

---

4   Churchill and Marshall met Eisenhower in Algiers three times between 29 May and 3 June. They discussed HOBGOBLIN (the capture of the tiny island of Pantelleria between Sicily and Tunisia), HUSKY, air attacks on Rome and what came after HUSKY.

5   British scientist Geoffrey Pike (1893-1948) suggested forming a commando force trained for fighting behind enemy lines in winter conditions. The elite American-Canadian 1st Special Service Force, nickname Devil's Brigade, was formed in 1942. The original plan to attack in Norway, eventually abandoned, was codenamed the PLOUGH scheme. They fought in the Aleutians, Italy and in France before they were disbanded in December 1944.

coming into action. It could be reassembled for its proper role before the winter. There were a number of possible places where the force might be utilized, such as the Aleutians, or post-HUSKY operations, or for commando raids from the United Kingdom or even in the Azores. It was a pity they had not been employed in the Attu operations, but another opportunity might occur in that area. Brooke agreed the value of the force would be greatly increased by early participation in battle. McNarney said the improved type of vehicle for use by the force would be ready about the middle of October.

Churchill said this force had been designed for a particular type of warfare and it would be a great pity to dissipate it if there was a chance of its real role coming to the fore. Nevertheless, he thought it would be quite easy to create an opportunity for its employment if it was sent to the United Kingdom. It might be possible, for example, to repeat a raid on the coast of Norway of the type of the raid on the Lofoten Islands.[1] Roosevelt said it would be necessary to consider using the Norwegian battalion in the United States first. Churchill agreed. He suggested the British Chiefs of Staff should make proposals to the Combined Chiefs of Staff. This was agreed to.

Consultations with the Russians

Roosevelt asked if steps had been taken to concert measures with the Russians in case Japan attacked.[2] Marshall said an attempt had been made to discuss this with the Russians and General Bradley had been sent to Moscow for the purpose.[3] After three months' negotiation, it had been agreed he should survey the Siberian airfields but the Russians then reversed the decision and the whole proposal had fallen through.

Roosevelt said the Russians did not wish to permit any act which might compromise them in the eyes of the Japanese. Nevertheless, it would be a pity if the occasion arose and no plans had been made. It might be desirable to send forces to help the Russians to hold Kamchatka.[4]

Churchill agreed but thought the Russians would be unlikely to be forthcoming. He suggested one way of making progress would be to say to the Russians they would be prepared to send them so many squadrons of aircraft so many days after the outbreak of the war with Japan. They could tell them they could count on this reinforcement in making their plans. This might lead them onto discussion. McNarney said this had been tried but the Russians asked them for the aircraft so they could fly them themselves. Admiral King said periodic studies were made of the possibilities presented by a Russo-Japanese war; the last review had been three months ago but little could be done without additional data.

The Trident Conference then adjourned. Churchill expressing his gratitude for the warm welcome he had received and his appreciation of the work which had been accomplished.

---

1   The Lofoten Islands are on the northwest coast of Norway.
2   Attacked the east coast of Russia.
3   Major-General Follet Bradley, USAAF (1890-1952).
4   The 1250-mile-long peninsula on the northeast side of the Sea of Okhotsk, north of Japan.

25 May: President and Prime Minister Press Conference

Roosevelt: We are awfully glad to have Mr. Churchill back here. I don't have to tell him that. All he has to do is read the papers and look into the faces of any American. He is very welcome. I don't think we have very much to tell you, except we are making exceedingly good progress, and taking up a matter which I spoke of the other day; the total war – the global war. Considering the size of our problems, these discussions have been done in practically record time. And so I am going to turn the meeting over to Mr. Churchill, and I think he will be willing to answer almost – with stress on the almost – any question (laughter).

Question: Mr. Prime Minister, in Australia there is a very great fear about the Japanese threat. What are your feelings about the matter?

Churchill: The threat is certainly less serious than it was when I saw you last in this room.[5]

Question: Mr. Prime Minister, can you tell us generally about the plans for the future, beginning with Europe?

Churchill: A very expansive topic (laughter) and one which leads very early to difficult country. But our plans for the future are to wage this war until unconditional surrender is procured from all those who have molested us and this applied equally to Asia and to Europe. It used to apply quite recently to Africa.

Roosevelt: I think that word molestation or molesting is one of the best examples of your habitual understatement I know (laughter).

Question: Mr. Prime Minister, could you say anything about how satisfied you are with the way things are going on the fighting fronts?

Churchill: I am very much more satisfied than l was when I was here last (laughter),[6] when the President handed me the telegram of the surrender of Tobruk. And as I have mentioned to him, I don't think there was anybody – any Englishman in the United States so unhappy, as I was that day, since Burgoyne surrendered at Saratoga (loud laughter).[7]

But the situation is very different now. The plans which were made and the movements of troops which were set in motion before June last enabled us to alter the balance of the affairs in Africa entirely. And we opened our offensive in Alamein on 23 October. The United States and British descent upon North Africa began on 8 November, and since then we have already had a very great measure of success, culminating in a decisive victory of proportions equal to any of the great victories that have been won: complete obliteration of the enemy. And while this has been going on, our Russian Ally, who in June last year was subject to the beginning of a very heavy and possibly deadly offensive by the Germans, and it seemed they might well lose the Caucasus, has gained another series of successes, culminating in Stalingrad.

Hitler has been struck with two immense blows, tremendous shattering blows: in Tunisia, and at Stalingrad. And from every point of view we must regard the last

---

5　On 23 December 1941, following the Arcadia Conference.
6　On 18 June 1942.
7　There were two battles of Saratoga (19 September and 7 October 1777), south of New York during the American War of Independence.

ten or eleven months as examples of highly successful war – a perfectly indisput-
able turning of the tide.

Question: Mr. Prime Minister, on the question of Russia. After you spoke to
Senator Chandler[1] you issued a statement saying while you promised Great
Britain would stay to fight Japan to the end, you could not promise Russia
would. Of course, there are reasons for this. But do you care to say anything? In
your opinion of Russia's self-interest, would it lead her to fight Japan after the
European war?

Churchill: Oh well, it is one of those oversights that I have not been placed in
the position to give directions to Russia (laughter). And I have this feeling, those
people have been doing such a tremendous job facing this enormous mass – they
have done what nobody else was in a position to do; torn a large part of the
guts out of the German army. And they have suffered very grievous losses. They
are battling with 190 German divisions – not up to strength, of course – and 28
satellite divisions from the different countries Hitler gathered around him in his
attack on Russia. They are bearing all that weight, and I certainly have not felt
I ought to suggest to my government asking more of them. But their strength
may grow as time goes on.

They must know Japan has watched them with a purely opportunist eye. But it
isn't for me to make any suggestions to them at all. They have been grand Allies;
and of course they have shown it in heroic fashion. They have struck blows no
one else could strike, and they have endured losses no one power has ever been
capable of enduring; and continue as an effective and even a growing factor in
the field.

Question: Mr. Prime Minister, what do you think of the dissolution of the
Comintern?[2]

Churchill: Well, I like it (laughter).

Question: To get back to Russia, sir, are you confident the Russians will be able to
hold out this year, as they have in past years?

Churchill: I certainly think they have a much better prospect of holding out this
year than they had the previous time. Indeed, I must express my full confidence
they will hurl back any attack which is made upon them.

Question: Mr. Prime Minister, in the light of developments since your speech to
Congress, would you care to make any general statement concerning the experiment of bombing Germany into submission?

Churchill: Well, I haven't had very much time to go on with the experiment
since I spoke to Congress (laughter). We have had the heaviest raid we have ever
had, the raid on Dortmund, where 2000 tons were cast down upon them with,

---

1   Senator Albert B. Chandler (1898-1991), Democrat of Kentucky; the longest living US Senator.
2   The Communist International, abbreviated as Comintern, was known as the Third International. It was an international comm
    unist organization initiated in Moscow in March 1919. Stalin dissolved it in 1943 probably to calm Roosevelt's and Churchill's
    suspicions that the Soviet Union was pursuing a policy to stir up revolution in other countries.

I believe, highly satisfactory results.[3] And also, it has been an extremely good week for the United States air forces in the United Kingdom. They made four heavy daylight attacks, which are judged to be extremely successful. Precision bombing in the daylight, of course, in proportion to the weight of bombs dropped, produces a more decisive effect – more than the night bombing, because it goes to more specific targets, precise and accurate.

Roosevelt: I think that is something that hasn't been brought out. The night bombing over Europe carries more weight of explosives; but of course being night-time the precision of the actual bombing can't be so great as the day bombing, which carries less explosives but with more precision, because it's daylight. On the whole, the combination of the two, day and night, is achieving a more and more satisfactory result.

Churchill: It's like running a 24 hour service (laughter).

Question: Mr. Prime Minister, have you any comment to make upon relations between General Giraud and General de Gaulle?

Churchill: Well, I am very glad to see apparently it's improved, and there is to be a meeting, judging only from what I read in the organs which you gentlemen sustain and serve (laughter). But certainly it will be very satisfactory if all this backchat comes to an end, and the Frenchmen who are fighting to relieve and liberate their country get together and look forward to the future instead of backward on the past, and think of the great duty they owe to France rather than to any factional interest.

Question: Mr. Prime Minister, the last time you spoke to us you used a term I have remembered, because you said you were not going to rely on an internal collapse of Germany, you would rather rely on an external knockout. Well, since then you have worked on Germany and the occupied countries a good deal, and there are constantly recurring evidences the German people may be getting close to "had enough". We still are working for this knockout but have you any further light on the internal collapse?

Churchill: I stand pat on the knockout (laughter).[4] But, of course, any windfall will be gratefully accepted (more laughter).

Question: Mr. Prime Minister, some quarters interpret your remarks to Congress on bombing to mean other methods, which you said should not be excluded, should be postponed until the termination of the experiment.

Churchill: Oh, no. That would be a most distorted deduction to draw. I said there is no reason why the experiment should not be continued, provided other simultaneous methods, or current methods, are not excluded.

Question: Mr. Prime Minister, whenever you and the President confer, the rumour always goes around you are about to pick an Allied commander for the European Theatre. Could you tell us whether you have done that?

Churchill: Well, we have an Allied commander in the Northwest Africa Theatre.

---

3   826 Lancasters successfully bombed Dortmund on the night of 23/24 May; 38 were reported missing and another 63 were damaged.

4   Churchill was sticking with a knockout result.

Question: I was thinking of the next one, sir (laughter).

Churchill: No step has been taken at the present moment. Because the great preparations going forward we haven't got to the point where the executive commander has to be chosen.

Miss May Craig:[1] Mr. Prime Minister, this may be an oversight, or you might not have been informed of this either, but I am curious to know what you think is going on in Hitler's mind now (much laughter)?

Churchill: I have very little doubt if he could have the past back he would probably play his hand a little differently. I think he would have hesitated long before he rejected all the repeated peace efforts made by Great Britain, which even brought the name of our government into disrepute, so far did we go on the path of trying to placate and appease.[2] But he then got out of the period where he was restoring his country to its place among the countries of Europe. He had achieved that; but that wasn't what he was after at all. Appetite unbridled, ambition unmeasured – all the world! There was no end to the appetite of this wicked man. I should say he repents now he did not curb his passion before he brought such a great portion of the world against him and his country.

Question: Mr. Prime Minister, do you think it's a sound assumption he still has a mind?

Churchill: I have no reason to suppose he isn't in control of his faculties and of the resources of his country. But, of course, I haven't the same facilities of acquainting myself with what is going on there, as I fortunately have on what is going on in the United States (laughter).

Question: Mr. Prime Minister, do you care to say anything about Mussolini and Italy? Is there any hint or news you can bring us on that?

Churchill: You know as much as I do about that. I think they are a softer proposition than Germany, but I wouldn't count on anything but the force of arms. It may be aided at any time by a change of heart on the part of the enemy's countries, a weakening of morale. Nobody proposes to take the native soil of Italy away from the Italian people. They will have their life in the new Europe. They have sinned by allowing themselves to be led by the nose by a very elaborate tyranny which was imposed upon them, so it gripped every part of their life. The one party totalitarian system, plus the secret police applied over a number of years, is capable of completely obliterating the sense of personal liberty. And thus they were led by intriguing leaders – who thought they had got the chance of 5000 years in aggrandizing themselves by the misfortunes of their neighbours who had not offended them in any way – into this terrible plight in which they find themselves. I think they would be very well advised to dismiss those leaders, and throw themselves upon the justice of those they have so grievously offended. We should not stain our names before posterity by cruel and inhuman acts. We have our own reputation to consider. But after all it really is a matter for them to settle among themselves, and settle with their leaders. All we can do is to apply

---

1 May Craig (1889-1975), a journalist who reported on World War II, the Korean War and politics. She was posted to France and gave eye-witness accounts on the liberation of the country.
2 Referring to the Munich Agreement in September 1938.

those physical stimuli (laughter) which in default of moral sanctions are sometimes capable of inducing a better state of mind in recalcitrant individuals and recalcitrant nations (more laughter).

Question: Mr. Prime Minister, there has been a lot of interest in the experts from India you brought with you. Would you care to comment about the situation in India, or China?

Churchill: Well, I am very anxious to increase the intensity of the war effort against Japan and brought these commanders-in-chief so they could meet the United States officers. Particularly meet those who have been serving with such effect in China, like General Chennault and General Stilwell, and the high officers here, because it is evident the war in that theatre must be prosecuted with the very greatest vigour. And we have been talking a great deal about that, and thinking a great deal, and have arrived at conclusions which I believe are good. When I saw you last in December 1941 or January 1942 – I forget which it was – the question of priority – which was first and which was second of the two great theatres and antagonists – assumed a much sharper form than at the present time. Our resources have greatly expanded. If the war continues on both fronts the war will be waged with equal force as our resources grow. Instead of being consecutive, our efforts will be concurrent, and that great degree of effort will be capable of being applied at the same time in both directions. They have been already applied. The forces we have are becoming very respectable in munitions, and in men trained to go to war of all kinds. But as I pointed out to Congress, the problem is one of application, and the problem of application is limited by distance, and the U-boat war, the amount of shipping, the character of the communications and the vast distances of the ocean. Our forces are growing and gathering their ambition, but to apply it is a matter of time, and it is exceedingly difficult to apply. But we follow out this principle; that all soldiers must be engaged, all ships and airplanes must be engaged on the widest possible fronts, the broadest possible superficies,[3] and maintain the fighting with the utmost intensity. Because we are the stronger animal; we are the stronger combination; we are shaking the life out of the enemy and as we are able to continue, we will not give him a moment's surcease. This is particularly true of the air, where they are already beginning to fail to keep up at all to the necessary strength on the various fronts. Neither Japan nor Germany is able to maintain equality with Britain, the United States and Russia on all the fronts. Still less are they able to do so in the field of production. Immense plurality – the superiority of production – is on our side. And although it takes a certain number of months after planes are made before they come into action – perhaps a good many months, having regard to all the distances to be covered and the large ground staffs to be transported. But in spite of that, at the end of certain periods, the great superiority in numbers of our manufacture and of our trading is bound to have an effect, which so far as the air war is concerned will be decisive. Whether the deciding of the air war will entail a similar ending of the other forms of warfare has yet to be seen. But the air was the weapon these people chose to subjugate the world. This was the weapon they struck at Pearl

---

Harbor with. This was the weapon with which the Germans boasted they would terrorize all the countries of the world. And it is an example of poetic justice that this should be the weapon in which they should find themselves most out-matched and first out-matched in the ensuing struggle.

Question: Mr. Prime Minister, have you anything to say about the submarine side of the situation?

Churchill: I am very much encouraged by all that has happened there since the turn of the year. Really, it has been very encouraging. The output from the United States' shipyards is prodigious and has fulfilled all hopes which, when the plans were first made and published, seemed to be excessive. But they have been made good. The movement of supplies across the ocean has been on an increasing scale. The surplus of new building over sinkings over the last six months has been substantial, especially in the later months. And the killings of U-boats by our forces has improved and reached a very high pitch; never better than in the last month. That is due, of course, to the increasing numbers of U-boats, but it is also due to the improved methods, and some wonderful things have been thought of on both sides of the Atlantic. And, of course, we interchange everything immediately. Anything we have we share and bring into action. A lot of clever people are thinking a lot about these things.

Question: Mr. Prime Minister, there is a great deal more confidence in the Allied commanders in the field than there was a year ago. Would you care to comment on that?

Churchill: Well, they have had a chance to come into action on reasonable terms. Indeed, on advantageous terms, because we struck with superior forces at the right spot. As your Confederate general used to say, "We got there firstest with the mostest" (laughter).[1] And also, our troops have been equipped with all the best weapons. You have only got to turn the industry of the United States and Britain over from peace to war. It undoubtedly takes a couple of years or more to get it running, but when it does run it gives you a flow of weapons which certainly neither Germany nor Japan possibly can beat.

Question: Mr. Prime Minister, would you make a prediction on the progress of the war for the rest of this year? I have in mind the statement you and the President made at Casablanca, on new and heavier blows against all of the Axis members in 1943.

Churchill: Well, I think that seems to be a very sound prediction, and couched in terms which are unexceptionable from the point of view of military security (laughter).

Question: Thank you very much, sir. Churchill: Thank you very much.[2]

Roosevelt: May I say one word, please? Don't get the idea the conferences are concluded. They are not. They are continuing.

Churchill: We have a lot of ground to cover.

---

1   Nathan Bedford Forrest (1821-1877), a Cavalry commander in the Civil War.
2   As the newspapermen left the room, the Prime Minister climbed on his chair and gave the V for Victory sign, accompanied by much applause.

The Quadrant Conference: 12–24 August 1943

Plans for a late summer conference were made at the end of the Symbol conference and in June the President recommended holding it in Quebec, Canada, where the climate was better than Washington DC. The plan was to hold Quadrant, a name chosen by Churchill, in September, but the early success of HUSKY meant it was brought forward so they could discuss their next move in the Mediterranean. It had been hoped to include Premier Stalin but he was again fully engaged with the summer offensive on the Eastern Front.

The Chiefs of Staff met for the first time at Chateau Frontenac, Quebec,[3] before the meeting of the Heads of State. Churchill met Roosevelt at his home, Hyde Park, 90 miles north of New York on 12 August and they had preliminary discussions over the next two days. They then proceeded to Quebec where the Quadrant meetings were held in the Citadel,[4] a 17th-century French fortification updated by the British in the 1820s.

There were two conferences and eleven Chiefs of Staff meetings between 17 and 24 August 1943. The chief representatives were President Roosevelt, Prime Minister Churchill and Prime Minister William L. Mackenzie King.[5]

14 August
First Chiefs of Staff Meeting
Conference Agenda; European Theatre.
Second Chiefs of Staff Meeting
War against Japan.

15 August
Third Chiefs of Staff Meeting
Making Rome an open city; Strategic concept for the defeat the Axis in Europe; Operation OVERLORD and Air and Naval command for OVERLORD; Synthetic harbours.

16 August
Fourth Chiefs of Staff Meeting
Strategic concept for the defeat the Axis in Europe; Operation POINTBLANK.

17 August
Fifth Chiefs of Staff Meeting
Strategic concept for the defeat the Axis in Europe; Italian peace feelers; Operations in the Pacific and Southeast; Operations from India against Japan.

---

3   A huge hotel built in the style of a French chateau at the end of the 19th century.
4   Or Citadelle of Quebec.
5   William L. Mackenzie King (1874-1950), Prime Minister of Canada on three occasions, notably from October 1935 to November 1948.

18 August
Sixth Chiefs of Staff Meeting
Italian peace feelers; Landing Craft production; Operations from India against Japan; Deception Plan for the War on Japan; The U-boat War; Operation ALACRITY; Southeast Asia command.

19 August
Seventh Chiefs of Staff Meeting
Habbakuks; Landing Craft; Use of the PLOUGH Force; Equipping Allies, Liberated Forces and Friendly Nations; Special operations in Sardinia.

19 August: First Quadrant Meeting
After welcoming the Combined Chiefs of Staff the President and Prime Minister agreed to read through the Progress Report.[1]
The U-boat War
They had encouraging reports from the Chiefs of the two Naval Staffs regarding the U-boat war. They had approved the Allied Submarine Board's recommendations which should result in further strengthening of their anti–U-boat operations. The Board has been directed to continue and expand its studies in search of further improvements.[2]

The facilities of the Azores Islands would be used for intensified sea and air operations against the U-boat. On the successful conclusion of the negotiations for the use of the Azores they had taken note that everything would be done by the British to make arrangements for their operational and transit use by US aircraft as soon as possible after actual entry had been gained.[3]
Discussion about the Azores
Roosevelt suggested sending Churchill a notice that a British and American convoy and some British and American air units were proceeding to the Azores a week or ten days after the British occupation of the Azores and they expected to use the islands' facilities. The British could then say to the Portuguese "they were frightfully sorry their cousins from overseas had descended upon them but having done so, there was little they could do about it."[4] Churchill agreed to the plan.[5]

---

1   The Overall Objective, the Overall Strategic Concept and the Basic Undertakings in Support of Overall Strategic Concept were the same as those stated at the Trident Conference.
2   Admiral King estimated that 429 U-boats were operating around the world, of which 166 were in the Atlantic. Refuelling U-boats had been targeted to limit their effectiveness and 10 of the original 12 U-boats had been sunk. The U.S. had deployed five auxiliary carriers and aircraft were being equipped with heavier weaponry to attack U-boats on the surface. King also reported that a large number of anti-submarine weapons were in the course of experiment and development.
3   Winter weather forced planes to fly farther south and the South Atlantic crossing was 5,400 miles more than the Azores route. It would speed up the movement of aircraft and air cargo and save an estimated 15 million gallons of gasoline over the winter.
4   A rather cheeky way of invading the island, designed not to arouse Axis suspicions.
5   The plan to occupy the Azores and use them as an airbase would be called Operation ALACRITY. Churchill attempted to justify the landing on the Azores by referring to the 1386 Anglo-Portuguese Treaty between Britain and Portugal; the oldest treaty in the world. Portugal approved Allied use of the islands in 1943.

The British were not at fault in failing to obtain the immediate use of these facilities for the United States; he had kept the President informed of events. He said the British had not given President Salazar[6] any assurance as to what forces would be sent to help Portugal in case of attack. The British had only committed themselves to declare war on Spain[7] if she attacked Portugal and to afford such help to Portugal as was in their power against an attack by the Germans.

Churchill said that, if on 8 October, the British had entered the islands and no attack against Portugal had resulted, President Salazar would feel much better about permitting United States use of the Azores' facilities. Immediately upon occupancy, the British would make every effort by diplomacy to obtain the permit for United States entry.[8] Mr. Eden[9] said it had always been visualized this would be done. He suggested the proposed American–British convoy might sail in about a fortnight after the British entry. He thought timing was an extremely important factor but was confident the situation could be handled to every-one's satisfaction.

The Bomber Offensive

The progressive destruction and dislocation of the German military, industrial and economic system, the disruption of vital elements of lines of communication, and the material reduction of German air combat strength by the successful prosecution of the Combined Bomber Offensive from all convenient bases was a prerequisite to OVERLORD.[10] This operation had to continue to have highest strategic priority.[11]

Discussion about the Bomber Offensive

Mr. Hopkins[12] asked if POINTBLANK included air operations from Italy. Air Marshal Portal said it did not but it might in the future. One of the chief objectives of the POINTBLANK operation was to destroy German fighter factories and some could be attacked better from Italy. General Arnold[13] contemplated part of the POINTBLANK forces would eventually move so they could operate from Italian bases when they became available.[14]

---

6 President Salazar of Portugal.
7 President Francisco Franco (1892-1975) met Hitler in October 1940 to discuss the possibility of Spain joining Nazi Germany. However, Franco's demands for territories, equipment and supplies were too high.
8 The plan was for British troops to occupy the islands under the terms of the medieval treaty. Germany's reaction would determine if American troops would follow.
9 R. Anthony Eden (1897-1977), Secretary of State for Foreign Affairs.
10 Barring an independent and complete Russian victory before OVERLORD could be mounted.
11 The number of German fighters was 2,260, an increase of 22% since 1 January 1943, and all new planes had been deployed in the west. It doubled the number facing the 921 U.S. and U.K. bombers flying missions across Nazi-occupied Europe. It meant the number of fighters facing Russia was falling. Squadrons were also being transferred from Russia and the Mediterranean and the Chief of the Air Staff believed that Germany faced "imminent disaster" if Operation POINTBLANK continued. He also urged the reinforcement of 8th Bomber Command or the Allies may "miss the opportunity to win a decisive victory against the German Air Force".
12 Harry L. Hopkins was Roosevelt's chief diplomatic advisor and trouble shooter.
13 General Arnold, Commander-in-Chief of the US Army Air Forces.
14 The imminent invasion of southern Italy presented opportunities for new airfields close to southern Europe. The distance from England's airfields to Bavaria and from southern Italy was 600 miles, however, most of Germany's anti-aircraft defences were in northwest Germany.

Roosevelt asked if the operation included attacks on Ploesti.[1] Arnold replied the oil industry was one of the major objectives in the third phase of the plan. Attacks on Ploesti, if not specifically mentioned in the plan, could be included in that phase provided suitable bases had become available. Roosevelt said if they reached bases as far north as Ancona in Italy[2] they would be within striking distance of Ploiesti.[3] It was then agreed the plan for the Combined Bomber Offensive would include attacks from all convenient bases.

Operation OVERLORD

The operation would be the primary US–British ground and air effort against the Axis in Europe.[4] After securing adequate Channel ports, exploitation would be directed toward securing areas to facilitate both ground and air operations against the enemy. Following the establishment of strong Allied forces in France, operations designed to strike at the heart of Germany and to destroy her military forces would be undertaken. There would be a balanced ground and air force build-up for OVERLORD. There would be continuous planning for, and maintenance of, those forces available in the United Kingdom in readiness to take advantage of any situation permitting an opportunistic cross-Channel move into France.[5]

Between Operation OVERLORD and operations in the Mediterranean, where there was a shortage of resources, available resources would be distributed and employed with the main object of ensuring the success of OVERLORD.[6] Operations in the Mediterranean would be carried out with the forces allotted at TRIDENT unless the Combined Chiefs of Staff varied them. They had approved the outline plan of General Morgan[7] for Operation OVERLORD and had authorized him to proceed with the detailed planning and full preparations.

Discussion about Operation OVERLORD

Churchill was in favour of the plan but they had to understand its implementation depended on certain conditions being fulfilled regarding relative strengths. One of these was there should be no more than twelve mobile German divisions[8] in northern France when the operation was mounted and they should not be capable of a build-up of more than fifteen divisions over the next two months.[9] If the German strength proved to be considerably greater than this, the plan should be revised by the Combined Chiefs of Staff.

---

1   By 1943 Ploesti's (now Ploiesti) oilfields in Romania (50 miles north of Bucharest) produced a third of the Axis oil supplies. Operation TIDAL WAVE on 1 August involved 178 American bombers flying from Benghazi and they were hit by hidden anti-aircraft guns. The raid was a disaster; 53 planes were shot down and the damage resulted in "no curtailment of overall product output".

2   150 miles northeast of Rome.

3   Ancona is 150 miles north northeast of Rome on Italy's east coast. Allied troops would not reach it until the summer of 1944.

4   Target date 1 May 1944.

5   COSSAC prepared Operation RANKIN in case Germany's situation deteriorated.

6   The main shortage of resources was landing craft, both in numbers and type. The possible rough sea conditions in the English Channel presented problems for COSSAC planners that the Mediterranean planners did not have to consider.

7   General Morgan, Chief of Staff to the Supreme Allied Commander, (COSSAC).

8   As opposed to static coastal divisions of a lower quality.

9   The Allies had to rely on shipping to bring troops across the Channel to the Normandy beaches until French ports were open. The two-month period suggested by Churchill covers this period.

Hopkins did not feel the Allies should take a rigid view of these limitations; there might be thirteen German divisions or even fifteen German divisions at two-thirds strength. It would be also difficult to assess what the German fighter strength would be and he felt General Morgan's report was inelastic.

Churchill agreed there should be elasticity in judgment in deciding whether or not the operation should be mounted but he wished to emphasize he strongly favoured OVERLORD for 1944. He had not been in favour of SLEDGEHAMMER in 1942 or ROUNDUP in 1943[10] but his objections to those operations had been removed. Every effort should be made to add at least 25% to the initial assault. This would mean an increase in landing craft but there were nine months available before the target date and much could be done in that time.

The beaches selected were good but it would be better if a landing was made on the inside beaches of the Cotentin Peninsula at the same time.[11] The initial lodgement must be strong because it largely affected later operations. Marshall agreed an increase in the initial assault would greatly strengthen the OVERLORD operation.

Roosevelt wanted the time of arrival of US troops in England stepped up. Marshall said a study was being made but he wished to emphasize the shortage of landing craft places was the greatest limitation on all of their operations.[12] He cited the case of the Mediterranean and how they could have made an earlier entry into Italy if landing craft had been available.

Churchill said Mr. Lewis Douglas,[13] Mr. Averill Harriman[14] and Lord Leathers[15] had made an intensive study of the shipping situation, which indicated a large increase would be available as a result of their success in anti-U-boat warfare. Admiral King said prospects were excellent and there would be more landing craft available than previously anticipated.

Roosevelt said a study on converting excess dry cargo ships into troop carriers was being carried out.[16] Conversion took about six months but he felt it should be done to bring cargo lift and troop lift into balance. Marshall reported General Somervell[17] was optimistic over the prospects of making up their present backlog in troop lift.

---

10 In April General Marshall suggested two plans for a cross-Channel invasion, both supported by the Soviets. SLEDGEHAMMER involved capturing Cherbourg in the autumn of 1942 and troops would build up in the Cotentin Peninsula over the winter ready for a spring 1943 offensive. ROUNDUP would be a large invasion in the spring of 1943. Both were later considered to be impractical.

11 At the time, the beaches selected stretched from the base of the Cotentin Peninsula to Caen. Churchill is suggesting what Eisenhower advocated in January 1944 and planners later adopted; the addition of UTAH beach on the southeast coast of the peninsula.

12 The shortage of landing craft would continue to be a major headache for the Allies until D-Day, contributing to the one-month delay from 1 May to early June.

13 Lewis Williams Douglas (1894-1974), deputy administrator of the United States War Shipping Administration responsible for managing the country's shipping needs.

14 W. Averell Harriman (1891-1986), United States ambassador to the Soviet Union and coordinator of the Lend-Lease program.

15 Minister of War Transport who negotiated the Lend-Lease of American ships to the United Kingdom.

16 Taking ships designed to carry dry goods and build accommodation inside so they could carry troops across the Atlantic.

17 General Somervell, Commander-in-Chief of the Army Services Forces.

They had also examined General Morgan's plans for an emergency operation to enter the Continent. They would keep the situation under continuous review, with particular reference to the attainment of air superiority and the number of troops necessary for success.

If circumstances rendered the execution of OVERLORD impossible, it might be necessary to consider JUPITER as an alternative.[1] Plans for the operation, with particular reference to an entry into southern Norway, had to be made and kept up-to-date.

Operations in Italy

First Phase: The elimination of Italy as a belligerent and the establishment of air bases in the Rome area, and, if feasible, further north.[2]

Second Phase: The seizure of Sardinia and Corsica.[3]

Third Phase: The maintenance of unremitting pressure on German forces in northern Italy.

Fourth Phase: The creation of the conditions required for OVERLORD and of a situation favourable for the eventual entry of our forces, including the bulk of the re-equipped French Army and Air Force into southern France.

Roosevelt asked where they contemplated using French troops and while it was desirable to use them against Corsica it was not in Sardinia.[4] General Brooke believed an attack against Sardinia depended entirely on what the Germans did with their forces on that island. There was a possibility the German force would be withdrawn in the case of a collapse of Italy. In that case, Sardinia would fall with Italy and a military operation to take it would not be necessary.[5]

Churchill wanted it understood that he was not committed to an advance beyond the Ancona-Pisa Line into northern Italy.[6] General Brooke doubted whether they would have enough troops to go beyond this line, it was not yet possible to say. Roosevelt asked if it was necessary to go farther into northern Italy to reach Germany with their aircraft. Portal replied it was not necessary but there was a distinct disadvantage in permitting the Germans to occupy the airfields south of the Alps. This had a particularly bad effect in improving the warning service for all raids into Germany.[7] Additionally, the airfields in northern Italy had a greater capacity than those in central Italy. The central Italian airfields needed considerable work before they could accommodate their big bombers.[8]

---

1   Operation JUPITER was a plan to invade Norway.
2   The airfields would allow Allied bombers to attack southern Germany.
3   Sardinia was (and is) Italian while Corsica was (and is) French.
4   French troops would lead the invasion of Corsica in September 1943.
5   General (later Field Marshal) Brooke's prediction became true. The Italian resistance forced the Germans to evacuate Sardinia and head for Corsica following the invasion of the Italian mainland in September 1943.
6   Between 200 and 100 miles northwest of Rome.
7   Fighters could intercept bombers as they flew towards, and returned from, targets north of the Alps.
8   While it took more troops to advance north up the Italian peninsula, the capture of the airfields north of Rome had many advantages for the Allies.

Operations in Southern France

Offensive operations against southern France[9] should be undertaken to establish a lodgement in the Toulon-Marseilles area and then exploit northward in order to create a diversion in connection with OVERLORD. Air-nourished guerrilla operations in the Southern Alps would, if possible, be initiated.

Churchill was hesitant about putting good divisions into southern France to meet the anticipated resistance and doubted if French divisions would be capable of an operation of the kind suggested. Brooke said such a diversion would depend on the German reaction and troops would only be landed in southern France if the Germans had been forced to withdraw a number of their divisions from that area.

There were two routes. Firstly, from Northwest Italy if they had been able to advance that far north; otherwise they would have to make an amphibious landing in southern France.[10] Eden asked if there would be adequate air cover for an amphibious operation against southern France. Air Marshal Portal replied it would not be good.

Churchill thought it would be well to consider, as an alternate plan, the possibility of flying supplies in for guerrillas operating in the mountains 30 miles from the coast. This mountain area would be an excellent rendezvous point for Frenchmen who objected to being sent into Germany and who might take refuge there. He described such an operation as "air-nourished guerrilla warfare." It was agreed the possibilities of this proposal should be explored.[11]

Operations in the Balkans

Operations in the Balkans would be limited to the supply of the guerrillas by air; sea transport for minor commando forces; and the bombing of strategic objectives.

Roosevelt asked if plans were being prepared in case the Germans withdrew from the Balkans to the line of the Danube.[12] Brooke replied action would depend on the forces available and he did not think there would be any surplus from their main operation.

Roosevelt said he was most anxious to have the Greeks and Yugoslav divisions they had trained operating in their own countries. He thought it would be advantageous if they could follow up, maintain contact, and harass the withdrawal of the Germans if they elected to withdraw to the Danube. Churchill suggested commando forces could also operate in support of the guerrillas on the Dalmatian coast.[13]

Mediterranean Garrisons and Lines of Communication

Defensive garrison commitments in the Mediterranean area would be reviewed from time to time, with a view to effecting economy of force.[14] The security of their

9   To include the use of French forces.
10   It would have to be an amphibious operation.
11   Plans were eventually made to drop French officers and NCOs along with French-speaking OSS personnel to help the guerrillas in southern France interrupt German troop movements from the south to the north.
12   The river Danube runs west to east past Vienna and Budapest before turning south to Belgrade; it then runs east to the Black Sea.
13   2nd Special Service Brigade was kept fully occupied from December 1943 onwards in Italy, the Adriatic Islands and the Balkans.
14   Assessing if troops could be redeployed as the front lines moved.

lines of communication through the Strait of Gibraltar would be assured by appropriate dispositions of their forces in Northwest Africa, so long as there remained even a remote possibility of the Germans invading the Iberian peninsula.

It was generally agreed there would be about 47 divisions available for operations in the Mediterranean. These included the French, Greeks, Yugoslavs, and Poles in addition to the divisions of the US and UK. Seven of the latter were due to be transferred to the UK for OVERLORD. Churchill said several British divisions had to be reconstituted and every effort was being made to do it as soon as possible.[1] One expedient was the sending of nine independent battalions to North Africa to take over guard duty from active formations.

Brooke said the operations now envisaged made use of all the available divisions but it was subject to fluctuation depending upon the enemy's reactions. He estimated 17 to 20 divisions would be required in Italy, one in Corsica and Sardinia, and these, together with garrison troops in Cyprus and North Africa, would limit those available for other offensive operations. There was also a shortage of anti-aircraft artillery. So long as the Germans occupied Crete and Sardinia,[2] anti-aircraft defence had to be maintained in North Africa and every effort was being made to remedy this deficiency.

Roosevelt reiterated his desire to use the Yugoslav and Greek divisions in the Balkans if the opportunity arose. Churchill believed it would be to the Germans' advantage to withdraw from the area, apart from the need to retain the oil output in the Balkans. Brooke said there were other raw materials the Germans secured from the Balkans, particularly bauxite,[3] which would cause them to hesitate to withdraw.

The War against Japan

They had made a preliminary study of the long-term strategy for the defeat of Japan and were of the opinion the following factors required particular emphasis:

a)   Japan's dependence upon air power, naval power, and shipping for maintaining her position in the Pacific and Southeast Asia.[4]

b)   The consequent need for applying the maximum attrition to Japan's air force, naval forces and shipping by all possible means in all possible areas.

c)   The advantage to be gained and the time to be saved by a more extensive use of the superior air resources at the disposal of the United Nations, both strategically and in conjunction with operations on land.

They considered great advantage could be obtained, by modern and untried methods, from the vast resources which, with the defeat of Germany, would become available to the United Nations. They had in mind:

---

1   Reconstituted means rebuilt after battle, absorbing new equipment and training replacement troops.
2   German airborne troops had spearheaded Operation MERCURY on 20 May 1941; the Greek island was taken in ten days.
3   Bauxite is the aluminium ore.
4   Japan's armies were spread across a huge area of the Far East, a large percentage of them on islands, including the Dutch East Indies and the Philippines. They needed naval and air support to keep them in touch and supplied.

1) A project to rapidly expand and extend the striking power of the United Nations air forces in China[5] by employing large numbers of load-carrying aircraft to open an 'air road' to China.[6]

2) The employment of lightly equipped jungle forces, largely dependent upon air supply lines.[7]

3) The use of special equipment, such as artificial harbours, Habbakuks, etc.,[8] to enable the superior power of the United Nations to be deployed in unexpected and undeveloped areas.

From every point of view, operations should be framed to force the defeat of Japan as soon as possible after the defeat of Germany. Planning should be on the basis of accomplishing this within twelve months. Decisions about specific operations which ensured a rapid course of events had to await further examination. They agreed the reorientation of forces from the European Theatre to the Pacific and Far East should be started as soon as the German situation allowed.

The principle had been accepted that the United States would provide forces to carry out operations from the east, including the Southwest Pacific, while Great Britain provided forces for operations from the west. This was except for special types not available to Great Britain, which would be provided by the United States. The employment of Dominion forces would be a matter of discussion between all governments concerned.

Specific Operations against Japan, 1943-44

They had found it impracticable during QUADRANT to arrive at all the necessary decisions for operations in the war against Japan in 1943-44. They proposed to hold, as soon as the necessary examinations had been made, a Combined Chiefs of Staff Conference.[9]

They were able to approve the US Chiefs of Staff proposals for the following Pacific operations in 1943-44:

1. The seizure and consolidation of the Gilbert Islands.[10]
2. The seizure of the Marshall Islands (including Wake and Kusaie) preparatory to a westward advance through the Central Pacific.[11]
3. The capture of Ponape.[12]

---

5 Including the ground troops for the defence of the air forces.

6 Tenth US Air Force had been established in India since February 1942 while Fourteenth US Air Force had been established in China since March 1943.

7 In particular, General Orde C. Wingate's Chindits, who were about to start operating in Burma.

8 Habbakuks were going to be aircraft carriers built out of pykrete (a mixture of wood pulp and ice) for use in arctic waters. The specification kept changing until the vessel became impossible to build; the plan was dropped at the end of the year. The carrier would allow planes to attack U-boats operating in the mid-Atlantic, out of range of land-based planes.

9 Unless agreement was reached through the ordinary channels.

10 The Gilbert Islands are a group of sixteen islands 2500 miles northeast of Australia and a similar distance southwest of Hawaii. The invasion of the main island, Tarawa, was codenamed GALVANIC and it was the first US offensive campaign in the Central Pacific. US Marines landed on 20 November 1943 and although the battle only lasted three days, over 6000 Americans and Japanese were killed.

11 The Marshall Islands are a group of 34 islands, northwest of the Gilbert Islands. US Marines landed on Kwajalein Island on 31 January 1944 while 7th Infantry Division landed on smaller islands. It took four days to clear them.

12 Pohnpei Island in the Caroline Islands was garrisoned by over 7000 Japanese. It was bypassed by the US naval and amphibious forces.

4. The seizure of the eastern Carolines (Truk Area) as far west as Woleai and the establishment of a fleet base at Truk.[1]
5. The capture of the Palaus Islands including Yap.[2]
6. The seizure of Guam and the Japanese Marianas.[3]
7. Consideration of operations against Paramushiru and the Kuriles.[4]
8. The seizure or neutralization of eastern New Guinea as far west as Wewak, including the Admiralty Islands and Bismarck Archipelago.[5] Rabaul would be neutralized rather than captured.
9. An advance along the north coast of New Guinea as far west as Vogelkop, by step-by-step airborne-waterborne advances.

Operations in India-Burma-China Theatre, 1943-44:

1. To carry out operations to capture Upper Burma; to improve the air route and establish overland communications with China; target date mid-February 1944.[6]
2. To continue preparations for an amphibious operation in the spring of 1944. Pending a decision on the particular operation, the scale of these preparations should be of the order contemplated at Trident for the capture of Akyab and Ramree.[7]
3. To continue preparing India as a base for operations in Southeast Asia Command.
4. To continue to build up and increase the air routes and air supplies of China, and the development of air facilities, with a view to:
    a) Keeping China in the war.
    b) Intensifying operations against the Japanese.
    c) Maintaining increased US and Chinese Air Forces in China.
    d) Equipping Chinese ground forces.

Their main effort should be put into offensive operations designed to establish land communications with China while improving and securing the air route. But priorities could not be rigid. They proposed to instruct the Supreme Commander to regard this decision as a guide and to consider the importance of the long term development of the lines of communication.

They had called for studies on the following operations and their relation one to another:

1) An operation against Northern Sumatra; target date spring 1944.
2) Operations southwards from Northern Burma; target date November 1944.

---

1   800 miles north of Papua New Guinea.
2   800 miles northwest of Papua New Guinea.
3   500 miles northeast of the Palaus Islands.
4   The Kurile Islands stretch in a long arc between Alaska and Russia. Paramushiru is the peninsula at the west end of the Kuriles.
5   The islands and archipelago at the east end of Papua New Guinea.
6   It was recognised that these operations were dependent upon the effects of recent floods on logistic considerations.
7   Akyab, now Sittwe, and Ramree Island, along the western coast of Burma.

3) Operations through the Moulmein[8] area or Kra Isthmus[9] in the direction of Bangkok; target date to be as early as practicable.

4) Operations through the Malacca Straits[10] and Malaya for the direct capture of Singapore; target date to be as early as practicable.

5) The capture of Akyab and Ramree to determine whether it was necessary to the success of operations in 1) to 4) above or the operations in Upper Burma.

Discussion about the War against Japan

Churchill understood work on the long term plan for the defeat of Japan had been proceeding ceaselessly since the last Conference. The plan was both strategical and technical. It would deal with such things as the best method to gain access to China, to secure airfields from which to bomb Japan, as well as the provision of synthetic harbours and Habbakuks.

Churchill had no doubt the combined resources of the United States and the British Empire could produce the special equipment required to concentrate the enormous air forces released to attack Japan after the defeat of Germany. But apart from such considerations, there were many political factors to be taken into account.

Great Britain would face difficulties moving her veterans into a new campaign, many of them had been on continuous service for several years. It might prove somewhat easier to arrange matters in the Navy and the Air Force, and the air war would be of vital importance in the war against Japan. These difficulties would, of course, be overcome.

Nevertheless Churchill hoped the planning staffs' work would only be taken as foundation data. With their comparatively circumscribed viewpoint, the planners could not be expected to produce final solutions to the problems confronting their two nations. He hoped the Combined Chiefs of Staff would not think themselves limited by the results of the planners' study of the war against Japan. Admiral King said the Chiefs of Staff never felt so limited.

Continuing, Churchill did not view with favour the idea of launching a great expedition to retake Singapore in 1945. He was most anxious not to set an aim for that year that would paralyse action in 1944. The campaign of 1942-43 had been most ineffective, and he felt ashamed that results in this theatre had not been better.

It was now proposed to extend the operation of the long-range penetration groups[11] in northern Burma over the coming winter, and this should be supplemented by the seizure of the tip of Sumatra. If a strong air force could be lodged there, the Japanese could be brought to action, their shipping could be bombed, and they would be forced to gather resources to react.[12] Options could be kept

---

8   Moulmein (now Mawlamyine) is 100 miles east of Rangoon (now Yangon).
9   The neck of the Malaysian Peninsula.
10 The stretch of water between Sumatra and the Malaysian Peninsula.
11 General Wingate's Chindits would help the General Stilwell's troops push the Ledo Road through northern Burma to link up with the Burma Road and re-establish an overland supply route to China.
12 An airbase in range of lucrative targets would force the Japanese air force into action and defeat it, the same as the strategy against the Luftwaffe. Planes could strike ground targets across Malaysia as well as naval targets in the Gulf of Thailand and the South China Sea.

open for subsequent action in either direction. Whatever happened, they must not let an ultimate objective paralyze intervening action.

Churchill earnestly hoped the Combined Chiefs of Staff would examine the possibilities in the Southeast Asia Theatre, with the object of doing the utmost possible to engage all forces against the Japanese. Only in this way would their overwhelming superiority achieve rapid results against the waning strength of the enemy.

Roosevelt looked at the problem from a rather different angle. The Japanese position compared to a slice of pie, with Japan at the apex and the island barrier forming the outside crust. One side of the piece of pie passed through Burma, the other led down to the Solomons. He quite saw the advantage of an attack on Sumatra, but he doubted whether there were sufficient resources for the opening of the Burma Road and the attack on Sumatra. He would rather see all their resources concentrated on the Burma Road, which represented the shortest line through China to Japan.

Roosevelt favoured attacks aimed at hitting the edge of the pie as near to the apex as possible, rather than attacks which nibbled at the crust. Provided Yunnan[1] could be held securely, an air force could be built up through Burma in China, which would carry out damaging attacks on Japanese shipping. At the same time the attack through the Gilberts and Marshalls to Truk would strike the opposite edge of the slice of pie. If they used the operations in the Solomon Islands as a yardstick, it would take many years to reach Japan. But the other side of the picture was the heavy attrition to which the Japanese forces were subjected in these operations.[2]

Churchill expressed his agreement with the President's simile, but asked whether the conquest of southern Burma was really necessary. The problem in Burma was not so much the finding of forces to deploy, but rather of overcoming the difficulties of an exiguous[3] line of communication and the monsoon, which limited operations to six months a year. Burma was the worst possible place to fight and operations could only be carried out by a comparatively small number of high-class troops.

There were large forces in the Southeast Asia Command and it was for this reason he hoped to see an attack on the Sumatran tip. An attack on Akyab could hardly be regarded as profitable. Roosevelt had also never thought much of the idea of taking Akyab or Rangoon. The Generalissimo had favoured the attack on Rangoon because he thought that it would interfere with the Japanese communications. But these probably now ran across land from Bangkok, and the Japanese were not as dependent on their line of communication as the Allied troops were.

Churchill favoured the extension of Wingate's operations in northern Burma, and the supporting advances; but he wished to emphasize his conviction that the attack on Sumatra was the great strategic blow which should be struck in 1944. CULVERIN[4] would be the TORCH of the Indian Ocean. In his opinion, it

---

1 The Chinese province adjoining Burma.
2 The offensive to retake the Solomons began on 30 June 1943; the Bougainville Campaign continued until the end of the war.
3 Slender.
4 CULVERIN was a plan to recapture the northern tip of Sumatra. Initially, a lack of resources stopped it being launched, while developments elsewhere made it unnecessary later on.

would not be beyond the compass of their resources. They should be striking and seizing a point of their own choice, against which the Japanese would have to beat themselves if they wished to end the severe drain on their shipping imposed by the air forces based in Sumatra.

Roosevelt suggested the Sumatra operation would be heading away from the main direction of their advance to Japan. Churchill said nevertheless it would greatly facilitate the direct advances. The alternative would be to waste the entire year, with nothing to show for it but Akyab and the future right to toil through the swamps of southern Burma. He earnestly hoped careful and sympathetic study would be given to the Sumatra project, which he was convinced was of the highest strategic importance. He compared it, in its promise of decisive consequences, with the Dardanelles operation of 1915.[5]

Churchill then read a recent telegram from General Auchinleck.[6] He reported Admiral Somerville's[7] opinion that more resources than previously deemed necessary would be required for the Akyab operation. Churchill said Akyab, the importance of which had apparently been overlooked in the retreat from Burma and which they had failed to take last winter, had now been turned into a kind of Plevna.[8] They proposed to employ all their amphibious resources in the Indian Ocean in 1943–44 against it. He did not believe this was right.

Roosevelt asked if the possession of Akyab was essential for an attack on Rangoon. Arnold said it would certainly be useful for improving the scale of air attack which could be brought to bear on Rangoon and possibly on Bangkok. He doubted whether it was essential. Admiral King had always understood Akyab was required so attacks could be made against the Japanese line of communication north of Rangoon. Marshall said the principal importance of Akyab was as a stepping stone to the conquest of Southern Burma.

The Air Route to China

The Chiefs of Staff had to study the potentialities and limitations of developing the air route to China on a scale sufficient to employ all the heavy bomber and transport aircraft likely to be available for the Southeast Asia Theatre and China in 1944–45.[9] It would specify the action required to implement the best possible plan without prejudicing other operations.[10]

Southeast Asia Command

The vigorous and effective prosecution of large scale operations against Japan in Southeast Asia, and the rapid development of the air route through Burma

---

5 The Gallipoli campaign was the invasion of the Dardanelles peninsula in April 1915, a project put forward by Churchill himself as First Sea Lord of the Admiralty. Hopes for a quick victory were dashed and after more than six months of stalemate the troops were evacuated, mainly due to winter weather preventing supplies reaching the beachhead.
6 General (later Field Marshal) Sir Claude J. E. Auchinleck, (1884-1981), Commander-in-Chief of the Indian Army; nickname the Auk.
7 Commander-in-Chief of the Eastern Fleet.
8 The Siege of Plevna was a major battle of the Russo-Turkish War (1877-1878). The Ottoman garrison held up the Russian advance south into Bulgaria, encouraging other great powers of the time to actively support the Ottoman cause. Eventually, superior Russian and Romanian numbers forced the garrison to surrender.
9 Assuming Germany was defeated in the autumn of 1944.
10 General Arnold reported that the figure of 7,000 tons on the air route to China was almost certain to be reached in August.

to China, necessitated the reorganization of the High Command in the Indian Theatre.[1] The administration of India as a base for the forces in Southeast Asia would remain under the control of the Commander-in-Chief, India.

Coordination of movement and maintenance[2] could be best carried out efficiently by one staff responsible to one authority with power to decide priorities. This machinery existed in India's Government and GHQ India. It was the only machinery which could meet the internal requirements of India and the requirements of Southeast Asia operations. The Supreme Allied Command in Southeast Asia should be set up as follows:

    a.   A combined British and American command and staff on the lines of the North African Command.

    b.   A British Supreme Allied Commander[3] with an American deputy.[4] He should have Naval, Army and Air Commanders-in-Chief and also a Principal Administrative Officer to coordinate the administrative planning of all three Services and of the Allied forces.

    c.   The Deputy Supreme Allied Commander and the Commanders of the three Services would control all operations and have under their command such Naval, Military and Air forces assigned to the Southeast Asia Theatre.

The boundaries generally included Burma, Ceylon, Thailand, the Malay Peninsula and Sumatra.

Conflicts of opinion over the priorities of the administration had to be anticipated. Someone on the spot had to resolve these differences as they occurred and the authority should be the Viceroy,[5] not in his statutory capacity as Governor-General but on behalf of the British War Cabinet.

The Supreme Commander would have direct access to the British Chiefs of Staff and he would be able to exercise this right if he was dissatisfied with the Viceroy's ruling. The Commander-in-Chief, India,[6] would continue to have direct access to the British Chiefs of Staff.

General Stilwell would be Deputy Supreme Allied Commander of the Southeast Asia Theatre and would command the Chinese troops operating into Burma and all US air and ground forces committed to the Southeast Asia Theatre. The operational control of the Chinese forces operating into Burma would be exercised, in conformity with the overall plan of the British Army Commander, by the Deputy Supreme Allied Commander who would be located with the troops. Stilwell would continue to have the same direct responsibility to

---

1   The Allies created the combined South East Asian Command in August 1943 to assume overall strategic command of all air sea and land operations of all national contingents in the theatre.

2   Both of the operational forces based in India and the internal garrison.

3   In August 1943, with the agreement of the Combined Chiefs of Staff, Winston Churchill appointed Admiral Lord Louis Mountbatten (1900-1979) as Supreme Allied Commander South East Asia; a post he held until 1946.

4   General Joseph Stilwell, US Army (1883-1946) was the deputy Supreme Allied Commander, a role he had to combine with being the commander of the US China Burma India Theatre (CBI) command.

5   Field Marshal Archibald P. Wavell (1883-1950) had recently been appointed Viceroy of India.

6   Field Marshall Auchinleck.

Generalissimo Chiang Kai-shek as before. His dual function under the Supreme Allied Commander and under the Generalissimo was recognized.[7]

The Coordination of American Agencies with Comparable British Organizations was required.[8] A Combined Liaison Committee would be set up in New Delhi to facilitate the free exchange of information and coordination between the US and British quasi-military agencies in India and Southeast Asia Command. There would be full and open discussion in the Combined Liaison Committee before any quasi-military activities involving operations in India or the Southeast Asia Theatre were undertaken. The concurrence of the government of India, the Commander-in-Chief, India, or the Supreme Commander, Southeast Asia Theatre, had to be obtained before plans for the operations in these areas were put into effect by US agencies.

Churchill said the agreed setup did not exactly coincide with the MacArthur model. He asked Marshall if it was possible to have a British liaison officer appointed to MacArthur's staff.[9] Marshall said arrangements were under way to accomplish this and he was taking the necessary steps to see the Southwest Pacific situation was reported to Churchill at frequent intervals.

Roosevelt asked what the relationship between the Generalissimo and the new Allied Commander-in-Chief of the Southeast Asia Command would be. He was told they would be two neighbouring Commanders-in-Chief. Liaison would be insured because Stilwell would be Deputy Commander-in-Chief, Southeast Asia Command, and the Chief of Staff to the Generalissimo. The arrangements for the new command guarded against the diversion of resources destined for China, unless they were agreed by the Combined Chiefs of Staff.[10]

Spain

The Chiefs of Staff suggested the general policy towards Spain should be to deny the enemy of his privileged position and take his place as much as possible, transferring their anxiety to the Germans. They suggested intensifying pressure by economic and political means to obtain the following objectives:

---

7 General Stilwell became increasingly disillusioned with the effectiveness of the British forces and his remarks became increasingly disparaging.

8 The Office of Strategic Services (OSS) was a US intelligence agency formed to coordinate espionage activities behind enemy lines. The Office of War Information (OWI) was a US government agency created to consolidate government information services. It established an overseas branch to deal with information and propaganda campaigns abroad. The Functional Capabilities Board (FCB) coordinated developments in the different arms and branches.

9 Lieutenant Colonel Gerald Wilkinson (1909-1965) had been an advisor on MacArthur's staff until recently. He reported to Churchill that MacArthur was "shrewd, selfish, proud, remote, highly strung and vastly vain. He has imagination, self-confidence, physical courage and charm, but no humour about himself, no regard for truth, and is unaware of these defects. He mistakes his emotions and ambitions for principles. With moral depth he would be a great man; as it is he is a near miss which may be worse than a mile... His main ambition would be to end the war as pan-American hero in the form of generalissimo of all Pacific Theatres... he hates Roosevelt and dislikes Winston's control of Roosevelt's strategy. He is not basically anti British, just pro-MacArthur."

10 General Stilwell faced a difficult task and his abrasive attitude towards the British and the Chinese meant he lived up to his nickname, Vinegar Joe. It would ultimately lead to his dismissal from the post.

1) Discontinuance of supplies of raw materials to Germany, the most important of which was wolfram.[1] Spain and Portugal supplied the largest proportion of German requirements.

2) Withdraw the Blue Division[2] from the ranks of the enemy.

3) A modification of the present distribution of Spanish forces in Morocco to remove any suggestion of distrust of the United Nations.

4) Stop using Spanish shipping to benefit their enemies.

5) Close down enemy secret intelligence facilities.

6) Provide facilities for civil aircraft of United Nations.

7) A more benevolent attitude towards escaped Allied prisoners of war.

8) Replacing objectionable anti-Allied propaganda with pro-Allied propaganda.

Turkey

The Chiefs of Staff believed the time was not ripe for Turkey to enter the war on their side. Their policy should be as follows:

1) They should ask Turkey to interpret the Montreux Convention strictly, stopping the passage of all German shipping of military value through the Straits.

2) Ask that supplies of chrome to Germany should be stopped.

3) Ask Turkey to continue:

    a) To improve her internal communications.

    b) To complete the airfields required for HARDIHOOD.[3]

    c) To install the full RDF and Sector Control facilities they required.[4]

    d) To complete the storage facilities required for the HARDIHOOD Plan.

    e) To raise the effectiveness of their fighting forces.

4) "Our policy on equipment to Turkey should be that we should continue to supply such equipment as we can spare and as the Turks can absorb."

Finally, Roosevelt said they needed a paragraph relating their action to the support of Russia and he was told one was already under consideration and would be included. The meeting adjourned.

20 August

Eighth Chiefs of Staff Meeting

Naval and Air Commanders for OVERLORD; Synthetic Harbours; Equipping Allies, Liberated Forces and Friendly Nations; Sardinia Fifth Column activities;

---

1   Wolfram is the ore used to create tungsten employed in machine tools and armour piercing shells.

2   The Blue Division, or División Azul, formed in Germany in the summer of 1941 and served on the Eastern Front until the Spanish Government ordered it to return in November 1943. Franco had been persuaded to recall it by the Allies and conservative Spaniards. Around 45,000 men served in the Blue Division; over 13,500 were casualties.

3   HARDIHOOD was the delivery of supplies to Turkey.

4   A chain of Radar Detection and Ranging (RDR) Stations would detect incoming air formations and report them to the Sector Control Stations, which in turn warned the Group Headquarters.

Immediate Mediterranean Operations; Military Consideration in Relation to Spain, Turkey and Russia; Plan for the Defeat of Japan.

21 August
Ninth Chiefs of Staff Meeting
Amendments to the Progress Report to the President and the Prime Minister.

22 August
Foreign Secretaries Meeting
Roosevelt and Churchill met their Foreign Secretaries.

August 22: Roosevelt and Churchill Meeting
Polish Statement
A statement was to be issued by the two Governments regarding the atrocities against Polish citizens in the Lublin area. The discussion hinged on the British text which would be used, even though it was not expected to have any real effect on the situation.[5]

Fraternization between US and British Soldiers in the British Isles
All possible steps should be taken to promote fraternization between the US and British forces in the British Isles. Eden would speak to Marshall, to General Devers and to Norman Davis as to methods for its accomplishment.

The King of Greece
Roosevelt and Churchill had just received a message from the King of Greece asking for advice. Certain Greek elements had asked him not to return to Greece until a plebiscite on the subject of the Monarchy had been held. Eden read the British Foreign Office's report on Greece's political situation. Sir Alexander Cadogan then read General Smuts' communication which advocated, as a matter of fair play, that the King should not be prohibited from entering his own country and resuming his former position, subject to a later decision by the people of Greece as to the future of the Greek regime. It was decided to support recognized governments and regimes until the defeat of the enemy.

Mr. Hull[6] said this attitude was in line with the one adopted on the administration of liberated areas. Roosevelt and Churchill agreed the British Foreign Office should reply to the King's telegram, supporting his intention to return to Greece and submit the question of the Royal House to a referendum. Roosevelt said the United States Government would not take a different position. Churchill said the British Government would instruct British agents in Greece to refrain from encouraging the guerrillas to put forward political claims to the future form of government.

---

5   It had no effect; 18,000 were executed in the man camp in the Lublin area during Operation Erntefest (Harvest Festival) on 3 November and many more in sub camps; it was the largest single day/single location mass killing of the Holocaust.
6   Cordell Hull, America's longest serving Secretary of State, from 1933 to 1944.

The French Committee of National Liberation

After some discussion Churchill said all the liberal elements in the world, including the governments-in-exile and the Soviet Government, were demanding full recognition of the French Committee of National Liberation.[1] Roosevelt said they all had to think of the future of France, which he felt would be in no way advanced by turning over the whole control of the French people to the French Committee. The President's suggestion was accepted.

23 August

Tenth Chiefs of Staff Meeting

Final Report to the President and the Prime Minister; Japanese treatment of prisoners; Pipeline from India to China, Operations from India; Movement of Queens; Amphibians for OVERLORD; Operation RANKIN; Equipping Allies, Liberated Forces and Friendly Nations; Rehabilitation of Occupied and Liberated Territories.

23 August: Second Quadrant Meeting

Brigadier Jacob[2] read a draft of the Combined Chiefs of Staff Final Report containing the conclusions of the Quadrant Conference.[3] Churchill asked if measures had been taken to prepare a combined British-US convoy for a move to the Azores about two weeks after the original British occupation on 8 October. Admiral King said arrangements would be made for one to leave the United States on or about 20 October.

Roosevelt asked if a study of an emergency entrance onto the Continent had been made; he wanted United Nations troops to be ready to get to Berlin as soon as the Russians. General Brooke said General Morgan's staff had prepared plans for such an entry and they were based on three contingencies: a weakening of German resistance, a withdrawal of German forces from France, or a complete German collapse.[4]

Operation OVERLORD

Churchill wanted it to be definitely understood that the British acceptance of the OVERLORD planning included the proviso that the operation could only be carried out if certain conditions regarding German strength were met.[5] These included the number of German divisions in France and a definite superiority over the German fighter force. If things developed so that the German ground

---

1   General de Gaulle was chairman of the French Committee of National Liberation. While the FCNL was opposed to the Vichy government and vowed to fight Nazi Germany, neither Churchill nor Roosevelt agreed with handing France over to de Gaulle.

2   Brigadier Ian C. Jacob (1899-1993), Military Assistant Secretary to the War Cabinet for the duration of the war. He worked closely with Churchill, implementing his communications during his thirteen wartime journeys outside the United Kingdom. Churchill valued Jacob's efforts enough to endorse his promotion from Colonel to Lieutenant-General.

3   Including continuing POINTBLANK against the German military, industrial and economic system and the material reduction of German air combat strength; pursuing OVERLORD with a target date of 1 May 1944; considering a landing in southern France; eliminating Italy from the war; establishing airfields north of Rome.

4   COSSAC had prepared the three RANKIN cases: Case A, substantial weakening of the German armed forces; Case B, a German withdrawal; and Case, C Germany's unconditional surrender.

5   Both in France at the time and reinforcements over the following 60 days.

or air fighter strength was greater, the Combined Chiefs of Staff would review whether or not the operations should be launched. He did not wish to imply he was not wholeheartedly in favour of OVERLORD but at the same time he wished to emphasize its launching was dependent upon certain conditions that gave it a reasonable chance for success.

Churchill suggested the United Nations needed a 'second string to their bow' in the form of a prepared plan to undertake JUPITER.[6] It was decided the Final Report to the President and Prime Minister should include a paragraph covering continued planning for JUPITER if OVERLORD had to be abandoned.

Churchill also discussed the moving of seven trained divisions from the Mediterranean to England. He agreed the decision to return the divisions was firm but it was subject to review by the Combined Chiefs of Staff. Churchill asked General Brooke if that was definitely understood. Brooke repeated the divisions would return to England for OVERLORD unless the Combined Chiefs of Staff had to reconsider this decision. It might be necessary to keep one or two divisions in the Mediterranean to create a better situation for OVERLORD or to avoid a setback in Italy. Churchill said other divisions could be moved between England and the Mediterranean without prejudice. For example, it might be necessary to send a second Canadian division to complete a Canadian Corps and bring home a British division in its place.

Churchill had heard Brigadier MacLean's[7] presentation of the OVERLORD plan and it seemed sound, but it should be strengthened. Marshall agreed and pointed out there would be 4½ divisions in the initial assault rather than the three divisions suggested at the last conference. Churchill asked if this included an attack on the inside of the Cotentin Peninsula.[8] Marshall said the present plans would not provide for such an operation but there was a possibility the landing would be included in the initial assault if more landing craft could be made available.

Churchill agreed with the choice of Air Commander-in-Chief[9] but he was surprised the Commander-in-Chief of Portsmouth had been designated Naval Commander; he had always thought he had administrative ability rather than outstanding tactical ability.[10] Admiral Pound said it was logical to give the Commander-in-Chief, Portsmouth, this command, particularly at this time. A lot of the naval planning and operations had to be accomplished between adjoining naval commands in Great Britain during the preliminary phases and he was the logical person to coordinate them.

---

6   An invasion of Norway.
7   Brigadier-General Kenneth G. McLean, (1896-1987), chief army planner at COSSAC and 21st Army Group's Chief Operations Officer.
8   Referring to what would become UTAH Beach. Both Eisenhower and Montgomery wanted to make the width of the landing larger when they started studying Operation OVERLORD in February 1944. UTAH Beach was added, placing ground troops either side of the Vire River and making it easier to cut off the Cotentin Peninsula and Cherbourg.
9   Air Chief Marshal Sir Trafford Leigh-Mallory, RAF (1892-1944).
10 Admiral Sir Charles James Colebrooke Little, RN (1882-1973).

Pound said there would be no difficulty in designating a new commander if later events indicated the desirability. Churchill had thought of giving the position to Admiral Ramsay[1] and would only accept the present arrangement if it was reviewed after the appointment of the Supreme Commander.[2]

Roosevelt said two light American passenger vessels, the *Harvard* and the *Yale*, had been sent to England in 1917 and had been utilized very successfully in transporting troops across the Channel.[3] He suggested combing the world to see if vessels of this type could not be made available to increase the troop lift from England to France. Admiral King said the United States had been pretty well explored in this connection but he would see what else could be done. Churchill suggested asking Canada to help out.

The Mediterranean Theatre

Churchill said there were rumours the Germans were planning to defend the Ravenna-Genoa Line in Italy, which was about 50 or 60 miles north of the Ancona-Pisa Line.[4] He thought their forces should proceed as far beyond their objective as possible with the troops allocated for the purpose. General Brooke said the Germans must defend the southern slope of the Apennines, in which case they would be somewhat south of the Ravenna-Genoa Line. Admiral King agreed and thought the terrain dictated a German defence on the Leghorn-Ancona position.[5] Churchill felt it would be easier to supply guerrillas who might assemble in the Maritime Alps, the further north the United Nations progressed in Italy. Roosevelt said guerrilla operations could be initiated in south central France as well as in the Maritime Alps.[6]

Churchill was pleased to see steps had been taken to investigate the possibility of intensifying fifth column activities in Sardinia. He thought organizations such as the OSS and the British SOE should certainly enter Sardinia at this time. However, he believed Sardinia would probably come into their hands without a struggle if Italy capitulated. Brooke said there were conflicting reports in this regard; either the Germans would attempt to hold Sardinia or they would assemble landing craft between Sardinia and Corsica ready for an evacuation.[7]

---

1 Ramsay had been in command of the British naval operations in the attack on Sicily under the Commander-in-Chief of the Mediterranean.
2 Admiral Little was replaced by Admiral Sir Bertram Home Ramsay, RN (1883-1945) in October. Ramsay had been responsible for Operation DYNAMO, the evacuation of Dunkirk and deputy naval commander of both TORCH and HUSKY.
3 USS *Harvard* (ID-1298) commandeered by the US Navy, refitted and sent to France. Between July 1918 and May 1919 she made 60 trips between Southampton and Le Havre or Boulogne. USS *Yale* (ID-1672) made 31 round trips between England and France between March 1918 and September 1919.
4 The Anacona-Pisa Line was called the Arno Line west of the Apennines and the Trasimene Line to the east. There was no line at Genoa on the west coast while the Ghengis Khan Line ran inland from Ravenna.
5 The two Generals were correct. The Germans would dig in along the Gothic Line (later called the Green Line) between Pisa and Rimini. Leghorn is the traditional English name of Livorno.
6 There were many French rural resistance groups, known as the Maquis. The Maquis des Glières and the Maquis du Grésivaudan were based in the French Alps, the Maquis du Limousin were based in the Massif Central.
7 The second speculation was true. Following the surrender of Italy in September 1943, German troops evacuated Sardinia and sailed to Corsica.

Churchill said if an advance into southern France appeared to be likely he thought Generals Giraud and de Gaulle should be brought into consultation by Eisenhower and French forces should be fully utilized.[8]

The War against Japan

Churchill was pleased to see the Chiefs of Staff believed plans should be made for the defeat of Japan within twelve months after the collapse of Germany. This was a target which they should work towards and it discouraged planning on the basis of a prolonged war of attrition. Churchill suggested bringing on a naval battle with the Japanese Fleet.[9] Admiral King replied that was one of their main purposes but he did not feel a large battle would develop until their forces had reached the Marianas.[10]

The India-Burma-China Theatre

Churchill asked for an explanation of the directive to the Commanding General, Southeast Asia Command, telling him to give priority to operations in northern Burma but at the same time keep in mind the long-term necessities for improving the lines of communication. Brooke said priority must be set between operations and maintaining the lines of communications.[11] The directive had been put forward to emphasize the importance of the Burma operations. At the same time it cautioned the Commanding General, Southeast Asia Command, to build up his lines of communication.

General Arnold told the President the delivery of supplies into China might be reduced if they gave priority to the operations in northern Burma. He did not disagree with the decision but he had been charged with the responsibility for the delivery of supplies to China and giving first priority to the reconquest of northern Burma might make it impossible to fulfil his responsibility.[12] Churchill said it would be largely a matter of judgment for the commander on the ground. He cited the need to send 2000 men to Yunnan as part of General Wingate's force to cover the Chinese advance. This would be result in a temporary, but justifiable, reduction in the delivery of supplies to China.

Roosevelt wanted a proviso to prevent commanders on the Chinese supply lines confiscating supplies intended for China for their own theatres. Marshall said the situation had been pretty well taken care of but it was necessary for someone with authority on the ground to make decisions regarding priorities. If

---

8   I French Corps was formed in August 1943 under Lieutenant General Martin and it landed on Corsica a month later in Operation VESUVE. Elba was next in June 1944 in Operation BRASSARD. I Corps, under Lieutenant General Antoine Béthouart (1889-1982), joined the battle in southern France in September 1944, fighting its way into Germany over the next ten months.

9   Detailing the planned advance through the Gilbert and Marshall Islands, the Caroline and Palau Islands, aiming to reach Guam and the Marianas.

10 Admiral King was correct. The Battle of the Philippine Sea in the Mariana Islands in June 1944 ended the Japanese navy's ability to conduct carrier actions. The Battle of Leyte Gulf in the Philippine Islands in October 1944 ended the Japanese navy's offensive capabilities.

11 Admiral Mountbatten had to plan to maintain his communications in the difficult Burmese terrain, a military operation in itself. In the Italian and European campaigns there was an existing network of roads, railways and bridges; in Burma's jungle everything had to be built.

12 There was only a limited number of planes and the amount needed for a new offensive would have to be deducted from the amount flown to China.

it was arbitrarily decided to use the entire capacity of the air transport route to supply General Chennault[1] with gasoline, it might jeopardize the success of the Burma operations essential for keeping China in the war.[2]

Churchill had no objection to a study being made on the capture of Singapore but he was very much opposed to such an operation being adopted for 1945 if it curtailed action in 1944. He would be quite unable to agree to an operation for the capture of Akyab and Ramree as the main amphibious operation for the Indian Ocean in 1944.

At the Trident Conference, the capture of Akyab had been the preliminary to operations in southern Burma en route to the capture of Rangoon. Rangoon was then dropped out for 1943-44, but Akyab had been retained, mainly to please Chiang Kai-shek. Later developments showed the capture of Akyab would be a dangerous, sterile and costly operation directed against a point where the Japanese would be expecting attack. They would hamstring operations in the Indian Ocean area to little purpose if they undertook it. Churchill was prepared for a study of the operation to be made, and it might well prove right to carry it out as a sequel to some more profitable operation elsewhere. But he would not subscribe to it as their main amphibious operation in the coming year.

Roosevelt said General Wingate had told him the capture of Rangoon would not cut the Japanese line of communications since they were now largely supplied overland from French Indochina and Thailand.[3]

Southeast Asia Command

Roosevelt asked if Thailand was included in the Chinese Theatre. Admiral Leahy replied that both French Indochina and Thailand had been included in the Chinese Theatre. It had been intended to include French Indochina but operations in this area were so far in the future that it was not necessary to include it in the new command.[4]

Thailand's situation was quite different because Southeast Asia Command's operations might envisage a conquest of the country. Southeast Asia Command's forces were in a position to carry out such an operation if it was desirable but Chinese forces could do nothing in the area. Thailand should definitely be included in Southeast Asia Command's area regardless of the Generalissimo's commitments. Admiral King would check to see if French Indochina and Thailand had been included in the Chinese Theatre in a more recent definition of bounds.

Churchill was anxious to make a public announcement regarding the formation of the Southeast Asia Command and its commander. It would signify the Quadrant Conference discussions had been about the war against Japan,

---

1 Commander of Fourteenth Air Force, operating from Chinese airfields.
2 A supply of ground and air forces in China had to be balanced against supplying offensives in Burma; they were mutually supporting.
3 French Indochina, now Vietnam. The Death Railway connecting Bangkok and Rangoon would open in October 1943. It meant the Japanese did not have to rely on shipping to supply their forces in Burma.
4 Burma and Thailand had to be dealt with first.

explaining why Russia had not been included in the deliberations. He asked General Ismay to make up a short statement for release to the press.

Roosevelt said the statement should make it clear Chiang Kai-shek still retained command of the Chinese Theatre. Marshall said it should be written in such a way as not to mention the use of Chinese troops in the Southeast Asia Command or give any indication of General Stilwell's place in the command setup. He said Stilwell was still the Generalissimo's Chief of Staff and it would be offensive to the Generalissimo if he had not been consulted before Stilwell was assigned his additional position.[5] Moreover, he might have expected a Chinese deputy. Actually, Stilwell was being made Deputy Supreme Commander to protect Chinese interests and to try and ensure Chinese forces would carry out their share of the plans devised by Southeast Asia Command.

Admiral King said the mere announcement of the formation of the Southeast Asia Command would indicate Stilwell's status at once. He thought the announcement should be delayed until after the Generalissimo had been informed. Mr. Hopkins said Dr. Soong[6] had just received a telegram from the Generalissimo saying the Supreme Allied Commander should be appointed immediately.

Churchill thought any difficulty could be overcome by making a brief announcement to the press. He suggested the following: "It has been decided to establish a combined separate Southeast Asia Command. The Supreme Commander will be…" He felt the shorter the better and there was agreement.

Spain

Churchill asked if the Chiefs of Staff's recommendations regarding Spain had been submitted to the Foreign Office. General Ismay replied they had, but no comments had been received.[7] Churchill wanted his government's advice before committing himself. He personally did not favour putting economic screws on Spain; the situation was still too critical. For instance, the negotiations with Portugal should be settled before a new attitude was adopted towards Spain.[8] Even though the recommendations of the Combined Chiefs of Staff were approved, the timing as to their execution would have to be determined by the governments.

Turkey

Churchill disagreed with the proposal to have the Commander-in-Chief, Middle East, empowered to determine how much supplies Turkey could absorb. The British Government should retain the decision. The time had come to ask Turkey for something in return for the aid the United Nations had been giving her. The Turks would be considerably relieved if they were only asked to carry out the

---

5   As Deputy Commander to the China-Burma-India Theatre.
6   Dr. Soong, Chinese Minister of Foreign Affairs.
7   1) Spain to stop supplying wolfram to Germany; 2) Withdraw the Blue Division; 3) Redeploy Spanish troops in Morocco; 4) Stop using shipping for the Axis benefits; 5) Remove Axis intelligence facilities; 6) Facilities for Allied planes, 7) A benevolent attitude to Allied POWs; 8) Stop anti-Allied propaganda and increase pro-Allied propaganda.
8   Britain and Portugal had signed a military co-operation agreement with Portugal in August 1939, accepting direct support in the effort of rearmament and modernization of the Portuguese Armed Forces. The agreement was only begun to be put into action in September 1943. In August 1943, Portugal signed the Luso-British agreement, which leased bases in the Azores to the British, allowing the Allies to provide air cover for the Atlantic convoys.

recommendations submitted by the Combined Chiefs of Staff rather than being asked to give up their neutrality and enter the war. The reference was deleted.

24 August

Eleventh Chiefs of Staff Meeting
Final Report to the President and Prime Minister; Atlantic Convoys; Mediterr-anean Operations; Relation of Resources to Plans; Southeast Asia Command; Propaganda Committee; Meeting with Dr. Soong; Message to Stalin.

24 August: Communiqué
The Anglo-American War Conference which opened at Quebec on 11 August, under the hospitable auspices of the Canadian Government, has now concluded its work. The whole field of world operations has been surveyed in the light of the many gratifying events which have taken place since the meeting of the President and the Prime Minister in Washington at the end of May. The necessary decisions have been taken to provide for the forward action of the Fleets, Armies and Air Forces of the two nations. Considering these forces are intermingled in continuous action against the enemy in several quarters of the globe, it is indis-pensable that the entire unity of aim and method should be maintained at the summit of the war direction.

Further conferences will be needed, probably at shorter intervals than before, as the war effort of the United States and British Commonwealth and Empire against the enemy spreads and deepens. It would not be helpful to the fighting troops to make any announcement of the decisions which have been reached. These can only emerge in action.

The military discussions of the Chiefs of Staff turned very largely upon the war against Japan and the bringing of effective aid to China. Mr. Soong, representing Generalissimo Chiang Kai-shek, was a party to the discussions. The President and the Prime Minister were able to receive and approve the unanimous recommen-dations of the Combined Chiefs of Staff. Agreement was also reached upon the political data underlying or arising out of the military operations.

It was resolved to hold another Conference before the end of the year between the British and American authorities, in addition to any tripartite meeting which it may be possible to arrange with Soviet Russia. Full reports of the decisions so far as they affect the war against Germany and Italy will be furnished to the Soviet Government.

Consideration has been given during the conference to the question of rela-tions with the French Committee of Liberation, and it is understood that an announcement by a number of governments will be made in the latter part of the week.

The Sextant Conference Part I: 22–26 November 1943

On 25 July 1943 the Allies heard the news they had been hoping for; Benito Mussolini had been deposed. On 8 September Pietro Badoglio's government surrendered Italy unconditionally and the following day Allied troops landed on the Italian mainland. It also meant Germany had to take over Italy's commitments on the Mediterranean shore, weakening their position on the Eastern Front.

Meanwhile, the Soviet Union was also on the offensive after stopping a massive German tank offensive at Kursk in July. Before long the Soviets had turned the tide and on 6 November they liberated the key city of Kiev. It was time for the three Heads of State to meet and discuss opening a new front in Northwest France.

The First Sextant Conference was held between 22 and 26 November in Cairo. The President had flown via Tunis to Cairo and stayed in the villa of the American Ambassador, Alexander Kirk, in Cairo. President Roosevelt and Prime Minister Churchill met Generalissimo Chiang Kai-shek of the Republic of China at the Mena House Hotel at the foot of the Pyramids of Giza to discuss Southeast Asia operations at the first meeting. Premier Stalin refused to attend because the Soviet-Japanese Neutrality Act of 1941 still stood and Stalin's attendance could have caused friction. The two Heads of State then continued their journey to Tehran, Iran, to meet Stalin.

22 November
First Combined Chiefs of Staff Meeting
Sextant Agenda; Eureka Agenda; Combined Chiefs of Staff relations with their Russian and Chinese counterparts.

23 November: First Sextant Meeting
Ambassador Harriman[1] met Mr. Vyshinsky.[2] The President extended a warm welcome to the Generalissimo, Madame Chiang Kai-shek, and the Chinese Delegation. It was an historic meeting and a logical consequence to the Four Power Conference recently concluded in Moscow.[3] He hoped the meeting would not only bear fruit that day and in the immediate future, but for decades to come.

Roosevelt asked Admiral Mountbatten to give a general survey of the intended operations in Southeast Asia. The ground to be covered mainly concerned land operations, since seagoing operations were in progress all the time. He felt sure there was unanimous agreement that every effort should be made to send more equipment to China, with a view to accelerating the process to launch an air offensive against the heart of Japan itself.

---

1 Ambassador W. Averell Harriman (1891-1986), US Ambassador to the Soviet Union.
2 Andrey Vyshinsky (1883-1954), Deputy People's Commissar for Soviet Foreign Affairs.
3 Twelve meetings in Moscow between 18 October and 23 November of the Foreign Ministers of the United Kingdom, United States, the Republic of China and the Soviet Union. The Moscow Declaration covered General Security, Italy, Austria and German atrocities. It also agreed to form the European Advisory Commission, which would make recommendations to the three joint governments.

Mountbatten outlined the proposed operations for the coming Burma campaign. Apart from the current air operations by British–US air forces and two Chinese divisions operating from Ledo,[1] the first land movement would take place in mid-January. XV British Indian Corps[2] would advance on the Arakan front, with a view to taking up an improved line. This Corps would not be restricted to a defensive role and would exploit success wherever possible. A West African brigade would be deployed on an outflanking movement for this purpose. At the same time IV British Indian Corps[3] would start operations with the object of capturing Minthami, Mawlaik, and Sittaung,[4] advancing as far southeast as possible.

Mountbatten explained the natural difficulties facing the Allied Forces. Their lines of communication ran through one of the most difficult countries in the world and it was served by a single one-metre gauge railway. Nevertheless, it carried 3100 tons a day and it was hoped that might be increased by a further 500 tons a day.

After leaving the railway and the Brahmaputra River, communication was by roads under construction, through thick jungle and across mountains. The Japanese in Burma were at the end of an excellent line of communication up the River Irrawaddy from Rangoon, with a railway running through Indaw to Myitkyina.[5] They had vast resources, adequate equipment and a force of some five divisions, which was likely to be strengthened by a sixth division. They were aiming to use large-scale air supply to supplement the inequality between the Allies' extremely difficult communications and the Japanese' relatively good communications.

In February General Wingate[6] intended to make three thrusts with his Long Range Penetration Groups. The first from Chittagong;[7] the second to support the 4th Group in the Tamu[8] area and the third to help the Chinese forces operating from Ledo.[9] It was hoped the 3rd Group would, by the use of gliders operating ahead of the Yunnan forces, disrupt and muddle the Japanese. Meanwhile, the Ledo forces would move down in the Myitkyina direction to link up at Bhamo with the main operations of the Yunnan forces advancing on Lashio.[10] In mid March 5th Indian Parachute Brigade would seize the airfield at Indaw, after which 26th Indian Division would be flown to Indaw by transport aircraft where it would be maintained by air.[11] The intention was to surprise the Japanese during

1 Ledo on the India-Burma border
2 Commanded by General (later Field Marshal) William J. Slim, (1891-1970), known as Bill.
3 The Imphal Force under Lieutenant General Sir Geoffrey A. P. Scoones (1893-1975).
4 The Sittaung River in northwest Burma.
5 Indaw and Myitkyina are in northeast Burma; Myitkyina would be captured in August 1944.
6 General Wingate, commander of the Chindits, who had carried out raids to knock out Japanese railways early in 1943. There were plans for more long-range missions in support of regular offensive.
7 Chittagong is a seaport on the Indian-Burma border (now the Bangladesh-Myanmar border).
8 Tamu is inland and north of Chittagong, on the India-Burma border.
9 Ledo is a small town on the India-Burma border, north of Tamu.
10 Myitkyina in north Burma, only 40 miles from the Chinese border. Bhamo is 75 miles south of Myitkyina. Lashio is 100 miles south-southeast of Bhamo.
11 The plan was to use Chindit groups to pave the way for the general offensive heading south from Ledo. Once Indaw airstrip had been taken, reinforcements would be flown in to continue the advance. Indaw is 75 miles west of Bhamo.

these operations by using novel methods of supply and by a bold advance through what they might consider to be impassable country.

Subject to the Generalissimo's permission, General Stilwell[12] had agreed the Ledo force should come under Fourteenth Army Commander[13] until it reached Kamaing,[14] after which it would revert to the command of General Stilwell. Mountbatten asked if this arrangement was agreeable to the Generalissimo. Kai-shek said he would like to see the proposals illustrated on a map before giving his decision.

Mountbatten then gave logistics information for the air route over the 'Hump'.[15] He had promised the Generalissimo to work the supply up to 10,000 tons a month over this route. For November and December the figure would be 9700 tons. For January and February it would drop to 7900 tons but it should rise again to 9200 tons in March. Twenty-five additional first-line transport aircraft were required and this demand had been put to the Combined Chiefs of Staff, with every prospect of it being met.[16]

Churchill said these were important military operations of a much greater magnitude than ever previously contemplated in the Theatre. The plans had not yet been examined by the Chiefs of Staff, but they would be at the earliest opportunity, possibly that day. In all, there was an Allied force of approximately 320,000 men who would apply pressure on the enemy. They would have a qualitative as well as a quantitative supremacy over the enemy. He had high hopes for these operations, the success of which largely depended on surprise and secrecy and ignorance on the part of the enemy as to the lines of approach and the points of attack.

Owing to the surrender of the Italian Fleet[17] and other naval events of a favourable character, a formidable British Fleet would be established in due course in the Indian Ocean. This would ultimately consist of no less than five modernised capital ships, four heavy armoured carriers, and up to twelve auxiliary carriers, together with cruisers and flotillas. This force would be more powerful than any detachment it was thought the Japanese could afford to make from their main fleet in the Pacific.[18] Mountbatten would have also formed an amphibious 'circus' by the spring for use in amphibious operations which might ultimately be decided upon.[19]

---

12 General Stilwell, Commander-in-Chief of the U.S. China-Burma-India Theatre of Operations would soon be made responsible for planning the invasion of northern Burma.

13 General Slim's Fourteenth Army, often referred to as the 'Forgotten Army' because Burma operations were overlooked in favour of Mediterranean and European campaigns.

14 Roughly midway between the Indian and Chinese borders.

15 The Hump was the eastern end of the Himalayan Mountains. Supplies for the Chinese war effort had to be flown from India over the mountains to China. The airlift was a real challenge, which the U.S. Tenth Air Force and then the USAAF's Transport Command (ATC) had to overcome.

16 Planes flew 650,000 tons of supplies over the Hump between April 1942 and November 1945.

17 Under the armistice terms, the *Regia Marina* sailed its ships to Malta while a few ships were captured in port by the Germans or scuttled by their crews. Between 8 and 10 September, 29 ships, including six battleships and eight cruisers, were surrendered; 33 submarines and other smaller ships were also handed over. The Italian Co-Belligerent Navy was formed to fight for the Allies but there was doubt about the loyalty of the crews, so the ships were interned in Egypt.

18 Considering what it had to keep in the Pacific Theatre to face the US Navy.

19 An amphibious 'circus' is a range of amphibious craft, from the large seagoing landing craft used to transport men, tanks and equipment long distances, down to the small landing craft used to ferry men and equipment to the shore.

Kai-shek said, in accordance with the view he had expressed at Chungking, the success of the operations in Burma depended not only on the strength of the naval forces in the Indian Ocean but on coordinated naval action with the land operations. Churchill said naval operations in the Bay of Bengal would not necessarily be coordinated with or linked to the land campaign.[1] Their naval superiority should ensure the security of their communications and a threat to those of the enemy. It had to be remembered the main fleet base would be anywhere from 2000 to 3000 miles away from the area where the armies were operating.[2] No comparison could be made with these operations and those carried out in Sicily, where it was possible for the fleet to work in close support of the army.

Kai-shek believed the enemy would reinforce Burma and this could only be stopped by vigorous naval operations. Churchill said it would be disastrous if they could do nothing to prevent the Japanese bringing large reinforcements by sea through the Malacca and Sunda Straits. They could not guarantee to cut off reinforcements by sea entirely, but they should do everything to prevent their arrival.

Kai-shek was not clear about the timing of the concentration of the naval forces in the Indian Ocean. He was convinced simultaneous naval and land operations gave the best chance of success for the operations. Burma was the key to the whole campaign in Asia. The loss of Burma would be a very serious matter to the Japanese and they would fight stubbornly and tenaciously to retain their hold on the country. After the enemy had been cleared out of Burma, his next stand would be in North China and finally in Manchuria.

Churchill did not believe the success of the land operations hinged entirely on a simultaneous naval concentration. The fleet could not be assembled by January or until some time later. The ships had to be tropicalized and fitted with special equipment. Some would be starting soon but the build-up to full strength would not be achieved until the late spring or early summer of 1944.[3] It seemed improbable the enemy would send naval forces of any strength to the Bay of Bengal in the meantime.

Roosevelt asked about the railway communications between Siam and Burma.[4] Mountbatten said the Japanese had recently completed the railway from Bangkok to Thanbyuzayat[5] and this would improve their facilities for maintaining forces in Burma to an appreciable degree. Churchill thought the Japanese were mainly relying upon road and rail communications from the Malay Peninsula in order to

1   The Bay of Bengal covered any amphibious operation on the west coast of Burma. The land campaign was planned to be far inland.

2   The main naval base was at Ceylon (a British colony until 1948), now Sri Lanka, while an additional base was established at Addus Atoll in the Maldive Islands 600 miles southwest of Ceylon.

3   It would take longer and the first amphibious assault would not take place until January 1945, when Ramree Island, off the west coast of Burma, was captured so the port and airfield could be used.

4   Now Thailand and Myanmar.

5   Thanbyuzayat (or Tin Shelter) was the western terminus of the Thailand-Burma Railway, or Death Railway. The 258-mile railway was started in October 1942 and completed in December 1943. Approximately 13,000 prisoners of war and 90,000 civilians died during the construction of the railway; 3,149 Commonwealth and 621 Dutch burials are in Thanbyuzayat War Cemetery.

maintain their forces in Burma. The Allies did not possess shore air bases, so they could not threaten the Japanese communications in the Gulf of Siam.[6]

Churchill wished to emphasize the great importance he attached to the operations in Southeast Asia, which would be driven forward with all vigour and dispatch. He hoped to have a further talk with the Generalissimo when some other details of the British naval situation would be communicated.

In conclusion, Roosevelt said the matter could not be carried any further that morning. He hoped the Generalissimo would take this opportunity to discuss these important problems with the Chiefs of the American and British Staffs.

23 November
Second Combined Chiefs of Staff Meeting
China's role in the defeat of Japan; Enemy situation in the Far East and Japan; Southeast Asia Operations; Situation in Southeast Asia.

24 November
Third Combined Chiefs of Staff Meeting
Thanksgiving Day Party; United Chiefs of Staff; Eureka Agenda; Southeast Asia command boundaries, Southeast Asia Operations discussed with Chinese.

24 November: Second Sextant Meeting
The President hoped there would be a preliminary survey of operations in the European Theatre, including the Mediterranean. Final decisions would depend on the way things went at the conference with Premier Stalin. Some reported Stalin had no thoughts beyond OVERLORD and he attached the highest importance to it as the only operation worth considering. Others thought Stalin was anxious the Germans should be given no respite throughout the winter and there should be no idle hands between now and OVERLORD. The logistic problem was whether they could retain OVERLORD in all its integrity and keep the Mediterranean ablaze at the same time. Roosevelt believed Stalin would be almost certain to demand continuation of action in the Mediterranean and OVERLORD.

As regards the Eastern Mediterranean, the question arose "Where would the Germans go from the Dodecanese?"[7] And the answer seemed to be "nowhere". If they applied the same question to themselves; the answer depended on Turkey's action. The entry of Turkey into the war would put quite a different complexion on the matter. This was another question for discussion with Stalin.

Churchill agreed with the President's views. They had had a year of unbroken success in North Africa and the Mediterranean, in Russia, and in the Pacific. Alamein and TORCH had paved the way for the extermination of large German

---

6   The Gulf of Siam, now the Gulf of Thailand, had Malaysia peninsula to the west, Thailand to the north and Cambodia to the east.

7   The Dodecanese Islands are 150 small Greek islands (only 26 are inhabited) off the southwest coast of Turkey. Following the surrender of Italy in September 1943, German and Allied troops had fought for control of the islands. The Germans won and Roosevelt is speculating as to their next move.

forces in Tunisia. They were followed by the highly successful Sicily operation, and subsequently by the daring amphibious landing at Salerno and the capture of Naples.[1] Then came Mussolini's fall, the collapse of Italy and the capitulation of the Italian Fleet.

In the whole history of warfare there had never been such a long period of joint Allied success, nor such a high degree of cooperation and comradeship between two Allies, extending from the High Command down to the troops in the field. They should be unworthy of these accomplishments and of the tasks lying ahead if they did not test their organization to see whether improvements could be made. That was the purpose of these periodical meetings.

As a contrast to the almost unbroken successes of the past year, the last two months had produced a series of disappointments. The Italian campaign had flagged. They did not have a sufficient margin of superiority to give them the power to force the enemy back.[2] The weather had been bad. It seemed the departure from the Mediterranean of certain units and landing craft had had a rather depressing effect on the soldiers left to fight the battle. The build-up of strategic air forces may have also contributed to the slow progress. The main objective was Rome, for "whoever holds Rome holds the title deeds of Italy." With Rome in their possession, the Italian Government would hold up its head. Moreover, they should then be in a position to seize the landing grounds north of the city.

Churchill had agreed with a heavy heart to the return of seven divisions from the Mediterranean Theatre. 50th and 51st British Divisions,[3] which were first-class troops, had had their equipment removed in preparation for embarkation. In the meantime, 3rd US Division had been no less than 49 days in constant contact with the enemy[4] while other US and British units had been fighting without rest for long periods.

Passing across the Adriatic to Yugoslavia, more trouble had brewed up. It was lamentable that virtually no supplies had been conveyed by sea to the 222,000 followers of Tito.[5] These stalwarts were holding as many Germans in Yugoslavia as the combined Anglo-American forces were holding south of Rome. The Germans had been thrown into some confusion after the collapse of Italy and the Patriots had gained control of large stretches of the coast. But the Allies had not

---

1   The Fifth Army of General Mark W. Clark (1896-1984) and Montgomery's Eighth Army landed at Salerno on 3 September 1943; the landing was codenamed AVALANCHE. Naples, 35 miles northwest of the beachhead, was entered on 1 October; the Germans badly damaged the city and port before withdrawing.

2   The troops of new Army Group C, serving under Field Marshal Albert Kesselring (1885-1960), were building a series of defensive lines south of Rome. The Volturno and Barbara Lines covered the main Gustav Line, with a key defensive point at Cassino. They were helped by the rugged terrain and winter weather.

3   Both 50th and 51st Divisions had been rebuilt after the disastrous battle for France in 1940 to serve in the North African, Sicily and Salerno campaigns.

4   First in Morocco, then as an assault division during the invasion of Sicily and at Salerno. In May 1944 they would begin training for the invasion of southern France.

5   Josip Broz Tito (1892–1980), Commander-in-Chief of partisan forces fighting across Yugoslavia during what was known as the National Liberation War.

seized their opportunity, the Germans had recovered and they were driving the partisans out bit by bit.[6]

The main reason for this was the artificial line of responsibility running through the Balkans. On the one hand, Middle East Command had the responsibility for operations but not the forces. On the other, General Eisenhower had the forces but not the responsibility. Considering the partisans and patriots had given such a generous measure of assistance at almost no cost to the Allies, it was of high importance to ensure their resistance was maintained and not allowed to flag.

Moving further east to the Aegean, the picture was equally black. When Italy fell, cheap prizes had been open to them and General Wilson[7] had been ordered to "improvise and dare". Although they had not been able to seize Rhodes they had occupied Kos, Leros, Samos and other smaller islands. It had been hoped that Rhodes would be taken in October, but when the time came only one Indian division was available for the task, and this had been insufficient to eject the 8000 Germans from the island.

The enemy reacted strongly to initial moves. He ejected the Allies from the islands one by one, ending up with the recapture of Leros where they had lost 5000 first-class troops, with four cruisers and seven destroyers either sunk or damaged. Nevertheless, taking into account the German soldiers drowned and those killed by air attack and in the battle, neither side could claim any significant superiority in battle casualties. The Germans were, however, now re-established in the Aegean.[8]

As stated by the President, the attitude of Turkey would have a profound effect on future events in that area. "With Rhodes once more in our possession and the Turkish airfields at our disposal, the other islands would become untenable for the enemy." It was hoped the Russians would share their view of the importance of bringing Turkey into the war.[9] They should see great possibilities would accrue and a chance to join hands with them by means of sending supplies through the Dardanelles.[10] The effect on Hungary, Romania and Bulgaria would also be profound. All this might be done at quite a small cost, say, two divisions and a few landing craft. Maybe a meeting with the Turkish Prime Minister could be arranged on the way back from meeting Stalin.

Passing now to the Southeast Asia Theatre, it was now clear CULVERIN would require many more ships and craft than the British alone could supply. If the US Chiefs of Staff thought CULVERIN was the best contribution to the Pacific war, then America would have to help. If, on the other hand, CULVERIN was

---

6   The German offensives nearly defeated the partisans in the winter of 1943.

7   General (later Field Marshal) Henry M. Wilson (1881-1965), Commander-in-Chief Middle East; nickname Jumbo.

8   Wilson was ordered to create a diversion during the invasion of Italy in September 1943 and he attempted to occupy the small Greek islands of Kos, Leros and Samos. The British forces suffered heavily and were repulsed, resulting in criticism of Wilson's handling of the campaign in Britain.

9   Having seen how easily the Germans fought off the British attacks on the Dodecanese Islands, the Turkish government was convinced it had been right to stay neutral.

10   The Dardanelles is a long narrow strait separating the Balkans, along the Gallipoli peninsula, from the Turkish mainland. It gives access to the Black Sea and southern Russian ports.

thought to be too costly, it might be better to bring back sufficient landing craft from the Southeast Asia Theatre to the Mediterranean for an attack on Rhodes.[1]

So the sequence was going to be, first Rome then Rhodes.[2] Churchill wished to make it clear the British had no idea of advancing into the Valley of the Po.[3] Their idea was the campaign in Italy should have the strictly limited objective of the Pisa-Rimini line.[4] No regular formations were to be sent to Yugoslavia.[5] All that was needed there was a generous packet of supplies, air support and possibly a few commandos. This stepping up of help to the patriots would not involve them in a large additional commitment. When they had reached their objectives in Italy, the time would come to decide whether to move to the left or to the right.[6]

Turning to the knockout blow, OVERLORD, Churchill emphasized he had in no way relaxed his zeal for this operation. They had profited very considerably in their experiences of amphibious operations and their landing appliances had improved out of all knowledge.[7] There would be an anxious period during the build-up, when the Germans might be able to concentrate quicker than the Allies could. Nevertheless, the sixteen British divisions would be ready when called upon.

The timing of the operation seemed to Churchill to depend more on the state of the enemy than on the set perfection of the Allied preparations. If the Germans had not thrown in the sponge by February he agreed they should expect heavy fighting throughout the summer. If so, it had to be realized sixteen British divisions were the limit of their contribution. The British could not meet any further calls on their manpower because it was now fully deployed on war service.

After reviewing all the various theatres of operations the relationships seemed to work out as follows. OVERLORD remained top of the bill, but this operation should not be such a tyrant as to rule out every other activity in the Mediterranean. For example, a little flexibility in the employment of landing craft ought to be conceded. Orders had been issued to build 70 additional LCTs in British shipyards but they had to see if they could do even better.

General Alexander[8] had asked for the return of the landing craft for OVERLORD to be deferred from mid-December to mid-January. The resources at issue between the American and British Staffs were probably no more than 10 per cent of the whole, excluding those in the Pacific. Surely some degree of elasticity could be arranged.[9]

---

1   The plan to capture the northern tip of Sumatra was first suggested at the Quebec conference in August 1943. By building an airbase the Allies would be able to attack Japanese lines of communications through Siam and Burma (Thailand and Myanmar). The Allies did not have the resources to carry out CULVERIN at this stage.
2   Capturing Rhodes would open the way to the Aegean Sea and ultimately the Dardanelles.
3   The Po Valley is at the north end of the Italian Peninsula, between the Apennines and the Alps. Milan is at the west end while Venice and Ravenna are at the east, either side of the Po estuary.
4   The Pisa-Rimini line, or Gothic Line, ran between the two cities and was Kesselring's last line of defence, 150 miles north of Rome.
5   Regular formations meaning divisions; instead, SOE and commandos would help the Yugoslav guerrillas.
6   In other words, left into France or right into Yugoslavia (now Slovenia and Croatia).
7   Experience gained on the shores of North Africa, Sicily and Italy.
8   General Alexander, commander of 15th Army Group in Italy.
9   A shortage of landing craft would continue to dog the planning for D-Day. Even after increasing construction the shortage would contribute to a delay of a month to D-Day.

Nevertheless, Churchill wished to remove any idea they had weakened, cooled or were trying to get out of OVERLORD. They were in it up to the hilt. To sum up, the program he advocated was Rome in January and Rhodes in February; supplies to the Yugoslavs, a settlement of the Command arrangements and the opening of the Aegean, subject to the outcome of an approach to Turkey. All the preparations for OVERLORD would go ahead full steam within the framework of the foregoing policy for the Mediterranean.[10]

Roosevelt could not tell what the state of German military capabilities would be from month to month. The Russian advance, if it continued at its present rate, would bring their ally to the boundaries of Romania in a few weeks. At the forthcoming conference, the Russians might ask what they intended to do in this event; they might suggest a junction of "our right with their left".[11] The Allies had to be ready to answer this question. The Russians might suggest staging an operation at the top of the Adriatic with a view to assisting Tito.[12]

Churchill said the staffs had been giving much thought to how to beat Japan when Hitler was finished.[13] He was determined to solve this problem and the British Fleet would be disposed wherever it could make the best contribution towards this end. The air force build-up would also be studied.[14]

Roosevelt shared Mr. Molotov's views[15] that the defeat of Japan would follow Germany's and more rapidly than was generally thought possible at present. The Generalissimo had been very satisfied with the previous day's discussion. There was no doubt China had wide aspirations, which included the re-occupation of Manchuria and Korea.[16]

Roosevelt then referred to the question of command, remarking he still received requests for the transfer of shipping and air forces from one theatre to another for a limited period of operations. In his view, their strategic air forces from London to Ankara[17] should be under one command. He cited the example of the command that Marshal Foch exercised in 1918.[18] Churchill said once they were across the Channel a united command would be established in the area of operations. He considered the Combined Chiefs of Staff system had worked reasonably satisfactorily in taking the decision referred to by the President. Churchill

---

10 Churchill did not get many items on his wish list. It would take until June 1944 to reach Rome while the invasion of Rhodes was cancelled. Supplies to Yugoslavia helped Tito's partisans hold on and they eventually drove the Germans out of their territory. Turkey would not declare war on the Axis and join the Allies until February 1945.

11 In Austria.

12 An invasion of the Istrian Peninsula, south of Trieste, from Italy, would allow the Allies to advance northeast towards Vienna and Budapest.

13 A case of when, not if, in Churchill's view.

14 A study of the building programme, making sure it matched planned operations.

15 Vyacheslav M. Molotov (1890–1986), the Soviet Union's People's Commissar for Foreign Affairs.

16 Japan had annexed Korea in 1910. It invaded Manchuria between September 1931 and February 1932 and established a puppet state called Manchuko.

17 Ankara is the capital of Turkey. Roosevelt is calling for one command covering the European and Mediterranean Theatres, particularly when it came to sea and air power.

18 Foch was given control of the Allied Armies at the Doullens Conference on 3 April 1918 during the German Spring Offensives on the Western front. He was later appointed Supreme Commander of the Allied Armies with the title of Généralissime (or Generalissimo; Supreme General).

then paid a tribute to the accuracy and effectiveness of the US daylight bombers operating from the United Kingdom.

Roosevelt and Churchill invited the staffs to study the scope and dates of the operations to be carried out in the European and Mediterranean Theatres in 1944. They had to arrive at an agreed view, if possible, before meeting the Russians.

25 November
Fourth Combined Chiefs of Staff Meeting
Southeast Asia Operations; Overall Plan for the defeat of Japan.
Thanksgiving Party
Civil Affairs Meeting
Ambassador Winant and Foreign Secretary Eden.
26 November
US Generals meet Chiang Kai-shek, where he demanded 10,000 tons of supplies a month.
Fifth Combined Chiefs of Staff Meeting
Reports from Eisenhower and Wilson; OVERLORD and the Mediterranean; Southeast Asia Operations; Collaboration with the USSR.

Roosevelt, Churchill and Chiang Meeting
No minutes but most of the discussion concerned the wording of the communiqué.

Sextant Communiqué
President Roosevelt, Generalissimo Chiang Kai-shek, and Prime Minister Churchill, and their respective military leaders, have completed a conference somewhere in Africa. They issued the following joint statement:

The military missions have agreed upon future operations directed against Japan from China and Southeast Asia. The plans, the details of which cannot be disclosed, provide for continuous and increasingly vigorous offensives against the Japanese. We are determined to bring unrelenting pressure against our brutal enemy by sea, land, and air. This pressure is already underway. Japan will know of its power.

We are determined the islands in the Pacific which have been occupied by the Japanese, many of them made powerful bases contrary to Japan's specific and definite pledge not to militarize them, will be taken from Japan forever.

The territory Japan has so treacherously stolen from the Chinese, such as Manchuria and Formosa, will of course be returned to the Republic of China. All of the conquered territory taken by violence and greed by the Japanese will be freed from their clutches.

We are mindful of the treacherous enslavement of the people of Korea by Japan, and are determined that country, at the proper moment after the downfall of Japan, shall become a free and independent country.

We know full well the defeat of Japan is going to require fierce and determined fighting. Our countries are pledged to fight together until we have received the unconditional surrender of Japan.

The Eureka Conference: 28 November–1 December 1943

Roosevelt and Churchill left Cairo and headed for Tehran, Iran, to meet Stalin for the Eureka Conferences. Stalin asked the President to stay at the Russian Legation because there were many Axis sympathizers in the city and there was a risk of an assassination attempt but he insisted on staying at the American Legation.

The three Heads of State met four times in the Russian Legation between 28 November and 1 December 1943. At the first meeting they were supported by their Chiefs of Staff. It was followed by a military meeting by the Chiefs of Staff of the three nations. The three heads of state then continued their discussions at two further meetings. The military conclusions of the conference were published on 2 December.

28 November: Roosevelt–Stalin First Meeting

The President greeted Marshal Stalin with "I am glad to see you. I have tried for a long time to bring this about." After returning the greeting, Stalin said he was to blame for the delay; he had been very occupied with military matters. Roosevelt asked about the situation on the Soviet battle front. Stalin answered the situation was not too good on part of the front; they had lost Zhitomir[1] and were about to lose Koresten, an important railroad centre in northern Ukraine, for which the capture of Gomel[2] could not compensate. The Germans had brought a new group of divisions into the area and they were exercising strong pressure on the Soviet front.

Roosevelt asked if the initiative remained with the Soviet forces. Stalin said it did but the situation was so bad it was only possible to make offensive operations in the Ukraine. Roosevelt wished it was within his power to bring about the removal of 30 or 40 German divisions from the Eastern front and that question was one of the things he wanted to discuss. Stalin said it would be of great value if it could be brought about.

Roosevelt wanted to talk over the possibility of part of the American-British merchant fleet being made available to the Soviet Union after the war. Stalin said an adequate merchant fleet would be of great value, not only to the Soviet Union, but for the development of relations between the Soviet Union and the United States, which he hoped would be greatly expanded. A plentiful supply of raw materials could be made available to the United States if equipment was sent from the United States to the Soviet Union.

Talk then turned to the Far East. Roosevelt referred to an interesting conversation with Chiang Kai-shek in Cairo, on the general subject of China. Stalin said the Chinese had fought very badly but, in his opinion, it was the fault of the Chinese leaders. Roosevelt told Stalin they were now supplying and training 30 Chinese divisions for operations in Southern China and were proposing to do the same for another 30 divisions. There was a new prospect of an offensive

---

1   Zhitomir in Ukrainian (or Zhytomyr in Russian) is in northern Ukraine.
2   Gomel or Homel is the second largest city in Belarus.

operation under Mountbatten's command to advance through North Burma and link up with China in Yunnan.

Stalin asked about the situation in the Lebanon. Roosevelt gave a brief description of the events leading up to the recent clashes and said they had occurred due to the attitude of the French Committee and General De Gaulle.[1] Stalin did not know General de Gaulle personally, but he thought he was very unreal in his political activities. While General de Gaulle represented the soul of sympathetic France, the real physical France was engaged in helping their common enemy Germany under Pétain,[2] by making French ports, materials and machines available for the German war effort.

Stalin said the trouble with de Gaulle's movement was it had no communication with the physical France, which should be punished for its attitude during this war. De Gaulle acted as though he was the head of a great state but it commanded little power. Roosevelt agreed and said no Frenchman over 40, and particularly no Frenchman who had ever taken part in the present French Government, should be allowed to return to a position in the future. General Giraud was a good old military type but he had no administrative or political sense whatsoever. There were approximately eleven French divisions, partly composed of Algerians and other North Africans, in training in North Africa.

Stalin continued at length about the French ruling classes and how they should not be entitled to share any of the benefits of the peace because of their past record of collaboration with Germany. Roosevelt said Churchill believed France would be quickly reconstructed as a strong nation but he did not share this view. He felt many years of honest labour would be necessary before France would be re-established. He said the first necessity for the French, not only for the Government but the people as well, was to become honest citizens. Stalin agreed and said he did not propose to have the Allies shed blood to restore Indochina to the old French colonial rule.

Stalin said the recent events in the Lebanon made public service the first step toward the independence of people who had formerly been colonial subjects. It was necessary to fight the Japanese in the political sphere in addition to military missions, particularly as the Japanese had granted extremely limited nominal independence to certain colonial areas. He repeated France should not get back Indochina and the French had to pay for their criminal collaboration with Germany.

Roosevelt was 100% in agreement with Marshal Stalin; after 100 years of French rule in Indochina, the inhabitants were worse off than they had been before.[3] Chiang Kai-shek had told him China had no designs on Indochina but the people of Indochina were not yet ready for independence. Roosevelt replied when the

---

1   Lebanon had recently held elections and became an independent state on 8 November 1943. It would declare war on Germany and Japan on 27 February 1945.

2   Marshal Phillippe Pétain (1856-1951), head of Vichy France.

3   France became involved in the area in the 18th century. French Indochina was formed in 1887 following its victory over China in the Sino-French War (1884-1885). The colony originally exported opium, salt and rice alcohol but the emergence of the motor industry in the early 20th century meant Indochina satisfied France's need for rubber; many new industries followed.

United States acquired the Philippines, the inhabitants were not ready for independence, but it would be granted without qualification when the war against Japan was over. He added he had discussed with Chiang Kai-shek the possibility of a system of trusteeship for Indochina that would prepare the people for independence within a definite period of time, perhaps 20 to 30 years. Stalin agreed.

Roosevelt said Mr. Hull[4] had taken a document to the Moscow Conference proposing annual visits by an International Committee to the colonies of all nations and they would use public opinion to correct abuses. Stalin saw merit in this idea. Roosevelt felt it would be better not to discuss the question of India with Mr. Churchill, since he had no solution for that question, and proposed to defer the entire question to the end of the war. Stalin agreed it was a sore point with the British.

Roosevelt wanted to talk with Stalin about India at some future date. The best solution would be reform from the bottom, somewhat on the Soviet line. Stalin replied the India question was a complicated one, with different levels of culture and the absence of relationship in the castes; reform from the bottom would mean revolution.

Roosevelt said he was glad to be in this house because of the opportunities to meet Marshal Stalin more often in completely informal circumstances.

28 November: First Eureka Meeting

The President said, as the youngest of the three Chiefs of State present, he had the privilege of welcoming Marshal Stalin and Prime Minister Churchill to the auspicious conference. They were sitting around the table for the first time as a family, with the one object of winning the war.

Regarding the conduct of naval and military meetings, it had been the habit, between the British and the United States, to publish nothing but to speak their minds very freely. In such a large family circle they hoped they would be very successful and achieve constructive accord so they would maintain close touch throughout and after the war. The General Staffs of the three countries should look after military matters. Marshal Stalin, the Prime Minister and the President had many things to discuss regarding matters pertaining to conditions after the war. If anyone of them did not want to talk about any particular subject brought up, they did not have to.

Roosevelt said perhaps Churchill would like to say something about the years to come before they came to the discussion of military problems. Churchill said they represented a concentration of great worldly power. They had perhaps the responsibility for the shortening of this war and the future of mankind in their hands. He prayed they may be worthy of this God-given opportunity. Roosevelt then turned to Stalin and said, "Perhaps our host would like to say a few words."

Stalin took pleasure in welcoming those present and thought history would show this opportunity had been of tremendous import. He thought the great opportunity they had and the power their people had invested in them could be

---

4 The Secretary of State.

used to take full advantage within the framework of their potential collaboration. He concluded "Now let us get down to business."

Roosevelt wanted to start with a general survey of the war and of the meaning of the war, from the American point of view. They earnestly hoped the completion of the war would come just as soon as possible. He wanted to begin with a subject affecting the United States more than either Great Britain or the USSR; the Pacific. It was most important to bring back to the United States those forces now in the Pacific. The United States was bearing a major part of the Pacific war and it had the greatest part of its naval power in the Pacific, plus about one million men.

They were proceeding on the principle of attrition as regards Japan, a policy presently accepted in the United States. They believed they were sinking many Japanese ships, both naval and merchant – more than they could possibly replace.[1] They had been moving forwards toward Japan from the south and were now moving towards Japan through the islands from the east.[2] There was very little more they could do regarding operations from the north.

To the west of Japan it was necessary to keep China in the war. They had arranged plans for operations through North Burma and in the Yunnan Province. That operation would advance far enough so China could herself strike in the Yunnan Province. In addition, they were still discussing an amphibious operation in order to strike at the supply lines from the Japanese base at Bangkok.[3] This base was a veritable storehouse for Japan. The whole operation covered a huge territory and large numbers of ships and men and planes were necessary to carry it out. They must definitely keep China actively in the war.

Roosevelt said by opening the Burma Road and increasing the transportation of supplies by plane into China,[4] they hoped they would be in a position to attack Tokyo from China by air that summer. All this concerned the Southeast Asia operations but they wanted to express to Stalin the very great importance, not only of keeping China in the war, but of being able to get at Japan with the greatest possible speed.

Roosevelt now came to the operations of immediate concern to the USSR and Great Britain. They had made many plans at the last three conferences at Casablanca, Washington and Quebec. About a year and a half ago the major part of their plans involved the consideration of an expedition against the Axis across the English Channel. Largely because of transportation difficulties they had not been able to set a definite date. Not only did they want to get across the English Channel but once they were across, they intended to proceed inland into Germany. But at Quebec they decided it would be impossible to launch such an

---

1   The Battle of Midway in June 1942 had been a major victory for the US Navy and was the high point of Japanese naval aspirations in the Pacific.

2   CARTWHEEL was launched in June 1943 as a two-pronged attack to cut off the Japanese base at Rabaul in Papua New Guinea. General Douglas MacArthur's forces, South West Pacific Area, or SWPA, advanced along the northeast coast of New Guinea. The forces of Admiral Chester W. Nimitz (1885-1966), Pacific Ocean Areas, or POA, advanced through the Solomon Islands toward Bougainville.

3   The problem with attacking Bangkok was getting access to the Gulf of Thailand.

4   Flying supplies over the Hump until the Burma Road was complete. It would take until January 1945 to finish the 717 miles of road through inhospitable terrain.

operation before about 1 May 1944. The Channel was such a disagreeable body of water but no matter how unpleasant it might be, they still wanted to get across it. Churchill said they were very glad it was an unpleasant body of water at one time.

They could not do everything they wanted to do in the Mediterranean or from the United Kingdom because there was definite 'bottleneck' in the matter of landing craft. If they were to conduct any large expedition in the Mediterranean, it would be necessary to give up the important cross-Channel operation. Certain contemplated operations in the Mediterranean might result in a delay in OVERLORD for one month or two or three. Therefore, he prayed for the benefit of the opinion of the two Soviet Marshals and asked how they could be of most help to the USSR.

Roosevelt said even though OVERLORD had been delayed, they could draw more German divisions from the Soviet front with this operation than any other. They had the troops in the Mediterranean but there was a shortage of landing craft.[5] They might help the USSR through certain immediate operations in the Mediterranean, but they had to avoid, if possible, delaying OVERLORD beyond May or June. There were several things they could do:

    a)   increase the drive into Italy;

    b)   undertake an operation from the Northeast Adriatic;[6]

    c)   carry out operations in the Aegean;

    d)   undertake operations from Turkey.

That was what the military conference was concerned with. They wanted to create a withdrawal of German divisions from the Western Front.[7]

Churchill wanted to know what they could do to most help what the Soviets were doing on their Western Front. They had tried to outline matters in the simplest terms. There were no differences between Great Britain and the United States in point of view except the "ways and means". They wanted to reserve any further comments until after they had heard from Stalin.

Stalin welcomed the successes in the Pacific. Unfortunately, they had not, so far, been able to help because they required too much of their forces on their Western Front and were unable to launch any operations against Japan. Their forces in the East were more or less satisfactory for defence but they would have to be increased about three-fold for offensive operations. This would not take place until Germany had been forced to capitulate. Then by their common front they would win.

Stalin had certain comments concerning Europe. Firstly he wanted to explain how the Soviets were conducting their own operations,[8] especially since they

---

5   Landing craft were needed both in the Mediterranean and the English Channel. It took time to switch between the two locations. Ideally there would be enough for both theatres. However, most of the larger landing craft were built in the US and it took time to sail them across the Atlantic. It also took time to train the crews how to use them and the troops how to sail on them.

6   An invasion of the Istrian Peninsula, south of Trieste.

7   The Soviet Western Front or the Allied Eastern Front. The Prime Minister interpolated "as soon as possible".

8   Stalin is referring to the Battle of Kursk in July and August 1943, the largest tank battle in history.

started their advance last July.[1] After the German defence had collapsed, they prepared their own offensive, accumulating sufficient munitions, supplies and reserves. They passed easily from the defensive to the offensive and had not expected the successes they achieved in July, August, and September.[2] Contrary to Soviet expectations, the Germans were considerably weakened.[3] At the present time the Germans had 210 divisions on the Soviet front.[4] In addition, there were 50 non-German divisions, including 10 Bulgarian, 20 Finnish, and 16 to 18 Romanian.

Roosevelt asked about the strength of these divisions. Stalin said the Germans considered a normal division to be 8000-9000 men, not counting the corps troops, anti-aircraft artillery and so forth. Including these special troops, the divisions totalled about 12,000. Last year the Germans had 240 divisions on the Soviet front, 179 of which were German, but this year they had 260 divisions, 210 of which are German.

The Red Army had 330 divisions opposing the Germans and the excess of 70 divisions was used for offensive operations. If the excess did not exist, no offensive operations would be possible. However, as time went on the difference between the German and Soviet strength decreased, due to the demolitions the Germans carried out during their withdrawals, which made supply difficult. As a result, operations slowed down. The Red Army still maintained the initiative but operations had come to a standstill in some sectors.

Stalin said the Germans had taken the initiative in the Ukraine, west and south of Kiev. In this sector they had three old and five new tank divisions, plus 22 or 23 infantry or motorized divisions for the purpose of capturing Kiev.[5] So some difficulties could be foreseen. All of these factors made it necessary for the Soviets to continue operations in the West and remain silent on the Far Eastern front. Stalin explained how the USSR believed the forces of the United States and Great Britain could best be used to help the Soviet front. It was possibly a mistake, but the USSR believed the Italian operations had been of great value, because it permitted ships to pass through the Mediterranean. But other large operations against Germany on the Italian front were not considered to be of great value. There was once a time when the Soviets tried to invade the Alps, but they found it a very difficult operation.[6] In the USSR it was believed the most suitable sector for a blow at Germany would be from some place in northwest or southern

1   The Marshal stopped to ask whether he would be taking too much time to discuss the operations on the Soviet front. The President and Prime Minister both replied emphatically in the negative and requested him to proceed.

2   The attack on the Kursk Salient was codenamed CITADEL. Ninth Panzer Army failed to break through in the north while Fourth Panzer Army was stopped by the 5th Guards Tank Army in the south. It was the Wehrmacht's last major offensive on the Eastern Front.

3   Casualties for the July-August period are estimated at roughly five to one in the Germans' favour. German: over 200,000 men, 700 tanks and assault guns and 650 planes. Soviet: over 850,000 men, over 6,000 tanks and assault guns and over 1600 planes.

4   Another six German divisions were in the process of moving to the front.

5   Kiev, the capital of the Ukraine, the southwest area of the Soviet Union. The city is a key crossing point over the Dnieper River south of the Pripyat Marshes.

6   General Alexander Suvorov (1730?-1800) and his Russian Army drove the French Revolutionary Army from Italy in 1799. Over the winter that followed he was forced to make a difficult crossing of the Alps following defeat at the hands of General (later Marshal) André Masséna (1758-1817) at Zürich.

France. It was thought Hitler was trying hard to contain as many Allied divisions in Italy as possible because he knew things could not be settled there. Germany was also protected by the Alps.[7]

It would be a good thing if Turkey could open the way to Germany and make it unnecessary to launch a cross-Channel operation.[8] Although the heart of Germany was far from the Balkans, it would be a better area to launch an attack from than Italy. The Soviet military authorities believed it would be better to invade northern France but it had to be expected the Germans would fight like devils to prevent such an attack.

Churchill said the British had long agreed with the United States to undertake an invasion of Northwest France across the Channel. At the present time preparations for such an operation were absorbing the major part of their energies and resources. It would take a long statement to explain why the United States and Great Britain had not been able to strike against France in 1943, but they were resolved to do so in 1944.

In 1943 operations in Africa and across the Mediterranean were the best they could accomplish because of the lack of shipping and landing craft. The United States and Great Britain had set the object of carrying an army into France in the late spring or early summer of 1944. While the forces set up for this operation amounted to 16 British divisions and 19 US divisions, they were almost twice as strong as the German divisions. The enterprise would involve a force of a million men being placed into France in 1944.

Stalin had not wished to imply the Mediterranean operations had been unimportant. Churchill said he was very grateful for the Marshal's courtesy but both he and the President had never regarded the Mediterranean operations as more than a stepping stone to the main offensive against Germany. But after the 16 British divisions had been committed, there were no more British divisions available for operations. The entire British manpower would be necessary to maintain the divisions committed in France and elsewhere throughout the world. The remaining build up for the offensive against Germany would rest with the United States.

Churchill again detailed the number of divisions for the OVERLORD build-up and said there were roughly 40,000 men each when you included their supporting troops. There would then be no more British divisions available but the United States would continue to pour divisions into France as fast as they could be shipped across the Atlantic until a total force of 50 to 60 divisions had been reached. Churchill said the summer of 1944 was far away and the operation was six months away. What more could be done to take more weight off the USSR in the meantime, without delaying OVERLORD more than a month or two? Already seven of the best divisions had been withdrawn from the Mediterranean for OVERLORD and many landing craft had already gone or were being collected together.

---

7 In other words, Kesselring's Army Group C could fall back into the Austrian Alps.
8 An assault across the Turkish border into Bulgaria would outflank the Eastern Front.

These withdrawals, plus bad weather, had resulted in their great disappoint-ment at not being in Rome already. However, they hoped to be there in January.[1] General Alexander[2] felt an offensive might cut off the ten or twelve divisions opposing the Anglo-American forces. This would result from amphibious opera-tions and flanking movements, which would cut off their lines of withdrawal.[3]

The United States and the British had not come to any decision regarding plans for going into the Valley of the Po or for trying to invade Germany from north-ern Italy. It was felt they could look towards southern France or the Adriatic after the Pisa-Rimini line[4] had been reached because sea power could open the way. But Churchill said these operations were not enough. Ways of doing much more were now being talked of. Splendid things had been accomplished in Yugoslavia by Tito and he was doing much more than Mihailović[5] had accomplished. There were no plans to put a large army into Yugoslavia, but a blow could be struck at the Germans by increasing supplies to Tito's forces.

Churchill said one of the greatest things under consideration was the bring-ing of Turkey into the war, opening the communications into the Dardanelles, Bosphorus and the Black Sea. Such operations would make possible an attack on Rhodes and other islands in the Aegean. This would have a very important effect because it would be possible for convoys to supply the USSR continuously through that route. While four convoys were presently scheduled to sail via the northern routes, it would be impossible to send more because the escorts were needed for the OVERLORD build-up.[6]

Churchill asked what should be done about bringing Turkey into the war? If Turkey should enter the war, should she be asked to attack Bulgaria or should her forces stop on the Thrace front?[7] What would be the effect of Turkey's action on Bulgaria? What did the Soviets think Bulgaria would do in the event of Turkey coming into the war? How would Turkey's entry into the war affect Romania and Hungary? Would not Turkey's entry into the war and consequent operations in the Aegean bring about a political 'turnover' and force a German evacuation of Greece? It would be appreciated if the Soviets would let them know their politi-cal and military opinions on the above questions.[8]

---

1   It would take until 4 June 1944 to reach Rome thanks to Kesselring's tenacious stand on the Winter Line, primarily the Gustav Line, which was anchored at Cassino in the Liri Valley.

2   General Harold Alexander, commander-in-chief of 15th Army Group under General Eisenhower.

3   Churchill is referring to SHINGLE, the proposed landing at Anzio on the west coast of Italy, behind the Gustav Line. The landing would take place on 22 January 1944.

4   Kesselring's last line of defence ran through Pisa and Rimini. It was originally named the Gothic Line but Hitler was later concerned the Allies would take too much notice of it and plan another amphibious operation to outflank it. So it was renamed the Green Line in June 1944.

5   Dragoljub Mihailović, (1893-1946), head of the Chetnik Detachments of the Yugoslav Army, later named the Yugoslav Army in the Homeland, nickname Uncle Draza. Allied support switched from Mihailović to Tito at the Tehran Conference.

6   Churchill is referring to the Arctic Convoys sailing to Murmansk and Archangel. They ran in the winter months, when the nights were long. The convoy escorts were needed for the Atlantic convoys bringing troops, equipment and supplies to the United Kingdom.

7   Advance into Bulgaria or stay behind its border.

8   In June, 1941, Bulgaria joined the Axis and allowed Germany to move troops through to invade Yugoslavia and Greece. Turkey then signed a non-aggression pact with Germany but it did sell chromite to Germany until April 1944.

Stalin said with regard to Churchill's remark as to whether Bulgaria would remember the Soviet action in freeing her from the Turks – "the liberation of Bulgaria had not been forgotten."[9]

Churchill said the objective of the contemplated operations in the Eastern Mediterranean was to support the Soviets, provided the USSR had sufficient interest in them; even if it meant up to two months delay in OVERLORD. The matter could not be decided until it was known how the Soviets felt about the Turkish and Aegean operations.

Roosevelt said a possible entry through the north eastern Adriatic for offensive operations against Germany in the direction of the Danube would be of value.[10] Such operations were being considered together with a movement into southern France but detailed plans had not been worked out. Such plans would be based on the assumption the Red Army would be approaching Odessa at the same time.[11]

Churchill said if the Anglo-American forces took Rome and broke up the German formation south of the Apennines they could either advance west into southern France or east across the Adriatic. Stalin understood it would require 35 divisions to invade France. Did these include the forces to be used in the Mediterranean? Churchill replied the Mediterranean forces were entirely separate from those included in the OVERLORD build-up. After the Italians had been defeated in Italy there remained the possibility of an attack against southern France or across the Adriatic in the direction of Hungary and the Danube. Entirely separate from the OVERLORD build-up there would be 22 divisions available in the Mediterranean; they should all be used. However, it was not possible to move more than seven of them to the OVERLORD build-up because of a lack of shipping.

Churchill also spoke of the large air forces being assembled in England and while the RAF had reached its maximum strength, it would be maintained at this strength.[12] It was hoped the American Air Forces in England would be doubled or tripled over the next six months.[13] The US had also already shipped a million tons of stores to the United Kingdom in preparation for the OVERLORD operation. Churchill said they would be delighted to present the OVERLORD build-up schedule to the Soviet authorities and answer any questions.

Stalin said it seemed to him that an operation in southern France was contemplated in addition to the operations to capture Rome and in the Adriatic. Churchill hoped an operation against southern France might be carried out as a diversion for OVERLORD but detailed plans had not been worked out. Stalin asked if Anglo-American forces would be allocated to Turkey if it entered the

---

9   Following the Russo-Turkish War of 1877-78 the Treaty of San Stefano of 3 March 1878 handed over large parts of the Ottoman Empire to Bulgaria.
10   The amphibious landing on the Istrian Peninsula followed by an advance northeast through what is now Slovakia towards Vienna and Budapest.
11   Odessa on the Black Sea coast.
12   The RAF reached its peak strength of 1,185,833 personnel (1,011,427 men and 174,406 women) on 1 June 1944; five days before D-Day.
13   Operation SICKLE involved the movement of 69 air groups to Britain and their build-up.

war. Churchill said, speaking for himself, that two or three divisions would be required to take the Aegean islands, which controlled communications to Turkey. Twenty squadrons of fighter aircraft and several regiments of anti-aircraft artillery could also be supplied by the British without seriously affecting other operations in the Mediterranean.[1]

Stalin said the Anglo-American presentation was clear to him and wanted to comment. It was not worthwhile scattering the British and American forces. The plans indicated part would be sent to Turkey, part to southern France, part to northern France and part for operations across the Adriatic. He suggested accepting OVERLORD as the basis for operations in 1944 while other operations were considered diversionary. After Rome had been captured there might be a chance for an operation against southern France from Corsica, in which event the OVERLORD forces could establish contact with an invasion force in southern France. This would be much better than scattering forces in several areas distant from each other. He thought France was the weakest of all the German-occupied areas.[2] Stalin had no hopes of Turkey entering the war and was convinced she would not, in spite of all the pressure they might exert. Churchill said he and the President understood the Soviet authorities wanted Turkey to come into the war. They were prepared to make every effort to persuade or force her to do so. Stalin wanted Turkey to enter the war but she could not be taken in by "the scruff of the neck".

Churchill agreed the Anglo-American forces should not be scattered but the Eastern Mediterranean operations only required three or four out of 25 divisions and this could be accomplished without seriously affecting the main operations of OVERLORD. Most of the operations would be done by divisions from the Middle East. The air power needed to assist Turkey would be taken from Egypt, bringing it into a better position to strike at the enemy. Churchill dreaded the six months of idleness between the capture of Rome and the mounting of OVERLORD; secondary operations should be considered to deploy the forces available.[3]

Stalin believed OVERLORD had the greatest possibilities; particularly if it was supported by another offensive movement from southern France. The Allies had to be prepared to remain on the defensive in Italy, releasing ten divisions for operations in southern France. Two or three months after operations in southern France had diverted the German forces, the time would be ripe to start an operation in the north of France such as OVERLORD. Under these conditions, the success of OVERLORD would be assured. Rome could be captured at a later date.[4]

Churchill said they would be no stronger if they did not capture Rome. It was impracticable to place enough aircraft for an attack on southern France if

---

1   While Turkey had troops, it did not have equipment or supplies. There were doubts if Turkish troops would be capable of operating outside their own country; they never did.

2   Stalin advocated a two-pronged invasion of France; one on the north coast and one on the south coast, to split the German reserves. The two Allied armies would be converging in their drive towards Germany. The Allied plan advocated sending troops to four different points.

3   Due to the German's dogged defence of the Gustav Line, the six-month period of idleness never happened. Rome was entered on 4 June and OVERLORD began two days later.

4   It would happen the other way round. The northern invasion was 6 June; the southern invasion was 15 August.

they did not secure the airfields north of the city.[5] It would be difficult for him to agree not to take Rome this January. Failure to do so would be considered as a crushing defeat, and the House of Commons would feel he was failing to use the British forces in full support of his Soviet ally. He said in this event he felt it would be no longer possible for him to represent his government.[6]

Stalin suggested an operation against southern France might be undertaken and given air cover from bases on Corsica. Churchill replied it would take considerable time to construct the necessary airfields on the island of Corsica.[7] Roosevelt said Stalin's proposals concerning southern France were of considerable interest to him. He wanted the planners to study the possibilities of this operation.[8]

Churchill said the relative timing of these operations in the Eastern Mediterranean posed a very serious question. Would it be better to go into the Eastern Mediterranean and delay OVERLORD for one or two months, or to attack southern France one or two months before 1 May[9] and then conduct OVERLORD on the original date? He was eager not to delay this operation if they could possibly to avoid it.

Stalin said as a result of the Soviet experiences over the past two years they had concluded that a large offensive from one direction was unwise. The Red Army usually attacked from two directions, forcing the enemy to move his reserves from one front to the other. When the two offensives converged, the power of the whole offensive increased. Such would be the case with simultaneous operations from southern and northern France.

Churchill agreed with Stalin but did not feel his proposals for Turkey and Yugoslavia were inconsistent with them. He wished to go on record as saying it would be difficult, even impossible to sacrifice all activity in the Mediterranean in order to keep an exact date for OVERLORD. Twenty divisions would be stuck in the Mediterranean due to a lack of shipping and they should be used to stretch Germany to the utmost. He hoped careful and earnest consideration would be given to make sure Mediterranean operations were not compromised solely for keeping the May date for OVERLORD.

Churchill said agreement between the three powers was necessary and would be reached but he hoped all factors would be given careful and patient consideration before decisions were made. He suggested meditating on the discussions of their first meeting before reviewing them at the next. Roosevelt thought it would be a good idea for the staff to study the operations against southern France immediately. Churchill agreed but added they should also work on Turkey. Stalin said they should

---

5   The plan would include an air campaign to knock out bridges and isolate the invasion area; it also included a large airborne landing.
6   Strong words indeed from Churchill. Rome would not be taken until 4 June 1944, despite the Anzio landing behind the Gustav Line on 22 January. Churchill did not resign.
7   Corsica had been taken by early October 1943. The dilemma was whether to capture the airfields north of Rome or build new airfields on Corsica. The failure to break the Gustav Line forced the Allies to change their plans and DRAGOON took place *after* D-Day.
8   Southern Group or DRAGOON Group was formed under the command of General Jake Devers (1887-1966) on Corsica on 1 August 1944 in preparation for DRAGOON. The official name, 6th Army Group, would be adopted soon.
9   Weather and sea conditions were calmer in the Mediterranean than the English Channel.

continue considering these matters the following day. He had not expected the conference to deal with purely military questions and they had not brought a large military staff. However, Marshal Voroshiloff[1] was available for military discussions.

Churchill asked how the question of Turkish entry into the war should be considered. If she could be brought in, what should she be expected to do and what would the cost of her entry be to the three powers concerned? Stalin said it was both a political and a military question. Turkey must take pride in her entry from the point of view of friendship. The British and the United States should use their influence to persuade Turkey to help. In this way it would be impossible for Turkey to maintain her position as a neutral and continue to play fast and loose between both sides.[2] If they could not induce Turkey to enter the war as a matter of friendship, she should not enter. Stalin said all neutral states, including Turkey, look upon belligerents as fools. They must prove to them if they do not enter this war they would not reap the benefits of the victory.[3] Churchill proposed presenting a paper before the conference, containing six or seven questions to clarify the Turkish situation. Roosevelt would do all he could to persuade the President of Turkey to enter the war but personally felt Turkey would ask such a high price for her entry as a belligerent that OVERLORD would be jeopardized.[4]

Stalin said the Turks had not answered previous proposals but he expected their reply would be in the negative. Churchill said Turkey would be mad not to accept the Soviet invitation to join the winning side. She would certainly lose the sympathy of the British people and almost certainly of the American people if she failed to align herself with the Allies. Stalin said "a bird in the hand is worth two in the bush."[5] The Turks were now inactive.[6]

It was agreed to hold a military conference the following morning and Marshal Voroshiloff would represent the USSR. Admiral Leahy[7] and General Marshall would represent the USA and General Brooke and Air Marshal Portal would represent Great Britain.

28 November: Roosevelt, Churchill, Stalin Dinner Meeting

During the first part of the dinner the conversation between the President and Marshal Stalin was general in character and dealt for the most part with a suitable

---

1   Marshal Kliment Voroshiloff (1881-1969), member of the State Defence Committee. During a ceremony to receive the 'Sword of Stalingrad' from Winston Churchill, he took the sword from Stalin but then dropped the sword from its scabbard onto his feet in front of the Big Three.
2   While Turkey was neutral it was still selling raw materials, particularly chromites, one of the two ores of chromium, to the Axis and the Allies.
3   The offer to attend the inaugural of the United Nations finally enticed Turkey to join the Allies, even though their armed forces did not operate outside their borders.
4   It would ask for supplies that would have to be directed away from the OVERLORD build-up.
5   In other words, it was better to stay neutral and know what the Axis response was than join the Allies and face possible invasion.
6   Turkey remained neutral. In February, 1945, the Allies invited Turkey to the inaugural meeting of the United Nations if it joined the war against the Axis. It did but no Turkish troops saw combat.
7   Admiral Leahy was President Roosevelt's personal Chief of Staff.

place for the next meeting. Both seemed to consider Fairbanks to be the most suitable spot.[8]

Stalin raised the question of the future of France and described at considerable length his reasons why France deserved no considerate treatment from the Allies and, above all, had no right to retain her former empire. The entire French ruling class was rotten to the core and had handed France over to the Germans and France was now actively helping their enemies. It would be not only unjust but dangerous to leave any important strategic points in French hands after the war.

Roosevelt partly agreed with Marshal Stalin. That was why he had earlier said it was necessary to eliminate anybody over 40 years old in the future government of France and particularly anybody who had formed part of the French Government.

Roosevelt specifically mentioned the question of New Caledonia and Dakar, the first of which he said represented a threat to Australia and New Zealand. Roosevelt said he was speaking for 21 American nations when he said Dakar in unsure hands was a direct threat to the Americas.

Churchill intervened to say Great Britain did not desire and did not expect to acquire any additional territory out of this war, but since the four great victorious nations[9] would be responsible for the future peace of the world, it was necessary to place strategic points throughout the world under their control.

Stalin said France could not be trusted with any strategic possessions outside her own border and described the ideology of the Vichy Ambassador to Moscow,[10] which he felt was characteristic of the majority of French politicians. This ideology definitely preferred an agreement with France's former enemy than with her former allies.

The conversation then turned to the treatment to be accorded Nazi Germany. Roosevelt said it was very important not to leave the concept of the Reich in the German mind and the very word should be struck from the language. Stalin replied it was not enough to eliminate the word; the very Reich itself had to be rendered impotent so it never again plunged the world into war. Unless the victorious Allies retained the strategic positions necessary to prevent any recrudescence of German militarism in their hands, they would have failed in their duty.

Stalin emphasized the measures for controlling Germany and her disarmament were insufficient to prevent the rebirth of German militarism. While he favoured even stronger measures, he did not specify what he had in mind except for favouring the dismemberment of Germany.

Stalin said Poland should extend to the Oder and the Russians would help the Poles to obtain a frontier on the Oder. Roosevelt was interested in securing the approaches to the Baltic Sea and had in mind some form of trusteeship with perhaps an international state to ensure free navigation through the Kiel Canal. Due to an error by the Soviet translator, Stalin thought the President was referring to

---

8   Fairbanks, the second largest city in Alaska.
9   The United States, the Soviet Union, Great Britain and China.
10 Gaston Bergery (1892-1974) ambassador of the Vichy regime in Moscow until the Germans invaded Russia in June 1941.

the Baltic States. He replied the Baltic States had by an expression of the will of the people voted to join the Soviet Union and the question was not for discussion. After the misapprehension had been cleared up he was in favour of ensuring free navigation to and from the Baltic Sea.[1]

Roosevelt returned to the question of outlying possessions and the possibility of a sovereignty fashioned in a collective body such as the United Nations; a concept which had never been developed in past history.

The President retired after dinner but Stalin and Churchill continued their conversation on the Germany treatment. Stalin favoured the strongest possible measures against Germany. Churchill said he supported no military or civilian aviation for Germany and the abolition of the German general staff system. He also proposed constant supervision over Germany industries and the territorial dismemberment of the Reich.

Stalin was doubtful if these measures would be effective. Furniture factories could be transformed into aircraft factories while watch factories could make fuses for shells. In his opinion, the Germans were an able and talented people who could easily revive and become a threat to the world within fifteen or twenty years. He had personally asked German prisoners in the Soviet Union why they had burst into Russian homes and killed Russian women. The only reply he had received was they had been ordered to do so.

Churchill could not look more than 50 years ahead and felt the grave responsibility of future measures to assure Germany would not again rise to plague the world rested on the three nations represented at Tehran. It was largely the fault of the German leaders and while no distinction could be made between the leaders and the people during war time, something might be done with the German people with a generation of self sacrifice, toil and education. Stalin disagreed and did not appear satisfied by any of Churchill's proposed measures.

Churchill asked if they could discuss the question of Poland later that evening. Great Britain had gone to war with Germany because it invaded Poland in 1939 and its government was committed to the reestablishment of a strong and independent Poland but not to any specific Polish frontiers. If Stalin had any desire to discuss Poland, he was prepared to do so and he was sure Roosevelt would as well. Stalin did not feel it was necessary or desirable to discuss the Polish question.[2]

Churchill had no attachment to any specific frontier between Poland and the Soviet Union; the consideration of Soviet security on their western frontiers was a governing factor. But the British Government was committed to the reestablishment of an independent and strong Poland, which he felt was a necessary instrument in the European orchestra.

Eden then asked if he understood Stalin correctly when he said the Soviet Union favoured the Polish western frontier on the Oder. Stalin replied he did favour such a frontier for Poland and the Russians were prepared to help the Poles achieve it. Churchill said it would be very valuable if the representatives of

---

1 A fine example of the importance of translators, who had to get complicated questions and answers right first time.
2 Stalin changed his mind after a few comments by Churchill.

the three governments could work out some agreed understanding on the Polish frontiers, which could then be taken up with the Polish Government in London.

Churchill wanted to see Poland moved westward in the same manner as soldiers at drill execute the drill 'left close' and illustrated his point with three matches representing the Soviet Union, Poland and Germany.[3] Stalin agreed it would be a good idea to reach an understanding but it was necessary to look further into the matter. The conversation then broke up.

29 November

First Combined Chiefs of Staff Meeting with Marshal Voroshilov

OVERLORD; Landing craft; air force strength for OVERLORD; Italian Front; Yugoslavia; Turkey; A landing in southern France; Mediterranean Air Force strength.

29 November: Roosevelt–Stalin Second Meeting

Roosevelt wished to lend Stalin a most interesting report from an American Army officer who had spent six months in Yugoslavia in close contact with Tito. This officer had the highest respect for Tito and the work he was doing. Stalin thanked the President and promised to return the report when he had read it.

Roosevelt said the American Delegation had introduced a proposal during the Moscow Conference to make air bases available in the USSR to the United States Air Forces for shuttle bombing between Great Britain and the Soviet Union.[4] He handed Stalin a memorandum and hoped he would give this project his support.

Roosevelt wished to tell Stalin how happy he would be to hear him speak on the defeat of Japanese forces and victory over Germany. They had to be prepared for the eventuality and had done some advance planning. Roosevelt emphasized the matter would be held in the strictest security and contacts between Soviet and American officers would be strictly secret. Stalin promised to study the documents.

Roosevelt had many other matters relating to the future of the world he wanted to obtain Stalin's view on. He hoped to discuss some of them before they left Tehran and was willing to discuss any military or political subject the Marshal desired. Stalin replied there was nothing to prevent them from discussing anything they wished.

Roosevelt said the question of a postwar organization to preserve peace had not been fully explained or dealt with and he wanted to discuss the prospect of some organization based on the United Nations with the Marshal. He then outlined the following plan: There would be a large organization of some 35 members of the United Nations which would meet periodically at different places to discuss and make recommendations to a smaller body.

---

3   Poland would give up its eastern territories to the Soviet Union while Germany gave up its eastern territories to Poland. It would rectify the situation established by the Treaty of Versailles after World War I.

4   The planes would fly from the United Kingdom or the Mediterranean, bomb targets in eastern Germany and then continue to airbases in the Ukraine. They refuelled and rearmed and made a second bombing raid on their return journey. It allowed the USAAF to reach targets outside their normal range. Operation FRANTIC lasted from June to September 1944.

Stalin asked whether this organization would be world-wide or European; Roosevelt replied world-wide. Roosevelt said there would be an executive committee composed of the Soviet Union, the United States, United Kingdom and China, together with two additional European states, one South American, one Near East, one Far Eastern country, and one British Dominion. Churchill did not like the proposal because the British Empire only had two votes.

This Executive Committee would deal with all non-military questions such as agriculture, food, health and economy, as well as establishing an International Committee. Stalin asked if it would have the right to make binding decisions on the nations of the world. Roosevelt replied, yes and no. It could make recommendations for settling disputes with the hope the nations concerned would be guided by them. But he did not believe the Congress of the United States would accept as binding a decision of such a body.

Roosevelt then turned to the third organization which he called 'The Four Policemen'; the Soviet Union, United States, Great Britain, and China. The organization would have the power to deal immediately with any threat to peace or sudden emergency. When Italy attacked Ethiopia in 1935,[1] the only machinery in existence was the League of Nations. He had personally begged France to close the Suez Canal but they referred it to the League, which disputed the question and in the end did nothing. The Italian Armies were able to go through the Suez Canal and destroy Ethiopia. Roosevelt said it would have been possible to close the Suez Canal if the machinery of the Four Policemen had been in existence. Roosevelt then summarized the idea he had in mind.[2]

Stalin did not think the small nations of Europe would like the organization because a European state would probably resent China having the right to apply certain machinery to it. In any event, he did not think China would be very powerful at the end of the war.[3] He suggested creating a European or a Far Eastern Committee and a European or a worldwide organization. He said there would be the United States, Great Britain, the Soviet Union and possibly one other European state in the European Commission.

Roosevelt said Stalin's idea was similar to Churchill's idea of a Regional Committee, one for Europe, one for the Far East, and one for the Americas. Churchill had also suggested the United States be a member of the European Commission, but he doubted if the United States Congress would agree to the United States' participation in an exclusively European Committee which might be able to force the dispatch of American troops to Europe. Roosevelt added it would take a terrible crisis such as at present before Congress would ever agree to that step.

Stalin said the world organization suggested by the President, and in particular the Four Policemen, might also require the sending of American troops to

---

1   The Second Italo–Abyssinian War, October 1935 to May 1936, illustrated the weakness of the League of Nations.
2   Britain would look after its Empire and Western Europe; the Soviet Union would look after the area inside its borders and Eastern Europe; the United States would look after the Western Hemisphere and the Eastern Pacific; China would look after the area inside its borders and the Western Pacific.
3   Chinese weakness would allow the United States to dominate its area.

Europe.[4] Roosevelt had only envisaged the sending of American planes and ships to Europe, and England and the Soviet Union would have to handle the land armies in the event of any future threat to the peace. He doubted if it had been possible to send any American forces to Europe if the Japanese had not attacked the United States.[5]

Roosevelt saw two methods of dealing with possible threats to the peace. If the threat arose from a revolution or development in a small country, it might be possible to apply the quarantine method, closing the frontiers of the countries in question and imposing embargoes. If the threat was more serious, the four powers would send an ultimatum to the nation in question and if refused, it would result in the immediate bombardment and possible invasion of that country.

Stalin had discussed the question of safeguarding against Germany with Churchill the day before and the Prime Minister believed Germany would not rise again. Stalin thought Germany would completely recover within 15 to 20 years unless stopped and they needed something more serious than the organization proposed by the President. The first German aggression had occurred in 1870[6] and then 44 years later in the First World War, whereas only 21 years elapsed between the end of the last war and the beginning of the present. He did not believe the period from defeat to the revival of German strength would be any longer in the future and did not think the President's organizations were enough. Stalin said the control of certain strong physical points was needed, either within Germany, along the German borders, or even further away, to ensure Germany would not start another course of aggression and he mentioned Dakar.[7] The same should apply to Japan and the nearby islands should remain under strong control to prevent Japan embarking on a course of aggression. Any commission or body set up to preserve peace should have the right to make decisions and occupy strong points against Germany and Japan. Roosevelt agreed 100%.

Stalin was still dubious about Chinese participation. Roosevelt insisted on the participation of China in the Four Power Declaration at Moscow, not because he did not realize the weakness of China, he was thinking further into the future. China was a nation of 400 million people and it was better to have them as friends rather than as a potential source of trouble.[8]

Roosevelt reverted to Stalin's statements about converting factories and said a strong and effective world organization of the Four Powers could move swiftly when factories were converted for warlike purposes. Stalin said the Germans had shown great ability at concealing such beginnings and Roosevelt accepted the

---

4   The Cold War intervened and the US armed forces never left Europe. There are still over 73,000 US troops stationed in Europe in 2013.

5   The United States followed an Isolationist Policy during the first half of the 20th century, preferring to avoid involvement in European conflicts; until it was under threat or attacked.

6   The Franco-Prussian War (1870-1871) led to the unification of Germany, shifting the balance of power in Europe. It also resulted in the loss of the French provinces of Alsace and Lorraine to the new Germany.

7   Dakar is on the Cap-Vert peninsula in what was French West Africa and is now Senegal.

8   Wise words indeed, when one considers China's position in the world today.

remark.[1] He agreed strategic positions across the world should be at the disposal of some world organization to prevent a revival of German and Japanese aggression.

29 November: Second Eureka Meeting

The President had no formal agenda for the meeting. He thought it would be a good idea if Marshal Stalin, the Prime Minister, and possibly Marshal Voroshiloff would give the meeting their ideas. General Brooke outlined the proceedings of the military conference. General Marshall had little to add but the problems concerning the United States were not those of troops or equipment but rather the problems of ships, landing craft and airfields close enough to the scene of the operations under consideration.

Brooke spoke of a special type of landing craft, which carried about 40 tanks or motor vehicles.[2] He made it clear the United States build-up for OVERLORD was proceeding according to schedule and one million tons of supplies and equipment had been assembled in the United Kingdom, in advance of the troops. The questionable factor was landing craft and the schedule of construction had been accelerated both in the United Kingdom and the United States for two reasons:[3]

1) the initial assault for OVERLORD;
2) operations in the Mediterranean, which could be carried out if additional landing craft could be made available.

In brief, the build-up of ground troops, air forces and equipment for OVERLORD was going according to schedule. Transfer of certain United States and British divisions from the Mediterranean to the United Kingdom was virtually complete[4] while discussions and problems were almost entirely related to landing craft. Voroshiloff said Brooke's and Marshall's information corresponded to the talks covering technical questions concerning OVERLORD.

It was hoped the ad hoc committee would deal with Italy, Yugoslavia, Turkey and southern France at the next meeting. Stalin asked who OVERLORD's commander was going to be. Roosevelt and Churchill said they had not decided yet. Stalin replied; "Then nothing will come out of these operations." Roosevelt replied they had decided on all the commanders except the Supreme Commander. Stalin asked who carried the moral and technical responsibility for this operation. Roosevelt and Churchill said General Morgan, the Chief of Staff to the Supreme Allied Commander (Designate)[5] was charged with the planning and preparations being made by a Combined US-British Staff. Stalin said Morgan might say everything was ready but the Supreme Commander might say he had not accom-

---

1   For example, the Nazis hid the formation of the Luftwaffe for two years, building planes for civilian purposes and training crews at flying and glider clubs.

2   Possibly referring to the Landing Ship Tank, which could carry eighteen 30-ton tanks or 22 × 25-ton tanks or 33 × 3-ton trucks and had berths for 217 men.

3   The addition of UTAH Beach added an extra division and extra landing craft to the invasion force. Extra landing craft would be obtained by postponing OVERLORD from 1 May to 1 June. The number of vehicles each division could take ashore during the assault also had to be cut to 2500.

4   Seven divisions were transferred.

5   COSSAC.

plished everything when he reported. There had to be one person in charge.[6] Churchill said His Majesty's Government had expressed its willingness to have OVERLORD undertaken under a United States commander. The United States would be concerned with the greatest part of the build-up, and this United States commander would have command in the field.[7]

Churchill said the British had large naval and air forces in the Mediterranean and they were under British command under the Allied Commander-in-Chief. The President and Prime Minister had not yet reached a decision regarding high command but decisions made at the conference would have a bearing on the choice. Therefore the President could name the Supreme Allied Commander for OVERLORD if he desired to accept the British orders to serve under a United States commander.[8]

Churchill also suggested giving Stalin an answer in confidence regarding the Supreme Allied Commander. Stalin did not want to take part in the selection of a commander for OVERLORD, he just wanted to know who he would be. He felt strongly he should be appointed as soon as possible and given responsibility for the OVERLORD preparations as well as the executive command of the operation. Churchill agreed and said an appointment would be made within a fortnight; he hoped it might be accomplished during the current meeting with the President.[9]

Churchill was concerned with the number and complexity of problems before the conference. He said the meeting was unique because the thoughts of more than 140 million people were centred upon it. He felt they should not separate until agreements on political, moral, and military problems had been reached. Churchill wished to present a few points which needed studying by a subcommittee. Both he and the British Staff had given long study to the Mediterranean position, where Great Britain had a large army. He wanted the British Mediterranean army to fight throughout 1944 and not be quiescent. He asked the Soviets to survey the field, examine the different alternatives put before them and then submit their recommendations.

Churchill asked what assistance the large Mediterranean force could give to OVERLORD. What were the possibilities of this force and what scale of operation could be launched from northern Italy into southern France? He did not feel such an operation had been studied in sufficient detail but he welcomed the opportunity to give it close examination. Churchill thought the US and UK staffs should consider the matter together, in the light of their knowledge of available resources. Stalin had stressed the value of pincer operations and said the timing for such operations was of great importance. A weak attack several months in

6   Stalin's point was that when the Supreme Commander took over, he might disagree with the plans made so far, resulting in delays.
7   General Eisenhower would be appointed Supreme Commander of the Allied Expeditionary Force (SCAEF) with Air Marshal Tedder as his deputy.
8   General Montgomery would return to the Britain in January 1944 to be commander of 21st Army Group, in command of all Allied ground forces during OVERLORD.
9   General Eisenhower was appointed on 23 December 1943.

advance might be defeated, allowing the enemy to turn his whole strength to meet the main attack.[1]

Churchill wanted landing craft to carry at least two divisions. With such an amphibious force it would be possible to do operations *seriatim*.[2] Firstly, an advance up the leg of Italy by amphibious turning movements,[3] possibly cutting off the enemy's withdrawal and capturing the entire German force in central Italy. Secondly, take Rhodes in conjunction with Turkey's entry into the war. Thirdly, attack the southern coast of France in six months time to assist OVERLORD.[4]

Churchill said none of the operations would be excluded but the timing would require careful study. This force of two divisions could not be supplied in the Mediterranean without setting back OVERLORD for six or eight weeks or without withdrawing landing craft from the Indian Ocean. This was one of the dilemmas the Anglo-American staffs had to balance in their minds. Churchill welcomed the views of Stalin and his officers because of his admiration for the military record of the Red Army. He suggested the military staffs continued studying these subjects.

Churchill said the second matter was political rather than military because of the small military forces involved. He referred to Yugoslavia and the Dalmatian Coast. There were 21 German divisions in the Balkans,[5] of which 54,000 troops were spread across the Aegean Islands.[6] There were also about 21 Bulgarian divisions; a total of 42 divisions in all.[7]

Churchill said if Turkey came into the war, the Bulgarian divisions would have to face the Turks on the Thrace front.[8] This withdrawal of Bulgarian divisions from the Balkans would leave the German divisions vulnerable to guerrilla operations. He did not suggest putting Anglo-American divisions into the Balkans; he proposed a continuous flow of supplies, frequent commando raids and air support.[9] Churchill felt it was short sighted to let the Germans crush Yugoslavia without giving those brave people now fighting under Tito weapons they might ask for. The Balkan operations would stretch the Germans, giving relief to the Russian front. The British had no exceptional or ambitious interests in the Balkans; all they wanted to do was to nail the 21 German divisions in the area and destroy them.

Roosevelt suggested sending all the aid they could to Tito without interfering with OVERLORD. They had to consider the value of the 40 German divisions in

---

1   If an early attack on the south coast was defeated, it would be a morale boost for Germany and would allow the German armed forces to concentrate on the northern landing.
2   Seriatim (Latin for in series) is a legal term used to indicate that multiple issues will be addressed in a certain order. In this case, a series of amphibious operations using the same landing craft and ships.
3   Amphibious landings behind the German lines, outflanking their defensive positions.
4   Keeping the landing craft busy throughout the winter of 1943 and into the spring of 1944.
5   Plus garrison troops.
6   The capitulation of Italy in September 1943 had left the Germans to garrison the Balkans alone and the guerrillas had taken advantage of the situation.
7   The Prime Minister later corrected these figures to indicate that there were 42 divisions in all, 12 of which were Bulgarian divisions in Bulgaria.
8   Thrace is the historical area which covers the southeast part of Bulgaria, the northeast coast of the Aegean Sea and the Turkish area on the northwest side of the Sea of Marmara.
9   The Balkan Air Force was formed in June 1944 to support SOE operations and Tito's guerrillas in Yugoslavia.

the Balkans and how they might no longer be of any value if they could do mini-mum effort operations.[10] Roosevelt felt commando raids should be undertaken and they should send all possible supplies to Tito, to keep the German divisions there. Stalin said the Germans only had eight divisions in Yugoslavia, five in Greece, and three or four in Bulgaria. The Prime Minister's figures were wrong.[11]

Churchill said the British were allies of Turkey and had accepted the responsi-bility of endeavouring to persuade or force Turkey into the war before Christmas. If the President would come in with the British or take the lead, it would be agreeable to him but he certainly wanted all possible help from the US and USSR. The British would go far in warning Turkey her failure to enter the war would jeopardize her political and territorial aspirations, particularly the Dardanelles, when they were discussed at the peace table. The military staffs had already dis-cussed the military aspects of Turkey's entry into the war but the question was largely political, since only two or three divisions were involved.[12] Churchill again asked how the USSR would feel about Bulgaria. Would they tell Bulgaria they would regard her as a foe if Turkey entered the war against Germany and Bulgaria helped Germany? Such a statement might have a great influence on Bulgaria's attitude because of her relationship with the Soviets.[13]

Churchill said Turkey had been an ally of Germany in the last war and it would have a profound effect on the remainder of the Balkans if she turned against her now. He pointed to Romania's desire to surrender unconditionally and other indications of unrest in the Balkans, as evidence Turkey's entry into the war would have a great effect. In conclusion, Churchill said the whole Mediterranean situation should be carefully examined to see what could be done to take the weight off the Soviet front.[14]

Stalin said as far as the question of the USSR versus Bulgaria was concerned, they could consider the matter closed when Turkey came into the war. The USSR would declare war on Bulgaria if Turkey declared war on Bulgaria but even then he believed Turkey would not enter the war.[15]

Stalin understood two or three divisions would be made available to help Turkey or help the partisan movement in Yugoslavia. There was no difference of opinion

---

10 In other words, forced to garrison the Balkans rather than fight on the Western or Eastern Front.
11 16 or 17 divisions rather than Churchill's 21.
12 Turkish divisions would not be deployed outside the country's borders.
13 Bulgaria joined the Axis in March 1941 and a month later joined the late stages of the invasion of Yugoslavia and Greece. It did not join the invasion of the Soviet Union in June, nor declare war on it. However, it was forced to declare war on Great Britain and the United States in December 1941. Bulgaria maintained diplomatic relations with the Soviet Union. When the Soviets crossed the Bulgarian border on 5 September 1944, its army was ordered not to resist; three days later Bulgaria switched to the Allied side.
14 By 1944 the Romanian economy was in tatters and by April the Soviet Armies were at its borders. They overran the border defences on 20 August and three days later King Michael I of Romania led a successful coup, with support from opposition politicians and the army. After an offer to retreat ahead of the German troops was refused, King Michael offered to turn the one-million-strong Romanian army over to the Allies, splitting the country's allegiances. Even so, the Soviets moved in so fast that 130,000 Romanian soldiers were captured and many died in captivity. The armistice was signed on 12 September.
15 The Soviet Union declared war on Bulgaria on 5 September and within three days had occupied the northeast part of the country, including the key ports of Varna and Burgas. The Bulgarian army offered no resistance and on 8 September joined the Soviet Union in the war on Germany.

on this point; they all wanted to help in Yugoslavia. But the Soviets did not think it was an important matter. Even the entry of Turkey into the war or the occupation of Rhodes was not the most important thing. Among all the military questions for discussion the USSR found OVERLORD the most important and decisive.

Churchill had one more word about Turkey. All were agreed she should enter the war but if she did not enter, that ended that. If she did enter, the only necessary thing to do would be to make an air attack from the Turkish bases in Anatolia[1] and an operation to take the Island of Rhodes. One assault division would be ready in the near future for the Rhodes operation and that would be sufficient.[2] Having occupied Rhodes and Turkish air bases, a course could be steered north and operations undertaken to drive and starve all German divisions out of the Aegean to open the Dardanelles.

Essentially, those specific operations were limited and could not be considered as military commitments of an indefinite character. If Turkey came into the war and they got the air bases, it would be a simple matter to open the Straits. If Turkey did not come in, they would not pay any further attention to the matter. If Turkey came into the war and they held Rhodes and the Aegean, they would be able to use the air squadrons based in Egypt where they were playing no part except defending the country. They could use the same troops guarding Egypt to drive the Germans back.

Churchill said they could all move forward and help the Soviets. It was a weighty matter and should not be considered lightly. Their future would suffer great misfortune if they did not get Turkey into the war, because troops and planes would stand idle. Stalin said it could not be helped if Turkey did not enter the war and Churchill replied he had no intention of asking for any troops for operations in Rhodes or Asia Minor if it did not.

Stalin wanted to call the attention of those present to the importance of not creating diversions from the most important operation to carry out secondary operations. He said the ad hoc committee[3] should be given a definite task to discuss. They always gave specific directive or instructions to a committee in the USSR. He said it was true the USSR needed help and that was why the Soviet representatives were at the conference. The Soviets expected help from those who were willing to fulfil OVERLORD.

Stalin asked what directive they would give to the ad hoc committee under General Brooke's guidance. First of all, the directive had to specify OVERLORD should not be postponed and must be carried out by the limiting date. Secondly, it should state OVERLORD must be reinforced by a landing in the south of France a month or two before the OVERLORD assault, or at the same time, or even a little later, depending on the available resources. Stalin thought that the

---

1 Anatolia is the western protrusion of Turkey, between the Black Sea to the north, the Aegean Sea to the west and the Mediterranean to the south.
2 The Italian garrison of the Dodecanese Islands (of which Rhodes is the largest) wanted to fight with the British or go home when Italy capitulated in September 1943. The Germans moved in fast to take over. The British attempt to seize the islands had ended in failure and Turkey had not been impressed.
3 The military representatives of the three nations.

operation in southern France would be an auxiliary or supporting operation and it would be considerably effective in contributing toward OVERLORD.[4] On the other hand, operations against Rhodes and other operations in the Mediterranean would be diversions, whereas operations in southern France would influence and contribute directly to OVERLORD.[5]

Churchill was not clear what the President's plans were but he was in favour of the continuance of the ad hoc committee if it could be done. Roosevelt then read a directive for the ad hoc committee:

1.   The committee will assume OVERLORD is the dominating operation.
2.   The committee recommends including a subsidiary operation in the Mediterranean, taking into consideration OVERLORD should not be delayed.

Stalin observed there was no mention regarding the date of OVERLORD. It was important for the USSR to know the date so the Soviets could prepare the blow on their side. He insisted on knowing the date.[6] Roosevelt replied it had been fixed at Quebec and only a much more important matter could possibly affect it.

Churchill believed they should take time drawing up a proper directive to the ad hoc committee. Roosevelt said his staff placed their emphasis on OVERLORD. While Churchill and his staff also emphasized OVERLORD, nevertheless the United States did not feel OVERLORD should be put off.

Roosevelt said if the three Chiefs of State were in agreement, the committee did not need a written directive because they had been confronted with every suggestion during the meeting. The staff would only have one directive if the Heads of State could agree on the conference proceedings.

Stalin said the ad hoc committee was unnecessary because it could not raise any new questions for the military conference. All there was left to do was select the commander and set the date for OVERLORD and agree on the supporting operation in southern France. He also approved of Churchill's proposal for a committee of Foreign Secretaries; the three of them could solve all matters.

Roosevelt asked if the ad hoc committee could go ahead with their deliberations without any further directive and produce an answer by tomorrow morning. Stalin questioned, "What can such a committee do? We Chiefs of State have more power and more authority than a committee. General Brooke cannot force our opinions and there are many questions which can be decided only by us."

Roosevelt said the directive had to state the Supreme Commander for OVERLORD would be appointed immediately. The decision should be made in Tehran but if not, it had to be done within a week at the latest. The Soviets

---

4   The Allied planners wanted to cancel ANVIL (later DRAGOON) as OVERLORD drew closer, owing to the shortage of landing craft. Roosevelt had to remind them he had made a pledge to carry out an invasion of southern France at the EUREKA conference. Eventually, OVERLORD was postponed by a month and DRAGOON took place five weeks later.

5   The landing would divert German ground and air forces away from northern France, forcing Army Group G to abandon southern France. On 10 September, the two Allied thrusts would meet in central France, cutting off 130,000 German troops in western France.

6   Stalin wanted to know so his armed forces could prepare for a summer offensive timed to coincide with the invasion of France, making it impossible for the Germans to concentrate their reserves on one front.

believed the organization of OVERLORD could not be expected to be a success until a commander had been appointed. Stalin added the USSR did not want to enter into the matter of selection but they definitely wanted to know who he would be. Stalin asked the conference to seriously consider his three points so OVERLORD would be successfully and rapidly accomplished.

Roosevelt was tremendously interested in hearing all angles of the subject, from OVERLORD to Turkey. If they are all agreed on OVERLORD, the next question would be the timing. The point was either to carry out OVERLORD at the appointed time or to agree to a postponement to some time in June or July. There were only one or two other operations in the Mediterranean that might use landing craft and air forces from some other theatre. Roosevelt warned that the use of two or three divisions in the eastern Mediterranean would delay OVERLORD and involve using landing craft for those operations, which could not be returned in time. Once they were committed to specific operations in the eastern Mediterranean, they would have to make it a supreme operation and they might not be able to pull out of it. Stalin said it might be necessary to utilize some equipment planned for OVERLORD to carry out operations in the eastern Mediterranean. Nothing would come out of the proposed diversions.

Roosevelt returned to the problem of OVERLORD's timing. It was believed it would be good for OVERLORD to take place about 1 May, or certainly not later than 15 May or 20 May, if possible. Churchill disagreed. In his opinion, OVERLORD should be done in May when there was suitable weather. Churchill considered the timing of OVERLORD in relation to any subsidiary operations would be most necessary as a condition for the success of OVERLORD. Furthermore, he believed the ad hoc staff committee should recommend what subsidiary operations should be carried out.

Churchill said their attitudes were not very far apart and he was going to do everything in the power of His Majesty's Government to begin OVERLORD at the earliest possible moment. However, he did not think the many great possibilities in the Mediterranean should be ruthlessly cast aside as valueless merely on the question of a month's delay in OVERLORD. Stalin said all the Mediterranean operations were diversions and he had no interest in any operations other than one into southern France. He accepted the importance of these other operations but definitely considered them as diversions. Churchill said their large armies in the Mediterranean should not be idle for six months but they should be, together with the United States, working toward the defeat of Germany in Italy and elsewhere. For the British to be inert for nearly six months would be a wrong use of forces and it would lay them open to reproach from the Soviets for letting them bear nearly all the burden of land fighting. Stalin did not want the British to think the Soviets wished them to do nothing.[1]

Churchill said if all the landing craft were taken away from the Mediterranean they would not affect the battle. Stalin had to remember the conditions under

---

1 Churchill is concerned about the British reputation and wanting a continuous contribution to the war effort. Britain would be in a poor position at the end of the war if its armies remained idle for lengthy periods.

which OVERLORD could be mounted were stated at Moscow and it would be launched under those conditions alone. OVERLORD was predicated on the assumption no more than 12 German mobile divisions would be located behind the coastal troops and no more than 15 reinforcement divisions could enter the fray within 60 days.[2] That was the basis on which he had stated the British would undertake OVERLORD. The Allies had to utilize as many divisions as necessary in the Balkans and other areas to contain German troops.[3] If Turkey came into the war, this would be particularly necessary.[4]

Stalin said there were 25 German divisions in France. Roosevelt replied they had to work out plans to contain them and on such a scale that did not divert means from OVERLORD. Stalin responded, "You are right, you are right." The German divisions in Italy had largely come from France and if there was a slackening off in Italy, they would withdraw and appear in southern France.[5] On the other hand, if they conducted operations in the eastern Mediterranean, they would contain more German divisions and create conditions indispensable to the success of OVERLORD.

Stalin asked "What if there were 13 divisions, not 12?" Churchill replied "Naturally." Stalin asked if the British were seriously thinking of OVERLORD only in order to satisfy the USSR. Churchill replied if the conditions specified at Moscow regarding OVERLORD should exist, he firmly believed it would be England's duty to hurl every ounce of strength she had across the Channel at the Germans.

Stalin asked how many French divisions were in the Allied Armies. Roosevelt understood there were five combat divisions and four more would be ready soon. Some were already engaged in Sardinia and Corsica. Marshall said the French Corps was to become a part of the US Fifth Army in Italy and it would occupy the left flank.[6] One division was en route to the front and would get a trial of battle. It would then be possible to judge how to employ the rest of the French divisions. All their equipment was in North Africa but there was some delay in bringing up to strength and completing the training of four or five divisions. The French divisions were training with US equipment and under the instruction of US officers and non-commissioned officers.

Stalin asked how many men were in these French divisions. Marshall replied the same number of men as the United States, 15,000 men per division. The men were mostly native troops with French officers and some non-coms. In the armoured command only one quarter were native troops.

Churchill agreed the chief problem was one of transportation across the water and it was largely a question of landing craft. The British were prepared to go into

2   The British would not agree to OVERLORD until the number of German divisions and the number of reinforcements had been reduced to a low level.
3   Churchill's desire to carry out Mediterranean operations has two motives. It keeps the British troops engaged in that area and draws German divisions away from the main offensive, OVERLORD.
4   The Allies could move divisions into Turkey to threaten the Thrace area, possibly diverting more German divisions from France.
5   Despite the difficult terrain and weather, the Allies had to keep the pressure on in Italy to hold the German divisions there.
6   The French Corps had 112,000 troops, 60 per cent of them North African troops. They were commanded by General Alphonse Juin (1888–1967). It was engaged in the First Battle of Monte Cassino in January 1944 and the breaking of the Gustav Line in May 1944; 31,500 were casualties.

the matter in great detail because a very small number of landing craft could make the subsidiary operations feasible. The technical committee should resolve the matter if they could not be kept in the Mediterranean because of OVERLORD, or could not be found from some other arrangement, such as the Indian Ocean. A landing in southern France required a great number of landing craft. Churchill said this important point should be carefully considered and accepted they had to draw up a directive for the technical committee.

Churchill suggested their three governments should draw up terms of reference and then he felt sure they would not be far apart. Roosevelt asked if the conference could be in session long enough for the staff to come to a conclusion on these matters. Churchill could give his own opinion on behalf of the British Government later that evening. Stalin asked how many more days the conference would continue. Roosevelt was willing to stay until the conference was finished. Churchill said he would stay there forever, if necessary, but he would be very glad to stay until 1 December and make a decision. Stalin had to leave on 1 December but he might stay until the 2nd if it had to be, then he must leave. He had to know when he could get away and Roosevelt would remember he had said he could come to the conference for three or four days.

The President said a very good dinner would be awaiting them in an hour and people would be very hungry. He suggested the Staffs could meet in the morning. Stalin believed it was unnecessary. The Staffs would not speed their work; they would only delay matters. It was proper to decide matters quicker. Marshal Stalin commented, "Then at 4.00 p.m. tomorrow we will have our conference again?" The President suggested the Heads of State had luncheon the following day.

29 November: Tripartite Dinner Meeting

The most notable feature of the dinner was Stalin's attitude towards Churchill; he lost no opportunity to jibe indirectly. Almost every remark addressed to the Prime Minister contained some sharp edge, although the Marshal's manner was entirely friendly. He apparently desired to put and then keep the Prime Minister on the defensive. On one occasion, he told Churchill just because Russians were simple people, it was a mistake to believe they were blind and could not see what was before their eyes.

Regarding the future treatment of Germans, Stalin strongly implied Churchill nursed a secret affection for Germany and desired to see a soft peace on several occasions. Stalin was obviously teasing him over his attitude during the afternoon session. He was also making known in a friendly fashion his displeasure at the British attitude on OVERLORD.[1]

Following Hopkins' toast to the Red Army, Stalin spoke with great frankness about the past and present capacity of the Red Army.[2] The Soviet Army had done very badly in the winter war against Finland and the entire army had been

---

1   The criteria Churchill laid down on the number of German divisions.
2   Stalin did not mention the Great Purge of 1937-1939, which removed three of five marshals, 13 of 15 army commanders, eight of nine admirals, 50 of 57 corps commanders and 154 of 186 division commanders. 30,000 officers were executed.

reorganized.[3] Even so, it could not be said the Red Army was a first class fighting force when the Germans attacked in 1941.[4] During the war with Germany, the Red Army had become steadily better from the point of view of operations and tactics and now he felt it was genuinely a good army.[5] The general opinion towards the Red Army had been wrong, because it was not believed the Soviet Army could reorganize and improve itself during time of war.

Stalin developed his ideas over the future treatment of Germany, namely, really effective measures to control Germany must be evolved or it would rise again within 15 or 20 years and plunge the world into another war. Two conditions had to be met:

1) At least 50,000 and perhaps 100,000 of the German Command Staff must be physically liquidated.

2) The victorious Allies must retain possession of the important strategic points in the world, so Germany could be rapidly stopped if she moved a muscle.

Roosevelt jokingly said he would put the figure of the German Commanding Staff which should be executed at 49,000 or more. Churchill took strong exception to what he termed the cold-blooded execution of soldiers who had fought for their country. He said war criminals must pay for their crimes and individuals who had committed barbarous acts had to stand trial at the places where the crimes were committed.[6] Churchill objected vigorously to executions for political purposes.[7]

Stalin said similar strong points now in the hands of Japan should remain in the hands of the Allies. Roosevelt said those bases and strong points close to Germany and Japan had to be held under trusteeship. Stalin agreed. Churchill stated Britain did not desire to acquire any new territory or bases, but intended to hold on to what she had. Nothing would be taken away from England without a war and specifically mentioned Singapore and Hong Kong. He said a portion of the British Empire might eventually be released but this would be done entirely by Great Britain herself, in accordance with her own moral precepts.[8] Great Britain might occupy certain bases under trusteeship, if asked to do so, provided others helped to pay for the occupation.

---

3   The Winter War lasted from 30 November 1939 to 13 March 1940. The Soviet forces had three times as many soldiers, 30 times as many aircraft, and 100 times as many tanks but their leaders were inexperienced. The highly motivated Finns inflicted heavy casualties on the Soviet troops.

4   Again, Stalin does not mention the Purge of 1940-1942 when the NKVD arrested, tortured and executed many senior officers. The German offensive steamrollered its way through the Soviet lines, cutting off and capturing tens of thousands of men; many of them were executed or worked to death in captivity.

5   The Soviet army suffered badly in BARBAROSSA. It was poorly led, partially mobilized and still in the process of reorganization. Many more officers were arrested and executed when their troops failed. Around 300 were executed on 16 October 1941 alone during the Battle of Moscow.

6   In accordance with the Moscow Document he had written.

7   During this part of the conversation Stalin continuously referred to Churchill's secret liking for the Germans.

8   For example, the Indian National Congress had been pushing for independence before the war and it resumed its final push for non-cooperation once it was over. A rise in Muslim nationalism was followed by a bloody partition and the formation of Pakistan following India's independence in 1947; 12.5 million people were displaced and tens of thousands killed.

Stalin replied England had fought well in the war and he, personally, favoured an increase in the British Empire, particularly the area around Gibraltar.[1] He also suggested Great Britain and the United States install more suitable governments in Spain and Portugal, since he was convinced Franco was no friend of Great Britain or the United States.

Churchill asked what territorial interests the Soviet Union had and Stalin replied "There is no need to speak at the present time about any Soviet desires, but when the time comes, we will speak."

Although the discussion between Stalin and Churchill remained friendly, the arguments were lively and Stalin did not let up on the Prime Minister all evening.

30 November
First Combined Chiefs of Staff Meeting[2]
OVERLORD date; a second landing in southern France; Mediterranean amphibious operations; Landing craft.

The President and the Shah of Iran
The Iranian economy and the US desire to aid the economy.

30 November: Tripartite Lunch
Roosevelt read the approved recommendations of the combined British and American Staffs before lunch. Stalin expressed his great satisfaction with this decision.[3] The Red Army would undertake offensive operations at the same time and would demonstrate by its actions the value it placed on this decision.

Stalin asked when the Commander-in-Chief would be named. Roosevelt had to consult his Staff but he was sure he would be named in three or four days, in other words immediately following his and the Prime Minister's return to Cairo. Roosevelt had to discuss a number of questions with Churchill, including under whose command the southern France operations would fall.[4] The OVERLORD Commander-in-Chief would operate from England and there would be a Commander-in-Chief for the Mediterranean area. Churchill interrupted to say the southern France operations should be under the Commander-in-Chief of OVERLORD.[5] The Italy operations, which had been intensified to coordinate with the operations in France, would be under the Commander-in-Chief of the Mediterranean Theatre. Stalin agreed and said it was sound military doctrine.

General conversation followed until Churchill asked Stalin whether he had read the proposed communiqué on the Far East. Stalin replied he had and although he could make no commitments he thoroughly approved it. It was right

---

1   To secure the entrance of the Mediterranean from Franco's Spain.
2   Just the US and British Chiefs of Staff.
3   The launching of OVERLORD in May 1944.
4   Southern Group or Dragoon Force would form in Corsica and be commanded by Lieutenant General Jacob L. Devers (1887-1979), nickname Jake. It would later be called 6th Army Group.
5   6th Army Group was subordinate to General Henry Wilson's Mediterranean Command to begin with. It would come under General Eisenhower's SHAEF command when it linked with 12th Army Group near Dijon, France, on 15 September 1944.

Korea[6] should be independent and that Manchuria,[7] Formosa[8] and the Pescadores Islands[9] should be returned to China. However, the Chinese had to be made to fight, which they had not done so far. Churchill and Roosevelt agreed.

After some discussion of the great size of the Soviet Union, during which Stalin admitted frankly that Russia's vast territory had stopped Germans from winning the victory, Churchill said such a large land mass as Russia deserved access to warm water ports. He said the question would of course form part of the peace settlement and it could be settled agreeably between friends.

Stalin replied the question could be discussed at the proper time but since Mr. Churchill had raised the question he would like to ask about the Dardanelles. Since England no longer objected, it would be well to relax that regime. Churchill replied England had no objections to Russia's access to warm water ports, although it had in the past.[10] He questioned the advisability of doing anything about the Straits while they were all trying to get Turkey to enter the war. Stalin said there was no need to hurry the question; he was merely interested in discussing it.

Churchill said Great Britain saw no objections to this legitimate question and they all hoped to see Russian fleets, both naval and merchant, on all seas of the world. Stalin said Lord Curzon had other ideas.[11] Churchill replied that was true and it would be idle to deny that Russia and England did not see eye to eye in those days. Stalin said Russia also was quite different in those days.

Roosevelt reverted to the question of the approaches to the Baltic Sea. He liked the idea of making the former Hanseatic cities[12] of Bremen, Hamburg and Lübeck into some form of a free zone, with the Kiel Canal under international control and guaranty, with free passage for the world's commerce. Stalin thought it was a good idea and asked what could be done for Russia in the Far East. Churchill replied it was for this reason he had been particularly glad to hear Stalin's views on the Cairo communiqué, since he was interested to find out the views of the Soviet government on the Far East and the question of warm water ports there.

---

6   At the end of the war Soviet troops occupied the area north of the 38th Parallel, while US troops occupied the area south of it. Korea remained divided because the two countries could not agree on the terms of Korean independence. They installed governments in line with their own ideologies.

7   After the atomic bombing of Hiroshima, the Soviet Union attacked Japan from Soviet Outer Manchuria. The Chinese communists and nationalists then fought for the control of Manchuria and the communists won and took control. With Soviet encouragement, Manchuria was used as a staging ground by the Communist Party of China during the Chinese Civil War; it emerged victorious in 1949.

8   Formosa (Portuguese for Beautiful), now Taiwan. Taiwan is officially the Republic of China (as opposed to the People's Republic of China the PRC), the last stronghold of the ROC following the Chinese Civil War.

9   The Penghu Islands, or Pescadores (from the Portuguese for fishermen) are off the west coast of Taiwan.

10 The Soviet Union's northern and eastern ports froze during the winter, making trade seasonal.

11 George Curzon, 1st Marquess of Curzon of Kedleston (1859-1925), Secretary of State for Foreign Affairs (1919-1924) had believed Russia was a threat to India and wanted Britain to make Iran a client state and use it as a buffer. His idea was rejected because Russia had the geographical advantage and the cost was too high.

12 Several cities along the northern Europe coast were part of the Hanseatic League to enhance their trading status. The League was formed to protect economic interests and diplomatic privileges. The cities were independent and had their own legal system and armies.

Stalin said the Russians had their views but it would better to wait until the Russians were actively represented in the Far Eastern war. However, all the ports in the Far East were closed off, since Vladivostok was only partly ice-free, while the Japanese controlled the Straits.

Roosevelt thought the idea of a free port might be applied to the Far East and mentioned Dairen[1] as a possibility. Stalin did not think the Chinese would like such a scheme and Roosevelt replied they would like the idea of a free port under international guaranty. Stalin said that would not be bad and Petropavlovsk on Kamchatka[2] was an excellent ice-free port but it had no rail connections. Russia had only one ice-free port, that of Murmansk.

Churchill said it was important the nations who would govern the world after the war, and who would be entrusted with the direction of the world, should be satisfied and have no territorial or other ambitions. He felt the world might indeed remain at peace if that question could be settled in an agreeable manner. Hungry nations and ambitious nations were dangerous and he wanted to see the leading nations of the world in the position of rich, happy men. Roosevelt and Stalin agreed.[3]

Foreign Ministers Meeting[4]
Future control of strongpoints and bases around the world; Bringing Turkey into the war; Yugoslavia; OVERLORD.

30 November: Third Eureka Meeting
Roosevelt assumed most of those present were familiar with what had transpired at the meeting of the British and American staffs earlier in the day. He suggested General Brooke read the conclusions of the meeting. Brooke said the British and American staffs recommended that Roosevelt and Churchill inform Stalin that the Anglo-American forces would launch OVERLORD during May. It would be in conjunction with a supporting operation against the south of France, on the largest scale permitted by the landing craft available at that time.

Churchill said they would keep in close touch with Stalin and the Soviet military authorities so operations could be coordinated.[5] The Anglo-American-Soviet forces would be closing in on Germany from all sections of a circle and it was essential they all exerted the pressure at the same moment. Churchill proposed to keep the Soviet authorities informed of the Anglo-American plans. It would be possible to hold eight to ten German divisions on the Italian front and he hoped the Yugoslavs could continue their good work in holding German divisions in

---

1   Dairen, now Dalian, is in Liaoning province, Northeast China. It has the Yellow Sea to the east and the Bohai Sea to the west and south.
2   Petropavlovsk-Kamchatsky is at the end of the peninsula between the Sea of Okhotsk and the Bering Sea.
3   Only six months after the end of the war, another war was brewing – the Cold War. By September 1946 the United States had decided to maintain an indefinite military presence in Europe.
4   Mr. Hopkins, US; Mr. Eden, Great Britain; Mr. Molotov, Soviet Union.
5   The Soviets launched a large attack against the Finnish lines across the Karelian Isthmus (which separates the Gulf of Finland from Lake Ladoga) on 9 June 1944, coordinated with the Allied Invasion of Normandy.

their country. If Turkey could be brought into the war, so much the better. He again emphasized the need for the three great powers to work together as a team.

Stalin understood the importance of the Anglo-American staffs' decision. He emphasized there would be difficulties in the beginning and dangers. The greatest danger would be from the Germans endeavouring to transfer divisions from the Eastern Front. In order to deny the Germans freedom of action and stop them moving their forces to the West, the Soviets would undertake to organise a large-scale offensive against the Germans in May, to contain the maximum number of German divisions on the Eastern Front. He had already made such a statement but felt it was necessary to repeat it.[6]

Roosevelt said Stalin's statement concerning the timing and coordination of operations was extremely satisfactory. He suggested it was essential the staffs of the three nations maintained close contact with each other now they were together. There had to be particular emphasis on making certain all future operations were timed with relation to each other.

Roosevelt had told Stalin the next step was the appointment of the Supreme Commander for OVERLORD. He and the Prime Minister would take up this matter with their staffs and make the decision within three or four days, certainly soon after their arrival in Cairo.[7]

Roosevelt said the only military matters remaining for consideration were the OVERLORD's details to be worked out between the combined British and American staffs. He suggested it might be more convenient for them to return immediately to Cairo for this purpose. Stalin understood the need for detailed staff planning and as he had nothing more to give them, Roosevelt and Churchill agreed they would return to Cairo the following day.

Churchill said there were many details to settle about OVERLORD. Landing craft had to be found, but he could not believe the two nations, with their great volume of production, could not make them available. He also wanted to add weight to the operation, especially in the initial assault.

Churchill wished to make sure the armed forces of the three nations would be in heavy action on the continent of Europe during the month of June; making it very difficult for "that man".[8] If Hitler attempted to meet the Soviet attack from the east, the Anglo-American forces will move in on him. On the other hand, if he attempted to stop the Anglo-American forces, the Soviet forces would be able to advance into Germany.

Churchill said the military business of the conference was concluded but there were some political matters of extreme importance to be decided. He hoped the three Heads of State could meet on 1 and 2 December and not leave Tehran until

---

6   The Soviets actually launched their largest summer offensive, codename BAGRATION, on 22 June 1944. Four Soviet army groups, totalling over 120 divisions, smashed Army Group Centre and in places advanced over 300 miles to the pre-war Polish border.

7   The decision to choose General Eisenhower rather than General Marshall was not taken until the winter. Eisenhower was appointed Supreme Commander Allied Expeditionary Force (SCAEF) in December 1943.

8   Adolf Hitler. Following the German invasion of the Soviet Union in June 1941, Churchill said in the House: "If Hitler invaded Hell I would make at least a favourable reference to the devil in the House of Commons."

3 December. It would be well if they remained until all the important questions had been decided. He was prepared to delay his departure and both Roosevelt and Stalin agreed to stay the extra day.

Roosevelt brought up the subject of the communiqué, particularly as it referred to the military decisions. He suggested the military staffs draft something for his and Churchill's approval. Stalin agreed. Churchill thought the communiqué should strike the note that all future military operations were to be concerted between the three great powers. Stalin said particularly those in Europe, from both the east and west.

Churchill said the preparations for OVERLORD were bound to be known to the enemy. Numerous depots were being constructed in southern England, the entire appearance of the coast was changing and photographs indicated these changes in detail. Stalin said it was difficult, if not impossible, to hide such a large operation from the enemy.[1]

Churchill asked if any arrangements had been made to provide a combined cover plan for the operations in May between the three great powers. Stalin said the Soviets had achieved success by the construction of false tanks, aircraft and airfields. They moved these items to sectors where no operations were being planned and German intelligence immediately picked up the movements.[2]

All movements were made quietly and mostly under cover of darkness in sectors where the blows were to be launched and they often succeeded in deceiving the Germans. At times up to 5000 false tanks and 2000 dummy aircraft had been used, and they constructed airfields they did not intend to use. Another method of deception practised by the Red Army was by the use of radio. Unit commanders communicated freely by radio giving the Germans false information and induced immediate attacks from the German air forces where they could do no harm.

Churchill said truth deserved a bodyguard of lies and Stalin replied "This is what we call military cunning." Churchill would rather call it military diplomacy. He suggested arrangements be made for liaison among the three great powers regarding the deception and propaganda methods to be adopted.[3] The conference:

1) Agreed the partisans in Yugoslavia should be supported by supplies and equipment to the greatest possible extent, and also by commando operations.

2) Agreed it was most desirable Turkey should come into the war on the side of the Allies before the end of the year.

---

1   FORTITUDE was the military deception plan to make the Germans think that the Allies were going to invade Norway (FORTITUDE NORTH) or the Calais area (FORTITUDE SOUTH). Fake infrastructure, controlled information leaks, wireless traffic, agents and the appearance of General George S. Patton, commander of the phantom 1st US Army Group (FUSAG) in the relevant areas.

2   There was plenty of activity in Kent to make the Germans believe the attack was going to be made against the Pas de Calais.

3   FORTITUDE was so successful that Hitler believed the invasion of Normandy was a feint and kept troops and armour in the Calais area.

3) Took note that if Turkey found herself at war with Germany and Bulgaria declared war on Turkey, the Soviet Union would immediately be at war with Bulgaria. This fact could be explicitly stated in the negotiations to bring Turkey into the war.

4) Took note that OVERLORD would be launched during May 1944, in conjunction with an operation against southern France in as great strength as the availability of landing craft permitted.[4]

5) Took note that Soviet forces would attack about the same time with the object of preventing the German forces from transferring from the Eastern to the Western Front.

6) Agreed the military staffs of the three Powers should keep in close touch with each other regarding the impending operations in Europe. It was agreed a cover plan to mystify and mislead the enemy as regards these operations should be determined between the staffs concerned.

30 November: Churchill's Birthday Dinner

Thirty-three members of the American, British and Russian delegations gathered for dinner on the occasion of Mr. Churchill's 69th birthday. It was clear those present had a sense that a historic understanding had been reached and this conception was brought out in the statements and speeches. Above all was the feeling that basic friendships had been established and there was every reason to believe they would endure. This strong feeling of optimism appeared to be based on the realization if the three nations went forward together, there was real hope for a better world future and their own most vital interests dictated such a policy. All the speeches took the form of toasts, following the Russian custom.

Roosevelt opened the proceedings with the first toast, and proposed the traditional toast to the King instead of the host. Roosevelt said that as an old friend of King George he had asked Mr. Churchill for the privilege of offering the toast. Churchill then paid a warm official and personal tribute to the President, whom he characterized as a man who had devoted his entire life to the cause of defending the weak and helpless, and to the promotion of the great principles that underlay their democratic civilizations. After a toast to Stalin, he said he was worthy to stand with the great figures of Russian history and merited the title of 'Stalin the Great'. Roosevelt spoke of his long admiration for Churchill and his joy in the friendship which had developed between them in the midst of their common efforts in this war.

Stalin said the honours which had been paid to him really belonged to the Russian people; it was easy to be a hero or a great leader, if one had to do it with people such as the Russians. The Red Army had fought heroically but the Russian people would have tolerated no other quality from their armed forces. Even persons of medium courage and cowards became heroes in Russia. Those who did not were killed.

---

4   DRAGOON would take place on 15 August, five-and-a-half weeks after the Normandy invasion.

Churchill spoke of the great responsibility resting on the three men who had the power to command some 30 million armed men, as well as the vast number of men and women who stood behind these men in their work in fields and factories. In a personal toast to Roosevelt, Churchill believed the President's courage and foresight in acting in 1933 prevented a revolution in the United States.[1] He expressed his admiration for the way the President had guided his country along the "tumultuous stream of party friction and internal politics amidst the violent freedoms of democracy".

Among the many toasts of the evening was one by Roosevelt to General Brooke. Stalin stood with the others but held his glass in his hand and after the others had drunk stayed on his feet. He wished to join in the toast of General Brooke, but wished to make certain observations. Acknowledging the General's greatness, Stalin said, with a twinkle in his eye, he regretted Sir Alan was unfriendly to the Soviet Union, and adopted a grim and distrustful attitude towards the Russians. He drank the General's health in the hope that General Brooke "would come to know us better and would find that we are not so bad after all".

Some time later, in reply to Stalin, General Brooke rose and with some stiffness of manner declared the Marshal had made note of the means used by the Russians in deceiving the enemy on the Eastern front. For the greater part of the war, Great Britain had adopted cover plans to deceive the enemy, and it was possible Stalin had mistaken the dummy tanks and aircraft for the real operations. Stalin interrupted dryly, "That is possible," bringing chuckles around the table. Brooke's real desire was to establish closer collaboration with the Russians. "That is possible, even probable," replied Stalin. And there were more chuckles. It was thought General Brooke would end with a toast to Marshal Voroshilov, but he proposed Admiral Leahy's health instead.

Churchill tried to soften the effect of the incident. In a subsequent toast he said he heard the suggestions concerning changing political complexions in the world. He could not speak with authority about the American people's political view in the coming year's elections and he would not discuss the changing political philosophy of the Russian nation. But as far as the British people were concerned, he could say very definitely their "complexions are becoming a trifle pinker".[2] Stalin spoke up instantly: "That is a sign of good health!"

In the concluding toast of the evening, Churchill referred to the great progress made towards the solution of world affairs and proposed a joint toast to Roosevelt and Stalin. But before the dinner broke up, Stalin requested the privilege of one more toast and Churchill nodded assent. Stalin wished to speak of the importance of "the machine" in the present war and expressed his great admiration for the produc-

---

1   Roosevelt entered office on 4 March 1933 and during his first 100 days his administration introduced major legislation and issued executive orders called the New Deal. The variety of programs known as the 3 Rs were designed to produce Relief (through government jobs for the unemployed), Recovery (through economic growth) and Reform (through regulation of Wall Street the banks and transportation). The economy improved rapidly from 1933 to 1937 before relapsing into a deep recession.

2   Churchill's Conservative Party was beaten by Clement Attlee's (1883-1967) Labour Party in the July 1945 landslide election. It took place during the Terminal Conference in Potsdam.

tive capacity of the United States. He had been told the United States would very soon be producing 10,000 planes every month. This compared with 2500 to 3000 planes the Soviet Union was able to produce, after making every effort to speed the task, and there were a similar number of planes being produced monthly by Great Britain. Stalin said the war would have been lost without these American planes. He expressed his gratitude and that of the Russian people for Roosevelt's great leadership, which had developed the great production of war machines and made possible their delivery to Russia. He wound up with a warm toast to the President.

Roosevelt said these meetings had raised their hopes the future would find a better world, an ordered world in which the ordinary citizen would be assured the possibility of peaceful toil and the just enjoyment of the fruits of their labours.

"There has been discussion here tonight of our varying colours of political complexion. I like to think of this in terms of the rainbow. In our country the rainbow is a symbol of good fortune and of hope. It has many colours, each individualistic, but blending into one glorious whole. Thus with our nations, we have differing customs and philosophies and ways of life. Each of us works out our scheme of things according to the desires and ideas of our own peoples. But we have proved the varying ideals of our nations can come together in a harmonious whole, moving together for the common good of ourselves and of the world. So as we leave this historic gathering, we can see in the sky, for the first time, that traditional symbol of hope, the rainbow."

1 December: Tripartite Luncheon Meeting

The telegram[3] inviting the President of Turkey to meet Roosevelt and Churchill in Cairo over the next few days was agreed. Mr. Hopkins said it was essential to agree what form of military assistance could be given to Turkey if she agreed to enter the war before they met the Turkish President. Roosevelt agreed and said the American staff had not worked out anything.

Churchill only intended to offer the Turks 20 fighter squadrons and three anti-aircraft regiments; he did not intend to offer any land forces. Stalin said if Turkey entered the war, only the air force and anti-aircraft force mentioned would be made available. Churchill agreed and spoke of the great assistance the Turkish air bases would be to the Allied cause, with the possibility of continual bombing of the Ploesti oil fields.

Churchill only wanted landing craft for the assault on the Island of Rhodes, a temporary operation in March 1944. Roosevelt said the problem was the number of landing craft in the Mediterranean; how many would be needed for the Italian, southern France and northern France operations, as well as the Indian Ocean operations? Roosevelt wanted advice on the subject, as he did not know whether it would be possible to sandwich an Aegean operation between the Italian and OVERLORD operations.

Churchill repeated he had made no promises to Turkey and would make none beyond the aircraft and anti-aircraft units. If the Turkish President was unable to

---

3   To be sent to the British and American Ambassadors in Ankara to deliver orally to the President of Turkey.

come to Cairo, he proposed to go to Ankara. He would present to him the ugly case resulting from the failure of Turkey to accept the invitation to join the war, and the unappetizing picture of what help could be afforded her if she did.

Hopkins said the US Chiefs of Staff had not yet considered the requirements of the Turkish operation. The whole of the Mediterranean would soon to come under the Combined Chiefs of Staff and the resources had to be examined in the light of that fact. They had to understand clearly the American side believed there were no landing craft available for an attack on Rhodes – and more important still – even if the landing craft were available, no decision had been made whether or not they could not be used to better advantage in some other operation. It had to be clearly understood no mention of an amphibious landing on Rhodes could be made to President Inonu, implied or otherwise.

Churchill thought they could have the information within three days; before meeting the Turkish President. Landing craft were the bottleneck and it might be possible to divert some from the Pacific Theatre. The only thing certain was OVERLORD must not suffer. Roosevelt said it was absolutely impossible to withdraw any landing craft from the Southwest Pacific. The distance alone from the Mediterranean made it impossible and all the landing craft were urgently needed for the operations in the Gilbert and Marshall Islands, and for the Burma campaign.

Mr. Eden then said he had only asked for bases when he spoke to the Turkish Foreign Minister in November in Cairo; he had made no mention of any assistance other than the air squadrons. He had said Turkey could make the bases available to the Allies without being attacked by Germany but the Foreign Minister disagreed.

Churchill repeated the advantages of acquiring bases in Turkey, as it would permit healthy battles with the German Air Force in that region and probably starve out the German garrisons on the Aegean Islands. It might not even be necessary to take Rhodes by assault. Stalin agreed and felt the German garrisons would be so demoralized following the loss of air superiority they would be easy prey. However, he thought bombers would be necessary for any such operations.

Roosevelt was in favour of meeting the Turkish Prime Minister but he did not intend to promise amphibious operations to Turkey and commitments should be confined to air forces. Churchill summed up the advantages to Turkey which would accrue if she accepted the invitation to join the war, particularly the possibility of sitting alongside the Soviet Union at the peace table.

Stalin said if Turkey declared war on Germany and Bulgaria, or if Bulgaria attacked or went to war with Turkey, the Soviet Union would break relations or declare war on Bulgaria. He asked what other assistance would be required of the Soviet Union. Churchill asked for nothing more but if the Soviet Armies approached Bulgaria, the pro-German Bulgarian circles would be greatly fearful.

Stalin asked what the Turkish Army lacked in the way of armaments. Churchill replied it was a good army at the end of the last war but then they had seen the modern Bulgarian equipment received from French arsenals, and realized their army was not a modern one. They had brave infantry but lacked anti-tank guns,

1. Churchill and Roosevelt smile for the cameras during the Symbol Conference.

2. Churchill and Roosevelt during the Trident Conference.

3. Churchill preparing to make a speech at the Quadrant Conference.

4. MacKenzie King, Churchill, Roosevelt and Field Marshal Dill at the Quadrant Conference.

5. All smiles during Churchill's 69th birthday party at the Eureka Conference.

6. The Big Three after the Eureka Conference.

7. The Big Three at the Yalta Conference, Roosevelt fading.

8. Representatives of the Pacific War Council.

9. Montgomery welcomes Churchill and Brooke to Normandy a few days after D-Day.

10. Generals Arnold, Eisenhower, Marshall and Bradley with Admiral King somewhere in France.

11. Churchill arriving for the Potsdam Conference.

12. Churchill, Truman and Stalin, the latter apparently in convivial mood.

13. Terminal: British delegation top left; American delegation bottom left; Soviet delegation, right.

14. The Foreign Ministers at Potsdam; Molotov (Soviet), Byrnes (American) and Eden (British).

15. Attlee takes his place alongside Truman and Stalin at the end of the Terminal Conference.

16. The Potsdam Conference table, where the future of the world was decided.

anti-aircraft and aircraft. £25 million[1] of military equipment, mostly American, had already been sent to Turkey.

Stalin said it was possible Turkey would not have to go to war if she granted bases to the Allies; she need not attack and it was possible neither the Bulgarians nor the Germans would do so. Roosevelt mentioned Portugal as an example of the granting of bases without involvement in the war.

With reference to Eden's remark that the Turkish Foreign Minister preferred to go right into war rather than to be dragged in by bases, Churchill said that was Turkey's usual behaviour. If you suggested a small move they preferred the big. If you suggested the big move, they said they were not ready. Churchill preferred to offer something substantial and then they could wash their hands of Turkey if they refused, both now and at the peace table. Stalin expected Turkey would only declare war on Germany, and not on Bulgaria. If Bulgaria attacked or declared war on Turkey, the Soviet Union would go to war with Bulgaria. But there was one other possibility. If Turkey declared war on Germany and Bulgaria refused to agree to German demands to go to war, the Germans might occupy Bulgaria. In which case Bulgaria might ask help from the Allies. What would be their position then? Churchill replied it would put great strain on Germany's strength and undoubtedly result in the removal of some German divisions from the Eastern front.

Molotov said two days earlier the Prime Minister had said if Turkey refused an invitation to enter the war, Great Britain would say her interests in the Straits and in the Bosporus would be adversely affected. What did that mean? Churchill replied he was far from his cabinet, but he personally favoured a change in the regime of the Straits if Turkey proved obdurate. Molotov said the Black Sea countries were very interested in the regime of the Straits.

Roosevelt wanted to see the Dardanelles free to the world's commerce and fleets, irrespective of whether Turkey entered the war or not. They agreed the Soviet Ambassador to Turkey and Mr. Vyshiasky[2] would come to Cairo if the Turkish president was attending.

Roosevelt wanted to help in every way to get Finland out of the war. Stalin said the Swedish Minister for Foreign Affairs, Boheman,[3] had recently asked the Soviet Ambassador in Stockholm what the Soviet Union's intentions were regarding Finland. The Finns were afraid the Russians intended to make good the Russian promise and destroy Finland's independence and said the Finns wanted an opportunity to talk to the Russians. The reply from Moscow was that Russia had no designs on the independence of Finland, if Finland by its behaviour did not force Russia to change her position.[4]

The Soviet Government also had no objection to the Finns coming to Moscow for conversations but it wanted to have the Finns' negotiating conditions in advance. They had had a Finnish reply through the Swedes that day but did not have the full text. The gist was that the Finns desired to take the 1939 frontier

---

1   Over £300 million today.
2   Andrey Vyshiasky remained in the Soviet Union to mind the shop during the Tehran Conference.
3   Erik Boheman (1895-1979), Swedish Minister for Foreign Affairs.
4   Finland had been on the defensive since December 1941 while the Soviets had been fully engaged fighting the Germans.

as a basis but it made no mention of disassociation from Germany. Stalin said this unacceptable reply indicated the Finns were not anxious to conduct serious negotiations, since they knew such conditions would be unacceptable.

Roosevelt said Stalin's statement was interesting but unsatisfactory. Stalin believed the Finnish ruling groups obviously still had hopes of a German victory. Roosevelt asked if Stalin thought it would help if the United States suggested the Finns send a delegation to Moscow. Stalin said he personally had no objections.

Churchill outlined the change in British feelings toward Finland from 1939 to the present as a result of the Finnish associations and the German attack on Russia. Great Britain was at war with Finland and the first consideration was to secure the city of Leningrad and the position of the Soviet Union as the leading naval and air power in the Baltic Sea. On the other hand, he would greatly regret seeing anything done to impair the independence of Finland, and welcomed Stalin's statement.

Churchill said an indemnity (compensation) would not be much good from a country as poor as Finland. Stalin disagreed; payments in kind over a period of five to eight years, such as timber, paper and other materials, would cover some of the damage done by Finland during the war and the Soviet Government intended to demand such reparation. Churchill explained at some length why he did not consider reparations from a country such as Finland either desirable or feasible. And he said in his ears there was an echo of the slogan "No Annexations and No Indemnities".[1] Stalin laughed and said he had already told Churchill he was becoming a Conservative. Churchill attached a great importance to Finland being out of the war and Sweden being in, at the moment of the great attack in May.[2] Stalin agreed.

Roosevelt asked if the Finns could expel the Germans from their country by their own efforts. Stalin said they had recently increased the number of divisions from 16 to 21 on the Soviet front while they were expressing their desire to negotiate. Stalin agreed it was desirable to get the Finns out of the war but not at the expense of the Soviet Union's interests. Molotov said the Finns and the Germans had kept Leningrad under artillery fire for 27 months.[3] According to Roosevelt's sources, the Finns were willing to move the frontier a long distance from Leningrad, but hoped to have Vyborg.[4] Stalin interrupted this was impossible. Roosevelt said Hango[5] should be demilitarized and made into a bathing beach.

---

1 Referring to the Petrograd Agreement, a peace formula written by the Bolshevik party in May 1918 that included the words: "peace without annexations or indemnities, on the basis of the self-determination of peoples".
2 It would mean the Baltic was controlled by the Allies when OVERLORD began.
3 The siege of Leningrad began on 8 September 1941 and would not end until 27 January 1944; lasting 872 days. There were over three million Soviet military casualties and one million civilian casualties; German casualties are unknown. Finnish troops did not take part, staying on their pre-Winter War line across the Karelian Isthmus, northwest of Leningrad, and did not shell or bomb the city.
4 Vyborg is 80 miles northwest of Leningrad, on the Karelian Isthmus. Finland relinquished her claims to the town during the 1947 Paris Peace Treaties.
5 Hango in Swedish and Hanko in Finnish is 80 miles west of Helsinki.

Churchill did not wish to press his Russian friends but he wanted to know what their conditions were because the British Government was leaving the initiative entirely in Russian hands. Stalin replied that the Soviet Government had told the United States and British Governments in February. However, the United States Government had not transmitted the terms to the Finns so they had not accepted them. Roosevelt agreed the Finns would not go along with any proposals at that time.

Stalin said the Treaty of 1940 had been broken but it had to be restored.[6] If Hango belonged to the Finns he was willing to accept Petsamo instead, which gave them a common boundary with Norway; Petsamo had been a gift from Russia to Finland.[7] Churchill said the British Government initially wanted to see the Soviet Government satisfied with the border in the west and secondly wanted to see Finland remain independent. Stalin thought it was all right to let the Finns live as they wished, but they had to pay half of the damages they had caused.

Roosevelt asked if it would help if the Finns went to Moscow without any reservations or conditions. Stalin believed such a move might play right into the hands of the Germans if there was no prospect of success, since the reactionary group in Finland would exploit such a failure and pretend it was impossible to talk with the Russians. Let the Finns come to Moscow if the President insisted; but who could they send?

Churchill said the British Government was not insistent on anything regarding the Finns. Stalin said allies could occasionally use pressure on one another, and repeated if the President thought it was worthwhile, an attempt might be made. Roosevelt believed the present Finnish Government was pro-German, and nothing could be done with them, but it might be possible to send other Finns. Stalin replied of course that would be better, they had no objection to anyone the Finns wanted to send, even Ryti,[8] or the devil himself. He then outlined the Soviet terms:

1) The restoration of the 1940 Treaty, with the possible exchange of Petsamo for Hango. Whereas Hango had been leased, Petsamo would be taken as a permanent possession.

2) Compensation for 50% of the damage done to the Soviet Union by the Finns.[9]

3) A break with Germany and the expulsion of the Germans from Finland.

4) A reorganization of the Finnish army.

Churchill and Stalin then discussed the advisability of reparations from Finland, and Stalin was adamant Finland should pay. The meeting adjourned.

---

6   Hanko was leased to the Soviet Union as a military base for a period of 30 years in the Moscow Peace Treaty at the end of the Winter War in March 1940. Soviet troops were forced to evacuate Hanko in early December 1941, during the Continuation War. The Soviet Union renounced the lease during the 1947 Paris peace treaty.

7   Bolshevist Russia ceded Pechenga, on the Barents Sea coast, to Finland and it was renamed Petsamo in 1921. It was ceded to the Soviet Union in 1944, giving it a border with Norway.

8   Risto H. Ryti (1889-1956), President of Finland December 1940 to August 1944.

9   The exact amount was to be discussed and agreed.

1 December: Third Roosevelt–Stalin Meeting

Roosevelt wanted to discuss a brief matter relating to internal American politics with Stalin. America had an election in 1944 and while he personally did not wish to run again, he might have to if the war was still in progress.[1] There were six to seven million Americans of Polish extraction in the United States, and as a practical man, he did not wish to lose their vote. He personally agreed with Stalin's views about restoring the Polish state but wanted to see the Eastern border moved farther to the west and the Western border moved even to the River Oder. He hoped Stalin understood he could not participate in any decision in Tehran or even next winter on this subject for the political reasons outlined above and he could not publicly take part in any such arrangement at the present time. Stalin understood.

Roosevelt said there were Lithuanians, Latvians, and Estonians, in that order, in the United States. He fully realized the three Baltic Republics had in history, and again more recently, been a part of Russia and jokingly added when the Soviet armies reoccupied these areas, he did not intend to go to war with the Soviet Union on this point.

Roosevelt said the big issue in the United States, insofar as public opinion went, would be the question of referenda and the right of self-determination. He thought world opinion would want some expression of the will of the people, perhaps not immediately after their reoccupation by Soviet forces, but some day, and he was personally confident the people would vote to join the Soviet Union.

Stalin replied the three Baltic Republics had no autonomy under the last Czar, an ally of Great Britain and the United States, and no one had raised the question of public opinion then and he did not quite see why it was being raised now. Roosevelt said the truth of the matter was the public neither knew nor understood. Stalin answered they should be informed and some propaganda work should be done. As for the expression of the will of the people, there would be lots of opportunities for that to be done in accordance with the Soviet constitution but he could not agree to any form of international control. Roosevelt replied it would be helpful for him personally if some public declaration could be made with regard to the future elections to which the Marshal had referred. Stalin repeated there would be plenty of opportunities for such an expression of the will of the people.

Roosevelt said there were only two matters which the three of them had not talked over. He had already outlined his ideas on the three world organisations but he felt it was premature to consider them here with Churchill. He referred particularly to his idea of the four great nations, the United States, Great Britain, the Soviet Union, and China, policing the world in the post-war period. He said it was just an idea, and the exact form would require further study.

Mr. Molotov said it had been agreed at the Moscow Conference that the three governments would give further study to the exact form of world organization and the means of assuring the leading role of the four great powers, in accordance

---

1   The election was due in November 1944. Roosevelt beat Republican candidate Thomas E. Dewey (1902-1971).

with the Four Power Declaration. Stalin agreed the world organization should be world-wide and not regional.

1 December: Fourth Eureka Meeting

Roosevelt thought there were two main questions to be discussed; the question of Poland and the treatment of Germany. Molotov asked if it would be possible to obtain any answer on the Soviet Union's request for Italian ships.

Italian War Ships for Russia

Roosevelt replied his position was very clear; the Allies had received a large number of Italian merchant ships and a lesser number of warships and he felt they should be used in the common cause until the end of the war when a division based on title and possession might be made. Molotov agreed. Churchill asked where the Soviet Union would like the ships delivered to. Stalin replied to the Black Sea if Turkey entered the war. If not, to the northern ports.

Churchill said it was a small thing to ask in the face of the tremendous sacrifices of Russia. Stalin said he knew how great the need for war vessels was on the part of England and the United States but he felt the Soviet request was modest. Both Roosevelt and Churchill accepted the Soviet suggestion. Churchill said it would require some time to work out the arrangements and he personally would welcome the sight of these vessels in the Black Sea and hoped some English war vessels could accompany them in action against the enemy in those waters.

Churchill said it would take a couple of months to work out the arrangements with the Italians, since they wished to avoid any possibility of mutiny in the Italian Fleet and the scuttling of the ships. It was agreed the ships would pass over to Soviet command around the end of January 1944. Churchill remarked it would be one of the advantages to be attained from Turkey even if she did not enter the war; namely to permit the passage of war vessels through the Dardanelles.

The Polish Question

Roosevelt hoped negotiations could be started for the reestablishment of relations between the Polish and Soviet Governments. They would facilitate any decisions at issue but he recognized the difficulties ahead. Stalin replied the Polish Government-in-Exile were closely connected with the Germans and their agents in Poland were killing partisans. It was impossible to imagine what was going on in Poland.

Churchill said the great question before the English was the fact they had declared war because of the German invasion of Poland. He had been astonished when Chamberlain had given the guarantee in April 1939 to Poland after refusing to fight for the Czechs; astonished but glad.[2] England and France had gone to war in pursuance of this guarantee and while he did not regret it, it was still difficult not to recognise the British people had gone to war because of Poland. Churchill had used the illustration of the three matches the other evening[3] in order to dem-

---

2 After Hitler sent his troops into Czechoslovakia, Chamberlain refused to say he had broken the Munich Agreement because the Czechs had invited them in. The British reacted furiously and Chamberlain countered by guaranteeing Poland's independence.

3 Churchill has used matches to demonstrate the proposed movement of borders.

onstrate one possible solution. The British Government was first of all interested in seeing absolute security for the Western frontiers of the Soviet Union against any surprise assault in the future from Germany.

Stalin said Russia, probably more than any other country, was interested in having friendly relations with Poland, since the security of Soviet frontiers was involved. The Russians were in favour of the reconstitution and expansion of Poland at the expense of Germany and they made a distinction between the Polish Government-in-exile and Poland. They broke relations with Poland not because of a whim but because the Poles had joined in slanderous propaganda with the Nazis.[1] What guarantee could there be this would not be repeated?

Stalin would like to have a guarantee the Polish Government-in-exile would stop killing partisans in Poland and secondly to urge the people to fight against the Germans and not to indulge in intrigues. The Russians would welcome relations with a Polish Government that led its people in the common struggle but it was not sure the Polish Government-in-exile could be such a government. The Russians would be prepared to negotiate with them if the Government-in-exile would go along with the partisans and sever all connections with the German agents in Poland.

Churchill wanted the Soviet Government's views on the frontier question. If some reasonable formula could be devised, he was prepared to take it up with the Polish Government-in-exile, but without telling them the Soviet Government would accept such a solution. He would tell them it was probably the best they could obtain. Great Britain would be through with the Polish Government if it refused and would certainly not oppose the Soviet Government under any condition at the peace table. The British Government wished to see a Poland strong and friendly to Russia.

Stalin replied this was desirable, but it was not just for the Poles to try and get back the Ukraine and White Russia; the frontiers of 1939 had returned Ukrainian soil to the Ukraine and White Russian soil to White Russia. The Soviet Government adhered to the 1939 line and considered it just and right. Eden said that was the Ribbentrop-Molotov Line. Stalin replied call it what you will, they still considered it just and right. Molotov interrupted to say the 1939 frontier was the Curzon Line. Eden said there were differences. Molotov replied not at any essential points.[2]

Roosevelt asked Stalin if East Prussia and the area between the old Polish frontier and the Oder was approximately equal to the former Polish territory acquired by the Soviet Union. Stalin did not know.

Churchill said if it was possible to work out some fair solution, it would be up to the Poles to amend it. Stalin replied the Soviet Union did not wish to retain any regions primarily occupied by Poles even though they were inside the 1939

1　The Soviet Union had broken relations with the Polish Government-in-exile at London on 26 April 1943, following the appeal by the latter to the International Committee of the Red Cross to investigate (accurate) German charges against the Soviet Union of the wholesale murder of Polish officers in the Katyn Forest.

2　They then identified the exact location of the Curzon Line on maps.

Line. Roosevelt asked if a voluntary transfer of peoples from the mixed areas was possible. Stalin said it was entirely possible.[3]

Germany's Future

Roosevelt said the next question was whether or not to split up Germany. Stalin preferred the dismemberment of Germany. Churchill said he was all for it but he was more interested in seeing Prussia, the evil core of German militarism, separated from the rest of Germany. Roosevelt said he had thought up a plan some months before which divided Germany into five self-governed parts:

1) All Prussia to be rendered as small and weak as possible.
2) The Hanover and Northwest section.
3) The Saxony and Leipzig area.
4) Hesse-Darmstadt, Hesse-Kassel and the area south of the Rhine.
5) Bavaria, Baden, and Württemberg.

There should be two regions under United Nations or some form of international control:

1) The area of the Kiel Canal and the city of Hamburg.[4]
2) The Ruhr and the Saar, the latter to be used for the benefit of all Europe.

Churchill said, to use an American expression, "The President had said a mouthful."[5] In his mind there were two considerations, one destructive and the other constructive.

1) Separate Prussia from the rest of the Reich.
2) Detach Bavaria, Baden, Württemberg and the Palatinate from the rest of Germany and make them part of the Confederation of the Danube.

Stalin said if Germany was going to be dismembered, it should be really dismembered, and it was not a question of the division of Germany in five or six states and two areas as the President suggested. But he preferred Roosevelt's plan to Churchill's suggestion. To include German areas within the framework of large confederations would merely offer an opportunity to the German elements to revive a great State. Stalin did not believe there was a difference among Germans; all German soldiers fought like devils and the only exception were the Austrians. The Prussian officers and staffs should be eliminated but he saw little difference between inhabitants in one part of Germany and another. He was against the idea of an artificial confederation, and one that would not last while providing the German elements the opportunity to control. Austria, for example, had existed as an independent state and should again; Hungary, Romania, and Bulgaria likewise.

Roosevelt agreed. There had been a difference in Germans 50 years before but it was no longer so since the last war. The only difference was in Bavaria and the southern part of Germany where there was no officer caste as there had been in Prussia. He agreed the Austrians were an exception.

Churchill did not wish to be considered as being against the dismemberment of Germany – quite the contrary – but to separate the parts above would merely

---

3   It was entirely possible; except the transfers would be forced.
4   Hamburg is at the mouth of the River Elbe and is now the second largest port in Europe after Rotterdam.
5   Meaning he had said something important.

mean sooner or later they would reunite into one nation and the main thing was to keep Germany divided, if only for 50 years.

Stalin repeated the danger of the re-unification of Germany and no matter what measures were adopted there would always be a strong urge on the part of the Germans to unite. It was a great mistake to unite Hungary with Germany since the Germans would merely control the Hungarians and create large frameworks within which the Germans could operate and that would be very dangerous.

Stalin felt the whole purpose of any international organisation to preserve peace would be to neutralize this tendency on the part of the Germans and apply against them economic and other measures to prevent their unification and revival. The victorious nations had to have the strength to beat the Germans if they ever started on the path of a new war.

Churchill asked if Stalin contemplated a Europe composed of little states, disjoined, separated and weak. Stalin replied not Europe but Germany. For example Poland would be a strong country, and France, and Italy likewise; Romania and Bulgaria would remain as they always had; small states. Roosevelt remarked Germany had been less dangerous to civilisation when it was 107 provinces. Churchill had hoped for larger units.

Churchill returned to the question of Poland and said he was not asking for any agreement nor was he set on the matter. He wanted Stalin to examine a statement suggesting Poland should obtain compensation in the West[1] to compensate for the areas which would be in the Soviet Union.

Roosevelt interrupted to say one question regarding Germany remained to be settled and that was what body should study the question of dismemberment of Germany. It was agreed the European Advisory Committee would undertake this task.[2]

Churchill said the Polish question was urgent. If they could work out a formula, he could go back to the Polish Government in London and urge them to attempt to reach a settlement along those lines, without indicating any commitment on the part of the Soviet Government.

Stalin said if the Russians were given the northern part of East Prussia[3] he would be prepared to accept the Curzon Line as the frontier between the Soviet Union and Poland. He said the acquisition of that part of Eastern Prussia would give the Soviet Union an ice-free port and a small piece of German territory, which he felt was deserved. Although nothing definite was stated, it was apparent the British were going to take this suggestion back to London to the Poles.

Eureka Communiqué

We, the President of the United States, the Prime Minister of Great Britain, and the Premier of the Soviet Union, have met these four days past in this, the capital

---

1   Including Eastern Prussia and frontiers on the Oder.
2   The European Advisory Committee had been agreed on 30 October 1943 at the Moscow meeting of Foreign Ministers and confirmed at Tehran. The Committee was to study postwar political problems and make recommendations to the three governments.
3   The area on the left bank of the Niemen, which included Tilsit and Königsberg.

of our ally, Iran, and have shaped and confirmed our common policy. We express our determination that our nations shall work together in war and in the peace that will follow.

As to war – our military staffs have joined in our round table discussions, and we have concerted our plans for the destruction of the German forces. We have reached complete agreement as to the scope and timing of the operations which will be undertaken from the East, West and South. The common understanding which we have here reached guarantees that victory will be ours.

And as to peace – we are sure our concord will make it an enduring peace. We recognize fully the supreme responsibility resting upon us and all the United Nations, to make a peace which will command the good will of the overwhelming mass of the peoples of the world, and banish the scourge and terror of war for many generations.

With our diplomatic advisors we have surveyed the problems of the future. We shall seek the cooperation and the active participation of all nations, large and small, whose peoples in heart and mind are dedicated, as are our own peoples, to the elimination of tyranny and slavery, oppression and intolerance. We will welcome them, as they may choose to come, into a world family of democratic nations.

No power on earth can prevent our destroying the German armies by land, their U-boats by sea, and their war plants from the air. Our attack will be relentless and increasing. Emerging from these friendly conferences we look with confidence to the day when all peoples of the world may live free lives, untouched by tyranny, and according to their varying desires and their own consciences. We came here with hope and determination. We leave here, friends in fact, in spirit and in purpose.

The Sextant Conference Part II: 2–7 December 1943

President Roosevelt and Premier Stalin left Tehran on 2 December and flew back to Cairo. Later that evening they heard that President Inonu of Turkey would meet them in Cairo on the 4th to discuss his country's position in the war. The conference was due to finish on 5 December but there was so much work it continued well into the night on the 6th.

3 December
First Combined Chiefs of Staff Meeting
Military Implications of the Eureka Conference; Agenda for the rest of the Sextant Conference; Turkey's entry into the war; Combined Bomber Offensive.

4 December: Third Sextant Meeting
Roosevelt had to leave Cairo on Monday morning so they had to sign all the conference reports by Sunday night. Apart from the Turkish participation in the

war, which he felt should be brought about at some date between 15 February and 1 April, the only outstanding problem was the comparatively small one of providing about twenty landing craft and their equipment. It was unthinkable to be beaten by a small item like that, and he felt bound to say that it had to be done.

Churchill did not wish to leave the conference in any doubt that the British Delegation viewed the early closure of the SEXTANT Conference with great apprehension. There were still many questions of primary importance to be settled. Two decisive events had taken place in the last few days.

In the first place, Marshal Stalin had voluntarily proclaimed the Soviet would make war on Japan the moment Germany was defeated. This gave them better bases than they ever could find in China and made it all the more important to concentrate on making OVERLORD a success. The Staffs had to examine how this new fact would affect operations in the Pacific and Southeast Asia.[1]

The second event of first class importance was the decision to execute OVERLORD during May. Churchill preferred the July date but he was determined to do all in his power to make the May date a complete success. OVERLORD was a task transcending all others. A million Americans were to be thrown in, and 500,000-600,000 British. Terrific battles were to be expected on a scale far greater than anything they had experienced before.[2]

Operation ANVIL[3] should be as strong as possible to give OVERLORD the greatest chance of success.[4] The critical time would come at about the 30th day and it was essential to make action elsewhere to prevent the Germans concentrating a superior force against their bridgeheads. As soon as the OVERLORD and ANVIL forces got into the same zone, they would come under the same Commander.

Churchill believed ANVIL should be planned for an assault force of at least two divisions. This provided enough landing craft to do the outflanking operations in Italy and capture Rhodes, if Turkey came into the war. He wished to say Rhodes no longer had the great importance he previously attached to it, in the face of the new situation. Admiral King[5] interrupted to say a two-division lift for ANVIL was in sight.[6]

Churchill said operations in Southeast Asia must be judged in their relation to the dominating importance of OVERLORD. He was astounded by the Supreme Commander's demands for BUCCANEER. Although there were only 5,000

---

1   Events would transpire quite differently. On 6 August 1945, the United States dropped an atomic bomb on the city of Hiroshima. Two days later, in accordance with the Yalta agreements, the Soviet Union declared war on Japan. Early on 9 August 1945 Soviet troops invaded the Imperial Japanese puppet state of Manchukuo. Later the same day the United States dropped a second atomic bomb on Nagasaki. The combined events caused Emperor Hirohito to order the Supreme Council for the Direction of the War to accept the Allies' terms for ending the war set down in the Potsdam Declaration on 26 July 1945.

2   A shortage of landing craft for OVERLORD meant the date had to be delayed from 1 May for an additional month's construction. Bad weather in the English Channel would delay it a few more days until 6 June.

3   ANVIL was the the invasion of southern France. SLEDGEHAMMER had been one of OVERLORD's predecessors.

4   There would be prolonged arguments over whether to carry out ANVIL or whether to make it a feint because the operations were fighting over some of the same resources.

5   Admiral Ernest J. King, Commander-in-Chief, United States Fleet, and Chief of Naval Operations.

6   If enough resources could be gathered for a two-division landing on the French Riviera, they could be used again to help the Italian campaign and to clear the Dodecanese islands, opening the route to the Dardanelles.

Japanese on the island, 58,000 men were required to capture it.[7] As he understood it, the Americans had been fighting the Japanese successfully at odds of two and a half to one.

In the face of Stalin's promise that Russia would come into the war, operations in the Southeast Asia Command had lost a good deal of their value; while on the other hand their cost had risen to a prohibitive extent. Churchill concluded there were still very large differences of opinion between the British and American Delegations and it was of the first importance they should be cleared away.

Brooke said the last stage of the Conference had always been the submission of a final report, followed by an examination of ways and means. SEXTANT had been a very different affair.

In the first place there had been meetings with the Generalissimo. Then the principal members of both delegations had gone to Tehran where there had been a number of Plenary Conferences on political as well as military matters. It meant the Combined Chiefs of Staff had had very few opportunities for discussion at SEXTANT.

The following matters were still outstanding: Firstly, an examination of the landing craft position, without which it was impossible to say which operations could or could not be undertaken. Secondly, the long-term plan for the defeat of Japan, which was affected by the decisions to undertake operations in Upper Burma next March. The plan was also seriously affected by Stalin's promise to make war on Japan as soon as Germany was finished.

It was essential to resolve these problems before the Combined Chiefs of Staff separated. The Mediterranean was of the greatest importance. It would be fatal to let up in that area. They should go on hitting the Germans as hard as possible and in every place they could. Finally, the question of ANVIL was still under examination and it was essential to decide how the necessary resources could be provided.

Admiral Cunningham said on preliminary examination their naval resources in cruisers, carriers, destroyers and escorts were not adequate to undertake more than two amphibious operations at the same time, namely OVERLORD and ANVIL. It might be possible to get some of the naval forces employed in BUCCANEER back in time for ANVIL but most of them would have to remain in the Indian Ocean.

Air Marshal Portal said, according to his information, there was only one good airfield in the Andamans and it was capable of operating squadrons of heavy bombers. There was another site which had been cleared by blasting the top off a hill, and a few landing strips might be made on the beach. It meant the value of the Andamans as a base for long-distance bombing was strictly limited.[8] Marshall agreed with Brooke's observations. There was no question there were a number of important points to be settled. It was impossible to say how long this settlement would take.

---

7   South East Asia Command was far more cautious than Churchill when it came to estimating its needs for amphibious operations. Churchill estimated BUCCANEER, the invasion of the Andaman Islands, only needed a single division of 14,000 men. Mountbatten also wanted almost all the Royal Navy's aircraft carriers until a land air base was established.

8   Admiral Mountbatten wanted nearly every aircraft available until the Andamans had been taken.

Churchill said he was leaving on Tuesday. Would it not be possible for the Staffs to stay for two or three days and work out their problems together? Admiral Leahy[1] said two or three days would not suffice; the problems they had to work out would take at least one or two weeks. Admiral King said the Staffs were unlikely to reach agreement on certain problems and they could only be resolved at the President–Prime Minister level. Churchill said the Generalissimo had left Cairo under the impression they were going to go through with BUCCANEER. The new facts were, firstly, the Soviets had declared themselves ready to go to war with Japan immediately Germany collapsed; secondly, it had been decided to go with OVERLORD in May; and, thirdly, ANVIL was also to be undertaken. He was very anxious lest the Russian promise should leak out. Roosevelt agreed but added it was impossible to tell the Chinese.

Continuing, Churchill said 18 to 20 additional landing craft must be provided by hook or by crook. As for the BUCCANEER assault, he thought 14,000 instead of 58,000 men would be ample. Mountbatten should be told he must do his best with the resources allocated to him. It should be possible for the staffs to settle their problems in principle, leaving the details to be worked out afterwards. They appeared already to have reached agreement on the objectives.

Brooke protested there were many questions. Shipping, landing craft and naval resources had to be examined in detail, as did the relation between ANVIL and BUCCANEER. ANVIL was being examined on the basis of a two-division assault, whereas the proper strategy might be to divert landing craft from BUCCANEER to the Mediterranean to increase it to a three-division assault. Admiral King said the landing craft and assault shipping for a two-division assault was already in sight, subject to certain complications. So long as the target date for OVERLORD was 1 May, it was necessary for the landing craft to be in the UK by 1 March.[2] Consequently, the intention had been to send all new construction of landing craft after that date to the Pacific. Now it had been decided to postpone OVERLORD by two to four weeks, this new construction would come to the UK. Nothing would be sent to the Pacific.[3] Churchill said this was a fruitful contribution.

Some discussion followed on the subject of LSI(L)s.[4] Churchill wanted to know if it was possible to adapt merchant ships instead of building special vessels. Admiral King said conversions of this character were in progress. The US Navy used ships of 6,000-10,000 tons for this purpose while monster liners were reserved for transportation of large bodies of troops across the Atlantic. Admiral Cunningham said the LSI(L)s could be more economically employed on the longer Mediterranean hauls than the short cross-Channel haul.

Discussion followed about the increase of Japanese fighter strength in Southeast Asia. Admiral King pointed to the interrelation between the attack on Rabaul

---

1 Admiral Leahy, senior American Representative on the Combined Chiefs of Staff.
2 Leaving two months for amphibious training and loading.
3 The shortage of landing craft would delay OVERLORD for one month, which in turn would result in a delay of one month for delivery of landing craft to the Pacific Theatre.
4 Landing Ship, Infantry (Small); British term for the Attack Transport Ship.

and BUCCANEER. The Japanese air force was going to be in difficulties at two widely separated points.[5]

Admiral Leahy said if it could be decided that a) ANVIL should be a two-division assault and b) Admiral Mountbatten should be instructed to do the best he could with the resources he already had, the picture would begin to be filled in. If Admiral Mountbatten said he could do nothing, some of his resources could be taken away from him for other purposes.[6]

Churchill suggested leaving BUCCANEER until after the monsoon; in fact this solution might be forced upon them by facts and figures. Admiral King said there was a definite commitment to the Generalissimo for an amphibious operation in the spring. Churchill recalled the Generalissimo had said it was essential to undertake an amphibious operation simultaneously with TARZAN.[7] Churchill had said quite firmly he could not agree. The Generalissimo could be under no illusion about this.

The President suggested the following plan of action:

    a)   Accept OVERLORD and ANVIL as the paramount operations of 1944.

    b)   Make every effort to get the additional 18 to 20 landing craft for the Eastern Mediterranean.

    c)   Tell Admiral Mountbatten he could keep what he has got, but he was going to get nothing else and he had to do the best he could.

Portal said ANVIL had only come seriously into the picture last week and nobody knew if a two-division assault would, or would not, be enough. It was merely a yardstick for the planning Staffs to work on. The proper strategy might be to get a lift for at least another division out of the Southeast Asia Command.

Brooke said the OVERLORD assault was only 3½ divisions while ANVIL was only a two-division assault at present. Surely it would be better to employ BUCCANEER's resources to strengthen the European front. Admiral Leahy agreed but BUCCANEER had been decided on a higher level than the Chiefs of Staff.

Churchill pointed to the great military advantages to be gained from operations in the Aegean. There would be great political reactions if Turkey entered the war. Bulgaria, Romania and Hungary might all fall into their hands. They had to try and make these German satellites work for them.

Eden thought Russia would probably agree to postponing the date for the Turkish entry into the war from 31 December 1943 to about 15 February 1944. As for Romania, the Russians had, in the first place, refused to have anything to do with the feelers put out by Maniu,[8] except on the basis of unconditional sur-

---

5   The Andaman Islands are west of Thailand; Rabaul is east of Papua New Guinea. They are 3500 miles apart.

6   BUCCANEER was finally dropped in the spring of 1945.

7   TARZAN was a plan for General Wingate's Chindits to go behind Japanese lines and seize airfields so the 26th Indian Division could be flown in.

8   Iuliu Maniu (1873-1953), President of the National Peasant's Party and Prime Minister on three occasions before the war. He was an opponent of Romanian Prime Minister General Ion Antonescu (1882-1946) who had aligned his army with the Germans. He was also against the Romanian Communist Party and the Soviet Union.

render. Maniu now said he was prepared to send a representative to negotiate on that basis. It was true he did not represent the Romania Government, but there was always the possibility of a coup d'état.

Churchill pointed out the great advantages to be gained by Romania's entry into the war. If they could get a grip on the Balkans, there would be a tremendous abridgement[1] of their difficulties. The next conference might perhaps be held at Budapest![2] All this would help OVERLORD. Churchill was not apprehensive about OVERLORD but the critical period would be about the 30th day. It was therefore essential to hold the Germans at every point and the whole ring should close in together. Discussion then followed about the conduct of the political conversations with President Inonu.[3]

Roosevelt summed up by asking if he was correct in thinking there was agreement on the following:

    a.   Nothing should be done to hinder OVERLORD.

    b.   Nothing should be done to hinder ANVIL.

    c.   By hook or by crook they should scrape up sufficient landing craft to operate in the Eastern Mediterranean if Turkey came into the war.

    d.   Mountbatten should be told to do his best with what had already been allocated to him.

Churchill said it might be necessary to withdraw resources from BUCCANEER to strengthen OVERLORD and ANVIL. Roosevelt disagreed. They had a moral obligation to do something for China and he was not prepared to forego the amphibious operation, unless there was a very great and readily apparent reason.

Churchill said this very good reason might be OVERLORD. At present the assault was only 3½ divisions, whereas they had put 9 divisions ashore on Sicily on their first day. The operation was at present on a very narrow margin. Field Marshal Dill[4] thought it was impossible for both OVERLORD and ANVIL to be strong. Admiral Leahy agreed there was everything to be said for strengthening OVERLORD and ANVIL at the expense of other theatres from a military point of view, but there were serious political issues at stake.

Marshall agreed with Dill and Leahy but said the difficulties in abandoning or postponing BUCCANEER were not merely political. If BUCCANEER was cancelled, the Generalissimo would not allow Chinese forces to take part in TARZAN. There would be no campaign in Upper Burma and this would have repercussions on Pacific operations. There would be revulsion in China; the effect on Japan would be bad and the line of communication between Indochina would be at hazard.

Churchill said he had never committed himself to the scale or timing of the amphibious operation in the Southeast Asia Theatre. Perhaps it might be advisable to revert to Akyab or Ramree.[5] Roosevelt said the Generalissimo was anxious

---

1   Shortening.

2   It was the Soviets who reached Budapest in December 1944 and the city surrendered in February 1945.

3   President Inonu of Turkey.

4   Field Marshal Dill, senior British Representative on the Combined Chiefs of Staff.

5   Akyab (now Sittwe) and Ramree Island, two ports on Burma's northwest coast.

to secure a base so they could bomb the supply line from Bangkok. Admiral King said he had no fear of the Japanese being able to retake the Andamans once they had occupied them but an increase in the scale of BUCCANEER was out of the question.

The meeting concluded with Roosevelt and Churchill commanding their respective staffs to meet. They had to try to reach agreement on the points at issue in the light of the discussion.

4 December

Second Combined Chiefs of Staff Meeting

Integrated command of US air forces in Europe and the Mediterranean; Mediterranean command; Operation RANKIN; Review of conditions in Europe; Occupation of Europe; Overall plan to defeat Japan.

President and Prime Minister meet President Inonu of Turkey

President Inonu was given the results of the Eureka Conference, particularly Stalin's pledges to declare war on Bulgaria if it took action against Turkey and to respect Iran. Roosevelt and Churchill discussed how Turkey could enter the war.

Quadripartite Dinner

There are no minutes of the dinner meeting but afterwards Churchill questioned President Inonu at length about Turkey joining the Allies.

5 December

Third Combined Chiefs of Staff Meeting

Draft agreements on operations; Amphibious operation against southern France; Integrated Command of US air forces in Europe and the Mediterranean; Mediterranean Command; Intensifying support for Yugoslav partisans.

5 December: Fourth Sextant Meeting

Roosevelt read out the Combined Chiefs of Staff report on European Theatre operations. Agreement still had to be reached on BUCCANEER and he wanted a document which could be signed. Churchill suggested advancing the date of BUCCANEER to January. Marshall said no. Roosevelt asked what date Mountbatten had given for the operation and General Arnold replied mid-March. Admiral Leahy said the landing craft could not return to the European Theatre until the beginning of May if mid-March was adopted.

Churchill was disturbed at the growth in the forces required for BUCCANEER. If a superiority of ten to one was required, it made the conduct of war impossible. Could BUCCANEER be postponed until after the monsoon and the Generalissimo be told, as a result of developments arising from the discussions with the Russians, BUCCANEER could not be carried out as originally contemplated? TARZAN would, of course, be carried out as arranged.

Roosevelt said the Generalissimo had left Cairo under the impression an amphibious operation would be carried out simultaneously with TARZAN. He was a little dubious about putting all their eggs in one basket. Suppose Stalin was unable to be as good as his word? They might have forfeited Chinese support without obtaining commensurate help from the Russians. Churchill said BUCCANEER would not really influence Chinese continuation in the war; it depended much more upon the supplies she received over the Hump.[1]

Hopkins asked if the landing craft and naval forces could leave the Indian Ocean for ANVIL if BUCCANEER took place on 1 March. Admiral Cunningham did not think so. Most of the naval forces had to remain in the vicinity of BUCCANEER for up to a month after the assault.[2] Admiral King agreed the follow-up for BUCCANEER might take up to four weeks before most of the ships could be released. This left no margin for fitting them into OVERLORD or ANVIL, even assuming they took place in late May. Hopkins asked if the Combined Staffs had examined the adequacy of a two-division assault for ANVIL. Brooke said this question had not yet been examined in detail.

Admiral King said the two-division lift for ANVIL was already in sight and it might even be possible to improve on it. However, the two-division lift entailed keeping back one month's production of landing craft output from the Pacific. Nothing at all was going to the Pacific now.

Churchill referred back to BUCCANEER, and said there was no question of providing any additional forces. Mountbatten was quite likely to say he could not do BUCCANEER and would revert to BULLFROG, an operation which found favour with no one.[3] The next step would be to discuss the possibilities of an amphibious operation in the Southeast Asia Theatre with the force commanders.

Field Marshal Dill asked what OVERLORD's earliest date was and it was agreed no specific date had been set. The full moon would be on 8 May and the new moon on 22 May. Marshall said ANVIL might take place at the same time as OVERLORD, or possibly a week later.

Hopkins understood there was nothing in any Combined Chiefs of Staff paper which said landing craft were not available for either OVERLORD or ANVIL. On the other hand, the Chiefs of Staff had never stipulated there should be a six-division assault for OVERLORD or a three-division assault for ANVIL.

Hopkins said there were probably sufficient landing craft for a two-division lift for ANVIL. There were also enough landing craft for BUCCANEER and for OVERLORD on the scale now planned; there might not be enough if OVERLORD was allocated the additional lift they hoped for. Unless the Chiefs of Staff determined there were sufficient landing craft for the assault on southern France, there would definitely not be enough landing craft for these operations. Hopkins summed up that OVERLORD and ANVIL were of such great importance they should be strengthened if possible.[4]

Admiral Leahy said while it was apparent there was sufficient lift for two divisions for ANVIL, it was unquestionably true a greater lift would be more likely to ensure the success of the operation. He felt if the Generalissimo could be persuaded to put his forces into TARZAN without accomplishing BUCCANEER,

1   The supplies were direct aid while the invasion of the Andaman Island was indirect aid.
2   Until a port had been taken and opened for ships.
3   BULLFROG was the plan to take Akyab Island first raised in March 1943.
4   Hopkins is all for the France campaign and wants their support.

it might be a good thing. Churchill felt there were a good many new, revolution-ary ideas recently injected regarding the relationship between BUCCANEER and TARZAN.[5]

Eden said it was unfortunate they could not separate BUCCANEER and TARZAN and continuously considered them connected. Admiral King said if the BUCCANEER operation was postponed, there would be no operations in Burma until after the monsoon, except possibly as a part of other incidental operations. Brooke said if they did TARZAN and it ran on into the monsoon, they could not sit still; they had to go on. There were two further steps; down to Mandalay and the Irrawaddy[6] and then on to Rangoon. Churchill said operations on land such as TARZAN would not cut into OVERLORD or ANVIL.

Air Marshal Portal asked if it was possible to carry amphibious operations instead of BUCCANEER because the Generalissimo had made a special point of naval operations. It might be possible to organize commando groups and make a descent on some part of the coast. He believed commando raids supported by naval forces would fulfil the Generalissimo's requirements. Operations of this kind would be suitable without making a definite commitment they had to con-tinue further.

Portal also believed the Generalissimo could be told that amphibious opera-tions on a large scale could be carried out after the monsoon. King said Portal probably meant some sort of 'hit-and-run' operations.[7] Roosevelt wanted to examine 'hit-and-run' raids.

Hopkins asked if the Chiefs of Staff would get any further if they sent Mountbatten a wire. Would the Chiefs of Staff recommend against the whole business if Mountbatten said he could not accomplish BUCCANEER with the means available? Would the Chiefs of Staff still tell Mountbatten to go ahead and do what he could with what he had? Churchill said both OVERLORD and ANVIL were known to be of great importance and they would be seriously affected by a diversion such as BUCCANEER.

Churchill said Southeast Asia Command had 50,000 men against 5,000 Japanese and they were now asking for more. Hopkins said it made no difference in the number of landing craft whether 30,000 men or 50,000 men were being used for BUCCANEER, the number of landing craft gauged the size of the initial assault.[8] He asked how many more men could be lifted if Mountbatten's landing craft were made available in the Mediterranean. Admiral Cunningham said Mountbatten's lift was about 25,000 men or an additional lift of about one division for ANVIL. He also believed the landing craft from the Indian Ocean could get to OVERLORD in time if necessary.

---

5   BUCCANEER was the capture of the Andaman Islands on the west coast of Burma; TARZAN was an advance into Northern Burma from India.

6   Mandalay, Burma's second largest city, stands on the River Irrawaddy in the centre of the country.

7   Portal is suggesting commando raids on the coast with a promise to make a larger landing when the monsoon ended in November.

8   Hopkins' point is that the number of landing craft determined the number of divisions that could be landed simultaneously on D-Day. It also determined the speed of the build-up until a port had been captured and opened.

Admiral King said the difficulty in lifting additional troops in the initial assault for OVERLORD was the available ports. Considerable port congestion was already anticipated in England with the contemplated lift of 4½ divisions.[1] King understood the number of troops in the initial OVERLORD assault was based on what could properly be used on the available landing front in France. Brooke believed the landing could be extended and use made of other beaches.[2]

Churchill said while he did not feel committed to an amphibious operation on any specific date in Southeast Asia; he realised the difficulty facing the President regarding the Generalissimo. Either Mountbatten should plan for BUCCANEER with the existing resources or start sending back the forces at once. He favoured TARZAN going ahead but he had not realized the amphibious operation was directly related to and bound up with TARZAN.

Churchill suggested the Generalissimo should be told Mountbatten wanted more forces than contemplated when the Generalissimo had been in Cairo. It was therefore proposed to postpone BUCCANEER until after the monsoon while TARZAN would go forward. The postponement of BUCCANEER would not affect TARZAN. If the Generalissimo expressed surprise and threatened to withhold the Yunnan forces, they should say they would go on without them. Alternatively, they could say the inaction of the Yunnan forces[3] would allow more supplies to go over the Hump. Brooke said if the Yunnan forces were withdrawn from TARZAN, the whole plan needed recasting.[4]

Cunningham said BUCCANEER's naval force would include battleships, cruisers, destroyers and one or two big carriers. No great difficulty should be encountered in doing a raid or raids. Admiral King had promised to help by providing American naval forces for ANVIL.

Churchill said assuming the President and US Chiefs of Staff were willing to extend their time at Cairo for a day or so, it would be necessary for the Combined Chiefs of Staff to get to work on the problems emerging from the discussion. First came ANVIL. A detailed study was required into the strength of the assault and the follow-up. Next, they ought to deal with the Turks. He had in mind a program on the following lines: at the end of January the Turkish airdromes should be fitted out with Radar and anti-aircraft defences. At the beginning of February the US and British squadrons should be ready to move to Turkey and medium bombers should start a softening-up process from airfields in Cyrenaica.[5] By 15 February the bombing attacks on the Dodecanese islands should be intensified. By this time they should expect some reactions from Germany, but as they grew progressively stronger, the Turks would have to face up to greater risks. Admiral

---

1   King's point is that more landing craft will not help OVERLORD because the ports on the southern English coast could not accommodate them or the extra troops.

2   On 18 January Eisenhower told Marshall that both he and Montgomery wanted to land on the east side of the Cotentin Peninsula (Utah Beach) so Cherbourg could be taken quicker. The extra beach would also allow First US Army to straddle the river Vire, rather than have to cross it.

3   The Chinese forces along the Burmese border.

4   The Yunnan Forces would advance south across the Burma-Chinese border while the British advanced east across the Burma-India border.

5   Libya's eastern territories.

Leahy said, as far as the US Chiefs of Staff were concerned, they were quite right to leave the Turkish program to the British Chiefs of Staff to decide upon.

Brooke said the adjustment of resources to plans, including particularly shipping, could not be worked out yet. The adjustment of resources depended on the decision about BUCCANEER and ANVIL. As regards the former operation, the right thing seemed to be to take what was required for the European Theatre, and then see what could be done with what was left in Southeast Asia.

Churchill suggested Mountbatten should be asked what he could do as an alternative to BUCCANEER, assuming the bulk of his landing craft and assault shipping were going to be withdrawn. They could not get away from the fact they were doing wrong strategically if they used vital resources such as landing craft on comparatively insignificant operations, instead of strengthening OVERLORD and ANVIL, which were working on a dangerously narrow margin.

General Arnold then explained the possibilities and capabilities of the very long range aircraft which would operate from Calcutta's four airfields. Churchill asked how the construction of these airfields was progressing. He called for a special report, to be followed by weekly progress reports.

The Conference:
a.   Invited the Combined Chiefs of Staff to initiate further studies concerning the scope of OVERLORD and ANVIL with a view to increasing both assaults.
b.   Invited the Combined Chiefs of Staff to consult with BUCCANEER's force commanders. They would then ask Mountbatten what smaller scale amphibious operations than BUCCANEER he could do if most of landing craft and assault shipping were withdrawn from Southeast Asia during the next few weeks.
c.   Agreed the British Chiefs of Staff should prepare a statement for presentation to the Turks showing what assistance they would receive if they entered the war.

Tripartite Meeting with Turkey
Roosevelt and Churchill discussed Turkey's entry into the war with President Inonu. They reached an impasse and Turkey would not join the Allies for the foreseeable future.

Fourth Combined Chiefs of Staff Meeting
Operations in Southeast Asia; Operation ANVIL; Directions to Combined Staff Planners and Shipping authorities; Future work.

6 December
Fifth Combined Chiefs of Staff Meeting
Southeast Asia Amphibious and other Operations; Overall plan to defeat Japan; Operations to defeat Japan; Strategic Air Forces in Europe and the Mediterranean; Draft Report to the President and Prime Minister; Relation of resources to plans; Message to Marshal Stalin and Generalissimo Chiang Kai-shek.

Tripartite Meeting with Turkey

Roosevelt and Churchill again met President Inonu and he was concerned that they were only proposing to provide anti-aircraft weapons in the way of support to begin with.

6 December: Fifth Sextant Meeting

The President read the Chief of Staffs' report of agreed conclusions.[1]

The U-boat War

The Combined Chiefs of Staff had encouraging reports from the Chiefs of the two Naval Staffs about the U-boat war.

The Combined Bomber Offensive

The Combined Chiefs of Staff had a most encouraging report covering the combined bombing operations against Germany. The progressive destruction and dislocation of the German military, industrial and economic system, the disruption of vital elements of lines of communication, and the material reduction of German air combat strength by the successful prosecution of the Combined Bomber Offensive from all convenient bases was a prerequisite for OVERLORD.[2] This operation continued to have the highest strategic priority.

They agreed the present plan for the Combined Bomber Offensive should remain unchanged except for periodic revision of the bombing objectives. The intensity of Eighth Air Force's operations should be limited only by the available aircraft and crews.

Eureka Decisions

In light of the military decisions of the Eureka Conferences approved by the President, the Prime Minister and Marshal Stalin, they had reached the following agreements regarding operations in the European Theatre:

a) OVERLORD and ANVIL were the supreme operations for 1944. They had to be carried out in May 1944. Nothing must be undertaken in any other part of the world which compromised the success of these two operations.

b) OVERLORD was at present planned on a narrow margin. Everything practicable should be done to increase its strength.

c) The examination of ANVIL would be pressed forward as fast as possible on the basis of not less than a two-division assault. Consideration would be given to the provision of additional resources if the examination revealed it required strengthening.

d) Operations in the Aegean, including the capture of Rhodes, were desirable, provided they could be fitted in without detriment to OVERLORD and ANVIL.

---

1   The Over-All Objective and the Over-All Strategic Concept for the Prosecution of the War were the same as for the Trident and Quadrant Conferences. The Basic Undertakings in Support of Over-All Strategic Concept were also the same apart from the following: a) Continue assistance to Italian forces as well as the French so they could fulfil an active role in the war against the Axis Powers; b) Prepare to reorient forces from the European Theatre to the Pacific and Far East as soon as the German situation allows.

2   Barring an independent and complete Russian victory before OVERLORD could be mounted.

e) Every effort had to be made, by accelerated building and conversion, to provide the essential additional landing craft for the European Theatre.

The Mediterranean Theatre

The Combined Chiefs of Staff had examined the operation against southern France. They had instructed the Supreme Allied Commander, Mediterranean Theatre[3] to submit, as a matter of urgency, an outline plan for the operation. He had been told it would take place at about the same time as Operation OVERLORD and he would be given assault shipping and craft for a lift of at least two divisions. He would inform the Chiefs of Staff what requirements he could not meet from the resources at his disposal in the Mediterranean.

The Combined Chiefs of Staff agreed the advance in Italy should continue to the Pisa-Rimini line. They had informed the Supreme Allied Commander, Mediterranean Theatre, he could keep the 68 LSTs due for return to the United Kingdom until 15 January 1944. This would allow them to reach the United Kingdom in time for OVERLORD.

The Combined Chiefs of Staff agreed to the unification of command in the Mediterranean Theatre and had issued the necessary directive to General Eisenhower. They had issued special instructions to the Supreme Allied Commander, Mediterranean Theatre, with regard to the assistance he should give to the Yugoslavian Partisans. They had also examined the role Turkey might adopt if she agreed to come into the war and the likely extent of their commitments.

Coordination with the USSR

The Combined Chiefs of Staff agreed the necessary coordination of effort with the USSR should be arranged through the United States and British Military Missions in Moscow. They agreed deception experts should proceed to Moscow to coordinate plans with the Soviet Staff.

An Emergency Return to the Continent

In developing the RANKIN plans,[4] COSSAC[5] recommended dividing the occupied territories into two spheres under the general direction of the Supreme Allied Commander. The British sphere, included northwest Germany, Belgium, Luxembourg, Holland and Denmark. The US sphere included southern Germany and France, with Austria a US sphere, initially under Mediterranean command.[6] COSSAC's planning was proceeding on this basis.

The United States Chiefs of Staff proposed to change the spheres as follows:

a) US sphere: The general area was the Netherlands and northern Germany as far east as the line Berlin-Stettin, Denmark, Norway and Sweden.[7]

---

3 Field Marshal Wilson in consultation with COSSAC as he planned OVERLORD.
4 RANKIN covered the possibility that Germany could a) be severely weakened; b) withdraw from France; c) capitulate.
5 General Morgan, Chief of Staff to the Supreme Allied Commander, (COSSAC).
6 COSSAC's plan was for the British to be on the left (north) flank of the invasion because their line of supply would be across the English Channel and then the North Sea as the advance into Germany developed. The Americans were on the right (south) flank of the invasion because their line of supply would ultimately be direct from American to French ports. The occupation of countries followed the same logic.
7 Following the Netherlands southern boundary, to Düsseldorf on the Rhine, down the Rhine to Mains, east to Bayreuth, north to Leipzig, northeast to Cottbus, north to Berlin (exclusive) and to Stettin (inclusive).

b) British sphere: The territory west and south of the American western boundary.

The Chiefs of Staff agreed to direct COSSAC to report on the implications of this new allocation.[1] They had also instructed the Combined Intelligence Committee[2] to keep the European situation under constant review in relation to RANKIN and to report to the Combined Chiefs of Staff on the first of each month.

Discussion on an Emergency Return to the Continent

Roosevelt understood objections had been raised to the United States proposals on the grounds they involved moving the United States forces from right to left, across the British lines of communication. In practice, this objection should not be a serious one, as the changeover would not take place until operations had been concluded. Churchill said he could not commit the British Government to these proposals. They would have to be put to the War Cabinet.

The War against Japan

Active study of the Overall Plan for the Defeat of Japan was continuing. The Combined Chiefs of Staff had directed the Combined Staff Planners to plan a campaign for the Chinese Theatre, together with an estimate of the forces involved. They had approved specific operations for the defeat of Japan in 1944 with the exception of references to BUCCANEER.

The Combined Chiefs of Staff agreed it was undesirable to enter into details of various operations in this theatre, but they had to decide which courses of action were to be undertaken and their sequence and timing.[3] They had agreed to delay major amphibious operations in the Bay of Bengal until after the next monsoon and to divert the BUCCANEER landing craft to ANVIL and OVERLORD. The Combined Chiefs of Staff had decided:

a) To prepare TARZAN as planned, less BUCCANEER. Instead of BUCCANEER there would be simultaneous naval carrier and amphibious raiding operations.[4] They would also bomb the Bangkok-Burma railroad and Bangkok harbour while maintaining naval control of the Bay of Bengal.

Or alternatively:

b) Postpone TARZAN and increase the air lift to China across the Hump to a maximum, intensifying the measures needed to bring B-29s to bear on the enemy at the same time.

The Combined Chiefs of Staff would choose between alternatives a) and b) at a later date[5] after hearing from the Generalissimo and the Supreme Allied Commander, Southeast Asia.[6]

---

1 The idea behind switching the areas was that US troops would be withdrawn from Europe as soon as Germany surrendered and sent to the Pacific to face the Japanese. So the American zone needed to include Germany's North Sea ports.

2 The Combined Intelligence Committee (CIC) consisted of the US Joint Intelligence Staff and the British Joint Intelligence Committee in Washington with a Subcommittee in London.

3 The Prime Minister commented that "this did not affect the decision taken at the QUADRANT Conference that the British Chiefs of Staff were to be the channel of communication with the Southeast Asia Command."

4 A land offensive in the northwest and amphibious raids limited to the coast.

5 Alternative b) was taken.

6 The Prime Minister suggested sending Field Marshal Wilson a copy of the President's recent signal to Generalissimo Chiang Kai-shek concerning operations in the Southeast Asia Command. The President agreed.

United Chiefs of Staff

The Combined Chiefs of Staff had studied the possible formation of a United Chiefs of Staff organization. They had also studied the possible representation of other powers on the Combined Chiefs of Staff. They agreed not to put forward either proposal.

The Combined Chiefs of Staff felt the difficulties of and objections to any kind of United Chiefs of Staff Committee should be frankly explained if the USSR or China raised the question. It would be pointed out the Combined Chiefs of Staff in Washington were responsible for the day-to-day conduct of the Anglo–American forces. They were closely integrated in accordance with the broad policy laid down at conferences such as Casablanca, Trident, Quadrant and Sextant. The USSR and/or Chinese governments would be invited to join any future conferences, to take part in the discussion of any military problems they were specifically concerned with.[7]

Conclusions

Roosevelt commended the Combined Chiefs of Staff while Churchill said the report was a masterly survey of the whole military scene. In his opinion, when military historians came to judge the decisions of the SEXTANT Conference, they would find them fully in accordance with the classic articles of war. Churchill expressed his deep sense of gratitude to his United States colleagues. The ANVIL operation had been their great contribution to the Conference. He was convinced this operation would contribute largely to the success of OVERLORD. The President and Prime Minister then initialled the report.

Churchill asked if the draft communiqué on the U-boat war had been approved. Admiral King said it had been cleared with the President and sent to Washington; it would be released on the 10th of the month. Churchill suggested the United States and the British alternately release the monthly communiqué. The British had prepared the present communiqué, so the next one should be prepared by the United States. The President agreed.

A draft message to Marshal Stalin was considered and modified; instructions to send it at once were given. A draft telegram to the Generalissimo was then read out. They agreed it would be undesirable to put so much secret information into a dispatch of this nature on grounds of security. It was decided not to dispatch a telegram to the Generalissimo until his reply had been received to the President's recent telegram on Southeast Asia Command's operations.

7 December

President Roosevelt flew from Cairo West Airport.

Churchill and Inonu

Churchill offered air support but while he believed Turkey's only threat was from the air, President Inonu believed the Axis could make a ground attack. Churchill disagreed because of Stalin's promise to declare war on Bulgaria if it attacked.

---

7   The President said the Chinese had asked for representation on the Combined Chiefs of Staff at SEXTANT. He made it clear it was not possible. The Chinese had also asked if a US-Chinese Committee could be set up to consider military operations that involved their troops.

Sixth Combined Chiefs of Staff Meeting

Command of US Strategic Air Forces in the Europe-Mediterranean area; Southeast Asia amphibious operations; Southeast Asia Operations; Draft Report to the President and Prime Minister; Relation of resources to plans; Developing the Azores facilities; Employment of French Forces; New command arrangements; Final remarks.

Sextant Communiqué

Mr. Roosevelt, President of the United States of America, Mr. Ismet Inonu, President of the Turkish Republic, and Mr. Winston Churchill, Prime Minister of Great Britain, met in Cairo on 4, 5 and 6 December 1943. The participation in this conference of the Head of the Turkish State, in response to the cordial invitation addressed to him by the United States, British and Soviet Governments, bears striking testimony to the strength of the alliance which unites Great Britain and Turkey and to the firm friendship existing between the Turkish Republic, the United States of America, and the Soviet Union.

Presidents Roosevelt and Inonu and Prime Minister Churchill reviewed the general political situation and examined the policy to be followed at length, taking into account the joint and individual interests of the three countries. The study of all problems in a spirit of understanding and loyalty showed the closest unity existed between the United States of America, Turkey and Great Britain in their attitude towards the world situation. The conversations in Cairo had been most useful and most fruitful for the future of the relations between the four countries. The identity of interest and of views of the American and British democracies, with those of the Soviet Union, and the traditional relations of friendship existing between these powers and Turkey, have been reaffirmed throughout the proceedings of the Cairo conference.

The Octagon Conference: 12–16 September 1944

The Allies continued on the offensive but the situation in Italy remained stagnant for some time, despite a landing at Anzio behind the Gustav Line in January 1944. The Germans finally cracked and on 4 June American troops entered Rome. However, the major event was the long awaiting opening of the second front, with the beginning of OVERLORD on 6 June. After a tough battle through the Normandy bocage, first the Americans and then the British broke out as German resistance collapsed. The second landing, codename DRAGOON, in the south of France was also a success and by mid-September most of France and parts of Belgium had been liberated. Meanwhile, on the Eastern Front, the Polish Home Army rose up and tried to liberate Warsaw while the Red Army regrouped on the River Vistula.

In the Far East the Japanese attacked in Assam and there was heavy fighting at Imphal and Kohima as well as in the Arakan; there were fierce battles on both fronts between March and July 1944. The Japanese eventually withdrew across the River Chindwin, harassed by the Chindits, but the death of General Wingate in a plane crash resulted in the attack stalling. In the Pacific, Kwajalein and Eniwetok were captured in February 1944 while the Mariana and Palau Islands campaign continued. Battles for Saipan and the Philippine Sea also began in June 1944.

The Citadel in Quebec, Canada, was again chosen as the venue for the Octagon conference. The chief representatives were President Roosevelt, Prime Minister Churchill and William L. Mackenzie King, Prime Minister of Canada.

12 September
First Chiefs of Staff Meeting
Personnel Shipping; Command of DRAGOON[1] Forces; European Situation Report;[2] Mediterranean Situation Report.[3]
Second Chiefs of Staff Meeting
Machinery for coordinating the west and east campaigns; Occupation zones of Germany; Control of the Strategic Bomber Force in Europe.

13 September
Third Chiefs of Staff Meeting
The Enemy Situation in and Progress Report on the Pacific; Strategy for the Defeat of Japan; Future Operations in the Mediterranean.

13 September: First Octagon Meeting
Churchill said the United Nations' affairs had taken a revolutionary turn for the good since SEXTANT. Everything they had touched had turned to gold and there had been an unbroken run of military successes during the last seven weeks.[4] The way the situation had developed since the Tehran Conference gave the impression of remarkable design and precision of execution.

First there had been the Anzio landing[5] and then on the same day as the launching of the great Operation OVERLORD they had captured Rome, which had seemed the most perfect timing. He wished to congratulate the US Chiefs of Staff on the success of DRAGOON,[6] which had produced the most gratifying results. It was already probable that 8000–9000 prisoners had been captured, while the south and western parts of France were now being systematically cleared of the enemy. He was firmly convinced future historians would give a great account of the period since Tehran. Roosevelt said no little of the credit for the conception

---

1 DRAGOON was the new name for the invasion of southern France.
2 General Eisenhower's situation report.
3 General Wilson's situation report.
4 Churchill is referring to the rapid advance across France.
5 SHINGLE began on 22 January 1944 but it had failed to break the deadlock in Italy. Churchill's comment at the time was "I had hoped we were hurling a wildcat into the shore, but all we got was a stranded whale."
6 DRAGOON began on 15 August when US troops landed on the French Riviera.

of DRAGOON should be attributed to Marshal Stalin. It was close to being his suggestion rather than theirs.[1]

Churchill was glad to be able to record, although the British Empire had now entered its sixth year of the war it was still keeping its end up with an overall population of only 70 million white people.[2] The British Empire effort in Europe, counted in terms of divisions in the field, was about equal to the United States. This was as it should be. He was proud the British Empire could claim equal partnership with their great ally, the United States, whom he regarded as the greatest military power in the world. But the British Empire effort had reached its peak, whereas their ally's was ever increasing.

There was complete confidence in General Eisenhower and his relations with General Montgomery were of the best, as were those between General Montgomery and General Bradley.[3] The part played by General Walter B. Smith[4] in directing and cementing the staffs was of the highest order. The control of operations in France was in capable hands. An efficient, integrated American-British staff machine had been built up and the battle was being brilliantly exploited.

Turning to Italy, Churchill said General Alexander had resumed the offensive at the end of August.[5] Since then Eighth Army had suffered about 8000 and the Fifth Army about 1000 casualties. Fifth Army had not been so heavily engaged, but they were expected to make a thrust that very day.

The British had a great stake in Italy. The largest British Empire Army in existence was in that theatre. There were sixteen British Empire divisions in all[6] but Churchill had been anxious lest Alexander be shorn of certain essentials for the vigorous prosecution of his campaign. He now understood the Combined Chiefs of Staff agreed there should be no withdrawals from Alexander's Army until either Kesselring's Army[7] had been beaten, or was on the run out of Italy. Marshall said there was no thought of withdrawing any forces until the outcome of Alexander's present operations was known. Churchill emphasized if the Germans were run out of Italy they should have to look for fresh fields and pastures new. It would never do for their armies to remain idle. He had always been attracted by a right-handed movement, with the purpose of giving Germany a stab in the armpit.

---

1   In February 1944 the US and British Chiefs of Staff were at loggerheads over DRAGOON. There were three options: no invasion, a fake invasion or an actual invasion. Eventually, the President had to remind the Combined Chiefs of Staff that he had made a commitment to DRAGOON to Marshal Stalin and he would have to refer its cancellation to Moscow.
2   Including the overseas Dominions and Colonies.
3   General Montgomery as commander of 21st Army Group on Eisenhower's left flank and General Bradley as commander of 12th Army Group in the centre. General Jake L. Devers commanded 6th Army Group on Eisenhower's right flank. Whatever the Generals thought of each other in private, they put their differences to one side to work together on a professional level. Some historians may disagree.
4   General Walter B. 'Beetle' Smith (1895-1961), Eisenhower's Chief of Staff at Supreme Headquarters Allied Expeditionary Force (SHAEF).
5   General Alexander, commander of 15th Army Group. OLIVE began on 25 August and although both Eighth and Fifth Armies penetrated the Gothic Line, no decisive breakthrough was made.
6   Eight British, two Canadian, one New Zealand, one South African and four British Indian divisions.
7   Field Marshal Kesselring's Army Group C.

Their objective should be Vienna.[8] If German resistance collapsed they should be able to reach Vienna quicker and easier. He had also given considerable thought to the capture of Istria, which would include the occupation of Trieste and Fiume.[9]

Churchill had been relieved to learn the US Chiefs of Staff were willing to leave come LSTs engaged in DRAGOON in the Mediterranean, to provide an amphibious lift if the Adriatic operation was found desirable and necessary. An added reason for this right-handed movement was the rapid encroachment of the Russians into the Balkans and the consequent dangerous spread of Russian influence in this area. He preferred to get into Vienna before the Russians, as he did not know what Russia's policy would be after she took it.

Churchill then reviewed the campaign in Burma which had been on a considerable scale. 250,000 men had been engaged, and the fighting for Imphal and Kohima had been extremely bitter.[10] General Stilwell was to be congratulated on his brilliant operation, resulting in the capture of Myitkyina.[11] There had been 40,000 battle casualties and 288,000 sick; the greater proportion of the latter had recovered and returned to duty. As a result of the campaign, the air line to China had been kept open and India rendered secure from attack. It was estimated the Japanese had lost 100,000 men in this, their largest land engagement.

In spite of these successes, it was most undesirable for the fighting in the jungles of Burma to go on indefinitely. For this reason, the British Chiefs of Staff had put forward DRACULA,[12] which would be preceded by CAPITAL Phase I and as much as was necessary of Phase II.[13] Difficulties were being experienced making the necessary forces available and transporting them to the Southeast Asia Theatre in time to carry out DRACULA before the 1945 monsoon beginning in May.

Churchill said the present situation in Europe, favourable as it was, did not permit the decision to withdraw forces to be taken. They had to keep an option open for as long as possible, and every effort was being directed to this end. There were certain elements inimical to Anglo–American good relations who were putting it about that Great Britain would take no share in the war against Japan once Germany had been defeated. Far from shirking this task, the British Empire was eager to play the greatest possible part. They had every reason for doing so.

Japan was as much the bitter enemy of the British Empire as of the United States. British territory had been captured in battle and grievous losses had been

---

8   Churchill is referring to an advance northeast through the Ljubljana Gap into Austria and Hungary. The Ljubljana Gap is between the east end of the Alps and the west end of the Dinaric Alps and connects Trieste and Ljubljana, the capital of Slovenia.

9   The Istrian Peninsula is on the northeast Adriatic coast between the Gulf of Trieste and the Bay of Kvaner. The large peninsula was ideal for an amphibious landing. It is now shared between Croatia to the south and Slovenia to the north (a tiny part belongs to Italy). Trieste is at the north corner and Fiume is at the east corner.

10 The Battle of Imphal took place around the capital of the state of Manipur in North-East India from March until July 1944. Japanese armies attempted to invade India but they were forced back into Burma with heavy losses. The simultaneous Battle of Kohima and the eventual relief of the encircled Allied forces at Imphal were the turning point of the Burma Campaign and the largest defeat to-date in Japanese history.

11 Myitkyina is in northeast Burma, 50 miles from the Chinese border.

12 DRACULA was a planned airborne and amphibious attack on Rangoon by British and Indian forces.

13 CAPITAL, or Operation Y, was a British offensive from Assam, India, into northeast Burma. It was planned to clear Japanese forces from northern Burma, reopen the Burma Road and stop Japanese forces transferring to the Pacific theatre.

suffered.[1] The offer Churchill wished to make was for the British Main Fleet to take part in the major operations against Japan under US Supreme Command. Roosevelt said the offer was accepted on the largest possible scale.

Churchill said there would be available a powerful and well balanced force, including, it was hoped, at the end of next year, their newest 15-inch battleship.[2] A fleet train[3] of ample proportions had been built up, which would render the fleet independent of shore base resources for a considerable time. The placing of a British fleet in the central Pacific would not prevent a detachment being made to work with General MacArthur in the Southwest Pacific if this was desired. This would include air forces. There was, of course, no intention to interfere in any way with MacArthur's command.[4]

As a further contribution to the defeat of the enemy, the Royal Air Force would like to take a part in the heavy bombardment of Japan. A bomber force of 1500 planes could be made available and he would like a proportionate share with the 4000 to 5000 American planes in striking at the heart of the enemy.

As regards land forces, it would probably be possible to move six divisions from the European Theatre to the East when Germany had been beaten, to be followed perhaps by a further six.[5] There were fifteen divisions in Burma who might ultimately be drawn upon. Churchill had always advocated an advance across the Bay of Bengal and operations to recover Singapore, the loss of which had been a grievous and shameful blow to British prestige that had to be avenged.[6] It would not be good enough for Singapore to be returned at the peace table. Churchill wanted to recover it in battle.

These operations would not debar the employment of small British Empire components with United States forces in the Pacific. There was nothing cast iron in these ideas. First they should go with DRACULA, and then survey the situation. If a better plan could be evolved, it should not be ruled out in advance. The keyword should be to engage the largest number of their own forces against the largest number of the enemy at the earliest possible moment.

Roosevelt thanked Churchill for his lucid and comprehensive review of the situation. It was a matter of profound satisfaction that there had been ever increasing solidarity of outlook and identity of basic thought at each succeeding conference between the American and British representatives. Added to this, there had always been an atmosphere of cordiality and friendship.

Their fortunes had prospered but it was still not quite possible to forecast the date of the end of the war with Germany. It seemed clear the Germans were

---

1 British forces had been forced out of Malaya, forced on the defensive in Burma and surrendered Hong Kong in December 1941 and Singapore in February 1942, along with 130,000 prisoners.

2 HMS *Vanguard* was launched in November 1944 but it was not ready until May 1946. It was the last Royal Navy dreadnought and the last battleship built in the world.

3 Support craft for the fleet.

4 General MacArthur's Southwest Pacific command was preparing to invade the Philippines.

5 There were twelve divisions in Northwest Europe.

6 Singapore was the major British military base in Southeast Asia but the 'Impregnable Fortress' fell on 15 February 1942 after only a week. Lieutenant General Arthur Percival's command of 80,000 British, Australian and Indian troops spent the rest of the war in captivity. Churchill called it the "worst disaster" and the "largest capitulation" in British history.

withdrawing from the Balkans and it appeared likely they would retire to the line of the Alps in Italy. The Russians were on the edge of Hungary. The Germans had shown themselves good at staging withdrawals and they had been able to save large numbers of personnel, although much material had been lost.

If the battle went well with Alexander, they should reach the Piave reasonably soon.[7] All forces in Italy should be engaged to the maximum intensity. In the west it seemed probable the Germans would retire behind the Rhine. The West Wall was the right bank of the Rhine and it would present a formidable obstacle.[8] He thought they should plan to force the barrier of the Rhine and then consider the situation. They should have to turn the line either from the east or from the west and their plans had to be flexible. The Germans could not yet be counted out and one more big battle would have to be fought.[9]

The operations in the East would to some extent depend on how the situation developed in Europe. They should not remain in Burma any longer than it was necessary to clean up the Japanese. The American plan was to regain the Philippines and to dominate the mainland of Japan from the Philippines or Formosa[10] and from bridgeheads seized in China. If forces could be established on mainland China, China could be saved. American experience was that the 'end run' method paid a handsome dividend.[11] Rabaul was an example of this bypassing technique, where it had been employed with considerable success at small cost of life. Would it not be equally possible to bypass Singapore by seizing an area to the north or east of it, for example, Bangkok? Singapore may be very strong and he was opposed to going up against strong positions.

Churchill suggested studying the seizure of localities such as Penang[12] and the Kra Isthmus[13] or Moulmein.[14] As far as Singapore was concerned he did not favour the bypassing method. There would undoubtedly be a large force of Japanese in the Malay Peninsula and it would help the American operations in the Pacific if they could bring these forces to action and destroy them, in addition to achieving the great prize of the recapture of Singapore. If Formosa was captured, would the Japanese garrisons to the south be completely cut off? Admiral King replied they would be strangulated and would ultimately perish. Churchill said all these projects were being examined and would be put in order. No decision could be taken until Rangoon[15] had been captured.

---

7   The River Piave started in the eastern Alps and ran south in a dog leg to the Adriatic Sea near Venice.

8   The West Wall, or Siegfried Line, ran 390 miles from Holland to the Swiss frontier. It was estimated to have over 18,000 bunkers and tank traps. After being ignored for several years, on 24 August 1944 Hitler directed work would restart on the fortifications and over 20,000 forced labourers and members of the Reich Labour Service were joined by thousands of local people.

9   The one big battle the Germans would soon be planning was an offensive in the Ardennes, starting on 16 December.

10   Now Taiwan. The island was bypassed during the American advance towards Japan.

11   The end run method (an American Football term) involved bypassing an enemy strongpoint to cut his lines of communication. The position could then be starved of supplies, forcing the enemy to either break out, organise a relief force or surrender.

12   Penang Island on the west coast of the Malaysia Peninsula.

13   Kra Isthmus is the narrow strip of land which connects the mainland of Asia and the Malay Peninsula; it is also known as the 'The Devil's Neck'.

14   Now Mawlamyine at the mouth of Thanlwin (Salween), at the midpoint of Burma's west coast.

15   Rangoon, now Yangon, is at the mouth of the river of the same name. It was then the capital of Burma.

They should not overlook Stalin's solemn undertaking at Tehran that Russia would enter the war against Japan the day Hitler was beaten. There was no reason to doubt he would be as good as his word, the Russians undoubtedly had great ambitions in the East. If Hitler was beaten by January and Japan was confronted with the three most powerful nations in the world, they would undoubtedly have cause to reflect whether they could continue the fight. Roosevelt referred to the almost fanatical Japanese tenacity; in Saipan, not only the soldiers but also the civilians had committed suicide rather than be taken.[1]

Air Marshal Portal hoped to have between 600 and 800 heavy bombers available for operations against the Japanese mainland. They could be supplemented by a considerable number of medium bomber squadrons.

Churchill asked about the employment of the British Fleet. Roosevelt wanted to use it in any way possible. Admiral King said a paper on the subject had been prepared for reference to the Combined Chiefs of Staff. The question was being actively studied. Churchill asked if it would not be better to employ the new British ships in place of battle-worn vessels of the United States. King said the matter was under examination. Churchill said the offer had been made and asked if it was accepted. Roosevelt said yes.

Churchill asked if an undertaking could be made that the British Air Force would participate in the main operations. Marshall said he and General Arnold were trying to see how best to get in the maximum number of aircraft for these operations. It was not so long ago they were crying out for airplanes and now they had a surplus.[2]

Marshall said if the British were heavily engaged in Southeast Asia and in Malaya they would require a large proportion of their air forces for these operations. Was there a distinction between these theatre operations and the envisaged heavy bombardment of Japan? Portal replied there was. The Lancaster bomber, if refuelled in the air, had a range nearly approaching that of the B-29;[3] they had a range of 800 or 900 miles without refuelling in the air.[4]

Roosevelt said there were certain groups in the United States, and he had no doubt similar groups existed in Great Britain, who evinced a kindly attitude towards the Germans.[5] Their theory was evil could be eradicated from the German make-up and the nation could be rejuvenated by kindness. Churchill said such sentiments would hardly be tolerated in Great Britain. The British people would demand a strong policy against the Germans.[6] The German working man should be allowed sufficient food for his bare needs and work, but no

1 Saipan is in the Mariana Islands and the battle lasted from 15 June to 9 July. Hirohito sent out an order encouraging the civilians to commit suicide at the end of June, promising them an equal spiritual status in the afterlife as soldiers who died in combat. 1,000 committed suicide, many jumping from 'Suicide Cliff' and 'Banzai Cliff'.

2 There were only a few islands and a limited number of suitable airfields in range of Japan.

3 The B-29 had a combat range of 3250 miles while that of the Lancaster was only 2530 miles.

4 Tokyo was 1500 miles north of the Mariana Islands and B-29s could use Saipan as an airbase to attack Japan; Lancasters needed to refuel.

5 Around one in six Americans had German ancestry. 300,000 German-born resident aliens who had German citizenship had to register under the Alien Registration Act of 1940, while some 11,000 were interned under the Alien Enemy Act of 1798.

6 Great Britain had endured the Blitz, rationing and other hardships which the United States had not.

more. The more virulent elements such as the Gestapo and the young fanatics should be deported to work in rehabilitating the devastated areas of Europe. Plans for the partition of Germany were now in the course of preparation but no final decisions had been taken.

14 September

Morgenthau and Cherwell
Discussed Lend–Lease and the economic plan for Germany.

Fourth Chiefs of Staff Meeting
British Participation in the Pacific; Operations in Southeast Asia; Planning date for the end of the war in Japan; Operations of the Twentieth Air Force; Communications to Marshal Stalin and Generalissimo Chiang Kai-shek.

15 September

Fifth Chiefs of Staff Meeting
Progress of the Pacific Campaign; Communicating Octagon's results to Stalin; Redeployment of troops from Europe; Operation HIGHBALL;[7] Final Report to the President and Prime Minister; Press Release.

Morgenthau and Cherwell
Policy towards Germany and Lend Lease.
The President met the Archduke Otto of Austria.

16 September

Sixth Chiefs of Staff Meeting
Allocating Occupation Zones in Germany; Situation in China; Press Communiqué.

Second Octagon Meeting, 16 September 1944
Admiral Leahy read out the Combined Chiefs of Staff's report to the President and Prime Minister.[8]

Control of Strategic Bomber Forces in Europe
The Supreme Commander had developed an air plan to support OVERLORD. Control of all air operations out of England by the Strategic Air Force and the RAF Bomber Command, had passed to the Supreme Commander, Allied Expeditionary Force (Eisenhower) in April 1944. The special conditions which made it desirable for the Supreme Commander, Allied Expeditionary Force to control all forces operating out of the United Kingdom no longer carried their original force.[9]

---

7   The bouncing bomb project. UPKEEP were cylindrical bombs used during CHASTISE, the Dambusters Raid, on the night of 16/17 May 1943. HIGHBALL was developed for use against ships, particularly the *Tirpitz* hiding in Norway's fjords. Development of both bombs continued at the same time but HIGHBALL had problems and the design was changed to a sphere. The problems were never solved and it was never used in action.

8   The Overall Objective, the Overall Strategic Concept and the Basic Undertakings in Support of Overall Strategic Concept were the same as those stated at the Sextant Conference. The Basic Undertakings in Support of Over-All Strategic Concept were also the same except for a commitment to continue operations leading to the earliest practicable invasion of Japan.

9   Supreme Commander of the Allied Expeditionary Force, General Eisenhower, had control of all the air forces before, during and after the invasion of Normandy. With the Allies pursuing the Germans across France, it was time for the USAAF and the RAF to resume strategic bombing activities.

They had agreed control of the Strategic Bomber Force in Europe should be exercised by the Deputy Chief of the Air Staff, Royal Air Force[1] and the Commanding General, United States Strategic Air Forces in Europe,[2] acting jointly for the Chief of the Air Staff, RAF and the Commanding General, United States Army Air Forces.[3] A directive[4] had been issued to the two officers.

Operations in Northwest Europe

General Eisenhower had reported[5] on the course of operations in France and the Low Countries and had given a review of his future intentions. His broad intention was to press on with all speed to destroy the German armed forces and occupy the heart of Germany. He considered his best opportunity for defeating the enemy in the West was in striking at the Ruhr and Saar,[6] since he was convinced the enemy would concentrate the remainder of his available forces to defend these essential areas.

The Supreme Commander's first operation would be to break the Siegfried Line and seize crossings over the Rhine. In doing this, his main effort would be on the left. He would then prepare logistically and otherwise for a deep thrust into Germany. They had approved Eisenhower's proposals and drawn his attention to:

a) the advantages of the northern line of approach into Germany, as opposed to the southern;[7]

b) the need to open up the northwest ports, particularly Antwerp and Rotterdam, before bad weather set in.[8]

Operations in Italy

The Chiefs of Staff had examined a report by General Wilson[9] on operations in his theatre. He considered operations in Italy would develop in one of two ways:

a) Kesselring's forces would be routed and it should be possible to undertake a rapid regrouping and a pursuit towards the Ljubljana Gap[10] and across the Alps via the Brenner Pass,[11] leaving a small force to clear up northwest Italy.

b) Kesselring's Army would succeed in effecting an orderly withdrawal; in which event it did not seem possible they could do more than clear the Lombardy Plains that year.[12]

---

1   Air Chief Marshal Sir Norman H. Bottomley RAF (1891-1970), assistant to Air Chief Marshal Sir Charles Portal.

2   General Carl A. 'Tooey' Spaatz (1891-1974), reporting to General Henry Arnold.

3   The latter acting as agents of the Combined Chiefs of Staff.

4   C.C.S. 520/6 noted that Eisenhower and Tedder were in France and far from General Spaatz's headquarters and the Air Ministry. Tedder's small staff was incapable of interpreting the results of bombing raids or assessing enemy opposition. At the time the US had 2970 heavy bombers in the UK and 1512 in the Mediterranean; 2980 were operational and each had two crews.

5   Cable SCAF 78.

6   The industrial and coal producing regions in western Germany.

7   Crossing the Rhine between Arnhem and Duisburg, heading for the open country north of the Ruhr.

8   Opening Antwerp involved clearing the Germans from either side of the River Scheldt (Schelde), a fifty-mile-long estuary.

9   Cable NAF 774.

10 The gap between the mountainous Alps and Dinaric Alps; it runs between Trieste and Ljubljana, the capital of Slovenia.

11 The principal pass connecting Italy and Austria.

12 The lowlands south of the Alps.

Difficult terrain and severe weather in the Alps during the winter would prevent another major offensive until the spring of 1945. The Chiefs of Staff agreed:

a)   No major units should be withdrawn from Italy until the outcome of Alexander's present offensive was known.

b)   The desirability of withdrawing formations from Fifth US Army should be reconsidered when they knew the results of General Alexander's present offensive, the German withdrawal in northern Italy and Eisenhower's views.

c)   To inform Wilson he could retain the amphibious lift in the Mediterranean for use in the Istrian Peninsula if he wished. He must submit his plan to the Combined Chiefs of Staff as soon as possible, and not later than 10 October.

They had instructed the Supreme Allied Commander accordingly.[13]

Churchill suggested the alternative developments in the operations in Italy postulated by General Wilson were rather too rigid. There might be many shades between the rout of General Kesselring's forces and the ability of the Germans to effect an orderly withdrawal. He suggested amending it to read "Kesselring's Army will succeed in effecting an orderly withdrawal, in which event it does not at present seem possible we can do more than clear the Lombardy Plains this year. Unless the enemy's resistance is markedly reduced, difficult terrain and severe weather in the Alps during the winter would prevent another major offensive until spring 1945."

Churchill asked for the precise implication of the statement referring to the outcome of General Alexander's offensive to be made perfectly clear. It would be quite unacceptable if the statement was intended to cover an offensive only as far as the Rimini Line. He assumed the contemplated offensive would include domination of the Po Valley. Marshall understood Alexander's present offensive included an invasion of the valley. Admiral Leahy agreed.

Churchill expressed his appreciation to Admiral King for his offer to provide an amphibious lift for possible operations against the Istrian Peninsula. Admiral King said the landing craft would have to proceed to the Southeast Asia Theatre for DRACULA after taking part in the Adriatic operations. It was important that General Wilson submitted his plan and a decision was taken before 15 October. Churchill agreed it was of the utmost importance to settle the matter promptly. There were certain other craft in the Mediterranean which were urgently required for the Pacific and General Laycock confirmed they would not be wanted for the Istrian operation.

Balkan Operations

General Wilson considered a situation could be anticipated in which the bulk of the German forces south of a line, Trieste–Ljubljana–Zagreb and the Danube,[14] would be immobilized and would remain so until their supplies were exhausted. They would then surrender to Alexander's army or be liquidated by partisans

---

13   Cable FAN 415.
14   In what is now Slovenia and Croatia, the area to the northeast of the Adriatic Sea.

or Russian forces. They had noted that as long as the battle in Italy continued there would be no forces available in the Mediterranean to employ in the Balkans except:

a) The small force of two British brigades from Egypt which was being held ready to occupy the Athens area. It would pave the way for the commencement of relief and establishment of law and order and the Greek Government.[1]

b) The small land forces in the Adriatic which were being actively used for commando type operations.[2]

Command of DRAGOON Forces

On 15 September command of the DRAGOON forces operating from southern France was transferred to the Supreme Commander, Allied Expeditionary Force.[3] Adjustments to the ground and air forces depended on the development of the campaign in Italy.

Coordination of the United States-Soviet-British Military Effort

Two months earlier Stalin had suggested improving the system of military coordination between the USSR, the US and the UK, to the US Ambassador in Moscow.[4] The Chiefs of Staff had instructed the heads of the US and British Military Missions in Moscow[5] to initiate action at once with the Soviet General Staff, with a view to the setting up a Tripartite Military Committee in Moscow. It would consist of senior representatives of the Russian General Staff, of the US Chiefs of Staff and of the British Chiefs of Staff.

They had instructed them to make it clear this Committee would be purely consultative and advisory, with no power to make decisions without reference to the respective Chiefs of Staff and the Russian General Staff. It had to be military in character and must not impinge upon the work being done by the European Advisory Commission, such as civil affairs.[6]

They had stressed the Russian representative on the Committee should be a senior member of the Russian General Staff to eliminate the delays in dealings between the Russians and the United States and British Military Missions. On the United States and British sides the heads of the present missions would represent the US and British Chiefs of Staff respectively.

The War against Japan

The Chiefs of Staff agreed the overall objective in the war against Japan should be expressed as follows. To force the unconditional surrender of Japan:

---

1   Greece was liberated soon after Octagon but British soldiers had to back government soldiers during a fight with supporters of the National Liberation Front (EAM) in December 1944.

2   Operations into the Balkans had been abandoned; it was more profitable to let the German divisions struggle to hold it than move troops in to fight them.

3   FACS 76. From General Devers to Eisenhower. At the same time, General Alexander 'Sandy' Patch (1889-1945) became commander of the new 6th Army Group, the right (south) wing of the Allied advance to the Rhine.

4   Ambassador W. Averell Harriman (1891-1986).

5   General John R. Deane (US) and Rear Admiral Ernest R. Archer (UK) were the military representatives in Moscow.

6   The European Advisory Commission (EAC) started work in January 1944 deciding how to divide Germany and Austria between the UK, US and Russia; the same division applied to Berlin and Vienna. It also drafted the instructions for the unconditional surrender of Germany and how to administer the occupied countries after the war ended.

a) By lowering the Japanese ability and will to resist, by establishing sea and air blockades, conducting intensive air bombardment and destroying Japanese air and naval strength;

b) By ultimately invading and seizing objectives in the industrial heart of Japan.

The Chiefs of Staff believed operations had to be devised to accomplish the defeat of Japan at the earliest possible date. Their plans had to retain flexibility and provision had to be made to take full advantage of possible developments in the strategic situation, which may permit taking all manner of short cuts. They proposed to exploit to the fullest the Allied superiority of naval and air power and to avoid, wherever possible, costly land campaigns. Unremitting submarine warfare against the enemy ships would be continued.

Very long range bomber operations against Japan would be continued from China's bases.[7] They would be started from bases being established in the Marianas[8] and from any seized in the future. The air forces in China would continue to support operations of the Chinese ground forces and would also provide the maximum practical support for the campaign in the Pacific.[9]

Operations were being conducted to effect the reconquest of the Philippines and the opening of a seaway to China.[10] They noted British operations against Japan[11] would require the allocation of resources. These requirements would be borne in mind when planning production.

The Chiefs of Staff agreed the British Fleet should participate in the main Pacific operations against Japan, with the understanding the Fleet would be balanced and self supporting. Its employment in Pacific operations would be decided from time to time in accordance with prevailing circumstances. They had invited the British Chiefs of Staff to put forward a general estimate of the contribution the Royal Air Force would be prepared to make against Japan.

Discussion about the War against Japan

Churchill said the Canadian Government was anxious for some assurance in principle that their forces would participate in the main operations against Japan. The Canadian Government preferred they should operate in the more northerly parts of the Pacific, as their troops were unused to tropical conditions. General Arnold said the need to secure suitable bases for all the forces operating in the Pacific might require employment of Canadian forces in the tropics.[12]

Churchill thought it quite possible that a heavy, sustained and ever-increasing air bombardment of the Japanese cities might cause Japan to capitulate. People could only stand heavy bombardment as long as they could hope it would come

---

7   Fourteenth Air Force operated from China.
8   The Marianas stretch for over 1500 miles from Guam in the south to Japan in the north. B-29s were operating from Saipan and Tinian and in there would be an air base on Iwo Jima in the future.
9   MATTERHORN involved XX Bomber Command's B-29s based in India and China bombing Japan.
10   General MacArthur's South West Pacific Area command was about to attack the Philippines, starting with Leyte on 20 October.
11   Operations which still needed approval.
12   The Prime Minister said the Canadian Government wanted some assurance that their forces would participate in the war against Japan although it preferred its forces were used in the north area of the Pacific because their troops were not used to tropical conditions. It was agreed a paragraph accepting Canadian participation in principle would be inserted in the report.

to some endurable end sooner or later. There could be no such hope for Japan and all they could look forward to was the prospect of an ever increasing weight of explosive on their centres of population.

Operations in Southeast Asia

The Chiefs of Staff agreed the object in Southeast Asia was the recapture of all Burma at the earliest date. It was understood these operations must not prejudice the security of the existing air supply route to China, including the air staging base at Myitkyina, and the opening of overland communications.[1] They approved the following operations:

a) The stages of CAPITAL necessary for the security of the air route and the realization of overland communications with China;[2]

b) The Chiefs of Staff attached the greatest importance to the execution of DRACULA before the monsoon in 1945, with a target date of 15 March. If DRACULA had to be postponed until after the monsoon of 1945, it was their intention to exploit CAPITAL as far as possible without prejudicing the preparations for DRACULA in November 1945.

Discussion about Southeast Asia Operations

With reference to the term "the opening of a seaway to China," Churchill assumed it meant the seaway from the United States. He did not contemplate a sea route being opened from the south, through the Sunda Strait. Admiral King agreed with his interpretation.

Churchill accepted the need to secure the air route and open overland communications with China. But any tendency to over ensure these operations would rule out DRACULA, which he and the British Chiefs of Staff were set on carrying out before the 1945 monsoon.[3] Churchill read out a note on the provision of forces for DRACULA and made suggestions about the timing of the movements of forces from the United States. If the United States authorities could see their way to assist the operations in Burma with one or two divisions, it would be better to move two divisions from the later schedules of the United States Army transportation to Europe than take two divisions from General Montgomery's Army which was fighting.

This change would bring additional troops into action against the Japanese quicker, without withdrawing any troops already fighting in Germany.[4] He did not ask for an immediate decision and asked if the US Chiefs of Staff would examine his suggestion. Marshall said there was only one light division available and it had been reorganized and allocated to the European Theatre at Eisenhower's special request.[5] Every division in the United States was already allocated either to Eisenhower or to the Pacific.

---

1   Myitkyina in north Burma. The Ledo Road opened in January 1945 at the end of three years of back breaking work; 1100 Americans and thousands more Burmese died building the road.
2   CAPITAL was the invasion of Northern Burma designed to clear the Burma Road and tie down Japanese forces.
3   In other words, if too many troops were allocated to CAPITAL, there would not be enough to carry out DRACULA.
4   Send two US Divisions direct from the United States to Burma rather than withdrawing two British divisions currently fighting in northwest Europe.
5   This was the 10th Mountain Division, organised and trained for mountain warfare.

The last divisions for the European Theatre of Operations were scheduled to sail during the final week in January or the first week in February. The only way of providing United States divisions for Burma was by taking them from approved allocations. General Stilwell had also asked for a division and would take two if he could get them.

Marshall had recently heard a rumour that the increase in DRACULA's requirements had been brought about by pressure from the United States authorities. After a thorough inquiry he found it was groundless; no United States authorities had advocated any such increase. Marshall then outlined certain developments regarding the Chinese forces. The Generalissimo contemplated withdrawing Y Force across the Salween[6] unless Stilwell's Ledo Force advanced on Bhamo.[7] No replacements had been provided for the Salween Force and it had now dwindled to 14,000 men. The Generalissimo had sent the President a note pointing out the consequences of the proposed action, stating the Generalissimo had to accept full responsibility.

Redeployment after the End of the War in Europe

The Chiefs of Staff considered the whole problem of the redeployment of forces after the end of the war in Europe, and of repatriation, needed a combined study to assure the optimum use of resources involved, including personnel and cargo shipping. They had to make certain the forces required for operations against Japan would reach the theatre of war at the earliest date.[8] They had instructed the combined staffs, in consultation with the combined shipping authorities, to study and report to the Combined Chiefs of Staff.

Discussion about Redeployment

Churchill pointed out their shipping situation would be greatly eased after the defeat of Germany by the cessation of the convoys, the end of the U-boat menace. Lord Leathers had said they should be able to get an additional lift of between 40 and 50 per cent. The ships would be faster on passage with a much quicker turn round at the terminal ports.

Duration of the War against Japan

The Chiefs of Staff felt it was important to agree and circulate a planning date for the end of the war against Japan. The date was necessary for planning production and the allocation of manpower. They recommended the date should be set at eighteen months after the defeat of Germany. The date could be adjusted to conform to the course of the war.[9]

Allocation of Zones of Occupation in Germany

Upon the collapse of organized resistance by the German Army, the following subdivision of the part of Germany not allocated to the Soviet Government was

---

6 The Salween River ('Angry River' in Chinese) forms the boundary between Burma and Thailand. The Salween Campaign was launched to open the Burma Road again and connect it to the Ledo Road. Y-Force was the Chinese Expeditionary Force advised by American Brigadier General Frank Dorn and his staff.
7 In northeast Burma, near the Chinese border.
8 Allied troops had to be moved to European ports and shipped to the Pacific, ready to join the war on Japan.
9 It would be in three months, following the dropping of the two atomic bombs on Hiroshima on 6 August and Nagasaki on 9 August.

acceptable to the Combined Chiefs of Staff from a military point of view. For disarmament, policing and preservation of order:

   a)   The British forces would occupy Germany west and east of the Rhine, north of the line from Koblenz. It would follow the northern border of Hessen and Nassau to the border of the Soviet area.

   b)   The United States forces would occupy Germany east of the Rhine, south of the line Koblenz to the northern border of Hessen-Nassau and west of the Soviet area.

   c)   Control of the ports of Bremen and Bremerhaven, and adjacent staging areas, would be vested in the Commander of the American Zone.[1]

   d)   The American area needed access through the west and northwest seaports and passage through the British-controlled area.[2]

Admiral Leahy said the Combined Chiefs of Staff had agreed on the provisional demarcation of zones of occupation in Germany. The details and implications would have to be worked out by the experts.

The Argonaut Conference, 4–11 February 1945[3]

The Allies had a tough time in Europe over the winter of 1944–45. While the opening of Antwerp port in November meant their supply line was safe, the Germans fought hard for the west bank of the Rhine. They struck back in the Ardennes on 16 December, creating the famous Bulge in the Allied line but by January it had virtually been erased. Meanwhile, on 12 January 1945, the Red Army launched a massive offensive in the east, liberating Warsaw and Krakow while closing in on Berlin.

While the Burma campaign stalled, the Pacific campaign went from strength to strength. The Battle of Peleliu ended in November 1944 while Leyte Gulf, Surigao Strait, Samar and Cape Engaño were all fought to a conclusion in October 1944. The invasion of Iwo Jima on the Bonin Islands was next, the first time American troops would be fighting on Japanese home soil.

President Roosevelt and his party embarked on USS *Quincy*,[4] on 23 January 1945 at Newport News, Virginia. They arrived on Malta on 2 February and after a preliminary meeting with the Prime Minister and other dignitaries, Roosevelt flew onto the Crimea by air to attend the Yalta Conference.[5] While he stayed in Livadia Palace, Churchill stayed in Vorontsoc Villa, 12 miles to the south.

The conferences were held in Livadia Palace, Yalta on the Crimea, on 4 February. The palace had been the Czar's summer residence and after the Revolution it had been turned into a rest home for tuberculosis patients. The Germans had looted

---

1   Bremen in northwest Germany and Bremerhaven, its seaport at the mouth of the River Wesser.
2   Access to the coast and the American controlled ports.
3   Also referred to as CRICKET during planning correspondence.
4   A Baltimore class heavy cruiser (CA-71).
5   Roosevelt had not wanted to spend too much time with Churchill in case Stalin thought they were ganging up on him.

the palace during their occupation but the Soviets had spent three weeks cleaning, redecorating and refurnishing the building.

30 January
First Combined Combined Chiefs of Staff Meeting
Conference agenda; Flying bomb and rocket attacks; Strategy in Northwest Europe; Coordination of operations with the Russians; Combined Bomber Offensive; End date of the war with Germany; the U-boat threat.

31 January
Second Combined Chiefs of Staff Meeting
Mediterranean operations; Bombing of U-boat assembly yards and operating bases; Enemy situation in Europe; Strategy in Northwest Europe; End date of the war with Germany; Southeast Asia operations, Resources for the India–Burma and China Theatres.

1 February
Foreign Ministers Meeting
Zones of occupation in Germany; Zones of occupation in Austria; Austro-Yugoslav Frontier; Poland's Situation; Polish–German Frontier; Warm water port for Russia; Conduct of the Russians in Eastern Europe; High Emergency Commission for Europe, Germany; China; Persia, Dumbarton Oaks Plan;[6]
Civil Supplies; Prisoners of War; War Criminals.
Third Combined Chiefs of Staff Meeting
Mediterranean Strategy; Strategy in Northwest Europe; Resources for the India–Burma and China Theatres, Pacific operations; Bombing of U-boat assembly yards and operating bases.

2 February
Fourth Combined Chiefs of Staff Meeting
Equipment for Allied and liberated forces; Transfer of tactical air forces from the Mediterranean to Europe; The U-boat threat; Review of cargo shipping; Interim report to the President and Prime Minister.

2 February: Preliminary Meeting between Roosevelt and Churchill
The meeting considered the Combined Chiefs of Staff interim report.[7] The President expressed his appreciation of the amount of progress made in the military discussions in so short a time.

Basic Undertakings in Support of Overall Strategic Concept[8]
  1)   Reorient forces from the European Theatre to the Pacific and Far East

---

6   Voting by the Big Powers and the creation of the World Organisation.
7   Interim Report to the President and Prime Minister C.C.S. 776/1
8   The new undertakings for Argonaut.

as a matter of highest priority as soon as the German situation allows.

2) Continue operations leading to the earliest practicable invasion of Japan.

3) Provide assistance to the forces of the liberated areas in Europe so they could fulfil an active and effective role in the war against Germany and/or Japan.

4) Assist other co-belligerents so they could help against enemy powers.

5) Provide supplies to liberated areas so they can effectively contribute to the war-making capacity of the United Nations against Germany and/or Japan.[1]

Discussion about Assistance for Liberated Areas

The wording was still under discussion and Marshall said the British Chiefs of Staff wording placed supplies for liberated areas in the same category as operational requirements.[2] This change in priority was at the expense of essential military requirements and the US Chiefs of Staff did not want to accept it.[3]

Churchill asked if the British import program would be affected because Great Britain had been receiving less than half her pre-war imports for over five years.[4] He was afraid some of the military requirements and all of the liberated area requirements would necessitate a reduction in Great Britain's imports in 1945.[5] General Brooke said the matter had not been submitted for consideration yet.

Churchill thought great efforts should be made to pass supplies to Russia via the Dardanelles. Admiral King said this was all in hand and the first convoy was expected to go through on 15 February.[6] The delay had been caused because the port of Odessa had not been ready to receive the supplies.[7]

The U-boat War

The Combined Chiefs of Staff were concerned German U-boats could again constitute a serious threat to the North Atlantic shipping lanes.[8] It was too early to assess the extent of a new U-boat offensive and they proposed to

---

1   In other words, help their allies and liberated areas so they could provide direct or indirect assistance. For example, if a liberated area was short of food, the population could riot, causing problems in an army's rear and require extra garrison troops to keep the peace.

2   Over and above those required for the prevention of disease and unrest.

3   Marshall's priorities were in order: 1) the needs of Allied armed forces; 2) the prevention of disease and unrest (which would place extra responsibilities on the Allied armed forces); 3) the liberated areas.

4   Churchill was concerned that the need to feed liberated areas, including Holland, Belgium and Germany, would reduce Britain's imports.

5   At the start of the war Great Britain imported 20 million long tons, 70 per cent of its food; principally meat, cheese, sugar, fruits, cereals and fats. Food rationing started in January 1940 and different foodstuffs were added at regular intervals. Families supplemented their diet with home-grown food and substitute foodstuffs while the government regularly suggested new recipes. Rationing did not end until 1954.

6   Turkey still remained neutral but President Inonu had met Roosevelt and Churchill at the Sextant Conference in December 1943. On 23 February 1945 it would join the Allies.

7   Odessa is a major seaport located on the northwest shore of the Black Sea.

8   Sir Andrew Cunningham explained that the Allies were in a similar position to that of 1918. U-boats were working closer to the United Kingdom's shore because they had learnt that the shallow water tides reduced the effectiveness of ASDIC. Steps had to be taken to force them back into deep water. The Chief of the Air Staff noted that U-boats were mounted with new radar devices which warned of approaching aircraft.

review the matter on 1 April 1945.[9] Meanwhile, they agreed on the following countermeasures:[10]

a) Build up the strength of surface hunting groups and anti–U–boat air squadrons;

b) Maintain and, if possible, increase the bomber effort on assembly yards, concentrating on Hamburg and Bremen;

c) Maintain the bomber effort on operating bases, increasing it when bases became crowded beyond the capacity of concrete pens;[11]

d) Increase, by 100% if possible, the air mining effort against U–boats and their training areas;

e) Mine other waters by using surface minelayers and carrier borne aircraft;

f) Intensify operations against enemy minesweepers;

g) Maintain and intensify operations against shipping supplying U–boat bases.

Operations in Northwest Europe

The Supreme Commander, Allied Expeditionary Force, had presented his appreciation and plan of operations for Northwest Europe in two telegrams:[12]

a) Immediately carry out operations north of the Moselle, with a view to destroying the enemy and closing the Rhine north of Düsseldorf.

b) Eliminate other enemy forces west of the Rhine, which still constituted an obstacle or potential threat to their Rhine crossing operations.

c) Seize bridgeheads over the Rhine in the north and the south.

d) Deploy the maximum number of divisions[13] which could be maintained east of the Rhine and north of the Ruhr. The force's initial task was to deny to the Ruhr industries to the enemy.[14]

e) Deploy east of the Rhine, on the axis Frankfurt–Kassel, with such forces available.[15] This force would draw enemy forces from the north by capturing Frankfurt and advancing on Kassel.[16]

The Combined Chiefs of Staff had taken note of the two cables and of the Supreme Commander's assurance he would seize the Rhine crossings in the north, as soon as it was a feasible operation and without waiting to close the

---

9   Two new types of U-boat were due to be launched: the deepwater Type 21, displacement 1,600 tons with greater submerged endurance and armed with 26 torpedoes; the coastal Type 23, displacement 180 tons and armed with 2 torpedoes.

10 The Prime Minister "thought the time had not yet come to take drastic measures at the expense of other operations, though it might be necessary to do so if the U-boat campaign developed in the way expected."

11 Attack when the pens were full and U-boats were anchoring in open water. The pens were concrete shelters that could survive all but the heaviest bombing attacks. There were six in Germany, five in France and two in Norway.

12 Cable SCAF 180 amended by Cable SCAF 194; both from General Eisenhower.

13 Estimated at some 35 divisions.

14 Montgomery's 21st Army Group would cross the Rhine either side of Wesel, north of the Ruhr. VARSITY would be launched on the night of 23/24 March.

15 After providing the 35 divisions for the north and maintaining a line along the rest of the Rhine.

16 12th Army Group of General Omar N. Bradley (1893-1981) would cross the Rhine either side of Frankfurt around 23/24 March. It would thrust northeast to Kassel, aiming to meet with 21st Army Group and cutting off the Ruhr, Germany's main industrial area.

Rhine throughout its length.[1] He assured them he would advance across the Rhine in the north with maximum strength and complete determination, immediately the situation in the south allowed him to collect the necessary forces[2] and do so without incurring unreasonable risks.[3]

Strategy in the Mediterranean[4]

The Combined Chiefs of Staff had reviewed their strategy in the Mediterranean, in the light of the development of the situation in Europe, and the fact the enemy was at liberty at any time to make a voluntary withdrawal in Italy. They agreed the primary object in the war against Germany was to build up the maximum possible strength on the Western Front and to seek a decision in that theatre. In accordance with this concept they agreed to withdraw certain forces from the Mediterranean Theatre and place them at the disposal of the Supreme Commander, Allied Expeditionary Force. They also agreed to redefine the tasks of the Supreme Allied Commander, Mediterranean.

Directive to Field Marshal Alexander, Supreme Allied Commander, Mediterranean[5]

It is our primary intention in the war against Germany to build up the maximum possible strength on the Western Front and to seek a decision in that theatre. We have reviewed your directive and decided as follows:

The earliest possible discharge of British obligations in Greece must be your constant aim. The object of the British presence and the operations in Greece is to secure that part of Greece which is necessary for the establishment of the authority of a free Greek Government.[6] This object must always be regarded in the light of the paramount need for releasing troops from Greece for use against the Germans. You should concentrate on building up a Greek force on a national basis as soon as possible.[7]

It has been decided to withdraw up to five divisions[8] from your theatre to the Western Front as follows:[9]

    a)   At the earliest possible date three Allied divisions drawn from the Allied Armies in Italy.

---

1   Units could spread out more when they were holding the bank of the Rhine, allowing Eisenhower to withdraw divisions into reserve and move them north to join 21st Army Group.

2   Montgomery had to wait until General Omar Bradley's 12th Army Group was in a position to release divisions for Ninth US Army, which would form his right wing.

3   Churchill stated he wanted plenty of divisions ready to support the main operation in the north, so that tired divisions could be replaced. Sir Alan Brooke said that ten divisions would be in reserve and others could also be taken from quieter parts of the front.

4   General Mark W. Clark (1896-1984) replaced General Alexander as Commander-in-Chief of 15th Army Group in December 1944 when Alexander was promoted to Supreme Commander of the Mediterranean.

5   Repeated to General Eisenhower.

6   The Prime Minister was concerned about weakening their strength in Greece because "it was necessary to build up a Greek National Army under a broad-based government."

7   The Supreme Allied Commander, Mediterranean, planned to help the Greek Government form their own army, releasing British troops for redeployment.

8   Of which not more than two should be armoured.

9   The President had been concerned about the reduction of forces on the Italian Front but Sir Alan Brooke assured him that Field Marshal Alexander had agreed to the withdrawal of three divisions, with two to follow from Greece.

    b)   Further complete formations as the forces in Greece are released.

    c)   It is intended to withdraw Canadian and British divisions.

Two fighter groups of Twelfth Air Force will be moved to France at once. The Combined Chiefs of Staff intend to move to France in the near future as much of the Twelfth Air Force as can be released without compromising your mission. There will be no significant withdrawal of amphibious assault forces.

We recognize these withdrawals will affect the scope of your operations in the Italian Theatre and therefore, redefine your objectives as follows:

    a)   Your first objective should be to ensure the front already reached in Italy is solidly held.

    b)   You should do your utmost, by means of such limited offensive action as may be possible and by the skilful use of cover and deception plans, to contain the German forces now in Italy and prevent their withdrawal to other fronts.

    c)   You should remain prepared to take immediate advantage of any weakening or withdrawal of the German forces.[10]

Discussion about Italy and Greece

Churchill expected it would be possible to start withdrawing troops from Greece by the time the first three divisions had moved. He was in agreement with the course proposed and was particularly glad Marshall had decided to withdraw Canadian and British troops. There were special reasons for wanting to transfer the Canadian Corps to France and he was also anxious the British contribution to the heavy fighting in Northwest Europe should be as great as possible.[11]

Air Marshal Portal said two groups would go now, while the Supreme Commanders would propose further moves.[12] Churchill agreed it was unwise to make any significant withdrawal of amphibious assault forces from Italy, because it would relieve the Germans of an ever-present anxiety.

Churchill attached great importance to a rapid follow-up of any withdrawal or of any surrender of the German forces in Italy. It was essential to occupy as much of Austria as possible because it was undesirable that more of Western Europe than necessary should be occupied by the Russians.[13]

Direction to the Supreme Allied Commander, Mediterranean, concerning Yugoslavia

Subject to the requirements of the Italian Theatre, Alexander should continue to give all possible support to the Yugoslav Army of National Liberation[14] until the territory of Yugoslavia had been completely cleared. "You will carry out such minor operations on the eastern shores of the Adriatic as your resources allow."

---

10 15th Army Group would attack on 9 April and advance quickly across the Po Valley.

11 Churchill was looking to Montgomery's 21st Army Group to make the main thrust across northwest Germany.

12 Portal as the RAF's Chief of the Air Staff is concerned about moving so much of the Allied air strength from Italy to France. If the Germans decided to withdraw from the Po Valley, a weak air force would not be able to stop them.

13 Churchill was anxious to advance as far east as the Anglo-American forces could to secure as much of Europe as possible before the war ended. He was concerned that the Soviets would seize both Berlin and Vienna, giving them greater bargaining powers.

14 Officially the National Liberation Army and Partisan Detachments of Yugoslavia, Josip Tito's communist resistance movement, renamed the Yugoslav Army on 1 March.

Discussion about Yugoslavia

Churchill presumed "the territory of Yugoslavia" meant the existing or lawful territory of Yugoslavia. Certain territories were claimed by both Yugoslavia and Italy and he was unwilling to give any suggestion of support to claims from either side.[1] For example, Trieste ought to be a valuable outlet to southern Europe and the question of sovereignty in that area should be entirely reserved. Roosevelt agreed and was unwilling to see either the Yugoslavs or the Italians in complete control.[2] General Brooke said the phrase applied to the present territory of Yugoslavia.

Operations in the Pacific Area

The agreed overall objective in the war against Japan was to force the unconditional surrender of Japan as follows:

   a) Lower the Japanese ability and will to resist by establishing sea and air blockades, conducting intensive air bombardment, and destroying Japanese air and naval strength;

   b) Invade and seize objectives in the industrial heart of Japan.[3]

The concept of operations for the main effort in the Pacific was:[4]

   a) Seize additional positions following the Okinawa[5] operation to intensify the blockade and air bombardment of Japan in order to create a situation favourable to –

   b) Make an assault on Kyushu[6] to reduce Japanese capabilities by containing and destroying major enemy forces and intensify the blockade and air bombardment to establish a tactical condition favourable to –

   c) Make a decisive invasion of the industrial heart of Japan through the Tokyo Plain.[7]

The following sequence and timing of operations had been directed by the US Chiefs of Staff and planned by theatre commanders:

Objectives	Target Date
Operations in the Philippines[8]	Continuing
Iwo Jima	19 February 1945
Okinawa and the Ryukyus	1 April–August 1945

Until a firm date could be established when redeployment from Europe could begin, planning would be continued for an operation to seize a position in the

---

1   The area from north of Trieste to the Mirna River in the south.
2   The United Nations Security Council created the city state of the Free Territory of Trieste in September 1947 and it was patrolled by peacekeeping American and British forces. It was taken over by its neighbours in 1954 and dissolved in 1975; the U.N. Security Council never ratified the decision so it still exists.
3   C.C.S. 417/11 stated the decisive invasion of the industrial heart of Japan would be through the Tokyo Plain.
4   C.C.S. 417/10 stated "Until a firm date can be established when redeployment from Europe will begin, planning will be continued for an operation to seize a position in the Chusan-Ningpo area and for invasion of Kyushu-Honshu in the winter of 1945-1946."
5   Okinawa is in the centre of the Ryukyu Islands that stretch between mainland Japan and Formosa (now Taiwan).
6   The invasion of Japan was codenamed DOWNFALL and it was split into two parts. OLYMPIC was the invasion of Kyushu Island (Japan's southern island) while CORONET was the invasion of Honshu (Japan's central island).
7   Around one third of the population of Japan lived on the Kanto Plain around Tokyo.
8   Luzon, Mindoro and Leyte, the main Philippine Islands.

Chusan-Ningpo area.[9] They would then draw up a plan to invade Kyushu-Honshu in the winter of 1945-1946.[10]

The need for and cost of operations to maintain and defend a sea route to the Sea of Okhotsk,[11] when the entry of Russia into the war against Japan was imminent, was being examined. So far, the possibility of seizing a position in the Kuriles during the favourable weather period of 1945 was remote, due to a lack of sufficient resources. The possibility of maintaining and defending a sea route from bases in Kamchatka alone was being further examined.

The US Chiefs of Staff had also directed the examination and preparation of a plan of campaign against Japan in case the prolongation of the European war required postponement of the invasion of Japan until well into 1946.

Operations in Southeast Asia Command

The Chiefs of Staff agreed the following policy for the deployment of United States resources in the India-Burma Theatre:

a) The primary military object of the United States in the China and India-Burma Theatres was the continuance of aid to China. It would be on a scale designed to permit the fullest utilization of the area and the resources of China for operations against the Japanese.

b) The US Chiefs of Staff contemplated no change to SACSEA's[12] use of resources of the US India-Burma Theatre in Burma. If there was any it must not prevent the fulfilment of their primary object, rendering support to China and the protection of the line of communications.[13]

Directive to Mountbatten, Supreme Allied Commander, Southeast Asia

a) Your first object is to liberate Burma at the earliest date.[14]

b) Your next main task is the liberation of Malaya and the opening of the Straits of Malacca.[15]

c) In view of your recent success in Burma, and of the uncertainty of the date of the final defeat of Germany, you must aim at the accomplishment of your first object with the forces at present at your disposal. This does not preclude the dispatch of further reinforcements from the European Theatre should circumstances make this possible.

d) You will prepare a program of operations for the approval of the Combined Chiefs of Staff.

---

9   Chusan (now Zhousan) is an island city port and Ningpo is another important port; both are in Zhejiang Province on the east coast of China.

10 OLYMPIC, the planned invasion of Kyushu in October 1945, was to be staged from Okinawa. CORONET, a landing south of Toyko, would be scheduled for 1 March 1946 or Y-Day. It would have been twice the size of operation OVERLORD and so obviously the largest amphibious operation ever planned.

11 The Sea of Okhotsk is off the east coast of Russia, between the Kamchatka Peninsula to the east, Sakhalin Island to the west and the Kurile Islands to the south.

12 Supreme Allied Commander, Southeast Asia.

13 The transfer of forces from the primary objective had to be discussed by the Combined Chiefs of Staff.

14 To be known as LOYALIST, formerly X-RAY, eventually called CAPITAL. The battles for Imphal and Kohima were the turning points in the Burma campaign. The port of Rangoon would be captured at the beginning of May, just after the monsoon broke.

15 To be known as BROADSWORD.

Discussion about Southeast Asia Operations

Churchill said the main object of the operations was to clear the enemy from Burma to liberate the important army engaged there for further operations against Japan.[1] He asked if the Staffs had decided what these further operations should be. Brooke said the directive to the Supreme Allied Commander, Southeast Asia Command, gave the liberation of Malaya and the opening of the Straits of Malacca as the next task.[2]

Churchill hoped there would be time to review the matter. For example, if the Japanese forces in Java or Sumatra[3] were greatly weakened, small detachments might be able to go in and liberate these countries. His object was to go where a good opportunity for fighting the Japanese presented itself, particularly in the air. This was the only way the British had been to help the main American operations in the Pacific. Brooke said the Supreme Allied Commander had been directed to submit his plans, and it would then be possible to review the matter. Churchill asked whether if there would be any help from United States air forces during operations in the Kra Peninsula and Malaya. Air Marshal Portal said any such help would be the subject of a separate agreement when the plan had been received.

Churchill asked if the President had been disappointed by the Chinese achievements, considering the tremendous American efforts to give them support. Roosevelt said three generations of education and training would be required before China became a serious factor.[4]

Marshall said the picture in China had changed considerably. In the first place certain well-trained Chinese troops were now in China, having been transferred there from Burma. Secondly, the opening of the Burma Road had allowed the first artillery for the Chinese Army to get through. Thirdly, if operations in Burma continued to go well, additional trained Chinese troops could move back to China, and it was hoped an effective reinforced Chinese corps would soon be in existence.[5]

Churchill said it appeared the American and British operations in this part of the world were now diverging. The American effort was going into China and the British effort was turning to the south. He asked if any consideration had been given to moving British or Indian divisions from Burma to take part in operations in China. Brooke said the facilities for sending equipment and supplies into China could support Chinese forces because they required a considerably lower scale of support than British troops. These facilities could not support British troops as well.

1　Referring to Lieutenant General William Slim's Fourteenth Army, the Forgotten Army.

2　Fourteenth Army would occupy Rangoon on 2 May 1945 and prepared for ZIPPER, an invasion of the west coast of Malaya. Although the dropping of the two atomic bombs ended the war quickly, the landing was carried out to enforce the Japanese surrender and rescue Allied prisoners of war.

3　Two of the largest Indonesian Islands; Java is south of Borneo while Sumatra is southwest of the Malaysian Peninsula and Singapore.

4　Both Churchill and Roosevelt were unimpressed by the returns for all the Allied aid and assistance given to China. It had, however, stopped China from falling to the Japanese.

5　Marshall was more optimistic about China's part in the final stages of the war against Japan. He expected that American-trained troops backed by artillery would be effective against Japanese troops.

Marshall agreed the maintenance of British forces in China was not a practical proposition. There was only one reinforced United States brigade in China, to act as a spearhead for critical operations. There was a reinforced Chinese corps, which had a stiffening of United States personnel in their tanks, armoured cars and tank destroyers, and there was an effective air force. These forces should be able to ensure the Japanese could no longer go where they pleased in China. The aid which these forces could give when the Americans arrived on the Chinese Pacific Coast would be important. A pincer movement against the Japanese could be initiated – one arm of the pincer being represented by the forces assaulting the selected spot on the Chinese Pacific Coast; this arm would be strong. The other arm of the pincer would be the Chinese and American forces in China; this arm would be weak, but nevertheless of value.

The progress of the main American operations in the Pacific and the campaign in the Philippines had changed the picture in Southeast Asia, and would make further operations by Mountbatten's forces much easier. He felt it was important that Mountbatten knew what forces would be available to him in these operations, so he did not plan on a false assumption. The American military authorities in Southeast Asia would know United States forces could not be supported logistically in China. These could be transferred to Mountbatten in Burma. It might even be possible to bring air forces back from China for specific operations. Mountbatten should be under no illusion concerning the forces he could count on for his operations.

Churchill repeated he would consider any American request for British troops to go into China. Admiral Leahy said all the available transportation was fully required for the forces now in China or earmarked for China.[6] Marshall agreed and did not think it would be practicable to increase the forces in China until a port had been secured. Up to the present it had only been possible to do very little in the way of equipping the Chinese ground army. Nearly all the transportation had been used to supply the American air forces. It would now be possible to handle the requirements of the Chinese ground forces.

Planning Dates for the End of the War

The Combined Chiefs of Staff said it was important to agree and circulate planning dates for the end of the war against Germany and Japan. These dates were necessary for the purpose of planning production and the allocation of manpower. They recommended the following planning dates for the end of the war against Germany:

a)   Earliest date: 1 July 1945.

b)   Date beyond which the war is unlikely to continue: 31 December 1945.[7]

They recommended setting the planning date for the end of the war against Japan at 18 months after the defeat of Germany.[8] The dates would be adjusted periodically to conform to the course of the war.

---

6   The amount of supplies that could be flown over the Hump and moved along the Ledo/Burma Road limited the number of Chinese troops the Allies could support. Although there were spare troops, they could not be supplied.

7   Actually 8 May 1945, eight weeks before the earliest estimate and nine months before the latest.

8   Actually August 1945, three months after the defeat of Germany; shortened by the use of the two atomic bombs.

Shipping

The Combined Chiefs of Staff had reviewed the overall cargo and troop shipping position for the remainder of 1945, assuming Germany was defeated on 1 July 1945. The principal difficulty during the first half of 1945 would be cargo shipping. It would be tight and the deficits would approach unmanageable proportions until VE Day. They had instructed theatre commanders to exercise strict control of shipping and agreed deficits would be adjusted as follows. In the event of a deficit in shipping resources, the first priority should be given to the basic undertakings in support of the overall strategic concepts.[1] Otherwise the appropriate Chiefs of Staff would be consulted before shipping was allocated.

The principal difficulty during the second half of 1945 would be troop shipping and it would become particularly acute in the last quarter of the year. They had agreed to review the matter and a report would be submitted to the Combined Chiefs of Staff not later than 1 April 1945. The report would take account of the possibility that the war against Germany could continue beyond 1 July 1945.[2]

Roosevelt–Stalin Meeting, 4 February

Roosevelt thanked Stalin for all the successful efforts made for his comfort and convenience. Roosevelt said the military situation was considerably improved since they had last met. Stalin replied this was true and the Soviet armies were moving very successfully onto the line of the Oder. Roosevelt had made a number of bets on board the cruiser coming over as to whether the Russians would get to Berlin before the Americans would get to Manila.[3] Stalin was certain the Americans would get to Manila before the Russians got to Berlin, since there was very hard fighting for the Oder line.

There followed a discussion about the climate and characteristics of the Crimea. Roosevelt had been struck by the extent of German destruction in the Crimea and he was more bloodthirsty regarding the Germans than be had been a year ago. He hoped Stalin would again propose a toast to the execution of 50,000 officers of the German Army. Stalin said because of the honest bloodshed in fighting the Germans, everyone was more bloodthirsty than they had been a year ago. The destruction in the Crimea was nothing compared to what occurred in the Ukraine. The Germans had been outflanked in the Crimea and had little time to carry out planned destruction,[4] whereas in the Ukraine they had done it with method and calculation. The Germans were savages and seemed to loathe with a sadistic hatred the creative work of human beings. Roosevelt agreed.

Stalin asked about the military situation on the Western Front. Roosevelt said General Marshall would give a detailed outline of the situation and plans at the

---

1 In other words, the defeat of Germany and then the defeat of Japan.
2 The problem was how to withdraw troops from Europe and transfer them to the Pacific and Southeast Asia in time to help the war against Japan. At the same time, troops had to be repatriated.
3 Elements of the 1st Cavalry Division entered Manila on 3 February. The battle for Berlin did not start until 20 April.
4 An assault across the Perekop Isthmus was made on 8 April 1944 and by the end of April the Germans were falling back into Sevastopol; it fell on 9 May. The Germans were forced to make a sea evacuation under Soviet air attack.

five o'clock meeting, but said there was an offensive planned for 8 February[5] and another on the 12th, but the main blow of the Anglo-American armies on the Western Front would take place in March.[6] Stalin was pleased with this news and said General Antonov would give a detailed review of the situation on the Eastern Front at the five o'clock meeting. If it was possible to capture the Ruhr and Saar regions, the Germans would be deprived of all sources of coal, since the Russians had already captured the Silesia basin. The Germans were already short of bread and there was a possibility the collapse would come before absolute military defeat if they were also deprived of coal.

Roosevelt felt the armies were getting close enough to have contact and hoped General Eisenhower could communicate directly with the Soviet Staff rather than through the Chiefs of Staff in London and Washington. Stalin thought it was very important and promised the staffs would work out the details. Roosevelt asked if the Soviet bridgeheads across the Oder were sufficient for further offensive action. Stalin said there were five or six bridgeheads and fierce battles were in progress on the Eastern front.[7] Roosevelt said one of the difficulties on the Western Front was they had no secure bridgeheads and the current was so strong with floating ice on the upper Rhine it made it very difficult for pontoon operations. General Eisenhower felt once he had reached the Rhine he would be able to cross it, but he did not expect this before March. The British had wanted to make a major crossing of the Rhine on the north sector in Holland, but since the Americans had four times the number of men in France than the British, they felt they were entitled to have an alternative, which would be either through Holland or around Mainz.

Roosevelt asked how Stalin had got on with General de Gaulle and he replied had not found him a very complicated person. De Gaulle was unrealistic, in the sense that France had not done very much fighting in this war, and he demanded full rights with the Americans, British and Russians who had carried the burden of the fighting.

Roosevelt described his conversation with de Gaulle in Casablanca two years ago when he compared himself with Joan of Arc as the spiritual leader of France and with Clemenceau[8] as the political leader. Stalin said de Gaulle did not seem to understand the situation in France and the fact the French contribution at the present time to military operations on the Western Front was very small and they had not fought at all in 1940.

Roosevelt replied he had recently decided to arm eight new French divisions composed of Frenchmen who had had previous military training. Stalin said that was good insofar as it helped the American armies but it was very weak at

---

5   VERITABLE began on 8 February when 1st Canadian Army advanced from Nijmegen, Holland. GRENADE was due to start the day after but the Germans destroyed the upstream dams on the Roer (Rur). 9th US Army eventually crossed the Roer on 23 February.

6   21st Army Group's crossing of the Rhine around Wesel, starting on 23 March.

7   The advance from the Oder began with a massive assault against Army Group Vistula and Army Group Centre on 16 April.

8   Georges Clemenceau (1841-1929), Prime Minister of France at the end of the First World War. He was one of the main participants in the Treaty of Versailles at the Paris Peace Conference, taking a harsh position on Germany's reparations.

present. Roosevelt said he had recently heard the French Government did not plan to annex outright any German territory but they were willing to have it placed under international control. Stalin replied that was not the story de Gaulle had told in Moscow – there he said the Rhine was the natural boundary of France and he wished to have French troops placed there permanently.[1]

Roosevelt said he would now tell the Marshal something indiscreet, since he would not wish to say it in front of Churchill. For two years the British had had the idea of artificially building up France into a strong power, which would have 200,000 troops on her eastern border, to hold the line for the period required to assemble a strong British army. He said the British were a peculiar people and wished to have their cake and eat it too.

Roosevelt understood the occupation zones of Germany were already agreed upon and Stalin agreed but one outstanding question was that of a French zone of occupation. Roosevelt had had a good deal of trouble with the British about the zones of occupation. He would have have preferred to have the northwest zone, which would be independent of communications through France. However, the British seemed to think the Americans should restore order in France and then return political control to the British.

Stalin asked if the President thought France should have a zone of occupation and for what reason. Roosevelt thought it was not a bad idea but only out of kindness. Both Stalin and Molotov spoke up vigorously to say that was the only reason to give France a zone. Stalin said the question would have to be considered at Yalta. As it was nearly five, the President suggested proceeding to the conference room where the military staffs were gathered.

First Argonaut Meeting, 4 February 1945

Stalin asked the President to open the meeting. The President was very happy to open such a historic meeting in such a lovely spot.[2] He thanked Stalin for all he had found time to do with the conveniences and comforts provided in the midst of the prosecution of the war. He said the United States, British and Russian delegations would understand each other better and better as they went along. They could therefore proceed informally to discuss frankly and freely amongst themselves the matters necessary to the successful prosecution of the common cause in which they all were engaged.

A lot required discussion, the whole map of Europe in fact. Today, however, the conversations concerned Germany. He felt sure the British and American people were viewing with as deep a satisfaction as the Soviet people the successful advances of the Soviet armies against their common enemy. Stalin replied that Colonel General Antonov, Deputy Chief of the Russian General Staff, would outline the situation existing on the Eastern Front. General Antonov made the following statement:[3]

---

1   American, Belgian, British and French troops had occupied the Rhineland following the end of World War I.
2   Livadia Palace, the summer retreat of the last Russian Tsar, Nicholas II and his family.
3   The commanders and objectives are listed from north to south, or right to left.

Soviet forces from 12 to 15 January went into attack between the Niemen River[4] and the Carpathians,[5] a distance of 700 kilometres. Forces of General Cherniakhovsky[6] advanced towards Königsberg; forces of Marshal Rokossovsky[7] along the north bank of the Vistula cutting off East Prussia from central Germany; forces of Marshal Zhukov[8] south of the Vistula against Poznan; forces of Marshal Konev[9] against Chenstokhov-Breslau; forces of General Petrov[10] in the area of the Carpathians against Novo Targ. The greatest blow was delivered by the army groups of Rokossovsky, Zhukov, and Konev on the 300-kilometre Ostrolenka-Krakow front.

Because of the unfavourable weather conditions, this operation was due to start at the end of January, when weather conditions were expected to improve. Since the operation was planned and prepared in full strength, it was hoped to carry it out under the most favourable conditions possible. Nevertheless, in view of the difficult circumstances on the Western Front in connection with the German attack in the Ardennes, the High Command of the Soviet Army had decided not to wait for an improvement in weather and ordered the attack to start no later than the middle of January.[11]

The enemy grouping, after the Soviet forces reached the Narev and Vistula Rivers, was concentrated in the central sector, since striking from this sector led their troops along the shortest route to the vital centres of Germany. The Supreme Soviet Command decided to extend the attack to the enemy's central group, to create more advantageous conditions. So the operation was conducted as a subsidiary against East Prussia, and the advance in Hungary toward Budapest was continued.

Both of these attacks were very painful for the Germans. They reacted quickly with a swift transfer of power onto the flank, at the expense of the central sector. Eleven out of 24 tank divisions[12] were drawn into the Budapest sector and six into the East Prussian;[13] so only four tank divisions remained in the centre. The aim of the Soviet High Command had been accomplished.[14]

The enemy had up to 80 divisions in the area of our greatest attack, between Ostrolenka to Krakow. They set up a grouping calculated on having infantry superiority of more than double and a decided superiority in artillery, tanks and

---

4   The Niemen (or Neman) River begins in Belarus and flows northwest through Lithuania to the Curonian Lagoon on the Baltic Sea.

5   The Carpathian Mountains straddle southern Ukraine and central Romania.

6   General Ivan D. Cherniakhovsky (1906-1945), commander of the 3rd Belorussian Front and the youngest Soviet General, at 39. He was mortally wounded in the attack on Königsberg and died on 18 February.

7   Marshal Konstantin Rokossovsky (1896-1968), commander of the 2nd Belorussian Front.

8   Marshal Georgy K. Zhukov (1896-1974), commander of the 1st Belorussian Front.

9   Marshal Ivan S. Konev (1897-1973), commander of the 2nd Ukrainian Front.

10 General Ivan Y. Petrov (1896-1958), commander of the 1st Ukrainian Front.

11 At this stage the Allies had contained the German attack in the Ardennes and were well on the way to eliminating the Bulge in their line. The early Soviet attack made sure the Germans could not move reserves from east to west to make a second attack.

12 Representing the principal German striking power.

13 Three tank divisions were located in Courland, Latvia.

14 Dividing the German armoured force, drawing the bulk away from the centre.

aviation. The massing of artillery on the sectors of the breakthrough amounted to 220-230 guns[1] on one kilometre of the front.

The advance began under extremely unfavourable weather conditions, which completely ruled out air operations and limited artillery observation to a few hundred metres. Due to good preliminary reconnaissance of the enemy positions and a powerful artillery advance, the fire power of the enemy was overwhelmed and his fortifications destroyed. This situation permitted their troops to move forward 10 to 15 kilometres during the first day of the advance, completely breaking through the entire tactical depth of the enemy defence.[2]

General Antonov then outlined the probable enemy action:

a) The Germans would defend Berlin and try to stop the movement of the Soviet troops along the Oder River. Their defence would be made by withdrawing troops from other areas and using reserves from all over Germany, Western Europe and Italy. They would try to use their Courland grouping for the defence of Pomerania, moving it by sea beyond the Vistula.

b) The Germans would probably reinforce the direction leading to Vienna, using troops now in action in Italy to strengthen the sector.

General Antonov expected an additional 35 to 40 divisions appear on their front.

Roosevelt asked whether the Russians proposed to change the gauge of the railroad rolling stock captured from the Germans or to widen the gauge of the lines. Antonov replied a lot of the equipment was unfit for use but they were widening the gauge of those lines most vital to supply. These lines were being widened only as a matter of necessity because they did not have the resources to widen all the railroads in Germany. The greater part of the German lines would remain intact.

Roosevelt pointed out the increasing need to coordinate the operations of the three Allies, now the British and American armies were getting so close to the Russians. The short distance separating the Western and Eastern Fronts meant the Germans could transfer their reserves quickly from one front to the other.

Marshall then gave a resumé of the operations planned for the Western Front. The German bulge in the Ardennes had been eliminated and the Allied forces had advanced beyond the line originally held in some areas.[3] During the past week General Eisenhower had been regrouping his forces and conducting operations designed to eliminate enemy pockets in the southern part of the line, north of Switzerland.[4] At the same time he had been maintaining pressure in the Ardennes area to determine whether the Germans were present in sufficient force to resist

1 75mm calibre guns and larger.
2 In summary, the Soviets advanced 500 kilometres to the Oder in 18 days, capturing the industry of Silesia. Around 68 German divisions were isolated and another 45 destroyed; 100,000 prisoners were taken and casualties were assessed at 300,000.
3 Army Group B launched Operation WATCH ON THE RHINE on 16 December 1944, breaking through First US Army's lines in the Ardennes. Sixth and Fifth Panzer Armies advanced up to sixty miles but failed to cross the River Meuse. The advance left a large bulge in the American line, one which took until mid-January to erase.
4 The Colmar Pocket was eliminated between 20 January and 9 February 1945.

a movement northeast towards Bonn. Because of the resistance encountered, it was decided four days before to cease operations and to transfer divisions further north.

At the southern end of the line, operations were being directed towards the elimination of the German positions in the vicinity of Mulhausen[5] and Colmar. Colmar had now been occupied but the advance of the First French Army north of Mulhausen had been very slow. The small German bridgeheads across the Rhine were being eliminated north of Strasbourg. As soon as the Rhine was reached, it would be possible to reduce the number of divisions in the front line and release them for other employments. Some released divisions were even now moving north in preparation for the larger operations.

Field Marshal Montgomery, in command of 21st Army Group and Ninth US Army, was preparing an operation designed to strike towards the southeast in order to reach the line of the Rhine from Düsseldorf north.[6] A complementary operation had been planned in a northeast direction towards the same objective, which it was hoped could be launched about a week later than the first operation.[7] By means of these two operations it was hoped to drive the Germans east of the Rhine north of Düsseldorf and then to cross the river north of the Ruhr. This crossing would constitute the main effort of the British and American armies and all of the divisions it was logistically possible to support would be put into it. In addition, airborne troops in large numbers would land east of the Rhine.

From the standpoint of weather, the passage of the Rhine was considered possible after 1 March. A crossing would be attempted as soon as the river was reached, but ice would make any crossing hazardous prior to 1 March. Three good crossing sites were available and a fourth might be attempted. However, the front of the assault would only accommodate five divisions initially.[8]

Plans had been made for a secondary effort in the vicinity of Frankfurt, which could be exploited if the main effort in the north failed to go through. The troops composing First US Army's left were now conducting an operation designed to capture the two dams controlling the water in the Roer River.[9] There was a danger the bridges established for the river crossing could be swept away by the release of the water, as long as these dams were in German hands.

The opening of the port of Antwerp had relieved the limitation on operations on the Western Front imposed by a lack of supplies.[10] It was now possible to bring in from 75,000 to 80,000 tons of dry cargo a day. The Germans had realized the importance of Antwerp in the Allied supply scheme and had made a continuous effort to interfere with the operations of that port through the use of 'robot'

5   Now Mulhouse in the Alsace region.
6   VERITABLE was 1st Canadian Army's advance southeast from Nijmegen along the west bank of the Rhine.
7   Operation GRENADE.
8   Operation VARSITY would have 21st Army Group crossing the Rhine either side of Wesel.
9   The Urft and Schwammenauel Dams.
10 Although the Allies liberated Antwerp on 4 September, it took until 8 November to secure the Scheldt Estuary; it then took several weeks to clear it of mines. The first cargo ship docked on 28 November and before long ½ million tons of supplies were being unloaded every month.

bombs and rockets.[1] This constituted a danger as there was always a chance of a lucky hit on the Antwerp lock gates.

Only scattered attacks had been made by air. US and British fighters and light bombers supporting the ground troops had destroyed a great deal of German transport. Considerable effort had been directed against trains operating in the vicinity of Cologne and on the east bank of the Rhine. Although definite final reports had not yet been received, there was every indication severe damage had been done to panzer divisions withdrawing from the Ardennes.

Heavy bombers had been employed primarily against German oil supplies to reduce the German supply of fuel for aircraft and motor transport. Present data indicated these operations had resulted in a reduction of German oil production to 20 per cent of the former capacity. Heavy bombers had also been used against German rail communications and assembly yards while a continuous effort had been maintained to destroy German fighter forces. These planes had also struck heavily at tank factories.

The air forces in these operations included US heavy bombers operating from the Italian Front. They were directed against communications leading into Germany when weather prevented profitable operations in the Po Valley. There were about 32 enemy divisions on the Italian Front, 27 German and 5 Italian. The number of Allied divisions was approximately equal. The Allied forces had great superiority in fighter aircraft and in good weather they were able to ravage the Po Valley. The destruction of rail lines and rolling stock had been heavy.

Indications pointed to a serious resumption of the German submarine war as the result of technical developments making the detection of the submarines increasingly difficult. The submarines had developed considerable skill in operating in shallow waters where the tide made it difficult for ASDIC to locate them.[2] In order to counter this submarine resurgence, heavy bombers were being employed to strike at submarine assembly points, whenever these operations did not interfere with the bombing of the German oil supplies.

Marshall said he would be glad to have Field Marshal Brooke amplify his remarks in any way he thought desirable. Churchill wanted Brooke to do so and also wanted Admiral Cunningham to say a word about the submarine operations. Churchill pointed out Danzig was the place where a lot of the submarines were assembled and was pleased the city was not far from the Russian front line, which was drawing closer daily.[3] In answer to a question from Stalin, the Churchill said other submarine assembling points were Kiel and Hamburg.[4]

Brooke said Marshall had fully covered the situation on the Western Front and the operations contemplated for the future. He said the British Chiefs of Staff were in full accord with the plans outlined by Marshall. Marshall explained the front of the main effort covered three crossings over a distance of 25 or 30 miles

---

1   Over 1600 V2 rockets were fired at Antwerp, half of all fired.
2   The underwater currents interfered with the ASDIC (known to the Americans as Sonar) transmitter-receiver.
3   The siege of Danzig lasted from 15 to 28 March; nearly 50,000 Germans were killed or captured.
4   Kiel is on the east side of the Danish Peninsula, in the Baltic Sea. Hamburg is south of the peninsula and its port is connected to the North Sea by the River Elbe.

and afforded room for not more than five divisions.[5] The front would eventually extend all along the Rhine down as far as Düsseldorf, a total of 50 or 60 miles. It would be necessary to assault on a narrow front but it would be expanded as rapidly as possible, as was the case in Normandy. The Ruhr was very heavily fortified and it would be bypassed; however, the attacking troops would soon get into good tank country.[6]

In answer to a question from Stalin, Marshall said the reserves available for the proposed attack were believed to be ample. Stalin asked the question because 9000 tanks were used up in the Russian central campaign.[7] He would like to know how many tanks the Allies expected to employ. Marshall said roughly one in every three divisions employed would be a tank division. Eisenhower would have 89 divisions at his disposal to cover the front from the Mediterranean to Holland on 1 March;[8] nine were French and the remainder were either British or American.

Marshall made it clear there were nearly 10,000 Allied tanks in the European Theatre. The British divisions numbered 18,000 men, the American divisions 14,000, and armoured divisions contained 10,000. There would be 4000 heavy bombers available, each carrying up to 3000 pounds of bombs.

Stalin said the Russians employed 100 divisions in their attack on the central German position, 20 more than the Germans had. He was interested in the preponderance the British and Americans would have over the Germans. Churchill said the British and American forces had an overwhelming preponderance in aircraft and armoured troops but not a great preponderance in infantry. He stressed the necessity of exploiting to the full such superiority in strength as existed.

Stalin said the British and Americans had asked the Russians to express their wishes. Now he wanted to know what the British and Americans wishes were. Churchill said his greatest wish was to express profound gratitude and admiration as he witnessed the marvellous advance of the Russian troops. He said the British and Americans recognized the difficult task lying before them in their impending operations but they had full confidence in their power to execute it. All they could ask from the Russians was to continue what they were doing now. Stalin said there had been no demand from the British and Americans for the Russian winter offensive and no pressure was exerted by them to bring it about.

Roosevelt wanted to give the information about the offensive to Eisenhower to assist him in his planning. Air Marshal Tedder[9] had asked for the Russian offensive to continue until the end of March but this was a request from the military leaders.[10] Stalin replied they had staged their winter offensive because they felt it was their duty as Allies to do it. They greatly appreciated the attitude manifested

---

5   Marshall is explaining VARSITY on the Wesel front, downstream from Düsseldorf.

6   The breakout northeast was codenamed Operation PLUNDER.

7   The Belorussian Offensive, BAGRATION, began when four Soviet army groups attacked on 22 June 1944. It was by far the largest attack of the war involving over 2.3 million Soviet troops, a ten to one superiority in tanks and seven to one superiority in planes. There were over 400,000 German casualties and while the Soviets suffered nearly twice as many, it had broken Army Group Centre.

8   Not including those on the Italian front.

9   Tedder had visited Moscow as General Eisenhower's representative.

10 As opposed to a request from Roosevelt and Churchill.

by both the President and the Prime Minister in this matter. Churchill said the reason neither the British nor Americans had made any attempt to bargain with Stalin was because of their faith in him and in the Russian people and the realization they could be depended on to do the right thing.

It was Churchill's opinion that, regardless of the discussions held with Air Marshal Tedder, matters should be discussed by the three Staffs to determine the best course to pursue and coordinate action on the Western and Eastern Fronts.[1] It was imperative the two offensives should be integrated to get the best results. Stalin agreed the offensives had not been fully synchronized at first and action should be taken to do this now. He thought it would be wise to consider a summer offensive, as he was not sure the war would be over by that time.

Cunningham said he would like to add something to Marshall's statement on submarine warfare. While the submarine threat was potentially great, it was not very serious at the moment. The point was the Germans were building large numbers of new types of U-boats. They would have a high underwater speed and embody all the latest technical devices, making it very difficult for the Allied air and surface craft to deal with them. The new submarines were being built by prefabrication methods in Bremen, Hamburg and Danzig. His greatest wish as a naval man was for the Russians to take Danzig as quickly as possible, because about 30 per cent of the U-boats were being constructed there. Stalin stated Danzig was not yet within artillery range of the Russian guns but it was hoped it soon would be.

Dinner Meeting, 4 February

The conversation was general and personal in character before and during most of the dinner. Stalin, Roosevelt and Churchill appeared to be in very good humour throughout. No political or military subjects of any importance were discussed until the last half hour of the dinner, when indirectly the subject of the responsibility and rights of the greater powers with relation to those of the small powers came up.

Stalin made it clear he felt the three Great Powers, which had borne the brunt of the war and had liberated the small powers from German domination, should have the unanimous right to preserve the peace of the world. He could serve no other interest than the Soviet state and people but the Soviet Union was prepared to pay its share in the preservation of peace in the international arena. He said it was ridiculous to believe Albania would have an equal voice with the three Great Powers who had won the war. Some of the liberated countries seemed to believe the Great Powers had been forced to shed their blood in order to liberate them and they were now scolding these Great Powers for failing to take into consideration the rights of these small powers.

Stalin was prepared to protect the rights of the small powers with the United States and Great Britain but he would never agree to any action of any of the Great Powers being submitted to the judgment of the small powers. Roosevelt

---

1   Eisenhower had sent Tedder to Moscow in January to seek help from the Soviets, to alleviate pressure on the Western Front.

agreed the Great Powers bore the greater responsibility and the peace should be written by the three. Churchill said there was no question of the small powers dictating to the big powers but the great nations of the world should discharge their moral responsibility and leadership and should exercise their power with moderation and great respect for the rights of the smaller nations.

Following Churchill's toast to the proletariat masses of the world, there was considerable discussion about the rights of people to govern themselves in relation to their leaders. Churchill was constantly being 'beaten up' as a reactionary but he was the only representative present who could be thrown out at any time by the universal suffrage of his own people and personally, he gloried in that danger.[2] Stalin ironically remarked Churchill seemed to fear these elections, to which Churchill replied not only did he not not fear them, he was proud of the right of the British people to change their government at any time they saw fit.[3] He felt the three nations represented were moving toward the same goal by different methods. Referring to the rights of the small nations, Churchill said: "The eagle should permit the small birds to sing and care not wherefore they sang."[4]

After Stalin and Roosevelt left, Churchill discussed the voting question in the Security Council[5] with Mr. Eden and Mr. Stettinius. Churchill was inclined to the Russian view on the voting procedure because he felt everything depended on the unity of the three Great Powers. Without that the world would be subjected to inestimable catastrophe; anything which preserved that unity would have his vote.

Eden took vigorous exception and pointed out there would be no attraction or reason for the small nations to join an organization based on that principle and he personally believed it would find no support among the English public. Churchill disagreed with Eden because he was thinking of the realities of the international situation.

Churchill asked about the American proposal to the solution of the voting question. Mr. Bohlen[6] said it reminded him of the story of the Southern planter who had given a bottle of whiskey to a Negro as a present. The next day he asked the Negro how he had liked the whiskey, to which the Negro replied it was perfect. The planter asked what he meant, and the Negro said it would not have been given to him if it had been any better and if it had been any worse he could not have drunk it. Churchill and Eden left in disagreement.

2   American Presidents are elected for a four year term. Stalin had eliminated all his opposition and served as Premier of the Soviet Union until he abolished the post in 1952, a few months before his death.

3   The British General Election was due in July 1945. Churchill's Conservative Party would suffer a landslide defeat at the hands of Clement Attlee's Labour Party.

4   The Big Three should let the small countries voice their opinions.

5   The United Nations Security Council would hold its first meeting on 17 January 1946 in London. The five permanent members were Britain, United States, Soviet Union, France and the Republic of China.

6   Charles E. Bohlen (1904-1974), United States diplomat in the Soviet Union and Truman's Russian interpreter.

5 February
First Tripartite Combined Chiefs of Staff Meeting
Coordination of offensive operations; Movement of German forces from Norway; Air and artillery in future operations; Liaison arrangements; Naval support of the land offensive; Date of the end of the war; Future business.

Second Argonaut Meeting, 5 February
The Surrender and Occupation of Germany
The first question concerned the zones of occupation agreed upon in the European Advisory Commission. One question was still open; France's desire to have a zone of occupation and French participation in the control machinery for Germany. He emphasized the question of zones did not relate to the permanent treatment of Germany. Roosevelt handed a map of the agreed tripartite zones to Stalin and although the zones had been agreed upon in the European Advisory Commission, they had not been signed by the three governments. Stalin wanted to include the following points.

They had exchanged views on the dismemberment of Germany at Tehran and at Moscow he had talked over the subject with Churchill. All were in favour of dismemberment but nothing had been decided; did Roosevelt and Churchill still adhere to the principle of dismemberment? Stalin asked if they proposed to set up a German government or would there be three governments for the various parts of Germany. Stalin then asked how the principle of unconditional surrender would operate in Germany. For example, if Hitler agreed to surrender unconditionally, would they deal with his government? Stalin's last point dealt with reparations.

Roosevelt understood the permanent treatment of Germany might grow out of the question of the zones of occupation, although the two were not directly connected. Stalin wanted to know if it was the joint intention to dismember Germany or not. At Tehran, Roosevelt proposed dividing Germany into five parts while Churchill suggested only two parts, separating Prussia from the southern part of Germany. He associated himself with Roosevelt's views but the Tehran discussion had only been an exchange of views.

At Moscow they had discussed with Churchill the possibility of dividing Germany with Prussia as one part and Bavaria and Austria the other; the Ruhr and Westphalia would be under international control. This plan was feasible but no decision had been taken because Roosevelt was not there. Had the time had not come to make a decision on the dismemberment of Germany?

Churchill said the British Government agreed in principle to dismemberment but he felt the final decision was too complicated to be done in four or five days. It would require elaborate searching by experienced statesmen on the historical, political, economic and sociological aspects of the problem and prolonged study by a subcommittee.

Churchill said the informal talks at Tehran and Moscow had been very general in character with no intention to lay down a precise plan. He was not in a position to state how Germany should be divided and would not commit himself to any definite plan for the dismemberment of Germany. Churchill felt the isolation of Prussia and the elimination of her might from Germany would remove the arch evil and German war potential would be greatly diminished. A south German state with perhaps a government in Vienna might indicate the line of great division. They agreed Germany should lose territories conquered by the Red Army and they would form part of the Polish settlement.[1] The question of the Rhine valley and the industrial areas of the Ruhr and Saar capable of producing armaments had not yet been decided. Should they go to one country, should they be independent, part of Germany, or under the trusteeship of the world organization that would delegate powers to see these areas were not used to threaten world peace?

Churchill said all this required careful study and the British Government did not yet have fixed ideas on the subject. It had not been decided if Prussia should be divided internally after being isolated from the rest of Germany. They might set up machinery to examine the best method of studying the question. Such a body could report to the three governments before any final decision was reached. They were well prepared for the immediate future, both as to thought and plans concerning the surrender of Germany. All that was required was a final agreement on the occupation zones and the question of a zone for France.

Stalin said the surrender was not clear to him. Suppose a German group declared they had overthrown Hitler and accepted unconditional surrender?[2] Would the three governments then deal with such a group as they had with Badoglio[3] in Italy? Churchill replied they would present the terms of surrender, but if Hitler or Himmler should offer to surrender unconditionally, the answer was clear – they would not negotiate under any circumstances with any war criminals and the war would go on.

Churchill added it was more probable they (Hitler and Himmler) would be killed or in hiding, but another group of Germans might indicate their willingness to accept unconditional surrender. In such a case the three Allies would immediately consult to see if they could deal with this group. If so, terms of unconditional surrender would immediately be submitted.[4] If not, the war would continue and they would occupy the entire country under a military government.

Stalin asked if the Allies should bring up dismemberment at the time of the presentation of the terms of unconditional surrender. Would it not be wise to add a clause to these terms saying Germany would be dismembered, without going into any details? Churchill said he did not feel there was any need to discuss with any German any question about their future – unconditional surrender gave them the right to determine the future of Germany and it could best be done

---

1   East Prussia, the Border Mark, Upper Silesia and parts of Brandenburg Pomerania and Lower Silesia.
2   Operation VALKYRIE, the General's plot to assassinate Hitler and take over, had failed on 20 July 1944.
3   General Pietro Badoglio, 1st Duke of Addis Abeba, 1st Marquess of Sabotino, (1871-1956), Italian Prime Minister from July 1943 (following Mussolini's arrest) to June 1944. Badoglio arranged the Italian surrender and after escaping to Allied-held Rome declared war on Germany.
4   Hitler committed suicide in his Berlin bunker on 30 April after appointing Admiral Karl Dönitz (1891-1980) as his successor.

after unconditional surrender.[1] They reserved under these terms all rights over the lives, property and activities of the Germans.

Stalin did not think the question of dismemberment was an additional question, but one of the most important. Churchill replied it was extremely important, but it was not necessary to discuss it with the Germans, only among themselves. Stalin agreed but felt a decision should be made. Churchill said there was not sufficient time, it needed careful study. Roosevelt said they were both talking about the same thing and what Stalin wanted to agree on was the principle of dismemberment of Germany. As stated by him at Tehran, he was in favour of dismemberment.

Forty years ago, when Roosevelt had been in Germany, the concept of the Reich had not really been known and communities dealt with provincial governments.[2] In the last twenty years everything had become centralized in Berlin. He still thought the division of Germany into five states or seven states was a good idea. Churchill interrupted "or less" and Roosevelt agreed. Churchill said there was no need to inform the Germans of future policy – they had to surrender unconditionally and await their decision. They were dealing with the fate of 80 million people and that required more than 80 minutes to consider. It might not be fully determined until a month or so after their troops occupied Germany.

Roosevelt thought Churchill had said it would be a great mistake to have a public discussion of the dismemberment of Germany as he would certainly receive as many plans as there had been German states in the past.[3] He suggested asking the three Foreign Ministers to discuss the best way to study the dismemberment of Germany and report back in 24 hours. Churchill replied the British Government accepted the principle of dismemberment of Germany but he could not agree to any specific method.

Stalin wanted to know what the intentions of the three governments were. Events in Germany were moving toward catastrophe for the German people and German defeats would increase in magnitude since the Allies intended to launch an important offensive on the Western Front. Germany was threatened with internal collapse because of the lack of bread and coal with the loss of Silesia and the potential destruction of the Ruhr. Such rapid developments made it imperative that the three governments kept up with events and were ready to deal with the question when the German collapse occurred. Stalin understood Churchill's difficulties in setting out a detailed plan and felt Roosevelt's suggestion might be acceptable:

1) agreement in principle that Germany should be dismembered;
2) to instruct the Foreign Ministers to work out the details;
3) to add to the surrender terms a clause stating Germany would be dismembered without giving any details.

---

1   Dönitz announced Germany was to continue the war against the 'Bolshevist enemy' and it would fight the British and Americans if they tried to stop her. The announcement allowed around 1.8 million German soldiers to avoid capture by the Soviets; however, it came at a high cost in lives.
2   Under the post World War I Weimar government.
3   There were 23 states and three free cities in the Weimar Republic (1919-1933).

This last point was important as it would definitely inform the group in power who accepted the surrender that the Allies intended to dismember Germany. This group by their signature would bind the German people to this clause. He thought it was very risky to follow Churchill's plan and say nothing to the German people about dismemberment. The advantage of saying it in advance would facilitate acceptance by the whole German people of what was in store for them.

Churchill then pointed out the Allied governments had full power and authority over the future of Germany. Roosevelt shared Stalin's idea of the advisability of informing the German people at the time of surrender of what was in store for them. Churchill said the psychological effect on the Germans might stiffen their resistance. Both Roosevelt and Stalin said there was no question of making the decision public and Stalin added the surrender terms that Italy had accepted had not yet been made public.

Roosevelt said the question of the French zone still had to be decided. He understood from Stalin the French definitely did not wish to annex outright the German territory up to the Rhine. Stalin replied this was not the case. During General de Gaulle's visit the French made it clear they intended to annex permanently the territory up to the Rhine.[4] Churchill did not want to discuss possible frontiers as they were only considering the zones of temporary military occupation.

Churchill was for giving the French a definite zone which could come out of the British and American zones. He wanted the Soviets to agree the British and American Governments should have the right to work out a French occupation zone. Stalin asked if it would set a precedent to other states. Churchill said the occupation of Germany might be a long one and the British Government was not sure it could bear the burden alone and the French might be of assistance.[5]

Stalin asked if it would change the Tripartite control of Germany to a four-nation control. Churchill replied the British Government expected if France were given a zone they would participate in the control machinery, but other nations who might assist in the occupation, such as Belgium or Holland, would take no part in the control machinery.

Stalin thought it would bring up many complications if they had four nations participating in the determination of German matters. Some method might be evolved whereby England could let the French, Belgians and Dutch assist in the occupation but without the right to participate in the decision making. If this was accepted the Soviet Government might ask other states to help in the occupation of the Soviet zone without participating in the control commission.[6]

Churchill felt this brought up the whole question of the future role of France in Europe and he believed it should play a very important role. France had had a long experience in dealing with the Germans; they were the largest naval power and could be of great help in the administration of Germany. Great Britain did

---

4   The Allies had temporarily occupied the Rhineland after the First World War. The last troops left in June 1930 and then the area had been demilitarized. Nazi Germany reoccupied it on 7 March 1936, violating the Treaty of Versailles.

5   France was given two areas in southwest Germany along the French border. One was the Saar Basin, an important coal producing region. Its governor was General Jean de Lattre de Tassigny (1889-1952).

6   The Allied Control Commission (ACC) for Germany was established on 5 June 1945.

not wish to bear the whole weight of an attack by Germany in the future and would like to see France strong and in possession of a large army. They did not know how long the United States forces would be able to stay in Europe and it was essential to rely upon France to assist in the long-term control of Germany.

Roosevelt did not believe American troops would stay in Europe much more than two years. He could obtain support in Congress and throughout the country for any reasonable measures designed to safeguard the future peace but he did not believe this would extend to the maintenance of an appreciable American force in Europe.[1]

Churchill felt France should have a large army since it was the only ally Great Britain had in the West, whereas the Soviet Union could count on Polish support.

Stalin appreciated the necessity of a strong France, which had recently signed an alliance treaty with the Soviet Union. He had discussed the matter with Daladier[2] before the war and recently in Moscow with General de Gaulle. Roosevelt felt France should be given a zone, but it would be a mistake to bring other nations into the general question of the control of Germany. Stalin said if France was given the right to participate in the control machinery for Germany, it would be difficult to refuse other nations. He wished to see France a strong power but he could not destroy the truth; France had contributed little to the war and it had opened the gate to the enemy. The control commission for Germany should be run by those who had stood firmly against Germany and made the greatest sacrifices in bringing victory. France did not belong on the list of such powers and it should be limited to the three nations.

Churchill replied every nation had had their difficulties at the beginning of the war and had made mistakes.[3] France had gone down before the attacks of the new German tank and air units and while it was true she had not been much help in the war, she was Germany's nearest neighbour and of great importance to Great Britain. It would be inconvenient to add France to the present group of major allies, but British public opinion would not understand why France was being excluded from a problem which was of such direct concern to her.[4] Churchill said the destiny of great nations was not decided by the temporary state of their technical apparatus. Sooner or later they would have to take France in. He had been against the participation of France in the present conference, which he understood was both Roosevelt's and Stalin's opinion. They had to provide for France in the future to stand guard on the left hand of Germany, otherwise Great Britain might again be confronted with the spectre of Germany at the Channel ports. Stalin would not like to see France as a participant in the control machinery for Germany, although he

---

1   The deepening Cold War crisis meant that the United States would make an indefinite commitment to maintaining a military presence in Germany.

2   Edouard Daladier (1884-1970), three times Prime Minister of France including from April 1938 to March 1940. He then became Minister of Defence. He fled to Morocco and was tried for treason by the Vichy government; he spent the rest of the war in prison.

3   For example, the German army advanced deep into the Soviet Union before the Red Army reacted in any meaningful way. As Stalin admitted, only the huge territories gave the Soviets enough time to regroup and counterattack.

4   Churchill was concerned about France's future participation in Europe, not its past failings in the war.

had no objection to her being given a zone within the British and American zones. Churchill said the control commission would be an extraordinary body under the orders of the governments concerned and there was no reason to fear that basic policy regarding Germany would be made by this commission.

Roosevelt said France was a full member of the European Advisory Commission, which was the only Allied body, apart from this Conference, considering the German problem. He favoured the acceptance of the French request for a zone, but agreed France should not take part in the control machinery, otherwise other nations would demand participation. For example, large sections of Dutch farmland had been inundated by salt water following the German destruction of the dykes and it would be necessary to give the Dutch farmers compensation from German territory for a temporary period.[5] It would be at least five years before the flooded lands would be suitable for cultivation. If this was done, the Dutch might claim a voice in the control machinery for Germany.

Eden said there was no question of any zones for any other power except France, but France would not accept a zone of occupation within the British and American zones without participation in the control commission. Stalin replied Great Britain could speak for France in the control commission. Churchill supported Eden's theories. If France got a zone they had to be given representation in the control commission, otherwise the administration of the French zone and its relation with the other zones would be impossible.

Churchill again said the control commission would be a subordinate body, similar to the European Advisory Council. Stalin said the control machinery for Germany would not be an advisory body but would be actively engaged in the everyday administration of Germany. French participation would serve as a precedent for others.[6] Churchill suggested asking the three Foreign Ministers to study the question. Molotov said the European Advisory Commission had already worked out a definite agreement on a tripartite administration of Germany. Eden replied there was no intention of reversing the decision but the relationship of the French zone to the control commission should be considered.

Churchill repeated there was no intention of giving the Belgians or Dutch a zone. Eden added the case of France was different and they would not accept a zone subordinate to British control. Stalin felt there was agreement on France being given a zone but not given participation in the control commission.

Reparations from Germany
Stalin wanted to discuss German reparations. Roosevelt said the desires and needs of the principal allies came first and then those of the smaller countries, such as Belgium, Holland, Norway. He wanted to bring up the question of the Russian desires with regard to the utilization of German manpower. Stalin replied they had a plan for reparations in kind but were not ready yet to present any plan

---

5   The German army had destroyed dykes and sluices to inundate large areas of northern Holland, making it easier to defend. The saltwater destroyed the crops and poisoned the earth, resulting in famine conditions for 4.5 million people. The winter of 1944-1945 was known as the Hunger Winter and 18,000 died.

6   Only the three major powers were on the Allied Control Commission. It broke down in March 1948 over disagreements and the stage was set for Germany to split into two parts.

concerning German manpower. Mr. Maisky[1] then outlined the Soviet plan for
reparations for Germany. It envisaged two categories:

1)   the removal of plants, machine tools, rolling stock, etc. to be com-
     pleted within a period of two years after the end of hostilities;
2)   yearly payments for ten years.

It would be necessary to reduce German heavy industry by 80% to restore the
Soviet economy, which had suffered so much from German aggression, and to
safeguard the future security of Europe. By heavy industry he meant iron and
steel, electrical power and chemical industries. 100% of specialized industry useful
only for military purposes, including aviation factories, synthetic oil refineries,
etc, should be removed. The Soviet Government felt Germany would be able to
cover their economic needs with 20% of her heavy industry. The list of goods to
be delivered during the 10-year period could be fixed later on.

Maisky also proposed Anglo-Soviet-American control over the German economy lasting beyond the reparations payments, for an orderly execution of the
reparations plan and for the security of Europe. Any German enterprises which
could be utilized for war purposes should be placed under international control,
with representatives of the Three Powers sitting on their boards.

Maisky said the calculation of losses as a result of German aggression had been
so astronomical it had been necessary to set a system of priorities for compensation. Even direct material losses, such as public and private property, factories,
plants, railroads, houses, institutions, confiscation of materials, etc. had been so
large that reparations could not cover their loss. Priorities had been established
according to indices:

1)   the proportional contribution of any one nation to the winning of the
     war;
2)   the material losses suffered by each nation.

Those countries which had made the highest contribution to the war and had
suffered the highest material losses would come into one category and all others
would fall into another. Maisky proposed setting up a special reparations committee
of the three governments in Moscow. The total reparations shown in withdrawals
and yearly payments which the Soviets required would reach $10 billion.[2]

Churchill recalled very well the end of the last war and although he did not
participate in the peace settlement he had been informed of the discussions. He
remembered only £2 billion[3] had been extracted from Germany in the form of
reparations by the Allies after the last war and even that was only possible because
the United States had given Germany credits.[4] For example, they had taken some

---

1   Ivan Maisky (1884-1975), Deputy Commissar of Foreign Affairs. His commission planned Soviet strategies to end the war
    and for the postwar world.
2   $128 billion in 2013.
3   £2 billion in 1918 is equivalent to £65 billion today.
4   While Germany's economy ailed, the American economy boomed and credits were given to Germany so it could pay its
    reparations. This all ended following the Wall Street Crash in 1929. The American economy crashed overnight, taking
    the frail German economy with it. The resultant economic crisis led to the Depression in America and the rise of the Nazis
    in Germany.

old Atlantic liners from the Germans and they immediately built new and better ships on credit. Churchill recognized the suffering which the Soviet Union had undergone in this war, it had been greater than any other power, but he felt the Soviet Union would get nowhere near the sum Maisky mentioned.

Churchill said the Allies had also indulged themselves with fantastic figures of reparations at the end of the last war but they had turned out to be a myth.[5] The British Isles had also suffered in the war and the British Government had disposed of the bulk of its assets abroad despite the generous help of Lend-Lease. The British Isles had to export goods to import food, since they were dependent on imports for half of their food supply. There would be no victorious country so burdened in an economic sense as Great Britain. If he could see any benefit to Great Britain in large reparations from Germany he would favour such a course but he very much doubted whether they were feasible.

Churchill said other countries, such as Belgium, Holland and Norway, also had claims against Germany. He was haunted by the spectre of a starving Germany, which would present a serious problem for the Allies since they could either say "it serves them right" or endeavour to help them.[6] In the latter case, who would pay for the help? Churchill concluded if you wanted a horse to pull a wagon you had to at least give it fodder. Stalin said that was right, but care should be taken to see the horse did not turn around and kick you.

Roosevelt said he had also been through the last war and he remembered very vividly the United States had lost a great deal of money. They had lent over $10 billion to Germany and this time they would not repeat their past mistakes. In the United States German property sequestered during the war had been returned to the German owners after the last war, but this time he would seek the necessary legislation to retain all German property in America. The Germans had no capital, factories or other equipment the United States needed but he did not want to have to contemplate the necessity of helping the Germans to keep from starving.

Roosevelt would willingly support any claims for Soviet reparations since the German standard of living should not be higher than the Soviet Union.[7] Just as they expected to help Great Britain expand her export trade, they would also help the Soviet Union retain the reparations in kind which she required, as well as German manpower to reconstruct the devastated regions. But the Germans should be allowed to live, so they might not become a burden on the world.

---

5   In January 1921 the reparations were set at 132 billion gold marks but the actual amount due to be paid was 50 billion marks; the rest was set to fool the public into thinking Germany had to pay more. Germany had paid 20 billion gold marks ($5 billion or £1 billion) when payments were suspended in 1931; 12.5 billion of it came from loans from New York banks.
6   In the end, the decision was made to help Germany and other European countries to stop the spread of Communism. The European Recovery Plan (or Marshall Plan, named after then Secretary of State George Marshall) gave $13 billion ($123 billion in 2013) of economic and technical assistance over four years, starting in 1948. Though there were significant limitations on the use of the aid and a lot of it flowed straight back to American industry.
7   United States Secretary of the Treasury Henry Morgenthau Jr. (1891-1967) proposed eliminating Germany's ability to wage war. The Morgenthau Plan looked at turning Germany into a country reliant on agriculture and Churchill drafted a new version, which became the version accepted by Roosevelt and Churchill. The plan aimed for industrial disarmament and a watered-down plan resulted in equipment being removed from over 700 manufacturing plants, while steel production was reduced to 6.7 million tons, the amount needed for peacetime reconstruction.

Roosevelt said despite his desire to see the devastated areas in all countries restored, reparations could not possibly cover the needs. He was in favour of extracting the maximum reparations from Germany but not to the extent that the people would starve.

Maisky appreciated Churchill's points concerning the experiences after the last war. He felt the failure had been due to the transfer problem, which was the rock on which the reparations policy was founded. The financial policies of the United States and Great Britain contributed to the German refusal to pay. The Germans had never paid more than one quarter of the total reparations figure and had received a great deal more in credits and loans.

Maisky said the purpose of reparations in kind was to avoid the problem of transfer. The amount desired by the Soviet Union was equal to only 10% of the present United States budget and equal to about six months of the British expenditures in the war. The Soviet demands for German reparations equalled about 1% of the United States budget in peace and about 2% times the British budget. Of course, there was no intention to force Germany into starvation but he did not feel the Germans had a right to a higher standard of living than Central Europe. Germany could develop her light industry and agriculture and since the Germans would have no military expenditures there was no reason why Germany could not give a modest but decent standard of living to her people.[1]

Churchill said the question of reparations should be examined by a sub-commission which should consider the claims of other countries who suffered Nazi aggression. In Roosevelt's opinion, the commission should be confined to the representatives of the Three Powers. Stalin and Churchill agreed.

Stalin felt the commission could accomplish nothing unless it they gave it general directives. Although the United States did not need machine tools she might well need raw materials, which she could receive from Germany. He mentioned the United States would take over German property in the United States as a part of her share. Roosevelt agreed.

Stalin said Germany's post-war resources should be also taken into consideration when calculating German capabilities. Then all factories and farms would work for peace, not war. The Three Powers who had made the most sacrifices and had been the organizers of victory should have first claim on reparations. He did not include France among these powers, since she had suffered less than Belgium, Yugoslavia, or Poland.

Churchill said the Allies had done a great deal of the damage in France.[2] Stalin replied France could not expect to get reparations from the Allies. He respected France but he could not ignore the truth and at the present moment France only had eight divisions in the war, Yugoslavia had twelve while the Poles had thirteen. The Foreign Ministers would decide directives for the reparations commission, which would sit in Moscow. The meeting adjourned.

---

1 Enforced limitations on German production resulted in an unhealthy deterioration of Europe's economy. The initial stages of the Marshall Plan called for the raising of Germany's steel quotas from 25 per cent to 50 per cent of pre-war capacity.
2 By bombing targets and during the Battle for France.

6 February

First Combined Combined Chiefs of Staff Meeting

Petroleum products in Northwest Europe; End date of the war with Germany; LVTs for the Mediterranean; Occupation Zones in Germany; Basic undertakings; Liaison with Soviets over strategic bombing of Eastern Germany

Second Tripartite Combined Chiefs of Staff Meeting

Bomb line and liaison arrangements; Coordination of offensive operations; River crossing techniques and equipment; US bomber bases around Vienna and Budapest; Soviet airfields for damaged British night bombers; Enemy intelligence; Pacific operations, Very Long Range (VLR) bomber operations against Japan; Operations in Burma and China.

Third Plenary Meeting, 6 February

Churchill said the importance of France in the future had been enhanced by the limitation which the President had placed on the length of time United States forces might stay in Europe.[3] Great Britain would not be strong enough alone to guard the Western approaches to the Channel.

Roosevelt had spoken on the basis of present conditions and he felt public opinion in the United States would be prepared to support an international organization along the lines of Dumbarton Oaks[4] and this might change their attitude in regard to the question of troops.

Roosevelt felt they should consider the United States proposal regarding Dumbarton Oaks. The nations of the world shared a common desire to see the elimination of war for at least 50 years. He was not so optimistic as to believe in eternal peace, but he did believe 50 years of peace were feasible and possible. Since neither he, Stalin, nor Churchill had been at Dumbarton Oaks, he asked the Secretary of State[5] to explain the United States position on voting in the Security Council and Stettinius read it out. Molotov said the Soviet Government attached great importance to the question and wished to study the proposal. Churchill said the President's proposals were satisfactory. World peace depended on the friendship and cooperation of the three Governments, but the British Government considered they would be committing an injustice if small countries were not allowed to state their grievances. It looked as though the three Great Powers were trying to rule the world, whereas they wanted to save it from a repetition of the horrors of the war.

Churchill felt the three Great Powers should make a proud submission because it would illustrate why the British Government did not think the President's proposal would harm British interests. For example, if China raised the question of the return of Hong Kong, both China and Great Britain would be excluded from voting from the controversy. Great Britain would be protected against any decision adverse to her interests by the exercise of the veto power.

---

3 Stated at no more than two years but actually indefinitely.
4 Talks on international peace and a security organization held at Dumbarton Oaks, Washington DC, between 22 August and 7 October 1944. Delegations from Britain, the United States, the Soviet Union and China agreed there was a need for an organization to replace the League of Nations.
5 Edward Stettinius (1900-1949), US Secretary of State (1944-1945), was chairman of the conference.

Stalin asked if Egypt would be on the assembly. Eden replied "Yes, but not on the Council unless elected." Stalin supposed Egypt raised the question of the return of the Suez Canal.[1] Churchill hoped Stalin would let him finish his illustration regarding Hong Kong. Great Britain had the right by their veto to stop all action against Great Britain by the Council of the World Organization. Great Britain would not need to agree to any decision contrary to her own interests and would not be required to return Hong Kong unless they felt it should be done. China should have the right to speak and the same considerations would apply to Egypt if that country had a complaint with regard to the Suez Canal.

Churchill said the same considerations applied if Argentina raised a complaint against the United States. Roosevelt recalled the Three Powers had stated in the Tehran Declaration: "We recognize fully the supreme responsibility resting upon us and all the nations to make a peace which will command good will from the overwhelming masses of the peoples of the world…" Roosevelt thought this Declaration was pertinent to the discussion.

Churchill saw no reason to fear the United States proposals and was pleased to associate the British Government with them. Because of their great power they should allow others to be heard. Stalin wanted to study the document, since it was impossible to understand all of the implications. The Dumbarton Oaks proposals already gave the right of discussion, but he did not believe any nation would be satisfied with expressing its opinion. They would want a decision.

If Churchill thought China would be satisfied with merely expressing her opinion over Hong Kong, he was mistaken; she would want a decision. The same was true of Egypt over the question of the Suez Canal. It was not a question of one power or three powers desiring to be masters of the world because the Dumbarton Oaks organization stopped that.

Stalin wanted further clarification on what powers Churchill had in mind when he spoke of a desire to rule the world. He was sure Great Britain had no such desire, nor did the United States and that only left the USSR. Churchill had spoken of the three Great Powers who could collectively place themselves so high over the others the whole world would say these three desired to rule. Stalin said ironically it looked as though two Great Powers had already accepted a document which would avoid any such accusation but the third has not yet signified its assent. In his opinion there was a more serious question than the voting procedure or the question of the domination of the world.

They all knew as long as the three of them lived none of them would involve their countries in aggressive actions, but none of them might be present in ten years time. A new generation would come into being not knowing the horrors of the present war.

Stalin felt there was an obligation to create for the future generation such an organization which would secure peace for at least 50 years. The main thing was to prevent quarrels in the future between the three Great Powers and the task was to secure their unity for the future. The covenant of the new World Organization

1   Stalin wants to compare the Suez Canal with the Dardanelles.

should have this as its primary task.[2] The greatest danger was conflict between the three Great Powers but if unity could be preserved there was little danger of the renewal of German aggression. Therefore, a covenant had to be worked out which would prevent conflicts between the three Great Powers.

Stalin apologized for not studying the Dumbarton Oaks proposals in detail; he had been busy. As he understood it, there were two categories of dispute:

1) conflicts which required the application of sanctions, economic, political or military;

2) conflicts which could be settled by peaceful means.

Permanent members had a right to vote under the first category even if they were parties to such disputes. But the parties in dispute would not be allowed to vote under the second category. He admitted the Russians were spending too much time on the technique of voting. But they attached great importance to this question, since all decisions were made by votes and they were interested in the decisions, not in the discussions.

Both Churchill and Stettinius said the power of the world organization could not be directed against any of the permanent members under the United States proposal. Stalin was afraid a conflict might break the unity of their united front. Churchill saw the force of that argument, but he did not believe the world organization would eliminate disputes between powers; that would remain the function of diplomacy. Stalin said his colleagues in Moscow could not forget the events of December 1939 during the Finnish war when at the instigation of England and France the League of Nations expelled the Soviet Union from the League and mobilized world opinion against the Soviet Union, even going so far as to speak of a crusade.[3]

Churchill said the British and French Governments were very angry at the Soviet Union and in any event such action was impossible under the Dumbarton Oaks proposals. Stalin was not thinking of expulsion but of the question of the mobilization of opinion against one country. Churchill thought this might happen to any nation but doubted very much if either Roosevelt or Stalin would lead a savage attack against Great Britain and he felt this applied to the other two countries.

Roosevelt felt the unity of the Great Powers was one of their first aims and the United States policy promoted rather than impaired this aim. Should there be any unfortunate differences between the Great Powers, it would become fully known to the world no matter what voting procedure was adopted.[4] In any event, there was no method of preventing discussions of differences in the assembly. Full and friendly discussions in the Council would in no sense promote disunity; they would serve to demonstrate the confidence the Great Powers had in each other and in the justice of their own policies.

---

2   There were 27 wars, civil wars, internal conflicts and revolutions in the ten years following World War II. There was also of course the Cold War, when the threat of nuclear war prevented the three Great Powers going to war.

3   The Soviet Union was expelled from the League of Nations for invading Finland. Although the League was the brainchild of President Woodrow Wilson (1856–1924), the United States never joined; isolationists in the Senate stopped it.

4   The unfortunate differences soon began. Soviet troops occupied the Eastern Bloc countries while the United States decided to keep its troops in Western Europe.

The Polish Question

Churchill was hoping for a start on the Polish question. Roosevelt said the United States was further away from Poland than anyone else and there were times when a long distance point of view was useful. At Tehran he believed the American people were favourably inclined to the Curzon Line as the eastern frontier of Poland. If the Soviet Government would consider a concession in regard to Lwow[1] and its oil deposits, it would have a very salutary effect.

Roosevelt wished to see the creation of a representative government composed of representatives of the principal parties of Poland that could have the support of all the great powers. One possibility was the creation of a Presidential Council of Polish leaders, which could create a government composed of the chiefs of the five political parties. Whatever happened, Poland should maintain the most friendly and cooperative relations with the Soviet Union. Stalin said Poland should also maintain friendly relations with the other Allies.

Roosevelt thought it would be a great help if they could solve the Polish question. He did not know any members of the London government or the Lublin government[2] but he had met Mr. Mikolajczyk,[3] who had made a deep impression on him as a sincere and an honest man. Churchill had consistently declared the British Government would support the Curzon Line, even leaving Lwow[4] to the Soviet Union. He and Eden had been criticized for this but after the burdens which Russia had borne in this war, the Curzon Line was not a decision of force but one of right.

Churchill added if the mighty Soviet Union could make some gesture to the much weaker country, such as the relinquishing of Lwow, this act of magnanimity would be acclaimed and admired. He was much more interested in sovereignty and independence of Poland than in the frontier line. He wanted the Poles to have a home where they could organize their lives as they wished. That was an objective he had often heard Stalin proclaim most firmly, and he put his trust in those declarations.

Churchill had not considered the question of the frontier vitally important. It could not be forgotten Great Britain had gone to war to protect Poland against German aggression when that decision was most risky and it had almost cost them their life in the world. Great Britain had no material interest in Poland, but the question was one of honour and his government would never be content with a solution which did not leave Poland a free and independent state.

The freedom of Poland did not cover any hostile designs or intrigue against the USSR. It was the earnest desire of the British Government for Poland to be mistress in her own house and captain of her soul. The British Government

---

1   Lwow, now Lviv in the western Ukraine.
2   The Polish Committee of National Liberation (PKWN), or Lublin Government, was a provisional government in opposition to the London-based Government-in-exile. The communist government was set up on 21 July 1944 and was fully supported by the Soviet Union; members had to be approved by the Soviet authorities.
3   Stanislaw Mikolajczyk (1901-1966) Prime Minister of the Republic of Poland July 1943 to November 1944.
4   Lwow Voivodeship and the city of Lviv became part of the Soviet Union in February 1946. Between 100,000 and 140,000 Poles were resettled and replaced by eastern Ukrainians; while the remaining Ukrainians discovered what Soviet rule entailed.

recognized the present Polish government in London[5] but did not have intimate contact with it. He had known Mr. Mikolajczyk, Mr. Grabski[6] and Mr. Romer[7] and had found them good and honest men. He asked if they could use these men to help form a government so it could be recognized as an interim government until the Polish people could form their own government by free vote. Churchill was interested in the President's suggestion.

Stalin understood the Polish question was one of British honour but it was a question of both honour and security for the Russians. It was a question of honour because Russia had many past grievances against Poland and desired to see them eliminated. It was also a question of strategic security because Poland was a bordering country and had been the corridor for attack on Russia. During the last 30 years Germany twice has passed through this corridor because Poland was weak. Russia wanted a strong, independent and democratic Poland.[8] Since it was impossible by the force of Russian armies alone to close this corridor from the outside, it could only be done by Poland's forces. It was very important to have Poland independent, strong and democratic. It was not only a question of honour for Russia, but one of life and death.

For this reason there had been a great change from the policies of the Czars who wanted to suppress and assimilate Poland.[9] With regard to the Curzon Line, concessions over Lwow and Churchill's reference to a magnanimous act on our part, it was necessary to remind them that Curzon and Clemenceau[10] fixed the line, not Russians. The Russians had not been invited and the line was established against their will.

Lenin had opposed giving Bialystok Province[11] to the Poles but the Curzon Line gave it to Poland. They had already retreated from Lenin's position regarding this province. Should they then be less Russian than Curzon and Clemenceau? They could not return to Moscow and face the people who would say Stalin and Molotov had been less sure defenders of Russian interests than Curzon and Clemenceau. It was impossible to agree with the proposed modification of the line.

Stalin preferred to have the war go on, although it would cost them blood, to compensate Poland with territory from Germany. When he was in Moscow, Mr. Mikolajczyk had been delighted to hear Poland's frontier would extend to the West Neisse River and he asked them to support it.

As to the question of the Polish government, Churchill had said it would be good to create one but he was afraid that was a slip of the tongue; it was quite

---

5   The Polish Government-in-exile.
6   Stanislaw Grabski (1871-1949), member of the Polish Government-in-exile.
7   Tadeusz Romer (1894-1978), Minister of Foreign Affairs of the Polish Government-in-exile.
8   Poland would become a satellite state of the Soviet Eastern Bloc in 1948 following fraudulent elections in January 1947. Between 1944 and 1952 around 200,000 people were executed and 400,000 were imprisoned or exiled for resisting the annexation of eastern Poland to the Ukraine.
9   Poland ceased to exist in 1795, divided between Prussia and Russia, but the people kept rising up against their rulers. The Allies agreed to reconstitute Poland during the First World War and it gained its independence in after the Armistice. It stopped the Russians retaking it during the Polish-Soviet War (1919-1921).
10 Lord Curzon, British Secretary of State for Foreign Affairs and Georges Clemenceau, Prime Minister of France.
11 Bialystok is 100 miles northeast of Warsaw.

impossible to create one without the Poles' participation. Stalin was called a dictator and not a democrat, but he had enough democratic feeling to refuse to create
a Polish government without the Poles being consulted; the question could only
be settled with the Poles' consent.

There had been a good chance for a fusion of the various Polish elements
last autumn in Moscow and various points of agreement were made between
Mikolajczyk, Grabski and the Lublin Poles,[1] as Churchill would remember.
Mikolajczyk left for London but did not return since he was expelled from office
precisely because he wanted agreement. Arciszewski[2] and Raczkiewicz[3] were
hostile to the agreement. Arciszewski had called the Lublin Poles bandits and
criminals and they paid him back in the same coin. It would be difficult to bring
them together.

The Warsaw Poles, Bierut[4] and Osobka Morawski,[5] did not even want to talk
with the London government about any fusion. Stalin asked what concessions
they might make in this respect and they said they could tolerate Zeligowski[6] or
Grabski[7] but they did not want to hear about Mikolajczyk being prime minister.
He was prepared to support any attempt to reach a solution that offered some
chance of success. Should they ask the Warsaw Poles to come to the conference
or to Moscow? The Warsaw government had a democratic base equal at least to
that of de Gaulle.

As a military man Stalin demanded no civil war in the rear from a country liberated by the Red Army. The men in the Red Army were indifferent to the type
of government, as long as it maintained order and they were not shot in the back.
The Warsaw, or Lublin, government had fulfilled this task.[8] There were agents of
the London government who claimed to be agents of the underground forces
of resistance. No good and much evil came from these forces. Up to the present
time, they had killed 212 of their military men. They attacked Soviet supply bases
to obtain arms.[9]

Although all radio stations had to register and obtain permission to operate,
agents of the London government were violating these regulations. They had
arrested some of them and would shoot them as military law required, if they
continued to disturb their rear. When he compared what the agents of the Lublin
government had done and what the agents of the London government had done,

1   The Lublin Poles were the Soviet-sponsored interim Polish government.
2   Tomasz Arciszewski (1877-1955), Prime Minister of the Polish Government-in-exile from 1944 to 1947.
3   Wladyslaw Raczkiewicz (1885-1947), President of the Polish Government-in-exile from 1939 to 1947.
4   Boleslaw Bierut (1892–1956), Polish Communist leader.
5   Edward Osobka-Morawski (1909-1997), Prime Minister of the Republic of Poland, 1944-1947.
6   General Lucjan Zeligowski (1865–1947), member of the Polish National Council.
7   Stanislaw Grabski (1871-1949), Polish economist and member of the Polish Government-in-exile.
8   The Red Army was fully engaged battling the Germans and it did not want a civil war to its rear, which would affect its lines of
    communications.
9   The Polish anti-Communist underground fought against the Soviet takeover from 1944 to 1946. They fought back against the
    People's Commissariat for Internal Affairs (the NKVD), attacking prisons and freeing political prisoners. They were known as
    the Cursed Soldiers and were hunted down by the security services and assassination squads.

he saw the first were good and the second were bad.[10] They wanted tranquillity in their rear and would support the government which gave them peace in the rear; as a military man he could not do otherwise. Without a secure rear there could be no more victories for the Red Army. Any military man and even the non-military man understood this situation.

Churchill said the British and Soviet Governments had different sources of information and obtained different views of the situation in Poland. Their reports could be mistaken as it was not always possible to believe everything. With the best of all their information he could not feel the Lublin government represented more than one third of the people and would be maintained in power if the people were free to express their opinion. One of the reasons why the British had so earnestly sought a solution had been the fear the Polish underground army would come into collision with the Lublin government, which would lead to great bloodshed, arrests and deportations, which could not fail to have a bad effect on the whole Polish question.[11] Churchill agreed anyone who attacked the Red Army should be punished but the British Government could not agree to recognizing the Lublin government of Poland. The conference adjourned.

7 February: Fourth Plenary Meeting

Molotov read the results of the Foreign Ministers' meeting and Roosevelt said they were all grateful for their productive work. Churchill also thanked the Committee for their fruitful work but he wished to study the English translation.

The French Question

Roosevelt asked if the document included Eden's reservation on France and Eden replied yes. Churchill said the British Government was unconvinced it would be possible to accord a zone to the French without their participation in the Control Commission. The French would cause endless trouble if they were given a zone without participation. If they were strict in their zones, they might be lenient in theirs and vice versa. It was of the utmost importance there should be uniformity in the treatment of Germany by the three, or four, Allies. The Control Commission for Germany would be a subordinate instrument, as was the case in Italy, although the German Commission would have more important tasks.

Churchill wished to make it clear he did not consider French participation in the Control Commission would give them any right to attend a conference such as this one, at least for the time being. He found the arguments on the subject somewhat futile since it was obvious France would accept no zone unless they were given participation in the Control Commission and he, for one, thought they were right. He felt it was no good to refer the question to the European Advisory Commission, which was a weaker body, particularly as France was represented on the Commission. A deadlock with the French and British on one

---

10　While the London government supported the anti-communist attacks, the Soviet-sponsored Polish Committee of National Liberation (Lublin government) were helping to put them down.

11　Churchill was right in his assessment.

side and the Russians and Americans on the other would result. He believed it should be settled now, but it still required further study.

Stalin asked if Churchill meant it should be settled now or later. Churchill answered it should be done now. Roosevelt asked would it not be better to postpone it for two or three weeks instead of two or three days? Churchill felt it would be difficult to settle the question once they had separated but Stalin replied they had been able to settle many things by correspondence.

Stalin then said they could at least have the benefit of the French opinion in the European Advisory Commission. Roosevelt agreed France should not join this body but he was doubtful whether it would keep them quiet. He suggested continuing with the Polish question.

The Polish Government

Roosevelt was less interested in frontier lines than the problem of the Polish Government. He did not attach any importance to the continuity or legality of any Polish Government because there had in reality been no Polish Government in some years.

Stalin had received Roosevelt's letter containing the suggestion they summon two representatives from the Lublin Government and two representatives from other elements of Polish public opinion. They should endeavour to settle the question of a new interim government for Poland, which would be pledged to hold free elections when conditions permitted. Three personalities from London, namely, Mr. Mikolajczyk, Mr. Grabski and Mr. Romer, were possible members of this new government.

Stalin had only received the President's letter an hour and a half before. He had tried to reach the Lublin Poles by telephone to ask their opinion but they were away in Krakow and Lodz. As to the others, he was not sure they could be located in time for them to come to the Crimea, especially Wincenty Witos[1] and Sapieha.[2]

Stalin said Molotov had worked out some proposals which approached the President's suggestions on the Polish question but they had not been typed up. He suggested proceeding to the Dumbarton Oaks proposal.

Dumbarton Oaks Conference[3]

Molotov had seen Stettinius's report and explanations of the President's proposals the day before. They had also followed Churchill's remarks closely. These proposals fully guaranteed the unity of the Great Powers in the preservation of peace. Since this had been the main Soviet purpose at Dumbarton Oaks and the new proposals fully safeguarded this principle, they were entirely acceptable. There was full agreement on this subject.

Soviet Republics Joining the World Organization

The Soviet views were based on constitutional changes made February last year and he did not think the Conference should ignore this request.[4] They would be

---

1   Wincenty Witos (1874-1945), three times premier of Poland in the 1920s.
2   Eustachy Sapieha (1881-1963), ex Minister of Foreign Affairs in exile.
3   Officially, the Washington Conversations on International Peace and Security Organization.
4   On 2 February 1944 changes included Article 18 (a): "Each Union Republic has the right to enter into direct relations with foreign states, to conclude agreements with them and exchange diplomatic and consular representatives with them."

satisfied with the admission of three, or at least two, of the Soviet Republics as original members; they were the Ukraine, White Russia and Lithuania.

Molotov said it was superfluous to explain the size, population and importance of the Ukraine, White Russia or Lithuania, or their importance in foreign affairs.[5] These three Republics had borne the greatest sacrifices in the war and were the first to be invaded by the enemy, so it was only fair they were original members. The Soviet Government hoped these proposals would be accepted.

Roosevelt asked if Molotov meant members of the Assembly. Molotov replied yes, they should be included. The Dominions of the British Commonwealth had gradually and patiently achieved their place in international affairs. He felt it was only right these Soviet Republics should find a worthy place among the members of the Assembly. Their sacrifices and contributions to the war earned them this place.

Molotov fully agreed with Roosevelt's proposals on voting but asked that the Soviet Republics be given a chance to become equal members of the World Organization. Roosevelt was happy to hear the agreement to his proposals. This was a great step forward which would be welcomed by all the peoples of the world. Roosevelt had been interested in the participation of the Soviet Republics.[6]

The British Empire, the USSR and the United States were very different in structure and in tradition. The British Empire, for example, had many large units, such as Canada and Australia. The USSR had a different national structure. The United States had one language and one Foreign Minister. It might prejudice the thesis of one vote for each member if the larger nations were given more than one.

While certain countries were large in area, they were small in population; Brazil was smaller than the USSR but larger than the United States. On the other hand, some countries were small in area but large in population, such as Honduras and Haiti. There were a number of nations associated with the United Nations, such as Chile, Peru, Paraguay, Iceland, and others, which had broken relations with Germany but which were not at war.[7]

Roosevelt felt the important thing was to proceed with the plans for a conference to set up the World Organization. The question of the admission of countries who were not members of the United Nations could be considered either at that time or after the organization was in operation. He suggested the Foreign Ministers studied Molotov's question.

Churchill expressed his heartfelt thanks to Stalin and Molotov for a great step forward that would bring joy and relief to the peoples of the world. The membership of the Soviet Republics had been put before them for the first time. He agreed the United States and the British Empire were different. Self-Governing Dominions had taken their place in world affairs and had worked for peace over the past 25 years and, if he could say so, for the furtherance of democratic processes.[8]

---

5   Basically, the Soviet Union's western border.
6   Belorussia and the Ukraine were invited.
7   Eventually, 45 nations were invited (including the four sponsors). Poland did not attend because its government had not been announced on 28 June 1945; it was added on 15 October 1945.
8   A pointed reference to the non-democratic processes of the Soviet Union.

The Dominions had come into the war when Great Britain declared war against Germany, knowing full-well the weakness of Great Britain at that time, Great Britain had no means of forcing them into this decision and into which they knew they could not often be consulted on major matters. Great Britain could not agree to any organization which reduced the status of the Dominions or excluded them from participation.

Churchill had great sympathy with the Soviet request. His heart went out to mighty Russia, which, though bleeding was beating down the tyrants in her path. He could understand their point of view, as they were represented by only one voice in comparison with the British organization, which had a smaller population if only the white people were considered. He was pleased Roosevelt had made an answer to the Soviet proposal which in no way constituted a final negation. Churchill added he could not exceed his authority; he had just heard the proposal and would like to discuss it with the Foreign Secretary and possibly communicate it to London.

Roosevelt said his recommendations had been somewhat different. He had meant the Foreign Ministers should study the question, the time and place of the conference and who should be invited. Churchill agreed but the Foreign Ministers had already had a good deal of work thrust upon them.

World Organization Conference

The conference could take place at the end of March, although it might be physically possible to do it within the next four weeks. Churchill foresaw difficulties in attempting to hold a meeting in March. The battle would be at its height and more soldiers would be involved than at any time of the war. British domestic problems would be very pressing and their Ministers, including the Foreign Secretary, would be greatly occupied in Parliament. He wondered if the state of the world and Europe in particular would make a meeting of the United Nations very difficult. He doubted if any representatives at the conference would have behind them the full thought of the vital forces of their countries.[1]

Roosevelt only had in mind a meeting to organize the setting up of the world organization, and the world organization itself would probably not come into being for three to six months after the conference.[2] Some nations would still be under the German yoke in March and would be represented by governments-in-exile whose authority would be questionable. Other countries would be starving and in misery, such as Holland. France would be there with a loud voice. There were other countries who had not suffered at all and had not lost a man in the war. He wondered how such a gathering could really undertake the immense task of the future organization of the world.

Roosevelt said the Foreign Ministers could consider the Soviet proposal on membership; the date and place of the conference and what nations should be invited. Churchill had no objection to the Foreign Ministers discussing this point

---

1　The opening meetings lasted from 25 April until 26 June 1945. The United Nations Charter was signed on the final day.
2　The United Nations came into existence on 24 October 1945; the event is still celebrated every year.

but this was no technical question; it was one of great moment. With this qualification, he agreed to Roosevelt's proposal.

Iran

Churchill proposed the Foreign Ministers should consider Iran and other matters of secondary importance. Roosevelt and Stalin agreed.[3] Roosevelt jokingly said he hoped forestry would be considered, since he had not seen a tree in his visit last year to Tehran. He thought Iran was a good example of the type of economic problem that might confront the world if they were to bring about expansion of world trade and greater exchange of goods. Persia did not have the purchasing power to buy foreign goods, and if expansion of world trade occurred, measures had to be considered for helping countries like Persia who did not have any purchasing power.

Persia had plenty of timber and water before the advent of the Turks and her people had been reasonably prosperous but he personally had never seen a poorer country than Persia. He hoped the new world organization would conduct a worldwide survey with a view to extending help to countries and areas that did not have sufficient purchasing power, either in cash or in foreign exchange.[4]

Roosevelt said there was a parallel in Europe where certain countries had adequate supplies of power, such as coal and water power, and had cheap and abundant electric power; other countries within 50 miles had neither. This situation was wrong. In the Soviet Union and its various republics consideration had been given to the problem of a country as a whole, and in the United States the TVA had the same idea. In the region of the TVA, electric current was sold at the same price throughout the area.[5]

Poland's Borders

Molotov read his proposals on the Polish question:

1) The Curzon Line should be the Eastern frontier of Poland.[6]
2) The Western frontier of Poland should be traced from Stettin, south along the River Oder and the western Neisse.
3) To add democratic leaders from Polish émigré circles to the Provisional Polish Government.
4) The enlarged Provisional Polish Government should be recognized by the Allied Governments.
5) The Provisional Polish Government should as soon as possible call the population of Poland to the polls.

---

3   Reza Khan (1878-1944) had been Shah since 1925 but he had ostensible ties with Germany. In fact, as argued by author Fariborz Mokhtari in his book *In the Lion's Shadow: The Iranian Schindler and his Homeland in the Second World War*, the ties were overwhelmingly economic and not political. In September 1941 the British and Soviet Union forced him to abdicate in favour of his son, Mohammed Reza Pahlavi (1919-1980), so a new Trans-Iranian railway could be built to move Lend-Lease supplies into the Soviet Union.
4   Iran was not exploiting its large reserves of petroleum and natural gas at this stage.
5   Tennessee Valley Authority engaged in one of the largest hydroelectric power schemes to produce aluminium for planes. 28,000 people worked on a dozen hydroelectric plants and Harry Truman is quoted as saying "I want aluminium. I don't care if I get it from Alcoa or Al Capone"; Alcoa owned the land. TVA also provided electricity for uranium enrichment, which was needed for the atomic bomb under the Manhattan Project.
6   With small digressions in favour of Poland.

6)   Mr. Molotov, Mr. Harriman[1] and Sir Archibald Clark Kerr[2] were entrusted with enlarging the Provisional Polish Government.

Roosevelt felt progress was being made but he did not like the word 'émigré'. He did not see any necessity to go to émigrés since you could find enough Poles in Poland for the purpose. He did not know any of the Poles in the Poland government in London and only knew Mr. Mikolajczyk.

Churchill shared Roosevelt's dislike of the word 'émigré'. It originated during the French revolution and in England it meant a person who had been driven out of their country by his own people. In the case of the Poles this was not true; they had left their country as a result of the brutal German attack. He preferred to refer to them as 'Poles temporarily abroad'.[3]

Churchill would always support the movement of Polish frontiers to the west since they should receive compensation, but not more than they could handle. It would be a pity to stuff the Polish goose so full of German food it got indigestion. There was a considerable body of British public opinion that would be shocked if it were proposed to move large numbers of Germans, and although he personally would not be shocked, he knew that view existed in England. If it were confined to East Prussia, six million Germans probably could be handled, quite aside from moral grounds, but the addition of the line west of the Neisse would create quite a problem.

Stalin said most of the Germans had already run away from the Red Army. Churchill said this simplified the problem. When it came to the question of space in Germany for these deported persons he felt Germany had six to seven million casualties and would probably have a million more, simplifying the problem. Stalin replied the Germans might well have one or possibly two million more casualties.[4]

Churchill was not afraid of the problem of transfer of populations provided it was proportional to the capacity of the Poles to handle them and the capability of the Germans to receive them. It needed study not only in principle but as a practical matter. In the Soviet proposal, some reference should be made to other democratic leaders from within Poland. Churchill agreed it would be well to sleep on the problem and take it up tomorrow, but he did feel some progress had been made. The meeting adjourned.

Roosevelt–Stalin Meeting, 8 February
Air Bases in the Far East

Roosevelt said the war in the Pacific was entering a new phase with the fall of Manila and they hoped to establish bases on the Bonins and on the islands near Formosa. The time had come to make plans for the additional bombing of Japan. He hoped it would not be necessary to invade the Japanese islands and would do so only if absolutely necessary. The Japanese had four million men in their army

---

1   W. Averell Harriman, US Ambassador to the Soviet Union.
2   Sir Archibald Clark Kerr, 1st Baron Inverchapel (1882-1951), Ambassador to the Soviet Union, 1942 to 1946.
3   Churchill does not mention the Soviet Union's occupation of the Eastern half of Poland.
4   There were over 300,000 casualties in the Battle of Berlin alone.

and he hoped to be able to destroy Japan and its army by intensive bombing to save American lives.[5]

Stalin did not object to the United States having bases at Komsomolsk or Nikolayevsk.[6] The first was on the lower reaches of the Amur River and the second at its mouth. He thought they would have to leave the bases on Kamchatka[7] until a later stage, since the presence of the Japanese Consul made it difficult to make arrangements. In any case, the other two bases in the Maritime Provinces were nearer.

Roosevelt handed Stalin a paper asking for the Soviet staff to enter into planning talks with the United States staff. Stalin said he would give the necessary instructions.

Use of airfields and survey of bomb damage in Eastern and Southeast Europe

Roosevelt asked if the United States Air Force could use airfields around Budapest to carry out bombing operations against the Germans. At the present time the American bombers based in Italy had to make a long and hazardous flight over the Alps to reach Germany. Roosevelt also asked if a group of United States experts could survey the effects of bombing in liberated or occupied areas by the Red Army in Eastern and South Eastern Europe, similar to the surveys made at Ploesti. He wanted the group to proceed at once, since it was important to examine the damage while the evidence was still fresh and the people who had been there during the bombing were still on the spot. Stalin granted both requests.

Sale of Ships to the Soviet Union

Stalin said Stettinius had told Molotov the United States would have surplus shipping after the war which might be sold to the Soviet Union. Roosevelt replied it would require changes in legislation so it could be transferred on credit without any interest after the war. The mistake after the last war had been to charge interest for the disposal of surplus property and it had not worked. His idea was to transfer the ships for a fixed sum on credit, which would include the cost of the ship less depreciation, so the credit would be paid in twenty years. The British never sold anything without commercial interest but he had different ideas.

Stalin was pleased with the President's statement and said the shipping would greatly ease the Soviet Union's task in the future. Roosevelt hoped the Soviet Union would interest itself in a large way in the shipping game. Stalin thought the President's idea was a very good one and Lend Lease was a remarkable invention, without which victory would have been delayed.

Stalin said in former wars some allies had subsidized others but this had offended the allies receiving the subsidies and led to difficulties. Lend Lease

---

5   For example, it would cost the Marine Corps 26,000 casualties to capture the tiny island of Iwo Jima. The Japanese garrison was only 22,000; just 216 had been captured, the rest died fighting or committed suicide. The thought of landing on the Japanese islands and the casualties involved was daunting.

6   Komsomolsk-on-Amur port on the river Amur is 1200 miles north of Tokyo. Nikolayevsk-on-Amur is 300 miles northeast of Komsomolsk.

7   The peninsula between the Sea of Okhotsk and the Bering Sea.

produced no such resentment and it had made an extraordinary contribution to the winning of the war. Roosevelt told him four years ago while resting on his small yacht he had been thinking of a way to help the Allies, while avoiding the difficulties inherent in loans, and had finally hit upon the scheme of Lend Lease.

Far East Russian Desires

Stalin wanted to discuss the political conditions under which the USSR would enter the war against Japan. He had spoken to Ambassador Harriman and Roosevelt had a report of the conversation. He felt there would be no difficulty in the southern half of Sakhalin[1] and the Kurile Islands[2] going to Russia at the end of the war.

Roosevelt recalled they had discussed a warm water port in the Far East at Tehran and had offered the port at the end of the south Manchurian railroad, possibly at Dairen[3] on the Kwantung peninsula. He had not yet spoken about it with Chiang Kai-shek, so he could not speak for the Chinese.

Roosevelt said there were two methods for the Russians to obtain the use of this port:

1) outright leasing from the Chinese;
2) making Dairen a free port under some form of international commission.

He preferred the latter because of the relation to the question of Hong Kong. He hoped the British would give the sovereignty of Hong Kong back to China and it would become an internationalized free port but Churchill would strongly object.[4]

Stalin said there was another question involving the Russian use of the Manchurian railways. The Czars had use of the line running from Manchouli to Harbin and from there to Dairen and Port Arthur, as well as the line from Harbin running east to Nikolsk-Ussurisk connecting there with the Khabarovsk to Vladivostok line.[5] Roosevelt repeated he had not spoke Chiang Kai-shek on the subject but there were two methods of bringing this about:

1) to lease it under direct Soviet operation;
2) place it under a commission composed of one Chinese and one Russian.

Stalin said if these conditions were not met it would be difficult to explain to the Soviet people why Russia was entering the war against Japan. They understood the war against Germany, which had threatened the very existence of the Soviet Union, but they would not understand why Russia would enter a war against a country with which they had no great trouble. However, if these political conditions were met, the people would understand the national interest involved and it would be much easier to explain the decision to the Supreme Soviet.[6]

1　Sakhalin Island is north of Japan and off the east coast of Russia.
2　The Kurile Islands stretch from the north end of Sakhalin Island across the Sea of Okhotsk to the Kamchatka Peninsula.
3　Dairen, now Dailan, was given to the Soviet Union. It was given to China in 1950.
4　China would not resume sovereignty of Hong Kong until 1997.
5　A short cut from the Trans-Siberian Line across northeast China to Port Arthur, now called Lüshunkou at the southern top of the Liaodong Peninsula, next to Darien (Dalian).
6　The Supreme Soviet of the Soviet Union was the highest legislative body with the power to pass constitutional amendments.

Roosevelt had not had an opportunity to talk to Chiang Kai-shek but one of the difficulties in speaking to the Chinese was anything said to them was known to the whole world in 24 hours. Stalin agreed but did not think it was necessary to speak to the Chinese yet and he could guarantee the security of the Supreme Soviet. He added it would be well to leave with these conditions agreed. Roosevelt thought this could be done.

Stalin said Soong[7] was expected to come to Moscow at the end of April. When it was possible to free a number of Soviet troops in the west and move 25 divisions to the Far East, he thought it would be possible to speak to Chiang Kai-shek about these matters. The Russians would not be difficult over the question of a warm water port and he would not object to an internationalized free port.

Trusteeships

Roosevelt had a trusteeship composed of a Soviet, an American and a Chinese representative in mind for Korea. The only experience they had in this matter was in the Philippines where it had taken about 50 years for the people to be prepared for self government.[8] In the case of Korea the period might be from 20 to 30 years. Stalin said the shorter the period the better and asked if any foreign troops would be stationed in Korea. Roosevelt replied no and Stalin approved.[9]

Roosevelt said there was one delicate question regarding Korea. Personally he did not feel it was necessary to invite the British to participate but they might resent this. Stalin replied they would most certainly be offended – the Prime Minister might "kill them". He felt the British should be invited.[10]

Roosevelt had in mind a trusteeship for Indochina. The British wished to give it back to the French, fearing it might affect Burma. Stalin said the British had lost Burma once through reliance on Indochina and he did not think Britain was a dependable country to protect this area.[11] He added Indochina was a very important area.

Roosevelt said the Indochinese were people of small stature, like the Javanese and Burmese and they were not warlike. France had done nothing to improve the natives since she had the colony. General de Gaulle had asked for ships to transport French forces to Indochina.[12] Stalin asked where de Gaulle was going to get the troops. Roosevelt replied he was going to find the troops when the President could find the ships, but to the present time he had been unable to find the ships.[13]

---

7   Dr. Soong, Chinese Minister of Foreign Affairs.
8   The Philippines came under US control following the Philippine-American War (1899-1902). It was granted Commonwealth status in 1935 but plans for independence were interrupted by the war. After being devastated during the war, it was given its independence on 4 July 1946.
9   Russian forces accepted the Japanese surrender north of the 38th Parallel while American troops did the same to the south. The superpowers could not agree on the terms for independence and installed governments following their own ideologies.
10 Neither wanted British involvement in the Korean question.
11 French Indochina fell when France was defeated and Germany gave it to the Japanese.
12 Indochina would return to France but the Viet Minh, a communist and nationalist liberation movement, emerged under Ho Chi Minh. The Viet Minh confronted the French Far East Expeditionary Corps in December 1946 and the fighting culminated in the battle of Dien Bien Phu in the spring of 1954. The country was split at the 17th Parallel with a Communist North Vietnam and pro-Western South Vietnam. The fighting never stopped; the Vietnam War followed, lasting until 1975.
13 In other words, Roosevelt was putting de Gaulle off.

Internal Conditions in China

Roosevelt said they had been trying to keep China alive for some time. Stalin believed it would remain alive. They needed some new leaders around Chiang Kai-shek and although there were some good people in the Kuomintang[1] he did not understand why they were not brought forward.

Roosevelt said General Wedemeyer[2] and the new Ambassador, General Hurley,[3] were having more success than their predecessors and had made more progress in bringing the communists in the north together with the Chungking government. The fault lay more with the Kuomintang and the Chungking Government than with the so-called communists.

Stalin did not understand why they did not get together since they should have a united front against the Japanese and Chiang Kai-shek should assume leadership. He recalled that some years ago there had been a united front and he did not understand why it had not been maintained.

8 February

Second Combined Combined Chiefs of Staff Meeting

Petroleum supplies; Cargo shipping; Prisoner of war reciprocal agreement; Equipment for Greek forces; Final Report to the President and Prime Minister; Western Front operations.

Third Tripartite Combined Chiefs of Staff Meeting

Far East military problems.

Fifth Plenary Meeting, 8 February

Roosevelt understood the Foreign Secretaries reported complete success and wished to congratulate them on their work; he then asked Mr. Eden to report.

The United Nations Conference

They recommended summoning the United Nations Conference on the proposed World Organization on 25 April 1945 in the United States.[4] Only the states who signed the United Nations Declaration would be invited and the UK and US Delegates supported admitting two Soviet Socialist Republics.[5] Eden did not think it was right for others to share the status of United Nations membership but understood the United States Delegation had other views.

Stalin said the Soviet Union did not have diplomatic relations with ten states at the conference. It was strange for the Soviet Government to attempt to build future world security with states which did not desire to have diplomatic relations with it. He asked what could be done. Roosevelt said most of these states wanted relations with the Soviet Union but had not got around to doing anything about it. A few had different reasons; some where the influence of the Catholic Church was very

---

1 The Chinese National Party; Chiang Kai-shek had assumed leadership of the party in 1926.
2 General Albert Wedemeyer (1897-1989), Mountbatten's Chief of Staff at Southeast Asia Command.
3 General Patrick J. Hurley (1883-1963), a personal envoy to Chiang Kai-shek who supported the replacement of Stilwell with Wedemeyer.
4 It would meet in San Francisco.
5 Belorussia and the Ukraine.

strong. The Soviet Union had sat down with these states at the Bretton Woods[6] and UNRRA[7] conferences. Stalin replied this was correct but they were to consider the vital question of the establishment of world security at this conference.

Roosevelt then explained the history behind the situation. Three years ago the then Acting Secretary of State, Mr. Welles,[8] had told these American Republics it was not necessary to declare war on Germany but only to break diplomatic relations. So six South American countries felt they had taken the United States' advice and were in good standing and they helped a great deal in the war effort. But the advice had been a mistake and a month ago the Secretary of State had brought the embarrassing question up. Roosevelt had sent letters to the presidents of these six countries urging them to declare war against the common enemy. Ecuador had done so, Peru's declaration was expected at any time and he hoped the others would before long.

Stalin asked about Argentina. Roosevelt said they were considering a conference of United Nations and Associated Nations who had helped in the war effort. Stalin had no love for Argentina but felt there was a contradiction in logic.[9] He asked what the criteria for the admission of states were and mentioned Turkey. He felt there were nations who had waged war and suffered, and there were others who had wavered and speculated on being on the winning side. Roosevelt's idea was only those Associated Nations who had declared war should be invited and suggested the time limit should be 1 March. Stalin agreed.

Churchill recommended the President's suggestion that only those countries who had declared war would be invited. He sympathized with Marshal Stalin's view and said many countries had played a poor part. There would be some advantage of having a new group of nations declaring war for the effect on German morale. Roosevelt mentioned Iceland, the newest of the United Nations Republics.[10]

Churchill said Egypt had wished to declare war on two occasions but had been advised not to by the British Government because it was more useful and convenient to have Egypt a non-belligerent to protect Cairo from systematic bombing.[11] The Egyptian army had rendered good service; they had maintained

---

6   In July 1944 730 delegates from 44 nations gathered in Bretton Woods, New Hampshire, for the United Nations Monetary and Financial Conference. They discussed rules, institutions and procedures to regulate the international monetary system and established the International Monetary Fund (IMF) and the International Bank for Reconstruction and Development (IBRD).

7   The United Nations Relief and Rehabilitation Administration (UNRRA) was an international relief agency representing 44 nations; it was dominated by the United States.

8   B. Sumner Welles (1892-1961), Under Secretary of State from 1937 to 1943.

9   Ramón Castillo (1873-1944) and his fraudulently elected government were overthrown in a coup d'état in June 1943. General Edelmiro Farrell (1887-1980) was de facto President at this time. Argentina declared war on the Axis a month before the end of the war in Europe.

10   Iceland had refused to enter the war so British Marines invaded it on 10 May 1940. It was soon garrisoned by 25,000 British troops and after July 1941 they were replaced by US troops; eventually, 40,000 would be stationed on the island. Iceland dissolved its union with Denmark and the Danish monarchy on 17 June 1944 and declared itself a republic. It remained neutral to the end of the war.

11   It also kept the Suez Canal neutral and open for shipping using the Mediterranean.

good order and guarded bridges. Egypt should have the opportunity to declare war if she desired.[1]

Iceland had rendered valuable service at a time when the United States had not entered the war and had permitted the entry of British and United States troops, violating her neutrality in a marked manner, assuring a vital lane of communications to the British Isles. Stalin said this did not apply to former enemy states who had recently declared war on Germany. Roosevelt and Churchill heartily agreed.

Churchill certainly did not include Eire among the possible candidates, since they still maintained German and Japanese missions.[2] He would refer to a new one that would not be greeted with universal approbation, namely, Turkey. Turkey had made an alliance with Great Britain at a very difficult time, but as the war progressed she discovered she was not up-to-date for modern war. Her attitude had been friendly and helpful, although she had not taken the chance to enter the war a year ago. Stalin replied if Turkey declared war before the end of February he agreed to her being invited to the conference. Churchill expressed gratitude.[3]

Roosevelt said there remained the question of Denmark; she had been overrun by the enemy in one night[4] and the King had been virtually a prisoner.[5] Only the Danish Minister in Washington, Mr. de Kauffman,[6] had voiced the sentiments which he knew all Danes felt and had repudiated the actions of his government. Stalin thought Denmark should wait. Roosevelt and Churchill agreed and the latter added once she was liberated she would certainly have the right to join the organization.[7] Stalin said Denmark had let the Germans in.[8]

Stalin hoped it would be possible to mention Ukrainian and White Russian Republics in the Foreign Ministers' recommendations. This was accepted. Molotov asked if it would make the admission of these two Soviet Republics easier if they signed the United Nations Declaration before 1 March. Roosevelt proposed inviting the United Nations, the Associated Nations and Turkey, provided it declared war before 1 March and signed the United Nations Declaration.

Churchill said it did not seem right to include small countries who had done so little and exclude the Ukraine and White Russia, bearing in mind their

---

1   Egypt had been granted its independence by Britain in 1922 but British troops were still stationed there. They stopped an Italian invasion over the winter of 1940-41, inflicting a defeat on the Italians in Operation COMPASS. King Farouk I had ascended the throne in 1936. The British wanted him to form a coalition government but he refused and in the following ministerial crisis, British troops forced him to capitulate on 4 February 1942; a new government was then formed.
2   The Irish Free State (it became the Republic of Ireland in 1949) was neutral throughout the war but it secretly offered to help defend Northern Ireland, even though it only had an army of 7,000. German spies were rounded up in September 1941. 100,000 Irishmen volunteered for the British forces; half from north of the border and half from the south.
3   Turkey eventually entered the war on the side of the Allies on 23 February 1945.
4   The Germans ignored a non-aggression pact with Denmark and crossed its border on 9 April 1940 in Operation Weserübung. The country was occupied in a day in what was virtually a bloodless coup.
5   King Christian X (1870-1947) was king of Denmark from 1912 to 1947 and the only King of Iceland from 1918 until it declared independence in 1944.
6   Henrik L.H. de Kauffman (1888-1963), the Danish ambassador to the United States. Nickname the King of Greenland for signing an agreement to defend Greenland on his own initiative on 9 April 1941, the anniversary of the German occupation of Denmark.
7   Denmark was a founding member of the United Nations.
8   Denmark had decided against opposing the Germans.

martyrdom and sufferings. Stalin agreed it was illogical. Although the three Powers agreed to recommend the Ukraine and White Russia as members of the assembly, they might be excluded because they had not signed the United Nations Declaration. Roosevelt and Stettinius assured Stalin this would not occur. Churchill preferred confining the conference to the United Nations but if others were going to be added, the Soviet Republics should also be added.[9]

Roosevelt had a technical question but it was an important one. Stalin said, "I don't want to embarrass the President, but if he will explain his difficulties we will see what can be done." It was the question of giving one of the Great Powers three votes instead of one. All three had to agree to support the Soviet request. Stalin asked what if the Ukraine and White Russia signed the United Nations Declaration; but Roosevelt did not think it would overcome the difficulty. Stalin withdrew his proposal and Roosevelt expressed his gratification.

Poland's Government

Roosevelt thought his proposals on Poland were very close to Molotov's but he wanted comments. Molotov asked if the President's proposal to recognize a Government of National Unity meant the London Government would disappear. Churchill confirmed it would. Stalin asked what would happen to the property and resources of the London Government. Churchill replied the withdrawal of recognition would take care of them; Roosevelt believed the property would go to the new government.

Churchill was prepared to accept the President's proposals if a decision in principle had been reached. Molotov said their proposals were based on certain realities existing in Poland. It was impossible to ignore the present Polish government and the Soviet Government felt it would be useful to discuss adding democratic elements from within Poland and abroad.

Molotov said the Lublin, or Warsaw, government stood at the head of the Polish people and enjoyed great prestige and popularity in the country. The Poles would never agree to a solution which changed the Provisional Government but they might succeed if they suggested enlarging it. The people in the Provisional Government had been closely connected with the liberation of Poland, but Messrs. Mikolajczyk, Grabski and Witos had not.[10] A practical result would be to enlarge the present government.

Molotov's observations also applied to the proposed presidential committee. It was a difficult question, which stemmed from the Polish people, and he had grave doubts about its feasibility. It might create additional difficulty because of the National Council,[11] which could be enlarged.

Both the National Council and Provisional Government were temporary and Molotov noted one common point in all three proposals; free elections in Poland. But during the temporary period pending such elections it was extremely important to ensure stable rule in Poland.

---

9   They were.
10 Being in London.
11 The National Council of Poland, or Rada Narodowa Rzeczypospolitej Polskiej.

Molotov was pleased to note the agreement on the Curzon Line but there was no unanimity on the western boundary. Even though they had to ask the Provisional Government, they knew it would support the western frontier outlined in the Soviet proposals. Molotov said Mr. Harriman and Sir Archibald Clark Kerr agreed it would be desirable to talk with the Poles in Moscow. The Provisional Government always sent three persons – Bierut, Osobka-Morawski, and General Rola-Zymierski.[1] As for the Poles from the other side, the President's proposals yesterday seemed more acceptable. Some Poles from abroad could be involved, but he was not at all sure about Mikolajczyk, especially after the autumn talks in Moscow.

Yesterday the President had proposed five names and he thought it would be a good idea to invite the three members of the Provisional Government and two from the President's list. Roosevelt asked if the presidential committee or an interim government should be avoided. Molotov said it was better to avoid the presidential committee but enlarge the National Council and the Provisional Government. He could discuss how to do this with Mr. Harriman and Sir Archibald.

Molotov said he had not touched on the Prime Minister's ideas. Churchill said they were now at the crucial point of this great conference and they would be found wanting by the world if they left it recognizing different Polish governments. This would be accepted by the world as evidence of a breach between Great Britain and the United States on the one hand and the Soviet Union on the other, with lamentable consequences in the future. It was stamping this conference with a seal of failure, and nothing else they did there would overcome it. Churchill admitted they had different views of the same facts. According to his information, the Lublin, or Warsaw, government did not commend itself to the overwhelming mass of the Polish people and it was certainly not accepted abroad as representative of the people.[2] If the British Government brushed aside the London government and went over to the Lublin government, there would be an angry outcry in Great Britain. There was also the problem of the Poles outside Poland.

Churchill reminded them there was a Polish army of about 150,000 men[3] on the Western and Italian fronts who had fought steadily and very bravely for their cause. He did not believe this army would accept the transfer of the British Government's support from the government it had dealt with since the beginning of the war.[4] It would be regarded as an act of betrayal.

As Stalin and Molotov knew, Churchill had no special feeling for the Polish government in London, which in his opinion had been foolish at every stage, but a formal act of transfer of recognition would cause the very gravest consequences. The group forming the Lublin Government was only about one year old. Churchill suggested it would be said the British Government had completely given away on matter of the frontiers, had accepted the Soviet view and had championed it.

1 Michal Rola-Zymierski (1890–1989), a Polish communist military commander.
2 But it was sponsored and supported by the Soviet Union.
3 Closer to 250,000.
4 The London-based Government-in-exile.

To break with the lawful Poland Government-in-exile, which had been recognized for five years of war, would be an act subject to the most severe criticism in England. It would be said they did not know what was going on in Poland – they could not even get anyone in there to find out what was going on and they had accepted the view of the Lublin government. Great Britain would be charged with forsaking the cause of Poland and he was bound to say the debates in Parliament would be most painful and most dangerous to Allied unity.

Churchill added all of the above supposed they agreed to Molotov's proposal. If they were to give up the London government it had to be clear a new start had been made on both sides from equal terms. Before such transfer of recognition His Majesty's Government would have to be convinced a new government, representative of the Polish people, had been created and pledged to an election.[5] When elections were held in Poland, Great Britain would salute the government which emerged but it was the interval before the elections that was difficult and alarming.[6]

Molotov suggested the talks in Moscow might yield some result, but it was very difficult to discuss the Polish question without participation of the Poles. Churchill said it was frightfully important agreement should be reached on the question. Roosevelt said they were agreed on the necessity of free elections and the only problem was how Poland was to be governed in the interval.

Stalin had heard Churchill complain he had no information regarding the situation in Poland. Churchill could get this information and he did not see why Great Britain and the United States could not send their own people into Poland. He assured the conference that the people running the government were popular. The three leaders, Bierut, Osobka Morawski and Rola-Zymierski, had not fled from Poland but had stayed on in Warsaw and had come from the underground. It was necessary to bear in mind the psychology of people under occupation – their sympathies were with those who stayed and not with those who left the country.

Stalin did not claim the men in the Provisional Government were geniuses – indeed, it is possible there were cleverer people in the Polish Government in London – he did not know. Perhaps the feeling of the Polish people was somewhat primitive, but it existed. What puzzled the Polish people was that a great event, the liberation of their country by the Red Army, had occurred and it had changed the mentality of the people. Stalin said for many years the Poles had hated the Russians and with reason; the Czarist government had participated in the partitioning of Poland.[7] With the advance of the Soviet troops the liberation of Poland had changed the attitude of the Polish people toward Russia, old resentments had disappeared and goodwill had taken their place. The driving out of the Germans

---

5   On the basis of universal sufferage, by secret ballot with the participation of all democratic parties who had the right to put up candidates.

6   The Polish Communists knew they did not have a majority, so they held a referendum called the 3 x Tak (Three Times Yes) referendum in 1946. It proved they had little support, so they set about repressing, imprisoning and executing their opponents. Parties to the right were also banned and the following year the election was rigged so they won. Democracy in Poland was over and opponents went into exile. Western governments did nothing.

7   The Polish-Lithuanian Commonwealth was divided in 1795, it reformed in 1918. It was again divided in 1939 following the Molotov-Ribbentrop Pact.

by the Red Army had been received by the Poles with a great national holiday and the people were surprised the Polish government in London had not had any part in it. They asked, "We of the National Council and Provisional Government participated in this holiday, but where are the London Poles?" This lay at the base of the great popularity of the members of the Provisional Government, although they may not be great men. Stalin did not think they could ignore these facts, nor fail to take into account the feelings of the people.

Churchill was worried they would leave without an agreement. So what could they do? They had different information so the best method was to summon the Poles and to learn from them. It would be better if free elections could be held but the war prevented it. But the day was drawing near when elections could take place and the people could express their view with regard to the Provisional Government.

Stalin saw little difference between the position of de Gaulle and the Polish Provisional Government.[1] Neither had been elected and he could not say which one enjoyed the greatest degree of popularity – yet they all had dealt with de Gaulle and the Soviet Government had concluded a treaty with him. Why should they be so different with the Polish Government and why could they not deal with an enlarged Polish government?

Stalin added de Gaulle had done nothing to arouse popular enthusiasm, whereas the Polish Government had carried out a number of popular land reforms. The situation was not as tragic as Churchill pictured it. The situation could be settled if they concentrated on the essential points. It would be better to deal with the reconstruction of the Provisional Government rather than set up a new one. Molotov was right and rather than a presidential committee they might agree on increasing the Provisional Government.

Roosevelt asked how long it would be before elections could be held in Poland. Stalin replied in a month, provided no catastrophes occurred on the front. Churchill welcomed free elections but not if they would hamper military operations. They agreed to refer the matter to the Foreign Ministers.[2]

Churchill asked for periodic meetings of the Foreign Ministers every three months. Roosevelt was in favour but he knew Stettinius was very busy with some of the Latin American countries and felt it would be best to say they would meet when necessary and not fix definite periods for the meetings. Churchill hoped the first meeting could be in London, to which the President and Stalin agreed.

Yugoslavia and Greece

Stalin wanted to know what was holding back the formation of a unified government in Yugoslavia and what was going on in Greece. He had no intention of criticizing British policy there but merely wanted to know what was going

---

1   General de Gaulle was head of the French Government-in-exile by the time of the Normandy invasion in June 1944. While the Allies planned to install a military government as they advanced across France, de Gaulle had other ideas. Most of his opponents had been discredited by their association with the Vichy government and the fact the Germans took them to Germany helped de Gaulle's case. There were concerns the communist elements of the guerrillas would seize control, so the General was the best option; he was accepted by the end of August 1944.
2   The elections would eventually take place in January 1947 and they would be rigged in favour of the communists.

on. Churchill said Greece would take a great deal of time to explain and would reserve it for the next meeting.[3] In Yugoslavia the King had been persuaded, or even forced, to agree to a regency. Subasic[4] was leaving soon, if he had not left already, for Yugoslavia to appoint the regents and form the government. Churchill said he had always made it plain, both privately and publicly, that the King would be bypassed if he would not agree to a regency.[5] If Stalin had said two words to Tito the matter would be settled. Stalin replied Tito was a proud man and a popular head of a regime who might resent advice. Churchill felt Stalin could risk this. Stalin answered he was not afraid.

Churchill hoped peace would come in Greece on the basis of amnesties except for those who committed crimes against the laws of war. He doubted a government of all the parties could be established since they hated each other so much. Stalin said the Greeks were not yet used to discussion and were cutting each other's throats.[6] Churchill would be glad to give information on Greece. Recently Sir Walter Citrine[7] and five members of the trades unions had gone to Greece and they might have their report. They had had rather a rough time in Greece and they were very obliged to Stalin for not having taken too great an interest in Greek affairs. Stalin repeated he had no intention of criticizing British actions there or interfering in Greece but merely wanted to know what was going on. The conference adjourned.[8]

Tripartite Dinner Meeting, 8 February

The atmosphere of the dinner was most cordial, and 45 toasts were drunk. Stalin was in excellent humour and even in high spirits. Most of the toasts were routine; to the armed forces of the representative countries, military leaders and the continuing friendships between the three great powers.

Stalin proposed a toast to the health of the Prime Minister. He characterized him as the bravest governmental figure in the world. Due in large measure to Churchill's courage and staunchness, England, when she stood alone, had divided the might

---

3   The Greek Government-in-exile had been unable to stop the emergence of various resistance groups. Problems started to emerge in December 1944 when government soldiers and British troops fired on a demonstration by the National Liberation Front (EAM), curbing its growth; the Greek People's Liberation Army (ELAS) also began to disband.

4   Ivan Subasic (1892-1955), a Croatian and Yugoslav politician known as the last Ban of Croatia (a Ban was a ruler's representative or viceroy). He was Prime Minister of Yugoslavia from July 1944, reaching a compromise with Tito that recognised the partisans as the country's legitimate armed forces in exchange for them taking part in the new government. He was succeeded by Tito in March 1945.

5   King George II of Greece (1890-1947) was in exile in Britain. The monarchists won an election on 31 March 1946, mainly because the communists were absent. A referendum on 1 September voted in favour of his return. He came back to find his palace looted and his country facing economic instability and political uncertainty. He died suddenly on 1 April 1947 and was succeeded by his son, Paul.

6   The Greek Civil War began in 1946 between the Greek government army, supported by the United Kingdom and the United States, and the Democratic Army of Greece or DSE, the military branch of the Greek Communist Party (KKE), supported by Bulgaria, Yugoslavia and Albania. It lasted until 1949.

7   Sir Walter Citrine (1887-1983), trade unionist.

8   Members of the Greek People's Liberation Army (ELAS) found a home with the Democratic Army of Greece (DSE), the armed wing of the Greek Communist Party (KKE). Believing it was no use using political means against the internationally recognized government, the KKE formed a provisional government while the DSE went on the attack. It resulted in three years of civil war, a split between Tito and Stalin, and failure for the Communists.

of Hitlerite Germany at a time when the rest of Europe was falling flat on its face before Hitler. Great Britain, under Churchill's leadership, had carried the light alone, irrespective of existing or potential allies. Stalin knew of few examples in history where the courage of one man had been so important to the future history of the world. He drank a toast to Churchill, his fighting friend and a brave man.[1]

Churchill toasted Stalin as the mighty leader of a mighty country, which had taken the full shock of the German war machine, had broken its back and had driven the tyrants from her soil. He knew in peace, no less than in war, Stalin would continue to lead his people from success to success.

Stalin then proposed the President's health. He and Churchill had had relatively simple decisions in their respective countries; they had been fighting for their very existence against Hitlerite Germany. But there was a third man whose country had not been seriously threatened with invasion, but who had had perhaps a broader conception of national interest. Even though his country was not directly imperilled, he had been the chief forger of the instruments which had led to the mobilization of the world against Hitler. Lend-Lease was one of the President's most remarkable and vital achievements in the formation of the Anti-Hitler combination and in keeping the Allies in the field against Hitler.

Roosevelt felt there was a family atmosphere at the dinner and he used those words to characterize the relations existing between their three countries. Great changes had occurred in the world over the past three years, and even greater changes were to come. Each leader was working in their own way for the interests of their people. 50 years ago there were vast areas of the world where people had little opportunity and no hope, but much had been accomplished, although there were still great areas where people had little opportunity and little hope, and their objectives were to give to every man, woman and child on earth the possibility of security and wellbeing.

In a subsequent toast to the alliance between the three great powers, Stalin said it was not so difficult to keep unity in time of war, since there was a joint aim to defeat the common enemy that was clear to everyone. The difficult task came after the war, when diverse interests tended to divide allies. He was confident the present alliance would also meet this test and it was their duty to see it would and their relations in peacetime should be as strong as they had been in war.[2]

Churchill felt they were all standing on the crest of a hill with the glories of future possibilities stretching before them. He said in the modern world the function of leadership was to lead the people out from the forests into the broad sunlit plains of peace and happiness. He felt this prize was nearer their grasp than any time before in history and it would be a tragedy for which history would never forgive them if they let this prize slip from their grasp through inertia or carelessness.

Justice Byrnes proposed a toast to the common man all over the world. He said there had been many toasts to leaders and officials and while they all shared these sentiments, they should never forget the common man or woman.

---

1 A remarkable toast by Stalin, considering the number of disagreements they had at the conferences.
2 Poignant words, when you consider that the Cold War and the Nuclear Age were imminent.

Miss Harriman replied for the three ladies present, then proposed a toast to those who had worked so hard in the Crimea for their comfort. Having seen the destruction wrought by the Germans, she fully realized what had been accomplished.

9 February

Second Combined Combined Chiefs of Staff Meeting

Final report to the President and Prime Minister; Liaison for strategic bombing in Eastern Germany.

US and Soviet Combined Chiefs of Staff Meeting

Far East operations.

9 February: The President and Prime Minister with the Chiefs of Staff

Churchill said it would be of great value if Russia could be persuaded to join the United States, the British Empire and China. They could issue a four-power ultimatum calling upon Japan to surrender unconditionally, or else be subjected to the overwhelming weight of all the forces of the four powers.

Japan might ask what mitigation of the full rigour of unconditional surrender would be extended to her if she accepted the ultimatum. In this event it would be for the United States to judge the matter. But there was no doubt some mitigation would be worthwhile if it led to the saving of a year or a year-and-a-half of a war in which so much blood and treasure would be poured out. Great Britain would not press for any mitigation but would be content to abide by the judgment of the United States. Whatever the decision, Great Britain would see the matter through to the end.

Roosevelt thought it might be good to mention it to Stalin. He doubted whether the ultimatum would have much effect on the Japanese; they did not seem to realize what was going on in the world outside. But he still seemed to think they might get a satisfactory compromise. They would be unlikely to wake up to the true state of affairs until all of their islands had felt the full weight of air attack.[3]

Churchill thanked the Combined Chiefs of Staff for their work. Without doubt they would be held up in years to come as a model of cooperation between Allies. He hoped they could be kept in being for three or four years more. There would be many problems affecting the security of the two nations in this period, the solution of which would be greatly facilitated if the Combined Chiefs of Staff continued to operate.[4]

Roosevelt agreed there would be many matters affecting the two countries, such as the use of bases, which would have to be effectively handled. Marshall agreed the continuance of the Combined Chiefs of Staff would be advantageous.

---

3 Japanese soldiers preferred to commit suicide than surrender while Kamikaze pilots had been making suicide attacks on ships since October 1944.

4 The years immediately after the war presented many problems, not least the developing Cold War between the superpowers.

Its existence had certainly simplified the solution of the problems which had confronted the two nations during the war.

Sixth Plenary Meeting, 9 February
Yugoslavia

Molotov wanted the Subasic-Tito agreement to be put into effect.[1] Churchill also wanted it putting immediately into effect irrespective of the King's wishes because he thought the Yugoslavia question was virtually settled. Churchill wanted to make suggestions he hoped would not affect the movements the President had in mind. In the general atmosphere of agreement, they should not put their feet in the stirrups and ride off.[2] It would be a great mistake to hurry this question; it was better to take a few days of latitude than to endanger bringing the ship into port. It was a great mistake to take hurried decisions on these grave matters. He wanted to study the Polish proposals before giving any opinion.[3]

Churchill felt the great prize should not be imperilled by too much haste but he definitely did not want to leave this conference without an agreement on the subject. He felt it was the most important they had to make.

It was agreed the British and Soviet representatives would draw up a statement on the Yugoslav situation. They would also reach agreement on the execution of the Subasic-Tito agreement. Churchill asked if the Soviets agreed Eden's amendments to the agreement.[4] Molotov said it had to be put into effect quickly and amendments meant delays. It would be better to ask Tito and Subasic about the amendments after the agreement had been made.[5]

Churchill asked if it was too much to ask to use democratic processes to confirm legislative acts. Stalin said delays were undesirable and if the British proposed two more amendments, the Soviet Government might propose some of their own.[6] In the meantime, the government of Yugoslavia was held in the balance. Churchill replied this was not the case: Tito was a dictator and could do what he wanted. Stalin replied Tito was not a dictator but the head of a national committee without any clear government and that was not a good situation.[7] Eden replied it was a request the amendments were adopted. Subasic was going to ask for them anyway and as Tito would agree, everything would be all right.

---

1   The first agreement, signed on 16 June 1944, provided for cooperation between Tito's National Committee for the Liberation of Yugoslavia (NKOJ), and the Subasic's Government-in-exile, as they fought to rid the country of the Germans and their collaborators. A second agreement was signed on 1 November 1944 for the formation of a united Yugoslav government to replace the NKOJ and the government-in-exile.
2   In other words, not move too fast.
3   The meeting adjourned for 30 minutes.
4   The Treaty of Vis attempted to merge the royal Yugoslav government-in-exile with the Communist-led partisans who were fighting the Germans.
5   Molotov is suggesting submitting the agreement without the amendments.
6   Delaying the situation even more.
7   Tito was a communist and would be President of Yugoslavia from 1953 to 1980. While his regime was authoritarian, he was considered to be a relatively benevolent dictator.

Stalin said the first British amendment stated that former members of the Skupshtina[8] who had not collaborated with the Germans should be included in the anti-Fascist Vetch.[9] The second suggested the legislative acts of the anti-Fascist Vetch should be confirmed by a regularly elected body. He agreed with the amendments but wanted the government to form first and then propose them. Eden felt if they could agree them, they could ask Tito to adopt them once the agreement was in force.

Stalin agreed and added it would be a good idea to send a telegram stating they had to put the agreement into effect irrespective of the King's wishes. Churchill and Eden explained the question of the King had been settled and was not important.[10] Subasic was on his way to Yugoslavia to put the agreement into effect. Churchill thought they should agree to advise adopting the amendments. Stalin replied he had already agreed, and as a man of his word he would not go back on it.

Reparations

Agreement had been reached on which countries should receive reparations and what type of reparations Germany should pay. The Soviet and American Delegations agreed the Reparations Commission should consider the Soviet suggestion of $20 billion,[11] 50% of it going to the Soviet Union. Eden was awaiting instructions from his Government. The Soviet Delegation said reparations payments would be based upon 1938 prices, possibly with increases of 10% to 15% on the price of delivered items.

Territorial Trusteeships and Dependent Areas

The Foreign Ministers agreed the five Governments on the Security Council should consult each other about providing machinery in the World Charter before the United Nations Conference.

Churchill interrupted with great vigour to say he did not agree with one single word of the report on trusteeships. He had not been consulted nor had he heard of this subject up to now. Under no circumstances would he ever consent to 40 or 50 nations thrusting interfering fingers into the existence of the British Empire. As long as he was Minister, he would never yield one scrap of their heritage. He continued in this vein for several minutes.

Stettinius explained the machinery did not refer to the British Empire. It was to take dependent areas out of enemy control; for example, the Japanese islands in the Pacific. Provision had to be made for machinery to handle trusteeship and he repeated it was not intended to refer to the British Empire.

Churchill thought it would be better to say it did not refer to the British Empire. Great Britain did not desire any territorial aggrandizement and had no objection to trusteeship of enemy territory. He asked how Stalin would feel if it was suggested the Crimea should be internationalized for use as a summer resort. Stalin said he would be glad to give the Crimea as a place to be used for meetings

---

8   The Skupshtina was the National Assembly.
9   Vetch was the Anti-Fascist Assembly.
10 King Peter II (1923-1970), last reigning member of the Karadordevic dynasty. He was deposed by Yugoslavia's Communist Constituent Assembly on 29 November 1945. He moved to the United States.
11 $319 billion in 2013.

of the three powers.[1] It was agreed Trusteeships should be discussed at the United Nations Conference.

Poland's Government

Mr. Stettinius reported on the Polish question. The Foreign Ministers had agreed to drop the question of the Presidential Committee but Molotov wished to present the American considerations to Stalin before making a final statement. He was very anxious to come to an agreement and could accept the proposal with certain amendments.

Roosevelt said Molotov's amendment meant they were close to an agreement and he felt the last sentence concerning Ambassadors' reports was important. The words 'Provisional Government' were difficult for those governments which still recognized the London government. He wanted to change them to 'the government now operating in Poland'. It was very important to make some gesture for the six million Poles in the United States concerning free elections.

Churchill agreed progress had been made but he had two points. He felt it was desirable to mention the liberation of Poland by the Red Army called for a broadly based government. This might be an ornament but nevertheless it was an important one. The second question was more important. One of the great difficulties while making decisions of great responsibility about Poland was the lack of accurate information. They knew there were bitter feelings among the Poles and fierce language had been used by Osobka-Morawski about the London government. He understood the Lublin government had declared it would try as traitors the members of the Polish Home Army[2] and the underground forces. These reports caused great anxiety and perplexity in England, and he hoped these two points would be considered with Stalin's usual patience and kindness.[3]

Churchill personally welcomed observers of the three powers in any area where they were needed. He felt the last sentence of the United States draft regarding Ambassadors' responsibilities was very important. He understood Tito would not object to foreign observers when elections were held in Yugoslavia. The British welcomed observers from the United States and the Soviet Union when elections were held in Greece and Italy. These were not idle requests; for example, whatever government held the elections in Egypt won.[4] King Farouk[5] refused to permit Nahhas Pasha[6] to hold an election while the latter was prime minister.

Stalin understood the very greatest politicians spent their time buying each other during the Egyptian elections. He would not compare them with Poland, since there was a high degree of literacy in Poland. He asked about literacy in

---

1   Stalin neatly sidestepped Churchill's question.
2   The Polish Home Army (Armia Krajowa) was formed in February 1942. It absorbed most underground organizations and had around 400,000 members involved in sabotage activities and occasional full-scale battles. It was disbanded on 20 January 1945, by which time Polish territory had been cleared by the Soviet armies.
3   Remarkable words about Stalin by Churchill.
4   In other words, the elections were rigged by the ruling party.
5   King Farouk I of Egypt (1920-1965), had been king since 1932. He was overthrown in 1952 and forced to abdicate by his son, Ahmed Fuad. He died in exile in Italy.
6   Mustafa el-Nahhas Pasha (1879-1965); Prime Minister of Egypt on five occasions between 1928 and 1952. He helped form the Arab League in 1944.

Egypt but neither Churchill nor Eden knew. Churchill did not mean to compare Poland with Egypt, but he had to assure the House of Commons free elections would be held. For instance, would Mikolajczyk[7] be allowed to take part? Stalin replied he was a member of the Peasant Party, which was not Fascist, and he could take part.

Churchill wanted the Foreign Ministers to consider observers while Stalin thought it should be discussed with the Poles. Churchill thought that was necessary and wanted to assure the House of Commons that free elections would be held in Poland. Stalin replied they were good people and in olden times many of them were scientists, such as Copernicus. He admitted they were still quarrelsome and there were Fascist elements in Poland and that was why 'non-Fascist' had been added to the term 'democratic parties'.

Roosevelt added the elections were the crux of the whole matter. Since it was true the Poles were quarrelsome people not only at home but also abroad, he wanted to assure the six million Poles in the United States there would be free elections. Such assurance would mean the elections would be held and there would be no doubt as to the sincerity of the agreement.

The Declaration on Liberated Europe

Stalin had before him the Declaration on Liberated Europe and Mr. Molotov had one small change to propose: "In this connection, support will be given to the political leaders of those countries who have taken an active part in the struggle against the German invaders." Stalin accepted the amendment. Roosevelt said the Declaration would apply to any areas or countries. Churchill did not disagree with the President's proposed Declaration as long as it was clearly understood the reference to the Atlantic Charter did not apply to the British Empire.[8] He had already made it plain in the House of Commons the principles already applied as far as the British Empire was concerned. He had given Mr. Willkie a copy of his statement on this subject. Roosevelt asked if that was what killed Mr. Willkie.[9]

Roosevelt said France had been included in earlier drafts but now it was absent. Stalin said three powers were better than four. Roosevelt suggested asking France to associate itself with the Declaration.

Greece

Stalin said Churchill need not worry about Molotov's amendment; it was designed to apply to Greece. Churchill was not anxious about Greece – he just thought everybody should to have a fair chance and do their duty. Stalin thought it would have been very dangerous if he had allowed other forces than his own to go into Greece.

Churchill would welcome a Soviet observer in Greece. Stalin said he had complete confidence in British policy in Greece and Churchill thanked him for the

---

7   Stanislaw Mikolajczyk, Prime Minister of the Polish Government-in-exile.
8   Referring to the statement "the right of all peoples to choose the form of government under which they will live – the restoration of sovereign rights and self-government to those peoples who have been forcibly deprived of them." Churchill did not want this applying to the British Empire.
9   Wendell Willkie (1892-1944), Republican Party nominee for president in 1940 against Roosevelt. He also stood in 1944 but his liberalism lost him support and he dropped out and then died of a heart attack.

statement. Stalin said they agreed the Tito–Subasic agreement should go into effect immediately. Churchill agreed. Stalin suggested sending a telegram to Tito but it was not pursued.

War Criminals

Churchill then spoke about war criminals whose crimes had no geographical limitation.[1] Molotov asked if his amendment was acceptable. Roosevelt thought it should be considered by the Foreign Ministers. Churchill reminded them he had drafted the Declaration on German atrocities issued by the Moscow Conference, which dealt with the main criminals whose crimes had no geographical location. It was an egg that he had laid himself and he thought they should draw up a list of the major criminals of this category.[2] He thought they should be shot once their identity was established.[3]

Stalin asked about Hess.[4] Churchill thought events would catch up with Hess. He believed these men should be given a judicial trial. Stalin agreed and asked if the war criminal question applied to prisoners of war. Churchill replied it did if they had violated the laws of war. They should just have an exchange of views and no publicity should be given to the matter.

The Allied Attack

Stalin asked if the offensive on the Western Front had begun. Churchill said yes, about 100,000 British launched an attack the morning before and advanced about 3000 yards on a five-mile front.[5] The defence had been weak except in two villages, and they were now in contact with the Siegfried Line. The second wave of the 9th US Army was to start tomorrow.[6] This offensive was to continue and grow in intensity. The meeting adjourned.

10 February: Seventh Plenary Meeting

Poland's Borders

Eden reported agreement on the future government of Poland; the Polish Provisional Government of National Unity.[7] Churchill said the document made no mention of frontiers. They all agreed on Poland's Eastern frontier and he agreed it should receive compensation in the West, up to the Oder if the Poles so

---

1　War crimes with geographical limitation were incidents at set places, such as ghettos and concentration camps. War crimes without geographical limitation referred to the men who had dictated policy; the men who issued the orders for others to follow; for example, crimes relating to the Holocaust and slave labour.

2　The main trial was held in Nuremberg between 20 November 1945 and 1 October 1946. 23 defendants were tried (Martin Bormann in absentia). Adolf Hitler, Heinrich Himmler and Joseph Goebbels were already dead. There were twelve subsequent trials including the Doctors Trial and the Judges Trial.

3　The preferred method of execution was hanging.

4　Rudolf Hess (1894-1987) was Deputy Leader of the Nazi Party. Just before the invasion of the Soviet Union in June 1941 he flew solo to Scotland in an attempt to negotiate a peace deal. He was arrested and after the war Churchill wrote, "He is a medical case and not a criminal case, and should be so regarded." Conspiracy theories about links between Hess and the English aristocracy, or "the Establishment", have survived to this day.

5　VERITABLE, an advance by the 1st Canadian Army southeast from Nijmegen, clearing the west bank of the Rhine.

6　GRENADE was postponed because the Germans blew the dams on the Roer River. 9th US Army crossed the river on 23 February and advanced towards the Rhine, on the west boundary of the Ruhr.

7　The new government was to hold free and unfettered elections on the basis of universal suffrage and secret ballot. The Allies would also open diplomatic relations with the new government.

desired. But he did not believe the War Cabinet would accept the Western Neisse. Some mention should be made of the territorial settlement, otherwise the whole world would wonder what they had decided. There would be some criticism but it would be better than no mention at all.[8]

Roosevelt said they should consult the Polish Government before any statement was made about the Western frontier. Stalin thought there should be a statement on the agreed Eastern frontier. Churchill agreed and repeated the people would want to know what they had decided.[9]

Molotov said it would be good to mention the Eastern frontier; it would clarify the situation for the Poles. There would be criticisms, but in general it would be beneficial. It was perhaps not necessary to be as specific about the Western frontier. Churchill had already gone on record to say Poland would receive a good slice of territory in the north and west but the opinion of the New Polish Government of National Unity would be needed. Roosevelt had no objection to such a statement but thought the Prime Minister should draft it.

Roosevelt proposed minor amendments necessary for American Constitutional reasons and they were accepted.[10] Molotov suggested including a comment on Poland's ancient frontiers in East Prussia and on the Oder. Roosevelt asked how long these lands had been Polish. Molotov said very long ago. Roosevelt said this might lead the British to ask for the return of the United States to Great Britain. Stalin replied the ocean prevented this. At present, the draft said nothing specific about frontiers, which was very important for the Poles.

Churchill preferred not to mention the west frontier since he shared the same difficulties the President had spoken of. Eden said they had always accepted a line up to the Oder. Churchill said there was no stopping place between what they proposed and the Oder, and there would be no answer if the question was asked about ancient territories. He was not against the line of the Oder in principle. Molotov thought it might be worthwhile considering this. Stalin would withdraw the Soviet amendment and leave the British draft. The draft regarding Polish frontiers was accepted.

The Declaration on Liberated Europe

Eden said the Soviet Delegation proposed the three Governments should immediately take measures to carry out of mutual consultations. Eden proposed they immediately consult on the joint responsibilities in the declaration. After some discussion on what had been agreed, Stalin accepted the British suggestion.

Eden wanted to invite the Provisional Government of France to associate themselves with the declaration. Roosevelt agreed it would be impossible to give France an area to administer in Germany unless they were members of the Control Commission. He thought it would be easier to deal with the French if they were on

---

8   There are two Neisse Rivers (Nysa in Polish). The Lusatian Neisse is the longer at 157 miles and is referred to as the Western Neisse. The Glatzer Neisse is 113 miles long and is the Eastern Neisse. Both start in the Sudeten Mountains and flow north into the Oder. The Polish-German border would be defined by the Western Neisse.

9   The Polish-Russian border roughly followed the Curzon Line, giving up previously Polish territories to Russia. It was bitterly contested by the Polish Government-in-exile.

10 Substituting the words 'three powers' with 'three heads of government'.

the Commission than if they were not. Stalin agreed. Churchill suggested sending a joint telegram to de Gaulle to inform him of the agreed decision.

Yugoslavia

Eden read a telegram to be sent to Tito and Subasic suggesting putting the agreement into effect immediately as the basis for the formation of a unified Government of Yugoslavia.[1] Stalin and Churchill wanted to put the two British amendments in the communiqué but Molotov disagreed. Churchill thought it would have a better reception if they were included. After discussion with Churchill and Eden, Stalin thought three points could be included in the telegram:

1)   the agreement should go immediately into force;
2)   the Skupstina members who had not collaborated with the Germans could be included into the Vetch;
3)   the actions of the Vetch[2] would be subject to confirmation by the Constituent Assembly.

Reparations

Eden said the British Government still had reservations over the Soviet proposals. The War Cabinet had instructed Churchill not to mention figures; they should be left to the reparations committee. Churchill was concerned the American people would believe reparations involved money if any figures were mentioned.[3] Stalin explained the sum was only an expression of the value of the reparations. Churchill added nothing would be published regarding reparations but he could not agree to the inclusion of a definite sum.

Stalin did not understand why there should be any confusion with regard to payment in money. The Soviet Union had concluded three treaties with Finland, Romania and Hungary in which the value of reparations was definitely stated and there had been no confusion. If the British felt the Russians should receive no reparations at all, it would be better to say so frankly. He had heard a great deal of talk about the Russians receiving reparations in the form of factories and plants but no decision had been reached. He thought two decisions might be:

1)   to agree in principle that Germany should pay reparations;
2)   that the Reparations Commission would sit in Moscow and should fix the amount and take into consideration the American-Soviet proposal of $20 billion of reparations, with 50 per cent to the Soviet Union.

Roosevelt feared the word reparations because the American people might think it meant reparations in cash. Someone replied this could be avoided by using the term "compensation for damages caused by Germany during the war".

Molotov said the Moscow Commission had a duty to find out what reparations would be paid, using the American-Soviet formula. Churchill replied the British Government could not commit itself to any figure. Stalin said there was no commitment but the Commission might use the American-Soviet formula.

---

1   The Tito-Subasic agreement recognised Tito's partisans as the legal armed force in Yugoslavia in return for the partisans recognising and taking part in the new government. Subasic would be Prime Minister until 30 January 1945 and then Tito took over when Subasic resigned over the communist policies of the new government.
2   The Anti-Fascist Assembly.
3   Figures would then be compared with the reparations following World War I, something they wanted to avoid.

Churchill read a telegram from the War Cabinet, which considered it inadmissible to state any figure until an investigation had been completed. At any rate, the figure of $20 billion was too great. It was equal to Germany's peacetime export trade and it was beyond Germany's capacity to pay. It was true some reparations would come from Germany's capital assets but it would make it more difficult for Germany to pay her bills. The payments would more than cover German imports. If these imports were not given priority ahead of reparations, it would mean some countries would in effect be paying for German reparations.

Stalin did not want to go into the circumstances of the Prime Minister's telegram. The experts may be right, but all they were doing was preparing a figure to use as a basis for discussions – it could be reduced or increased by the Moscow Commission. Roosevelt suggested leaving the whole matter to the Moscow Commission. Stalin felt Germany should pay reparations in principle and they could all say that. Stettinius had reported full agreement on the first two points of the Soviet proposal. The question was which countries should receive reparations and what type. The only difference between them was the sum. Eden said rightly or wrongly, the British Government felt naming a sum would commit them. He proposed getting the Moscow Commission to examine Mr. Maisky's report.[4] Molotov and Maisky both thought referring the question to a lesser body was utterly illogical. Churchill repeated no agreement had been reached about a sum. Eden added Molotov's first two points were agreed and Stalin proposed the following formula:

1) Germany must pay compensation for the damage caused to the Allied nations as a result of the war;

2) the Moscow Commission would be instructed to consider the amount.

This was agreed.

Dardanelles

Stalin again said the Montreux Convention was outmoded. The Japanese Emperor had played a big part in the treaty, even greater than the Soviet Union. It was linked with the League,[5] which did not exist, just as the Japanese Emperor was not present at this Conference.

Stalin also reminded them that the Turks could close the Straits in time of war or if she felt threatened. The treaty was made when the relations between Great Britain and the Soviet Union were not perfect but he did not think Great Britain wished to strangle Russia with the help of the Japanese. The treaty needed revising but he did not know how and did not wish to prejudge any decisions; but he felt Russian interests should be considered. Stalin said it was impossible to accept Turkey having a hand on Russia's throat but changes should not harm Turkey's legitimate interests. He thought the three Foreign Ministers might consider the matter.

Roosevelt said the United States had a frontier of over 3000 miles with Canada and there was no fort and no armed forces. This situation had existed for over 100

---

4   Maisky's report was made at the Crimean Conference.
5   The League of Nations.

years and it was his hope that other frontiers in the World would eventually be without forts or armed forces on any part of their national boundaries.

Churchill said Stalin had reminded them of the question of the Straits when they met in Moscow last autumn. They agreed to a revision of the treaty but they were waiting for the Soviet Government to send a note on the subject. He thought Stalin's method was a wise one. The British felt Russia's great interests in the Black Sea should not be dependent on the narrow exit. He hoped the Russians would make their proposals known when the Foreign Ministers discussed it.

They should tell the Turks the Montreux Convention would be under consideration, particularly if they wanted them to come into the war on their side. It was advisable to give the Turks some assurance their independence and integrity would be guaranteed. Stalin said it was impossible to keep anything secret from the Turks and such assurance should be expressed. Roosevelt agreed.[1]

Stalin said the Foreign Ministers could discuss the Straits at the United Nations Conference. Churchill thought it affected the position of Great Britain in the Mediterranean more than it did the United States position and he felt London was the proper place to discuss this question.[2]

Churchill went on to say some years ago he had tried very hard to get through the Dardanelles and the Russian Government had made available an armed force to help but it did not succeed.[3] Stalin said the Prime Minister had been in too much of a hurry to withdraw his troops, since the Germans and Turks were on the verge of surrender.[4] Churchill replied he was out of the government by that time because of the Dardanelles campaign and had had nothing to do with that decision.[5]

Summing Up

Roosevelt said he had to leave Yalta the following afternoon. Churchill doubted they could get all the work done by then. Roosevelt, Churchill, Stettinius and Eden discussed the communiqué before the time set for the President's departure. Stalin said there was little time and felt it was impossible to complete the work and suggested cancelling the dinner. Arrangements were made for the drafting committee to report that night. The meeting adjourned.

---

1   The Turks would be anxious to know if the Big Three had discussed the Dardanelles and what the outcome was. The Allies wanted to keep them onside because they wanted them to enter the war.

2   Great Britain used the Mediterranean and the Suez Canal as a conduit to the Empire.

3   Referring to the Gallipoli campaign in 1915, a military operation advocated by Winston Churchill when he was First Sea Lord of the Admiralty. The campaign was to open the Dardanelles to open a trade route to Russia; the northern route through the Baltic Sea was blocked by the German Navy. Troops landed on 25 April 1915 but they failed to take the peninsula and trench warfare ensued.

4   By December 1915 the winter weather made it impossible to supply the troops on Gallipoli while rain and snow made life unbearable. With disaster looming, 14 divisions were evacuated from the beachheads without interference; the last troops were evacuated on 9 January 1916.

5   Churchill was sacked from the post of First Sea Lord and commanded a battalion in the trenches on the Western Front before returning to government.

10 February: Tripartite Dinner Meeting[6]

The conversation was general to begin with. Churchill proposed a toast to the King George VI, the President of the United States, and Mr. Kalinin, President of the Supreme Soviet of the Soviet Union,[7] and he asked the President as the only Head of State present to reply to this toast. Roosevelt replied that the Prime Minister's toast brought back many memories and he recalled his first year as President of the United States in the summer of 1933. His wife had gone down in the country to open a school, and on the wall there had been a map on which there had been a great blank space. The teacher had told his wife it was forbidden to speak about this place, and it was the Soviet Union. He decided to write a letter to Mr. Kalinin asking him to send someone to the United States to open negotiations for the establishment of diplomatic relations.

Stalin, in his conversation with Churchill, emphasized the unsatisfactory nature of the reparations question. He did not want to go back and tell the Soviet people they were not going to get any reparations because the British were opposed to it. Churchill said he very much hoped Russia would receive reparations in large quantities, but he remembered the last war when they had placed the figure at more than the capacity of Germany to pay. Stalin said it would be a good idea to mention the Reparations Commission and the intention to make Germany pay for the damage it had caused the Allied Nations in the communiqué. Churchill and Roosevelt agreed.

Churchill then proposed a toast to the health of Marshal Stalin. He hoped the Marshal had a warmer feeling for the British than he had had, and he felt the great victories which his armies had achieved had made him more mellow and friendly than he had been during the hard times of the war. He hoped the Marshal realized he had good and strong friends in the British and American assembled representatives. They all hoped, Churchill continued, the future of Russia would be bright, and he said he knew Great Britain, and he was sure the President, would do all they could to bring this about. He felt the common danger of war had removed impediments to understanding and the fires of war had wiped out old animosities. He envisaged a Russia which had already been glorious in war as a happy and smiling nation in times of peace.[8]

Stettinius proposed a toast to his predecessor, Mr. Cordell Hull,[9] who had been an inspiration to them all in his labours for the creation of a peaceful and orderly world. He concluded by saying that Mr. Hull was a great American and great

---

6   Held at the Vorontsov Villa with Churchill acting as host.
7   Mikhail I. Kalinin (1875-1946), known as Kalinych, was nominal head of state of Russia and then the Soviet Union from 1919 to 1946.
8   On 12 May 1945 Churchill wrote to Truman "an iron curtain is drawn down on their front. We do not know what is going on behind." Then on 5 March 1946 in a famous speech at Westminster College, Fulton, Missouri, he repeated the metaphor: "From Stettin in the Baltic to Trieste in the Adriatic, an Iron Curtain has descended across Europe."
9   Cordell Hull (1871-1955), the longest serving Secretary of State (1933-1944), received a Nobel Peace for his role in establishing the United Nations. President Roosevelt called him the "Father of the United Nations".

statesman. Roosevelt recalled there had been an organization in the United States called the Ku Klux Klan that hated the Catholics and the Jews.[1] Once when he had been on a visit in a small town in the South he had been a guest of the president of the local Chamber of Commerce. He sat between an Italian and a Jew and had asked the president of the Chamber of Commerce whether they were members of the Ku Klux Klan, to which the president replied they were. They were considered all right since everyone in the community knew them. The President remarked it was a good illustration of how difficult it was to have any prejudices – racial, religious or otherwise – if you really knew people. Stalin said he felt that this was very true.

There was considerable discussion about English politics between Churchill and Stalin, in which the latter said he did not believe the Labour Party would ever be successful in forming a government in England.[2]

Roosevelt said any leader of a people must take care of their primary needs. When he became President the United States was close to revolution because the people lacked food, clothing and shelter, but he had said, "If you elect me President I will give you these things". Since then had been little problem in regard to social disorder in the United States.[3]

Roosevelt then proposed a toast to the Prime Minister. He had been 28 years old when he entered political life but even then Mr. Churchill had had long experience in the service of his country. Churchill had been in and out of the government for many, many years, and it was difficult to say whether he had been of more service to his country within the government or without. The President personally felt Mr. Churchill had been perhaps of even greater service when he was not in the government, since he had forced the people to think.[4]

Churchill said he would face difficult elections in the near future in England, since he did not know what the Left would do. Stalin felt that Left and Right now were parliamentary terms. For example, under classical political concepts, Daladier,[5] who was a radical socialist, had been more to the left than Mr. Churchill, yet Daladier had dissolved the trades unions in France, whereas Churchill had not in England. He asked who could be considered more to the left.

Roosevelt said in 1940 there had been eighteen political parties in France and within one week he had dealt with three different prime ministers.[6] He had asked de Gaulle last summer how this had happened in French political life and

1   The Ku Klux Klan enjoyed a resurgence of membership in the 1920s but by the time of the Second World War it was in decline. A claim by the Internal Revenue Service (IRS) for back taxes resulted in the organization being dissolved in 1944.
2   It would in July 1945, when Clement Attlee's Labour Party defeated Churchill's Conservative Party.
3   Roosevelt had introduced the New Deal between 1933 and 1936, a raft of measures to get the United States back to work after the Depression. Historians call it the 3 Rs; Relief, Recovery, and Reform; relief for the unemployed and poor, recovery of the economy and reform of the financial system to prevent another depression.
4   Meaning he could be more radical and outspoken when he was in opposition than when he was Prime Minster.
5   Edouard Daladier (1884-1970), three times Prime Minister of France; January to October 1933, January to February 1934 and April 1938 to March 1940.
6   The French Prime Minister changed fifteen times (nine different men) between March 1933 (Roosevelt's appointment) and June 1940 (the Fall of France).

he replied it was based on a series of combinations and compromises, but he intended to change all that. Churchill remarked Stalin had a much easier political task since he only had one party to deal with. Stalin replied experience had shown one party was of great convenience to a leader of a state.[7]

Churchill said if he could get full agreement of all the British people it would greatly facilitate his task but he had lost two votes during the Greek crisis and the opposition had only eleven votes against him. He had accosted those Members of Parliament who had deserted him and had asked them to have the courage of their convictions. He had been very unhappy they had made this stand against the government. He concluded he didn't know what would be the result of the election in England but he knew he and Mr. Eden would continue to support the interests of Russia and the United States no matter who was in power.

Churchill said although he had had great difficulty with Mr. Gallacher,[8] the Communist member in the House of Commons, he nevertheless had written him a letter of sympathy when he lost his two foster children in the war. He felt British opposition to Communism was not based on any attachment to private property[9] but to the old question of the individual versus the state. In war the individual is subordinate to the state of necessity, and any man or woman between the ages of 18 and 60 was subject to the government in England. Stalin still did not believe the Labour Party could ever form a government.

Stalin asked the President whether there was any labour party in a political sense in the United States. Roosevelt replied labour was extremely powerful in the United States but there was no one specific party. Stalin thought more time was needed to consider and finish the business of the conference. Roosevelt answered he had three Kings waiting for him in the Near East, including Ibn Saud.[10]

Stalin said the Jewish problem was a very difficult one. They had tried to establish a national home for the Jews in Birobidzhan[11] but they had only stayed there two or three years and then scattered to the cities. The Jews were natural traders but much had been accomplished by putting small groups in some agricultural areas. Roosevelt said he was a Zionist[12] and asked if Marshal Stalin was one. Stalin said he was one in principle but he recognized the difficulty.[13]

---

7   Stalin, of course, executed opponents.

8   Willie Gallacher (1881-1956) a founding member of the Communist Party of Great Britain and one of only three Communist members of Parliament elected without Labour Party endorsement.

9   Manifesto of the 1848 Communist Party: "The Communist theory is summed up in a single sentence. Abolition of private property."

10   Ibn Saud (1876-1953), the first monarch of Saudi Arabia, the third Saudi state, from 1932 to 1953. He had 45 sons, all subsequent kings of Saudi Arabia among them.

11   Birobidzhan is the administrative centre of the Jewish Autonomous Oblast. It is at the east end of the Trans-Siberian railway, near the China border. It was planned in 1931 and granted town status in 1937.

12   In supporting a Jewish nation state in the territory defined as the Land of Israel.

13   Anti-Semitic measures were associated with Nazi Germany so Stalin's Soviet Union distanced themselves from the name and used the term 'anti-Zionism' for their anti-Semitic policies; the Jewish community was referred to as the 'rootless cosmopolitan'. Despite the different labels, Communist and Fascist anti-Semitism had many common factors.

Stalin said the Soviet Government would never have signed a treaty with the Germans in 1939[1] had it not been for Munich and the Polish–German treaty of 1934.[2]

11 February: Eighth Plenary Meeting

There are no full minutes of this meeting. Most of the conversation dealt with the language of the communiqué.

11 February: Tripartite Luncheon Meeting

Roosevelt acted as host at Livadia Palace. The conversation was general and personal. At one point, Stalin made an obvious reference to Iran, stating that any nation which kept its oil in the ground and would not let it be exploited was "working against peace".

13 February: Publication of the Yalta Agreement

World Organization

It was decided:

1)   A United Nations conference on the proposed world organization should be summoned on 25 April, 1945 in the United States.

2)   The nations to be invited should be:

     a)   The United Nations on 8 February 1945;

     b)   Associated Nations who have declared war on the common enemy by 1 March, 1945.[3] The United Kingdom and United States delegates would support a proposal to admit two Soviet Socialist Republics to the original membership, the Ukraine and White Russia.

3)   The United States Government should consult the Chinese Government and the French Provisional Government about the proposed world organization.

Territorial Trusteeship

The five nations on the Security Council would consult each on the question of territorial trusteeship. Territorial trusteeship would only apply to:

a)   Existing League of Nations' mandates;

b)   Territories detached from the enemy due to the present war;

c)   Any other territory placed voluntarily under trusteeship.

The Declaration of Liberated Europe

The Premier of the USSR, the Prime Minister of the UK and the President of the US declare their mutual agreement to work together during the temporary period

---

1   The Treaty of Non Aggression between Germany and the Soviet Union was signed on 23 August 1939. It was also known as the Molotov-Ribbentrop Pact and secretly divided Eastern Europe into spheres of influence. It opened the way for an invasion of Poland on 1 September.

2   The German-Polish Non Aggression Pact was signed on 26 January 1934. Both sides agreed to forego armed conflict for ten years caused by border disputes resulting from the Treaty of Versailles. Germany broke the pact when they invaded Poland on 1 September 1939.

3   The date enticed Turkey to enter the war on the Allied side after five years of neutrality.

of instability in liberated Europe in assisting the peoples liberated from the domination of Nazi Germany and the peoples of the former Axis satellite states of Europe to solve by democratic means their pressing political and economic problems.

The establishment of order in Europe and the rebuilding of national economic life must be achieved by processes that will enable the liberated peoples to destroy the last vestiges of Nazism and fascism and to create democratic institutions of their own choice. This is a principle of the Atlantic Charter – the right of all people to choose the form of government under which they will live – the restoration of sovereign rights and self-government to those peoples who have been forcibly deprived of them by the aggressor nations. To foster the conditions in which the liberated people may exercise these rights, the three governments will jointly assist the people in any European liberated state or former Axis state in Europe where, in their judgment conditions show the requirement:

a)   to establish conditions of internal peace;

b)   to carry out emergency relief measures to relieve distressed peoples;

c)   to form interim governments representative of the democratic elements of the population;

d)   for the earliest possible establishment through free elections of governments;

e)   to facilitate the holding of such elections.

The three Governments will consult the other United Nations and provisional authorities or other Governments in Europe when matters of direct interest to them are under consideration.

When, in the opinion of the three Governments, conditions in any European liberated state or former Axis satellite in Europe make such action necessary, they will immediately consult together on the measures necessary to discharge the joint responsibilities set forth in this declaration.

By this declaration we reaffirm our faith in the principles of the Atlantic Charter, our pledge in the Declaration by the United Nations and our determination to build, in cooperation with other peace-loving nations, world order, under law, dedicated to peace, security, freedom and general well-being of all mankind. The three powers also express the hope that the Provisional Government of the French Republic may be associated with them.

The Dismemberment of Germany

The United Kingdom, the United States of America and the Union of Soviet Socialist Republics will possess supreme authority with respect to Germany. They will dismember Germany as they deem requisite for future peace and security.

The French in Germany

A zone in Germany should be allocated to France and occupied by the French forces. This zone would be formed out of the British and American zones. The French Provisional Government would also be invited to join the Allied Control Council for Germany.

Reparations

1)   Germany must pay in kind for the losses caused by her to the Allied nations in the course of the war. Reparations are to be received in the

first instance by those countries which have borne the main burden of the war, have suffered the heaviest losses and have organized victory over the enemy.

2) Reparation is to be exacted from Germany in the three following forms:

    a) Removals within two years from the surrender of Germany, or the cessation of organized resistance, from the national wealth of Germany located on the territory of Germany herself as well as outside her territory,[1] these removals to be carried out chiefly for the purpose of destroying the war potential of Germany.

    b) Annual deliveries of goods from current production for a period to be fixed.

    c) Use of German labour.

3) For the working out on the above principles of a detailed plan for exacting reparation from Germany an Allied reparation commission will be set up in Moscow. It will consist of three representatives – one from the Union of Soviet Socialist Republics, one from the United Kingdom and one from the United States of America.

4) With regard to the fixing of the total sum of the reparation, the Soviet and American delegations agreed a figure of $22 billion[2] and 50 per cent should go to the USSR. The British delegation did not want to mention any figures until the Moscow reparation commission had met.

Poland

A new situation in Poland, resulting from her liberation by the Red Army, calls for the establishment of a Polish Provisional Government. The Provisional Government now functioning in Poland should be reorganized on a broader democratic basis, including Poles abroad. This new Government should then be called the Polish Provisional Government of National Unity.

The Foreign Ministers are authorized to consult with the present Provisional Government and other Polish democratic leaders in Moscow, with a view to reorganizing the Government. This Polish Provisional Government of National Unity shall be pledged to the holding of free and unfettered elections as soon as possible on the basis of universal suffrage and secret ballot. All democratic and anti-Nazi parties have the right to put forward candidates and take part.

The Governments of the USSR, the UK and the US will establish diplomatic relations with the new Polish Provisional Government of National Unity, and will exchange Ambassadors to keep them informed about the situation in Poland.

The three heads of Government consider the eastern frontier of Poland should follow the Curzon Line.[3] They recognize Poland must receive substantial accessions in territory in the north and west and the opinion of the new Polish

---

1   Equipment, machine tools, ships, rolling stock, German investments abroad, shares of industrial, transport and other enterprises in Germany, etc.

2   Around $265 billion today.

3   As mentioned earlier, with small digressions in favour of Poland.

Provisional Government of National Unity should be sought. The final delimitation of the western frontier of Poland should await the peace conference.

Yugoslavia

It was agreed to recommend to Marshal Tito and to Dr. Ivan Subasic:

1) That the Tito-Subasic agreement should immediately be put into effect and a new government formed on the basis of the agreement.

2) That as soon as the new Government has been formed it should declare:

   a) The Anti-Fascist Assembly of the National Liberation will be extended to include previous members of the Yugoslav Skupstina (Assembly) who have not compromised themselves by collaboration with the enemy;

   b) Legislative acts passed by the Anti-Fascist Assembly of the National Liberation will be subject to ratification by a Constituent Assembly.

Japan

Two or three months after Germany surrenders, the Soviet Union shall enter into war against Japan on condition that:

1) The status quo in Outer Mongolia is preserved.[4]

2) Russia's former rights violated by the treacherous attack of Japan in 1904 shall be restored:

   (a) The southern part of Sakhalin shall be returned to the Soviet Union;[5]

   (b) The commercial port of Dairen shall be internationalized, the pre-eminent interests of the Soviet Union in this port safeguarded and the lease of Port Arthur as a naval base of the U.S.S.R. restored;

   (c) The Chinese-Eastern Railroad and the South Manchurian Railroad, which connect with Dairen, shall be operated by a joint Soviet-Chinese company;[6]

3) The Kurile Islands shall be handed over to the Soviet Union.

The heads of the three great powers have agreed that these claims of the Soviet Union shall be unquestionably fulfilled after Japan has been defeated.

The Soviet Union was ready to agree a pact of friendship and an alliance with China to help it liberate itself from the Japanese yoke.

The Terminal Conference: 16 July–2 August 1945

There had been many changes since the ARGONAUT Conference. The Allies crossed the Rhine at Remagen on 7 March 1945 and then at many more places

---

4 The Mongolian People's Republic.
5 Including the adjacent islands.
6 Soviet Union interests would be safeguarded and China would retain sovereignty in Manchuria.

towards the end of the month; the advance across Germany then began in earnest. The Red Army was also advancing rapidly, reaching the suburbs of Berlin on 23 April and two days later they met American troops on the River Elbe, cutting the German armed forces in two. Hitler committed suicide eight days later and on 8 May 1945 the war in Europe was over.

However, there was still the ongoing war against Japan to consider, a war in which casualties were mounting as the Japanese fought to the death to hold onto their territory. Early in 1945, Fourteenth Army advanced onto the plains of upper Burma, capturing Mandalay in March before crossing the Irrawaddy. Arakan was cleared next and Rangoon was taken on 3 May; but morale plummeted when Mountbatten relieved General Slim as commander of Fourteenth Army. Meanwhile, the bloody battle of Iwo Jima came to a close in March and an even harder battle for Okinawa followed in April 1945. All that was left was the invasion of the main Japanese islands; a prospect no one was relishing.

Thirteen formal meetings were held in the Cecilienhof Palace, the former palace of Crown Prince Wilhelm of Prussia. The building is in the New Garden, Potsdam, in southeast Berlin. At the same time meetings were held by the Combined Chiefs of Staff, the Foreign Ministers and the Economic Subcommittee.

There were a number of personnel changes at the meetings. The first was due to the recent death of President Roosevelt and he was replaced by President Harry S. Truman. On 25 July Prime Minister Churchill attended his last meeting and returned to London to hear the results of the British general election. He was beaten in a landslide victory by Clement Attlee's Labour Party. Attlee joined the meetings on 28 July. There was a short break on 29 and 30 July because Stalin was ill. The final meeting was on 1 August, bringing to an end ten momentous conferences by the Heads of State of the Allies.

16 July

First Combined Chiefs of Staff Meeting
Plan for the meetings; Chairmanship; Policy on Lend-Lease; French colonial divisions in the Far East.

Second Combined Chiefs of Staff Meeting
Estimate of the enemy situation; Progress report on Pacific and Southeast Asia operations; Army Air Operations in the war against Japan.

17 July

Third Combined Chiefs of Staff Meeting
Military aspects of the Unconditional Surrender of Japan; Retention of US forces in Italy; US policy on the Dardanelles and the Kiel Canal; British participation in the war on Japan; Command and control in the war on Japan.

Fourth Combined Chiefs of Staff Meeting
British participation in the war on Japan.

17 July: First Terminal Meeting

Premier Stalin proposed President Truman[1] preside over the meetings and Churchill seconded it. Truman accepted and asked if it was proper to propose items for the agenda. Stalin agreed and Eden asked if all members would have the power to add to the agenda. Truman said they would.

Truman read the document on the Council of Foreign Ministers and Churchill proposed referring it to the meeting of the Foreign Ministers. Stalin agreed but he was not clear about including China because he thought the Council would discuss European problems. Truman's second memorandum related to Germany and he proposed the Control Council should begin to function immediately. Churchill said the Heads of State should discuss it and Stalin said they could the following day.

Truman read the 'Yalta Declaration on Liberated Europe'. In view of the recent Italian declaration of war on Japan he hoped they would support the Italian entry into the United Nations Organization. Churchill said it was important but their positions were not the same. The British were attacked by Italy in 1940, when France was going down; President Roosevelt had described it as "a stab in the back" at the time.[2] The British then fought the Italians for some time before the United States came in.[3]

At a most critical time Britain was obliged to send sorely needed troops to Africa and for two years they fought on those shores before the arrival of the American forces.[4] Britain also suffered very heavy naval losses in the war with Italy in the Mediterranean. They provided 14 out of the 15 vessels, which was the equivalent to the Russian share of the Italian fleet. Churchill said the question must be given very careful consideration and suggested Truman gave his presentation on Italy. Stalin agreed.

Truman appreciated the honour of being made Chairman and while he came gladly to the conference, he had some trepidation because he succeeded a man who could not be replaced,[5] one who was on the friendliest terms with the Prime Minister and Premier Stalin. He hoped he would merit the same friendship.

Churchill expressed his gratitude to Truman for undertaking the Presidency of this momentous conference. He thanked him for presenting so clearly the views of his mighty republic. They would renew the warm and ineffaceable sentiments they had had for President Roosevelt with him. Churchill wished to express his most cordial respect. He trusted the bonds not only between their countries but also between them personally would increase. The more they came to grips with

---

1 President Harry S. Truman (1884-1953), 33rd President of the United States 1945–1953. He was Roosevelt's running mate in 1944 and succeeded to the presidency on 12 April 1945, when Roosevelt died after months of poor health.

2 Following Germany's invasion of France in May 1940, Benito Mussolini declared war on France and Britain on 10 June. Roosevelt declared "the hand that held the dagger has struck it into the back of its neighbor."

3 Mussolini declared war on the United States on 11 December 1941, the same day as Hitler did the same and four days after Pearl Harbor.

4 American troops landed on North African soil in November 1942 during Operation TORCH.

5 President Roosevelt died from a stroke on 12 April 1945. His health had been deteriorating for some time due a combination of several medical issues brought about by the polio paralysis he had suffered since 1921, smoking, and the stress of being President.

the world's momentous problems the closer their association would become. Stalin shared Churchill's sentiments.

Churchill then proposed they start on the agenda and either deal with items or refer them to the Foreign Ministers.[1] The agenda was not complete but they had a program. Truman wanted Churchill and Stalin to add any questions they wished while Stalin said they should set forth the questions they wanted to discuss. The British wished to add the Polish problem while the Soviets wanted to discuss dividing the German merchant fleet and navy. They also wanted to discuss reparations from Germany and Italy. Churchill asked what about Bulgaria and Romania? Molotov said they were already taken care of.

Stalin proposed the question of territories to be placed under trusteeship. Churchill asked if he was referring to areas in Europe or throughout the world. Stalin replied it could be discussed. The Soviets had already mentioned they would like territories of defeated states and they also wished to raise the question of relations with satellite states.

Another question the Soviet delegation wished to discuss was Franco's Spain. The regime did not originate in Spain; it had been imported and forced on the Spanish people by Germany and Italy. It was a danger to the United Nations and Stalin thought it would be good to create conditions which enabled the Spanish people to establish the regime they wanted.

Stalin said the question of Tangier[2] should be brought up, as well as Syria and Lebanon. Churchill pointed out the question could only be discussed provisionally in the absence of the French.[3] Stalin replied it would be interesting to clarify their views.

Stalin proposed discussing the Polish question and the émigré Polish Government. Churchill agreed. Sensible progress had been made since Yalta, while the winding up of the Polish Government-in-exile was part of the question. Stalin and Truman knew Britain had been the government's home and the base from which the Polish Armies were maintained and paid. Churchill thought their objectives were the same but the British task was harder because they had to handle the details. They did not wish to release large numbers of soldiers into their midst without making proper provision for them.[4] They could handle the problem in a satisfactory manner but it was important to carry out the Yalta agreement and he attached great importance to the Polish elections. Churchill said the broad presentation had been made and they would address themselves to the most agreeable questions or perhaps he should say, the least disagreeable, at the next meeting. Stalin said they could not escape the disagreeable ones; they had a duty to prepare for the peace conference. The war was over in Europe and they had to deal with its effects.

---

1   The Foreign Ministers discussed matters to reduce the work on the three Heads of State. They stated their nation's position and settled as many issues as possible, leaving the Heads of State to deal with the contentious issues.
2   Tangier is in Morocco, at the western entrance of the Mediterranean.
3   Syria and Lebanon were French territories. British troops had taken control when France was defeated in 1940.
4   The Polish armed forces in the west numbered over 250,000.

Churchill said there did not seem to be any difficulty in reconciling the objects they were pursuing. They ought to set up a peace conference but they should not replace the two useful bodies already set up: the Foreign Ministers and the European Advisory Commission.[5] It was a matter of selecting the correct body to use. He would be sorry to see these existing organizations destroyed.

Churchill suggested the world peace treaty would be settled by the Five Powers but European problems would be dealt with by the Four Powers directly concerned.[6] Meanwhile, the meeting of the three Foreign Ministers and the European Advisory Commission would continue. For example, Churchill could not see China advising them on the Rhineland; she would only have an intellectual interest. He saw difficulties in a Power having full representation when its interests were not directly concerned. Truman had no objection to excluding China from the Council and the question would be referred to the Foreign Ministers. Stalin replied they would have nothing to do if all the questions were discussed by the Foreign Ministers.

Churchill suggested the Foreign Ministers looked into the question of there being four or five members of the Council. Stalin interrupted "or three members."[7] Churchill also suggested the Council stuck to questions of peace while the meetings of the three Foreign Ministers and the European Advisory Commission continued. The Foreign Ministers could pick the questions for the Heads of States to discuss.

Stalin asked if it was a question of a peace treaty or a peace conference. Churchill said the Council would prepare a plan for the peace and submit it to the three Heads of States. Stalin suggested the Foreign Ministers should decide whether to preserve the European Advisory Commission and the Foreign Ministers meetings.

Stalin had one question before they adjourned. Why did Churchill refuse to give Russia her share of the German fleet? Churchill exclaimed, "Why, because the fleet should be destroyed *or* shared; weapons of war are horrible things." Stalin replied, let us divide it. "If Mr Churchill wishes, he can sink his share." The meeting adjourned.

18 July

Fourth Combined Chiefs of Staff Meeting
French and Dutch participation in the war on Japan; Staff conversations with Portugal; Captured German passenger ships.

First Foreign Ministers Meeting
Forming the Council of Foreign Ministers; London Polish Government; Control Council for Germany; Disposing of the German Fleet; German economic problems.

Fifth Combined Chiefs of Staff Meeting
Southeast Asia and Southwest Pacific area; Command and control in the war on Japan.

---

5 The European Advisory Commission (EAC) was confirmed at the Tehran conference in November 1943. It would study postwar political problems in Europe for the Foreign Ministers to discuss. It would be dissolved after the Potsdam conference.
6 The fifth power was China.
7 Stalin did not want France included. Truman and Churchill did because of her proximity to Germany.

18 July: Second Terminal Meeting

Churchill raised the question of the press. At Tehran it had been difficult for the press to gain access; at Yalta it had been impossible. Here there were many press representatives outside the well guarded fortress. They were raising a great outcry in the world press about the inadequacy of their access to information.

Stalin asked who had let them in and Churchill replied they were outside the compound. He recognized secrecy and quiet were necessary for the work of the conference. If his colleagues agreed, he was willing to talk with the press; not to explain the work of the meeting but why they must be excluded. Alternatively, the President or someone else could do it. Truman said each delegation had a press representative and suggested they handle them; this meeting had to be kept secret as the others had always been. He was not worried about the correspondents who were mostly American. This was agreed to. Churchill said he had only offered himself as the lamb and in any event he would only go if Stalin agreed to rescue him.

Germany's Borders

Churchill said the word Germany was used repeatedly but what was Germany? Was it pre-war Germany?[1] If so, he agreed. Stalin said Germany was what she had become after the war. No other Germany existed now. For example, Austria was not now a part of Germany. Truman proposed considering Germany as it existed in 1937.[2] Stalin proposed adding "minus what Germany had lost in 1945".[3] Truman observed Germany had lost everything in 1945. Stalin replied he was speaking geographically and it was impossible to get away from the results of the war. Truman agreed but said it was necessary to have a line from which to start.

Stalin suggested fixing the western frontier of Poland and the question would become clear. Truman replied this could best be done when they had decided what to do with Germany. Stalin said Germany had no government, no definite frontier and no frontier guards but it had four occupied zones. Truman still suggested 1937 Germany as a starting point from which to operate. Stalin and Churchill agreed.

Churchill drew attention to the section covering the destruction of arms, implements of war and so forth. There were many things they should not destroy, such as wind tunnels and other technical facilities; would it not be well to have some use of them? Truman pointed out the report said "seized or destroyed". Stalin said they were not barbarians and they would not destroy research institutions. Churchill meant they could share them and use them together. Stalin agreed this could be done.[4]

---

1   Germany under the Third Reich had first included Austria under the Anschluss in March 1938 and then the Sudetenland in October; the rest of Czechoslovakia was occupied in March 1939.

2   Before the Anschluss with Austria.

3   Stalin is talking about East Prussia and eastern Germany.

4   There had been a race at the end of the war between the Allies and the Soviets to seize German research facilities, equipment and technicians. The German rocket scientist Werner von Braun (1912-1977) was a key member of the V-2 rocket development program. He was seized by the Americans under Project Paperclip and worked on the US Army's intermediate range ballistic program that came under the National Aeronautics and Space Administration (NASA). Braun was the architect of the Saturn V launch vehicle and booster rocket, which was used to land men on the Moon in July 1969. There was no cooperation between the United States and the Soviet Union during the Space Race.

The Polish Question

Churchill said the burden of this matter was with the British Government. Great Britain received the Poles when Hitler drove them out of Poland.[5] There was no property of any worth belonging to the London Polish Government, which the British had now disowned. There was about £20 million in gold, the ultimate asset of the Central Polish Bank, which had been frozen and they had to follow whatever was the normal course of such transfers.[6] But the Polish Government-in-exile did not control this gold.

Churchill said Raczkiewicz[7] had vacated the Polish Embassy in London and it was available for the Polish Provisional Government's representative.[8] The Ambassador of the Polish Provisional Government[9] could have it when he wanted and the sooner he arrived, the better. Churchill said the British Government had financed the Polish Government-in-exile and it had cost about £120 million[10] to finance the Polish Army and look after Poles who had fled the German scourge and taken refuge on British shores – the only asylum available to them in Europe.[11] When the Polish Government-in-exile had been disowned, the British dismissed its employees and gave them three months salary so they could look around to see what they would do. This expense fell on the British Government.[12]

Churchill asked for the President's understanding in pointing out the unique British position. They had to deal with the transfer, or liquidation, of the Polish forces which had fought with them. Some Poles had got out of France; others had escaped from Switzerland to Italy. They had got 40,000–50,000 out of France before the French capitulation and had built a Polish Army of about five divisions based in England. There were a great many Poles in a Polish corps of three divisions in Italy and they were also in a very excited frame of mind.

This Polish Army of about 200,000 had fought with great bravery and discipline in Germany and Italy.[13] They had suffered heavy losses and held the line

---

5　Great Britain pledged support to Poland and France on 31 March 1939, in response to the recent German occupation of Slovakia. The Agreement of Mutual Assistance between Britain and Poland was signed on 25 August, two days after the Ribbentrop-Molotov non-aggression pact between Nazi Germany and the Soviet Union. In a secret protocol Britain offered Poland assistance if she was attacked by Germany. The Ribbentrop-Molotov pact also included a secret protocol to divide Poland between them. Germany invaded western Poland on 1 September and the Soviets invaded eastern Poland on 17 September.

6　The equivalent of over £700 million, $1.13 billion or 3.58 billion zloty today.

7　Wladyslaw Raczkiewicz (1885-1947) was the first president of the Polish Government-in-exile from 1939 until his death in 1947. Until 1945 he was internationally recognized as the Polish head of state and the Polish Government-in-exile was recognized as the continuum of the Polish government.

8　The Provisional Government of the Republic of Poland was set up by the State National Council on 1 January 1945. It did not recognise the Government-in-exile and was initially only recognised by the Soviet Union; this changed after the Yalta Conference.

9　Also called the Lublin Government.

10　The equivalent of over £4.2 billion, $6.8 billion or 21.56 billion zloty today.

11　Even though the Soviet Union was much nearer.

12　During 1943 and 1944, the Allied leaders, particularly Winston Churchill, tried to get Stalin and the Polish Government-in-exile to talk. The Katyn massacre of Polish army officers by the Soviets, Poland's postwar borders and the refusal to accept a communist government in postwar Poland prevented this.

13　Nearer 250,000; 89,000 deserted from the Wehrmacht, 83,000 were evacuated from the USSR, 35,000 escaped from France, 21,750 were liberated from POW camps, 14,200 escaped from occupied Europe, 7000 were recruited in France, 2300 were ex-pats from South America and Canada and 1800 ex-pats in the UK.

with distinction.[1] Relations with these men involved His Majesty's Government's honour. While pledges had been given in Parliament they would feel obliged to treat them in a way which the whole world would approve. Stalin interrupted with "Of course."

Churchill said these men had taken an oath to President Raczkiewicz and British policy was to persuade as many of them as possible to return to Poland. He had been very angry when he heard General Anders,[2] who was a good soldier but who Marshal Stalin knew was anti-Russian, had told his troops they would probably be sent to Siberia if they returned to Poland.[3] Disciplinary action would be taken against this officer. This was the British policy but they needed a little time. Of course, the better things were in Poland, the quicker they would go.

Churchill wished to rejoice in the improvement in the Polish situation and expressed his wish for the success of the new Polish Provisional Government. He referred to Mikolajczyk's[4] contribution to its establishment. He had wanted more in the setting up of this Government but the progress so far was a splendid example of the collaboration of the great powers.

Churchill had pledged in Parliament that soldiers who had fought for Britain would be received in the British Empire if they did not wish to return to Poland, because feeling on the Polish question was high after the Crimea Conference.[5] They could not cast adrift men who had been brothers in arms but he hoped as few as possible would remain and they would be encouraged to return to Poland. It would be of great help if the Provisional Government[6] could assure them they would be well received when they returned to their homes, which the Red Army's victory had freed.

Stalin appreciated the British Government's difficulties. They had sheltered the former rulers of Poland but they had caused them much trouble.[7] The Soviet draft was not intended to complicate the British position; it was intended to end

---

1   195,000 Polish troops fought with the Allies; memorably at Tobruk in North Africa, Normandy in France, Cassino in Italy and Arnhem in Holland. Around 19,400 Poles served in the RAF. Three Polish destroyers fought with the Royal Navy.

2   General Wladyslaw Anders (1892-1970) was commander of the Polish Armed Forces in the East, nickname Anders' Army. The Army was created in the USSR in 1941 and in March 1942 left because the Soviets refused to help it. The Poles made their way through Iran to Palestine, and became II Polish Corps. It fought in Italy, at Monte Cassino in 1944. The Soviet-installed communist government in Poland in 1946 deprived Anders of Polish citizenship and of his military rank; he remained in Britain unwilling to return in case he was jailed or executed. General Anders was buried alongside his men at Monte Cassino. His citizenship and military rank were posthumously reinstated after the collapse of communist Poland in 1989.

3   Sent to the Gulag labour camps in Siberia because they would have ideas of democracy, unacceptable to the Soviets, after serving their country.

4   Stanislaw Mikolajczyk (1901–1966), Prime Minister of the Polish Government-in-exile from July 1943 to November 1944. Encouraged to return to Poland and become Prime Minister of the Provisional Government from June 1945 until 1947. He was fired from the government in 1949 when the Soviets took control.

5   Stalin had insisted that territories annexed by the Soviets in 1939 should remain in Soviet hands while Poland should be compensated with lands to be annexed from Germany.

6   On 28 June, the Provisional Government of the Republic of Poland was transformed into the more coalition-like Provisional Government of National Unity. This had been promised by Stalin at Yalta and done as gesture of goodwill towards the Allies and Polish Government-in-exile.

7   The Polish Government-in-exile was of course concerned about the Soviet Union's influence in Polish politics. While they wanted it to be an independent state, leading communists wanted it to become a republic of the Soviet Union.

the existing position. Arciszewski's[8] government continued to exist, it had the means to conduct activities and it had agents and press representatives. This made an unfavourable impression on public opinion in all allied nations.[9] If Churchill pointed out the items which complicated the British position, he was prepared to withdraw them from the Soviet draft.

Churchill agreed with Stalin but when you cut off money and end a government you could not prevent – in England – individuals from going on talking and this included members of Parliament. He had never seen the members of this Government nor had the Foreign Secretary after the departure of Mikolajczyk.[10] But what could be done if Arciszewski wandered through the streets of London and talked with journalists? Churchill repeated the British Government had nothing to do with these men and was giving them no facilities.

They had to be careful about the Army, if they were to prevent mutiny and possibly bloodshed; in which case their own people would be killed.[11] Many of them were in Scotland and they wanted to be rid of them.[12] The British had the same objectives as the Soviets. They asked for help, a little time and for Poland to be made an attractive place for Poles to return to. Churchill asked for time to prepare the Polish soldiers for their return to Poland. Stalin agreed to withdraw any points in the Soviet draft that would complicate the British Government's position.

Truman was also interested in the Polish question. He recalled the Yalta Agreement had been reached agreement on the holding of free and secret[13] Polish elections as soon as possible. Stalin said the Polish Government had never refused to hold elections.

Churchill was impressed by the question of political principles to be applied to Germany and it was good to discuss it at the next meeting. It was, however, a very big question. Were there to be uniform or different practices in the different zones? Stalin understood they were all in favour of a uniform policy.[14] Truman agreed. Churchill said he only wished to emphasize the point. The meeting adjourned.

19 July

Sixth Combined Chiefs of Staff Meeting
Information for the Russians on the war with Japan.

Second Foreign Ministers Meeting
Agenda; Council of Foreign Ministers; Poland; Germany's economic problems.

---

8   Tomasz Arciszewski (1877-1955), Prime Minister of the Polish Government-in-exile in London from 1944 to 1947.

9   As long as the Government-in-exile in London functioned, it undermined the Soviet Union's new communist government of Poland.

10 Mikolajczyk had resigned in November 1944 and returned to Poland to take office in the new government. He later lost in a rigged election and returned to London where Churchill remarked "I am surprised you made it out alive." He emigrated to the United States.

11 The Polish contingent had swelled to 250,000 as the Allies released over 90,000 Poles from POW camps and labour camps.

12 Polish troops had been based across Scotland through the war and many were still there.

13 Secret, as in hidden ballots carried out without political pressure.

14 Of course there was nothing 'uniform' about the democratic West Germany and East Germany as part of the communist-run Eastern Bloc.

First Economic Subcommittee Meeting
Decentralisation of the German economy.

Seventh Combined Chiefs of Staff Meeting
Information for the Russians on the war with Japan; Planning date for the end of the war with Japan.

19 July: Third Terminal Meeting

The German Merchant and Naval Fleets
Truman said the first thing to consider was the difference between reparation and war booty.[1] The merchant fleet was to be classified as reparations and the United States wanted it to operate in the Japanese war zone. Stalin said war material taken by armies in the course of a war was booty. Armies laid down their arms, surrendered and turned in their arms; these arms were booty. The same applied to the navy. The Three Powers' military proposals stipulated the navy surrendered, so it was booty. No questions had been raised when the Italian naval and merchant fleets had been treated as booty.

Churchill and Truman agreed they did not want to approach the matter from a juridical standpoint.[2] Churchill was not opposed to a division of the German fleet. It was better to discuss the Italian fleet in connection with the Italian settlement but the replacement of losses was relevant to this matter. The British had suffered immense naval losses in the war. Speaking from memory, they had lost about ten capital ships and aircraft carriers, twenty cruisers and literally hundreds of destroyers, submarines and various kinds of small craft.

The question of U-boats stood on a different footing because they had a limited legal use and the Germans had used them in contravention of the international agreements.[3] As many of them as possible should be destroyed.[4] But the latest German U-boats might contain valuable information for the future and should be shared by the three Powers. Churchill did not look at the matter solely from a naval point of view because he was aware of the tremendous sacrifices the Russians had made in the field.

Churchill thought the other naval vessels should be divided equally. He had no objection to the Soviet proposal to divide the German naval fleet. He did not feel a nation as great and mighty as Russia should be denied this. She should have her flag welcomed. As it took so long to build new vessels, the German ships would be a means of developing the Russian navy and training personnel and would facilitate showing the Russian flag on the ocean.

---

1   War booty is seized military equipment and it belongs to the country that captures it. Reparations are put into the pot to be divided as payment for damages; the term refers to goods or money rather than territory.
2   A legal standpoint.
3   Article 22 of the 1930 London Naval Treaty declared that international law applied to submarines in the same way as surface vessels. Only merchant vessels that persistently refused to stop or actively resisted could be sunk without the ship's crew and passengers being first delivered to a place of safety.
4   Of 154 U-boats that were surrendered, 121 were sunk off the coast of Northern Ireland or Scotland over the winter of 1945–46. The scuttling was codenamed DEADLIGHT.

Churchill felt all captured German merchant ships should play their role to the full and contribute to the ending of the Japanese war. The limiting factor in the Japanese war was shipping. They had sufficient men, planes and naval ships but merchant ships were needed for the movement of men and materials. There was also the difficulty of feeding the British Isles and liberated Europe. Every ton was needed during this critical period. They had all placed all of their shipping in the shipping pool. He would be sorry if the German fleet was not used to conclude the war with Japan.

The only international agreement governing the conduct of submarines in wartime to which Germany was a party[5] was the 1930 Treaty on Limitation and Reduction of Naval Armament.[6] Allied shipping was pooled and controlled through the operations of the United Maritime Authority and the Combined Shipping Adjustment Boards.[7]

Churchill said the Finns had a merchant fleet of some 400,000 tons, which had passed into the hands of their Russian ally.[8] Two Romanian troop ships had also fallen into Russian hands. If the German fleet was to be separated into three, the Romanian and Finnish fleet should be also. Stalin interrupted to say the Russians had not taken a single merchant ship from Finland and had taken only one ship from the Romanians to carry wounded troops.

Churchill said there were others besides the three at the meeting who had suffered heavy losses. The Norwegian oil tanker fleet had been very valuable and it had been used freely but it had suffered terrible losses. Perhaps the German fleet should be divided into four and the fourth part used for Powers not represented at this meeting. He only threw in the suggestions so they could be considered.

Truman was agreeable to a three-way division of the German merchant and naval fleets but he wanted to do it after the Japanese war. They needed the ships for the conduct of the war and to haul food and supplies for the rehabilitation of Europe, their great ally, Russia, Greece, and others. They would need every bomb and every ton of food. Stalin asked what about the navy? Truman said he was not ready to dispose of the craft now. The United States would have merchant and naval ships for sale when the Japanese war was over but he did not want to upset the war against Japan. Stalin asked "Are not the Russians to wage war against Japan?" Truman replied Russia would join the shipping pool when she was ready to fight Japan. Stalin said he was interested in the question of principle.

---

5   And in effect at the outbreak of World War II.
6   The London Naval Treaty was agreed between the UK, the US, France, Italy and Japan on 22 April 1930. It was an extension of the Washington Naval Treaty, which regulated submarine warfare and limited naval shipbuilding. The new treaty restricted displacements and gun calibres of submarines. It also defined heavy cruisers (8-inch guns) and light cruisers (6-inch guns) and limited the number of heavy cruisers a country could have and the tonnage of light cruisers.
7   The United Maritime Authority ensured maximum use was made of ships and shipping routes while the Combined Shipping Adjustment Boards ensured that ships carried cargoes in an efficient way.
8   Finland had initially defended its territory against the Soviet Union but in late 1944 it signed a peace treaty with Russia and drove the German troops out. She would have to cede 10 per cent of her territory and her second largest city, Vyborg, to keep her independence.

Churchill said they could earmark vessels; if they had any ears when the Japanese war was over.[1] If any were damaged they could be made good from their general resources. He supported Stalin's request for a share of these war and merchant vessels. The only alternative was to sink them and this would be harsh when one of their trusty allies wanted them. Truman said they were not far apart on this question. Stalin asked if he meant the merchant ships. Churchill answered he did.

Stalin said it was impossible to make out that the Russians intended to interfere with the war against Japan. It should not be put in a way to imply they were going to receive a gift from the Allies. They were not after a gift. Both Churchill and Truman said they had not said that. Stalin wanted to know if Russia was going to have a claim to one third of the German merchant and naval fleet and if his colleagues thought otherwise, they should say so. Truman did not think otherwise.[2]

Stalin asked if his Commission could see the German fleet or a list of the vessels. Churchill replied it was possible but the British wanted reciprocal facilities to see the German installations in the Baltic. He believed the Russians had obtained 45 German U-boats in Danzig. They could arrange an exchange. Stalin replied these submarines were out of use but they could agree to an exchange of visits. Churchill said all they were asking for was fair play and equality. Truman said the Russians were at liberty to see anything they wanted but they expected it would be reciprocal.

Churchill had made a distinction between U-boats and other ships. He knew Stalin would appreciate the sensitiveness of an island power which grew two-thirds or less of its own food. They had suffered much from the U-boats and the submarine was not a popular form of naval vessel in Great Britain. He strongly suggested the bulk of them be sunk. Great Britain had very nearly perished from them twice.[3] Those who lived with a large population on a small island did not welcome any nations of the world extending their construction of submarines. His consent depended on how many would be divided and how many would be sunk; but he agreed to divide them equally. German submarines had damaged them severely in the war and had eaten up a large part of their war-making capacity.[4] Stalin was also in favour of sinking a large proportion of the U-boats. Truman said that was sufficient discussion on the subject.

The Spanish Question

Churchill said his Government had a strong distaste for General Franco and his government.[5] He had been misrepresented as being friendly to this gentleman. All he had said was there was more to Spanish policy than drawing rude cartoons of Franco. The taking out of prisoners who had been in jail for years and shooting

---

1   In other words, they may be damaged or destroyed.
2   When Germany surrendered only three cruisers were left. *Prinz Eugen* was used in A-bomb trials in the Pacific, *Leipzig* was loaded with poison gas munitions and scuttled in the North Sea and *Nurnberg* was given to Russia. Around a dozen destroyers were also shared out.
3   At the beginning of the war Allied ships were vulnerable because there was no air cover in the middle of the Atlantic, leaving convoys exposed to attack. The U-boats' most successful year was 1942, when they sunk over 6 million tons in the Atlantic.
4   U-boats sank around 2,779 ships, or 14.1 million tons; 70% of Allied shipping losses.
5   General Francisco Franco (1892-1975) had ruled Spain since October 1936.

them for what had happened long before indicated Spain was not a democracy in accordance with British ideas. When Franco had written a letter proposing he and Churchill organize the western states against that terrible country, Russia, he had[6] sent him a chilly reply. Copies had been sent to Molotov and the President. British feeling was against the Franco regime.

Churchill saw some difficulty in Stalin's proposal to break off all relations with Spain. Taking such a step against a nation having a character like Spain, which was proud and touchy, might rally those elements now deserting Franco around him. The breaking of relations was not a satisfactory process. It would be a pleasure to do so but after that they would have no contact. Ambassadors were needed in difficult times most of all. If they took this action it would be a shock and might strengthen Franco's position. If it did, it would be necessary to consider whether to take a rebuff or to intervene with force. Spain had an army, although it was not very good. Churchill was against the use of force and interfering with countries which had a different regime, unless they were molested by them. They had set up democratic governments in the countries they controlled. They could not allow a Fascist regime to be set up in liberated areas. But there should be no exchange of cannon fire in countries that had not taken part in this war.

His Majesty's Government had to give Stalin's proposal to break relations with Spain prolonged consideration. Churchill was prepared to take every measure by all proper diplomatic means to speed the departing guest. But the breaking of relations with a state because of its internal conduct of affairs was a dangerous principle. He would greatly deplore anything that would lead Spain into civil war. Spain had suffered terribly from its civil war, in which two million people had been killed.[7] But the British would be sorry to intervene in the Spanish affair. Forces there were working for a change for the better.

Churchill said the World Organization, which had just been agreed upon at San Francisco,[8] had a provision against interference in domestic affairs.[9] It would be inconsistent to resort to action which would be prohibited under the San Francisco charter. Truman said he had no love for Franco but he had no desire to have any part in starting another civil war in Spain. There had been enough wars in Europe. He would be happy to recognize another government in Spain but Spain had to settle that question.

Stalin said everything would be unchanged in Spain, the Franco regime was gaining strength in his opinion and this was not an internal affair.[10] It was feeding semi-fascist regimes in other countries. The Spanish regime had been imposed on the Spanish people by Hitler and Mussolini, and they were in the process of

---

6   With the approval of the British Cabinet.
7   The Spanish Civil War lasted from July 1936 to April 1939. While the victorious Nationalists were supported by Nazi Germany and Italy, the Soviet Union had supported the Republicans. Around half a million were killed in the war while another 450,000 fled the new regime. Over 200,000 were executed in the bloody civil war; another 114,000 were executed over the next ten years.
8   The United Nations.
9   It was one of the United Nations' principles.
10   It would last until Franco's death in November 1975.

destroying their regimes.[1] While he believed his colleagues had no love for Franco, they should prove it in deeds. Stalin was not proposing military intervention, nor that civil war be let loose, but he wanted the Spanish people to know the three governments had taken a stand on the side of the democratic forces among the Spanish people. They should have grounds to believe they were against Franco. There was a diplomatic way of showing they were against Franco and they were for the democratic Spanish people.

Stalin said if the means of breaking relations was too severe, there must be a better way of letting the Spanish people know the three governments were in sympathy with the Spanish people and not with Franco. It was dangerous to let the Spanish regime remain unchanged. Public opinion in Europe and in America was not in sympathy with Franco and if the three governments passed by this cancer in Europe in silence, it might be believed they sanctioned Franco. That would be a grave charge.

Stalin had the right to raise and settle this question; why should they be silent? People presumed the Big Three could settle such a question and he was one of them, just as Churchill was. Must they keep silent about what was going on in Spain, as well as refrain from action against a Spain which was giving shelter to Fascists?[2] They could not shut their eyes to the grave danger of Franco's Spain. Churchill said individuals were not enjoined by governments from expressing opinions. The Soviet Union press also spoke very freely on this matter, as did the British and sometimes the American press.

His Majesty's Government had frequently spoken to Franco and his Ambassador but they did not want to break relations. Churchill also referred to the valuable trade relations Britain maintained with Spain. Spain sent them many useful products and received British manufactured goods in return.[3] He did not want this old and well established trade stopped unless he was convinced it would bring about the desired result. Churchill fully understood Stalin's feelings. Franco had had the audacity to send the Spanish Blue Division[4] to Russia. Russia was in a different position, having been molested.[5] But they had refrained from taking action against the British at a time it could have been disastrous.[6] Churchill said merely opening fire on the ships and air units concentrated around Gibraltar during TORCH would have done them great harm.[7] Stalin interrupted to say

---

1   Both Italy and Germany had sent troops to Spain to fight on the side of the Nationalists. There were up to 50,000 Italian troops fighting in Spain at one time and a total of 16,000 Germans. Both countries supplied a large amount of military hardware.
2   Thousands of Nazis would eventually flee prosecution in Germany and settle in Spain.
3   Spain and Portugal were the two largest tungsten suppliers in the world. The Allied strategy had been to buy enough tungsten to satisfy the export need and prevent the rest reaching the enemy. As a result of Allied economic measures and German defeats, Spain had adopted a more genuinely neutral policy by 1943.
4   Franco gave permission for men to join the German Army on the proviso they only fought the Bolshevists (the Soviet Army). The Blue Division, or División Azul, served on the Eastern Front from the summer of 1941 until the Spanish Government ordered it to return in November 1943.
5   Spain's official status was non-belligerent instead of neutral because of its alignment with the Axis Powers.
6   For example, a Spanish seizure of Gibraltar would have seriously compromised the North African and Italian campaigns.
7   There had been concerns at the time that German troops might invade Spain during TORCH, with a view to seizing airfields so the Luftwaffe could attack Allied troops in French North Africa.

the Spaniards were afraid. They would have been doomed if they had dared to take such action.

Churchill said Britain had not been specifically injured by the Spaniards. No one doubted Stalin had no love for the Franco regime and he had no doubt the majority of the English people shared this view. Churchill only wanted to emphasize the Russians had been injured in a way in which others had not.

Stalin thought Great Britain had also suffered from Spain, because it had provided bases on its shores for German submarines. All Allied Powers had suffered in this way but he did not wish to look at the question from this point of view. What was important was the danger to Europe. This should be remembered. Some steps should be taken, even if the breaking of diplomatic relations was too severe. They should say the aspirations of the Spanish people were just; they had only to say this and nothing would be left of Franco. Churchill did not think this was advisable. It was a question of principle. To interfere in the domestic affairs of other countries was very dangerous. He might not like some things in the United States, but he did not consider it wise to attempt to intervene.

Stalin said this was not a domestic affair; the regime of Franco was of external origin. Churchill stated anyone could say this about any country. Stalin replied no other country in Europe had such a regime. Churchill said Portugal might be considered as being under a dictatorship.[8] Stalin replied it was not the dictatorship that mattered. The Portuguese regime resulted from internal developments, whereas the Franco regime had resulted from intervention by Hitler and Mussolini. Franco's behaviour was provocative. He gave shelter to Nazis.[9]

Churchill was not prepared to interfere in the internal affairs of other states; this had always been the British policy. To push things might make matters worse. He would be very pleased, although he knew the idea would not be received with enthusiasm, if the regime was overthrown and replaced by a constitutional monarchy with free democratic principles and elections.[10] If he or any British Government pushed this proposal, all in Spain would turn against it. No country liked to be told how it was to be run. There was intervention on both sides in the Spanish Civil War. The Soviet Union intervened on one side and then Hitler and Mussolini came in on the other but that was long ago. Action taken at the Conference was more likely to rivet Franco in his place. The British Government did not give the slightest support to Franco's Spain other than trade, which they had always carried on.

Truman was happy for the Foreign Ministers to discuss the matter to see if agreement could be reached. Stalin fully appreciated the British difficulties but felt the matter could be facilitated by action at the Conference. He proposed

8   The Portuguese Republic was an authoritarian political regime under António de Oliveira Salazar and the *Estado Novo* was often regarded as being pro-fascist.

9   One French report claimed 100,000 Nazis and collaborators fled to Spain at the end of the war. The Soviet Union declared there were 200,000 Nazis in the country.

10   Churchill's wish would come about in 1975 when General Franco died, King Juan Carlos I was crowned King of Spain and democratic elections were once again held. (The claim that the British policy had always been not to interfere in the internal affairs of other states sits uneasily alongside the fact of an empire on which the sun never set.)

preparing an appraisal of Franco's regime, including observations made by Churchill on the trend of developments in Spain. This would be one of the items in the declaration to be made on Europe.

Churchill had not agreed to any declaration on Spain and he gathered the President had not either. Stalin said it was not a question of a declaration on Spain alone, but on all countries. Churchill said the line he had taken was not to interfere in the domestic affairs of all countries involved in this war. It was a question of principle. There were many things Churchill did not like about Yugoslavia and Romania[1] but they were involved in a war that gave them greater freedom there. If there had to be a declaration of the principles on which democratic governments were founded – he personally had always liked the statement in the American Constitution – they could consider a statement on what governments had not fulfilled these principles.[2] But many governments in Europe did not now fulfil these principles. Churchill did not know what the Spanish people thought. There were many shades of opinion in Spain but most of them would doubtless like to get rid of Franco without interference from outsiders. Truman said there appeared to be no chance for agreement and suggested coming back to the Spanish question later. The meeting adjourned.

20 July
Seventh Combined Chiefs of Staff Meeting
Basic objectives, strategy and policies; Air route between the United States and Moscow.

Second Economic Subcommittee Meeting
Eliminating the German war economy while maintaining a regulated economy to pay reparations.

Third Foreign Ministers Meeting
Council of Foreign Ministers; the agenda; Yalta declaration on liberated Europe.

Eighth Combined Chiefs of Staff Meeting
Directive to the Southeast Asia Commander; Disposal of war material in Germany and Austria.

20 July: Fourth Terminal Meeting
A Policy towards Italy
The President said it was proper to recognize the Italian contribution to the defeat of Germany. He suggested terminating the short terms of surrender and the obsolete long-term clauses and proposed the following undertakings:

    1)   The Italian Government would refrain from any hostile action against any of the United Nations, pending the conclusion of the peace treaty.

---

1   So while Stalin objects to the pro-fascist regimes of Spain and Portugal, Churchill objects to the pro-communist regimes of Yugoslavia and Romania.

2   The Preamble to the United States Constitution states the government would be just and it would protect its citizens from internal strife and from attack from the outside. The First Amendment states that it would protect the people's right to practise religion, to speak freely, to assemble, to petition the government and the rights of the press to publish.

2) The Italian Government would maintain no military, naval or air forces or equipment[3] and would comply with all instructions on them.

3) Control of Italy should be retained only so far as is necessary:

   a) To cover Allied military requirements, as long as Allied forces remain in Italy.

   b) To safeguard the equitable settlement of territorial disputes.

Stalin had no objections but it might need amendments and improvements.[4] There was no doubt Italy was the first to surrender, but she had helped Germany. It was true she had only supplied small forces but they had helped. She now proposed to come into the war against Japan, which counted in her favour. The day after their surrender, Romania and Bulgaria had moved their troops into action against Germany. Bulgaria had sent eight divisions against Germany[5] while Romania[6] had sent ten or twelve. He was bound to say these divisions had fought well. Finland had not given much support against Germany but her behaviour had been acceptable,[7] so it would be good to improve her position. The same applied to Hungary.[8] If they were going to improve Italy's position, they should also improve the position of the other satellite states and throw them all together.

Truman had raised the question of Italy because it was the first to surrender and its armistice terms had been harsher than those imposed on other satellite states. He agreed that the question of the other satellite states should be taken up. Churchill said the British position regarding Italy was not quite the same as his two honoured colleagues. Italy had attacked the British in June 1940. They had suffered very heavy naval losses in the Mediterranean and heavy losses in North Africa, at a moment when they were in very grave danger. They had also undertaken the campaign in Abyssinia,[9] which had restored the Emperor to his country, without help. Detachments of Italian planes had also bombarded London.

It should also not be forgotten that Italy had made a dastardly attack upon Greece[10] and a lawless attack upon Albania[11] just before the war began. All this occurred when the British were alone. Churchill said all this should be remembered, so it could not be said they had not suffered most grievously at the hands

---

3 Except those authorized by the Allies.

4 He suggested the Foreign Ministers look it over and also discussed preliminary policies with regard to Finland, Hungary, Romania and Bulgaria.

5 Bulgaria deployed three armies over 450,000 strong in September 1944, entering Yugoslavia and helping to stop German troops withdraw from Greece, Serbia and Macedonia. They advanced through Hungary to enter Austria and meet British troops on 8 May 1945.

6 Romania deployed around 250,000 troops against the Axis in August 1944, advancing through Hungary into Czechoslovakia by May 1945.

7 Finland joined the Soviets in September 1944 and fought the Germans in the Lapland war for nickel mines in the Petsamo area. There was an informal agreement to let German troops withdraw into Norway but the Soviets pushed the Finns to fight.

8 Hungary fought for the Axis on the Eastern Front; around 300,000 soldiers and 80,000 civilians died. Around half a million Hungarian Jews and gypsies perished in Auschwitz-Birkenau extermination camp.

9 Abyssinia, now Ethiopia. Haile Selassie I was crowned in November 1930 but independence did not last long. Italian troops invaded in October 1935 and the League of Nations failed to act. The Second Italo-Ethiopian War was over by May 1936.

10 Italian troops invaded Greece in October 1940 but after a winter-long stalemate, German troops joined the battle in April 1941, and by 3 May the fighting was over. Crete, an important base for air attacks, was also captured.

11 Italian troops invaded Albania in April 1939, forcing King Zog I into exile and absorbing the country into the Italian Empire.

of Italy. He was bound to state they could not acquit the Italian people of responsibility any more than they could acquit Germany, because she had come under the control of Hitler. Nevertheless, they had endeavoured to keep alive the idea of the renewal of Italy as one of the important powers in Europe and the Mediterranean. When Churchill went there a year ago he had made a series of proposals to Roosevelt, the bulk of which were embodied in a joint declaration.[1] Churchill wanted to show he was not against Italy or motivated by a feeling of vengeance. For example, it was agreed at Tehran either to divide the Italian fleet among the three powers or give the Soviet Union a corresponding number to the fifteen ships[2] and four submarines of a new type.

Churchill was illustrating the injuries they had received but they were still prepared to proceed in a broad manner with respect to Italy's future. He had seen it said they were hostile to Italy and they had wished to see Italy plunged into misfortune when they spoke against Count Sforza.[3] He rejected these press statements. He spoke in the name of his government and with a clean heart. He was anxious to join the President and the Marshal in the principle of making a gesture to an Italian people who had suffered terribly and who had helped expel the Germans from their land.

They did not oppose the proposal to make a peace with Italy but the work would take several months. Churchill also noted the Italian Government had no democratic foundation derived from free and unfettered elections; it consisted of politicians calling themselves leaders of different political parties. But it was the intention of the Italian Government to hold elections before the winter. While he agreed the Foreign Ministers should start preparing the peace treaty, it was not advisable to make a final conclusion until the Italian Government rested on a democratic foundation.

Churchill was against the American memorandum calling for an interim arrangement. No government could carry out its undertakings if it did not have a democratic foundation chosen by its people. If Italy's existing rights were abolished, the long and short armistice terms withdrawn, and there was a considerable interval before the peace settlement, they could only protect their rights through the use of force and no one wanted to do that. They were entitled to get Italy's compliance with various terms. There would be a gap between the withdrawal of the armistice terms and when Italy had a responsible government that could conclude a peace treaty.

Churchill said the American proposal did not cover the future of the Italian fleet, the Italian colonies, the question of reparations and other important points. If the Italian Government lost their existing rights under the surrender in the interval, they would not have the power to secure the peace they were entitled to.

Finally, Churchill said the terms of surrender had been signed by a great many

---

1   With improvements made by the President.
2   Provided the British had contributed fourteen, including HMS *Royal Sovereign*.
3   Count Carlo Sforza (1872-1952) was an Italian diplomat and anti-Fascist politician.

other people. Australia and New Zealand had lost many dead on African soil, so had the Greeks; other countries had signed the armistice terms as well. He did not wish today to go further than to agree in principle to a peace treaty and he would be pleased if it received the Foreign Ministers' priority.

With regard to the other countries, Churchill was bound to say Bulgaria had no claim from Britain. It had struck them a blow and had done them all the harm it possibly could. It was not for him to say what the Bulgarians had done against the Russians. Bulgaria had hardly suffered at all in this war. She lay crouching in the Balkans, fawning on German aid.[4] She also committed many cruelties in Greece and Yugoslavia[5] and she had prevented Turkey's entry into the war when it would have been most helpful.

There had been no proposal to disarm Bulgaria; on the contrary, Churchill believed Bulgaria had some fifteen divisions. No arrangements had been made for reparations from Bulgaria. She had also ill treated British and American prisoners of war. Their sympathies lay much more with concluding a peace with Italy than with Bulgaria. Churchill thanked his colleagues for listening to him as he differed in some points from Truman and Stalin. He also thought it was important to have all the facts before them.

Stalin said the question regarding Italy and other satellite states was how to separate these countries from Germany. This could be done by two methods. One was the use of force, which had been successfully applied by the Allies in Italy and by the Soviet forces in other satellite states. But the use of force alone was not enough and there was a danger they would create a favourable medium for the association of these countries to Germany. It was beneficial to improve the position of these satellites to supplement force. This seemed to be the only way to rally the satellites around them and to detach them once and for all from Germany. The questions of revenge and complaints paled compared with these considerations of high policy. He felt the President's paper was in full harmony with this policy of detaching the satellites from Germany by easing their position, so he had no objection in principle.

Stalin said Italy had committed great sins; it had committed sins against the Russians but not great ones. They had fought Italy on the Don and in the Ukraine, because they had penetrated far into his country. However, it would be incorrect to be guided by the remembrance of injuries. The feeling of revenge, hatred or the desire for redress was a bad advisor in politics.

Stalin said it was not for him to teach, but he thought they should be guided in politics by the weighing of forces. The question was did they wish to have Italy on the side of the United Nations, to isolate all possible forces which might arise against them from Germany? This determined everything and the same principle applied to the other satellites. Stalin said the satellite states had caused many difficulties and sacrifices. Romania had used 22 divisions against them, Hungary had

---

4   Although Bulgaria joined the Axis in April 1941 she followed a course of military passivity and maintained diplomatic links with the Soviet Union. She was forced to declare war on Britain and the United States on 13 December 1941. As soon as the Soviet forces crossed the Bulgarian border, she changed sides in September 1944.
5   While Bulgaria saved her own Jews from the Germans, she stood by while they deported the Greek Jews.

26 divisions at the end of the war and still greater injuries had been caused by Finland. Without Finland's help, Germany could not have maintained the blockade at Leningrad. Finland had moved 24 divisions against Soviet troops. Smaller injuries had been caused by Bulgaria. She helped Germany against Russia but she had not sent troops against them. On the other hand, she had caused harm to the Allies, Yugoslavia and Greece. Bulgaria should be punished for this and he was not opposed to punishing her. The armistice terms provided for reparations to be paid to these two countries. Stalin said not to worry; the Russians would compel this payment.[1]

It was contemplated that Bulgaria would provide troops to fight Germany in the armistice terms[2] signed by the United States and the United Kingdom. They said the Bulgarian army would be reduced to normal after the end of hostilities against Germany. Bulgaria had no right to resist the execution of the armistice terms and the Soviets would see to it they did not resist. Such were the sins committed by the satellite states against the Allies and the Soviet Union particularly.

Stalin was against taking revenge against the satellite states for their brazen behaviour and the losses they had caused. It was time to ease the position of these countries and to dig a channel between the Germans and the satellite states. Truman's proposals did not suggest preparing an immediate peace treaty with Italy. He proposed covering the situation between the end of the armistice terms and the conclusion of a peace treaty. It was difficult to oppose because it was practical and right.

Stalin did not propose signing peace treaties with the satellites, nor even some intermediate position. They should start by resuming diplomatic relations. Although there were no freely elected governments in the satellite states, no such government existed in Italy and in spite of this they had resumed diplomatic relations with Italy. The same thing was true of France and Belgium.[3] Churchill said they were Allies. Stalin understood this but democracy was democracy everywhere, no matter whether it was a question of allies or satellites.

Truman stated he had made a concrete proposal. The armistice agreement with Italy had been signed by the three governments and the same was true of the other armistice arrangements. He had made a proposition regarding Italy and Stalin had made a proposal regarding the others.

Truman said the United States policy was to bring about a feeling of peace in the world and this did not have to wait for a final peace conference for the world

---

1   Hungary paid $200 million to the Soviet Union and $100 million each to Czechoslovakia and Yugoslavia. Romania paid $300 million to the Soviet Union. Bulgaria paid $50 million to Greece and $25 million to Yugoslavia.
2   Although Bulgaria had joined the Axis in March 1941, it had not invaded the Soviet Union and had maintained diplomatic relations. On 5 September 1944 Soviet troops crossed the Bulgarian border and occupied the key ports of Varna and Burgas; the Bulgarian armed forces were ordered not to resist. Three days later Bulgaria signed an armistice and joined the Soviet Union in its war on Nazi Germany.
3   Nazi Germany had of course replaced France and Belgium's democratic governments with their own administrations.

as a whole.[4] The United States was having to spend enormous sums of money on countries in Europe. With reference to the reparations from Italy, the United States was spending from $750 million to $1 billion to feed Italy that winter.[5] The United States was rich but it could not pour out its resources forever for the help of others without getting something in return.[6]

Unless they were able to get these governments on a self-supporting basis, and there was no prospect of that, the United States would be unable to maintain them indefinitely the way things were going. They had to try to prepare conditions which in which these countries could help themselves.[7]

Churchill thought they had agreed the preparation of a peace with Italy should be forwarded to the Foreign Ministers. He had only deprecated tearing up the surrender terms, removing their right to obtain a proper peace. Truman was not proposing to sweep away that right. Churchill agreed to the easing of the burden on Italy and supposed there was no objection to a declaration of policy on Italy. Truman thought they should include the other satellite states.

Churchill agreed with not allowing the future to be governed by a spirit of revenge. It had been a great pleasure for him to hear these words from his colleagues. He had great sympathy for Italy. He had mentioned reparations but the British did not want them for themselves. They were thinking of Greece. It was agreed the Foreign Ministers could prepare a treaty and consider the armistice terms for Italy and the satellites.

The Austrian Situation

Churchill regretted appearing to be arguing against the Soviet view today. The situation in Austria was very unsatisfactory. Two months ago they had humbly asked if British officers could go to Vienna to look at accommodation. This had been arranged with the greatest difficulty and he had addressed several communications to Stalin. There had been no satisfactory results from this inspection. The British had no one in Vienna and they were not allowed to take up their positions.

The entry of British troops into Styria[8] had not been allowed, although it had been agreed to. The Soviets had liberated Austria three or four months ago. Field Marshal Alexander had submitted a very unsatisfactory report on the situation.[9]

---

4   The Paris Peace Conference 29 July–15 October 1946 resulted in the Paris Peace Treaties being signed on 10 February 1947. The Allied powers negotiated treaties with Italy, Romania, Hungary, Bulgaria, and Finland. It allowed those countries to reassume their responsibilities as sovereign states in international affairs and to qualify for membership of the United Nations.

5   $9.67 billion to $12.9 billion today.

6   Meanwhile, Italy had to pay $125 million to Yugoslavia, $105 million to Greece, $100 million to the Soviet Union, $25 million to Ethiopia and $5 million to Albania; $360 million in total ($4.64 billion today).

7   Eventually the European Recovery Program (better known as the Marshall Plan, after Secretary of State George C. Marshall) would be introduced in April 1948. The four-year plan was started to prevent the spread of Soviet Communism and the United States' goals were to rebuild a war-devastated region, remove trade barriers and modernise industry. It would make Europe, one of its main trading partners, prosperous again.

8   Styria (or Steiermark) is the southeast state of Austria.

9   Field Marshal Alexander had been Supreme Commander Allied Forces Headquarters, Mediterranean Theatre, since December 1944.

The British did not have a foothold. He thought they should be allowed to go to Austria and take up their zone.[1]

At the meeting yesterday Marshal Stalin had raised the question of a visit to the German ships. He proposed they proceed in a reciprocal manner and asked that cities occupied by the Russians should also be opened up.

The British had retreated to their occupation line in the north of Germany while the United States forces had retreated from an enormous territory to occupy their zone,[2] but they had not been allowed to set foot in their zone in Austria. Stalin said the zones in Austria had been agreed but not the zones in Vienna. It had taken time to hold negotiations and an agreement had only been reached the day before. Truman added he had only signed the document today.

Stalin said there was also the question of airfields. Agreement had also been reached on this matter, but the French had only communicated their agreement yesterday. For some reason the French were always late. They agreed to fix the date for the Allied troops to enter Vienna and the date for the Soviet troops to leave. The movement of troops could begin today or tomorrow. He said Churchill appeared to be indignant and he wondered why. The Soviets had not been allowed into the United Kingdom zone in Germany and they had not complained. They knew how hard it was to move troops and they had no intention of violating an obligation. If only Austria and Vienna were in question, this was settled.

A wiser action was taken in the case of Berlin and the question of occupation was settled quicker. Alexander had acted less skilfully and this had delayed matters. He had behaved as if Russian troops were under his control. The British and American commanders in the German zone had behaved well and everything was all right there.[3] There was no objection to each army occupying its zone, whether in Vienna or in Austria. That agreement had been reached only yesterday.

Churchill was very pleased to hear that matters were now settled. He really did not think Alexander had been able to give sufficient attention to all of these matters. Stalin had no complaints against Alexander, although he had not checked on the matter. Churchill would be happy to receive complaints, if there were any. Stalin did not wish to institute an investigation.[4] Churchill was bound to say that in the absence of any complaint, Alexander retained the complete confidence of His Majesty's Government. Stalin understood this; he had no complaint. He had only stated what his commanders had told him and this was one of the factors causing the delay. Churchill said the British were not the only people involved. There were American deputies involved and the United States had been far from satisfied. The President agreed. The meeting adjourned.

---

1   In the immediate aftermath of the war, Austria was divided into four zones occupied by the United States, Soviet Union, United Kingdom and France. Vienna was also divided and the central district was jointly administered by the Allied Control Council.
2   The dividing line was the Oder-Neisse River. The British Army had withdrawn from Mecklenburg in the north and the US armies had withdrawn from Saxony and Thuringia in the south.
3   Field Marshal Montgomery with 21st Army Group in the north and General Bradley with 12th Army Group in the centre.
4   Field Marshal Brooke claimed Alexander needed an able chief of staff to think for him, while Montgomery (Alexander's subordinate during the African and Italy campaigns) claimed he was incompetent.

Third Meeting of the Economic Subcommittee
Discussion of the Russian suggestion to internationalise the Ruhr industrial area.

21 July
Fourth Foreign Ministers Meeting
Council of Foreign Ministers meeting; German economic questions; Polish question; Italian declaration; Agenda for the Big Three meeting.
Ninth Combined Chiefs of Staff Meeting
Basic objectives, strategy and policies.

21 July: Fifth Terminal Meeting
Polish Elections
Stalin said the freedom of the press in Poland had already been confirmed. There was no use repeating the fact because the Poles were very touchy and would be hurt. They would suspect the Allies were accusing them of being unwilling to accord a free press. Stalin suggested stating all democratic and anti-Nazi parties had the right to take part in the elections.[5] Churchill said this was in no way a compromise but Stalin replied it was, as far as the Polish Provisional Government was concerned. Churchill had hoped to strengthen the declaration rather than weaken it.[6]

Truman said the United States was very interested in the Polish elections because there were six million Poles in the United States. A free election in Poland reported to the United States by a free press would make it much easier to deal with them. Truman believed the Polish Provisional Government knew the Three Powers would expect the press to report the elections.

Polish Western Frontiers
Truman said as the Crimean Declaration[7] read, Germany would be occupied by the Soviet Union, the United Kingdom, the United States and France. While the Polish frontiers would be favourably considered by them, the final settlement would occur at the peace conference. The three governments had decided the zones, their boundaries had been set[8] and the Americans and British had gone back to their zones.[9] Poland was now being assigned a zone without consultation and it should have been agreed on.[10] Truman could not see how reparations could be decided if Germany was being carved up. While he was very friendly toward the Polish Provisional Government, and they could probably agree on what the

---

5   There were still pro-Fascist elements in Poland, which Stalin wanted to exclude. There were also strong communist elements that he wanted to include and support.
6   Stalin had promised free elections but the Polish Communists knew they lacked support. Intimidation and ballot rigging resulted in nationalisation of industry, land reform and a one-house senate (unicameral rather than bicameral). The communists then reduced their opponents' rights, often using persecution and execution to remove them.
7   Made at the Yalta Conference (Argonaut) in February 1945.
8   The zones had been set by the European Advisory Commission (EAC) in 1944.
9   The Americans in southeast Germany and the British in northwest Germany.
10 The Polish-occupied Pomerania, Border Mark, Brandenburg, and Upper and Lower Silesia along the eastern border with Germany. They also occupied West Prussia and Danzig (now Gdansk) on the Baltic coast.

Soviet Government desired, he wanted consultation.[1] Stalin replied the Crimean declaration stated Poland's eastern frontier should follow the Curzon Line[2] and it should receive cessions of territory in the north and west. The Crimean declaration also stated a new Polish government should be consulted on the western frontiers at the appropriate time.

Truman said this was correct, but it was not correct to assign a zone. Stalin replied the Polish Provisional Government had already stated its views regarding the western frontiers. He proposed expressing an opinion on the Polish Government's wishes while the final settlement was left to the peace conference. Stalin also said it was not quite true the Russians had given the Poles a zone of occupation without agreement. The American and British Governments had sent communications saying the Polish should not establish an administration until the western frontiers had been set. But the Soviet Union could not accept the suggestion, because the German population in these areas had followed the German army to the west and the Poles had remained.[3] The Red Army needed administration in this territory, since it was not accustomed to setting up an administration while fighting and clearing out enemy agents. The Soviet Government was ready to allow a Polish administration because it could not see what harm was being done by establishing of a Polish administration where only Poles remained.[4]

Truman had no objection to an expression of opinion regarding the western frontiers but he wanted it understood the occupation zones would be as established. Any other course would make reparations very difficult, particularly if part of the German territory had gone before an agreement had been reached.[5] Stalin replied the Soviet Union was not afraid of the reparations question and would if necessary renounce them. Truman said the United States would get no reparations anyhow so it made no difference to them. America just wanted to try to keep from paying more, as they had done before.[6]

Stalin said everything the President spoke of was interpretative since no frontiers had been agreed at Crimea, only a provision that Poland would receive

1　The reparations were going to be determined by the zones each nation held and the Polish were holding a large part of the Soviet zone.

2　The Curzon Line was suggested by the Allied Supreme Council after World War I as a demarcation line between the Polish Republic and Bolshevik Russia. It ran north-south, to the east of Bialystok and Lublin. In the wake of the Russian Revolution and the end of World War I, Poland declared its independence and pushed its border with Russia 160 miles east; this was agreed under the Treaty of Riga. The Curzon Line was named after British Foreign Secretary Lord Curzon of Kedleston.

3　The western area of Poland had been taken over by Germany as part of the Nazis Living Space (Lebensraum) program. Polish Nationals were displaced while the Jews were first moved into ghettoes and then exterminated as part of the Holocaust. The Germans who moved into the area left ahead of the Soviet armies' advance fearing (quite rightly) revenge for atrocities committed during the invasion of the Soviet Union.

4　The Allies had planned to install a temporary administration in France back in the summer of 1944, until elections could be held. However, with many pre-war leaders and parties discredited by their associations with the Vichy Government, there was little opposition to General Charles de Gaulle. Poland faced a similar situation, only she had to deal with the Soviets rather than the United States and Great Britain.

5　They had to assess Germany's value and determine what was needed to keep the economy going to work out what counted as reparations. It changed all the calculations if part of Germany had already been 'handed over' to the Poles.

6　Giving loans to Germany so it could pay reparations after World War I.

territory. The western frontier question was open and the Soviet Union was not bound. The President repeated: "You are not?" Stalin replied: "No."

Churchill had a good deal to say about the actual line, but gathered it was not the time for saying it. Truman said it was not possible for them to settle the question because it was a matter for the peace conference. Stalin countered it would be very difficult to restore a German administration to this area.[7]

Stalin wanted the President to understand the Russian conception, which it adhered to both in war and occupation. An army cared only for its efforts in fighting a war but it needed a quiet rear so it could win and advance. An army could not fight the enemy *and* the rear. It fought well if the rear was quiet and better if the rear was friendly.[8] Even if the Germans had not fled, it would have been difficult to set up a German administration in these areas since the majority of the population were Polish.[9] He asked the President to imagine the establishment of a German administration that would stab one in the back, while the Poles received the Soviet army enthusiastically. Since such a situation existed, it was natural the Soviet Government set up an administration of friends.

Truman agreed but pointed out there were other aspects to the matter. Stalin insisted there was no other way out. Soviet action did not imply the Russians had settled the question themselves and if the President did not agree, the question should be suspended. Churchill asked whether the question could be suspended because there was the urgent question of supply. The region in question was an important source of food for Germany. Stalin asked who would work to produce the grain and who would plough the fields; this had to be borne in mind.[10]

Truman said each of them was stating his own point of view in a friendly way. The question was not one of who occupied an area, but a question of the occupation of Germany. The Americans occupied their zone, the British theirs, the French theirs, and the Soviet Union should occupy theirs. There was no objection to a discussion on the western frontier. The President did not believe they were far apart on this matter.

Stalin insisted the areas constituted German territory on paper, but practically, they were Polish territories since there was no German population. Truman remarked that nine million Germans was a lot but Stalin replied they had all

---

7   The Polish administration had been removed in the autumn of 1939 (and in many cases members had been executed). Members of the German administration had left ahead of the Soviet armies, fearing for their lives.

8   Stalin may have been remembering over half a million men and women who fought as partisans behind the Axis lines between 1941 and 1945. Not only did they engage in acts of sabotage on supply lines, they also tied up tens of thousands of troops. Their sabotage and intelligence-gathering activities were often linked to large-scale offensives during the later stages of the war.

9   In the aftermath of World War I the Greater Polish Uprising, starting in December 1918 and ending when the Treaty of Versailles was signed in June 1919, resulted in the creation of the state of Poland. It received Posen, the eastern part of Upper Silesia, most of West Prussia and a small part of East Prussia (creating the Polish Corridor).

10 The areas occupied by the Poles were agricultural and the traditional areas for producing a lot of Germany's grain. However, the Germans had either left or died and the Poles were not likely to want to hand over the harvest.

fled.[1] Churchill said if this was true, they had to consider how to feed them in the regions where they had fled, because the produce of the land they had left was not available to nourish Germany.[2] There were figures showing there were about 2½ million Germans left in the area and the figures had to be explored.

Churchill's understanding was that a quarter of the total arable land of 1937 Germany[3] would be alienated from the German area under the Soviet plan for Poland; that was a tremendous amount. While three to four million people would be moved from east of the Curzon line, the pre-war population of the German territory to be transferred amounted to 8½ million. It was a serious matter to carry out wholesale transfers of German populations, burdening the remainder of Germany with their care while cutting off their food supply.

Truman asked where they would be if they gave the Saar and the Ruhr to France.[4] Stalin replied the Soviet Government had not made a decision regarding French claims but had done so on the western frontier of Poland. Stalin said the questions of frontiers had been up for discussion but they were now talking about food supplies; he had no objection.[5] Churchill said he was only pointing out the implications of the question. Stalin said the Soviet Union fully appreciated the burden and admitted there were difficulties arising from the transfer of this territory but the German people were principally to blame for these difficulties.[6]

Churchill quoted the figure of 8½ million but there had been several call-ups during the war and the rest of the population had left before the Soviet Army. For example, only 8,000 remained out of a population of 500,000 in Stettin.[7] The majority of the Germans had gone west but some had moved to Königsberg.[8] They had heard the Russians would be in Königsberg and they preferred to deal with the Russians rather than the Poles. Not a single German remained in the territory to be given to Poland. Between the Oder and the Vistula the Germans had left their fields and they were are now being cultivated by the Poles. It was unlikely the Poles would agree to the return of these Germans. The situation had to be borne in mind.[9]

Truman again declared the occupation zones should be occupied as agreed. Whether the Poles should have part of Germany could not be settled at the

1　The Germans had dealt with civilians in a brutal manner during their advance across the Soviet Union. German civilians had been led to believe by Nazi propaganda that they would face the same terror. The propaganda actually proved to be accurate in some areas where troops went on the rampage. And then the killings and deportations of those thought to be enemies of the state began.

2　They had fled ahead of the Soviet advance and moved into the British and American zones, increasing the food and fuel shortages in those areas. A lot of Germany's food came from its eastern areas, which were now under Soviet control.

3　The amount of land on which food and reparations were based.

4　Germany's two main industrial areas.

5　While Truman is trying to draw a parallel example in the West, Stalin is not prepared to discuss hypothetical arguments.

6　Stalin has no sympathy for the problems of the German people.

7　Stettin (now Szczecin, a port on the northwest Polish border with Germany) still only has a population of 400,000.

8　Named Kaliningrad in 1946 in memory of Mikhail I. Kalinin (1875-1946), nominal head of state of Russia and later of the Soviet Union, from 1919 to 1946. All Germans were expelled after the war and the city was repopulated with Russians.

9　The occupying Soviet and Polish Communist military authorities started to relocate people from the east to the west even before the Potsdam Conference; they were known as the wild expulsions. The Polish Communists stated "We must expel all the Germans because countries are built on national lines and not on multinational ones."

Conference. Churchill agreed to compensation for Poland at the expense of Germany for the territory taken from the east of the Curzon Line. However, he had thought a balance would be maintained. Poland was now taking far more territory than she had lost and that was not good for Europe. Millions of people would be moved across the Curzon Line and other millions would be moved elsewhere. These vast transfers constituted a great shock to the country. It brought about a position not possible for him and he did not believe it was good for Poland.[10] If it was true the Germans had run away, they should be encouraged to come back. Poland, which owed all to the Great Powers, had no right to bring about a catastrophe. Truman emphasized these things because he wanted Stalin to see their difficulties; they saw his. They did not want to be left with a German population deprived of sources of food supply. Take the immense population of the Ruhr in the British zone. They could be confronted with a condition similar to the German concentration camps if they did not find food, only on a far larger scale.[11]

Stalin said Germany had always imported food and it would have to continue. Churchill replied they would if their feeding grounds were taken and Stalin countered they could buy food from the Poles. Churchill insisted he did not admit the territory was Polish. Stalin said it was inhabited by Poles who cultivated the fields, not by Germans. It was impossible to ask the Poles to cultivate the fields and give the food to the Germans.

Churchill said conditions in this great area where the Poles had been introduced were most peculiar. He understood the Poles were selling Silesian coal to Sweden while England was facing a fireless winter.[12] Great Britain stood on the general principle that food supplies from the 1937 German territories should be available to the whole German people in proportion to their number, irrespective of where the food was produced.

Stalin said the Soviet Union was purchasing coal from Poland because it had coal shortages. He then asked who would produce the coal; the Germans would not, the Poles were producing the coal. Churchill said, "You mean the Silesians?"[13] Stalin replied they had all fled. Churchill remarked they had fled from fright and could now return. Stalin said they were reluctant to return and the Soviet Union was not in sympathy with them. He was afraid the Poles would hang them if they returned.[14]

Churchill had been deeply impressed by Stalin's statement about the mistake of letting past bitterness influence future problems. They should not have a mass of people dumped on them, while the Poles acquired the food the Germans needed. Stalin

---

10 In August the communist-dominated Polish government ceded eastern Poland to the Ukrainian Soviet Socialist Republic and the Byelorussian Soviet Socialist Republic. 600,000 people were deported and another 170,000 were killed in partisan battles between the Ukrainian Insurgent Army and the Soviet Army from 1944 to 1952.

11 Thousands of deaths through starvation, diseases and bad weather come the winter. The Allies already had tens of thousands of prisoners of war held in makeshift camps and they were struggling to house and feed them; many died from malnutrition and disease.

12 The winter of 1947 would be one of the harshest on record. Coal stocks at the power stations were already low and snow stopped supplies getting through, resulting in power cuts. Widespread flooding followed in the thaws and the Army and foreign aid agencies had to help with humanitarian aid.

13 As parts of Silesia were still officially part of 1937 Germany.

14 Strong words indeed, but true.

replied what he had said yesterday did not apply to war criminals. Churchill said surely 8½ million people were not war criminals. Stalin had in mind the proprietors.[1]

Truman said it seemed to be an accomplished fact that a large piece of Germany has been given to the Poles. The United States was short of coal but had made arrangements to ship considerable quantities to Europe. The Silesian mines were a part of Germany for reparations and feeding purposes. Under these conditions they could talk about boundaries but the Poles had no right to take the territory and remove it from the German economy. Truman asked if the zones were only valid until the peace conference; or were they giving Germany away piecemeal?

Stalin insisted no one could exploit the region but the Poles. Russia was short of labour and there were no Germans there; apparently German propaganda had carried the day.[2] Either all production would stop or the Poles would operate it. The Poles had their own rich coal areas and Silesia had been added. The Poles were now working the mines and they could not take their coal for nothing. Churchill said large numbers of Polish miners had always worked in the Silesian mines. There was no objection to the mines being operated as an agency of the Soviet Government but not for the Polish Government. Stalin said this was impossible because it would disturb normal relations between the two states.

Stalin wanted to draw Churchill's attention to the serious German shortage of labour. Most enterprises during the advance of the Soviet army employed foreign labour.[3] When Russian troops entered, the foreign labour was freed and went home. He asked, "Where had the German workers gone? They had either been killed or captured."

A vast German industry existed with few German labourers and everything had fallen to pieces before the Soviet Army. Either enterprises remained closed or the local Poles should be given a chance to work. This was not a result of deliberate policy but the result of the situation. No one but Germany was to blame.

Stalin agreed the Polish Provisional Government's proposal for territory on its western frontier would create difficulties for Germany. Churchill interrupted with "For us all". Stalin said their policy was to create difficulty for the Germans and to make it difficult for German power to rise again. It was better to make difficulties for the Germans than for the Poles.

Truman said it was bad to create difficulties for the Allies. Stalin said the less industry Germany had, the greater the market would be for American and British goods. He asked, "What was the best?" They had brought the state which competed with their countries to its knees. Germany was a dangerous business rival because she lowered living standards.[4] Churchill said they did not wish to be confronted by a mass of starving people. Stalin replied, "There will be none."

---

1   In other words, the administrators of the regime.
2   Nazi propaganda stating that the Soviet hordes would seek revenge; and in many cases it was right.
3   Slave labour under the concentration camp system. Tens of thousands of people had been taken from their homes to work for the Nazi regime while Germans had joined their armed forces. The forced labourers who had survived were now considered Displaced Persons (DPs), free to return home. The Germans who had joined the armed forces were either dead, injured or in POW camps. No one was left to work in the industries, particularly those producing food and coal.
4   An interesting insight into Stalin's view of Germany as an economy.

Churchill said Mr. Attlee[5] wished to make a statement. Attlee said that aside from the boundaries between Germany and Poland, they were faced with a country in chaos and one which depended to a considerable extent for coal and food on the eastern area partly inhabited by Poles. Pending the final settlement, the resources of 1937 Germany would have to bear a first charge on the sustenance of the whole people. If part of Germany was detached, it would be a very heavy burden on the powers charged with the occupation of the western and southern zones.[6] Any labour needed to exploit the eastern areas should be made available from the rest of Germany, including released army forces (POWs). They should be directed to where they could work most usefully. The Allies should not be confronted by an impossibly difficult situation.

Stalin reminded Attlee that Poland was also an ally. Attlee replied it was true but it should not be compensated at the expense of the rest of the Allies. Truman could not agree to the separation of the eastern part of Germany under these circumstances. It had to be considered in connection with reparations and the supply problems of the whole German people.

Stalin said "Are we through today?" Truman replied the Conference had reached an impasse. Churchill said while they were not through, there were more agreeable things to come and he suggested later consideration. The President announced the Conference adjourned.

Fourth Meeting of the Economic Subcommittee
No record of the meeting.

22 July
Fifth Foreign Ministers Meeting
Implementation of the Yalta Agreement on liberated Europe; German economic questions; Industrial equipment in Romania; Agenda for the Big Three.

22 July: Sixth Terminal Meeting
Stalin announced that the withdrawal of the Soviet troops in Austria had begun. They would withdraw about 100 kilometres and the movement would be completed by July 24. Churchill was pleased Stalin had carried out his agreement so quickly. Truman was also appreciative. Stalin replied it had merely been their duty.

The Western Frontier of Poland
All delegations maintained their views, so Stalin said the question remained unsettled. Truman proposed to proceed to the next question but Churchill asked if this meant nothing would be done. Truman said it could be brought up again, while Churchill said they had to hope it would be ripe for discussion before their departure. Stalin suggested they complied with the Polish Government's request but Churchill said it was totally unacceptable. Stalin asked why and Churchill listed the following:

---

5   Clement Attlee, leader of the British Labour Party and Deputy Prime Minister to Churchill in the wartime coalition government.
6   The British and American zones.

1) It had been agreed boundaries should be determined at the peace conference.

2) It was not advantageous for Poland to take so much German territory.

3) It would rupture the Germany's economic position and throw an undue burden on the occupying powers.

4) They would have a grave moral responsibility for the transfer of enormous populations. The British accepted in principle the transfer of the population from the east of the Curzon line. However, it would be wrong to transfer another 8½ million people.

5) The number of people living in the area in question was not agreed.

The British understood there were around 8 million Germans in this area but the Soviet delegation said they had already gone. This had to be cleared up.

Stalin did not intend to oppose all of Churchill's points but two were important. Germany had fuel in the Ruhr and the Rhineland, so the loss of the Silesian coal caused no great difficulty.[1] The second point was the transfer of populations. There were neither 8 nor 6 nor 3 million Germans in this area. There had been several call-ups of troops and many of these people had been killed. The few Germans left had fled before the Red Army. This could be checked.

They could arrange for representatives of the Polish Provisional Government[2] to come to the Conference and they could hear what they had to say. Stalin proposed letting the Foreign Ministers hear the Polish representatives and Truman agreed. Churchill said the Council would not meet until 1 September and Stalin replied they would have collected information by then.

Churchill said it merely transferred the problem to the Foreign Ministers and asked if the President agreed. Truman said further discussion could be had and they could take up something else while they could not agree. Churchill said he would regret sending such a grave matter to a body of less importance. Stalin suggested inviting the Poles to the meeting, something Churchill preferred because the matter was urgent, but he was concerned they would ask for more than he could accept. Stalin said if they invited the Poles, they could not accuse the Big Three of not hearing them.

Truman did not see the urgency of the matter and while it would be helpful to have a preliminary discussion, the matter would not be settled until the peace conference.[3] Churchill wanted to explain the urgency of the matter, because the situation would consolidate if the question was delayed. The Poles would be digging themselves in and making themselves the sole masters of this territory. The longer the problem remained, the harder it would be to settle. They should at least see where they stood. It was no use the Poles coming to London when the great powers did not even know the broad outline.

---

1 Silesia is a coal-rich area that was in Germany before 1945 and is now in Poland. It is on the northeast side of the Czech Republic.

2 Headed by Prime Minister Edward Osóbka-Morawski (1909-1997).

3 However, if an agreement between the three Heads of State could be made, the work of the peace conference would be much easier.

Meanwhile, the food problem remained unsettled while the burden of feeding fell upon the British and Americans. The British zone had the largest concentration of people and the smallest supply of food.[4] He was anxious to meet the practical difficulties resulting from the movement of troops. He was ready to suggest a compromise solution to cover the period until the final conclusion of peace.

Churchill had in mind a line and the Poles would occupy the territory to the east of it as a part of Poland. They would work as agents of the Soviet Government west of the line, dealing with the problem in accordance with the zones of occupation in Germany.[5]

Churchill had had several talks with Stalin since the Tehran meeting[6] and they were broadly in agreement on the line of the Oder.[7] Of course the matter could not be so simply expressed. He did not want to go as far as Stalin but they agreed the Poles should have a large amount of territory.

To wait until September to have long discussions with the Poles would leave the matter unsettled and winter would be upon them. Churchill wanted an agreement on principle and wanted the Foreign Ministers to come to a general understanding. Otherwise, the three powers would be left with all of their difficulties unsolved and a solution would be virtually impossible after several months.[8] Churchill asked what would happen in Berlin if the matter was referred to the Foreign Ministers; it obtained part of its coal from the Silesian mines. Stalin interrupted to say Berlin drew its coal from Zwickau in Saxony.[9] They should let the Ruhr supply the coal but he thought Zwickau would be enough. There was good coal there and they made briquettes out of brown coal.[10] Churchill repeated that only a portion of the Berlin coal came from the Silesian mines.

Truman read the part of the Yalta Declaration concerning Poland's western frontier. Poland had been assigned a zone of occupation in Germany and there were now five occupying powers. They could assign a zone to Poland but he did not like how Poland had occupied a zone without any discussion between the three powers. Truman believed the main problem was the Poles' occupation of Germany and that was his position yesterday, that was his position today, and that would be his position tomorrow.[11] Stalin said not only the Poles were to blame – circumstances and the Russians were to blame.[12] Truman agreed.

Stalin said if they were not bored with the question of frontiers, he would like to make a further statement based on the Crimean Conference decision.

---

4   The northwest part of Germany included the heavily populated Ruhr area.
5   A compromise in which the Poles were allowed to administer the area they would definitely be given by the peace conference and an area they would administer on behalf of the Soviets. The actual border would be decided at the peace conference.
6   The EUREKA Conference in Iran at the end of November 1943.
7   The Oder River would form nearly 150 miles of the border between postwar Germany and Poland, as part of the Oder-Neisse Line.
8   The longer the decision was postponed, the harder it would be to change how the area was being administered.
9   Southwest of Dresden, near the Czech Republic border.
10 Brown coal, or lignite, has characteristics somewhere between coal and peat. It is the 'lowest' form of coal but 25 per cent of Germany's power still comes from lignite-fuelled plants.
11 Poland getting territory was not the problem; it was the manner in which it had assumed authority in the area.
12 The Germans leaving the area, the needs of the Soviet army there and the Poles making the most of the grain harvest and coal mines had all contributed. It did of course work in the Soviets' favour rather than the Western Allies.

They were bound to hear the Government of National Unity's[1] opinion about its western frontiers, after it had been formed. They could either approve the Polish proposal or hear the Poles and settle the question. Churchill agreed. Stalin thought it was beneficial to settle the matter now. Stalin reminded Truman and Churchill that they wanted the western frontier along the Oder to where the Eastern Neisse joined the Oder and he disagreed.[2] It left Stettin, Breslau, and the region west of Breslau on the German side. Stalin insisted on the Western Neisse. They could settle the matter or they could put it off, but they could not ignore it.

Churchill withdrew any objection to the Poles attending, so they could reach a temporary practical solution until the peace conference. Truman agreed but did not wish to go into the matter. Stalin said this was satisfactory. Churchill said the Foreign Ministers should report to the Big Three and they all agreed.

Trusteeship[3]

Molotov said the trusteeship system had been settled in principle by the San Francisco Charter and they now had to make progress on specific territories.[4] They could discuss Italy's colonies in Africa and the Mediterranean first and they had two alternative proposals that could be referred to the Foreign Ministers.

Secondly, there was the question of territories under mandate from the League of Nations.[5] Eden asked which ones he had in mind, there were only a few left to England and France.[6] Molotov replied it was worthy of their attention and thought they should also exchange views on Korea.[7] Churchill was ready to exchange views on any subject, but if they reached no agreement there would have simply been an interesting discussion. His impression was the existing mandates had been dealt with at San Francisco.[8]

---

1   The Provisional Government of National Unity (Tymczasowy Rzad Jednosci Narodowej, or TRJN) had been formed by the State National Council (Krajowa Rada Narodowa) on 28 June 1945. It was a coalition government of the Polish communists and the Polish Government-in-exile as agree during the Yalta Conference (ARGONAUT) in February 1945. However, the Polish Government-in-exile didn't recognize the TRJN and the Polish communists had no intention of sharing power or carrying out free elections.

2   South from Stettin (now Szczecin) on the Baltic Sea coast, 120 miles south along the River Oder to Frankfurt. The River Oder then heads west but the border follows the tributary, the River Neisse, another 130 miles south to the Czechoslovakian border (now the Czech Republic).

3   The United Nations trusteeships replaced the mandates of the League of Nations. Trusteeships would ensure the territories were administered in the best interests of the population, and international peace and security.

4   At the end of the first meeting of the UN the United Nations Charter (or San Francisco Conference Charter) was signed on 28 June 1945 by 50 of the original 51 members (Poland signed it two months later). It was split into nineteen Chapters. It called for the maintenance of peace, international security and respect for human rights with the United Nations acting as a mediator of disputes and imposer of sanctions.

5   Following World War I the League of Nations had transferred the control of some territories from one country to another. They were colonies of the Axis nations in the Middle East, Africa and the Pacific. Following the disbandment of the League of Nations in 1945, the mandates were placed under the United Nations' trusteeship subject to new agreements.

6   French-controlled Syria and Lebanon, British-controlled Palestine (now Israel), Transjordan (now Jordan) and Mesopotamia (now Iraq) in the Middle East.

7   The unconditional surrender of Japan led to Korea being divided into two occupation zones on 8 September 1945. The United States administered the southern half of the peninsula while the Soviet Union took over the area north of the 38th Parallel. The Provisional Government was ignored. The temporary arrangement became permanent because of deadlock over the decision to establish a national government and in September 1947 the Korean question was submitted to the United Nations General Assembly.

8   By the United Nations.

Truman read Article 77 of the proposed Charter of the United Nations which dealt with the question of trusteeships. He understood the Soviet Government wished to discuss the matter under section 2 of the Article.[9] He was ready to refer it to the Foreign Ministers. Churchill said they had agreed to raise the project at San Francisco and nothing more. He doubted their opinion would be the best way to deal with it, if it was in the hands of the World Organization. Truman said it was just as appropriate to discuss the matter as it was to discuss Poland or anything else. Churchill said Poland was not being dealt with by the International Organization. Truman replied it would be.

Molotov said the matter should be considered but the final decision should be taken at the peace conference, the same as Poland's case. Churchill said their position had been settled secretly at Yalta and publicly at San Francisco and it could not be changed. Truman told Churchill the British position was amply protected by another Article of the Charter and he did not see why it could not be discussed. Molotov had learned Italy had lost its colonies once and for all from the foreign press.[10] The question was, who had received them and where had this matter been decided? Churchill referred to the heavy losses the British had suffered and the victories the British Army had achieved, conquering all of the Italian colonies except Tunisia. Truman inquired "All?" Molotov reminded them the Red Army had conquered Berlin.[11]

Churchill said he meant Libya, Cyrenaica[12] and Tripoli. They had conquered them at a time when they were under heavy attacks and were without help, at least during the early stages. Stalin said no one denied this. Churchill replied they were not expecting to gain out of the war and they had suffered terrible losses. Their losses had not been so heavy in human life as those of their gallant Soviet allies but they came out of the war a great debtor to the world.

Britain would not regain naval equality with the United States because they had built only one capital ship during the war and had lost ten or twelve. But in spite of the heavy losses, they had made no territorial claims; no Königsberg, no Baltic states – nothing. So they approached the question of the Italian colonies with complete rectitude. Eden regarded Italy as having lost the colonies, that meant Italy had no claim of right to these colonies. This did not stop the peace conference considering if some of the colonies should be restored to Italy.[13]

Churchill did not favour the proposal but it was entirely open for discussion in the Council of Foreign Ministers and the final peace settlement. Having visited Tripoli and Cyrenaica, he had seen the admirable reclamation work done by the

---

9   Article 77, Section 1: The trusteeship system shall apply to such territories in the following categories: a) territories now held under mandate; b) territories which may be detached from enemy states as a result of the Second World War; and c) territories voluntarily placed under the system by states responsible for their administration.
10 Libya and Abyssinia. Albania, Yugoslavia and the Dodecanese had been captured by Germany when Italy switched to the Allies in September 1943.
11 So if the British were getting the Italian territories they had captured, would the Soviets get Berlin?
12 Cyrenaica is the eastern coastal region of Libya.
13 Italy had lost its territories and while she could not ask for them back, she could be given them back.

Italians.[1] While they did not declare themselves in favour of restoration, neither had they excluded it from the discussion.

At present, the British held these colonies. Who wanted them? If there were claimants they should put forward their claims. Truman said the United States did not want them, nor want a trusteeship over them; they had enough poor Italians to feed. Churchill had wondered if any of these colonies were suitable as a place of settlement for the Jews, but those he had discussed the matter with had not been interested.[2] Churchill said the British had great interests in the Mediterranean and any marked alteration in the status quo there would need long and careful examination.

Molotov wanted the Conference to consider the Soviet proposals. Churchill could not see what their Soviet allies wanted. Did Stalin wish to put a claim on one of these Italian colonies? Stalin wanted to know if Italy would lose her colonies and whether they could decide what states they would be transferred to for trusteeship. They could wait if it was too early to deal with the matter. Churchill had not considered the possibility of the Soviet Union wanting a large tract of the African shore. If so, it would have to be considered in relation to many other problems.

Stalin said the Soviet delegation at San Francisco had indicated they were anxious to receive mandates for certain territories in a communication to Secretary Stettinius.[3] Churchill said the British did not seek territory. Stalin again asked who would receive the colonies. Churchill said they had to decide if they should be taken, as they had a right to do, and then decide who they would be assigned to. This question belonged to the peace treaty. The ultimate administration belonged to the United Nations Organization.[4]

Stalin asked if Churchill was suggesting they were not competent to settle the question. Churchill replied no; it was for the peace conference but it would facilitate matters if they agreed. Stalin said they were proposing to consider the matter and Churchill replied that is what they were doing. Stalin asked why Churchill objected to the Soviet proposal. Churchill replied he was not objecting and if Stalin could say what he wanted, he would address himself to the question. Stalin said the matter did not lie with him; the question was set forth in the Soviet paper.

Truman said the Soviet proposal was for the Foreign Ministers to discuss the matter and he did not object. Churchill did not object but thought they were throwing a lot of work on the Foreign Ministers. But there were many more urgent matters to discuss and it was agreed to refer the matter to the Foreign Ministers.

---

1   Italian Libya had been a unified colony of Cyrenaica, Tripolitania and Fezzan since 1934. The Italians had seized power by repressing the Libyan resistance movement, executing its leaders and incarcerating 100,000 people in concentration camps.
2   Britain had been made aware of its dependence on Arab oil during the war and this made her more interested in improving relations with the Arabs than with helping the Jews establish a new homeland. The new Labour government decided to maintain restrictions on immigration to Palestine but illegal immigration continued. Many Jews came from Europe (over 100,000 from Poland) and from Arab countries determined to secure their land, fighting a guerrilla war against the British.
3   Edward R. Stettinius Jr. (1900-1949), US Secretary of State.
4   Tripolitania and Cyrenaica were under British administration, while the French controlled Fezza from 1943 to 1951. Libya declared its independence in December 1951 as the United Kingdom of Libya, a constitutional and hereditary monarchy under King Idris (1889-1983), Libya's only monarch. A British invasion in January 1941 of Italian East Africa restored Ethiopian independence.

Turkey

Churchill said this was not the first time he had discussed Turkey with Stalin. But it had become important because of the need to modify the Montreux Convention. He agreed revisions had to be made with all the signatories except Japan. Churchill was ready to welcome an arrangement for the free movement of Russian ships, naval or merchant, through the Black Sea and opened the discussion on the basis of a friendly agreement.

Churchill also wished to impress the importance of not alarming Turkey on Stalin. Undoubtedly, Turkey was alarmed by a strong concentration of Bulgarian and Soviet troops in Bulgaria[5] and by the continuous attacks in the Soviet press and radio. They were also alarmed by conversations between the Turkish Ambassador and Molotov over the modifications of Turkey's eastern frontier and a new Soviet base in the Straits. Turkey had been left fearing for the integrity of her empire and questioning her power to defend Constantinople.[6]

Churchill understood the Soviet Government was not making demands on Turkey but the Turks had asked for an alliance. Molotov had no objection to an alliance subject to certain conditions but there were two questions. Firstly, they each undertook to defend the frontiers of both states. Churchill had mentioned sections of their frontiers which they considered unjust. A portion of their territory had been torn from Soviet Armenia and Soviet Georgia in 1921.[7] The second question concerned the Black Sea Straits. The Soviet Union had repeatedly told their allies they were not satisfied with the Montreux Convention. The rights of the Soviet Union under this Convention were equal to those of the Japanese Emperor and this did not correspond to the present situation.[8] Molotov had made it clear the Russians were ready to conclude an alliance if these issues were settled. They were prepared to settle any questions the Turks had and would agree on the Straits alone if the Turkish Government was not prepared to settle both questions.

Churchill said this was an important document, which went far beyond the conversations between Eden and himself and Stalin and Molotov. But different questions were raised when they asked for a Russian base in the Straits. The document also said that no one had anything to do with the Bosphorus and the Dardanelles except Russia and Turkey. He was certain Turkey would never agree to the proposal.

Molotov said similar treaties had existed in the past between Russia and Turkey. Churchill asked if he meant the question of a Russian base in the Black Sea

---

5   Soviet troops had entered Bulgaria in September 1944 and shortly afterwards Bulgarian troops helped liberate parts of Serbia, Macedonia and Hungary. A communist regime headed by Georgi Dimitrov (1882-1949) succeeded the Fatherland Front headed by Kimon Georgiev (1882-1969) in 1946.

6   Now Istanbul. Soviet ships would have to sail through the Dardanelles and then along the Bosphorus River to reach the Black Sea. The Bosphorus separated the two halves of the Turkish capital. The Bosphorus had been closed during the Second World War until Turkey joined the Allies in February 1945.

7   The Treaty of Kars in October 1921 handed over territories to Turkey. Most of them had been taken by Imperial Russia from the Ottoman Empire following the war in 1877–1878.

8   The Japanese had been on the Allied side and had signed the Montreux Treaty. So even though Russia needed access to its southern ports in the Black Sea and Japan had no need of it, they had the same rights over the Straits.

Straits, but Molotov meant the treaties of 1805 and 1833, which had settled the Straits question between Turkey and Russia.[1] Churchill would have to ask his staff to look up these ancient treaties but the British were not prepared to push Turkey to accept these proposals. He stood by his conversations with Stalin when he expressed his willingness to press for a revision of the Montreux Convention. That agreement still stood, but he felt quite free with regard to these new proposals. Stalin said yes, he was free. Truman was not ready to express an opinion and suggested deferring the question. This was agreed to.

Treatment of Soviet Prisoners in a British Camp in Italy

Molotov said Camp 5 near Rimini, which was under British control, contained Ukrainians.[2] The first British statement said there were only 150 prisoners but their representatives had found 10,000 and 665 were willing to return to their native country. Churchill asked where he had obtained the figures because the British did not make false statements. Molotov understood the British had formed a division of twelve regiments of these Ukrainians, with officers selected from those who served in the ranks of the German army.

Churchill welcomed the Russians to inspect all of their camps but perhaps some of the men were Polish. Molotov replied there were only Ukrainians in the camp and added they had received a telegram from General Golikov,[3] who was in charge of repatriating Soviet prisoners, that day. Churchill promised to investigate the matter. The meeting adjourned.

23 July

Sixth Foreign Ministers Meeting

Reparations; Trusteeships; Directives to Allied commanders-in-chief in Germany; Solving urgent European economic problems; Iran; Tangier; Invitations to China and France; Agenda for the Big Three.

Tenth Combined Chiefs of Staff Meeting

Captured passenger ships and British troop ships in the US trans-Atlantic program; Command of Allied ships in the Seventh US Fleet.

Informal Foreign Ministers Meeting

War booty, reparations and the cost of feeding the German people.

---

1 The 1805 treaty allowed Russian and Turkish warships through the Straits but prohibited others. Turkey revoked the right the following year and the Russo-Turkish War (1806-1812) followed soon afterwards. The 1833 Treaty of Unkiar Skelessi (Hunkar Iskelesi) obligated Turkey to close the Dardanelles to warships of other countries if Russia wanted; it virtually restored the Russo-Turkish alliance.

2 The POWs were from the 1st Ukrainian Division of the Ukrainian National Army (UNA). Until recently it was known as the 14th Waffen SS Grenadier-Division (previously the Galizien Division). They were interned at Camp 5 near Rimini, Italy, until 1947.

3 General Filipp I. Golikov (1900-1980) Assistant Minister of Defence, responsible for the repatriation of Soviet prisoners of war. The Nazis' treatment of Soviet POWs resulted in the deaths of around 3.4 million, or 60 per cent. Many were worked to death or executed in the concentration and extermination camps system. Of the 1.8 million who survived, between 230,000 and 360,000 were accused of collaborating with the enemy and were sent to labour battalions or the Gulag, corrective labour camps.

23 July: Seventh Terminal Meeting
Turkey and the Black Sea

Truman did not think Churchill had finished on the subject. Churchill replied he had finished when he said he could not consent to a Russian base in the Straits; he did not think Turkey would agree. Stalin stated Churchill had said the Russians had frightened the Turks by concentrating too many troops in Bulgaria but his information was out-of-date. Russia had fewer troops in Bulgaria than the British had in Greece.[4] Churchill asked how many troops Stalin thought the British had in Greece. He said five divisions; Churchill replied only two. Stalin asked how strong the British divisions were. Churchill said there were about 40,000 troops altogether and Stalin replied they had about 30,000.

Churchill hoped the meeting would hear Field Marshal Alexander give the figures. Stalin was not seeking accuracy and believed Churchill 100%; General Antonov[5] could make a detailed report if necessary. The Turks had about 23 divisions and they had nothing to be afraid of.

As to rectifying the frontiers, perhaps the possible restoration of the pre-war frontiers which existed under the Czar had frightened the Turks.[6] The subject was brought up because the Turks raised the question of an alliance. An alliance meant the Soviet Union would defend Turkey's frontiers, just as Turkey would defend the Soviet Union's frontiers. But the frontiers were incorrect in the Soviet opinion and they had told the Turks the frontiers had to be rectified if there was to be an alliance. If not, the question of an alliance would be dropped. What was there to be afraid of?

The third question was that of the Straits and the position of such a great state as the Soviet Union was the following. The Montreux Convention[7] had been decided against Russia and they considered it inimical. Turkey had the right to block the Straits to any shipping, not only if Turkey was at war but if there was a threat of war; the Convention also let Turkey decide when this threat appeared.[8] It left the Russians with the same rights in the Straits as the Japanese Emperor.[9] This was ridiculous, but it was a fact. The result was a small state supported by Great Britain held a great state by the throat and gave it no outlet. Stalin said they could imagine what commotion there would be in England if a similar regime existed in Gibraltar or in the Suez Canal, or in the United States if such a regime existed in the Panama Canal.[10] So the point at issue was to allow Soviet shipping to pass freely to and from the Black Sea. Turkey was too weak to guarantee the

---

4 Bulgaria's southeast border was with Turkey.
5 General Aleksei I. Antonov (1896–1962), Chief of Staff of the Soviet Army.
6 Two areas in northeast Turkey; the area of Kars, formerly in Armenia, as well as Ardahan (now called Göle), formerly in Georgia.
7 The 1936 Montreux Convention gave Turkey control of the Bosphorus Straits and the Dardanelles. It also allowed Turkey to remilitarise the Straits. While civilian access to the Black Sea was unrestricted, military access was restricted to the Black Sea states.
8 Turkey could effectively close access to the Black Sea when she wanted.
9 The Japanese had signed the Montreux Convention and their rights had not been changed.
10 The Panama Canal Zone was owned and controlled by the United States from 1903 to 1979. It gives rapid access between the western and eastern seaboards of North America.

possibility of free passage if complications arose, so the Soviet Union wanted to see the Straits defended by force, as the American navy defended the Panama Canal and the British navy guaranteed the Suez Canal.

Stalin said if naval bases in the Straits were unacceptable to the Turks, then let the Soviet Union have another base where the Russian fleet could repair and refuel.[1] She could also protect the Straits in cooperation with her allies. It was ridiculous to let the situation continue.

Truman wanted to revise the Montreux Convention but the Straits should be a free waterway open to the whole world and should be guaranteed by all of them. After a long study of history, he had come to the conclusion that all the wars of the last 200 years had originated in the area from the Black Sea to the Baltic and from the eastern frontier of France to the western frontier of Russia.[2] In the last two instances, the peace of the whole world had been overturned; by Austria in the case of the previous war,[3] and by Germany in the case of this war.

Truman thought it should be for them and the coming peace conference to see it did not happen again. This could be accomplished by arranging for the free passage of goods and vessels through the Straits, the same as in American waters. He wanted all countries to have free access to all the seas of the world. Truman then read his paper on the free and unrestricted navigation of inland waterways.

Truman did not want another war 25 years from then over the Straits or the Danube. Their ambition was to have an economically sound Europe that could support itself. He wanted a Europe which made Russia, England, France and all other countries in it happy and with which the United States could trade and be happy as well as prosperous. He thought his proposal was a step in that direction. Truman said the question of territorial concessions was a Turkish and Russian dispute that they had to settle themselves and which Stalin had said he was willing to do. But the question of the Black Sea Straits concerned the United States and the whole world.

Churchill strongly supported Stalin's wish for a revision of the Montreux Convention, to secure free and unrestricted navigation of the Straits by merchant and war ships alike in peace or war. He agreed with Truman, that it should be guaranteed by all of them. A guarantee by the Great Powers and the interested powers would certainly be effective. He earnestly hoped Stalin would consider this alternative instead of a base in close proximity to Constantinople.[4]

With regard to the other waterways, they were in full accord with Truman's general line: that the Kiel Canal[5] should be free and open and guaranteed by all the Great Powers. He also attached great importance to the free navigation of the

---

1   A base in the Mediterranean where Soviet ships could refuel and carry out maintenance without having to pass through the Straits.

2   For example the Napoleonic Wars (1803–1815), the Russo-Turkish War (1828–1829), the Austro-Prussian War (1866) the Franco-Prussian War (1870–1871), to name but a few. But discounting the American Civil War of course.

3   With reference to the assassination of the heir to the Austro-Hungarian throne, Archduke Franz Ferdinand of Austria (1863-1914), in Sarajevo, Bosnia, on 28 June 1914.

4   The Soviet Union had several naval bases in the eastern Mediterranean during the Cold War. It still has a maintenance naval base at Tartus in Syria.

5   In northern Germany, across the base of the Danish Peninsula.

Danube and the Rhine. He felt there was a great measure of agreement between the Three Powers represented at the Conference.

The Transfer of Königsberg to the Soviet Union

Stalin said the Russians complained that all the Baltic ports froze and it was necessary to have at least one ice-free port at the expense of Germany. Stalin's argument was the Russians had lost so much blood they were anxious to have some piece of German territory to give some small satisfaction to the tens of millions of their inhabitants who had suffered. Neither Roosevelt nor Churchill had raised any objections and this question had been agreed upon by the three of them. They were anxious to see this agreement approved at this Conference. Truman agreed in principle.[6]

Churchill said the matter had been raised at Tehran and he had also discussed it with Stalin in October 1944 in Moscow. He had spoken about the Soviet wish to secure Königsberg in Parliament and His Majesty's Government was in sympathy with their wish. The only question was the legality behind the transfer. They all had to admit East Prussia did not exist and Königsberg was not under the authority of the Allied Control Council in Germany. They also had to recognize the incorporation of Lithuania into the Soviet Union. All these matters really belonged to the final peace settlement.

His Majesty's Government supported the Soviet wish to have the port incorporated into the Soviet Union but they had not examined the Soviet line on a map. This could be examined at the peace conference. Stalin replied they were suggesting nothing more at the present time.[7]

Syria and Lebanon

Churchill said the burden of defending Syria and Lebanon had fallen on the shoulders of the British but they did not wish to receive any advantage there not enjoyed by other powers. At the time, they entered Syria and Lebanon to throw out the Germans and Vichy troops.[8] They had made an arrangement with the French in which they both recognized Syria and Lebanon. The British did not object to France having a favoured position with the new independent governments of those countries because of their long historical connections.

The British had told General de Gaulle they would withdraw their troops the moment he made a satisfactory treaty with Syria[9] and Lebanon.[10] If they withdrew

---

6 He wanted ethnic issues studied first.

7 Königsberg was transferred to the Soviet Union and renamed Kaliningrad in July 1946. The German population was deported to the Western Zones of occupied Europe or to the Siberian labour camps, where half died from starvation and disease. The nearby port of Pillau was renamed Baltiysk.

8 Syria and Lebanon had been under the control of Vichy French since the fall of France in the summer of 1940. The British and Free French took control of the country following the Syria–Lebanon campaign in the summer of 1941, codename EXPORTER.

9 Syria proclaimed its independence in 1941 but it was not recognized as an independent republic until 1 January 1944. There were protests in 1945 over the slow French withdrawal, until pressure from Syrian nationalist groups forced the French to evacuate the last of their troops in April 1946.

10 In November 1941 General Georges Catroux (1877-1969) announced Lebanon would become independent under the authority of the Free French government. Elections were held in November 1943 and the new Lebanese government unilaterally abolished the mandate. The French threw the new government members into prison but they were released due to international pressure and France accepted Lebanon's independence. The Allies kept the region under control until the last French troops withdrew in 1946.

their troops now, there would be a massacre of the French civilians and the small number of troops there. They would not like to see this because it would lead to great excitement throughout the Arab world. Churchill said it would affect their task of keeping the peace in Saudi Arabia and Iraq and there would be a great outbreak of turbulence and warfare, which might affect Egypt. There could not be a worse moment for creating such a disturbance in the Arab world. It would endanger their lines of communication through the Suez Canal while the United States and Great Britain were using it in the war against Japan.

General de Gaulle had acted very unwisely in this region. Against their advice and entreaties, about 500 men had been sent to Syria and caused a serious disturbance, which had still not died away. How silly this was, for what could 500 men do? But there had been a spark and the uprising had followed immediately.[1] Iraq then wanted to go to the help of the Syrians while the entire Arabic world was convulsed with excitement. General de Gaulle later agreed to hand over the so-called Troupes Spéciales[2] to the Syrian Government.

Churchill trusted they could reach a settlement with de Gaulle, guaranteeing the independence of Syria and Lebanon; one which would reserve some recognition of the French cultural and commercial interests they had built up over such a long time. Churchill repeated Great Britain had no wish to remain there one day longer than necessary. They would be delighted to withdraw from a thankless task assumed in the interest of the Allies. But the matter rested between them and the French, and of course Syria and Lebanon. The burden had been shouldered by the British and they would not welcome the matter being reviewed by a body of this kind. Churchill said it would be a different matter if the United States wanted to take their place. Truman replied, no thank you.

Churchill said the British had sufficient troops to keep the peace and stop the outbreak of war in the area when the controversy arose. Truman asked the British to do so immediately because the United States was very interested in the line of communications through the Suez Canal to the Far East.

Truman thought no country should have special privilege. The French did not deserve a special position after the way they had stirred up all the trouble; they should all have equal rights. Stalin asked if they did not recognize any privileged position of the French in the area. Churchill replied the British did and he had promised this to the French at a time when the British were weak.[3] This was only a promise as far as the British were concerned. They had no power to bind others to it, nor had they tried to obtain special rights for the French. The British would not object if they got them and would smile benignly on the achievement.

Stalin asked who the French would obtain these special rights from. Churchill replied from Syria and Lebanon. Stalin queried, "Them alone?" and Churchill replied yes. He added the French had many schools and archaeological institutes

---

1   The Syrians were complaining about the slowness of the French withdrawal.
2   The Special Troops of the East (Troupes Spéciales du Levant) were an ethnic army under French command. Following the Allied takeover they were renamed the Levantine Force (Troupes du Levant) and there were 5000 Syrians serving in it in 1945.
3   When France had fallen to the Germans, leaving the British to take control of Syria and Lebanon, to protect the Suez Canal.

there. Many French lived there and the French even had a song which went "Nous partout pour La Syrie". Their claims dated back to the Crusades.

Churchill said the British were not embarking on a serious quarrel with the great powers on this matter. Truman replied the United States stood for equal rights for all. Churchill asked Truman if he would try and prevent the Syrians giving the French special rights. Truman had no qualms because he was sure the Syrians would not want to. Stalin said they were reluctant. Stalin thanked Churchill for his information and withdrew his proposal. Churchill and Truman thanked Stalin for this.

Iran

Stalin said the British proposals presumed the term for the presence of Allied troops in Iran had expired. The Soviets assumed it had not and would do so only until after the termination of the war against Japan; as stipulated by the treaty.[4] Truman said they had been ready to withdraw for a long time but they had many supplies in Iran and they were guarding them ready to use in the war against Japan.[5] Stalin had no objection to the presence of American and British troops in Iran but agreed troops could be withdrawn from Tehran.[6]

Churchill said only 2½ months had elapsed since the end of the war against Germany. The British wanted both sides to continue removing troops because they had promised they would go when the German war was over. Stalin wanted time to think it over. The treaty said the troops should be withdrawn not later than six months after the end of the war with Germany and her associates and that included Japan. They had until six months after the completion of the war with Japan. That gave them plenty of time.

Churchill suggested accepting the proposal to withdraw and let the Foreign Ministers discuss the matter. Truman said they were withdrawing their troops because they needed them in the Far East and they expected to be out within 60 days. Stalin said the United States was fully entitled to look after their supplies. He added, "So as to rid the United States of any worries, we promise no action will be taken by us against Iran." Truman thanked him.

Occupation of Vienna

Churchill said it appeared there were 500,000 people in Vienna. Vienna's food sources lay to the east so they would not be able to feed them. He suggested a provisional arrangement where the Russians fed them until a permanent arrangement could be worked out.

Field Marshal Alexander did not have the food to send from Italy; there was a small reserve in Villach[7] in the Klagenfurt area but there was only enough for

---

4   The Anglo-Soviet invasion of Iran in August 1941 was codenamed COUNTENANCE. It secured the Iranian oilfields and the Allied supply route to the Soviet Union. Iran was neutral but its monarch, Reza Shah Pahlavi (1878-1944), was seen as friendly towards the Axis; he was replaced by his son, Mohammad Reza Pahlavi (1919-1980).

5   Over five million tons of supplies were moved through the Persian Corridor to the Soviet Union and the British troops in the Middle East.

6   The Shah signed an alliance to supply non-military support to Britain and the Soviet Union in January 1942 but it had to end six months after the end of hostilities. In September 1943 Iran declared war on Germany.

7   Villach is near the border of Austria and Italy in what is now Slovenia.

three or four weeks. The food would have to come from the United States, if they agreed to feed these people. Churchill said this would be in addition to the population in the United States zone of Vienna. Truman replied there were about 375,000 in their zone.

Truman said their transport was almost totally engaged in transporting supplies in the Japanese war and in supplying Italy, France, Russia, and other countries in Europe. Stalin asked about the French zone but Truman did not know. Stalin said he would talk to Marshal Konev;[1] he was acquainted with the matter.

Stalin wanted to know what period they had in mind; was it until the next harvest? Churchill said the difficulty was the people in Vienna had always drawn their food from the east. Stalin said they had made an arrangement with the Austrian Government to pay for a small quantity of food until the next harvest. This would continue until August or September but he had to talk with Marshal Konev.

Churchill said Alexander's troops were entering Styria but were reluctant to enter Vienna because of the difficulty with food. Stalin asked if the food situation in Vienna was so bad now. Churchill replied they had not been there. Stalin said it did not seem to be, as far as the population was concerned.

Alexander said they were ready to go forward and take up their work if Stalin could help them with food. Stalin would let them know that evening or the next day. Churchill thanked him. Stalin said it would be good if the British and American Governments agreed to extend the authority of the Renner Government[2] to their zones. This would not imply diplomatic recognition but it would be placed in the same position as Finland. The Renner Government's authority should be extended to the British and American zones to help them collect food.[3] Truman thought they could agree as soon as they had moved in and looked into the matter.

Churchill referred to earlier in the day when he had said they had two divisions in Greece and he proposed to ask Alexander to speak on this subject. Stalin demurred; a Churchill statement could not be disputed, as he had said at the previous meeting. Churchill then wished to raise a question of procedure. He had already warned them that Mr. Attlee and he had interests to attend to in London on Thursday.[4] They had to leave by lunchtime on Wednesday, taking the Foreign Secretary with them, but they would be back for the evening sitting on the 27th. He added, "Or some of us will be back."[5] They agreed to meet on the morning before his departure. Churchill suggested the Foreign Ministers could continue

---

1   Marshal Konev has commanded the 1st Ukrainian Front as it advanced into Austria at the end of the war.
2   Karl Renner (1870-1950) was President of the Austrian Parliament before the Anschluss in 1938. He set up a provisional government just before the Third Reich collapsed, made sure Austria separated from Germany and campaigned for his country to be an independent republic.
3   The Western Allies were suspicious that the Russians in Vienna had been first to accept the Renner Government and waited until October 1945 before they recognized it.
4   There had been a General Election in Britain and the results were expected.
5   Against all (or most) expectations, Attlee's Labour Party won a landslide victory on 26 July. Attlee would attend the rest of the meetings in Churchill's place.

to meet and Sir Alexander Cadogan[6] would represent Mr. Eden in his absence. This was agreed to. The meeting adjourned.

24 July
Seventh Foreign Ministers Meeting
German economic questions and German reparations; Romanian oil equipment; European oil supplies; Implementation of the Yalta Declaration; Admission of Italy and non-admission of Spain into international organisations; Agenda for the Big Three; Poland's western frontier.

24 July: Combined Chiefs of Staff with the President and Prime Minister[7]
Truman and Churchill examined a draft of the Combined Chiefs of Staff's final report.[8]

Overall Objective
Bring about at the earliest possible date the unconditional surrender of Japan.

Overall Strategic Concept
Bring about at the earliest possible date the defeat of Japan by:
   a)   Lowering the Japanese ability and will to resist by establishing sea and air blockades, conducting intensive air bombardment, and destroying Japanese air and naval strength;
   b)   Invading and seizing objectives in the Japanese home islands as the main effort;
   c)   Conducting operations against other objectives to contribute to the main effort;
   d)   Establishing absolute military control of Japan;
   e)   Liberating Japanese-occupied territory if required.

Establish and maintain, as necessary, military control of Germany and Austria.

Basic Undertakings and Policies
   a)   Maintain the security and war-making capacity of the Western Hemisphere and the British Commonwealth.
   b)   Support the war-making capacity of forces in all areas, with first priority given to those forces in, or designated for, employment in combat areas in the war against Japan.
   c)   Maintain vital overseas lines of communication.

First priority will be given to the provision of forces and resources of the United States and Great Britain, including reorientation from the European Theatre to the Pacific and Far East. The invasion of Japan and connected operations are the supreme operations in the war against Japan. Forces and resources will be allocated to assure invasion can be accomplished at the earliest practicable date. No

---

6   Sir Alexander G.M. Cadogan (1884-1968), Permanent Under-Secretary for Foreign Affairs in the British Parliament, 1938-1946.
7   Held At 2 Kaiserstrasse, Babelsberg.
8   CCS 900/2.

other operations which could hazard the success or delay these main operations will be undertaken.

The following additional tasks will be undertaken:

a)   Encourage Russian entry into the war against Japan and provide aid to her war-making capacity.

b)   Undertake measures in order to aid the war effort of China as an effective ally against Japan.

c)   Provide assistance to co-belligerents and forces of liberated areas so they can fulfil an active and effective role in the present war.

d)   Provide supplies to liberated areas so they will effectively contribute to the capacity of the United Nations to prosecute the war against Japan.

e)   Conduct operations in cooperation with other Allies to liberate enemy-occupied areas.

Discussion about Basic Undertakings and Policies

Admiral Leahy said there was a difference of opinion on two or three points. The US Chiefs of Staff believed the basic commitment should be confined to the war against Japan while the British Chiefs of Staff felt it should be extended to include the occupation of Germany and Austria. Churchill said the holding down of Germany and Austria was a very vital matter and Truman agreed it was quite definitely a part of the war. After all, they were still technically at war with Germany and Austria. Marshall said the US Chiefs of Staff accepted the British Chiefs of Staff proposal and both Truman and Churchill agreed.

Churchill said British industrial effort was interwoven with the United States and many British units worked with US equipment.[1] Nothing had been done to replace it from British sources and it would take time to make such provision. He hoped Truman would make it possible for him to pass smoothly from this position of dependence to one in which British forces could be independent.

Churchill was concerned a rigid interpretation of an undertaking to maintain the British war-making capacity only in connection with the war against Japan would place him in great difficulties. He hoped the rules covering Lend Lease equipment would not limit British sovereign rights over British equipment. He had to be free to give British equipment, for example, to the Belgians, if His Majesty's Government felt it was desirable. He hoped this would not result in the drying up of supplies from the United States.

Truman was handicapped by the latest renewal of the Lend-Lease Act. As Vice President, he had worked out its clauses with Senator George,[2] who had explained to Congress how the Act was only intended as a weapon of war. Truman was now striving to give to the Act the broadest interpretation possible and he had no intention of causing the British any embarrassment. Truman asked Churchill to be patient as he wished to avoid any embarrassment with Congress over the

---

1   For example, while over 20,000 M4 Shermans were issued to US Army and Marine Corps units, over 17,000 were also supplied to Great Britain; some of which were issued to Commonwealth and Polish units.

2   Senator Walter F. George (1878-1957), Democrat, chairman of the Senate Foreign Relations Committee and then of the Senate Finance Committee.

interpretation of the Act while additional legislation might be needed to clear the matter up.[3]

Churchill attached great importance to the United Kingdom import program and did not wish to see it lose its status. Truman was not clear how far he could accept liability for the reconstruction and rehabilitation of the United Kingdom under existing United States law. Therefore, his acceptance of the paragraph was on the understanding the necessary authority did exist.

Lord Leathers[4] said the United Kingdom import program had been included in the basic undertakings at previous conferences. Shipping requirements for military and civilian needs were closely interlocked and the United Kingdom import program would be properly associated with military requirements if it was linked to them. Churchill asked whether the United Kingdom import program would be swept aside. Truman gave his word it would not suffer.

The War against Japan

a) The US Chiefs of Staff will control operational strategy in the Pacific Theatre.

b) The US Chiefs of Staff will provide the British Chiefs of Staff with full and timely information as to their future plans and intentions.

c) The US Chiefs of Staff will consult the British Chiefs of Staff on matters of general strategy but the final decision will lie with the United States Chiefs of Staff.

d) If the British Chiefs of Staff decide they cannot commit British troops in support of any US Chiefs of Staff decision, they will give advance notice to permit timely rearrangements.

e) If the USSR enters the war against Japan, the strategy to be pursued should be discussed between the parties concerned.

Churchill hoped they did not think the British Chiefs of Staff wished to take advantage of this arrangement because what was good enough for the United States was good enough for the British. Admiral King said the US Chiefs of Staff did not expect the British Chiefs of Staff to invoke this paragraph while Marshall said he suggested putting it in. For example, if the British Chiefs of Staff did not agree with the action proposed by the United States Chiefs of Staff after OLYMPIC,[5] they would be free to take such action they thought fit. Churchill thanked the US Chiefs of Staff for their explanation and the spirit in which this provision had been made. Truman and Churchill approved the report.

---

3 Large quantities of undelivered goods were in Britain or in transit when Lend-Lease ended on 2 September 1945. Britain wanted to keep some of this equipment and it was sold to Britain at 10% of its nominal value in 1946; £1 billion for the Lend Lease portion of the post-war loans alone. The first payment was deferred until 1951 with 2% interest. The final payment of £42.5 million was paid in 29 December 2006.
4 British Minister of War Transport.
5 The proposed invasion of Japan was codenamed DOWNFALL and it was split into two parts. OLYMPIC was the invasion of the southern part of Kyushu (Japan's southern island). CORONET was the invasion of Honshu (Japan's central island) and the capture of Tokyo.

Operations in the Pacific

We have taken note of the plans and operations proposed by the United States Chiefs of Staff.[1] We have considered the scope and nature of British participation in operations in the Pacific area:

a)   The British Pacific Fleet will participate as planned.

b)   A British very long range bomber force of ten squadrons[2] will participate. There is little prospect there will be enough airfield space for more than this before 1 December 1945 at the earliest.

c)   We have agreed in principle that a Commonwealth land force[3] should take part in the final phase of the war against Japan. In addition, some units of the British East Indies Fleet may also take part.

We have agreed the appropriate British commanders and staff should visit Admiral Nimitz and General MacArthur[4] to draw up plans for submission to the Combined Chiefs of Staff.

Operations in Southeast Asia Command

We have agreed the directive to be issued to the Supreme Allied Commander, Southeast Asia.[5]

Reorganizing the Southwest Pacific and Southeast Asia Areas

We have agreed the southern part of the Southwest Pacific Area should pass from United States to British command as soon as possible. The British Chiefs of Staff had undertaken to obtain the agreement of the Australian, New Zealand, and Dutch Governments and to report on the earliest practicable date the transfer can be made.

We consider it desirable for Admiral Mountbatten to initially control operations undertaken in southern Indochina as they are closer to Southeast Asia Command than the China Theatre. The best arrangement would be to transfer Indochina south of latitude 16° into Southeast Asia Command.[6] This arrangement continues General Wedemeyer's control of the part of Indochina covering the flank of Chinese operations. It would enable Mountbatten to prepare the ground in the southern half of Indochina where his operations would develop. We recommend approaching Generalissimo Chiang Kai-shek to secure his agreement. It may be desirable to transfer more of Indochina to Southeast Asia Command at a later date.

---

1   To intensify the blockade and air bombardment of Japan from bases in Okinawa, Iwo Jima, Marianas, and the Philippines. Curtail expansion in the Ryukyus to accelerate the development of Okinawa. Then assault on Kyushu followed by a decisive invasion of Honshu.

2   Increasing to 20 squadrons when more airfields became available.

3   And a small tactical air force if possible.

4   Admiral Nimitz Commander-in-Chief Pacific Ocean Areas (POA); General MacArthur Commander-in-Chief Southwest Pacific Area (SWPA).

5   Open the Straits of Malacca between the Malay Peninsula and Sumatra, allowing British and Commonwealth troops to be moved into the South China Sea.

6   The 16th Parallel was eventually used to separate Indochina. The French would eventually take control of the south while the Viet Minh occupied the north. War ensued and lasted until the French defeat at Dien Bien Phu. The 1954 Geneva Accords used the 17th Parallel to split the country into North and South Vietnam.

French and Dutch Participation in the War

While it is at present impracticable[7] for French or Netherlands armed forces to take part in the immediate operations in the Far East, their assistance will be taken into account. The use of such forces will depend solely on military considerations. French or Netherlands forces must operate under the complete control of the Commander-in-Chief concerned and their representatives will be given timely information of our intentions.

We have considered and agreed to an offer of a French corps of two infantry divisions to serve in the Pacific war. However, pressing shipping and other requirements for operations in the Pacific mean the corps cannot be moved for at least several months so it will not be possible to commit it before the spring of 1946.[8]

Portuguese Participation in the War

We have examined a report on Portuguese participation in future operations to expel the Japanese from Portuguese Timor.[9] We have informed the State Department and the Foreign Office of our views.[10]

Information for the Russians Concerning the Japanese War

The US and British Chiefs of Staff will pass operational information and intelligence to the Russians regarding their theatres as they wish and without bargaining. They will consult each other before passing anything to the Russians. Neither party will pass information or intelligence to the Russians without the other party's consent.

Planning Date for the End of Organized Resistance by Japan

For the purpose of planning production and the allocation of manpower, the planning date for the end of organized resistance by Japan will be 15 November 1946; it will be adjusted periodically to conform to the course of the war.[11]

24 July

First Tripartite Chiefs of Staff Meeting

Proposed Russian operations against Japan; Proposed Allied operations against Japan; US order of battle and dispositions; Japanese order of battle and dispositions.

Truman-Bierut Meeting[12]

The President discussed Poland's claims over Germany's eastern territories with President Bierut.

---

7   Due chiefly to logistical difficulties.
8   The Far East Expeditionary Force ended up fighting the Chinese- and Soviet-backed Viet Minh for over eight years.
9   Now East Timor.
10 Portugal was offering a regimental combat team of 4,000, or a battalion combat team of 2,200, both including 400 native troops.
11 The use of the atom bomb on Hiroshima and Nagasaki shortened this to August 1945.
12 Boleslaw Bierut (1892-1956), President of the Provisional National Council, and future President of the Soviet-backed regime.

24 July: Eighth Terminal Meeting
The Admission of Italy and the Satellite States[1]
into the United Nations Organization

Byrnes[2] understood the US and British delegations had reached an agreement. Eden said the second draft agreed to reconstruct the Italian Government before Italy could be admitted to the United Nations. He questioned the effect of this on the present Italian Government.

Stalin said if the point was to ease the position of the satellite states then they should be mentioned. The position of the Italian Government would be eased and it would be difficult to object to. But an abnormal position was being created for the other satellite states and an artificial distinction was being drawn between them. It appeared Romania, Bulgaria, Hungary, and Finland were being categorized as leprous states and the Soviet delegation saw a danger that attempts would be made to discredit the Soviet Union.[3]

So what were the merits of Italy compared to the other satellite states? While it had been the first to capitulate, it had done more harm and its behaviour had been worse than the others. There was no doubt Romania, Bulgaria, Hungary and Finland had done less harm to the Allies than Italy.[4] Was the Italian Government more democratic or more responsible than the governments of these countries? There had been no democratic elections in Italy or the other satellite countries, so he did not understand the benevolent attitude towards Italy compared to the others.[5] The position of Italy had been eased when the first step had been taken, the resumption of diplomatic relations. While Stalin agreed to take the second step with Italy, he also wanted to take the first step with the satellite states. Italy would still occupy first place because it had been first to surrender, in spite of the fact she had done more harm.

Churchill said the British agreed with the US delegation. Truman had a different point of view about Romania, Bulgaria, and Hungary than he did about Italy. They had not had free access to the satellite states and had not been able to get information about them. Everybody had free access to Italy. They would recognize them when they had free access but not sooner.[6] The language in the

---

1   The Axis satellite states of Romania, Bulgaria, Hungary and Finland.
2   James F. Byrnes (1882-1972), US Secretary of State. Following Roosevelt's death on 12 April 1945, President Truman relied heavily on Byrnes's council and appointed him US Secretary of State on 3 July 1945.
3   Italy surrendered in September 1943. Romania signed an armistice with the Soviet Union in August 1944, while Hungary and Finland signed an armistice in September 1944.
4   While the British and US were closer to the Italian situation, the Soviets were experts and almost sponsors of the other satellite countries. They would blame the Soviet Union for not achieving the same status for them.
5   The problem with Italy was it had taken over 18 months to capture. While the Fascist regime capitulated in September 1943, the north part of the country did not fall into Allied hands until April 1945. Romania, Bulgaria and Hungary fell in a matter of days.
6   The Soviet authority and the beginnings of its communist influence were stopping the Western Allies checking on the satellite states.

American document regarding Romania,[7] Bulgaria,[8] and Hungary[9] had been made the same as Italy's to meet the Soviet position.

Molotov said Italy already had diplomatic relations with the other powers. Truman replied the satellites could as well, if they complied with their requirements but they had not done so. Stalin asked what requirements; satellite governments could not stop allied agents moving freely or getting access to information. Truman replied they did. Molotov countered there were also restrictions on the Soviet representatives in Italy.

Truman was asking for the reorganization of the other satellite governments along democratic lines, as agreed upon at Yalta.[10] Stalin wished to assure him the governments in those countries were more democratic than Italy's and they were closer to the people than the Italian Government.[11] Truman said they would have the same status for the Council of Foreign Ministers and Molotov replied that meant maintaining diplomatic relations. Truman thought this was not the case and they could not recognize them until they had been set up on democratic lines. Molotov said his proposal was for the satellites to be placed in a position of equality.

Byrnes said the proposal to ease Italy's situation was to give support to its entry into the United Nations Organization. "The conclusion of such a peace treaty with the democratic and responsible Italian Government will make it possible for the three Governments to fulfil their desire to support the admission of Italy into the United Nations Organization." The same language was used for the other satellite states.[12] The wording had been chosen to do what Stalin had asked, namely, to express a view on Franco's government.

Stalin wanted the words "responsible and democratic governments" deleted as it discredited the satellite countries. Truman said the language showed the only way to get their support for entry into the United Nations Organization was to have a democratic government. Stalin replied they were not Fascist governments. There was a far less democratic government in Argentina and it had been admitted to

---

7 Romania's communists took control by manipulating elections, forcing their opponents to flee, and merging their party with others; all while the Soviet Army was in occupation.

8 Bulgaria was ruled by the Bulgarian Communist Party from the start.

9 The Soviets authorised the only free election in Eastern Europe in November 1945 in Hungary and while the Smallholder's Party won, the Soviet commander, Marshal Voroshilov, forced them to form a coalition government with the Communist Party and the communists forced their opponents to leave the country over the months that followed. The communists used fraud at the next election in August 1947 but still did not get a majority. Instead, the communists forced the Social Democrats to merge with them in 1948, forming the People's Front, while other parties were declared illegal.

10 According to the principle of the Atlantic Charter — "the right of all peoples to choose the form of government under which they will live" — the Big Three agreed that all liberated European countries and former Axis satellite states would hold free elections. They promised to rebuild occupied countries by processes that would allow them "to create democratic institutions of their own choice."

11 Although Italy had surrendered in September 1943, fighting had continued in Italy until the end of April 1945 and many Italians had fought on alongside the Germans. General Pietro Badoglio (1871-1956) headed the government for nine months, despite being accused of war crimes committed in Africa. He was replaced by Ivanoe Bonomi (1873-1951), leader of the Labour Democratic Party, in June 1944. Bonomi was in turn replaced by Ferruccio Parri (1890-1981), an anti-fascist partisan released by the Germans at the end of the war as evidence of good faith.

12 Romania, Hungary, Bulgaria and Finland would join the United Nations in December 1955.

the United Nations.[1] He said "If a government was not Fascist, a government was democratic."[2] The word "responsible" would discredit these governments.[3]

Molotov proposed adding a paragraph concerning the resumption of diplomatic relations with those countries. While the United States and the Soviet Union had diplomatic relations with Italy, Great Britain and France only had political representatives who did not hold the rank of ambassador. Churchill considered the British ambassador in Italy to be fully accredited[4] but Molotov replied he was not called an ambassador. Churchill said this was because the British were at war with Italy and while their ambassador did not have full formality he was an ambassador for practical purposes; the distinction was made for technical reasons. Molotov repeated he was not called an ambassador and Churchill replied he was and he was also 90 per cent a full ambassador. Stalin said he was still not the same as the Soviet Union and United States ambassadors and he suggested sending the same kind of ambassador to Romania and Bulgaria as the British had in Italy.

Truman said the United States was making every effort to send an ambassador and he had already stated the difficulties preventing this. Stalin said that was in the past and there were no difficulties now. Generally speaking, it was hard for the Soviet delegation to adhere to the resolution, as they would be discredited by it. Truman said they had no such intention. Stalin admitted this but insisted it would happen. Churchill said they wanted no words which would be a slur on any of them.

Churchill wanted to put in a plea for Italy and not just because Italy was first out of the war. Nearly two years had passed since Italy went out of the war while the other satellites had been fighting against them only a short time before.

Stalin said diplomatic relations with Italy had been resumed seven to ten months after Italy's surrender. Churchill replied Italy had been out of the war for two years and had been fighting on their side all of that time. They had been living in Italy and knew all about the political conditions there. That was not the case in Bulgaria and Romania. But Italy had not been a united country. The great democratic north had been under the enemy until two months ago.[5] Italy had given a great measure of help but it had always been recognized it could not have a democratic government until the north was liberated.

Churchill agreed with Stalin but disagreed with the Americans about holding onto Badoglio[6] longer, but the march of events had carried things in a different way. They had built up considerable sympathy for Italy. There was no censorship

---

1   When it looked as if Argentina was going to join the Allies in June 1943, there was a military coup. De facto President Pedro P. Ramirez (1884-1962) broke relations with the Axis and refused Lend Lease to remain neutral. Ramirez appointed Edelmiro J. Farrell (1887-1980) in February 1944 and he made a late declaration of war so his country would be on the winning side.

2   Stalin is claiming that the satellite countries' communist governments were democratic. Military pressure, intimidation, vote-rigging, the forcing of opponents into exile and the outlawing of opposition parties in these countries was being ignored.

3   They would be considered irresponsible if they were not admitted.

4   Sir Noel H. H. Charles (1891-1975).

5   Different parts of Italy had very different experiences. While the southern half of Italy had been liberated by the end of 1943, it had taken until June 1944 to reach Rome. A dogged German resistance in northern Italy had kept the Po valley under Nazi rule until they surrendered at the end of April 1945.

6   General Badoglio was replaced by Ivanoe Bonomi of the Labour Democratic Party in June 1944.

and he had frequently been attacked in the Italian newspapers only a few months after Italy had surrendered. There was a considerable growth of freedom in Italy. Now the north was liberated, they could have democratic elections. He did not see why they could not discuss peace with them.

They knew nothing about Romania and Bulgaria. Their mission in Bucharest had been penned up with a closeness approaching internment. Stalin asked how he could cite unverified facts. Churchill replied their representatives informed them; Stalin would be astonished to read the long catalogue of difficulties encountered by their mission there. An iron fence had come down around them.[7] Stalin interrupted with, "All fairy tales." Churchill said of course they could call each other's statements fairy tales but he had complete confidence in his representatives there. He had known Stevenson for many years.[8]

The conditions in the British mission had caused them great distress, even their motor cars were followed by other cars which supervised their every movement. There had been complaints from their Soviet friends with regard to the size of their mission even though it had not been large. The Control Commission, which was supposed to have three representatives, almost always met as two. The Soviet representative sometimes saw the American representative, sometimes the British, but he rarely both together. In Italy, Soviet representatives were welcomed and many Russians had visited. Stalin broke in to say this was not the case. The Russians had no rights in Italy. Vyshinski[9] had never been on the Control Commission, he sat on the Advisory Council.

Churchill said the Russians were welcome to go to Italy and visit anywhere. The position there was the same as in the other satellite states. Truman said the American mission had encountered difficulties in Romania and Bulgaria and this had caused much concern. However, they had no intention to cast any aspersion upon Stalin or his government at this Conference.[10]

Byrnes suggested substituting the word 'recognize' for the word 'responsible' and while Stalin said it was more acceptable, he wanted to add an amendment, which Molotov read out. "The three governments agree to consider the establishment of diplomatic relations with Finland, Romania, Bulgaria and Hungary separately." Churchill said this did not reflect what they had been saying. Stalin replied it was wrong to say this. They had decided to prepare peace treaties with Romania, Bulgaria, and the other satellites. This could not be done if they did not have diplomatic relations.

Truman had no objection to Molotov's amendment and Stalin replied that then they had no objections to the draft as a whole. Churchill said they were

---

7   As noted earlier, Churchill would use the term more than once. His famous 'Sinews of Peace' address of March 1946 used the term "iron curtain" in the context of Soviet-dominated Eastern Europe.

8   Ralph S. Stevenson (1895–1977), British diplomat and Envoy Extraordinary and Minister Plenipotentiary to the Kingdom of Yugoslavia 1943–1946.

9   Andrey Vyshinski (1883-1954), Soviet diplomat who arranged for a communist regime to take control of Romania before the Potsdam conference.

10 Truman is acknowledging the difficulties of the American mission but is careful to make it clear he is not placing the blame on Stalin or his government.

using words to cover a difficulty they had not removed around the conference table and it would be read by the whole world. He thought the President had said he would not recognize the present governments of Romania and Bulgaria. Truman said that was correct; they were only agreeing to examine the question. Churchill said this did not remove the disagreement and it would mislead the public. Stalin asked why.

Churchill replied the statement claimed there would be immediate recognition of these governments, whereas, he understood this was not the position of the American and British Governments. Stalin suggested Truman could speak for himself. The statement had already been accepted by the British and the Council of Foreign Ministers were tasked with preparing peace treaties with Romania, Bulgaria, Hungary and Finland. But a peace treaty could only be concluded after recognition; so the question of recognition was on the agenda. If they made no mention of the resumption of diplomatic relations then the paragraph on peace treaties should be left out.

Stalin asked if Truman thought the Romanian and Bulgarian representatives would come to the Council of Foreign Ministers in the autumn to discuss a peace treaty. Truman replied they could only deal with a government they recognized.[1] Stalin agreed. Churchill said the present governments would not be recognized and there could be no peace treaty with them until they were. Stalin could not see how that followed. Churchill said it should follow but Stalin replied it did not. A peace treaty with them would be considered when they had been recognized.

Churchill said no one would realize the United States did not recognize the governments of Romania and Bulgaria. If other governments were created which they could recognize, then they would begin preparing peace treaties. They would have to say they would make treaties with governments they recognized when they did not intend to recognize these governments. That was almost meaningless. Truman proposed referring the question back to the Foreign Ministers.

The Dardanelles

Truman asked if anyone had considered his paper on inland waterways. Stalin replied it did not deal with the question of Turkey and the Straits, only with the Danube and the Rhine.[2] He wanted a reply on the Black Sea Straits.[3] Truman wanted to consider the two questions together. Stalin was afraid they would not be able to reach an agreement over the Straits, because their views differed so widely. Perhaps they should postpone the question and take up the next question.

Churchill understood they agreed free movement in the Black Sea Straits should be approved and guaranteed, a remarkable and important fact. Truman had clearly stated the United States' position and this was a big step. Stalin said this was correct with respect to freedom of passage, because the British were in favour

---

1 The United States did not recognise the communist governments in place.
2 Both rivers passed through more than one country. The Rhine starts in Switzerland, follows the Franco-German border, through Germany and then Holland. The Danube starts in Germany, through Austria, Hungary, Yugoslavia (now Serbia) and along the Romanian-Hungarian border.
3 Russia wanted free access to their Black Sea ports, allowing her to trade into the Mediterranean and beyond.

of freedom for all traffic. Churchill hoped the proposed guarantee was more than a substitute for the fortification of the Straits.[4]

Molotov asked if the Suez Canal was under the same principle. Churchill replied it was open in war and peace to all. Molotov asked if it was under the same international control proposed for the Black Sea Straits. Churchill said this question had not been raised and Molotov replied he was asking; if it was such a good rule, why not apply it to the Suez? Churchill said they had a satisfactory arrangement that had operated for some 70 years with no complaints. Molotov said there had been a lot of complaints; they should ask Egypt. Eden replied Egypt had signed the treaty with them.[5]

Molotov said the British claimed international control was better. Churchill replied their suggestion meant Russia could move freely in and out of the Black Sea and they would join in a guarantee with other nations and press it upon Turkey. Would Turkey resist when the three Great Powers agreed and took an interest in the matter? This way freedom could be attained without trouble for Turkey. Churchill agreed the question had to be put off, but he hoped the agreement on freedom in the Black Sea Straits would not be underestimated by their Russian friends.

Truman said his understanding of an international guarantee for the freedom of the Straits was that any nation would have free access for any purpose. He did not contemplate any fortifications of any kind. Churchill fully sympathized and agreed with Stalin. A great power, such as the Soviet Union, must not have to go to a smaller power, like Turkey, cap in hand, each time it wanted to send ships through the Straits. He did not oppose Stalin's complaint in this respect.

Stalin said the question had been raised by Great Britain but it was evident they differed in their views. They had many more urgent questions before them and this one could be put off. Churchill said the question had been brought up following their conversations regarding the Montreux Convention. Stalin said the question was not yet ripe; talks had to take place with the Turks. Churchill inquired "With Turkey, by whom?" Stalin replied they had interrupted their conversations with the Turks but the United States could talk with them as well as Great Britain. He was not certain whether Turkey would agree to international control. Churchill replied they would be more likely to agree to it than to the construction of fortifications in the Straits. Stalin said that might be, he did not know.

The President drew attention to the word 'control'. If the Straits were free there would be no control. They would endeavour to make Turkey see their point of view. Stalin then proposed they each work on the matter.

Soviet Prisoners of War in a British Prison Camp in Italy

Churchill said it was true there were 10,000 persons in the camp but it had to be remembered they had just taken one million prisoners. They were in the process

---

4   The Soviet Union wanted a fortified base to stop any ship entering the Black Sea. Turkey was nervous of a large Russian base in the Straits.

5   The 1888 Convention of Constantinople declared the Suez Canal a neutral zone under the protection of the British, who had occupied Egypt and Sudan to suppress the 'Urabi Revolt (or revolution). The UK insisted on retaining control over the canal under the Anglo-Egyptian Treaty of 1936. It did so until Egypt repudiated the treaty in 1951 and the UK agreed to remove its troops in 1954.

of being sifted by the Russian Mission at Rome, which had full access to the camps. They were chiefly non-Soviet Ukrainians and a few Poles who had lived inside the 1939 Polish frontiers.

Among their number, 665 wanted to return to their native Soviet Union and their return was being arranged. The British would hand over any others who would go without the use of force. The question of how much force would be used must be considered and it had to be carefully handled. The 10,000 had surrendered almost intact as an enemy division. They had retained the division as organized under their own general for administrative reasons exclusively. They would have been happy if General Golikov[1] had made his complaints to Field Marshal Alexander's headquarters.

Alexander said he had always given the Russian representatives in Italy complete freedom of movement and assistance to see anything and everything they wished to see at any time. It was a great help to receive their advice when they had a great number of Russian soldiers on their hands. He hoped Stalin agreed, so facilities could continue to be made available.

Stalin said under the treaty they were bound to give each other admission to such camps and not to obstruct the return of Soviet nationals to their own country. If Alexander thought this was possible he would be grateful. Churchill said if Stalin would send his generals they would examine the situation and see if it could be done. Stalin replied, "All right."[2]

Occupation of Vienna

Stalin had talked to Marshal Konev[3] and they were ready to issue rations to all zones in Vienna until the British and Americans found it possible to make some other arrangements. Churchill said as soon as they got to Vienna, one of the first things they would examine would be the extension of the administrative control of the Renner Government[4] in the American and British zone.[5] Stalin said that was a good thing to do. Truman agreed with Churchill. The meeting adjourned.

Truman Advises Stalin about a New Weapon

At the end of the meeting Truman walked around the large circular table to Stalin and "casually mentioned they had a new weapon of unusual destructive force. Stalin showed no special interest, he was pleased to hear it and hoped they would make good use of it against the Japanese."[6] He was referring to the atomic bomb. Truman later said that Stalin showed no special interest and did not seem to

---

1 General Filipp I. Golikov, (1900-1980), Assistant Minister of Defence responsible for the repatriation of Soviet POWs.
2 The Ukrainian soldiers were held in an area controlled by the Polish II Corps. Ukrainian National Army commander Pavlo Shandruk (1889-1979) asked Polish General Wladyslaw Anders to protect the soldiers against deportation to the Soviet Union because they were citizens of the Second Republic of Poland. Due to Vatican intervention, their status was changed from POW to surrendered enemy personnel and they were not deported. Instead, around 7000 were allowed to emigrate to the United Kingdom and a similar number to Canada. Around 175 joined the Polish army.
3 Ivan S. Konev (1897-1973), commander of the 1st Ukrainian Front, which had advanced across Hungary and Austria during the final weeks of the war.
4 Karl Renner's Provisional Government.
5 Vienna, like Berlin, would be partitioned into British, American and Russian zones.
6 *Year of Decisions*, President Harry S. Truman, William Konecky Associates (1999).

understand what he was talking about. As it later transpired, spies had made Stalin aware of the bomb.

Eleventh Combined Chiefs of Staff Meeting

Operations in Southeast Asia.

25 July: Ninth Terminal Meeting

The Transfer of Germans out of Poland and Czechoslovakia

Churchill had spoken with President Bierut[7] while Eden had seen the Polish delegation for two hours. The Poles agreed about 1.5 million Germans were left in the area in the west under discussion. Many Germans also had to move out of Czechoslovakia and they had to consider where they would go.[8] Stalin said the Czechs had evacuated these Germans and they had gone to Leipzig, Dresden, and other cities. Churchill understood there were 2.5 million Germans in the Sudetenland and about 150,000 Reich Germans in Czechoslovakia. The British understood only a few thousand had left Czechoslovakia so it was a big question.[9]

Churchill asked if they were being moved into the Russian zone and Stalin said yes. Churchill added the British did not want them; they brought their mouths with them. Stalin was not suggesting the British take them. Churchill understood emigration had not begun on a large scale yet but Stalin understood the Czechs had only given the Germans two hours notice and then thrown them out.

Stalin said the Poles had retained 1.5 million Germans to help with the harvest but they would be evacuated as soon as it was over. Churchill did not think they should but Stalin replied the Poles did not ask; they did as they liked.[10]

Churchill said Czechoslovakia's situation was different to Poland's. The Poles were evacuating Germans from the Russian zone;[11] they were driving them out. It should not to be done without consideration for food supply or reparations. The Poles had little food and fuel while the British had a mass of population thrown on them.[12]

Stalin said they had to appreciate the Poles' position. They were taking revenge on the Germans for the injuries they had caused over the course of centuries. Churchill said their revenge took the form of throwing the Germans into the American and British zones and they had to be fed. Truman agreed this should not be done. He was sympathetic with the Poles and Stalin with regard to the

---

7   Boleslaw Bierut (1892–1956) Communist leader, NKVD agent, and Stalin supporter. He was President of Poland from 1947 until the post was abolished in 1952 and then President until his suspicious death during a visit to Moscow in 1956.

8   Between May and August many were moved in 'wild expulsions' carried out by the army or by armed volunteers. Many died in violent confrontations or of hunger or illness as they looked for new homes.

9   Stalin believed over 2.5 million Germans had been forced out of Czechoslovakia and across the German border. Churchill believed they were still in Czechoslovakia.

10 The Poles were using the Germans as slave labour. The following season soldiers and prisoners would have returned to collect their own harvest. (For the tragic human story behind the expulsion of the Germans westwards, see *East of the Oder: A German Childhood under the Nazis and Soviets* by Luise Urban.)

11 After the Germans defeated the Polish Army, they designated central and southern Poland (including Warsaw and Krakow) the General Government. The government and administration was manned by Germans and they made no attempt to include the Polish in the running of the country. Eastern Galicia was added to the General Government following the invasion on the Soviet Union in June 1941.

12 Into the British zone in northwest Germany.

difficulties they were up against but he had made his position very clear. The occupying powers of Germany were Great Britain, the Soviet Union, France, and the United States. If the Poles were to have a zone, they were responsible to the Soviet Union for it.

Eden said they had received a message from Dr. Beneš[1] asking them to examine the transfer of populations. Stalin asked if they should summon the Czechs to the Conference and Churchill said he would be pleased to see his old friend Dr. Beneš. Stalin said would they not be serving the mustard after supper because the transfers had already taken place.[2]

Eden thought the Czechs had sent a note to all three Governments, asking for the question to be discussed and he thought they ought to do so. Churchill thought the Soviets and the Czechs had agreed no more than 1000 Germans would depart at one time and the transfer would take a long time because there were 2.5 million of them. Stalin said there had been no such agreement. Churchill proposed the Foreign Ministers ascertain the facts first. This was agreed to.[3]

The United States Position on Peace Treaties

Truman wished to clarify his powers regarding the peace treaty. A peace treaty could only be concluded with the consent of the United States Senate under the United States Constitution. When he supported a proposal at the Conference they could be sure he would support it in the Senate. But he had to consider the standpoint of the United States people and wanted to be in a position to get the best arrangements approved by the Senate. In conclusion, he was convinced world peace could only be maintained by the three of them present at the table.

Stalin asked if his remarks referred only to the peace treaties or to the whole discussion. Truman replied only agreements or treaties had to be ratified by the Senate. He had wide powers, the same as his colleagues, but he did not wish to abuse these powers; he had to have the support of the American people for his policies. Stalin understood.[4]

Food and Coal for Germany

Stalin said coal and steel were much more important than food in the question of supplies for Germany. 90 per cent of Germany's metal and 80 per cent of its coal came from the Ruhr. Churchill said if supplies from the Ruhr were to be given to the Russian and Polish zones, they would have to be paid for with food from the Russian zone. He could not take the position that everything behind the Russian line was to be disposed of by the Russians, while the Russians could demand plants and materials from them. Stalin replied the Ruhr had to supply the whole of Germany if it remained in Germany. Churchill asked then why not

---

1   Edvard Beneš (1884-1948) was the Czechoslovakian President politician who opposed the Nazis and went into exile in London when they occupied the Sudetenland in October 1938. He returned home following the Prague uprising in May 1945 and was confirmed President in October.

2   The uselessness of offering something after the need for it has passed.

3   1.6 million Germans were moved out of Czechoslovakia between January and October 1946 under the expulsion agreed at the Potsdam Conference.

4   Truman could not agree a peace treaty, only agree to put a peace treaty before the US Senate. He would therefore argue for a peace treaty he believed the Senate would agree to.

food? Stalin said this could be discussed. There were two points, the Ruhr and food.[5] Churchill asked how the miners would get the coal out without food and where would the food come from. Stalin said it was a question of imports and exports; Germany had always imported large amounts of food and exported to pay for its imports. Churchill asked how Germany could pay reparations. Stalin replied it would be able to pay.

Churchill would not agree to anything which would lead to starvation conditions in the British zone that winter, while the Poles had the feeding grounds to themselves. Stalin said the Poles had asked the Russians for bread because they were short of food until the next harvest.[6]

Churchill said they would have the most fireless winter of the war this year in England because coal was short. Stalin replied England had always exported coal and suggested making their prisoners of war work; the Russians were working theirs in the mines. The British were short of coal because they were exporting to Holland, France, and Belgium. Churchill said they were denying themselves but found it odd the Poles sold coal, taken from ground which they did not recognize as Polish, to Sweden and other countries. Stalin said the Poles were not selling coal from the territory in question but from other sources.[7]

Stalin was not accustomed to make complaints but the Russian situation was worse than the British; they had lost over five million men in this war. He was afraid if he started complaining about the difficult situation in Russia Churchill would burst into tears.[8] Churchill said they were eager to barter coal from the Ruhr in exchange for food for the German population. The British position would be more difficult after the war than it had been during it, although it might be less deadly.[9] Stalin said they had tackled the war properly and they would tackle the peace.

German Troops in Norway

Stalin said the British had 400,000 German soldiers in Norway who had not been disarmed and no one knew what they were waiting for. Churchill said they intended to disarm them. He did not know exactly what the situation was but SHAEF had made arrangements; he would inquire.[10] He assured them these troops would be disarmed immediately; they did not want to keep them up their sleeves. He would have a report made. The meeting adjourned.

Eighth Foreign Ministers Meeting

Inland waterways; Transfer of populations.

---

5   Germany's industrial area was in the British Zone while foodstuffs such as grain were produced in the Russian and Polish zones. Stalin wants to share the Ruhr's steel but he was reluctant to share the grain from eastern Germany.

6   The population shifts caused by the end of the war meant the Poles were struggling to gather the harvest, leaving them short of grain.

7   All of Poland's modern coalfields are in areas occupied since the end of the war; Lower Silesia, Upper Silesia and Lublin.

8   Between 8.8 and 10.7 million soldiers and between 12.7 and 14.6 million civilians perished.

9   A bad harvest in 1946 and a harsh winter in 1946-1947 added to the British people's hardships. Rationing of petrol ended in 1950 but rationing of foodstuffs did not end until 1954.

10 An Allied military mission supervised the surrender of 400,000 German soldiers on 8 May 1945 in Oslo. 13,000 Norwegian troops and 30,000 British and American troops were then sent to Norway to secure the country, which only had a population of three million.

27 July
Ninth Foreign Ministers Meeting
Italy; Reparations; Reparations from Austria and Italy; Oil for Western Europe.

28 July
Second Tripartite Chiefs of Staff Meeting
Establishing US Weather Stations in eastern Russia; Coordination of US and Soviet naval operations; Coordination of US and Soviet air operations; Coordination of US and Soviet operations against Japan; Emergency facilities for US planes and ships in eastern Russia.

28 July: Tenth Terminal Meeting
Stalin said the Russian Delegation had received a new proposal from Japan. Prince Konoe's[1] mission asked the Soviet Government to take part in mediation to end the war and to transmit the complete Japanese case. He would be empowered to negotiate with respect to Soviet–Japanese relations during the war and after the war. Prince Konoe was especially charged by His Majesty, the Emperor, to convey to the Soviet Government that it was the desire of His Majesty to avoid more bloodshed by the parties engaged in the war. The Prince hoped the Soviet Government would give favourable attention to his request and would give its consent to the arrival of the mission.

Stalin said there was nothing new in this, except it was more definite than the previous approach.[2] It would receive a more definite answer than last time and the answer would be in the negative.[3] Truman thanked Stalin.

The Admission of Italy and the Satellite States into the United Nations Organization
Stalin said there was no difference in the arrangements for Italy on the one hand and the other satellite states on the other. None of these countries had democratic governments (except Finland)[4] because they had not held elections. Churchill said Great Britain recognized Italy 90 per cent. Stalin replied the proposal did not provide for establishing full diplomatic relations; only consideration of the question. He still did not understand the distinction between Italy and the other satellites. Mr. Bevin[5] replied they knew about the Italian government but they did not know about the other governments.

Stalin proposed recognizing them when they obtained information. Bevin asked why they were being asked to commit themselves first. Stalin replied the

---

1   Prince Fumimaro Konoe (1891-1945), Prime Minister of Japan on three occasions between 1937 and 1941. He resigned the third time after failing to find a diplomatic solution to avoid war with the United States following the Japanese occupation of French Indochina in July 1941. In February 1945 he advised Emperor Hirohito to begin negotiations to end World War II; Hirohito refused. Konoe committed suicide in December 1945 after being accused of war crimes.

2   The first approach was made on 13 July 1945 in Moscow.

3   The Allies were seeking unconditional surrender, not mediation.

4   Finland was led by its elected President (and parliament) throughout the war. This was Risto H. Ryti (1889-1956) from 1940-1944 and then Baron Carl G. E. Mannerheim (1867-1951) when it was clear Germany was losing the war. Mannerheim supervised the peace negotiations with the Soviet Union and the Allies.

5   Ernest Bevin (1881-1951), Foreign Secretary.

Russians had known little about the Italian Government when they had established diplomatic relations with them; perhaps even less than the British knew about the other satellites. But the first step with Italy had been the resumption of diplomatic relations six to eight months after their surrender. The proposal to admit Italy into the United Nations Organization was a second step. They should now give the other satellite governments hope that relations would resume with them eleven months after capitulation. If they agreed to ease the situation of Italy, something should be done for the other satellites.

Attlee[6] said it was impossible to enter into diplomatic relations with countries until they were at peace with them. One question in Parliament would bring out the real difficulty. Stalin said the British could study the proposal, accept it and lose nothing. Bevin said Parliament would ask what they meant by what they had done and he wanted to be perfectly straight with the British people. If he was going to recognize these governments, he would recognize them and he did not want to clothe things with words. He would rather take the latest American view and leave the whole question to a later date. Stalin agreed.

Italian Reparations

Truman said the United States and Great Britain had to contribute $500 million to feed and rehabilitate Italy and much more would be needed to stop her from starving to death.[7] As he had made plain, the United States did not intend to provide money for the payment of reparations. If the Soviet government needed war plants, they should take them, but contributions made to support Italy should be a first claim on exports.

Stalin said the Soviet people would understand why they were not exacting reparations from Austria but not from Italy. Italy had sent armies to the Volga[8] but Austria did not have her own armed forces. Truman said if reparations could be obtained from Italy he was perfectly willing, but the United States could not spend money to rehabilitate Italy just to allow it to pay reparations to other countries. Stalin understood this. Stalin referred to the moral right of the Soviet Union to reparations because her territory had been occupied for 3½ years and much devastation had been caused. Truman said if equipment was available in Italy, it could be used for reparations. He did not want to ask too much. It was necessary to find out what the sum would be. It had been $300 million from Romania, Hungary and Finland, so what should Italy pay? While the President was perhaps not ready to answer, he wanted to know but the answer could be postponed.

Bevin asked if the supplies furnished by the United States and Great Britain would be protected. Stalin did not wish to ignore American interests. Attlee agreed with the President and he had full sympathy for the Russian people's suffering but Britain had also suffered from Italian attacks. Britain also had ravaged lands and they could imagine the British people's feelings if Italy paid reparations

---

6   Attlee was back at the table as Britain's new Prime Minister after his Labour Party had won a landslide victory.
7   Equivalent to $6.4 billion in 2013.
8   The Italian Army in Russia (*Armata Italiana in Russia*, or ARMIR) served on the Eastern Front and by the end of 1942 it had over 230,000 men organised in 12 divisions. It was attacked as part of the Battle of Stalingrad in December 1942 and by February it ceased to exist, having suffered nearly 115,000 casualties. The survivors returned to Italy.

which had come from Britain and America. The fact was, Italy had to receive help in order to live.

Stalin agreed to take reparations in the form of military equipment. Attlee asked if they would be once and for all removals and not levies on war production. Stalin said they would. Bevin asked if they would take military equipment with no peace time value. Stalin said military factories could be used for any purpose, the same as equipment taken from Germany. Attlee said the equipment should have no peace time usefulness and Stalin replied all equipment could be adjusted for peace time production, they were adjusting theirs now. There was no such equipment that had no peace time use. Bevin said it was so difficult to tell what the Russians would take away. Stalin said of course they could not say now, he wanted only a decision in principle.

Truman thought Stalin wanted a decision in principle that Italy would pay reparations. Stalin said they could be reduced. Truman replied they were not far apart on the principle and he only wanted to protect the help they were giving. Stalin agreed the Russians did not want to touch the advances the United States was making to Italy. Bevin asked was it not then a question of priorities; what Great Britain and the United States supplied had first priority and reparations came next. Stalin wanted to give no bonus to aggressors without their paying for a small part of the damage they had caused. Truman agreed.[1] Stalin reminded Attlee not to forget what Italy had done to Britain. Attlee said they would not forget. The meeting adjourned.

29 July: Truman-Molotov Meeting
Stalin was ill so Molotov attended the meeting in his place. Truman, Byrnes and Molotov discussed the Polish Western frontier, reparations and the German fleet.

30 July
Tenth Foreign Ministers Meeting
Inviting France and China to the Council of Foreign Ministers; Notifying France about decisions on Germany; Reparations from Germany, Austria and Italy; Yugoslavia; German fleet and merchant navy; First stage of Germany's control period; War crimes; Fascist activities in Germany and Austria; The Ruhr; The agenda for the Big Three.

Eleventh Terminal Meeting, 31 July 1945
Reparations from Germany
The US proposal was to deliver 25 per cent of the Ruhr's[2] industrial capital equipment to the Soviet Union in exchange for commodities. An additional 15 per cent of capital goods[3] would be delivered without any payment or exchange.

---

1   Italy would have to pay a total of $360 million in reparations ($4.78 billion today) as follows. Yugoslavia $125 million ($1.66 billion today); Greece $105 million ($1.39 billion); Soviet Union $100 million ($1.33 billion); Ethiopia $25 million ($330 million); Albania $5 million ($66 million).

2   Surplus to the requirements of a peacetime economy.

3   Again, unnecessary for a peacetime economy.

The British Delegation of Foreign Ministers wanted to make the transfer from all three western zones rather than just the Ruhr.[4] Byrnes thought the proposal was better for the French, British and American zones and also advantageous to their Soviet friends. Stalin agreed.[5]

Byrnes suggested the Control Commission[6] could calculate the surplus equipment when there was a peacetime economy. Removals of industrial capital equipment should be completed within two years while the USSR should deliver the products within five years.[7] Reparations claims of other countries should be met from the western zones of occupation.

Stalin said Byrnes wanted to link the three questions on Germany's reparations, the Polish western frontier and the economic principles of Germany.[8] While Byrnes could use any tactics he wanted, he would not reply with the same tactics and the Soviet Delegation would vote separately on these questions. Germany's reparations were the most debatable question.[9]

Stalin had heard the British and Americans had removed 11,000 railroad cars from the western zones and he did not know their fate.[10] Would they be returned to the Russian zone or would they be compensated? Truman believed there should be a central transport administration.

Stalin said the Soviets did not remove railroad equipment from the American zone, although the Americans had charged the Russians with taking everything. He mentioned this to illustrate the British and Americans had sinned as well as the Russians. Truman said the removals had been made by the American Army but not under the instructions of the American Government; they would be accounted for. He would address a communication to General Eisenhower instructing him to undertake an investigation. He added no people had been removed by the American Army.[11]

Stalin suggested a three-month time limit to determine which equipment should be removed. While Truman agreed, Bevin thought it was not enough. Stalin said make it three, four or five, but there should be a time limit. Bevin suggested six and both Stalin and Truman agreed. They agreed not to mention a definite

---

4 The percentages would be halved (with respect to the Ruhr) to 12 per cent and 7 per cent but this did not affect the Soviet Union's total.

5 The Morgenthau Plan was an early plan to transform post-war Germany into an agrarian society. The French Monnet Plan would have transferred the Ruhr Area to France. Neither was carried out.

6 The Reparations Commission would decide which industries related to the peacetime economy, subject to the final approval of the Commander of the zone.

7 Although the Allies started dismantling the remnants of German industries, they abandoned the plan in favour of the European Economy Plan, better known as the Marshall Plan (after Secretary of State George C. Marshall). It started in April 1948 and lasted four years. The United States spent $13 billion ($172 billion today) starting the rebuilding of the war-devastated region, in removing trade barriers, modernising industry and getting Europe, one of their greatest trade partners, working again.

8 Byrnes wanted to define the border between Germany and Poland before defining the reparations, which in turn were calculated from Germany's economy.

9 The reparations exceeded the aid from the Marshall Plan but Germany managed to pay them.

10 Taken as the British and American troops withdrew from the Soviet zone into their own zones; probably used to move supplies and equipment.

11 People as in railway staff.

figure for reparations but they agreed to set a percentage.[1] Stalin hoped the British and Americans would meet the Soviet wishes and Bevin had to remember the Russians had lost a lot of equipment and they should receive a small part of it back. Bevin said they first had to determine how much equipment was needed for the maintenance of the economy but they had in mind which equipment could be removed. Stalin said they had 15 per cent in mind. Bevin agreed.[2]

Byrnes said the only remaining differences were the percentages of shares of German companies and gold holdings proposed by the Russians. It might turn out the gold belonged to others and had to be returned. Stalin said the Russians meant German gold. Byrnes said it was all looted gold and the question was, would they return it to the countries from which it was removed?[3]

Byrnes asked if the Soviet Delegation was insisting on an increase on the 30 per cent of German foreign assets and the shares of German companies. Stalin wanted it if possible. Byrnes asked what he had in mind. Stalin wanted to freeze Germany's overseas foreign assets, including those in America. Byrnes said that required action by Congress in America and it had already fixed the manner of establishing claims. There was no doubt many people, including refugees, had valid claims.[4] The US Delegation could not agree to the disposing of these assets in the US. Meanwhile, many countries in Latin America had claims against Germany for shipping and other losses and no doubt they would use these assets to satisfy their claims.

Bevin believed they had agreed on 12 per cent in the Foreign Ministers' meeting and thought they had treated the claim liberally. Stalin said it was the opposite of liberal but Bevin replied it was generous and they had different points of view. Bevin said the Soviet proposal for the gold was difficult for the British. He asked if Stalin would agree to limit their claim on foreign assets to neutral territory and Stalin agreed. Byrnes said the American position did not agree with the Soviet proposals. Truman added if the Russians would leave off their claim for assets in the United States and Latin America, he would agree to the percentage. Bevin agreed to 12½ per cent–10 per cent. He also had to satisfy France.

Stalin said the US was willing to meet the Soviet wishes, so why was Britain unwilling? Bevin replied it was because they were responsible for the zone from where the Soviet claims would be taken (the Ruhr). They were also responsible for satisfying the claims of France and other countries. Stalin replied France had signed an armistice with Hitler and had suffered no real occupation. France should be satisfied with a small amount. 150 divisions had been sent to Russia from France or had been supplied from France.[5] Bevin repeated they had to

---

1 That meant they could agree how much should be removed before they knew how much there was.
2 The process was to determine how much Germany had, then determine how much Germany needed in peacetime and then divide the surplus as reparations.
3 American troops had found $250 million ($3.3 billion today) in gold and many other valuables in Kaiseroda Salt Mine, near the town of Merkers, Germany, on 11 April 1945. It was virtually the entire gold and currency reserves of the Reichsbank.
4 Refugees who had fled the Third Reich before the war, many of them Jewish, and refugees who had fled during it.
5 German divisions which had conquered France were transferred to the Eastern Front in time for the invasion of the Soviet Union in June 1941. Stalin's argument is that collaboration by the Vichy government and a lack of resistance allowed these divisions to be moved.

satisfy France, Belgium, Czechoslovakia and Holland. The British wanted nothing except some raw materials.

Bevin said the percentage the Soviets wanted, plus the reparations from their own zone, gave them over 50 per cent. Stalin insisted it was less than 50 per cent and said they were also supplying goods equivalent to 15 per cent. The Soviet proposal was a minimum. The Soviets received only 10 per cent – the others got 90 per cent. He agreed to 15 per cent and 10 per cent and thought it fair. The Americans agreed. He hoped Bevin would support them. Bevin said "All right then," and Stalin expressed his thanks.

The Polish Western Frontier

Bevin said his instructions were to stand for the Eastern Neisse and asked what the new proposal involved. Would the zone be handed over to the Poles entirely and would the Soviet troops withdraw? He had asked the Poles what their intention was because he had to defend any decision in Parliament. Bevin had also asked the Poles their intentions about free and secret elections on the basis of the 1921 Constitution.[6] They assured him they would be held as soon as possible, and they hoped not later than early 1946, subject to conditions making them possible.[7]

The Poles also agreed to freedom of the press and to foreign correspondents sending reports abroad without interference. They also assured him regarding the freedom of religion. An important matter was the return of the troops under Allied command as well as the return of civilians. He had asked the Poles to make a declaration to ensure these people would be treated equally with those in the country.[8]

The US document stated this territory would be under the Polish state and not part of the Soviet zone of occupation and it would pass out of Soviet responsibility. Even though the zone would be under Polish administration, it would technically remain under Allied military control. Otherwise they would be transferring territory before the peace conference and it would have to be approved by the French. Stalin replied it was in the Russian zone and the French had nothing to do with it.

Bevin asked if the British could give away pieces of their zone without approval from the other governments. Stalin replied it could be done because the Poland state had no western border, the only such situation in the world. Bevin said the authority of the Control Commission was to extend over the whole of 1937 Germany. Byrnes said they all understood the cession of territory was left to the peace conference. The three powers agreed Poland was administering a good

---

6   The Second Polish Republic adopted the March Constitution on 17 March 1921, after beating German troops in the 1918 Greater Poland Uprising and Soviet troops in the 1920 Polish-Soviet War. The Constitution was democratic and modelled on the French one. It expressly ruled out discrimination on racial or religious grounds. In April 1935 it was replaced with a more authoritarian version and a presidential system. It limited the power of the lower house of Parliament in favour of Presidential powers.

7   A referendum by the communist Polish Worker's Party made sure it dominated the country's politics. The elections held in January 1947 were then controlled by the communists and violence, intimidation and fraud helped them get into power. A forced amalgamation of the Worker's party and the Socialist Party secured power while other parties were banned and opponents were forced to leave the country or face imprisonment or execution.

8   250,000 Polish troops under Allied command and thousands more civilians who had fled following the Nazi and Soviet occupation in September 1939.

part of this territory with Soviet consent, so there would be no further dispute between them.[1]

Byrnes asked what would happen in this zone now. Would the Poles take over and the Soviet troops withdraw? Stalin replied they would withdraw but this territory was on the line of communications of their army in Germany. There were only two roads, one to Berlin to the north and the other to the south. They were how Marshal Zhukov's troops were kept supplied; the same as Holland and Belgium were used by the British. Bevin asked if these troops would be limited to the lines of communication and Stalin replied they would. The Soviets had already removed 80 per cent of their troops from Poland and they were contemplating a further reduction. The territory was already administered by Poles, there was no Russian administration. Truman concluded they were all agreed on the Polish question and they agreed to inform the French of the changes in the Polish arrangement.

1 August: Twelfth Terminal Meeting
German Reparations

Byrnes asked if the Big Three had reached agreement after the Soviet delegate withdrew the claim to 30 per cent of German gold, foreign assets, and shares. Stalin said the Russians would not claim the gold the Allies had found in Germany. With regard to shares and foreign investments, he suggested the demarcation line between the Soviet and western zones of occupation as the dividing line. Truman asked if he meant a line running from the Baltic to the Adriatic. Stalin agreed; everything west of the line would go to the Allies and everything east of the line to the Russians. For example, German investments in Romania and Hungary would fall to the Russians.

Bevin asked if German investments in other countries would be theirs. Stalin replied they would and mentioned France, Belgium, and America as examples. Bevin agreed and asked if Greece would belong to Britain. Stalin said the questions only related to Austria and Yugoslavia and suggested the Allies took Yugoslavia, while Austria was divided into zones. Byrnes understood the Russians would make no claim to shares of enterprises located in the American zones. Stalin agreed.

Byrnes asked what percentage of German foreign assets the Russians wanted. Stalin replied it would be very small because most were west of the demarcation line. Bevin understood the Russians had renounced all claims to German foreign assets but Stalin said not those in Romania, Bulgaria, Finland and Hungary. He added those in Norway, Switzerland, Spain and other countries in the west would fall to the Allies. Bevin asked if the Russian claim was limited to the zone occupied by the Russian Army. Stalin replied yes. Bevin assumed it was clear that assets owned by British and Americans in those areas would not be touched. Stalin replied of course not, they had not been at war with Great Britain. Truman said

---

1   The area under question had been German but the Germans had fled. The Poles had started to administer the area with Soviet consent, on the assumption it would be given to Poland.

Yugoslavia and Czechoslovakia and other countries would claim assets in their territory. Stalin replied Yugoslavia and Czechoslovakia were in the Allied zone for this purpose. Truman and Bevin agreed.[2]

Invitation to France to Join the Reparations Commission

Attlee proposed inviting the French government to become a member of the Reparations Commission. Stalin suggested inviting Poland, as it had suffered greatly. Attlee understood it had been agreed to invite France and Stalin replied, why not invite Poland? Truman said they had agreed the Soviet government could take care of Poland with respect to reparations and the Allies could take care of the others. Why mix other hands in the pie? Attlee pointed out France had a zone of occupation in Germany. Stalin asked if Attlee was anxious for France to participate. Attlee said yes and Stalin said he would agree.

Supplies for Berlin

Attlee read an agreement on the Soviet delivery of 40,000 tons of food per month and 2,400 tons[3] of coal per day to the British and American zones in Berlin for 30 days starting on 15 July. He proposed the Control Commission should draw up a six-month program of food, coal, and fuel to be imported into the greater Berlin area. Stalin did not think it was possible to have a high standard of living for Germany in the near future. Attlee replied it was not a question of a high standard of living, deliveries of capital goods from the Ruhr were to about to begin and the supply of necessary food should also begin.[4]

Stalin said there should be an agreement in principle but it was impossible to discuss figures. The military people on the Control Commission could arrange such matters. Attlee said that was what he was asking for.[5] The British wanted to agree the Soviet Government would supply the goods in principle. Attlee understood the Russians wanted regular deliveries of capital goods from the Ruhr and they were proposing the same from the Russian side. Stalin said there was no similarity between the agreements to supply capital equipment and food since they were to be completed within different time periods.

Attlee said the Russians were asking for advance deliveries before the value of the equipment had been set. Stalin replied they could refuse to make those advance deliveries. Bevin did not wish to do that; they wished to accommodate each other. Stalin asked what he could do if he was not ready to decide the matter. Bevin said then they would postpone it.[6]

---

2 The Soviet Union secured reparations from countries in its zone, including Bulgaria, Hungary and Romania.
3 Possibly 24,000 tons a day, the minutes state both.
4 The Ruhr made goods, including steel, to give to the Soviet Union in return for food. The Allies had deliberately not destroyed the vast industries across Ruhr during the latter stages of the war. It meant they could now be used to create goods to be exchanged for food.
5 A temporary agreement was in place but agreement had to be made on a permanent agreement, so the Control Commission could work out precise figures.
6 On 24 June 1948 the Soviet Union blocked rail, road and canal access to Berlin, hoping to get control over the entire city. The Western Allies organised the Berlin Airlift and over the next 12 months the US Air Force and RAF flew over 200,000 flights delivering 4700 tons of food and fuel a day. The Soviets finally realised the blockade could not work and lifted it in May 1949. Two German states were the outcome, the Federal Republic of Germany (West Germany) and the German Democratic Republic (East Germany); Berlin was also split.

1 August: Thirteenth Plenary Meeting

After discussions over the wording in a number of documents, it was agreed representatives would be appointed to check the text. The conference was then brought to a close. Stalin asked about the publication time. Bevin wanted to release the communiqué for publication in the Friday morning papers. It would be given out the next day. Stalin agreed.

Attlee expressed his thanks to Stalin for the excellent arrangements for this meeting and for their comfort and also to Truman for presiding over this conference. He hoped the Conference would be a milestone on the road the three nations were pursuing together towards a permanent peace and the friendships between the three would be strengthened. Stalin said this was the Soviet desire.

Truman expressed his appreciation to Stalin for his kind treatment and also joined in all that Attlee had said. Stalin thanked Truman for presiding over the conference. Truman appreciated the privilege and hoped it had been satisfactory to the Marshal and the Prime Minister. Stalin expressed his personal thanks to Mr. Byrnes, who seemed to work harder than anyone else. Byrnes expressed his appreciation and hoped he and his two colleagues had been able to make a contribution to the conference. Truman also thanked the other Foreign Ministers and others who had worked to get the three to agree. The meeting adjourned.

Communiqué[1]

Important decisions and agreements were reached. Views were exchanged on a number of other questions and consideration of these matters will be continued by the Council of Foreign Ministers established by the conference. President Truman, Generalissimo Stalin and Prime Minister Attlee leave this conference, which has strengthened the ties between the three governments and extended the scope of their collaboration and understanding, with renewed confidence that their governments and peoples, together with the other United Nations, will ensure the creation of a just and enduring peace.[2]

Postscript

On 26 July the United Kingdom, the United States and the Republic of China called for a surrender of Japan in the Potsdam declaration. Japan ignored the threat of "prompt and utter destruction". The Terminal Conference ended on 1 August and an atomic bomb was dropped on Hiroshima on 6 August; between 45,000 and 83,000 people died. The second atomic bomb was dropped on Nagasaki on 9 August; between 40,000 and 60,000 died. As many more died in the two cities over the months that followed from radiation sickness, injuries, burns and illness.

On 15 August Japan announced her surrender to the Allies; the Japanese signed the Instrument of Surrender on 2 September, bringing World War II to an end. The justification for dropping the two atomic bombs is still argued over today.

---

1 The communiqué opened with a list of attendees, how many meetings were held and the location.
2 The communiqué then listed the topics covered and the agreements made.

INDEX